INVESTIGATION OF THE PEARL HARBOR ATTACK

REPORT

OF THE

JOINT COMMITTEE ON THE INVESTIGATION OF THE PEARL HARBOR ATTACK

CONGRESS OF THE UNITED STATES

PURSUANT TO

S. Con. Res. 27, 79th Congress

A concurrent resolution to investigate the attack on Pearl
Harbor on December 7, 1941, and events and
circumstances relating thereto

W9-BPJ-760

This book is a copy, without changes, of the *Report of the Joint Committee on the Investigation of the Pearl Harbor Attack,* Congress of the United States, pursuant to a concurrent resolution to investigate the attack on Pearl Harbor on December 7, 1941, and the events and circumstances relating thereto.

The original report was published by the Government Printing Office in 1946.

The publisher has included in this edition a complete personality index. This index provides an alphabetical listing of every name which appears in the report and its location in the text. In addition, this edition includes a recently obtained "Memorandum for the Director of Central Intelligence," which provides a study of the cited Joint Committee Report from the viewpoint of ascertaining the role, achievements, and shortcomings of intelligence in connection with the attack on Pearl Harbor.

AEGEAN PARK PRESS Edition — May 1994

ISBN: 0-89412-234-7

AEGEAN PARK PRESS
P.O. Box 2837
Laguna Hills, CA 92654
(714) 586-8811
FAX (714) 586-8269

JOINT COMMITTEE ON THE INVESTIGATION OF THE PEARL HARBOR ATTACK

ALBEN W. BARKLEY, Senator from Kentucky, *Chairman*

JERE COOPER, Representative from Tennessee, *Vice Chairman*

WALTER F. GEORGE. Senator from Georgia

SCOTT W. LUCAS, Senator from Illinois

OWEN BREWSTER, Senator from Maine

HOMER FERGUSON, Senator from Michigan

J. BAYARD CLARK, Representative from North Carolina

JOHN W. MURPHY, Representative from Pennsylvania

BERTRAND W. GEARHART, Representative from California

FRANK B. KEEFE, Representative from Wisconsin

COUNSEL

(Through January 14, 1946)

WILLIAM D. MITCHELL, *General Counsel*

GERHARD A. GESELL, *Chief Assistant Counsel*

JULE M. HANNAFORD, *Assistant Counsel*

JOHN E. MASTEN, *Assistant Counsel*

(After January 14, 1946)

SETH W. RICHARDSON, *General Counsel*

SAMUEL H. KAUFMAN, *Associate General Counsel*

JOHN E. MASTEN, *Assistant Counsel*

EDWARD P. MORGAN, *Assistant Counsel*

LOGAN J. LANE, *Assistant Counsel*

LETTER OF TRANSMITTAL

UNITED STATES SENATE AND
HOUSE OF REPRESENTATIVES,
Washington, D. C., July 16, 1946.

Hon. KENNETH McKELLAR,
 President pro tempore of the Senate.
Hon. SAM RAYBURN,
 Speaker of the House of Representatives.

DEAR MR. PRESIDENT AND MR. SPEAKER: Pursuant to Senate Concurrent Resolution No. 27 (as extended), Seventy-ninth Congress, first session, the Joint Congressional Committee on the Investigation of the Pearl Harbor Attack has completed its work with a view to a full and complete investigation of the facts relating to the events and circumstances leading up to or following the attack made by Japanese armed forces upon Pearl Harbor in the Territory of Hawaii on December 7, 1941.

The committee has endeavored faithfully to discharge the duties assigned and respectfully submits herewith its report.

Sincerely yours,

ALBEN W. BARKLEY,
 Chairman.
JERE COOPER,
 Vice Chairman.

CONTENTS

FOREWORD

On Sunday morning, December 7, 1941, the United States and Japan were at peace. Japanese ambassadors were in Washington in conversation with our diplomatic officials looking to a general settlement of differences in the Pacific.

At 7:55 a. m. (Hawaiian time) over 300 Japanese planes launched from 6 aircraft carriers attacked the island of Oahu and the American Pacific Fleet at Pearl Harbor in the Territory of Hawaii. Within a period of less than 2 hours our military and naval forces suffered a total of 3,435 casualties in personnel and the loss of or severe damage to: 188 planes of all types, 8 battleships, 3 light cruisers, and 4 miscellaneous vessels.

The attack was well planned and skillfully executed. The Japanese raiders withdrew from the attack and were recovered by the carriers without the latter being detected, having suffered losses of less than 100 in personnel, 29 planes, and 5 midget submarines which had been dispatched from mother craft that coordinated their attack with that of the planes.

One hour after Japanese air and naval forces had struck the Territory of Hawaii the emissaries of Japan delivered to the Secretary of State a reply to a recent American note, a reply containing no suggestion of attack by Japan upon the United States. With the benefit of information now available it is known that the Japanese military had planned for many weeks the unprovoked and ambitious act of December 7.

The Pyrrhic victory of having executed the attack with surprise, cunning, and deceit belongs to the war lords of Japan whose dreams of conquest were buried in the ashes of Hiroshima and Nagasaki. History will properly place responsibility for Pearl Harbor upon the military clique dominating the people of Japan at the time. Indeed, this responsibility Premier Tojo himself has already assumed.

We come today, over 4 years after the event, not to detract from this responsibility but to record for posterity the facts of the disaster. In another sense we seek to find lessons to avoid pitfalls in the future, to evolve constructive suggestions for the protection of our national security, and to determine whether there were failures in our own military and naval establishments which in any measure may have contributed to the extent and intensity of the disaster.

INTRODUCTORY STATEMENT

On November 15, 1945, the Joint Congressional Committee on the Investigation of the Pearl Harbor Attack held its first public hearings pursuant to Senate Concurrent Resolution No. 27, Seventy-ninth Congress, first session, as follows:[1]

IN THE SENATE OF THE UNITED STATES

SEPTEMBER 6, 1945

Mr. BARKLEY submitted the following concurrent resolution; which was considered, modified, and agreed to

SEPTEMBER 11, 1945

House concurs

CONCURRENT RESOLUTION

Resolved by the Senate (the House of Representatives concurring), That there is hereby established a joint committee on the investigation of the Pearl Harbor attack, to be composed of five Members of the Senate (not more than three of whom shall be members of the majority party), to be appointed by the President pro tempore, and five Members of the House of Representatives (not more than three of whom shall be members of the majority party), to be appointed by the Speaker of the House. Vacancies in the membership of the committee shall not affect the power of the remaining members to execute the functions of the committee, and shall be filled in the same manner as in the case of the original selection. The committee shall select a chairman and a vice chairman from among its members.

SEC. 2. The committee shall make a full and complete investigation of the facts relating to the events and circumstances leading up to or following the attack made by Japanese armed forces upon Pearl Harbor in the Territory of Hawaii on December 7, 1941, and shall report to the Senate and the House of Representatives not later than January 3, 1946, the results of its investigation, together with such recommendations as it may deem advisable.

SEC. 3. The testimony of any person in the armed services, and the fact that such person testified before the joint committee herein provided for, shall not be used against him in any court proceeding, or held against him in examining his military status for credits in the service to which he belongs.

SEC. 4. (a) The committee, or any duly authorized subcommittee thereof, is authorized to sit and act at such places and times during the sessions, recesses, and adjourned periods of the Seventy-ninth Congress (prior to January 3, 1946), to require by subpena or otherwise the attendance of such witnesses and the production of such books, papers, and documents, to administer such oaths, to take such testimony, to procure such printing and binding, and to make such expenditures as it deems advisable. The cost of stenographic services to report such hearings shall not be in excess of 25 cents per hundred words.

(b) The committee is empowered to appoint and fix the compensation of such experts, consultants, and clerical and stenographic assistants as it deems necessary, but the compensation so fixed shall not exceed the compensation prescribed under the Classification Act of 1923, as amended, for comparable duties.

(c) The expenses of the committee, which shall not exceed $25,000, shall be paid one-half from the contingent fund of the Senate and one-half from the con-

---

[1] The authority of the committee is to be found in S. Con. Res. No. 27, 79th Cong., 1st sess., passed by the Senate on September 6, 1945, and concurred in by the House of Representatives on September 11, 1945, and as extended by both Houses under S. Con. Res. No. 49, 79th Cong., 1st sess., and by S. Con. Res. No. 54, 79th Cong., 2d sess.

tingent fund of the House of Representatives, upon vouchers signed by the chairman.

Passed the Senate September 6, 1945.

Attest: LESLIE L. BIFFLE,
                                                                    Secretary.

Passed the House of Representatives September 11, 1945.

Attest:
                                                                SOUTH TRIMBLE,
                                                                    Clerk.

On 70 days subsequent to November 15 and prior to and including May 31, 1945, open hearings were conducted in the course of which some 15,000 pages of testimony were taken and a total of 183 exhibits received incident to an examination of 43 witnesses.

Of assistance to the committee and its work were the testimony and exhibits of seven prior investigations concerning the Pearl Harbor attack, including inquiries conducted by the Roberts Commission.[2] Admiral Thomas C. Hart,[3] the Army Pearl Harbor Board,[4] the Navy Court of Inquiry,[5] Col. Carter W. Clarke.[6] Maj. Henry C. Clausen,[7] and Admiral H. Kent Hewitt.[8] For purposes of convenient reference there has been set forth in appendix A to this report a statement concerning the scope and character of each of these prior proceedings, the records of which total 9,754 printed pages of testimony from 318 witnesses and the attendant 469 exhibits. The records of these proceedings have been incorporated as exhibits to the record of the committee which encompasses approximately 10,000,000 words.

All witnesses appeared under oath and were afforded the fullest opportunity to offer any and all information which was regarded as having any relationship whatever to the disaster. In the course of examination by committee counsel and the committee members themselves, an effort was made to elicit all facts having an immediate or remote bearing on the tragedy of December 7, 1941. It is believed the committee has succeeded through its record in preserving for posterity the material facts concerning the disaster.

The figures and witnesses in the drama of Pearl Harbor ran the gamut of officials of the executive branch of the Government. The principal personalities in the picture were the President of the United States, Franklin D. Roosevelt; the Secretary of State, Cordell Hull; the Secretary of War, Henry L. Stimson; the Secretary of Navy, Frank Knox; the Chief of Staff, George C. Marshall; the Chief of Naval Operations. Harold R. Stark; the commander in chief of the Pacific Fleet, Husband E. Kimmel; and the commanding general of the Hawaiian Department, Walter C. Short. In appendix B to this report there are set forth the names and positions of the ranking Army and Navy officials in Washington and at Hawaii at the time of the attack along with the principal witnesses in the various proceedings.

The committee's investigation has extended to the files of all pertinent branches of the Government. Instructions in this regard from the President of the United States, Harry S. Truman, to various departments will be found in appendix C to this report. The committee through its counsel requested Miss Grace Tully, custodian of the files of the late President Roosevelt, to furnish the committee all

[2] For proceedings of the Roberts Commission, see committee exhibit No. 143.
[3] For proceedings of the Hart Inquiry, see committee exhibit No. 144.
[4] For proceedings of the Army Pearl Harbor Board, see committee exhibit No. 145.
[5] For proceedings of the Navy Court of Inquiry, see committee exhibit No. 146.
[6] For proceedings of the Clarke investigation, see committee exhibit No. 147.
[7] For report of investigation conducted by Major Clausen, see committee exhibit No. 148.
[8] For proceedings of the Hewitt inquiry, see committee exhibit No. 149.

papers in these files for the year 1941 relating to Japan, the imminence of war in the Pacific, and the general Far Eastern developments. She furnished such papers in response to this request as she considered might be involved and stood ready to testify before the committee at any time.

All parties in interest have attested to the fact that they have been afforded a full, fair, and impartial public hearing before the committee. All witnesses who retained counsel—Admiral Stark, Admiral Kimmel, and General Short—were given the opportunity to be examined by their counsel if they so desired, and to submit questions to committee counsel to be asked other witnesses.

The following action was not taken by the committee for the reasons indicated:

(1) Former Secretary of War Henry L. Stimson was not called before the committee as a witness for the reason that his health would not permit. Mr. Stimson did, however, submit a statement under oath for the committee's consideration and the answers supplied by him to interrogatories propounded were considered by the committee. He supplied the portions of his personal diary requested by committee counsel and informed the committee that the portions of his diary now in evidence are the only portions thereof having any relationship to the Pearl Harbor investigation.

(2) Former Ambassador to Japan Joseph Grew appeared before the committee as a witness and testified to material appearing in his personal diary having a relationship to the events and circumstances of the Pearl Harbor attack. On the basis of his personal representation that no additional material pertinent to the subject of the committee's inquiry appeared in his diary beyond that to which he had testified, the committee did not formally request or otherwise seek to require the production of Mr. Grew's complete diary.

(3) A request by one member of the committee for the appearance of the former Prime Minister of England, Mr. Winston Churchill, was disapproved by a majority of the committee. At the time Mr. Churchill was a guest in the United States and it was not felt that he should with propriety be requested to appear as a witness.

(4) A request by one member of the committee for production by the State Department of all papers relating to the so-called Tyler Kent case was disapproved by a majority of the committee. The State Department had advised that these papers were in no way pertinent to the subject of the committee's inquiry, and, additionally, members of the committee had discussed the question with Mr. Kent who advised that he possessed no facts that would in any way have relationship to the Pearl Harbor attack.

Former Secretary of State Cordell Hull appeared before the committee but was forced to retire by reason of failing health before completion of the examination by all members of the committee. Mr. Hull subsequently responded to interrogatories propounded by the committee.

The committee has conceived its duty to be not only that of indicating the nature and scope of responsibility for the disaster but also of recording the pertinent considerations relating to the greatest defeat in our military and naval history. Only through a reasonable amount of detail is it possible to place events and responsibilities in their proper perspective and give to the Nation a genuine appreciation of the salient facts concerning Pearl Harbor. For this reason our report is of somewhat greater length than was initially believed necessary. It is to be recalled in this connection, however, that the over-all record of the committee comprehends some ten million words. It was felt therefore that the story of the antecedent, contemporaneous, and succeeding events attending the disaster could not be properly encompassed within a report any more concise than that herewith submitted.

We believe there is much to be learned of a constructive character as a result of the Japanese attack from the standpoint of legislation and, additionally, for guidance in avoiding the possibility of another military disaster such as Pearl Harbor. Accordingly, in the section devoted to recommendations there are set forth, in addition to the recommendations proper, a series of principles, based on errors revealed by the investigation, which are being commended to our military and naval services for their consideration and possible assistance.

Our report does not purport to set forth or refer to all of the enormous volume of testimony and evidence adduced in the course of the Pearl Harbor investigation. It is believed, however, that the material facts relevant to the disaster have been outlined in the report. The committee's record and the records of all prior investigations have been printed and are available for review and study. It is to be borne in mind that the findings and conclusions are based on the facts presently in our record after an exhaustive investigation.

We desire to acknowledge particular gratitude to those who have acted as counsel to the committee for their excellent work during the course of the investigation and for their magnificent assistance in compiling the facts for the committee in order that we might draw our conclusions, which are necessarily those of the committee only.

In the following pages an effort has been made to present a review of the diplomatic and historical setting of the Pearl Harbor attack followed by a picture of the Japanese attack itself. Set forth thereafter are separate treatments of responsibilities in Hawaii on the one hand and responsibilities in Washington on the other. Situations existing in our Army and Navy establishments having a proximate or causative relationship to the disaster have been distinguished from those which, while not to be condoned, are regarded as having no direct or reasonable bearing on the conditions prevailing at Hawaii, preceding and in the wake of the Japanese attack on Sunday morning, December 7, 1941. To assist in following and better appreciating the story of the attack there has been outlined in appendix F the geographical considerations and military installations playing a role in and relating to the disaster.

Throughout the report italics have been freely employed to facilitate reading and to bring out more clearly matters regarded as of particular importance.

PART I

DIPLOMATIC BACKGROUND OF THE
PEARL HARBOR ATTACK

Japanese Record of Deceit and Aggression

For several months prior to December 7, 1941, the Governments of the United States and Japan had been engaged in conversations with a view to settlement of fundamental differences existing in the Far East. To appreciate the realistic basis upon which the Government of the United States participated in the negotiations it is necessary to consider briefly the course of modern Japanese history in order to gauge her diplomatic and military purposes. These purposes become apparent through an outline review of Japanese aggression: [1]

Upon the conclusion of a successful war against China in 1895 Japan annexed Formosa and indicated her purpose, not then realized, of establishing herself in China.

Following the Russo-Japanese War, Japan in 1905 effected a foothold in Manchuria through acquisition of a lease of the Kwantung territory and ownership of the South Manchuria Railway, at the same time acquiring southern Sakhalin.

In 1910, after many years of encroachment, Japan annexed Korea. (In 1904 she had guaranteed Korea's independence and territorial integrity.)

In the midst of the First World War Japan in 1915 took advantage of the situation to present to China her notorious Twenty-one Demands.

In 1918 Japan entered into an inter-Allied plan whereby not exceeding some 7,000 troops of any one power were to be sent to Siberia to guard military stores which might subsequently be needed by Russian forces, to assist in organizing Russian self-defense, and to aid in evacuating Czechoslovakian forces in Siberia. Seizing upon this opportunity the Japanese conceived the idea of annexing eastern Siberia, in which she was unsuccessful, and sent more than 70,000 troops.

Japan participated in the Washington Conference of 1921–22 and became a party to the agreements concluded. One of these agreements was the Nine Power Treaty which was designed to provide for China full opportunity to develop and maintain a stable government. Japan pledged herself to the principles and policies of self-restraint toward China which was the cornerstone of the Nine Power Treaty. Japan agreed to respect the sovereignty, independence, and territorial and administrative integrity of China, and agreed to use her influence to establish the principle of equal opportunity in that country. Following the advent of the Cabinet of General Tanaka in 1927 Japan adopted a positive policy toward China and manifested an increasing disposition to interfere in Chinese internal affairs. In 1931 Japan invaded Manchuria, subsequently establishing the puppet regime of Manchukuo. (This action was a flagrant violation of her agreements

SEE APPENDIX D FOR A DETAILED REVIEW OF THE DIPLOMATIC CONVERSATIONS BETWEEN THE UNITED STATES AND JAPAN FROM THE ATLANTIC CONFERENCE THROUGH DECEMBER 8, 1941

[1] See committee record, pp. 1076–1085. Committee record references throughout this report are to page numbers of the official transcript of testimony, which are represented in the printed Hearings of the Committee by italic numerals enclosed in brackets.

at the Washington Conference, and was in complete disregard of her obligations under the Kellogg-Briand Pact of 1928 for the renunciation of war as an instrument of national policy.) [2] The Japanese delegate to the League of Nations had stated on November 21, 1931: "We want no more territory." The end of 1932 saw Japanese occupying the whole of Manchuria. Later they moved southward and westward occupying vast areas of China. When the League of Nations adopted the report of the Lytton Commission appointed by the League to investigate the Manchurian situation, Japan walked out of the Assembly on February 24, 1933. On March 27 of the same year Japan gave notice of her intention to withdraw from the League.[3]

On February 21, 1934 the Japanese Minister for Foreign Affairs dispatched a note to the American Secretary of State expressing the conviction that no question existed between the United States and Japan "that is fundamentally incapable of amicable solution".[4] Yet on April 17, 1934 a spokesman of the Japanese Foreign Office issued the "hands off China" statement making clear a purpose to compel China to follow the dictates of Japan and to permit only such relations with China by other countries as the Japanese Government saw fit.

In a formal declaration Japan on December 29, 1934 announced her purpose to withdraw at the end of 1936 from the Naval Limitation Treaty signed at Washington on February 6, 1922.[5] Thereafter she prepared her armaments with a view to launching the invasion of China.

Conversations between Japan and Nazi Germany culminated in the Anti-Comintern Pact of November 25, 1936, to which Italy adhered in 1937. The pact marked the genesis of the "Axis." Thus the parallel courses of aggression being followed by these countries blended in an expression of their common designs in foreign policy.[6]

Seizing upon the negligible Marco Polo Bridge incident between Japanese and Chinese forces near Peiping, Japan in July of 1937 began wholesale invasion of China. The lawless acts of the Japanese military in carrying forward the invasion was a disgusting and degrading episode of rape, theft, and murder. In the outrages attending the occupation of Nanking on December 13, 1937, the Japanese military wrote a particularly ignoble page in history. Yet on July 27, 1937, the Japanese Premier, Prince Konoye, stated, "In sending troops to North China, of course, the Government has no other purpose, as was explained in its recent statement, than to preserve the peace of East Asia." Again on October 28, 1937, the Japanese Foreign Office said: "Japan never looks upon the Chinese people as an enemy." As observed by Secretary Hull: "Japan showed its friendly feeling for China by bombing Chinese civilian populations, by burning Chinese cities, by making millions of Chinese homeless and destitute, by mistreating and killing civilians, and by acts of horror and cruelty."

[2] Peace and War, United States Foreign Policy. 1931–41 (State Department publication), p. 4. committee exhibit No. 28.
[3] Id., at p. 7.
[4] Id., at p. 18.
[5] Id., at p. 12.
[6] Id., at p. 41.

On December 12, 1937, Japanese aircraft bombed and sank the U. S. S. *Panay* in the Yangtze River.[7]

(A proposal made by the Japanese Prime Minister, Baron Hiranuma, on May 18, 1939 to the Secretary of State, contained the thesis that world peace could only be obtained through assuring to nations their "proper places in the world". It was suggested subsequently that Hiranuma was prepared to sound out Germany and Italy with regard to the holding of a conference if the President were prepared at the same time to sound out Great Britain and France on the settling of European problems.[7a] The proposal was received by the American Government with interest. The suggestion was made that Japan could assist in attaining the objective of world peace by settling the "armed conflict and consequent political disturbances in the Far East today." This suggestion reminded the Japanese Government of "the methods of Japan in relations with China", which perturbed American opinion. In consequence, the proposal of Hiranuma withered with the Japanese refusal to settle her "incident" with China, and to indicate her good faith in proposing a search for world peace.)

On April 15, 1940, the Japanese Minister for Foreign Affairs stated that the "Japanese Government cannot but be deeply concerned over any development * * * that may affect the status quo of the Netherlands East Indies." But following the occupation of the Netherlands by Germany, Japan sent a commercial commission to the Indies asking far-reaching concessions, the effect of which, if acceded to, would have made the Indies a virtual Japanese colony. In August and September of 1940 with German assistance Japan extorted from Vichy France an agreement whereby Japanese forces moved into northern Indochina. On September 27, 1940, Japan entered into the Tripartite Pact along with Germany and Italy—an alliance pointed directly at the United States.[8] As stated by Secretary Hull: "It was designed to discourage the United States from taking adequate measures of self-defense until both Japan and Germany had completed their program of conquest in Asia and Europe, when they could turn on the United States then standing alone." Commenting on the Tripartite Pact, Premier Konoye was quoted in the press of October 1940, as having said:

If the United States refuses to understand the real intentions of Japan, Germany, and Italy and continues persistently its challenging attitude and acts * * * those powers will be forced to go to war. Japan is now endeavoring to adjust Russo-Japanese political and economic relations and will make every effort to reduce friction between Japan and Russia. Japan is now engaged in diplomatic maneuvers to induce Russia, Britain, and the United States to suspend their operations in assisting the Chiang regime.

On July 30, 1941 Japanese aircraft bombed the U. S. S. *Tutuila* at Chungking and struck within 400 yards of the American Embassy at that place. On the following day Japan assured the Government of the United States that her military would discontinue bombing the city area of Chungking. Yet only 11 days later on August 11 the American Embassy reported that during

---

[7] Id., at pp. 52, 53.
[7a] Committee exhibit No. 177.
[8] The pact provided that Germany, Italy, and Japan would assist one another with all political, economic, and military means when one of the powers was attacked *by a power not then involved in the European war or in the Chinese-Japanese conflict.* Peace and War, p. 84.

the preceding 4 days Chungking had been delivered unusually heavy and prolonged Japanese air raids. Repeatedly Japan gave assurances that American lives and property in China would be respected. Despite her pledges ever increasing numbers of cases were reported of bombing of American property with consequent loss or endangering of American lives. Secretary Hull summarized the picture in the following words: "Time and again the Japanese gave assurances that American treaty rights in China would be respected. Unnumbered measures infringing those rights were put into effect in Japanese occupied areas. Trade monopolies were set up, discriminatory taxes were imposed, American properties were occupied, and so on. In addition, American nationals were assaulted, arbitrarily detained, and subjected to indignities."

Fundamental Differences Between American and Japanese Policies

The bold aggression launched by Japan in 1931 in complete violation and disregard of treaty obligations stands in irreconcilable conflict with the policy [9] voiced by the President-elect, Mr. Roosevelt, on January 17, 1933:

I am * * * wholly willing to make it clear that American foreign policies must uphold the sanctity of international treaties. That is the cornerstone on which all relations between nations must rest.

In his inaugural address on March 4, 1933, President Roosevelt dedicated the Nation to the policy of the good neighbor:

* * * the neighbor who resolutely respects himself and, because he does so, respects the rights of others—the neighbors who respects his obligations and respects the sanctity of his agreements in and with a world of neighbors.

From that time forward, despite repeated efforts and discussions on the part of the Government of the United States to incline the Government of Japan to a peaceful policy in the Orient, she proceeded in July of 1937 to invade China. In consequence of this policy of aggression by the Empire of Japan, the Secretary of State made public a statement of fundamental principles of international policy with a view to rallying all countries to the support of peaceful processes. The Secretary said on July 16, 1937:[10]

I have been receiving from many sources inquiries and suggestions arising out of disturbed situations in various parts of the world.

Unquestionably there are in a number of regions tensions and strains which on their face involve only countries that are near neighbors but which in ultimate analysis are of inevitable concern to the whole world. Any situation in which armed hostilities are in progress or are threatened is a situation wherein rights and interests of all nations either are or may be seriously affected. There can be no serious hostilities anywhere in the world which will not one way or another affect interests or rights or obligations of this country. I therefore feel warranted in making—in fact, I feel it a duty to make—a statement of this Government's position in regard to international problems and situations with respect to which this country feels deep concern.

This country constantly and consistently advocates maintenance of peace. We advocate national and international self-restraint. We advocate abstinence by all nations from use of force in pursuit of policy and from interference in the internal affairs of other nations. We advocate adjustment of problems in international relations by processes of peaceful negotiation and agreement. We advo-

---

[9] Committee record, pp. 1084–1094.
[10] Foreign Relations of the United States, Japan: 1931–41. (State Department publication), vol. 1, pp. 325–326. Committee exhibit No. 29.

cate faithful observance of international agreements. Upholding the principle of the sanctity of treaties, we believe in modification of provisions of treaties, when need therefor arises, by orderly processes carried out in a spirit of mutual helpfulness and accommodation. We believe in respect by all nations for the rights of others and performance by all nations of established obligations. We stand for revitalizing and strengthening of international law. We advocate steps toward promotion of economic security and stability the world over. We advocate lowering or removing of excessive barriers in international trade. We seek effective equality of commercial opportunity and we urge upon all nations application of the principle of equality of treatment. We believe in limitation and reduction of armament. Realizing the necessity for maintaining armed forces adequate for national security, we are prepared to reduce or to increase our own armed forces in proportion to reductions or increases made by other countries. We avoid entering into alliances or entangling commitments but we believe in cooperative effort by peaceful and practicable means in support of the principles hereinbefore stated.

The principles announced in the statement of July 16, 1937, were given express application to the Chinese situation in a statement of the Secretary of State on August 23, 1937: [11]

The situation in Shanghai is in many ways unique. Shanghai is a great cosmopolitan center, with a population of over three million, a port which has been developed by the nationals of many countries, at which there have prevailed mutually advantageous contacts of all types and varieties between and among the Chinese and people of almost all other countries of the world. At Shanghai there exists a multiplicity of rights and interests which are of inevitable concern to many countries, including the United States.

In the present situation, the American Government is engaged in facilitating in every way possible an orderly and safe removal of American citizens from areas where there is special danger. Further, it is the policy of the American Government to afford its nationals appropriate protection primarily against mobs or other uncontrolled elements. For that purpose it has for many years maintained small detachments of armed forces in China, and for that purpose it is sending the present small reinforcement. These armed forces there have no mission of aggression. It is their function to be of assistance toward maintenance of order and security. It has been the desire and the intention of the American Government to remove these forces when performance of their function of protection is no longer called for, and such remains its desire and expectation.

The issues and problems which are of concern to this Government in the present situation in the Pacific area go far beyond merely the immediate question of protection of the nationals and interests of the United States. The conditions which prevail in that area are intimately connected with and have a direct and fundamental relationship to the general principles of policy to which attention was called in the statement of July 16, which statement has evoked expressions of approval from more than 50 governments. This Government is firmly of the opinion that the principles summarized in that statement should effectively govern international relationships.

When there unfortunately arises in any part of the world the threat or the existence of serious hostilities, the matter is of concern to all nations. Without attempting to pass judgment regarding the merits of the controversy, we appeal to the parties to refrain from resort to war. We urge that they settle their differences in accordance with principles which, in the opinion not alone of our people but of most of the world, should govern in international relationships. We consider applicable throughout the world, in the Pacific area as elsewhere, the principles set forth in the statement of July 16. That statement of principles is comprehensive and basic. It embraces the principles embodied in many treaties, including the Washington Conference treaties and the Kellogg-Briand Pact of Paris.

From the beginning of the present controversy in the Far East we have been urging upon both the Chinese and the Japanese Governments the importance of refraining from hostilities and of maintaining peace. We have been participating constantly in consultation with interested governments directed toward peaceful adjustment. The Government does not believe in political alliances or entanglements, nor does it believe in extreme isolation. It does believe in international cooperation for the purpose of seeking through pacific methods the achievement of those objectives set forth in the statement of July 16. In the light of our well-

[11] Id., at pp. 355-356.

defined attitude and policies, and within the range thereof, this Government is giving most solicitous attention to every phase of the Far Eastern situation, toward safeguarding the lives and welfare of our people and making effective the policies—especially the policy of peace—in which this country believes and to which it is committed.

On October 6, 1937, a release by the Department of State stated, among other things: [12]

The Department of State has been informed by the American Minister to Switzerland of the text of the report adopted by the Advisory Committee of the League of Nations setting forth the Advisory Committee's examination of the facts of the present situation in China and the treaty obligations of Japan. The Minister has further informed the Department that this report was adopted and approved by the Assembly of the League of Nations today, October 6.

Since the beginning of the present controversy in the Far East, the Government of the United States has urged upon both the Chinese and the Japanese Governments that they refrain from hostilities and has offered to be of assistance in an effort to find some means, acceptable to both parties to the conflict, of composing by pacific methods the situation in the Far East.

The Secretary of State, in statements made public on July 16 and August 23, made clear the position of the Government of the United States in regard to international problems and international relationships throughout the world and as applied specifically to the hostilities which are at present unfortunately going on between China and Japan. Among the principles which in the opinion of the Government of the United States should govern international relationships, if peace is to be maintained, are abstinence by all nations from the use of force in the pursuit of policy and from interference in the internal affairs of other nations; adjustment of problems in international relations by process of peaceful negotiation and agreement; respect by all nations for the rights of others and observance by all nations of established obligations; and the upholding of the principle of the sanctity of treaties.

On October 5 at Chicago the President elaborated these principles, emphasizing their importance, and in a discussion of the world situation pointed out that there can be no stability or peace either within nations or between nations except under laws and moral standards adhered to by all; that international anarchy destroys every foundation for peace; that it jeopardizes either the immediate or the future security of every nation, large or small; and that it is therefore of vital interest and concern to the people of the United States that respect for treaties and international morality be restored.

In the light of the unfolding developments in the Far East, the Government of the United States has been forced to the conclusion that the action of Japan in China is inconsistent with the principles which should govern the relationships between nations and is contrary to the provisions of the Nine Power Treaty of February 6, 1922, regarding principles and policies to be followed in matters concerning China, and to those of the Kellogg-Briand Pact of August 27, 1928. Thus the conclusions of this Government with respect to the foregoing are in general accord with those of the Assembly of the League of Nations.

Pursuant to the provisions of the Nine Power Treaty of 1922, the United States in November of 1937 with 18 other nations participated in a conference convened at Brussels with a view to "study peaceable means of hastening the end of the regrettable conflict which prevails" in the Far East. The Government of Japan refused repeatedly to participate in the conference which prevented bringing the conflict in China to an end and resulted in the conference suspending its work on November 24.[13]

The President late in 1937, exercising the discretion provided by law, refrained from applying the provisions of the Neutrality Act to the conflict between China and Japan. This position was assumed in recognition of the fact that the arms-embargo provisions of the act worked to the detriment of China and to the benefit of Japan.[14]

[12] Id., at pp. 396–397.
[13] See statement of Secretary Hull, committee record, pp. 1087, 1088; also Peace and War, pp 51, 52.
[14] See statement of Secretary Hull, committee record, p. 1088.

On July 26, 1939, the following notification was given the Japanese Ambassador by the Secretary of State: [15]

EXCELLENCY: During recent years the Government of the United States has been examining the treaties of commerce and navigation in force between the United States and foreign countries with a view to determining what changes may need to be made toward better serving the purpose for which such treaties are concluded. In the course of this survey, the Government of the United States has come to the conclusion that the Treaty of Commerce and Navigation between the United States and Japan which was signed at Washington on February 21, 1911, contains provisions which need new consideration. Toward preparing the way for such consideration and with a view to better safeguarding and promoting American interests as new developments may require, the Government of the United States, acting in accordance with the procedure prescribed in Article XVII of the treaty under reference, gives notice hereby of its desire that this treaty be terminated, and, having thus given notice, will expect the treaty, together with its accompanying protocol, to expire six months from this date.

In explaining the foregoing action Secretary Hull testified [16] that the Treaty of Commerce and Navigation was not affording adequate protection to American commerce either in Japan or in Japanese-occupied portions of China, while at the same time the operation of the most-favored-nation clause of the treaty was a bar to the adoption of retaliatory measures against Japanese commerce. With the termination of the treaty on January 26, 1940, the legal impediment to placing restrictions upon trade with Japan was removed.

In the face of widespread bombings of Chinese civilians by the Japanese, the Government of the United States placed into effect "moral embargoes," adopted on the basis of humanitarian considerations.[17] On July 1, 1938, the Department of State notified aircraft manufacturers and exporters that the United States Government was strongly opposed to the sale of airplanes and aeronautical equipment to countries whose armed forces were using airplanes for attack on civilian populations. In 1939 the "moral embargo" was extended to materials essential to airplane manufacture and to facilities for production of high-quality gasoline.[18] Following passage of the act of July 2, 1941, restrictions were imposed in the interests of national defense on an ever-increasing number of exports of strategic materials. These measures had the additional purpose of deterring and expressing the opposition of the United States to Japanese aggression.[19]

On April 15, 1940, when questioned by newspapermen concerning Japan's position with regard to possible involvement of the Netherlands in the European war and its repercussion in the Netherlands East Indies, the Japanese Foreign Minister replied: [20]

With the South Seas regions, especially the Netherlands East Indies, Japan is economically bound by an intimate relationship of mutuality in ministering to one another's needs. Similarly, other countries of East Asia maintain close economic relations with these regions. That is to say, Japan, these countries and these regions together are contributing to the prosperity of East Asia through mutual aid and interdependence.

Should hostilities in Europe be extended to the Netherlands and produce repercussions, as you say, in the Netherlands East Indies, it would not only interfere with the maintenance and furtherance of the above-mentioned relations of economic interdependence and of coexistence and coprosperity, but would also give rise to an undesirable situation from the standpoint of the peace and stability of East Asia. In view of these considerations, the Japanese Government cannot

---

[15] Foreign Relations, vol. II, p. 189; also committee record, p. 1088.
[16] Committee record, p. 1088.
[17] Id.
[18] Peace and War, p. 89.
[19] See statement of Secretary Hull, Committee Record, pp. 1088, 1089.
[20] Foreign Relations, vol. II, p. 281.

but be deeply concerned over any development accompanying an aggravation of the war in Europe that may affect the status quo of the Netherlands East Indies.

Referring to the foregoing statement the Secretary of State made the following comments on April 17, 1940: [21]

I have noted with interest the statement by the Japanese Minister for Foreign Affairs expressing concern on the part of the Japanese Government for the maintenance of the status quo of the Netherlands Indies.

Any change in the status of the Netherlands Indies would directly affect the interests of many countries.

The Netherlands Indies are very important in the international relationships of the whole Pacific Ocean. The islands themselves extend for a distance of approximately 3,200 miles east and west astride of the Equator, from the Indian Ocean on the west far into the Pacific Ocean on the east. They are also an important factor in the commerce of the whole world. They produce considerable portions of the world's supplies of important essential commodities such as rubber, tin, quinine, copra, et cetera. Many countries, including the United States, depend substantially upon them for some of these commodities.

Intervention in the domestic affairs of the Netherlands Indies or any alteration of their status quo by other than peaceful processes would be prejudicial to the cause of stability, peace, and security not only in the region of the Netherlands Indies but in the entire Pacific area.

This conclusion, based on a doctrine which has universal application and for which the United States unequivocally stands, is embodied in notes exchanged on November 30, 1908, between the United States and Japan in which each of the two Governments stated that its policy was directed to the maintenance of the existing status quo in the region of the Pacific Ocean. It is reaffirmed in the notes which the United States, the British Empire, France, and Japan—as parties to the treaty signed at Washington on December 13, 1921, relating to their insular possessions and their insular dominions in the region of the Pacific Ocean— sent to the Netherlands Government on February 4, 1922, in which each of those Governments declared that "it is firmly resolved to respect the rights of the Netherlands in relation to their insular possessions in the region of the Pacific Ocean."

All peaceful nations have during recent years been earnestly urging that policies of force be abandoned and that peace be maintained on the basis of fundamental principles, among which are respect by every nation for the rights of other nations and nonintervention in their domestic affairs, the according of equality of fair and just treatment, and the faithful observance of treaty pledges, with modification thereof, when needful, by orderly processes.

It is the constant hope of the Government of the United States—as it is no doubt that of all peacefully inclined governments—that the attitudes and policies of all governments will be based upon these principles and that these principles will be applied not only in every part of the Pacific area, but also in every part of the world.

The situation existing during 1940 was summarized by Secretary Hull in his testimony before the committee: [22]

Throughout this period the United States increasingly followed a policy of extending all feasible assistance and encouragement to China. This took several different forms, including diplomatic actions in protest of Japan's aggression against China and of Japan's violation of American rights. Loans and credits aggregating some $200,000,000 were extended in order to bolster China's economic structure and to facilitate the acquisition by China of supplies. And later lend-lease and other military supplies were sent to be used in China's resistance against Japan.

During the winter of 1940 and the spring of 1941 I had clearly in mind, and I was explaining to Members of Congress and other Americans with whom I came in contact, that it was apparent that the Japanese military leaders were starting on a mission of conquest of the entire Pacific area west of a few hundred miles of Hawaii and extending to the South Seas and to India. The Japanese were out with force in collaboration with Hitler to establish a new world order, and they thought they had the power to compel all peaceful nations to come in under that new order in the half of the world they had arrogated to themselves.

[21] Id., at p. 282.
[22] Committee Record, pp. 1089–92.

I was saying to those Americans that beginning in 1933 I had commenced a systematic and consistently earnest effort to work out our relations with Japan. I had been trying to see whether it was humanly possible to find any new way to approach the Japanese and prevail on them to abandon this movement of conquest. We had been urging the Japanese to consider their own future from the standpoint of political, economic, and social aspects. The people of China were living on a very low standard. Japan, if it should conquer China, would keep China bled white and would not have the capital to aid in restoring purchasing power and social welfare. It meant everything for the development of that half of the world's population to use the capital of all nations, such as the United States and other countries, in helping China, for example, to develop internal improvements and increase its purchasing power. We had reminded the Japanese of our traditional friendship and our mutually profitable relations.

During these years we had kept before the Japanese all these doctrines and principles in the most tactful and earnest manner possible, and at all times we had been careful not to make threats. I said that I had always felt that if a government makes a threat it ought to be ready to back it up. We had been forthright but we had been as tactful as possible.

I was pointing out in these conversations that if we had not, by previously modifying our Neutrality Act, been in a position to send military aid to Great Britain in the early summer of 1940 there might well have been a different story. Our aid assisted Britain to hold back the invaders for 7 months, while we had that 7 months in which to arm, and everybody knew that no country ever needed time in which to arm more than we did in the face of the world situation.

In his address to Congress on January 6, 1941, President Roosevelt declared [23] that "at no previous time has American security been as seriously threatened from without as it is today." He observed that the pattern of democratic life had been blotted out in an appalling number of independent nations with the aggressors still on the march threatening other nations, great and small. The national policy of the Government of the United States was outlined by the President as committed to an all-inclusive national defense, to full support of resolute peoples everywhere who were resisting aggression and thereby were keeping war away from our hemisphere, and to the proposition that principles of morality and considerations for our own security would "never permit us to acquiesce in a peace dictated by aggressors."

In a statement on January 15, 1941, in support of the Lend-Lease Act before the Committee on Foreign Affairs in the House of Representatives, Secretary Hull said: [24]

It has been clear throughout that Japan has been actuated from the start by broad and ambitious plans for establishing herself in a dominant position in the entire region of the Western Pacific. Her leaders have openly declared their determination to achieve and maintain that position by force of arms and thus to make themselves master of an area containing almost one-half of the entire population of the world. As a consequence, they would have arbitrary control of the sea and trade routes in that region.

As Secretary Hull testified [25]—

I pointed out that mankind was face to face with an organized, ruthless, and implacable movement of steadily expanding conquests and that control of the high seas by law-abiding nations "is the key to the security of the Western Hemisphere.'"

The hope of the United States, therefore, for mediation and conciliation based on peaceful processes was overshadowed by an uncompromising and relentless aggressor who had cast her lot with the Axis in the Tripartite Pact of September 1940 and voiced her slogan of domination by force in the "Greater East Asia Co-prosperity Sphere."

---

[23] See Committee record, pp. 1092, 1093.
[24] Committee record, p. 1093.
[25] Id.

The backdrop of activity by Japan's partners left little doubt as to the program and methods of the Axis: [26]

> On October 14, 1933, Germany withdrew from the Disarmament Conference coincidentally giving notice of withdrawal from the League of Nations.
>
> On October 3, 1935, Italian armed forces invaded Ethiopia.
>
> In violation of the Locarno Pact Hitler proceeded in March of 1936 to occupy and fortify the demilitarized Rhineland.
>
> On March 11, 1938, German forces entered Austria and 2 days later proclaimed the union of Germany and Austria.
>
> At Munich on September 29, 1938, Hitler and Mussolini extorted a settlement by which Germany acquired the Sudetenland.
>
> In violation of pledges given at Munich, Germany invaded Czechoslovakia on March 14, 1939.

With further German aggression, war broke out in Europe on September 1, 1939, which as Secretary Hull stated "weakened the position of all countries, including the United States, opposed to Japanese banditry in the Pacific." He presented the picture in the following terms:

In the early summer of 1940 France's effective resistance collapsed. Britain was virtually under siege. Germany's vast and powerful military machine remained intact.

Nazi submarines and long-range bombers were taking a heavy toll of ships and materials in the North Atlantic. Shipping was inadequate. The countries resisting aggression desperately needed supplies to increase their defenses.

It was clear that any aggravation of the situation in the Far East would have a serious effect on the already dangerous situation in Europe, while conversely, an easement of the Far Eastern tension would aid enormously the struggle against the Nazis in Europe.

Steps Taken by the United States To Meet the Threat of Axis Aggression

With each threatened "annexation" or "occupation" of countries bordering on Germany up to the invasion of Poland, President Roosevelt had made an appeal for the settlement of differences without recourse to force or the threat of force; but the United States in line with its traditional aloofness in European affairs had adopted no positive measures to deter Hitler's course of aggression. In the face of the inexorable trend of Axis militarism, however, progressive steps were taken by the Government of the United States to build our defenses and throw our weight on the side of France and Great Britain. For purposes of convenient reference it would be well to review briefly these steps.

Addressing the Congress in extraordinary session on September 21, 1939, the President recommended that the arms embargo be repealed and that our citizens and our ships be restricted from dangerous areas in order to prevent controversies that might involve the United States in war. On November 4 the arms embargo was repealed, thereby permitting large shipments of aircraft and other implements of war, much of which had been ordered by Great Britain and France before the outbreak of war, to be shipped across the Atlantic for use in combating Nazi aggression.[27]

---

[26] See committee record, pp. 1093–1095.
[27] Peace and War, pp. 69, 70.

In an address on June 10, 1940, at Charlottesville, Va., the President announced the policy of extending the material resources of the United States to the opponents of force. He said:

We will extend to the opponents of force the material resources of this Nation and, at the same time, we will harness and speed up the use of those resources in order that we ourselves in the Americas may have equipment and training equal to the task of any emergency and every defense.[28]

With a view to strengthening the defenses of the Western Hemisphere an agreement was made on September 2, 1940, between the United States and Great Britain whereby the latter received 50 over-aged destroyers and the United States acquired the right to lease naval and air bases in Newfoundland, in British Guiana, and in the islands of Bermuda, the Bahamas, Jamaica, St. Lucia, Trinidad, and Antigua. Referring to this agreement, the President stated that the value to the Western Hemisphere "of these outposts of security is beyond calculation." He considered them essential to the protection of the Panama Canal, Central America, the northern portion of South America, the Antilles, Canada, Mexico, and our eastern and Gulf seaboards.[29]

On September 16, 1940, the Selective Training and Service Act was enacted, marking another important step for national defense. The act included a provision that persons inducted into the land forces should not be employed beyond the Western Hemisphere except in United States Territories and possessions. It marked, for the first time in the history of the United States, the adoption of compulsory military training of manpower when the Nation was not at war.[30]

President Roosevelt, in an address of December 29, 1940, observed that the Nazi masters of Germany had made it clear they intended not only to dominate all life and thought in their own country but also to enslave the whole of Europe and to use the resources of Europe to dominate the rest of the world. He pointed out that although some of our people liked to believe that wars in Europe and Asia were of no concern to us, it was a matter of most vital concern that European and Asiatic war makers should not gain control of the oceans which led to the Western Hemisphere. He pointed out that if Great Britain went down the Axis Powers would control the continents of Europe, Asia, Africa, and the high seas, and would then be in a position to bring enormous military and naval resources against this hemisphere. Warning of the danger ahead, the President stated the Government was planning our defense with the utmost urgency and in it we must "integrate the war needs of Britain and the other free nations resisting aggression." Referring to the need for increased production, the President said we must have more ships, more guns, more planes; we must be the great "arsenal of democracy." [31]

With the signature of the President on March 11, 1941, the lend-lease bill became law. This bill provided the machinery enabling the United States to make the most effective use of our resources for our own needs and for those whom, in our own self-defense, we were determined to aid. Secretary Hull expressed the belief that this act would make it possible for us to allocate our resources in ways best

[28] Id., at p. 76
[29] Id., at p. 83
[30] Id., at p. 84.
[31] Id., at pp. 86, 87.

calculated to provide for the security of the United States and of this continent.[32]

On April 10, 1941, the Department of State announced an agreement regarding Greenland, recognizing that as a result of a European war there was danger that Greenland might be converted into a point of aggression against nations of the American Continent. This agreement accepted the responsibility on behalf of the United States of assisting Greenland in the maintenance of its existing status, and granted to the United States the right to locate and construct airplane landing fields and facilities for the defense of Greenland and this continent.[33]

In an address on May 27, 1941, the President declared an "unlimited national emergency," stating that our whole program of aid for the democracies had been "based on a hard-headed concern for our own security and for the kind of safe and civilized world in which we wished to live." He stated that every dollar of material that we sent helped to keep the dictators away from our own hemisphere and every day they were held off gave us time in which to build more guns and tanks and planes and ships.[34]

On July 7, 1941, the President announced that in accordance with an understanding reached with the Prime Minister of Iceland, forces had arrived in Iceland in order to supplement and eventually to replace the British forces which had been stationed there to insure the adequate defense of that country. The President pointed out that the United States could not permit the occupation by Germany of a strategic outpost in the Atlantic to be used as air or naval bases for eventual attack against the Western Hemisphere.[35] Subsequently, there was instituted an escort to Iceland of United States and Iceland shipping.[36]

In a joint declaration by President Roosevelt and Prime Minister Churchill, the principles of the Atlantic Charter were enunciated on August 14, 1941.[37]

In a message of August 15, 1941, in which he was joined by Prime Minister Churchill, the President advised Premier Stalin that the United States and Great Britain had consulted together as to how best they could help the Soviet Union; that they were cooperating to provide the Soviet Union with the very maximum of supplies most urgently needed and that many shiploads had already left for the Soviet Union and more would leave in the immediate future.[38]

On September 11, 1941, as a result of several incidents fully demonstrating a grave menace to the vital interests of the United States, the President warned that from that time forward, if German or Italian vessels of war entered the waters the protection of which was necessary for American defense, they would do so "at their own peril."[39]

Despite the announcement of the "shooting orders", ships of the United States and other American Republics continued to be sunk in the Atlantic Ocean by Nazi submarines. In view of this situation and in view of the fact that the Neutrality Act of 1939 prohibited the arm-

[32] Id., at p. 100.
[33] Id., at pp. 103, 104
[34] Id., at p. 111.
[35] Id., at p. 111.
[36] See committee record, p. 6111.
[37] "Peace and War," p. 111.
[38] Id., at p. 113.
[39] Id., at pp. 113–115.

ing of United States merchant ships engaged in foreign commerce and prevented United States merchant ships from carrying cargoes to belligerent ports, it became increasingly difficult to obtain shipping for the carriage of lend-lease supplies to Great Britain and other nations whose defense was considered vital to the defense of the United States. Accordingly, on October 9, 1941, the President asked Congress to modify the Neutrality Act. On November 17, 1941, in a joint resolution of the Congress, sections of the act were repealed permitting United States vessels to be armed and to carry cargoes to belligerent ports anywhere.[40]

In contrast with our historic aloofness in European affairs, it was the traditional policy of the United States, based upon territorial, commercial, and humanitarian interests, to maintain a concern in the Pacific. This policy had its inception in the enunciation of the Hay open-door policy toward China in 1899 which formed the cornerstone of the Nine-Power Treaty, adopted concurrently with the Washington Naval Treaty of 1922.[41]

To implement this policy Japan's course of aggression was countered by a series of deterrent measures in addition to those relating generally to the Axis or applying more specifically to the European situation. These measures included material aid to China, curtailment of trade with Japan, and basing of the Pacific Fleet at Hawaii.

Initial United States-Japanese Negotiations, 1941

Admiral Nomura, the new Japanese Ambassador, was received by the President on February 14, 1941, at which time reference was made to the progressive deterioration of relations between Japan and the United States. President Roosevelt suggested that Ambassador Nomura might desire to reexamine and frankly discuss with the American Secretary of State important phases of American-Japanese relations. Secretary Hull made the following observations concerning the initial conversations with the Japanese Ambassador: [42]

On March 8 (1941) in my first extended conversation with the Japanese Ambassador I emphasized that the American people had become fully aroused over the German and Japanese movements to take charge of the seas and of the other continents for their own arbitrary control and to profit at the expense of the welfare of all of the victims.

On March 14 the Japanese Ambassador saw the President and me. The President agreed with an intimation by the Ambassador that matters between our two countries could be worked out without a military clash and emphasized that the first step would be removal of suspicion regarding Japan's intentions. With the Japanese Foreign Minister Matsuoka on his way to Berlin, talking loudly, and Japanese naval and air forces moving gradually toward Thailand, there was naturally serious concern and suspicion.

On April 16, I had a further conversation with the Japanese Ambassador. I pointed out that the one paramount preliminary question about which our Government was concerned was a definite assurance in advance that the Japanese Government had the willingness and power to abandon its present doctrine of conquest by force and to adopt four principles which our Government regarded as the foundation upon which relations between nations should rest, as follows:

    (1) Respect for the territorial integrity and the sovereignty of each and all nations;

    (2) Support of the principle of noninterference in the internal affairs of other countries;

---

[40] Id., at pp. 115-117.
[41] Id., at p. 168.
[42] Committee record, pp. 1103, 1104.

(3) Support of the principle of equality, including equality of commercial opportunity;

(4) Nondisturbance of the *status quo* in the Pacific except as the *status quo* may be altered by peaceful means.

I told the Japanese Ambassador that our Government was willing to consider any proposal which the Japanese Government might offer such as would be consistent with those principles.

JAPANESE PROPOSAL OF MAY 12

The Japanese Ambassador on May 12 presented a proposal for a general settlement the essence of which was (1) that the United States should request Chiang Kai-shek to negotiate peace with Japan and, if the Generalissimo should not accept the advice of the United States, that the United States should discontinue its assistance to the Chinese Government; (2) that normal trade relations between Japan and the United States should be resumed; and (3) that the United States should help Japan acquire access to facilities for the exploitation of natural resources (including oil, rubber, tin, and nickel) in the Southwest Pacific area.[43]   This proposal contained an affirmation of Japan's adherence to the Tripartite Pact with specific reference to Japan's obligations thereunder to come to the aid of any of the parties thereto *if attacked by a power not at that time in the European war or in the Sino-Japanese conflict, other than the Soviet Union which was expressly excepted.*   In referring to the proposal Secretary Hull said:[44]

The peace conditions which Japan proposed to offer China were not defined in clear-cut terms.   Patient exploring, however, disclosed that they included stipulations disguised in innocuous-sounding formulas whereby Japan would retain control of various strategic resources, facilities, and enterprises in China and would acquire the right to station large bodies of Japanese troops, professedly for "joint defense against communism," for an indefinite period in extensive key areas of China proper and inner Mongolia.

Notwithstanding the narrow and one-sided character of the Japanese proposals, we took them as a starting point to explore the possibility of working out a broadgage settlement, covering the entire Pacific area, along lines consistent with the principles for which this country stood.

The Japanese Minister of Foreign Affairs advised Ambassador Grew on May 14, 1941, that he and Prince Konoye were determined that Japan's southward advance should be carried out only by peaceful means *"unless circumstances render this impossible."*   Replying to the inquiry as to what circumstances he had in mind the Foreign Minister referred to the concentration of British troops in Malaya and other British measures.   When it was pointed out by Ambassador Grew that such measures were defensive in character, the Japanese Minister observed that the measures in question were regarded as provocative by the Japanese public which might bring pressure on the Government to act.[45]

President Roosevelt on May 27, 1941, as has been indicated, proclaimed the existence of an "unlimited national emergency" and declared in a radio address on the same day that our whole program of aid for the democracies had been based on concern for our own security.[46]

---

[43] There were also other provisions, which Japan eventually dropped, calling for joint guaranty of Philippine independence, for the consideration of Japanese immigration to the United States on a nondiscriminatory basis, and for a joint effort by the United States and Japan to prevent the further extension of the European war and for the speedy restoration of peace in Europe.

[44] Committee record, pp. 1104–1106.

[45] See committee record, pp. 1106, 1107.

[46] Id., at p. 1107.

Secretary Hull commented as follows with respect to preliminary conversations with Ambassador Nomura: [47]

During the next few weeks there were a number of conversations for the purpose of clarifying various points and narrowing areas of difference. We repeatedly set forth our attitude on these points—the necessity of Japan's making clear its relation to the Axis in case the United States should be involved in self-defense in the war in Europe; application of the principle of noninterference in the internal affairs of another country and withdrawal of Japanese troops from Chinese territory; application of the principle of nondiscrimination in commercial relations in China and other areas of the Pacific; and assurance of Japan's peaceful intent in the Pacific. I emphasized that what we were seeking was a comprehensive agreement which would speak for itself as an instrument of peace.

The Japanese pressed for a complete reply to their proposals of May 12. Accordingly, on June 21, the Ambassador was given our views in the form of a tentative redraft of their proposals. In that redraft there was suggested a formula which would make clear that Japan was not committed to take action against the United States should the latter be drawn by self-defense into the European war. It was proposed that a further effort be made to work out a satisfactory solution of the question of the stationing of Japanese troops in China and of the question of economic cooperation between China and Japan. There also was eliminated any suggestion that the United States would discontinue aid to the Chinese Government. Various other suggested changes were proposed in the interest of clarification or for the purpose of harmonizing the proposed settlement with our stated principles.

JAPANESE REACTION TO GERMAN INVASION OF RUSSIA

In violation of the August 23, 1939, nonaggression pact, Germany attacked the Soviet Union on June 22, 1941. The invasion of Russia removed the restraining influence on the western flank of Japan and the life-and-death struggle of the Soviet Union for existence was seized upon by the Government of Japan to realize its dreams of empire in the Far East.

In an intercepted message of July 31, 1941, from Tokyo to its Washington Embassy the reaction of Japan to the war between Germany and Russia was unequivocally expressed:[48]

Needless to say, the Russo-German war has given us an excellent opportunity to settle the northern question, and it is a fact that we are proceeding with our preparations to take advantage of this occasion.

The opportunist disposition of Japan was cogently expressed much earlier in a dispatch of September 12, 1940, from Ambassador Grew to the State Department:[49]

Whatever may be the intentions of the present Japanese Government, there can be no doubt that *the army and other elements in the country see in the present world situation a golden opportunity to carry into effect their dreams of expansion;* the German victories have gone to their heads like strong wine; until recently they have believed implicitly in the defeat of Great Britain; they have argued that the war will probably (*) in a quick German victory and that it is well to consolidate Japan's position in greater East Asia while Germany is still acquiescent and before the eventual hypothetical strengthening of German naval power might rob Japan of far-flung control in the Far East; they have discounted effective opposition on the part of the United States although carefully watching our attitude. *The ability of the saner heads in and out of the Government to control these elements has been and is doubtful.* * * *

Diplomacy may occasionally retard but cannot effectively stem the tide. Force or the display of force can alone prevent these powers from attaining their objectives. Japan today is one of the predatory powers; *she has submerged all moral and ethical sense and has become frankly and unashamedly opportunist, seeking at every turn to profit by the weakness of others.* Her policy of southward expansion

---

[47] Id., at pp. 1108, 1109.
[48] Committee exhibit No. 1, p. 9.
[49] Committee exhibit No. 26.

is a definite threat to American interests in the Pacific, and is a thrust at the British Empire in the east.

Following an Imperial Conference at Tokyo on July 2 at which "the fundamental national policy to be taken toward the present situation was decided" Japan proceeded with military preparations on a vast scale. From one to two million reservists and conscripts were called to the colors. Japanese merchant vessels operating in the Atlantic Ocean were suddenly recalled; restrictions were imposed upon travel in Japan; strict censorship of mails and communications was effected; and conditions were generally imposed throughout the Empire presaging a major military effort. The Japanese press dwelt constantly on the theme that Japan was being faced with pressure directed against it never before approached in its history. The United States was charged with using the Philippine Islands as a "pistol aimed at Japan's heart." The Japanese press warned that if the United States took further action in the direction of encircling Japan, Japanese-American relations would face a final crisis.[50] This false propaganda was clearly designed to condition the Japanese public for further military aggression.

In an intercepted dispatch of July 2, 1941, from Tokyo to Berlin for the confidential information of the Japanese Ambassador and staff, the policy of Japan was expressed in the following terms: [51]

1. Imperial Japan shall adhere to the policy of contributing to world peace by establishing the Great East Asia Sphere of Coprosperity, regardless of how the world situation may change.
2. The Imperial Government shall continue its endeavor to dispose of the China incident, and shall take measures with a view to advancing southward in order to establish firmly a basis for her self-existence and self-protection.

In a second part of the same message Japan outlined the "principal points" upon which she proposed to proceed:

For the purpose of bringing the Chiang Regime to submission, increasing pressure shall be added from various points in the south, and by means of both propaganda and fighting plans for the taking over of concessions shall be carried out. Diplomatic negotiations shall be continued, and various other plans shall be speeded with regard to the vital points in the south. *Concomitantly, preparations for southward advance shall be reenforced and the policy already decided upon with reference to French Indo-China and Thailand shall be executed.* As regards the Russo-German war, although the spirit of the Three-Power Axis shall be maintained, every preparation shall be made at the present and the situation shall be dealt with in our own way. In the meantime, diplomatic negotiations shall be carried on with extreme care. Although every means available shall be resorted to in order to prevent the United States from joining the war, if need be, *Japan shall act in accordance with the Three-Power Pact and shall decide when and how force will be employed.*

Temporary Cessation of Negotiations

During July of 1941 reports were received that a Japanese military movement into southern Indochina was imminent. The Government of the United States called to the attention of Japan the incompatibility of such reports with the conversations then under way looking to an agreement for peace in the Pacific. Asked concerning the facts of the situation, the Japanese Ambassador on July 23 explained the Japanese movement into southern as well as northern Indochina by observing that Japan feared, first, that vital supplies including rice, foodstuffs, and raw materials from Indochina might be cut off by

---

[50] Foreign Relations, vol II, pp. 339, 340.
[51] Committee exhibit No. 1, pp. 1, 2.

de Gaullist French agents and Chinese agitators in southern Indochina and, second, that Japan believed certain foreign powers were determined to encircle Japan militarily and for that reason occupation of southern Indochina was undertaken purely as a precautionary measure.[52]

The explanation of Ambassador Nomura is in interesting contrast with an intercepted dispatch of July 14, 1941, from Canton to Tokyo: [53]

Subsequent information from the military officials to the Attachés is as follows:

1. The recent general mobilization order expressed the irrevocable resolution of Japan to put an end to Anglo-American assistance in thwarting her natural expansion and her indomitable intention to carry this out, if possible, with the backing of the Axis but, if neccessary, alone. Formalities, such as dining the expeditionary forces and saying farewell to them, have been dispensed with. That is because we did not wish to arouse greatly the feelings of the Japanese populace and because we wished to face this new war with a calm and cool attitude.

2. The immediate object of our occupation of French Indo-China will be to achieve our purposes there. *Secondly, its purpose is, when the international situation is suitable, to launch therefrom a rapid attack.* This venture we will carry out in spite of any difficulties which may arise. We will endeavor to the last to occupy French Indo-China peacefully but, if resistance is offered, we will crush it by force, occupy the country and set up martial law. *After the occupation of French Indo-China, next on our schedule is the sending of an ultimatum to the Netherlands Indies. In the seizing of Singapore the Navy will play the principal part.* As for the Army, in seizing Singapore it will need only one division and in seizing the Netherlands Indies, only two * * *.

In commenting on the observations made by Ambassador Nomura, Acting Secretary of State Sumner Wells on July 23, 1941, pointed out that any agreement which might have been concluded between the French Government at Vichy and Japan could only have resulted from pressure exerted on Vichy by Germany; and in that consequence this agreement could only be looked upon as offering assistance to Germany's policy of world domination and conquest. He further observed that conclusion of the agreement under discussion by the Secretary of State and Ambassador Nomura would bring about a far greater measure of economic security to Japan than she could secure through occupation of Indochina; that the policy of the United States was the opposite of an encirclement policy or of any policy which would be a threat to Japan; that Japan was not menaced by the policy of Great Britain and if an agreement had been concluded, Great Britain, the British Dominions, China, and the Netherlands would have joined the United States and Japan in support of the underlying principles stood for by the United States. He pointed out that the United States could only regard the action of Japan as constituting notice that the Japanese Government intended to pursue a policy of force and conquest, and, since there was no apparent basis calling for filling Indochina with Japanese military and other forces as a measure for defending Japan, the United States must assume that Japan was taking the last step before proceeding on a policy of expansion and conquest in the region of the South Seas. Finally, the Acting Secretary said that in these circumstances the Secretary of State—with whom he had talked a few minutes before—could not see any basis for pursuing further the conversations in which the Secretary and the Ambassador had been engaged.[54]

On July 24 Mr. Welles made a statement to the press in which he characterized the Japanese action in Indochina in substantially the

---

[52] Foreign Relations, vol. II, p. 340.
[53] Committee exhibit No. 1, p. 2.
[54] See Foreign Relations, vol. II, p. 341.

same terms as in his statement of the previous day to the Japanese Ambassador. He further pointed out that the actions of Japan endangered the use of the Pacific by peaceful nations; that these actions tended to jeopardize the procurement by the United States of essential materials such as tin and rubber, which were necessary in our defense program; and that the steps being taken by Japan endangered the safety of other areas of the Pacific, including the Philippine Islands.[55]

Also, on July 24, 1941, in the face of a progressive movement by Japan into southern Indochina, the President proposed to the Japanese Government that French Indochina be regarded as a "neutralized" country. This proposal contemplated that Japan would be given the fullest and freest opportunity of assuring for itself a source of food supplies and other raw materials which on the basis of Japan's own representations she was seeking to obtain. The Japanese Government did not accept the President's proposal. The answer of Japan was characteristically pragmatic and well described in the following language: [56]

> Large Japanese forces, however, soon were moved into southern Indochina. Japan's constant expansion of her military position in the southwest Pacific had already substantially imperiled the security of the United States along with that of other powers. By this further expansion in southern Indochina, Japan virtually completed the encirclement of the Philippine Islands and placed its armed forces within striking distance of vital trade routes. *This constituted an overt act directly menacing the security of the United States and other powers that were at peace with Japan.* It created a situation in which the risk of war became so great that the United States and other countries concerned were confronted no longer with the question of avoiding such risk but from then on with the problem of preventing a complete undermining of their security. No sooner were Japanese military forces moved into southern Indochina than there began to appear evidence that there was in progress a vigorous under-cover movement of Japanese infiltration into Thailand. With Japan's armed forces poised for further attacks, the possibility of averting armed conflict lay only in the bare chance that there might be reached some agreement which would cause Japan to abandon her policy and procedure of aggression. Under those circumstances and in the light of those considerations, the Government of the United States decided at that point, as did certain other governments especially concerned, that discontinuance of trade with Japan had become an appropriate, warranted and necessary step— as an open warning to Japan and as a measure of self-defense.

With the unsuccessful attempt to bring to a halt Japanese aggression in Indochina no further conversations were held on the subject of an agreement until August of 1941.

FREEZING OF ASSETS

It was clear that positive action must be taken under the circumstances for reasons well expressed by Secretary Hull in his testimony: [57]

> The hostilities between Japan and China had been in progress for four years. During those years the United States had continued to follow in its relations with Japan a policy of restraint and patience. It had done this notwithstanding constant violation by Japanese authorities or agents of American rights and legitimate interests in China, in neighboring areas, and even in Japan, and notwithstanding acts and statements by Japanese officials indicating a policy of widespread conquest by force and even threatening the United States. The American Government had sought, while protesting against Japanese acts and while yielding no rights, to make clear a willingness to work out with Japan by peaceful processes a basis for continuance of amicable relations with Japan. It had desired to give the Japanese every opportunity to turn of their own accord from their program of conquest toward peaceful policies.

---

[55] Id.
[56] Id., at p. 342.
[57] Committee record, pp. 1111-1113.

The President and I, in our effort to bring about the conclusion of an agreement, had endeavored to present to the Japanese Government a feasible alternative to Japan's indicated program of conquest. We had made abundantly clear our willingness to cooperate with Japan in a program based upon peaceful principles. We had repeatedly indicated that if such a program were adopted for the Pacific, and if thereafter any countries or areas within the Pacific were menaced, our Government would expect to cooperate with other governments in extending assistance to the region threatened.

While these discussions were going on in Washington, many responsible Japanese officials were affirming in Tokyo and elsewhere Japan's determination to pursue a policy of cooperation with her Axis allies. Both Mr. Matsuoka and his successor as Minister for Foreign Affairs had declared that the Three Power Pact stood and that Japanese policy was based upon that pact. Large-scale preparation by Japan for extension of her military activities was in progress, especially since early July. Notwithstanding our efforts expressly to impress upon the Japanese Government our Government's concern and our objection to movement by Japan with use or threat of force into Indochina, the Japanese Government had again obtained by duress from the Vichy Government an authorization and Japanese armed forces had moved into southern Indochina, occupied bases there, and were consolidating themselves there for further southward movements.

Confronted with the implacable attitude of Japan, President Roosevelt issued an Executive Order on July 26, 1941, freezing Japanese assets in the United States. This order brought under control of the Government all financial and import and export trade transactions in which Japanese interests were involved. The effect of the order was to bring to virtual cessation trade between the United States and Japan.[58]

It should be noted that shortly before large Japanese forces went into French Indochina, late in July, a change was effected in the Japanese Cabinet whereby Admiral Toyoda took over the portfolio of Foreign Affairs from Mr. Matsuoka. Thereafter the Japanese Prime Minister, the new Japanese Foreign Minister and Ambassador Nomura made emphatic and repeated protestations of Japan's desire for peace and an equitable settlement of Pacific problems. Despite these representations of peaceful intentions, the Japanese Government continued with mobilization in Japan, and dispatched increasing numbers of armed forces to Manchuria, Indochina, and south China. Bombing of American property in China continued, including bursts which damaged the American Embassy and the U. S. S. *Tutuila* at Chungking.[59] An intercepted message of July 19, 1941, from Tokyo to Berlin presented a candid estimate of the change in the Japanese Cabinet:[60]

The Cabinet shake-up was necessary to expedite matters in connection with National Affairs and has no further significance. Japan's foreign policy will not be changed and she will remain faithful to the principles of the Tripartite Pact

RESUMPTION OF NEGOTIATIONS AND PROPOSED MEETING OF PRESIDENT ROOSEVELT AND PREMIER KONOYE

The Japanese Government did not reply to the President's proposal of July 24, but on August 6 the Japanese Ambassador presented a proposal which, so he stated, purported to be responsive to that of the President. This proposal provided among other things:

(1) For removal of restrictions which the United States had imposed upon trade with Japan;

---

[58] Foreign Relations, vol. II, p. 343.
[59] Id., at p. 343.
[60] Committee exhibit No. 1, p. 3.

(2) For "suspension of its (the United States') military measures in the southwest Pacific area";

(3) For the exercise of good offices by the United States for the initiation of direct negotiations between Japan and China;

(4) For withdrawal of Japanese troops from Indochina *after* a settlement between Japan and China;

(5) For recognition by the United States of Japan's special position in Indochina even after the withdrawal of Japanese troops.

Throughout the negotiations it had been specified or implied that Japan would expect the United States, in the proposed exercise of its good offices between China and Japan, to discontinue aid to China. The Japanese proposal of August 6 completely ignored the proposal of the President to which it was allegedly responsive. It asked either expressly or by implication that the United States remove the restrictions it had imposed upon trade with Japan; suspend its defensive preparations in the Philippines; discontinue furnishing military equipment to Great Britain and the Netherlands for the arming of their far eastern possessions; discontinue aid to the Chinese Government; and acquiesce in Japan's assertion and exercise of a special military position and a permanent preferential political and economic status in Indochina, involving, as this would, assent to procedures and disposals which menaced the security of the United States and which were contrary to the principles to which this Government was committed. The Japanese Government in return offered not to station Japanese troops in regions of the southwestern Pacific other than Indochina. It proposed to retain its military establishment in Indochina for an indeterminate period. There thus would still have remained the menace to the security of the United States, already mentioned, as well as the menace to the security of British and Dutch territories in the southwestern Pacific area.

On August 8 Secretary Hull informed Japan's Ambassador that the Japanese proposal was not responsive to the President's proposal of July 24. Ambassador Nomura thereupon inquired whether it might be possible for President Roosevelt and Premier Konoye to meet with a view to discussing means for reaching an adjustment of views between the two Governments.[61] This suggestion was made pursuant to a dispatch from Tokyo to Ambassador Nomura which related in pertinent part:[62]

We are firm in our conviction that the only means by which the situation can be relieved is to have responsible persons representing each country gather together and hold direct conferences. They shall lay their cards on the table, express their true feelings, and attempt to determine a way out of the present situation.

In the first proposal made by the United States mention was made of just such a step. If, therefore, the United States is still agreeable to this plan, Prime Minister Konoye himself will be willing to meet and converse in a friendly manner with President Roosevelt.

Will you please make clear to them that we propose this step because we sincerely desire maintaining peace on the Pacific.

The sincerity of Japan's desire for peace and the appraisal of any hopes for a satisfactory settlement from such a meeting necessarily had to be viewed in the light of a statement only 7 days earlier in an intercepted dispatch from Tokyo to Ambassador Nomura:[63]

---

[61] Foreign Relations, vol. II, p. 344.
[62] Committee exhibit No. 1, p. 12.
[63] Id., at p. 10.

Thus, *all measures which our Empire shall take will be based upon a determination to bring about the success of the objectives of the Tripartite Pact.* That this *is* a fact is proven by the promulgation of an Imperial rescript. We are ever working toward the realization of those objectives, and now during this dire emergency is certainly no time to engage in any light unpremeditated or over-speedy action.

On August 18, the Japanese Minister for Foreign Affairs orally observed to Ambassador Grew that the only way to prevent the strained relations between the United States and Japan from further deterioration would be through a meeting of President Roosevelt and the Japanese Prime Minister. Strict secrecy concerning the proposal was urged upon our Ambassador for the reason that premature announcement of the meeting would result in the project being "torpedoed" by certain elements in Japan. The Japanese Government's concern for preserving the secrecy of the proposed meeting between the President and Premier Konoye is fully evinced in an intercepted dispatch from Tokyo to Washington on September 3, 1941:[64]

Since the existence of the Premier's message was inadvertently made known to the public, *that gang that has been suspecting that unofficial talks were taking place, has really begun to yell and wave the Tripartite Pact banner.*

In the midst of this confusion at home Fleisher's story in the Herald-Tribune relating the rumor of a proposed conference between the Premier and the President broke, which was unfortunate, to say the least, as you can well imagine.

The government is not afraid of the above-mentioned confusion; nor does it feel that that condition will destroy the fruits of the said conference. It is only that the government wished to keep the matter a secret until the arrangements had been completed. I am sure that you are aware that such a policy is not limited to just this case.

Because of the circumstances being what they are, we would like to make all arrangements for the meeting around the middle of September, with all possible speed, and issue a very simple statement to that effect as soon as possible. (If the middle of September is not convenient, any early date would meet with our approval.)

Will you please convey this wish of the government to Hull and wire us the results. If an immediate reply is not forthcoming, we plan to issue a public statement describing our position in this matter. We feel that this should be done from the viewpoint of our domestic situation. Please advise the United States of this plan.

The fact that the Konoye Cabinet desired the suggested meeting between the President and the Japanese Premier to be strictly secret for the reason that premature disclosure would result in frustration of the move by hostile elements in Japan would indicate beyond doubt that there existed in Japan a formidable opposition to efforts designed to achieve an improvement in relations with the United States.[65] Further, secrecy with respect to such a meeting would accomplish the additional purpose from the Japanese viewpoint of disguising from her Axis partners, Germany and Italy, the fact that steps might be undertaken which would in any way compromise Japan's commitments under the Tripartite Pact.

[*There will be found in Appendix D a detailed and comprehensive review of the diplomatic conversations between the United States and Japan, and related matters, during the critical period from the Atlantic Conference through December 8, 1941, in the light of the facts made public by this committee, to which reference is hereby made.*]

In connection with the proposed meeting it should be noted that President Roosevelt returned to Washington on August 17 from the

[64] Id., at p. 25.
[65] See Memoirs of Prince Fumimaro Konoye, committee exhibit No. 173.

Atlantic Conference at which the far eastern situation had been discussed with Mr. Churchill. It had been agreed by both the President and Prime Minister Churchill that more time was needed by both the United States and Britain to prepare their defenses against Japanese attack in the Far East. It was further agreed that steps should be taken to warn Japan against new moves of aggression. The President and Mr. Churchill were in agreement that this Government should be prepared to continue its conversations with the Government of Japan and thereby leave open to her a reasonable and just alternative to the aggressive course which she had mapped out for herself.

Upon his return to Washington from the Atlantic Conference, the President on August 17 handed the Japanese Ambassador two documents, one pointing out that the principles and policies under discussion in conversations between the two Governments precluded expansion by force or threat of force and that if the Japanese Government took any further steps in pursuance of a program of domination by force or threat of force of neighboring countries, the Government of the United States would be compelled to take any and all steps necessary toward insuring the security of the United States.[66] In the second document reference was made to the desire expressed earlier in August by the Japanese Government to resume conversations and to the Ambassador's suggestion of August 8 that President Roosevelt and the Japanese Minister meet with a view to discussing means for adjustment of relations between the United States and Japan. Reaffirmation was made of this Government's intention not to consider any proposals affecting the rights of either country except as such proposals might be in conformity with the basic principles to which the United States had long been committed and of its intention to continue to follow its policy of aiding nations resisting aggression.

It was pointed out that informal conversations with the Japanese Government relative to a peaceful settlement would naturally envisage the working out of a progressive program involving the application to the entire Pacific area of the principle of equality of commercial opportunity and treatment, thus making possible access by all countries to raw materials and other essential commodities; and that such a program would contemplate cooperation by all nations of the Pacific toward utilizing all available resources of capital, technical skill and economic leadership toward building up the economies of each country and toward increasing the purchasing power and raising the standards of living of the nations and peoples concerned. The opinion was expressed that if Japan was seeking what it affirmed to be its objectives the program outlined was one that could be counted upon to assure Japan satisfaction of its economic needs and legitimate aspirations with a far greater measure of certainty than could any other program. The statement was made that, in case Japan desired and was in a position to suspend its expansionist activities, to readjust its position, and to embark upon a peaceful program for the Pacific along the lines of the program and principles to which the United States was committed, the Government of the United States was prepared to consider resumption of the informal exploratory discussions which had been interrupted in July and would be glad to endeavor to arrange a suitable time and place to

---

Foreign Relations, vol. II, p. 556.

exchange views. It was also stated that, before renewal of the conversations or proceeding with plans for a meeting of the heads of the two Governments, it would be helpful if the Japanese Government would furnish a clearer statement than had as yet been given of its present attitude and plans. If the Japanese Government continued its movement of force and conquest, "we could not," the President said to the Ambassador, "think of reopening the conversations."

On August 28 the Japanese Ambassador handed the President a message from Premier Konoye urging a meeting between the heads of the Governments of the United States and Japan to discuss all important problems in the Pacific. This message was accompanied by a statement of the Japanese Government in which assurances were given, with several qualifications, of Japan's peaceful intentions and her desire to seek a program for the Pacific area consistent with the principles to which the United States had long been committed. The qualifications were voiced in the following terms: the Japanese Government was prepared to withdraw its troops from Indochina "as soon as the China incident is settled or a just peace is established in east Asia"; Japan would take no military action against the Soviet Union as long as the Soviet Union remained faithful to the Soviet-Japanese neutrality treaty and did "not menace Japan or Manchukuo or undertake any action contrary to the spirit of said treaty"; the Japanese Government had no intention of using "without provocation" military force against any neighboring nation.[67]

On September 3 the President handed the Japanese Ambassador the following "oral statement." [68]

Reference is made to the proposal of the Japanese Government communicated on August 28, 1941, by the Japanese Ambassador to the President of the United States that there be held as soon as possible a meeting between the responsible heads of the Government of Japan and of the Government of the United States to discuss important problems between Japan and the United States covering the entire Pacific area in an endeavor to save the situation and to the reply of the President of the United States, in which the President assured the Prime Minister of the readiness of the Government of the United States to move as rapidly as possible toward the consummation of arrangements for such a meeting and suggested that there be held preliminary discussion of important questions that would come up for consideration in the meeting. In further explanation of the views of the Government of the United States in regard to the suggestion under reference observations are offered, as follows:

On April 16, at the outset of the informal and exploratory conversations which were entered into by the Secretary of State with the Japanese Ambassador, the Secretary of State referred to four fundamental principles which this Government regards as the foundation upon which all relations between nations should properly rest. These four fundamental principles are as follows:

1. Respect for the territorial integrity and the sovereignty of each and all nations.

2. Support of the principle of noninterference in the internal affairs of other countries.

3. Support of the principle of equality, including equality of commercial opportunity.

4. Nondisturbance of the *status quo* in the Pacific except as the *status quo* may be altered by peaceful means.

In the subsequent conversations the Secretary of State endeavored to make it clear that in the opinion of the Government of the United States Japan stood to gain more from adherence to courses in harmony with these principles than from any other course, as Japan would thus best be assured access to the raw materials and markets which Japan needs and ways would be opened for mutually bene-ficial cooperation with the United States and other countries, and that only upon

[67] Id., at pp. 346, 347.
[68] Id., at pp. 589–591.

the basis of these principles could an agreement be reached which would be effective in establishing stability and peace in the Pacific area.

The Government of the United States notes with satisfaction that in the statement marked "Strictly Confidential" which was communicated by the Japanese Ambassador to the President of the United States on August 28 there were given specific assurances of Japan's peaceful intentions and assurances that Japan desires and seeks a program for the Pacific area consistent with the principles to which the Government of the United States has long been committed and which were set forth in detail in the informal conversations already referred to. The Government of the United States understands that the assurances which the Japanese Government has given in that statement exclude any policy which would seek political expansion or the acquisition of economic rights, advantages, or preferences by force.

The Government of the United States is very desirous of collaborating in efforts to make effective in practice the principles to which the Japanese Government has made reference. The Government of the United States believes that it is all-important that preliminary precautions be taken to insure the success of any efforts which the Governments of Japan and of the United States might make to collaborate toward a peaceful settlement. It will be recalled that in the course of the conversations to which reference has already been made, the Secretary of State on June 21, 1941, handed the Japanese Ambassador a document marked "Oral, Unofficial, and Without Commitment" which contained a redraft of the Japanese Government's proposal of May 12, 1941. It will be recalled further that in oral discussion of this draft it was found that there were certain fundamental questions with respect to which there were divergences of view between the two Governments, and which remained unreconciled at the time the conversations were interrupted in July. *The Government of the United States desires to facilitate progress toward a conclusive discussion, but believes that a community of view and a clear agreement upon the points above-mentioned are essential to any satisfactory settlement of Pacific questions.* It therefore seeks an indication of the present attitude of the Japanese Government with regard to the fundamental questions under reference.

It goes without saying that each Government in reaching decisions on policy must take into account the internal situation in its own country and the attitude of public opinion therein. The Government of Japan will surely recognize that the Government of the United States could not enter into any agreement which would not be in harmony with the principles in which the American people—in fact all nations that prefer peaceful methods to methods of force—believe.

The Government of the United States would be glad to have the reply of the Japanese Government on the matters above set forth.

The formal reply of the President to the Japanese Prime Minister was handed Ambassador Nomura on September 3, and follows: [69]

I have read with appreciation Your Excellency's message of August 27, which was delivered to me by Admiral Nomura.

I have noted with satisfaction the sentiments expressed by you in regard to the solicitude of Japan for the maintenance of the peace of the Pacific and Japan's desire to improve Japanese-American relations.

I fully share the desire expressed by you in these regards, and I wish to assure you that the Government of the United States, recognizing the swiftly moving character of world events, is prepared to proceed as rapidly as possible toward the consummation of arrangements for a meeting at which you and I can exchange views and endeavor to bring about an adjustment in the relations between our two countries.

In the statement which accompanied your letter to me reference was made to the principles to which the Government of the United States has long been committed, and it was declared that the Japanese Government "considers these principles and the practical application thereof, in the friendliest manner possible, are the prime requisites of a true peace and should be applied not only in the Pacific area but throughout the entire world" and that "such a program has long been desired and sought by Japan itself."

I am very desirous of collaborating with you in efforts to make these principles effective in practice. Because of my deep interest in this matter I find it necessary that I constantly observe and take account of developments both in my own country and in Japan which have a bearing upon problems of relations between our two countries. At this particular moment I cannot avoid taking cognizance of indications of the existence in some quarters in Japan of concepts which, if

⁶⁹ Id., at pp. 591, 592.

widely entertained, would seem capable of raising obstacles to successful collaboration between you and me along the line which I am sure we both earnestly desire to follow.' Under these circumstances, I feel constrained to suggest, in the belief that you will share my view, that it would seem highly desirable that *we take precaution, toward ensuring that our proposed meeting shall prove a success, by endeavoring to enter immediately upon preliminary discussion of the fundamental and essential questions on which we seek agreement.*   The questions which I have in mind for such preliminary discussions involve practical application of the principles fundamental to achievement and maintenance of peace which are mentioned with more specification in the statement accompanying your letter.   I hope that you will look favorably upon this suggestion.

The decision to defer any meeting between the President and the Japanese Prime Minister pending preliminary discussions of fundamental and essential questions was deliberate and well considered. Secretary Hull testified fully concerning the considerations attending the decision: [70]

A meeting between the President and Prince Konoe [70a] would have been a significant step.   Decision whether it should be undertaken by our Government involved several important considerations.

We knew that *Japanese leaders were unreliable and treacherous.*   We asked ourselves whether the military element in Japan would permit the civilian element, even if so disposed, to stop Japan's course of expansion by force and to revert to peaceful courses.   Time and again the civilian leaders gave assurances; time and again the military took aggressive action in direct violation of those assurances.   Japan's past and contemporary record was replete with instances of military aggression and expansion by force.   *Since 1931 and especially since 1937 the military in Japan exercised a controlling voice in Japan's national policy.*

Japan's formal partnership with Nazi Germany in the Tripartite Alliance was a hard and inescapable fact.   The Japanese had been consistently unwilling in the conversations to pledge their Government to renounce Japan's commitments in the alliance.   They would not state that Japan would refrain from attacking this country if it became involved through self-defense in the European war.   *They held on to the threat against the United States implicit in the alliance.*

Our Government could not ignore the fact that throughout the conversations the Japanese spokesmen had made a *practice of offering general formulas* and, when pressed for explanation of the meaning, had consistently narrowed and made more rigid their application.   This suggested that when military leaders became aware of the generalized formulas they insisted upon introducing conditions which watered down the general assurances.

A meeting between the President and the Japanese Prime Minister would have had important psychological results.

It would have had a *critically discouraging effect upon the Chinese.*

If the proposed meeting should merely endorse general principles, the Japanese in the light of their past practice could have been expected to utilize such general principles in support of any interpretation which Japan might choose to place upon them.

If the proposed meeting did not produce an agreement, the Japanese military leaders would then have been in a position to declare that the United States was responsible for the failure of the meeting.

The Japanese had already refused to agree to any preliminary steps toward reversion to peaceful courses, as, for example, adopting the President's proposal of July 24 regarding the neutralization of Indochina.   Instead they steadily moved on with their program of establishing themselves more firmly in Indochina.

It was clear to us that *unless the meeting produced concrete and clear-cut commitments toward peace, the Japanese would have distorted the significance of the meeting in such a way as to weaken greatly this country's moral position and to facilitate their aggressive course.*

The acts of Japan under Konoe's Prime Ministership could not be overlooked.

He had headed the Japanese Government in 1937 when Japan attacked China and when huge Japanese armies poured into that country and occupied its principal cities and industrial regions.

He was Prime Minister when Japanese armed forces attacked the U. S. S. *Panay* on the Yangtze River on December 12, 1937.

---

[70] Committee record, pp. 1120–1124.   For a thoroughgoing discussion of events and circumstances attending the proposed meeting between President Roosevelt and Prince Konoye, see Appendix D.
[70a] It is to be noted that except in those instances where the name appears in direct quotations, the Japanese Prime Minister's name is spelled *Konoye*, rather than *Konoe*.

He was Prime Minister when Japanese armed forces committed notorious outrages in Nanking in 1937.

He as Prime Minister had proclaimed in 1938 the basic principles upon which the Japanese Government, even throughout the 1941 conversations, stated that it would insist in any peace agreement with China. Those principles in application included stationing large bodies of Japanese troops in North China. They would have enabled Japan to retain a permanent stranglehold on China.

He had been Prime Minister when the Japanese Government concluded in 1940 with the Chinese Quisling regime at Nanking a "treaty" embodying the stranglehold principles mentioned in the preceding paragraph.

Prince Konoe had been Japanese Prime Minister when Japan signed the Tripartite Pact with Germany and Italy in 1940.

As a result of our close-up conversations with the Japanese over a period of months, in which they showed no disposition to abandon their course of conquest, *we were thoroughly satisfied that a meeting with Konoe could only result either in another Munich or in nothing at all, unless Japan was ready to give some clear evidence of a purpose to move in a peaceful direction.* I was opposed to the first Munich and still more opposed to a second Munich.

Our Government ardently desired peace. It could not brush away the realities in the situation.

Although the President would, as he said, "have been happy to travel thousands of miles to meet the Premier of Japan," it was felt that in view of the factors mentioned the President could go to such a meeting only if there were first obtained tentative commitments offering some assurance that the meeting could accomplish good. Neither Prince Konoe nor any of Japan's spokesmen provided anything tangible.[71]

JAPANESE PROPOSALS OF SEPTEMBER 6 AND 27

On September 6 Ambassador Nomura handed Secretary Hull the following proposal:[72]

The Government of Japan undertakes:

(a) that Japan is ready to express its concurrence in those matters which were already tentatively agreed upon between Japan and the United States in the course of their preliminary informal conversations;

(b) that Japan will not make any military advancement from French Indochina against any of its adjoining areas, and likewise will not, without any justifiable reason, resort to military action against any regions lying south of Japan;

(c) that the attitudes of Japan and the United States towards the European War will be decided by the concepts of protection and self-defense, and, in case the United States should participate in the European War, the interpretation and execution of the Tripartite Pact by Japan shall be independently decided;

(d) that Japan will endeavour to bring about the rehabilitation of general and normal relationship between Japan and China, upon the realization of which Japan is ready to withdraw its armed forces from China as soon as possible in accordance with the agreements between Japan and China;

(e) that the economic activities of the United States in China will not be restricted so long as pursued on an equitable basis;

---

[71] The Konoye Memoirs reflect that the Japanese Navy approved the idea of a meeting between the President and the Japanese Prime Minister whereas the Army viewed such a meeting as of questioned desirability. After outlining his ideas with respect to such a meeting Prince Konoye observed: "Both the War and Navy Ministers listened to me intently. Neither could give me an immediate reply but before the day (August 4, 1941) was over, the Navy expressed complete accord and, moreover, anticipated the success of the conference. The War Minister's reply came in writing, as follows:

" 'If the Prime Minister were to personally meet with the President of the United States, the existing diplomatic relations of the Empire, which are based on the Tripartite Pact, would unavoidably be weakened. At the same time, a considerable domestic stir would undoubtedly be created. For these reasons, the meeting is not considered a suitable move. The attempt to surmount the present critical situation by the Prime Minister's offering his personal services is viewed with sincere respect and admiration. *If, therefore, it is the Prime Minister's intention to attend such a meeting, with determination to firmly support the basic principles embodied in the Empire's revised plan to the N plan and to carry out a war against America if the President of the United States still fails to comprehend the true intentions of the Empire even after this final effort is made, the army is not necessarily in disagreement.*

" 'However, (1) it is not in favor of the meeting if, after making preliminary investigations, it is learned that the meeting will be with someone other than the President, such as Secretary Hull or one in a lesser capacity; (2) *you shall not resign your post as a result of the meeting on the grounds that it was a failure; rather, you shall be prepared to assume leadership in the war against America.'*

"The War Minister was of the opinion that 'failure of this meeting is the greater likelihood.' " See committee exhibit No. 173, pp. 30, 31.

[72] Foreign Relations, vol. II, pp. 608, 609.

(f) that Japan's activities in the Southwestern Pacific Area will be carried on by peaceful means and in accordance with the principle of nondiscrimination in international commerce, and that Japan will cooperate in the production and procurement by the United States of natural resources in the said area which it needs;

(g) that Japan will take measures necessary for the resumption of normal trade relations between Japan and the United States, and in connection with the above-mentioned, Japan is ready to discontinue immediately the application of the foreigners' transactions control regulations with regard to the United States on the basis of reciprocity.

The Government of the United States undertakes:

"(a) that, in response to the Japanese Government's commitment expressed in point (d) referred to above, the United States will abstain from any measures and actions which will be prejudicial to the endeavour by Japan concerning the settlement of the China Affair;

"(b) that the United States will reciprocate Japan's commitment expressed in point (f) referred to above;

"(c) that the United States will suspend any military measures in the Far East and in the Southwestern Pacific Area;

"(d) that the United States will immediately [upon settlement] reciprocate Japan's commitment expressed in point (g) referred to above by discontinuing the application of the so-called freezing act with regard to Japan and further by removing the prohibition against the passage of Japanese vessels through the Panama Canal."

Secretary Hull made the following comments with respect to the foregoing Japanese proposal: [73]

On September 6 the Japanese Ambassador presented a new draft of proposals. These proposals were much narrower than the assurances given in the statement communicated to the President on August 28. In the September 6 Japanese draft the Japanese gave only an evasive formula with regard to their obligations under the Tripartite Pact. There was a qualified undertaking that Japan would not "without any justifiable reason" resort to military action against any region south of Japan. No commitment was offered in regard to the nature of the terms which Japan would offer to China; nor any assurance of an intention by Japan to respect China's territorial integrity and sovereignty, to refrain from interference in China's internal affairs, not to station Japanese troops indefinitely in wide areas of China, and to conform to the principle of nondiscrimination in international commercial relations. The formula contained in the draft that "the economic activities of the United States in China will not be restricted *so long as pursued* on an equitable basis" [italics added] clearly implied a concept that the conditions under which American trade and commerce in China were henceforth to be conducted were to be a matter for decision by Japan.[74]

From time to time during September of 1941 discussions were held between Secretary Hull and the Japanese Ambassador. On September 27, Ambassador Nomura presented a complete redraft of the Japanese proposals of September 6, following the form of the American proposals of June 21. On October 2, Secretary Hull replied to the proposals made by the Japanese Ambassador during September, handing the Ambassador an "oral statement" reviewing significant developments in the conversations and explaining our Government's attitude toward various points in the Japanese proposals which our Government did not consider consistent with the principles to which this country was committed. He said: [75]

Disappointment was expressed over the narrow character of the outstanding Japanese proposals, and questions were raised in regard to Japan's intentions regarding the indefinite stationing of Japanese troops in wide areas of China and regarding Japan's relationship to the Axis Powers. While welcoming the Japanese suggestion of a meeting between the President and the Japanese Prime

[73] Committee record, pp. 1118, 1119.
[74] The Konoye Memoirs reveal that on September 6 an imperial conference was held at which were determined the basic principles of the Japanese Empire's national policy. Among these principles was the understanding that in case there was no way found for attainment of Japanese demands by early in October of 1941, the Empire should at once determine to make up its mind to get ready for war against the United States, Great Britain, and the Netherlands. Committee exhibit No. 173.
[75] Committee record, pp. 1124–1126.

Minister, we proposed, in order to lay a firm foundation for such a meeting, that renewed consideration be given to fundamental principles so as to reach a meeting of minds on essential questions. It was stated in conclusion that the subject of the meeting proposed by the Prime Minister and the objectives sought had engaged the close and active interest of the President and that it was the President's earnest hope that discussion of the fundamental questions might be so developed that such a meeting could be held.

During this period there was a further advance of Japanese armed forces in Indochina, Japanese military preparations at home were increased and speeded up, and there continued Japanese bombing of Chinese civilian populations, constant agitation in the Japanese press in support of extremist policies, and the unconciliatory and bellicose utterances of Japanese leaders. For example, Captain Hideo Hiraide, director of the naval intelligence section of Imperial Headquarters, was quoted on October 16 as having declared in a public speech:

"America, feeling her insecurity * * * , is carrying out naval expansion on a large scale. But at present America is unable to carry out naval operations in both the Atlantic and Pacific simultaneously.

"*The imperial navy is prepared for the worst and has completed all necessary preparations. In fact, the imperial navy is itching for action, when needed.*

"In spite of strenuous efforts by the government, the situation is now approaching a final parting of the ways. The fate of our empire depends upon how we act at this moment. It is certain that at such a moment our Navy should set about on its primary mission."

It is of interest to note the Japanese estimate of Secretary Hull's position in the negotiations, reflected in an intercepted message of September 15 from Nomura to Tokyo:[76]

Whatever we tell to Secretary Hull you should understand will surely be passed on to the President if he is in Washington. It seems that the matter of preliminary conversations has been entrusted by the President to Secretary Hull, in fact he told me that if a matter could not be settled by me and Secretary Hull it would not be settled whoever conducted the conversations. Hull himself told me that during the past eight years he and the President had not differed on foreign policies once, and that they are as "two in one."

Advent of the Tojo Cabinet

The Konoye Cabinet fell on October 16, 1941, and was replaced on the following day by a new cabinet headed by General Hideki Tojo.[76a] On October 17 a dispatch from Tokyo to Washington was intercepted manifesting a disposition by the Tojo Cabinet to continue the negotiations: [77]

The Cabinet has reached a decision to resign as a body. At this time I wish to thank Your Excellency and your entire staff for all the efforts you have made.

The resignation was brought about by a split within the Cabinet. It is true that one of the main items on which opinion differed was on the matter of stationing troops or evacuating them from China. However, regardless of the make-up of the new Cabinet, negotiations with the United States shall be continued along the lines already formulated. There shall be no changes in this respect.

Please, therefore, will you and your staff work in unison and a single purpose, with even more effort, if possible, than before.

The situation existing from the advent of the Tojo Cabinet to the arrival of Saburo Kurusu in Washington on November 15 to assist Ambassador Nomura in the conversations was depicted by Secretary Hull as follows: [78]

On October 17 the American press carried the following statement by Maj. Gen. Kiyofuku Okamoto:

"Despite the different views advanced on the Japanese-American question, our national policy for solution of the China affair and establishment of a common coprosperity sphere in East Asia remains unaltered.

---

[76] Committee exhibit No. 1, p. 27.
[76a] For a complete discussion of the fall of the Konoye Cabinet, see Appendix D.
[77] Id., at p. 76.
[78] Committee record, pp. 1127–34.

"For fulfillment of this national policy, this country has sought to reach an agreement of views with the U. S. by means of diplomatic means. There is, however, a limit to our concessions, and the negotiations may end in a break with the worst possible situation following. The people must therefore be resolved to cope with such a situation."

Clearly the Japanese war lords expected to clinch their policy of aggrandizement and have the United States make all the concessions.

On October 30, the Japanese Foreign Minister told the American Ambassador that the Japanese Government desired that the conversations be concluded successfully without delay and he said that "in order to make progress, the United States should face certain realities and facts," and here thereupon cited the stationing in China of Japanese armed forces.

The general world situation continued to be very critical, rendering it desirable that every reasonable effort be made to avoid or at least to defer as long as possible any rupture in the conversations. From here on for some weeks especially intensive study was given in the Department of State to the possibility of reaching some stopgap arrangement with the Japanese so as to tide over the immediate critical situation and thus to prevent a break-down in the conversations, and even perhaps to pave the way for a subsequent general agreement. The presentation to the Japanese of a proposal which would serve to keep alive the conversations would also give our Army and Navy time to prepare and to expose Japan's bad faith if it did not accept. We considered every kind of suggestion we could find which might help or keep alive the conversations and at the same time be consistent with the integrity of American principles.

In the last part of October and early November messages came to this Government from United States Army and Navy officers in China and from Generalissimo Chiang Kai-shek stating that he believed that a Japanese attack on Kunming was imminent. The Generalissimo requested that the United States send air units to China to defeat this threat. He made a similar request of the British Government. He also asked that the United States issue a warning to Japan.

At this time the Chinese had been resisting the Japanese invaders for 4 years. China sorely needed equipment. Its economic and financial situations were very bad. Morale was naturally low. In view of this, even though a Chinese request might contain points with which we could not comply, we dealt with any such request in a spirit of utmost consideration befitting the gravity of the situation confronting our hard-pressed Chinese friends.

I suggested that the War and Navy Departments study this Chinese appeal. In response, the Chief of Staff and the Chief of Naval Operations sent a memorandum of November 5 to the President giving an estimate concerning the Far Eastern situation. At the conclusion of this estimate the Chief of Staff and the Chief of Naval Operations recommended:

"That the dispatch of United States armed forces for intervention against Japan in China be disapproved.

"That material aid to China be accelerated consonant with the needs of Russia, Great Britain, and our own forces.

"That aid to the American Volunteer Group be continued and accelerated to the maximum practicable extent.

"That no ultimatum be delivered to Japan."

I was in thorough accord with the views of the Chief of Staff and the Chief of Naval Operations that United States armed forces should not be sent to China for use against Japan. I also believed so far as American foreign policy considerations were involved that material aid to China should be accelerated as much as feasible, and that aid to the American Volunteer Group should be accelerated. Finally, I concurred completely in the view that no ultimatum should be delivered to Japan. I had been striving for months to avoid a show-down with Japan, and to explore every possible avenue for averting or delaying war between the United States and Japan. That was the cornerstone of the effort which the President and I were putting forth with our utmost patience.

On November 14 the President replied to Generalissimo Chiang Kai-shek, in line with the estimate and recommendations contained in the memorandum of November 5 of the Chief of Staff and the Chief of Naval Operations. The Generalissimo was told that from our information it did not appear that a Japanese land campaign against Kunming was immediately imminent. It was indicated that American air units could not be sent and that the United States would not issue a warning but there were outlined ways, mentioned in the memorandum of the Chief of Staff and the Chief of Naval Operations, in which the United States would continue to assist China.

On November 7, I attended the regular Cabinet meeting. It was the President's custom either to start off the discussion himself or to ask some member of the Cabinet a question. At this meeting he turned to me and asked whether I had anything in mind. I thereupon pointed out for about 15 minutes the dangers in the international situation. I went over fully developments in the conversations with Japan and emphasized that in my opinion relations were extremely critical and that we should be on the lookout for a military attack anywhere by Japan at any time. When I finished, the President went around the Cabinet. All concurred in my estimate of the dangers. It became the consensus of the Cabinet that the critical situation might well be emphasized in speeches in order that the country would, if possible, be better prepared for such a development.

Accordingly, Secretary of the Navy Knox delivered an address on November 11, 1941, in which he stated that we were not only confronted with the necessity of extreme measures of self-defense in the Atlantic, but we were "likewise faced with grim possibilities on the other side of the world—on the far side of the Pacific"; that the Pacific no less than the Atlantic called for instant readiness for defense.

On the same day Under Secretary of State Welles in an address stated that beyond the Atlantic a sinister and pitiless conqueror had reduced more than half of Europe to abject serfdom and that in the Far East the same forces of conquest were menacing the safety of all nations bordering on the Pacific. The waves of world conquest were "breaking high both in the East and in the West," he said, and were threatening, more and more with each passing day, "to engulf our own shores." He warned that the United States was in far greater peril than in 1917; that "at any moment war may be forced upon us."

Early in November the Japanese Government decided to send Mr. Saburo Kurusu to Washington to assist the Japanese Ambassador in the conversations.

On November 7, the Japanese Ambassador handed me a document containing draft provisions relating to Japanese forces in China, Japanese forces in Indochina, and the principle of nondiscrimination. That proposal contained nothing fundamentally new or offering any real recessions from the position consistently maintained by the Japanese Government.

In telegrams of November 3 and November 17 the American Ambassador in Japan cabled warnings of the possibility of sudden Japanese attacks which might make inevitable war with the United States.

In the first half of November there were several indeterminate conversations with the Japanese designed to clarify specific points. On November 15 I gave the Japanese Ambassador an outline for a possible joint declaration by the United States and Japan on economic policy. I pointed out that this represented but one part of the general settlement we had in mind. This draft declaration of economic policy envisaged that Japan could join with the United States in leading the way toward a general application of economic practices which would give Japan much of what her leaders professed to desire.

On November 12 the Japanese Foreign Office, both through Ambassador Grew and through their Ambassador here, urged that the conversations be brought to a settlement at the earliest possible time. In view of the pressing insistence of the Japanese for a definitive reply to their outstanding proposals, I was impelled to comment to the Japanese Ambassador on November 15 that the American Government did not feel that it should be receiving such representations, suggestive of ultimatums.

On November 15 Mr. Kurusu reached Washington. On November 17 he and the Japanese Ambassador called on me and later on the same day on the President.

ARRIVAL OF SABURO KURUSU

Mr. Kurusu in his initial conversation with President Roosevelt and Secretary Hull indicated that Prime Minister Tojo desired a peaceful adjustment of differences. At the same time it was clear that Kurusu had nothing new to suggest concerning Japan's participation in the Tripartite Pact or the presence of her troops in China. The President reiterated the desire of the United States to avoid war between the two countries and to effect a peaceful settlement of divergent positions in the Pacific. The Secretary of State, setting forth his comments at the conference, stated: [79]

---

[79] Foreign Relations, vol. II, pp. 740, 741.

Ambassador Kurusu made some specious attempt to explain away the Tripartite Pact. I replied in language similar to that which I used in discussing this matter with Ambassador Nomura on November fifteenth, which need not be repeated here. I made it clear that any kind of a peaceful settlement for the Pacific area, with Japan still clinging to her Tripartite Pact with Germany, would cause the President and myself to be denounced in immeasurable terms and the peace arrangement would not for a moment be taken seriously while all of the countries interested in the Pacific would redouble their efforts to arm against Japanese aggression. I emphasized the point about the Tripartite Pact and self-defense by saying that when Hitler starts on a march of invasion across the earth with ten million soldiers and thirty thousand airplanes with an official announcement that he is out for unlimited invasion objectives, this country from that time was in danger and that danger has grown each week until this minute. The result was that this country with no other motive except self-defense has recognized that danger, and has proceeded thus far to defend itself before it is too late; and that the Government of Japan says that it does not know whether this country is thus acting in self-defense or not. This country feels so profoundly the danger that it has committed itself to ten, twenty-five, or fifty billions of dollars in self-defense; but when Japan is asked about whether this is self-defense, she indicates that she has no opinion on the subject—I said that I cannot get this view over to the American people; that they believe Japan must know that we are acting in self-defense and, therefore, they do not understand her present attitude. I said that he was speaking of their political difficulties and that I was thus illustrating some of our difficulties in connection with this country's relations with Japan.

In a further conversation with Ambassador Nomura and Mr. Kurusu on November 18, Secretary Hull's observations were related in the following terms: [80]

The Secretary of State conferred again with the Japanese Ambassador and Mr. Kurusu on November 18. The Secretary expressed great doubt whether any agreement into which we entered with Japan while Japan had an alliance with Hitler would carry the confidence of our people. He said that a difficult situation was created when, for example, telegrams of congratulation were sent to Hitler by Japanese leaders when he commits some atrocity, and he emphasized that we would have to have a clear-cut agreement making clear our peaceful purpose, for otherwise there would be a redoubled effort by all nations to strengthen their armaments. He pointed out that we were trying to make a contribution to the establishment of a peaceful world, based on law and order. He said that this is what we want to work out with Japan; that we had nothing to offer in the way of bargaining except our friendship. He said that frankly he did not know whether anything could be done in the matter of reaching a satisfactory agreement with Japan; that we can go so far but rather than go beyond a certain point it would be better for us to stand and take the consequences.

During the discussion Ambassador Nomura and Mr. Kurusu suggested the possibility of a *modus vivendi* or a temporary arrangement to tide over the abnormal situation.[81] They offered as a possibility return to the status prevailing prior to July 26, 1941, when Japanese assets in the United States were frozen following Japan's entry into southern French Indochina. To this suggestion, Secretary Hull replied: [82]

I said that if we should make some modifications in our embargo on the strength of such a step by Japan as the Ambassador had mentioned, we would not know whether the troops to be withdrawn from French Indochina would be diverted to some equally objectionable movement elsewhere. I said that it would be difficult for our Government to go a long way in removing the embargo unless we believed that Japan was definitely started on a peaceful course and had renounced purposes of conquest. I said that I would consult with the representatives of other countries on this suggestion. On the same day I informed the British Minister of my talk with the Japanese about the suggestion of a temporary limited arrangement.

---

[80] Id., at p. 363.
[81] See committee record, p. 1135.
[82] Id.

Negotiations *versus* Deadlines

In a conversation with the Secretary of State on November 19, the Japanese emissaries made it clear that Japan could not abrogate the Tripartite Alliance and regarded herself as bound to carry out its obligations. Through all of the discussions it was evident that Japan was pressing for an early decision. In a series of "deadlines" (now known to have been keyed to the contemplated departure of the task force that struck Pearl Harbor) contained in intercepted messages from Tokyo to Washington the urgency of the negotiations was explained:

November 5, 1941, circular No. 736.[83]

Because of various circumstances, *it is absolutely necessary that all arrangements for the signing of this agreement be completed by the 25th of this month.* I realize that this is a difficult order, but under the circumstances it is an unavoidable one. Please understand this thoroughly and tackle the problem of saving the Japanese-U. S. relations from falling into chaotic condition. Do so with great determination and with unstinted effort, I beg of you.

This information is to be kept strictly to yourself only.

November 11, 1941, circular No. 762.[84]

Judging from the progress of the conversations, there seem to be indications that the United States is still not fully aware of the exceedingly criticalness of the situation here. *The fact remains that the date set forth in my message #736 is absolutely immovable under present conditions. It is a definite dead-line and therefore it is essential that a settlement be reached by about that time.* The session of Parliament opens on the 15th (work will start on [the following day?]) according to the schedule. The government must have a clear picture of things to come, in presenting its case at the session. You can see, therefore, that the situation is nearing a climax, and that time is indeed becoming short.

I appreciate the fact that you are making strenuous efforts, but in view of the above mentioned situation, will you redouble them. When talking to the Secretary of State and others, drive the points home to them. Do everything in your power to get a clear picture of the U. S. attitude in the minimum amount of time. *At the same time do everything in your power to have them give their speedy approval to our final proposal.*

We would appreciate being advised of your opinions on whether or not they will accept our final proposal A.

November 22, 1941, circular No. 812.[85]

To both you Ambassadors.

It is awfully hard for us to consider changing the date we set in my No. 736. You should know this, however, I know you are working hard. Stick to our fixed policy and do your very best. Spare no efforts and try to bring about the solution we desire. There are reasons beyond your ability to guess why we wanted to settle Japanese-American relations by the 25th, but if within the next three or four days you can finish your conversations with the Americans; *if the signing can be completed by the 29th* (let me write it out for you—twenty-ninth); if the pertinent notes can be exchanged; if we can get an understanding with Great Britain and the Netherlands; and in short if everything can be finished, we have decided to wait until that date. This time we mean it, that the dead line absolutely cannot be changed. *After that things are automatically going to happen.* Please take this into your careful consideration and work harder than you ever have before. This, for the present, is for the information of you two Ambassadors alone.

Japanese Ultimatum of November 20 and the *Modus Vivendi*

During a conversation with Secretary Hull on November 20 the Japanese Ambassador presented a proposal which was in fact an ultimatum, reading as follows: [86].

---

[83] Committee exhibit No. 1, p. 100.
[84] Id., at p. 116.
[85] Id., at p. 165.
[86] Foreign Relations, vol. II, pp. 366, 367.

1. Both the Governments of Japan and the United States undertake not to make any armed advancement into any of the regions in the Southeastern Asia and the Southern Pacific area excepting the part of French Indo-China where the Japanese troops are stationed at present.

2. The Japanese Government undertakes to withdraw its troops now stationed in French Indo-China upon either the restoration of peace between Japan and China or the establishment of an equitable peace in the Pacific area.

In the meantime the Government of Japan declares that it is prepared to remove its troops now stationed in the southern part of French Indo-China to the northern part of the said territory upon the conclusion of the present arrangement which shall later be embodied in the final agreement.

3. The Government of Japan and the United States shall cooperate with a view to securing the acquisition of those goods and commodities which the two countries need in Netherlands East Indies.

4. The Governments of Japan and the United States mutually undertake to restore their commercial relations to those prevailing prior to the freezing of the assets.

The Government of the United States shall supply Japan a required quantity of oil.

5. The Government of the United States undertakes to refrain from such measures and actions as will be prejudicial to the endeavors for the restoration of general peace between Japan and China.

In his testimony Secretary Hull observed with respect to the foregoing proposal: [87]

On November 20 the Japanese Ambassador and Mr. Kurusu presented to me a proposal which on its face was extreme. I knew, as did other high officers of the Government, from intercepted Japanese messages supplied to me by the War and Navy Departments, that this proposal was the final Japanese proposition—*an ultimatum.*

The plan thus offered called for the supplying by the United States to Japan of as much oil as Japan might require, for suspension of freezing measures, for discontinuance by the United States of aid to China, and for withdrawal of moral and material support from the recognized Chinese Government. It contained a provision that Japan would shift her armed forces from southern Indochina to northern Indochina, but placed no limit on the number of armed forces which Japan might send to Indochina and made no provision for withdrawal of those forces until after either the restoration of peace between Japan and China or the establishment of an "equitable" peace in the Pacific area. While there were stipulations against further extension of Japan's armed force into southeastern Asia and the southern Pacific (except Indochina), there were no provisions which would have prevented continued or fresh Japanese aggressive activities in any of the regions of Asia lying to the north of Indochina—for example, China and the Soviet Union. The proposal contained no provision pledging Japan to abandon aggression and to revert to peaceful courses.

There can now be no question that Japan intended her proposal of November 20 as an ultimatum. It was their final proposal [88] and a deadline of November 25, subsequently changed to November 29, had been set for its acceptance. It was a proposal which the Government of Japan knew we could not accept. It was the final gesture of the Tojo Cabinet before launching the vast campaign of aggression which the military overlords of Japan had long before decided upon.

The critical situation culminating in consideration of a *modus vivendi* was revealed by Secretary Hull: [89]

On November 21 we received word from the Dutch that they had information that a Japanese force had arrived near Palao, the nearest point in the Japanese Mandated Islands to the heart of the Netherlands Indies. Our Consuls at Hanoi and Saigon had been reporting extensive new landings of Japanese troops and equipment in Indochina. We had information through intercepted Japanese messages that the Japanese Government had decided that the negotiations must

[87] Committee record, pp. 1136–1138.

[88] In an intercepted dispatch from Tokyo to Washington on November 19, the Japanese Government stated, in referring to the ultimatum presented to the United States on the following day: "If the United States consent to this cannot be secured, the negotiations will have to be broken off: therefore, with the above well in mind put forth your very best efforts." Committee exhibit No. 1, p. 155.

[89] Committee record, pp. 1138–1141.

be terminated by November 25, later extended to November 29. We knew from other intercepted Japanese messages that the Japanese did not intend to make any concessions, and from this fact taken together with Kurusu's statement to me of November 21 making clear that his Government had nothing further to offer, it was plain, as I have mentioned, that the Japanese proposal of November 20 was in fact their "absolutely final proposal."

The whole issue presented was whether Japan would yield in her avowed movement of conquest or whether we would yield the fundamental principles for which we stood in the Pacific and all over the world. By midsummer of 1941 we were pretty well satisfied that the Japanese were determined to continue with their course of expansion by force. We had made it clear to them that we were standing fast by our principles. It was evident, however, that they were playing for the chance that we might be overawed into yielding by their threats of force. They were armed to the teeth and we knew they would attack whenever and wherever they pleased. If by chance we should have yielded our fundamental principles, Japan would probably not have attacked for the time being—at least not until she had consolidated the gains she would have made without fighting.

There was never any question of this country forcing Japan to fight. The question was whether this country was ready to sacrifice its principles.

To have accepted the Japanese proposal of November 20 was clearly unthinkable. It would have made the United States an ally of Japan in Japan's program of conquest and aggression and of collaboration with Hitler. It would have meant yielding to the Japanese demand that the United States abandon its principles and policies. It would have meant abject surrender of our position under intimidation.

The situation was critical and virtually hopeless. On the one hand our Government desired to exhaust all possibilities of finding a means to a peaceful solution and to avert or delay an armed clash, especially as the heads of this country's armed forces continued to emphasize the need of time to prepare for resistance. On the other hand, Japan was calling for a showdown.

There the situation stood—the Japanese unyielding and intimidating in their demands and we standing firmly for our principles.

The chances of meeting the crisis by diplomacy had practically vanished. We had reached the point of clutching at straws.

Three possible choices presented themselves.

Our Government might have made no reply. The Japanese war lords could then have told their people that the American Government not only would make no reply but would also not offer any alternative.

Our Government might have rejected flatly the Japanese proposal. In that event the Japanese war lords would be afforded a pretext, although wholly false, for military attack.

Our Government might endeavor to present a reasonable counter-proposal.

The last course was the one chosen.

Full consideration was given by officials of our Government to a counterproposal to the Japanese note of November 20, including the thought of a possible *modus vivendi*. It was recognized that such an arrangement would demonstrate the desire of the United States for peace and at the same time afford a possible opportunity for the Army and Navy to continue its preparations. From November 22 to 26 the President, State Department, and the highest military authorities discussed a *modus vivendi*, a first draft being completed on November 22. Revised drafts were prepared on November 24 and 25. The final draft of November 25, which is being set forth in its entirety in view of the testimony that has been adduced concerning it, was as follows: [90]

The representatives of the Government of the United States and of the Government of Japan have been carrying on during the past several months informal and exploratory conversations for the purpose of arriving at a settlement if possible of questions relating to the entire Pacific area based upon the principles of peace, law and order, and fair dealing among nations. These principles include the principle of inviolability of territorial integrity and sovereignty of each and all nations; the principle of non-interference in the internal affairs of other countries; the principle of equality, including equality of commercial opportunity and

[90] See Committee Exhibit No. 18.

treatment; and the principle of reliance upon international cooperation and conciliation for the prevention and pacific settlement of controversies and for improvement of international conditions by peaceful methods and processes.

It is believed that in our discussions some progress has been made in reference to the general principles which constitute the basis of a peaceful settlement covering the entire Pacific area. Recently, the Japanese Ambassador has stated that the Japanese Government is desirous of continuing the conversations directed toward a comprehensive and peaceful settlement in the Pacific area; that it would be helpful toward creating an atmosphere favorable to the successful outcome of the conversations if a temporary *modus vivendi* could be agreed upon to be in effect while the conversations looking to a peaceful settlement in the Pacific were continuing; and that it would be desirable that such *modus vivendi* include as one of its provisions some initial and temporary steps of a reciprocal character in the resumption of trade and normal intercourse between Japan and the United States.

On November 20, the Japanese Ambassador communicated to the Secretary of State proposals in regard to temporary measures to be taken respectively by the Government of Japan and by the Government of the United States, which measures are understood to have been designed to accomplish the purposes above indicated. These proposals contain features which, in the opinion of this Government, conflict with the fundamental principles which form a part of the general settlement under consideration and to which each Government has declared that it is committed.

The Government of the United States is earnestly desirous to contribute to the promotion and maintenance of peace in the Pacific area and to afford every opportunity for the continuance of discussions with the Japanese Government directed toward working out a broad-gauge program of peace throughout the Pacific area. With these ends in view, the Government of the United States offers for the consideration of the Japanese Government an alternative suggestion for a temporary *modus vivendi*, as follows:

MODUS VIVENDI

1. The Government of the United States and the Government of Japan, both being solicitous for the peace of the Pacific, affirm that their national policies are directed toward lasting and extensive peace throughout the Pacific area and that they have no territorial designs therein.

2. They undertake reciprocally not to make from regions in which they have military establishments any advance by force or threat of force into any areas in Southeastern or Northeastern Asia or in the southern or the northern Pacific area.

3. The Japanese Government undertakes forthwith to withdraw its forces now stationed in southern French Indochina and not to replace those forces; to reduce the total of its force in French Indochina to the number there on July 26, 1941; and not to send additional naval, land, or air forces to Indochina for replacements or otherwise.

The provisions of the foregoing paragraph are without prejudice to the position of the Government of the United States with regard to the presence of foreign troops in that area.

4. The Government of the United States undertakes forthwith to modify the application of its existing freezing and export restrictions to the extent necessary to permit the following resumption of trade between the United States and Japan in articles for the use and needs of their peoples:

(a) Imports from Japan to be freely permitted and the proceeds of the sale thereof to be paid into a clearing account to be used for the purchase of the exports from the United States listed below, and at Japan's option for the payment of interest and principal of Japanese obligations within the United States, provided that at least two-thirds in value of such imports per month consist of raw silk. It is understood that all American-owned goods now in Japan, the movement of which in transit to the United States has been interrupted following the adoption of freezing measures shall be forwarded forthwith to the United States.

(b) Exports from the United States to Japan to be permitted as follows:

(i) Bunkers and supplies for vessels engaged in the trade here provided for and for such other vessels engaged in other trades as the two Governments may agree.

(ii) Food and food products from the United States subject to such limitations as the appropriate authorities may prescribe in respect of commodities in short supply in the United States.

(iii) Raw cotton from the United States to the extent of $600,000 in value per month.

(iv) Medical and pharmaceutical supplies subject to such limitations as the appropriate authorities may prescribe in respect of commodities in short supply in the United States.

(v) Petroleum.   The United States will permit the export to Japan of petroleum, within the categories permitted general export, upon a monthly basis for civilian needs.   The proportionate amount of petroleum to be exported from the United States for such needs will be determined after consultation with the British and the Dutch Governments.   It is understood that by civilian needs in Japan is meant such purposes as the operation of the fishing industry, the transport system, lighting, heating, industrial and agricultural uses, and other civilian uses.

(vi) The above-stated amounts of exports may be increased and additional commodities added by agreement between the two Governments as it may appear to them that the operation of this agreement is furthering the peaceful and equitable solution of outstanding problems in the Pacific area.

The Government of Japan undertakes forthwith to modify the application of its existing freezing and export restrictions to the extent necessary to permit the resumption of trade between Japan and the United States as provided for in paragraph 4 above.

6. The Government of the United States undertakes forthwith to approach the Australian, British, and Dutch Governments with a view to those Governments taking measures similar to those provided for in paragraph 4 above.

7. With reference to the current hostilities between Japan and China, the fundamental interest of the Government of the United States in reference to any discussions which may be entered into between the Japanese and the Chinese Governments is simply that these discussions and any settlement reached as a result thereof be based upon and exemplify the fundamental principles of peace, law, order, and justice, which constitute the central spirit of the current conversations between the Government of Japan and the Government of the United States and which are applicable uniformly throughout the Pacific area.

8. This *modus vivendi* shall remain in force for a period of 3 months with the understanding that the two parties shall confer at the instance of either to ascertain whether the prospects of reaching a peaceful settlement covering the entire Pacific area justify an extension of the *modus vivendi* for a further period.

The tentative *modus vivendi* was submitted for consideration to the Governments of Great Britain, Australia, the Netherlands, and China. The ultimate decision to abandon it was made for reasons best set forth in Secretary Hull's testimony: [91]

On the evening of November 25 and on November 26 I went over again the considerations relating to our proposed plan, especially the *modus vivendi* aspect.

As I have indicated, all the successive drafts, of November 22, of November 24, and of November 25, contained two things: (1) The possible *modus vivendi*; and (2) a statement of principles, with a suggested example of how those principles could be applied—that which has since been commonly described as the 10-point proposal.

I and other high officers of our Government knew that the Japanese military were poised for attack.   We knew that the Japanese were demanding—and had set a time limit, first of November 25 and extended later to November 29, for—acceptance by our Government of their extreme, last-word proposal of November 20.

It was therefore my judgment, as it was that of the President and other high officers, that the chance of the Japanese accepting our proposal was remote.

So far as the *modus vivendi* aspect would have appeared to the Japanese, it contained only a little chicken feed in the shape of some cotton, oil, and a few other commodities in very limited quantities as compared with the unlimited quantities the Japanese were demanding.

It was manifest that there would be widespread opposition from American opinion to the *modus vivendi* aspect of the proposal especially to the supplying to Japan of even limited quantities of oil.   *The Chinese Government violently opposed the idea.   The other interested governments were sympathetic to the Chinese view and fundamentally were unfavorable or lukewarm.   Their cooperation was a part of the plan.   It developed that the conclusion with Japan of such an arrangement would have been a major blow to Chinese morale.*   In view of these considerations it became clear that the slight prospects of Japan's agreeing to the *modus vivendi* did not warrant assuming the risks involved in proceeding with it, especially the serious

⁹¹ Committee Record, pp. 1145-1147.

risk of collapse of Chinese morale and resistance, and even of disintegration of China. It therefore became perfectly evident that the *modus vivendi* aspect would not be feasible.

The Japanese were spreading propaganda to the effect that they were being encircled. On the one hand we were faced by this charge and on the other by one that we were preparing to pursue a policy of appeasing Japan. In view of the resulting confusion, it seemed important to restate the fundamentals. We could offer Japan once more what we offered all countries, a suggested program of collaboration along peaceful and mutually beneficial and progressive lines. It had always been open to Japan to accept that kind of a program and to move in that direction. It still was possible for Japan to do so. That was a matter for Japan's decision. Our hope that Japan would so decide had been virtually extinguished. Yet it was felt desirable to put forth this further basic effort, in the form of one sample of a broad but simple settlement to be worked out in our future conversations, on the principle that no effort should be spared to test and exhaust every method of peaceful settlement.

In the light of the foregoing considerations, on November 26 I recommended to the President—and he approved—my calling in the Japanese representatives and handing them the broad basic proposals while withholding the *modus vivendi* plan. This was done in the late afternoon of that day.

The very serious reaction of the Chinese to the suggested *modus vivendi* is clearly set forth in a dispatch dated November 25, 1941, from an American adviser to Generalissimo Chiang Kai-shek in Chungking: [92]

After discussion with the Generalissimo the Chinese Ambassador's conference with the Secretary of State, I feel you should urgently advise the President of the Generalissimo's very strong reaction. I have never seen him really agitated before. Loosening of economic pressure or unfreezing would dangerously increase Japan's military advantage in China. A relaxation of American pressure while Japan has its forces in China would dismay the Chinese. Any "modus vivendi" now arrived at with Japan would be disastrous to Chinese belief in America and analogous to the closing of the Burma Road, which permanently destroyed British prestige. Japan and Chinese defeatists would instantly exploit the resulting disillusionment and urge oriental solidarity against occidental treachery. It is doubtful whether either past assistance or increasing aid could compensate for the feeling of being deserted at this hour. The Generalissimo has deep confidence in the President's fidelity to his consistent policy but I must warn you that even the Generalissimo questions his ability to hold the situation together if the Chinese national trust in America is undermined by reports of Japan's escaping military defeat by diplomatic victory.

There is no possibility whatever that the *modus vivendi* would have been accepted by the Japanese. In an intercepted dispatch of November 19 [93] the Japanese Ambassadors suggested to Tokyo that there were three courses open to the Empire: (1) maintain the status quo, (2) break the "present deadlock" by an advance under force of arms, or (3) devise some means for bringing about a mutual nonaggression arrangement. In favoring the third alternative it was stated:

* * * as I view it, the present, after exhausting our strength by 4 years of the China incident following right upon the Manchuria incident, is hardly an opportune time for venturing upon another long-drawn-out warfare on a large scale. I think that it would be better to fix up a temporary "truce" now in the spirit of "give and take" and make this the prelude to greater achievement to come later * * *.

Replying to the foregoing suggestion, Tokyo advised on November 20 [94] that "under the circumstances here, we regret that *the plan suggested by you, as we have stated in our message would not suffice for*

---

[92] Communication from Owen Lattimore in Chungking to Lauchlin Currie, Presidential Assistant handling Chinese matters, in Washington. See committee exhibit No. 18.
[93] Committee exhibit No. 1, p. 158.
[94] Id., at p. 160.

saving the present situation. We see no prospects for breaking the deadlock except for you to push negotiations immediately along the lines of the latter part of our No. 798.[95] Please understand this. The Premier also is absolutely in accord with this opinion."

It is significant to note that when Mr. Kurusu suggested the possibility of a *modus vivendi* to Secretary Hull on November 18, the Japanese ambassadors very obviously had not consulted their Tokyo superiors. When they did on November 19, Tokyo replied the following day rejecting the idea completely, as indicated above.

Writing in his diary for November 25, 1941, Secretary Stimson, in referring to the tentative draft of a *modus vivendi*, clearly indicated an appreciation of the fact that it would not be acceptable to the Japanese: [96]

At 9:30 Knox and I met in Hull's office for our meeting of three. Hull showed us the proposal for a 3 months' truce, which he was going to lay before the Japanese today or tomorrow. It adequately safeguarded all our interests, I thought as I read it, but *I don't think there is any chance of the Japanese accepting it, because it was so drastic.* In return for the propositions which they were to do, namely, to at once evacuate and at once to stop all preparations or threats of action, and to take no aggressive action against any of her neighbors, etc., we were to give them open trade in sufficient quantities only for their civilian population. This restriction was particularly applicable to oil.

Had our Government submitted the tentative *modus vivendi*, it is clear that Japan would have rejected it, and Chinese morale and resistance would very probably have been seriously impaired if not destroyed.

United States Memorandum of November 26

The *modus vivendi* was designed to accompany a statement of principles with a suggested example of how the principles could be applied. With the decision not to propose a *modus vivendi*, the Secretary of State on November 26 presented to the Japanese Ambassador its accompanying material which was as follows: [97]

The representatives of the Government of the United States and of the Government of Japan have been carrying on during the past several months informal and exploratory conversations for the purpose of arriving at a settlement if possible of questions relating to the entire Pacific area based upon the principles of peace, law and order and fair dealing among nations. These principles include the principle of inviolability of territorial integrity and sovereignty of each and all nations; the principle of noninterference in the internal affairs of other countries; the principle of equality, including equality of commercial opportunity and treatment; and the principle of reliance upon international cooperation and conciliation for the prevention and pacific settlement of controversies and for improvement of international conditions by peaceful methods and processes.

It is believed that in our discussions some progress has been made in reference to the general principles which constitute the basis of a peaceful settlement covering the entire Pacific area. Recently the Japanese Ambassador has stated that the Japanese Government is desirous of continuing the conversations directed toward a comprehensive and peaceful settlement in the Pacific area; that it would be helpful toward creating an atmosphere favorable to the successful outcome of the conversations if a temporary *modus vivendi* could be agreed upon to be in effect while the conversations looking to a peaceful settlement in the Pacific were continuing. On November 20 the Japanese Ambassador communicated to the Secretary of State proposals in regard to temporary measures to be taken respec-

---

[95] See committee exhibit No. 1, p. 155.
[96] See committee record, pp. 14417, 14418.
[97] Foreign Relations, vol. II, pp. 766–770.

tively by the Government of Japan and by the Government of the United States, which measures are understood to have been designed to accomplish the purposes above indicated.

The Government of the United States most earnestly desires to contribute to the promotion and maintenance of peace and stability in the Pacific area, and to afford every opportunity for the continuance of discussions with the Japanese Government directed toward working out a broad-gauge program of peace throughout the Pacific area. The proposals which were presented by the Japanese Ambassador on November 20 contain some features which, in the opinion of this Government, conflict with the fundamental principles which form a part of the general settlement under consideration and to which each Government has declared that it is committed. The Government of the United States believes that the adoption of such proposals would not be likely to contribute to the ultimate objectives of ensuring peace under law, order and justice in the Pacific area, and it suggests that further effort be made to resolve our divergences of views in regard to the practical application of the fundamental principles already mentioned.

With this object in view the Government of the United States offers for the consideration of the Japanese Government a plan of a broad but simple settlement covering the entire Pacific area as one practical exemplification of *a program which this Government envisages as something to be worked out during our further conversations.*

The plan therein suggested represents an effort to bridge the gap between our draft of June 21, 1941, and the Japanese draft of September 25 by making a new approach to the essential problems underlying a comprehensive Pacific settlement. This plan contains provisions dealing with the practical application of the fundamental principles which we have agreed in our conversations constitute the only sound basis for worthwhile international relations. We hope that in this way progress toward reaching a meeting of minds between our two Governments may be expedited.

OUTLINE OF PROPOSED BASIS FOR AGREEMENT BETWEEN THE UNITED STATES
AND JAPAN

SECTION I—DRAFT MUTUAL DECLARATION OF POLICY

The Government of the United States and the Government of Japan both being solicitous for the peace of the Pacific affirm that their national policies are directed toward lasting and extensive peace throughout the Pacific area, that they have no territorial designs in that area, that they have no intention of threatening other countries or of using military force aggressively against any neighboring nation, and that, accordingly, in their national policies they will actively support and give practical application to the following fundamental principles upon which their relations with each other and with all other governments are based:

"(1) The principle of inviolability of territorial integrity and sovereignty of each and all nations.

"(2) The principle of non-interference in the internal affairs of other countries.

"(3) The principle of equality, including equality of commercial opportunity and treatment.

"(4) The principle of reliance upon international cooperation and conciliation for the prevention and pacific settlement of controversies and for improvement of international conditions by peaceful methods and processes."

The Government of Japan and the Government of the United States have agreed that toward eliminating chronic political instability, preventing recurrent economic collapse, and providing a basis for peace, they will actively support and practically apply the following principles in their economic relations with each other and with other nations and peoples:

"(1) The principle of nondiscrimination in international commercial relations.

"(2) The principle of international economic cooperation and abolition of extreme nationalism as expressed in excessive trade restrictions.

"(3) The principle of nondiscriminatory access by all nations to raw-material supplies.

"(4) The principle of full protection of the interests of consuming countries and populations as regards the operation of international commodity agreements.

"(5) The principle of establishment of such institutions and arrangements of international finance as may lend aid to the essential enterprises and the continuous development of all countries and may permit payments through processes of trade consonant with the welfare of all countries."

SECTION II—STEPS TO BE TAKEN BY THE GOVERNMENT OF THE UNITED STATES AND BY THE GOVERNMENT OF JAPAN

The Government of the United States and the Government of Japan propose to take steps as follows:

1. The Government of the United States and the Government of Japan will endeavor to conclude a multilateral nonaggression pact among the British Empire, China, Japan, the Netherlands, the Soviet Union, Thailand, and the United States.

2. Both Governments will endeavor to conclude among the American, British, Chinese, Japanese, the Netherlands, and Thai Governments an agreement whereunder each of the Governments would pledge itself to respect the territorial integrity of French Indochina and, in the event that there should develop a threat to the territorial integrity of Indochina, to enter into immediate consultation with a view to taking such measures as may be deemed necessary and advisable to meet the threat in question. Such agreement would provide also that each of the Governments party to the agreement would not seek or accept preferential treatment in its trade or economic relations with Indochina and would use its influence to obtain for each of the signatories equality of treatment in trade and commerce with French Indochina.

3. The Government of Japan will withdraw all military, naval, air, and police forces from China and from Indochina.

4. The Government of the United States and the Government of Japan will not support—militarily, politically, economically—any government or regime in China other than the National Government of the Republic of China with capital temporarily at Chungking.

5. Both Governments will give up all extraterritorial rights in China, including rights and interests in and with regard to international settlements and concessions, and rights under the Boxer Protocol of 1901.

Both Governments will endeavor to obtain the agreement of the British and other governments to give up extraterritorial rights in China, including rights in international settlements and in concessions and under the Boxer Protocol of 1901.

6. The Government of the United States and the Government of Japan will enter into negotiations for the conclusion between the United States and Japan of a trade agreement, based upon reciprocal most-favored-nation treatment and reduction of trade barriers by both countries, including an undertaking by the United States to bind raw silk on the free list.

7. The Government of the United States and the Government of Japan will, respectively, remove the freezing restrictions on Japanese funds in the United States and on American funds in Japan.

8. Both Governments will agree upon a plan for the stabilization of the dollar-yen rate, with the allocation of funds adequate for this purpose, half to be supplied by Japan and half by the United States.

9. Both Governments will agree that no agreement which either has concluded with any third power or powers shall be interpreted by it in such a way as to conflict with the fundamental purpose of this agreement, the establishment and preservation of peace throughout the Pacific area.

10. Both Governments will use their influence to cause other governments to adhere to and to give practical application to the basic political and economic principles set forth in this agreement.

The foregoing reply was clearly not an ultimatum from the standpoint of the Government of the United States. On the contrary it was an admirable statement of every honorable principle for which the United States has stood for many years in the Orient. Ambassador Grew characterized the November 26 note of Secretary Hull as follows : [98]

NOVEMBER 29, 1941.

Our Government has handed to the Japanese a 10-point draft proposal for adjusting the whole situation in the Far East. It is a broad-gauge objective, and statesmanlike document, offering to Japan practically everything that she has ostensibly been fighting for if she will simply stop her aggressive policy. By adopting such a program she would be offered free access to needed raw materials, free trade and commerce, financial cooperation and support, withdrawal of the freezing orders, and an opportunity to negotiate a new treaty of commerce with us. If she wants a political and economic stranglehold on the countries of East Asia (euphemistically called the New Order in East Asia and the East Asia

[98] Grew, Ten Years in Japan (1944), pp. 482, 483. Committee exhibit No. 30.

Co-Prosperity Sphere)—which most of her extremists do want—and if she pursues her southward advance by force, she will soon be at war with all of the A B C D powers and will unquestionably be defeated and reduced to the status of a third-rate power. But if she plays her cards wisely, she can obtain without further fighting all of the desiderata for which she allegedly started fighting—strategic, economic, financial, and social security.

Referring to the November 26 note Secretary Stimson said: [99]

I personally was relieved that we had not backed down on any of the fundamental principles on which we had stood for so long and which *I felt we could not give up without the sacrifice of our national honor and prestige in the world.* I submit, however, that no impartial reading of this document can characterize it as being couched in the terms of an ultimatum, although the Japanese were of course only too quick to seize upon it and give that designation for their own purposes.

As suggested by Mr. Stimson, Japan did choose to regard it as an ultimatum consistent with her purposes. Her note of November 20, it is apparent, was the final diplomatic move and failing to secure the concessions demanded the November 26 reply of the United States was seized upon by the war lords of Japan in subsequent propaganda as their excuse for the attack on Pearl Harbor which they had planned for many weeks. It is to be noted in this connection that the Japanese task force was enroute for its attack on Pearl Harbor before the American note of November 26 was delivered to the Government of Japan. At the time of receiving the note from Secretary Hull, Kurusu stated the Japanese Government would be likely "to throw up its hands" when it received the proposal; that he felt the response which had thus been given to the Japanese proposal of November 20 could be interpreted as tantamount to meaning the end of the conversations.[100] A dispatch from Ambassador Grew to the State Department on December 5 reflected the strong reaction in Japan.[101]

Secretary Hull said: [102]

It is not surprising that Japanese propaganda, especially after Japan had begun to suffer serious defeats, has tried to distort and give false meaning to our memorandum of November 26 by referring to it as an "ultimatum." This was in line with a well-known Japanese characteristic of utilizing completely false and flimsy pretexts to delude their people and gain their support for militaristic depredations and aggrandizement.

In press conferences on November 26 and 27, Secretary Hull outlined the status of American-Japanese relations.[103]

The decision to stand by basic American principles was the only honorable position under the circumstances.[104] To have acceded to the Japanese ultimatum of November 20 would have been indefensible. Firmness was the only language Japan understood. As Ambassador Grew had stated in his celebrated "green light" dispatch of September 12, 1940, to the State Department:[105]

Force or the display of force can alone prevent these powers (including Japan) from attaining their objectives * * *.

If then we can by firmness preserve the status quo in the Pacific until and if Britain emerges successfully from the European struggle, Japan will be faced with a situation which will make it impossible for the present opportunist philosophy to maintain the upper hand * * *.

In the present situation and outlook I believe that the time has come when continued patience and restraint on the part of the United States may and probably will lead to developments which will render Japanese-American relations progressively precarious.

---

[99] See committee record, p. 14393.
[100] Foreign Relations, vol. II, p. 375.
[101] Committee Record, p. 1821-24.
[102] Committee Record, p. 1153.
[103] See statement of Secretary Hull, Committee Record, pp. 1153 et seq.
[104] Id., p. 1155.
[105] Committee exhibit No. 26.

That firmness, the only language the Japanese understood, failed to dissuade them cannot redound to our regret but only to the ignominy of the Empire of Japan.

Fraudulent Nature of Japanese Diplomacy—November 28 to December 7

An intercepted dispatch No. 844 from Tokyo to its Washington Embassy on November 28 left little doubt of the fraudulent character of the negotiations thereafter and is a classic example of Japanese deceit and duplicity:[106]

Well, you two Ambassadors have exerted superhuman efforts but, in spite of this, the United States has gone ahead and presented this humiliating proposal. This was quite unexpected and extremely regrettable. The Imperial Government can by no means use it as a basis for negotiations. Therefore, with a report of the views of the Imperial Government on this American proposal which I will send you in two or three days, the negotiations will be *de facto* ruptured. This is inevitable. *However, I do not wish you to give the impression that the negotiations are broken off.* Merely say to them that you are awaiting instructions and that, although the opinions of your Government are not yet clear to you, to your own way of thinking the Imperial Government has always made just claims and has borne great sacrifices for the sake of peace in the Pacific. Say that we have always demonstrated a long-suffering and conciliatory attitude, but that, on the other hand, the United States has been unbending, making it impossible for Japan to establish negotiations. Since things have come to this pass, I contacted the man you told me to in your #1180 [107] and he said that under the present circumstances what you suggest is entirely unsuitable. From now on do the best you can.

The following dispatch, while the attack force was en route to Pearl Harbor, was sent from Tokyo to Washington on December 1:[108]

The date (November 29) set in my message #812 [109] has come and gone, and the situation continues to be increasingly critical. However, to prevent the United States from becoming unduly suspicious we have been advising the press and others that though there are some wide differences between Japan and the United States, the negotiations are continuing. (The above is for only your information) * * *.

After November 26 Ambassador Nomura and Mr. Kurusu conferred with the President and Secretary Hull on several occasions but with nothing new being developed looking to a peaceful settlement.

On the morning of December 6 a dispatch from Tokyo to Washington was intercepted advising that the Japanese reply to the American note of November 26 was being transmitted:

I will send it in fourteen parts and I imagine you will receive it tomorrow· However, I am not sure. The situation is extremely delicate, and when you receive it I want you to please keep it secret for the time being.

This dispatch indicated that subsequent instructions would be forthcoming concerning the time for presenting the reply to the Government of the United States. By approximately 9 p. m. on the evening of December 6 the first 13 parts of the 14-part Japanese memorandum had been intercepted, decoded, and made ready for distribution to authorized recipients by our military. These 13 parts were a long recapitulation of the negotiations with the purposes of Japan colored with pious hue and those of the United States perverted into a base and ulterior scheme "for the extension of the war." The thirteenth part concluded on the note that—

therefore, viewed in its entirety, the Japanese Government regrets that it cannot accept the proposal (American proposal of November 26) as a basis of negotiations.

[106] Committee exhibit No. 1, p. 195.
[107] See committee exhibit No. 1, p. 181.
[108] Committee exhibit No. 1, p. 208.
[109] See committee exhibit No. 1, p. 165, setting the date November 29 as the deadline for effecting an understanding.

The fourteenth part was intercepted early on the morning of December 7 and was available for distribution at approximately 8 a. m. It stated that—[110]

obviously it is the intention of the American Government to conspire with Great Britain and other countries to obstruct Japan's efforts toward the establishment of peace through the creation of a New Order in East Asia, and especially to preserve Anglo-American rights and interests by keeping Japan and China at war.

With the observation that this intention had been revealed during the course of the negotiations and the "earnest hope of the Japanese Government * * * to preserve and promote the peace of the Pacific through cooperation with the American Government has finally been lost", the Japanese memorandum closed with the statement:

The Japanese Government regrets to have to notify hereby the American Government that in view of the attitude of the American Government it cannot but consider that it is impossible to reach an agreement through further negotiations.

Nowhere in the memorandum was there any indication or intimation of an intention to attack the United States nor, indeed, that formal diplomatic relations were to be broken—merely that it was impossible to reach an agreement through the then current negotiations. Coincident with the receipt of the full reply, instructions were issued to Japan's representatives for its delivery to the American Government at an hour keyed to the time set for the assault on Pearl Harbor. On the previous evening, President Roosevelt had dispatched an earnest appeal to the Emperor of Japan for the preservation of peace in the Pacific.[111] The infamous character of the Japanese reply was voiced by Secretary Hull to the Japanese ambassadors who were making delivery 1 hour after [112] the first bombs had fallen on Pearl Harbor:[113]

I must say that in all my conversations with you (the Japanese ambassador) during the last nine months I have never uttered one word of untruth. This is borne out absolutely by the record. In all my fifty years of public service I have never seen a document that was more crowded with infamous falsehoods and distortions—infamous falsehoods and distortions on a scale so huge that I never imagined until today that any Government on this planet was capable of uttering them.

Diplomatic and Military Liaison in Washington

With a view to effecting the fullest liaison between the diplomatic and military arms of the Government, there was created in the light of the approaching emergency a body familiarly referred to as the War Council. This Council consisted of the President, the Secretary of State, the Secretary of War, the Secretary of Navy, the Army Chief of Staff, the Chief of Naval Operations, and, on occasion, the Chief of the Army Air Forces.[114] It met at the call of the President, and during the fall of 1941 it was in frequent session. Secretary Hull said:

[110] See committee exhibit No. 1, pp. 239–245.
[111] See Foreign Relations, vol. II, pp. 784–786. Several hours after the Pearl Harbor attack had begun Ambassador Grew was informed by the Japanese Foreign Minister that the Japanese 14-part memorandum replying to the American note of November 26 was to be regarded as the Emperor's reply to the President's appeal. See Peace and War, p. 148.
[112] The Japanese Ambassadors were instructed to deliver the Japanese note to the American Secretary of State at 1 p. m. on Sunday, December 7. They made the appointment pursuant to the instruction; however, they later postponed for 1 hour their previous appointment, stating the delay was due to the need of more time to decode the message they were to deliver.
[113] Foreign Relations, vol. II, p. 787.
[114] For a rather full discussion of liaison between the various departments, see testimony of Secretary Stimson, Army Pearl Harbor Board Record, p. 4041 et seq.

"The War Council, which consisted of the President, the Secretaries of State, War, and Navy, the Chief of Staff, and the Chief of Naval Operations, was a sort of clearing house for all the information and views which we were currently discussing with our respective contacts and in our respective circles. The high lights in the developments at a particular juncture were invariably reviewed at those meetings." [115]

In addition to the War Council, another liaison body, consisting of the Secretary of State, the Secretary of War, and the Secretary of Navy, was created during 1940, with a view to holding weekly meetings, which were scheduled for 9:30 each Tuesday morning. Secretary Stimson said: [116]

> They were perfectly informal and unofficial meetings, but they were very regular, and we met once a week regularly; and * * * just before Pearl Harbor, we had extra meetings. In fact, we were in such a meeting on the Sunday morning that the Japanese attacked. The meetings took place in the State Department, Mr. Hull's office, and during that time the Secretary of State, the Secretary of Navy, and myself were in constant contact.

And again: [117]

> During this entire period I kept in constant and close touch with Mr. Hull and Mr. Knox, as well as having frequent meetings with the President.

During 1941 Rear Adm. R. E. Schuirmann was the Director of the Central Division, Office of the Chief of Naval Operations, and had as one of his duties liaison with the State Department. He made the following observations concerning State Department liaison: [118]

> A "Liaison Committee" consisting of the Chief of Naval Operations, the Chief of Staff, U. S. Army, and the Under Secretary of State was set up while Admiral Leahy was Chief of Naval Operations. This Committee was mainly occupied with questions other than the Far East, but occasionally questions relating to the Far East were discussed. About the middle of May 1941, the practice of having a stenographer present to record the discussion was commenced; prior to that time I would take notes of the meetings in order to be able to follow up such matters as required action, and I believe one of Mr. Welles' assistants made a *precis* of the meetings. At times there were "off the record" discussions at these liaison committee meetings. I made notes of some of these "off the record" discussions. Aside from the meetings of the Liaison Committee, Secretary Hull held meetings with various officials of the Navy Department, and I maintained liaison with Dr. Hornbeck and Mr. Hamilton of the Far Eastern Division of the State Department by visit and by telephone. I know of no official record of these meetings and discussions. Fragmentary notes of some are in the files of the Central Division as are such records of the Liaison Committee as are in the possession of the Navy Department. It is possible that the State Department representatives may have made notes of some of these meetings and discussions with Secretary Hull and other State Department officials.

Admiral R. K. Turner, Director of War Plans Division in the Office of the Chief of Naval Operations, summarized the liaison with the State Department as follows: [119]

> The Chief of Naval Operations had a close personal association with the Secretary of State and Under Secretary of State. *He consulted them frequently and they consulted him, I might say invariably, before making any particular diplomatic move.* In the Office of Naval Operations, the Chief of the Central Division was appointed as liaison officer with the State Department. He visited the State Department and discussed problems with them practically every day. There was a weekly meeting in the State Department conducted by the Under Secretary of State, Mr. Welles, usually attended by the Chief of Naval Operations, the Chief of Staff of the Army, Chief of the War Plans of the Army, Chief of War

[115] Committee record, p. 1144.
[116] Roberts record, pp. 4051–4053, 4078–4079.
[117] Committee record, p. 14386.
[118] Hart record, p. 405.
[119] Id., at p. 257.

Plans of the Navy, the Chief of the Central Division of the Office of Naval Operations, an officer of the General Staff not in the War Plans Division, and two or three representatives of the State Department. The matters discussed at these meetings usually related to events in Western Hemisphere countries. The Army was building a lot of air fields in the Caribbean and South America. The Navy and the Army, both, had sent missions to those countries and at the meetings with the Under Secretary it was chiefly American affairs that were discussed. Occasionally, possibly once a month, the Secretary of State would hold a conference with representatives of the War and Navy Departments, and at these meetings events outside of the Americas were discussed. From time to time the Secretary of State would call individuals from the War and Navy Departments to discuss particular aspects of world events. There were other unscheduled conferences between the State and War and Navy Departments. I participated in a great many such conferences. From time to time, informal memoranda were exchanged between individuals of the State and Navy Departments or exchanged between the Secretary of State and the Chief of Naval Operations. *I would say that relations between the State and War and State and Navy Departments were very close and were characterized by good feeling.*

At a regular Cabinet meeting on November 7 the President inquired of Secretary Hull as to whether he had anything in mind. In replying Secretary Hull testified: [120]

I thereupon pointed out for about 15 minutes the dangers in the international situation. *I went over fully developments in the conversations with Japan and emphasized that in my opinion relations were extremely critical and that we should be on the lookout for a military attack anywhere by Japan at any time.* When I finished, the President went around the Cabinet. All concurred in my estimate of the dangers. It became the consensus of the Cabinet that the critical situation might well be emphasized in speeches in order that the country would, if possible, be better prepared for such a development.[121]

Secretary Stimson stated: [122]

On Friday, November 7, we had the usual weekly Cabinet meeting. The Far Eastern situation was uppermost in many of our minds. Mr. Hull informed us that relations had become extremely critical and that we should be on the outlook for an attack by Japan at any time. [123]

At a meeting of the war council on November 25 Secretary Hull pointed out that the leaders of Japan were determined and desperate, and, in his opinion, the Japanese military was already poised for attack; that they might attack at any time and at any place. He emphasized the probable element of surprise in Japanese plans, that "virtually the last stage had been reached and that the safeguarding of our national security was in the hands of the Army and Navy." [124]

At the same meeting of the council the President warned that we were likely to be attacked, perhaps as soon as the following Monday, for "the Japanese are notorious for making an attack without warning." [125]

On the morning of November 26, Secretary Hull advised Secretary Stimson that he had about decided not to make the proposition of the 3-month truce, the *modus vivendi*, that he had discussed with Secretaries Knox and Stimson on November 25—"the Chinese, for

[120] Committee record, p. 1131.

[121] In an address delivered on November 11, 1941, Secretary Knox warned that the Nation was confronted not only by the necessity for extreme measures of self-defense in the Atlantic but was "likewise faced with grim possibilities on the other side of the world—on the far side of the Pacific." See committee record at pp. 1131, 1132.

[122] Committee record, pp. 14387, 14388.

[123] In an address on November 11, Under Secretary of State Sumner Welles stated that beyond the Atlantic a sinister and pitiless conqueror had reduced more than half of Europe to abject serfdom and that in the Far East the same forces of conquest were menacing the safety of all nations bordering on the Pacific. He said that the waves of world conquest were "breaking high both in the East and in the West" and were threatening "to engulf our own shores"; that the United States was in far greater peril than in 1917 and "at any moment war may be forced upon us." See committee record, p. 1132.

[124] Id., at p. 1144. See also statement of Mr. Stimson, committee record, p. 14390.

[125] See statement of Mr. Stimson, committee record, p. 14390.

one thing, had pointed out strong objections to the proposal, particularly the effect on the morale of their own people."[126] Secretary Stimson said: [127]

Early that morning (November 27) I had called up Mr. Hull to find out what his final word had been with the Japanese—whether he had handed them the proposal for three months' truce, or whether he had told them he had no other proposition to make. He told me that he had broken the whole matter off. His words were: "*I have washed my hands of it, and it is now in the hands of you and Knox—the Army and the Navy.*" I then called up the President, who gave me a little different view. He said that it was true that the talks had been called off, but that they had ended up with a magnificient statement prepared by Hull. I found out afterwards that this was the fact and that the statement contained a reaffirmation of our constant and regular position without the suggestion of a threat of any kind.

With reference to his remarks before the War Council on November 28, Secretary Hull stated: [128]

* * * I reviewed the November 26 proposal which we had made to the Japanese, and pointed out that there was practically no possibility of an agreement being achieved with Japan. *I emphasized that in my opinion the Japanese were likely to break out at any time with new acts of conquest and that the matter of safeguarding our national security was in the hands of the Army and the Navy.* With due deference I expressed my judgment that any plans for our military defense should include an assumption that the Japanese might make *the element of surprise a central point in their strategy* and also might attack at various points simultaneously with a view to demoralizing efforts of defense and of coordination.

Addressing a public rally in Japan on November 30, Premier Tojo stated: [129]

The fact that Chiang-Kai-shek is dancing to the tune of Britain, America, and communism at the expense of able-bodied and promising young men in his futile resistance against Japan is only due to the desire of Britain and the United States to fish in the troubled waters of East Asia by putting [pitting?] the East Asiatic peoples against each other and to grasp the hegemony of East Asia. This is a stock in trade of Britain and the United States.

For the honor and pride of mankind we must purge this sort of practice from East Asia with a vengeance.

Following a conference with military leaders concerning the Japanese Premier's address, Secretary Hull called the President at Warm Springs, Ga., urging him to advance the date set for his return to Washington. The President accordingly returned to Washington on December 1.[130]

In testifying before the Navy inquiry conducted by Admiral Hart, Admiral Schuirmann stated in reply to a query as to whether the State Department's estimate of the situation *vis-a-vis* Japan as conveyed to the Navy Department was in accord with the statements contained "on page 138 of the book *Peace and War*": [131]

I was not present at any meeting that I recall where the Secretary expressed the element of surprise so strongly or if at all, or the probability of attack at various points. However, the particular meetings which he mentioned, I do not know if I was present. I cannot make any positive statement that he did not make such a statement. However, on Wednesday or Thursday before Pearl Harbor, Secretary Hull phoned me saying in effect, "*I know you Navy fellows are always ahead of me but I want you to know that I don't seem to be able to do anything more with these Japanese and they are liable to run loose like a mad dog and bite anyone.*" I assured him that a war warning had been sent out. I reported the conversation to Admiral Stark.

---

[126] Committee record, pp. 14391, 14392.
[127] Id., at pp. 14392, 14393.
[128] Committee record, pp. 1160, 1161.
[129] See committee record, p. 1162.
[130] Id., at p. 1163.
[131] Hart record, p. 412.

Referring to a meeting at the State Department on the morning of December 7, Mr. Stimson said: [132]

On December 7, 1941, Knox and I arranged a conference with Hull at ten-thirty, and we talked the whole matter over. *Hull is very certain that the Japs are planning some deviltry, and we are all wondering where the blow will strike.* We three stayed together in conference until lunchtime, going over the plans for what should be said and done.

Considering all of the observations made by Secretary Hull to Army and Navy Officials in the days before December 7, 1941, it is difficult to imagine how he could have more clearly and forcefully depicted the manner in which relations between the United States and Japan had passed beyond the realm of diplomacy and become a matter of cold military reality.[133] This thought was expressed by General Marshall when he testified to a distinct recollection of Mr. Hull's saying: *"These fellows mean to fight; you will have to be prepared."* [133a]

That there was the fullest exchange of information between the diplomatic and military arms of the Government is further indicated by the manner in which intercepted and decoded Japanese diplomatic messages were distributed. These messages, familiarly referred to as "Magic" and discussed in detail elsewhere in this report, contained detailed instructions and proposals from Tokyo to its Washington Embassy and the comments concerning and contents of American proposals as forwarded to Tokyo by its ambassadors. This material not only indicated what Japan and her ambassadors were *saying* but literally what they were *thinking*. This material was available to the Secretaries of War and Navy, the Chief of Staff, the Chief of Naval Operations, the Directors of War Plans in both the Army and Navy, and the heads of the intelligence branches of both the services, among others.

CONCLUSIONS

Beginning in 1931 Japan embarked on a career of conquest no less ambitious nor avowed than that of the Nazis. Despite American protests she overran and subjugated Manchuria. In 1937, bulwarked by her Anti-Comintern Pact with Germany of the preceding year, she invaded China. In 1940 she seized upon the struggle for survival of the western powers against Hitler's war machine to conclude an iron-clad alliance with Germany and Italy aimed directly at the United States. Thereupon she set about to drive the "barbarians" from the Orient and to engulf the Far East in her Greater East Asia Co-prosperity Sphere which was to be her bastion for world conquest. As early as January of 1941 the dominating military clique prepared for war on the United States and conceived the attack on Pearl Harbor.

Hailing the German invasion of Russia on June 22, 1941, as a "divine wind" securing her northern flank, Japan within a period of 20 days adopted a crucial policy followed by an all-out mobilization for war. Almost immediately thereafter she invaded Southern French Indochina for the purpose "when the international situation is suitable, to launch therefrom a rapid attack." She boldly declared in an intercepted dispatch of July 14, 1941:

---

[132] Army Pearl Harbor Board record, p. 4081. See also committee record, p. 14428.

[133] For a record of Mr. Hull's conferences, consultations, and telephone conversations (as entered in engagement books) with representatives of the War and Navy Departments, November 20 to December 7, 1941, and arrangements for contacts between the Departments of State, War, and Navy in 1940 and 1941. see committee record, pp. 1166–1176. See also committee record, p. 1180.

[133a] Committee record, p. 3079.

After the occupation of French Indochina, next on our schedule is the sending of an ultimatum to the Netherlands Indies. In the seizing of Singapore the Navy will play the principal part.

The invasion of southern Indochina resulted in the freezing of assets and virtual cessation of trade between the United States and Japan.

On November 20, 1941, the Empire of Japan delivered an ultimatum to the Government of the United States. It required that the United States supply Japan as much oil as she might require; that we discontinue aid to China, withdrawing moral and material support from the recognized Chinese Government. It contained no provision pledging Japan to abandon aggression and to resort to peaceful methods. The ultimatum contained no tenable basis for an agreement, a fact well known to and contemplated by the Tojo Cabinet.

During all of the negotiations, Japan qualified and restricted every intimation of her peaceful purposes. With each succeeding proposal it became abundantly apparent that she did not intend to compromise in any measure the bellicose utterances and plans of conquest of her military masters. She uniformly declared her purpose to fulfill her obligations under the Tripartite Pact—aimed directly at the United States. She refused to relinquish the preferential commercial position in the Orient which she had arrogated to herself. She demanded a victor's peace in China and would give no effective recognition to the principle of noninterference in the internal affairs of other countries. Her clear purpose was to maintain a military and economic overlordship of China.

The story of our negotiations with the Empire of Japan during the year 1941 epitomizes the traditional purpose of the United States to seek peace where compatible with national honor. Conversations were carried forward with the representatives of that nation in the hope of bringing to an end the frightful aggression that had brought sorrow, death, and degradation to the Orient for almost a decade. At the same time it was realistically recognized that the negotiations afforded precious time to improve our own capacity for self-defense, the appalling need for which was becoming daily more apparent as the Axis dreams of world conquest pushed relentlessly toward realization.

That there were elements in Japan who desired peace is unquestioned. But for many years the Government of that nation had been divided into two schools of thought, the one conceivably disposed to think in terms of international good will with the other dominated by the militarism of the war lords who had always ultimately resolved Japanese policy.[134] It was this monstrous condition which, from the time of Japan's emergence as a power in world affairs, resulted in her military acts invariably belying her diplomatic promises. The United States therefore in looking to any final settlement had properly before it the substantial question of whether those in Japan who might wish peace possessed the capacity and power to enter a binding and effective agreement reasonably designed to stabilize conditions in the Far East. It was for this reason that our Government insisted Japan offer some tangible proof of her honest purpose to abandon a policy of aggression. No such proof or disposition to provide it was at any time forthcoming.

---

[134] See testimony of Mr. Hull, committee record, p. 1120.

In considering the negotiations in their entirety the conclusion is inescapable that Japan had no concessions to make and that her program of aggression was immutable. When the Konoye Cabinet could not secure an agreement giving Japan an unrestrained hand in the Orient it was replaced by a Cabinet headed by General Tojo. Tojo made one gesture in the form of an ultimatum to realize Japan's ambitions without fighting for them. When he realized such a price for peace was too high even for the United States, his Government launched the infamous attack on Pearl Harbor while instructing her ambassadors in characteristic duplicity to maintain the pretense of continuing negotiations.[135]

It is concluded that the diplomatic actions of the United States provided no provocation whatever for the attack by Japan on Pearl Harbor. It is further concluded that the Secretary of State fully informed both the War and Navy Departments of diplomatic developments and that he in a timely and forceful manner clearly pointed out to these Departments that relations between the United States and Japan had passed beyond the stage of diplomacy and were in the hands of the military.

---

[135] The Japanese force to strike Pearl Harbor actually left Hitokappu Bay for the attack at 7 p. m., November 25, Washington time, before the United States note in reply to the Japanese ultimatum of November 20 was delivered to Japan's ambassadors on November 26.

PART II

THE JAPANESE ATTACK AND ITS AFTERMATH

PART II. THE JAPANESE ATTACK AND ITS AFTERMATH

Formulation of the Plan and Date for Execution [1]

The evidence tends to indicate that a surprise attack on Pearl Harbor was originally conceived and proposed early in January of 1941 by Admiral Isoroku Yamamoto, commander in chief of the combined Japanese Fleet, who at that time ordered Admiral Onishi, chief of staff of the Eleventh Air Fleet, to study the operation. Admiral Yamamoto is reported to have told Onishi about February 1,[2] "If we have war with the United States we will have no hope of winning unless the United States Fleet in Hawaiian waters can be destroyed."[3] During the latter part of August 1941, all fleet commanders and other key staff members were ordered to Tokyo by Yamamoto for war games preliminary to formulation of final operation plans for a Pacific campaign which included a surprise attack on Pearl Harbor. A war plans conference was held continuously at the Naval War College, Tokyo, from September 2 to 13, and on September 13 an outline incorporating the essential points of a basic operation order, which was later to be issued as *Combined Fleet Top Secret Operation Order No. 1*, was completed. On November 5, 1941, this operation order, which included detailed plans for the surprise attack on Pearl Harbor, was promulgated to all fleet and task force commanders. The date, November 5, is in consequence properly to be regarded as the date on which the plan for the attack on Pearl Harbor was completed.

Under the heading "Preparations for the outbreak of war," operation order No. 1 provided that "when the decision is made to complete over-all preparations for operations, orders will be issued establishing the *approximate* date (Y-day) for commencement of operations and announcing 'first preparations for war.' " The order further provided that "the time for the outbreak of war (X-day) will be given in an imperial general headquarters order." The details of the plan with respect to the Pearl Harbor attack were worked out by members of the naval general staff operations section, combined fleet operations staff, and first air fleet operations staff.

Admiral Yamamoto on November 7 issued combined fleet top secret operation order No. 2 relating: "First preparations for war. Y-day will be December 8." Consistent with the definition of Y-day as given in operation order No. 1, December 8 (December 7, Honolulu time) was thus established only as the approximate date for commencement of operations. The imperial general headquarters,

---

[1] The chief sources of information concerning the attack are translations of captured Japanese documents, interrogations of prisoners of war, and reports submitted by general headquarters, supreme commander for the Allied Powers, comprising questionnaires filled out since VJ-day by former members of the Japanese naval high command. See committee exhibits Nos. 8, 8A, 8B, 8C, and 8D.

For purposes of convenience, the term Hawaii is used throughout this report as synonymous with the Territory of Hawaii.

[2] Unless otherwise stated the time indicated is Tokyo time. To obtain the corresponding time in Washington and Honolulu, 14 hours and 19½ hours, respectively, should be subtracted from Tokyo time. See committee exhibit No. 6, item 4.

[3] See committee exhibit No. 8D.

53

however, issued an order on December 2 stating, "The hostile actions against the United States of America shall be commenced on December 8," thereby announcing X-day as defined in operation order No. 1. The tentative approximate date for the attack selected on November 7 and defined as Y-day in consequence became the final precise date, X-day.

The Japanese imperial headquarters navy section, in discussions prior to November 7, generally recognized December 8 as a propitious date from an operational viewpoint and decided upon this date in conjunction with the leaders of the combined fleet. It was noted that from the standpoint of a dawn attack in the Hawaiian area December 10 would have been suitable in view of the dark of the moon. But it was expected the United States Pacific Fleet, in accordance with its custom during maneuvers, would enter Pearl Harbor on Friday and leave on Monday. Sunday, December 8, was therefore decided upon with the understanding that, to assure the success of the attack and still avoid a night attack, the take-off time of the attacking planes was to be set as near to dawn as possible; that is, approximately 1 hour before sunrise. An imperial naval order issued on December 1 stated: "*Japan * * * has reached a decision to declare war on the United States of America, British Empire, and the Netherlands.*" [4]

NATURE OF THE PLAN

Three possible avenues in approaching Hawaii for the attack presented themselves: The northern course, which was used; a central course which headed east following the Hawaiian Islands; and a southern route passing through the Marshall Islands and approaching from the south. Because of the absolute requirement that the element of surprise be a factor in the attack, the northern course was selected since it was far from the United States patrol screen of land-based aircraft, and there was little chance of meeting commercial vessels.

Screening destroyers were to be sent ahead of the Japanese Fleet and in the event any vessels were encountered the main body of the force was to make a severe change in course and endeavor to avoid detection. If the striking force was detected prior to the day before the attack, it was planned to have the force return to Japanese waters without executing the attack. On the other hand, should the force be detected on the day before the attack, the question of whether to carry home the attack or to return was to be resolved in accordance with local conditions.[5] If the attack should fail, the main force of the Japanese Navy, located in the Inland Sea, was to be brought out to the Pacific in order to return the striking force to home waters.

According to Japanese sources interviewed since the defeat of Japan, the sources of information employed in planning the attack included public broadcasts from Hawaii; reports from naval attachés in the Japanese Embassy, Washington; public newspapers in the United States; reconnaissance submarines in Hawaiian waters prior to the attack; and information obtained from crews and passengers

---

[4] See committee exhibit No. 8D.
[5] Had the American Fleet left port it is reported that the Japanese force would have scouted an area of about 300 miles around Oahu and was prepared to attack. If the American Fleet could not be located the striking force was to withdraw. See committee exhibit No. 8.

of ships which had called at Honolulu in mid-November.[6] It also appears that Japan was receiving the same type of espionage information from its Honolulu consul as from other Japanese diplomatic establishments.[7]

The Japanese plan of operation was predicated on certain assumptions with respect to the United States Pacific Fleet: (1) That the main body of the fleet would be at anchor within Pearl Harbor on Sunday, December 7, Hawaii time; (2) that a carrier could be moved from Japanese home waters across the Pacific to within striking distance of the main islands of the Hawaiian group without undue risk of detection by American defensive reconnaissance; (3) that should the two foregoing assumptions be in error, a reserve group of heavy naval units could sortie from the Inland Sea to give support to the carrier striking force in a decisive engagement with the American Fleet; (4) that a powerful carrier air strike against the American forces based in Hawaii could, if tactical surprise were effective, achieve the strategic result of crippling the American Fleet, and (5) that such a strike could achieve also the destruction of American land-based air power and thus permit the Japanese striking force to withdraw without damage.

Incident to preparations and discussions on September 6 and 7 relating to operation order No. 1, it was decided that no landing on the island of Oahu should be attempted since (1) it would have been impossible to make preparations for such a landing within less than a month after the opening of hostilities; (2) it was recognized that the problems of speed and supply for an accompanying convoy would have rendered it unlikely that the initial attack could be accomplished without detection; and (3) insuperable logistic problems rendered landings on Oahu impractical. In formulating the final plans it was determined that a torpedo attack against ships anchored in Pearl Harbor was the most effective method of putting the United States Pacific Fleet in the Hawaiian area out of action for a long period of time. Two obstacles to a torpedo attack were considered: The fact that Pearl Harbor is narrow and shallow; and the fact that it was probably equipped with torpedo nets. In order to overcome the first difficulty it was decided to attach stabilizers to the torpedoes and launch them from extremely low altitude. Since the success of an aerial torpedo attack could not be assured because of the likelihood of torpedo nets a bombing attack was also to be employed.

---

[6] It is reported that Japanese agents in Hawaii played no part in the attack. See committee exhibit No. 8.

The location of the anchorages shown on the maps recovered from the attacking force was determined on the basis of the indicated sources beginning in the early part of 1941.

It has been reported that the intelligence section of the Japanese naval general staff was having a most difficult time judging the habits, strength, and security situations of the American Fleet in the Hawaiian area. Because of this, the intelligence section had been for years compiling material by carefully collecting, making into statistics, and analyzing bits of information obtained from naval officers at Washington, newspapers and magazines published in America, American radio broadcasts, signal intelligence, passengers and crews of ships stopping over at Honolulu, other foreign diplomatic establishments, commercial firms, and similar sources. According to the signals of the American ships, the number of ships and small craft of the Pacific Fleet anchored in Pearl Harbor or out on training was deduced. By combining the flying time (judged according to signal situations) of airplanes shuttling between bases and aircraft carriers out on training missions, and the location of United States Fleet units as seen by passengers and crews of ships stopping over at Honolulu, the training areas of the fleet were determined. The zone, time, etc., of airplanes at Hawaii were deduced in the same way. From newspapers and magazines published in the United States, material was obtained for deduction of America's war preparation, progress and expansion of military installations, location and capabilities of warships and airplanes, Army strength at Hawaii, Panama, the Philippines, and other places.

It is reported from Japanese sources that the reports from foreign diplomatic establishments and commercial firms in foreign countries were regarded as not important enough from the standpoint of intelligence to have a "special write-up, and were considered on their own merits." See committee exhibit No. 8C.

[7] See committee exhibit No. 2.

The complete plan of the attack was known in advance to members of the Navy general staff, the commander in chief and chiefs of staff, and staff members of the combined fleet headquarters and first air fleet headquarters. Portions of the plan were known to the Navy Minister, the Navy Vice Minister, and other ranking naval officers. It has been reported that the Japanese Emperor knew in advance only the general outline of the plan and that none of the Japanese officials in the United States, including Ambassadors Nomura and Kurusu, knew anything concerning the plan prior to the attack.

The aims of the entire Japanese campaign, including the attack on Pearl Harbor, were based on the desire for military conquest, security, and enhancement of the Empire by occupation of areas rich in natural resources. With respect to the Pearl Harbor attack, operation Order No. 1 stated: "In the east the American Fleet will be destroyed and American lines of operation, and supply lines to the Orient, will be cut. Enemy forces will be intercepted and annihilated. Victories will be exploited to break the enemy's will to fight." [8]

Departure for the Attack

On or about November 14 [9] units of the Pearl Harbor attacking force were ordered to assemble in Hitokappu Bay, located in the Kurile Islands, [10] this operation being completed by November 22. On November 25 the commander in chief of the combined Japanese Fleet issued the following order: [11]

(a) The task force, keeping its movements strictly secret and maintaining close guard against submarines and aircraft, shall advance into Hawaiian waters and upon the very opening of hostilities, shall attack the main force of the United States Fleet in Hawaii and deal it a mortal blow. The first air raid is planned for dawn of X-day (exact date to be given by later order).

Upon completion of the air raid the task force, keeping close coordination and guarding against enemy counterattack, shall speedily leave the enemy waters and then return to Japan.

(b) Should it appear certain that Japanese-American negotiations will reach an amicable settlement prior to the commencement of hostile action, all the forces of the combined fleet are to be ordered to reassemble and return to their bases.

(c) The task force shall leave Hitokappu Bay on the morning of November 26 and advance to 42° N. and 170° E. (standing-by position) on the afternoon of December 4, Japan time, and speedily complete refueling. (The actual time of departure was 9 a. m., November 26, Japan time—1:30 p. m., November 25, Hawaii time.)

Since the American Fleet and air power based in the Hawaiian area were the only obstacles of consequence, a major task force built around a carrier striking group was considered essential to conducting a successful surprise attack. Accordingly, the striking force consisted of 6 aircraft carriers, including the *Akagi*, the flagship of Admiral Nagumo; 2 battleships, 2 heavy cruisers, 9 destroyers, 3 submarines, 8 train vessels, and approximately 360 planes, which

---

[8] Other factors included (1) rendering impotent the United States Pacific Fleet in order to gain time and maintain freedom of action in the South Seas operation, including the Philippine Islands, and (2) the defense of Japan's mandated islands. See committee exhibit No. 8.

[9] Other information obtained indicates that the commander in chief of the combined fleet issued the following order on November 7: "The task force, keeping its movements strictly secret will assemble in Hitokappu Bay by November 22 for refueling." Committee exhibit No. 8.

[10] Also referred to as Tankan Bay (Etorfu Islands, Kuriles), and Tankappu-Wan.

[11] See committee exhibit No. 8.

participated in the attack. Other submarines had proceeded from the Inland Sea independent of the striking force.[12]

At 9 a. m., November 26,[13] the Japanese Fleet departed under complete radio silence from Hitokappu Bay for its destination 200 miles north of Oahu. Held down by the low speed of the train vessels and the need for fuel economy, the force cruised eastward at 13 knots. Lookouts were posted, but no searches or combat air patrols were flown.[14] The anticipated difficulty in refueling at sea because of weather conditions did not materialize, since the weather proved uniformly calm. On or about December 2 all ships were darkened, and on December 4 the rendezvous point (42° north; 170° east) was reached and the combat ships fueled to capacity from the tankers. The cruise had been entirely uneventful, no planes or ships having been sighted.[15]

The green light to execute the attack had been sent by Admiral Yamamoto from his flagship, the *Yamato*, on December 2. The message was "Niita Kayama Nobore," translated "Climb Mount Niitaka," which was the code phrase meaning "proceed with attack." [16]

EXECUTION OF THE ATTACK [17]

AIR PHASE

On the night of December 6–7 (Hawaii time) the "run-in" to a point 200 miles north of Oahu was made at top speed, 26 knots. Beginning at 6 a. m. and ending at 7:15 a. m., December 7, a total of 360 planes were launched in three waves. The planes rendezvoused to the south and then flew in for coordinated attacks. In addition to the attack planes, it is reported that two type Zero reconnaissance

[12] The following allocation of forces for the attack was made (see committee exhibit No. 6, item 17):

STRIKING FORCE

Commanding Officer: CinC 1st Air Fleet, Vice Admiral Chuichi NAGUMO.
BatDiv 3 (1st Section) (HIEI, KIRISHIMA), 2 BB.
CarDiv 1 (KAGA, AKAGI).
CarDiv 2 (HIRYU, SORYU).
CarDiv 5 (SHOKAKU, ZUIKAKU), 6 CV.
CruDiv 8 (TONE, CHIKUMA), 2 CA.
DesRon 1 (ABUKUMA, 4 DesDivs), 1 CL, 16 DD.
8 Train Vessels.

ADVANCE EXPEDITIONARY FORCE

Commanding Officer: CinC 6th Fleet, Vice Admiral Mitsumi SHIMIZU.
ISUZU, YURA, 2 CL.
KATORI, 1 CL-T.
I-class submarines (including SubRons 1, 2, 3) (I-1, 2, 3, 4, 5, 6, 7, 16, 17, 18, 20, 22–24, 68, 69, 74), 20 SS.
Midget submarines, 5 M-SS.
6 Train Vessels.

[13] The corresponding time in Washington would be 7 p. m. November 25.
[14] A very close watch was kept on Hawaiian broadcasts by Commander Ono, staff communication officer of the striking force. Admiral Nagumo and his staff believed that they could sense from these broadcasts whether or not the forces on Oahu had an inkling of the impending attack. They felt they could judge the tenseness of the situation by these broadcasts. Since stations KGU and KGMB were going along in their normal manner, Admiral Nagumo felt that American forces were still oblivious of developments. For several days prior to the attack the Jap force had been intercepting messages from our patrol planes. They had not broken the code, but they had been able to plot in their positions with radio bearings and knew the number of our patrol planes in the air at all times and that they were patrolling entirely in the southwestern sector from Oahu. Committee exhibit No. 8D.
[15] To disguise the move against Pearl Harbor the main Japanese force in the Inland Sea area and the land-based air units in the Kyushu area carried on deceptive communications, and deceptive measures were taken to indicate that the task force was still in training in the Kyushu area. See committee exhibit No. 8
[16] Committee exhibit No. 8D.
[17] The time hereafter indicated is Hawaiian time unless otherwise specified.

seaplanes were launched at approximately 5 a. m., December 7, to execute reconnaissance of Pearl Harbor and Lahaina Anchorage just before the attack, reaching their destination about 1 hour before arrival of the attack planes.[18]

The Japanese aircraft participating in the operation included 81 fighters, 135 dive bombers, 104 horizontal bombers, and 40 torpedo bombers. Five distinct phases were noted in the execution of the attack, as recounted from the Navy point of view: [19]

Phase I: Combined torpedo plane and dive bomber attacks lasting from 7:55 a. m. to 8:25 a. m.

Phase II: Lull in attacks lasting from 8:25 a. m. to 8:40 a. m.

Phase III: Horizontal bomber attacks extending from 8:40 a. m. to 9:15 a. m.

Phase IV: Dive bomber attacks between 9:15 a. m. and 9:45 a. m.

Phase V: Warning of attacks and completion of raid after 9:45 a. m.

The primary objectives of the Japanese during the raid were the heavy combatant ships and aircraft. Damage to the light forces and the industrial plant was incidental to the destruction or disablement of the heavy ships and aircraft based ashore. In the statement submitted for the consideration of the committee and in his testimony, Rear Adm. R. B. Inglis set forth a review of the various phases of the attack: [20]

Phase I: 7:55–8:25 a. m.—Combined Torpedo Plane and Dive Bomber Attacks

The beginning of the attack coincided with the hoisting of the preparatory signal for 8 o'clock colors. At this time (namely, 7:55 a. m.) Japanese dive bombers appeared over Ford Island, and within the next few seconds enemy torpedo planes and dive bombers swung in from various sectors to concentrate their attack on the heavy ships moored in Pearl Harbor. It is estimated that nine planes engaged in the attack on the naval air station on Ford Island and concentrated on the planes parked in the vicinity of hangar No. 6.

At the time of the attack Navy planes (patrol flying boats, float planes, and scout bombers, carrier type) were lined up on the field. These planes caught fire and exploded. Machine-gun emplacements were set up hastily and manned, although the return fire from shore on Ford Island was pitifully weak. Then, as suddenly as they had appeared, the Japanese planes vanished. No further attack on this air station was made during the day. Except for a direct hit on hangar No. 6 resulting from a bomb which was apparently aimed at the battleship *California* and which fell short, the damage to the station itself was comparatively slight. However, 33 of the Navy's best planes out of a total of 70 planes of all types were destroyed or damaged.

As soon as the attack began, the commander of patrol wing 2 broadcasted from Ford Island the warning: "Air raid, Pearl Harbor. This is *not* drill." This warning was followed a few minutes later by a similar message from the commander in chief, United States Fleet.

At approximately the same time that the Japanese dive bombers appeared over Ford Island, other low-flying planes struck at the Kaneohe Naval Air Station on the other side of the island. The attack was well executed, with the planes coming down in shallow dives and inflicting severe casualties on the seaplanes moored in the water. Machine guns and rifles were brought out, and men dispersed to fire at will at the low-flying planes. After a period of 10 to 15 minutes, the attacking planes drew off to the north at a low altitude and disappeared from sight. Several other contingents of bombers passed over, but none dropped bombs on Kaneohe Bay.

About 25 minutes after the first attack, another squadron of planes, similar to one of the Navy's light bomber types, appeared over Kaneohe and commenced bombing and strafing. No. 3 hanger received a direct hit during this attack, and

[18] See committee exhibit No. 155.
[19] For a description of the attack as obtained from Japanese sources since VJ-day, see committee exhibits Nos. 8 and 8B. p. 10.
[20] Committee record, pp. 85–103.

four planes in the hangar were destroyed. The majority of the casualties suffered at Kaneohe resulted from this attack. Most of the injured personnel were in the squadrons attempting either to launch their planes or to save those planes not as yet damaged. When the enemy withdrew, some 10 to 15 minutes later, salvage operations were commenced, but it was too late to save No. 1 hangar, which burned until only its steel structural work was left. Only 9 out of the 36 planes at Kaneohe escaped destruction in this attack; 6 of these were damaged, and 3 were in the air on patrol south of Oahu.

Meanwhile, the Marine air base at Ewa was undergoing similar attack. Apparently the attack on Ewa preceded that at Pearl Harbor by about 2 minutes. It was delivered by 2 squadrons of 18 to 24 single-seater fighter planes using machine-gun strafing tactics, which came in from the northwest at an altitude of approximately 1,000 feet. These enemy planes would descend to within 20 to 25 feet of the ground, attacking single planes with short bursts of gunfire. Then they would pull over the treetops, reverse their course, and attack from the opposite direction. Within less than 15 minutes, all the Marine tactical aircraft had been shot up or set on fire. Then the guns of the enemy fighters were turned upon Navy utility aircraft, upon planes that had been disassembled for repair, and upon the marines themselves.

Effective defense measures were impossible until after the first raid had subsided. Pilots aching to strike at the enemy in the air viewed the wreckage which until a few minutes before had been a strong air group of Marine fighters and bombers. Altogether 33 out of the 49 planes at Ewa had gone up in smoke. Some marines, unable to find anything more effective, had tried to oppose fighter planes with pistols, since the remaining 16 planes were too badly damaged to fly.

Although in phase I of the attack on the ships at Pearl Harbor Japanese dive bombers were effective, *the torpedo planes did the most damage*. They adhered strictly to a carefully laid plan and directed their attacks from those sectors which afforded the best avenues of approach for torpedo attack against selected heavy ship objectives. Thus they indicated accurate knowledge of harbor and channel depths and the berths ordinarily occupied by the major combatant units of the fleet. At least in the great majority of cases, the depth of water in Pearl Harbor did not prevent the successful execution of this form of attack. Shallow dives of the torpedoes upon launching were assured by the use of specially constructed wooden fins, remnants of which were discovered on enemy torpedoes salvaged after the attack.

Four separate torpedo plane attacks were made during phase I. The major attack was made by 12 planes, which swung in generally from the southeast over the tank farm and the vicinity of Merry Point. After splitting, they launched their torpedoes at very low altitudes (within 50 to 100 feet of the water), and from very short distances, aiming for the battleships berthed on the southeast side of Ford Island. All the outboard battleships (namely, the *Nevada*, *Arizona*, *West Virginia*, *Oklahoma*, and *California*) were effectively hit by one or more torpedoes. Strafing was simultaneously conducted from the rear cockpits. A recovered unexploded torpedo carried an explosive charge of 1,000 pounds.

During the second of these attacks, the *Oklahoma* was struck by three torpedoes on the port side and heeled rapidly to port, impeding the efforts of her defenders to beat off the attackers.

The third attack was made by one torpedo plane which appeared from the west and was directed against the light cruiser *Helena* and the minelayer *Oglala*, both of which were temporarily occupying the berth previously assigned to the battleship *Pennsylvania*, flagship of the Pacific Fleet. One torpedo passed under the *Oglala* and exploded against the side of the *Helena*. The blast stove in the side plates of the *Oglala*. Submersible pumps for the *Oglala* were obtained from the *Helena* but could not be used since no power was available because of damage to the ship's engineering plant.

The fourth wave of five planes came in from the northwest and attacked the seaplane tender *Tangier*, the target ship *Utah*, and the light cruisers *Raleigh* and *Detroit*. The *Raleigh* was struck by one torpedo, and the *Utah* received two hits in succession, capsizing at 8:13 a. m. At first it was feared that the *Raleigh* would capsize. Orders were thereupon given for all men not at the guns to jettison all topside weights and put both airplanes in the water. Extra manila and wire lines were also run to the quays to help keep the ship from capsizing.

The *Utah*, an old battleship converted into a target ship, had recently returned from serving as a target for practice aerial bombardment. As soon as she received her torpedo hits, she began listing rapidly to port. After she had listed to about 40 degrees, the order was given to abandon ship. This order was executed with some difficulty, as the attacking planes strafed the crew as they went over the side. Remnants of the crew had reached Ford Island safely. Later knocking was heard within the hull of the *Utah*. With cutting tools obtained from the *Raleigh* a volunteer crew succeeded in cutting through the hull and rescuing a fireman, second class, who had been entrapped in the void space underneath the dynamo room.

An interesting sidelight on Japanese intentions and advance knowledge is suggested by the fact that berths F–10 and F–11 in which the *Utah* and *Raleigh* were placed, were designated carrier berths and that a carrier was frequently moored in nearby F–9.

The *Detroit* and *Tangier* escaped torpedo damage, one torpedo passing just astern of the *Detroit* and burying itself in the mud. Another torpedo passed between the *Tangier* and the *Utah*.

It is estimated that the total number of torpedo planes engaged in these 4 attacks was 21.

In the eight dive-bomber attacks occurring during phase I, three types of bombs were employed—light, medium, and incendiary.

During the second of these attacks, a bomb hit exploded the forward 14-inch powder magazine on the battleship *Arizona* and caused a ravaging oil fire, which sent up a great cloud of smoke, thereby interfering with antiaircraft fire. The battleship *Tennessee* in the adjacent berth was endangered seriously by the oil fire.

The *West Virginia* was hit during the third of these attacks by two heavy bombs as well as by torpedoes. Like the *California*, she had to be abandoned after a large fire broke out amidships. Her executive officer, the senior survivor, dove overboard and swam to the *Tennessee*, where he organized a party of *West Virginia* survivors to help extinguish the fire in the rubbish, trash, and oil which covered the water between the *Tennessee* and Ford Island.

The total number of dive bombers engaged in this phase is estimated at 30. While a few fighters were reported among the attackers in the various phases, they were no doubt confused with light bombers and accordingly are not treated as a distinct type.

Although the major attack by high-altitude horizontal bombers did not occur until phase III, 15 planes of this type operating in 4 groups were active during phase I.

Most of the torpedo damage to the fleet had occurred by 8:25 a. m. All outboard battleships had been hit by one or more torpedoes; all the battleships had been hit by one or more bombs with the exception of the *Oklahoma*, which took four torpedoes before it capsized, and the *Pennsylvania*, which received a bomb hit later. By the end of the first phase, the *West Virginia* was in a sinking condition; the *California* was down by the stern; the *Arizona* was a flaming ruin; the other battleships were all damaged to a greater or lesser degree.

Although the initial attack of the Japanese came as a surprise, defensive action on the part of the fleet was prompt. All ships immediately went to general quarters. Battleship ready machine guns likewise opened fire at once, and within an estimated average time of less than 5 minutes, practically all battleship and antiaircraft batteries were firing. The cruisers were firing all antiaircraft batteries within an average time of about 4 minutes. The destroyers, although opening up with machine guns almost immediately, averaged 7 minutes in bringing all antiaircraft guns into action.

During this phase of the battle there was no movement of ships within the harbor proper. The destroyer *Helm*, which had gotten under way just prior to the attack, was just outside the harbor entrance when, at 8:17 a. m., a submarine conning tower was sighted to the right of the entrance channel and northward of buoy No. 1. The submarine immediately submerged. The *Helm* opened fire at 8:19 a. m., when the submarine again surfaced temporarily. No hits were observed.

Phase II: 8:25–8:40 a. m.—Lull in Attacks

This phase is described as a lull only by way of comparison. Air activity continued, although somewhat abated, with sporadic attacks by dive and horizontal bombers. During this phase an estimated total of 15 dive bombers participated in 5 attacks upon the ships in the navy yard, the battleships *Maryland*, *Oklahoma*, *Nevada*, and *Pennsylvania*, and various light cruisers and destroyers.

Although three attacks by horizontal bombers occurred during the lull, these appear to have overlapped into phase III and are considered under that heading.

At 8:32 a. m. the battleship *Oklahoma* took a heavy list to starboard and capsized.

During phase II there was still relatively little ship movement within the harbor. The ready-duty destroyer *Monaghan* had received orders at 7:51 a. m. (Pearl Harbor time) to "proceed immediately and contact the *Ward* in defensive sea area." At about 8:37, observing an enemy submarine just west of Ford Island under fire from both the *Curtiss* and *Tangier*, the *Monaghan* proceeded at high speed and at about 8:43 rammed the submarine. As the enemy vessel had submerged, the shock was slight. The *Monaghan* thereupon reversed engines and dropped two depth charges.

The *Curtiss* had previously scored two direct hits on the conning tower. This submarine was later salvaged for inspection and disposal. The *Monaghan* then proceeded down the channel and continued her sortie. At the same time that the *Monaghan* got under way, the destroyer *Henley* slipped her chain from buoy X-11 and sortied, following the *Monaghan* down the channel.

Phase III: 8:40–9:15 a. m.—Horizontal Bomber Attacks

The so-called "lull" in the air raid was terminated by the appearance over the fleet of eight groups of high-altitude horizontal bombers which crossed and re-crossed their targets from various directions, inflicting serious damage. Some of the bombs dropped were converted 15- or 16-inch shells of somewhat less explosive quality, marked by very little flame. According to some observers, many bombs dropped by high-altitude horizontal bombers either failed to explode or landed outside the harbor area.

During the second attack (at 9:06 a. m.) the *Pennsylvania* was hit by a heavy bomb which passed through the main deck amidships and detonated, causing a fire, which was extinguished with some difficulty.

The third group of planes followed very closely the line of battleship moorings. It was probably one of these planes that hit the *California* with what is believed to have been a 15-inch projectile equipped with tail vanes which penetrated to the second deck and exploded. As a result of the explosion, the armored hatch to the machine shop was badly sprung and could not be closed, resulting in the spreading of a serious fire.

Altogether, 30 horizontal bombers, including 9 planes which had participated in earlier attacks, are estimated to have engaged in phase III. Once more it was the heavy combatant ships, the battleships and cruisers, which bore the brunt of these attacks.

Although phase III was largely devoted to horizontal bombing, approximately 18 dive bombers organized in 5 groups also participated.

It was probably the second of these groups which did considerable damage to the *Nevada*, then proceeding down the South Channel, and also to the *Shaw*, *Cassin*, and *Downes*, all three of which were set afire.

During the fifth attack, a Japanese dive bomber succeeded in dropping 1 bomb on the seaplane tender *Curtiss* which detonated on the main deck level, killing 20 men, wounding 58, and leaving 1 other unaccounted for.

During this same phase, the *Curtiss* took under fire one of these bombers, which was pulling out of a dive over the naval air station. Hit squarely by the *Curtiss'* gunfire, the plane crashed on the ship, spattering burning gasoline and starting fires so menacing that one of the guns had to be temporarily abandoned.

Considerable ship movement took place during phase III. At 8:40 a. m. the *Nevada* cleared berth F-8 without assistance and proceeded down the South Channel. As soon as the Japanese became aware that a battleship was trying to reach open water, they sent dive bomber after dive bomber down after her and registered several hits. In spite of the damage she had sustained in the vicinity of floating drydock No. 2, and although her bridge and forestructure were ablaze, the ship continued to fight effectively. At 9:10, however, while she was attempting to make a turn in the channel, the *Nevada* ran aground in the vicinity of buoy No. 19.

Meanwhile the repair ship *Vestal*, also without assistance, had gotten under way at about 8:40, had cleared the burning *Arizona*, and at about 9:40 anchored well clear northeast of Ford Island.

Soon after the *Nevada* and *Vestal* had cleared their berths, tugs began to move the *Oglala* to a position astern of the *Helena* at 10–10 dock. The *Oglala* was finally secured in her berth at about 9, but shortly thereafter she capsized.

At 8:42, the oiler *Neosho* cleared berth F-4 unaided and stood toward Merry Point in order to reduce fire hazard to her cargo and to clear the way for a possible sortie by the battleship *Maryland*.

Phase IV: 9:15-9:45—Dive Bomber Attacks

During phase IV an estimated 27 dive bombers conducted 9 strafing attacks directed against ships throughout the entire harbor area. In all probability the planes were the same ones that had conducted previous attacks. These attacks overlapped by about 10 minutes the horizontal bomber attacks described in phase III.

Phase V: 9:45—Waning of Attacks and Completion of Raid

By 9:45 all enemy planes had retired. Evading Navy aerial searches, both shore-based and from carriers at sea, the Japanese striking force retired to its home waters without being contacted by any American units.

An outline review of the Japanese attack on Army planes and installations is as follows:[21]

Hickam Field

(Army planes at the time of the attack were lined up on the warming-up aprons three or four abreast with approximately 10 feet between wing tips, and approximately 135 feet from the tail of one plane to the nose of another.)

First attack (lasting about 10 minutes): At about 7:55 a. m. nine dive bombers attacked the Hawaiian Air Depot buildings and three additional planes attacked the same objectives from the northwest. Several minutes later nine additional bombers bombed Hickam Field hangar line from the southeast. Immediately thereafter, seven more dive bombers attacked the hangar line from the east.

Second attack (lasting between 10 and 15 minutes): At about 8:25 a. m. between six and nine planes attacked the No. 1 Aqua System,[21a] the technical buildings, and the consolidated barracks. During and immediately after this bombing attack, Army planes on the parking apron were attacked with gunfire. About 8:26 a. m. a formation of five or six planes bombed the baseball diamond from a high altitude, possibly believing the gasoline storage system to be in that area.

Third attack (lasting about 8 minutes): At 9 a. m. from six to nine planes attacked with machine gun fire the technical buildings behind the hangar lines and certain planes which by then were dispersed. At about the same time from seven to nine planes bombed the consolidated barracks, the parade ground and the post exchange.

Wheeler Field

(Army planes were parked in the space between the aprons in front of the hangars, generally in a series of parallel lines approximately wing tip to wing tip, the lines varying from 15 to 20 feet apart.)

First attack (lasting approximately 15 minutes): At 8:02 a. m. 25 planes dive-bombed the hangar lines; machine-gun fire was also employed during the attack.

Second attack (lasting less than 5 minutes): At 9 a. m. seven planes machine-gunned Army planes being taxied to the airdrome.

Bellows Field

(The P-40's were parked in line at 10 to 15 feet intervals; the reconnaissance planes were also parked in a line at slightly greater intervals.)

First attack: At 8:30 a single Japanese fighter machine-gunned the tent area.

Second attack (lasting about 15 minutes): At about 9 a. m. nine fighters machine-gunned the Army planes.

Haleiwa Field was not attacked and after 9:45 a. m. there were no further attacks on Army installations. The evidence indicates that a maximum of 105 planes participated in the attacks on the airfields, it being noted that some of the planes included in this number may have taken part in more than one attack.

SUBMARINE PHASE

Prior to completion of the surprise attack the advance Japanese expeditionary force of submarines was under the command of the striking force commander, Admiral Nagumo. The precise move-

---

[21] See testimony of Col. Bernard Thielen, Committee Record, pages 104-111.
[21a] A hydrostatic pass for the fuel-pumping system. See committee record, p. 105.

ments of the participating submarines are not known, but it is believed that most of these units departed from Japanese home waters in late November and proceeded to the Hawaiian area by way of Kwajalein. A few of the submarines, delayed in leaving Japan, proceeded directly to Hawaii. The functions assigned to the submarines in operations order No. 1 were:[22]

 (a) Until X-day minus 3 some of the submarines were to reconnoiter important points in the Aleutians, Fiji, and Samoa, and were to observe and report on any strong American forces discovered.

 (b) One element was assigned to patrol the route of the striking force in advance of the movement of that force to insure an undetected approach.

 (c) Until X-day minus 5, the remaining submarines were to surround Hawaii at extreme range while one element approached and reconnoitered without being observed.

 (d) On X-day the submarines in the area were to "observe and attack the American Fleet in the Hawaii area; make a surprise attack on the channel leading into Pearl Harbor and attempt to close it; if the enemy moves out to fight, he will be pursued and attacked."

With orders not to attack until the task force strike was verified, the force of I-class submarines took up scouting positions on the evening of December 6 in allotted patrol sectors covering the waters in the vicinity of Pearl Harbor. Between 50 and 100 miles off Pearl Harbor, five midget submarines were launched from specially fitted fleet submarines as a special attacking force to conduct an offensive against American ships within the harbor and to prevent the escape of the Pacific Fleet through the harbor entrance during the scheduled air raid. Available data indicates that only one of the five midget submarines penetrated into the harbor, discharging its torpedoes harmlessly. None of the five midget submarines rejoined the Japanese force.[23]

The I-class submarines maintained their patrols in the Hawaiian area after the attack and at least one of the group (the *I–7*) launched its aircraft to conduct a reconnaissance of Pearl Harbor to ascertain the status of the American Fleet and installations. In the event of virtual destruction of the American Fleet at Pearl Harbor, the operation plan provided that one submarine division or less would be placed between Hawaii and North America to destroy sea traffic. At least one submarine (the *I–7*) was dispatched to the Oregon coast on or about December 13.

WITHDRAWAL OF THE STRIKING FORCE

Upon completion of the launchings of aircraft at 7:15 a. m., December 7, the fleet units of the Japanese striking force withdrew at high speed to the northwest. Plane recovery was effected between 10:30 a. m. and 1:30 p. m., whereupon the force proceeded by a circuitous route to Kure, arriving on December 23. En route two carriers, two cruisers, and two destroyers were detached on December 15 to serve as reinforcements for the Wake Island operation. The

[22] See committee exhibit No. 8.
[23] All midget submarine personnel were prepared for death and none expected to return alive. Committee exhibit No. 8.

original plans called for the retiring force to strike at Midway if possible but this strike was not made, probably because of the presence of a United States task force south of Midway.[24]

DAMAGE TO UNITED STATES NAVAL FORCES AND INSTALLATIONS AS A RESULT OF THE ATTACK

Of the vessels in Pearl Harbor on the morning of December 7,[25] the following were either sunk or damaged:[26]

Type	Name	Extent of damage
Battleships	Arizona	Sunk.
	California	Do.
	West Virginia	Do.
	Oklahoma	Capsized.
	Nevada	Heavily damaged.
	Maryland	Damaged.
	Pennsylvania	Do.
	Tennessee	Do.
Light cruisers	Helena	Heavily damaged.
	Honolulu	Damaged.
	Raleigh	Heavily damaged.
Destroyers	Shaw	Do.
	Cassin	Heavily damaged (burned).
	Downes	Do.
Repair ship	Vestal	Badly damaged.
Minelayer	Oglala	Sunk.
Seaplane tender	Curtiss	Damaged.
Miscellaneous auxiliaries	Utah	Capsized.

The Navy and Marine Corps suffered a total of 2,835 casualties, of which 2,086 officers and men were killed or fatally wounded. Seven hundred and forty-nine wounded survived. None were missing.[26a]

A total of 92 naval planes (including 5 scout planes from the carrier *Enterprise*) were lost and an additional 31 planes damaged.[27] At the Ford Island Naval Air Station one hangar was badly damaged by fire and another suffered minor damage. A complete hangar, in which planes were stored, was destroyed at Kaneohe Naval Air Station along with the planes therein and the seaplane parking area was damaged. At the marine base at Ewa a considerable amount of damage was suffered by material, installations, machinery, tentage, and buildings. Damage at the base to aircraft was extremely heavy inasmuch as the primary objective was aircraft on the ground, the attacks being made on individual aircraft by enemy planes using explosive and incendiary bullets from extremely low altitudes.[28]

---

[24] The Japanese attack on Pearl Harbor cannot be separated from the wide-scale operations of which it was a part. On the evening of December 7, Japanese forces struck Hong Kong, Guam, the Philippine Islands, Wake and, on the morning of December 8, Midway.

[25] The vessels in Pearl Harbor included 8 battleships; 2 heavy cruisers; 6 light cruisers; 29 destroyers; 5 submarines; 1 gunboat; 8 destroyer minelayers; 1 minelayer; 4 destroyer minesweepers; 6 minesweepers; and 24 auxiliaries. Committee exhibit No. 6.

Units of the Pacific Fleet not in Pearl Harbor at the time of the attack included: (1) Task Force 8 under Admiral Halsey, consisting of one aircraft carrier, the *Enterprise*, three heavy cruisers, and nine destroyers, was about 200 miles west of Oahu en route to Pearl Harbor after having ferried Marine Corps fighter planes to Wake Island. (2) Task Force 12 under Admiral Newton, consisting of one aircraft carrier, the *Lexington*, three heavy cruisers, and five destroyers, was about 460 miles southeast of Midway en route to Midway from Pearl Harbor with a squadron of Marine Corps scout bombers. (3) Task Force 3 under Admiral Wilson Brown, consisting of one heavy cruiser and five destroyer minesweepers, had just arrived off Johnston Island to conduct tests of a new type landing craft. (4) Other units of the fleet were on isolated missions of one type or another. See testimony of Admiral Inglis, committee record, pp. 52–55.

[26] See committee exhibit No. 6.

[26a] See testimony of Admiral Inglis, committee record, p. 131.

[27] See testimony of Admiral Inglis, committee record, pp. 128, 135, 136.

[28] See committee exhibit No. 6.

Damage to United States Army Forces and Installations as a Result of the Attack

The Army suffered a total of 600 casualties, including 194 killed in action and 360 wounded.[29]

A total of 96 Army planes were lost as a result of enemy action, this figure including aircraft destroyed in depots and those damaged planes which were subsequently stripped for parts.[30]

In addition, extensive damage was inflicted on Army installations as reflected by photographic evidence submitted to the committee.[31]

Japanese Losses

It has been estimated by our own sources, that the Japanese lost a total of 28 planes, most of them being dive-bombers and torpedo planes, as a result of Navy action. Three Japanese submarines of 45 tons each, carrying two torpedoes, were accounted for; two were destroyed by Navy action and one was grounded off Bellows Field and recovered. From reports available it is estimated that the Japanese lost, due solely to Navy action, a minimum of 68 killed. One officer, an ensign, was taken prisoner when he abandoned the submarine which grounded off Bellows Field.[32]

General Short reported that 11 enemy aircraft were shot down by Army pursuit planes and antiaircraft fire.[33]

Information developed through Japanese sources indicates, however, that a total of only 29 aircraft were lost and all of the 5 midget submarines.[34]

Summary Comparison of Losses

As a result of the December 7 attack on Hawaii, military and naval forces of the United States suffered 3,435 casualties; Japan, less than 100. We lost outright 188 planes; Japan, 29. We suffered severe damage to or loss of 8 battleships, 3 light cruisers, 3 destroyers, and 4 miscellaneous vessels; Japan lost 5 midget submarines. The astoundingly disproportionate extent of losses marks the greatest military and naval disaster in our Nation's history.[35] The only compensating feature was the many acts of personal valor during the attack.[36]

---

[29] In addition 22 were missing in action, 2 died (nonbattle), 1 was declared dead (Public Law 490), and 21 died of wounds. Committee exhibit No. 5.

[30] See testimony of Colonel Thielen, committee record, p. 130. In a statement by General Short concerning events and conditions leading up to the Japanese attack, a total of 128 Army planes are indicated as having been damaged in the raid. See Roberts (Army) exhibit No. 7.

[31] See committee record, p. 130; exhibits Nos. 5 and 6.

[32] See testimony of Admiral Inglis, committee record, p. 128.

[33] See testimony of Colonel Thielen, committee record, p. 130.

[34] Committee exhibit No. 8B.

[35] The Japanese estimate of losses inflicted was: 4 battleships, 1 cruiser, and 2 tankers sunk; 4 battleships heavily damaged; 1 battleship lightly damaged; and 260 planes destroyed. Committee exhibit No. 8.

[36] In the accounts of some 90 ships under attack, commanding officers have recorded hundreds of acts of heroism in keeping with the highest traditions of the naval service. No instance is recorded in which the behavior of crews or individuals left anything to be desired. References to individual valor are replete with such acts as:

    (1) Medical officers and hospital corpsmen rendering aid and treatment while they themselves needed help.

    (2) Officers and men recovering dead and wounded through flame and from flooded compartments.

    (3) Fighting fires while in actual physical contact with the flames.

    (4) Handling and passing ammunition under heavy fire and strafing.

    (5) Repairing ordnance and other equipment under fire.

    (6) Remaining at guns and battle stations though wounded or while ships were sinking.

    (7) Reporting for further duty to other ships after being blown off their own sinking vessels.

For deeds of extreme heroism on December 7, 15 Medals of Honor have been awarded and 60 Navy crosses. (Testimony of Admiral Inglis, committee record, pp. 131, 132.)

On the Army side, too, acts of heroism were numerous. Five Distinguished Service Crosses and 65 Silver Stars were awarded to Army personnel for heroism displayed during the December 7 attack. (Testimony of Colonel Thielen, committee record, p. 133.)

State of Readiness to Meet the Attack

ATTACK A SURPRISE

The Japanese attack came as an utter surprise to the Army and Navy commanders in Hawaii. The Army was on an alert against sabotage only with the planes, which were on 4 hours' notice, lined up side by side as perfect targets for an attack. The state of readiness aboard naval vessels was the usual state of readiness for vessels in port. Fifty percent of the Navy planes were on 4 hours' notice. Although the Hawaiian forces were completely surprised, two significant events occurred on the morning of December 7 which indicated a possible attack.

The first indication came at 3:50 a. m. when the United States coastal minesweeper *Condor* reported sighting the periscope of a submerged submarine while approximately 1¾ miles southwest of the Pearl Harbor entrance buoys, an area in which American submarines were prohibited from operating submerged.[37] The Navy destroyer *Ward* was informed and, after instituting a search, sighted the periscope of an unidentified submarine apparently trailing a target repair ship en route to Honolulu harbor. This submarine was sunk shortly after 6:45 a. m. No action was taken apart from dispatching the ready-duty destroyer U. S. S. *Monaghan* to proceed to sea, to close the net gate to Pearl Harbor, and to attempt to verify the submarine contact report. The presence of the submarine was not interpreted as indicating the possibility of an attack on Pearl Harbor.[38]

The second indication of an attack came at approximately 7:02 a. m., December 7, when an Army mobile radar unit detected a large number of planes approaching Oahu at a distance of 132 miles from 3° east of north.[39] These planes were the Japanese attacking force. The aircraft warning information center, which closed down at 7 a. m. on the morning of December 7, was advised of the approaching planes at 7:20 a. m. An Army lieutenant, whose tour of duty at the information center was for training and observation and continued until 8 a. m., took the call and instructed the radar operators in effect to "forget it." His estimate of the situation appears to have been occasioned by reason of a feeling that the detected flight was either a naval patrol, a flight of Hickam Field bombers, or possibly some B–17's from the mainland that were scheduled to arrive at Hawaii on December 7.

PERSONNEL

A summarized statement of Navy personnel actually on board ship at the beginning of the attack is as follows:[40]

	On board
Commanding officers of battleships	5 out of 8.
Commanding officers of cruisers	6 out of 7.
Commanding officers of destroyers	63 percent.
Damage control officers of battleships	6 out of 8.

---

[37] See committee exhibit No. 112, p. 96.
[38] See discussion, *infra*, of the submarine contact on the morning of December 7.
[39] See committee exhibit No. 155.
[40] See testimony of Admiral Inglis, committee record, p. 103.

Average percentage of officers:		On board
Battleships (approximate)		60 to 70 percent.
Cruisers, battle force (approximate)		65 percent.
Destroyers, battle force (approximate)		50 percent.

Average percentage of men:
Battleships		95 percent.
Cruisers, battle force		98 percent.
Destroyers, battle force		85 percent.

There were ample personnel present and ready to man all naval shore installations.

In the case of the Army, a summary report compiled by the Adjutant General of the Hawaiian Department indicates that at least 85 percent of the officers and men were present with their units at 8 a. m., December 7.[41]

ANTIAIRCRAFT

All naval antiaircraft batteries, consisting of 780 guns, were ship-based; that is, located on the ships in Pearl Harbor. At the time of the attack, roughly one-fourth of all antiaircraft guns were manned, and within 7 to 10 minutes, all antiaircraft batteries were manned and firing. It appears that all naval batteries were in operating condition; the number of temporary gun stoppages during action was so low as to be negligible. All ships had the full service allowance of ammunition on board, except in a few instances where removal was necessary because of repairs in progress, and ammunition was ready at the guns in accordance with existing directives. Ready antiaircraft machine guns opened fire immediately and within an average estimated time of under 5 minutes practically all battleship antiaircraft batteries were firing; cruisers were firing all antiaircraft batteries within an average time of 4 minutes; and destroyers, though opening up with machine guns almost immediately, averaged 7 minutes in bringing all antiaircraft guns into action. Minor combatant types had all joined in the fire within 10 minutes after the beginning of the attack.[42]

In the case of the Army, the following table reflects the places and times at which antiaircraft units were in position:[43]

Regiment	Battery	In position and ready to fire
Sixty-fourth (alerted at 8:15 a. m.)	A (searchlight) at Honolulu	10:00 a. m.
	B (3-inch) at Aiea	10:00 a. m.
	C (3-inch) at Aliamanu	10:30 a. m.
	D (3-inch) south of Aliamanu	11:00 a. m.
	E (searchlight) at Ewa-Pearl Harbor	(Time not known.)
	F (3-inch) at Pearl City	11:05 a. m.
	G (3-inch) at Ahua Point	10:30 a. m.
	H (3-inch) at Fort Weaver	11:45 a. m.
	I (37-mm.) at Aliamanu	(Known only that batteries were in position before 11:45 a.m.)
	K (37-mm.) at Hickam Field	
	L (37-mm.) at Hickam Field	
	M (37-mm.) at Wheeler Field	11:55 a. m.
Ninety-seventh (alerted between 7:55 and 8:10 a. m.).	A (searchlight) at Fort Kamehameha	8:34 a. m.
	F (3-inch) at Fort Kamehameha	8:55 a. m.
	G (3-inch) at Fort Weaver	8:30 a. m.
	H (3-inch) at Fort Barrett	10:20 a. m.
Ninety-eighth	A (searchlight) at Schofield Barracks	(Time not known.)
	B (3-inch) at Schofield Barracks	9:55 a. m.
	C (3-inch) at Schofield Barracks	10:30 a. m.
	D (3-inch) at Puuloa dump, south of Ewa	11:45 a. m.
	F (3-inch) at Kaneohe Naval Air Station	1:15 p. m.
	G (3-inch) at Kaneohe Naval Air Station	1:15 p. m.
	H (3-inch) at Waipahu High School	1:30 p. m.

41 See testimony of Colonel Thielen, committee record, p. 114.
42 See testimony of Admiral Inglis, committee record, pp. 123, 124
43 See committee exhibit No. 5.

Regiment	Battery	In position and ready to fire
Two Hundred and Fifty-first	A (searchlight) at Ewa	(Time not known.)
	B (3-inch) at West Loch	11:45 a. m.
	C (3-inch) at Ewa Beach	11:45 a. m.
	D (3-inch) at South of Ewa	11:45 a. m.
	E (50-caliber) at Navy Yard, Pearl Harbor	12:41 p. m.
	F (37-mm.) at Navy recreation area	12:30 p. m.
	G (37-mm.) at tank farm, Schofield Barracks	11:00 a. m.
	H (37-mm.) at Navy Yard	12:05 p. m.

One antiaircraft detachment was located at Sand Island when the attack started and engaged the enemy with 3-inch guns at 8:15 a. m., shooting down two enemy planes at that time.

The foregoing table reflects that of 31 army antiaircraft batteries, 27 were not in position and ready to fire until after the attack and in several instances not for a considerable period of time after the attack.

The extraordinary lack of readiness of Army antiaircraft units appears to have been occasioned largely by the time required for moving into position and the fact that ammunition was not readily accessible to the mobile batteries.[44]

AIRCRAFT

Seven Navy patrol flying boats were in the air at the time of the attack. Three of these planes were engaged in a routine search of the fleet operating area approximately 120 miles south of Oahu and the remaining four were engaged in intertype tactical exercises with United States submarines near Lahaina Roads. Eight scout bombers that had been launched from the carrier *Enterprise*, which was 200 miles west of Pearl Harbor at the time of the attack, for the purpose of searching ahead of the ship and then landing at Ewa, arrived during the attack and engaged Japanese aircraft. Three of these planes landed after the attack while the remaining five were lost.[45] The majority of the Navy planes were on 4 hours' notice.[46]

In the case of the Army, planes were generally on 4 hours' notice. Between 25 and 35 planes, these being fighters, took off after the attack began and before it was concluded.[47]

ACTION TAKEN FOLLOWING THE ATTACK

An effort was made in the course of and after the attack, through planes already in the air and those that could get into the air during

[44] Colonel Thielen stated: "* * * only a limited amount of ammunition was in the hands of troops of the Hawaiian Department. The Coast Artillery Command had previously been authorized to draw, and had drawn, ammunition for its fixed positions only, including antiaircraft. However, at these installations, the shells were kept in boxes in order to keep the ammunition from damage and deterioration. The ammunition for the mobile guns and batteries was in storage chiefly at Aliamanu Crater and Schofield Barracks. The Infantry and Artillery units of the Twenty-fourth and Twenty-fifth Divisions had only a small amount of machine gun and rifle ammunition. All divisional artillery ammunition, grenades, and mortar shells were in the ordnance storage depots, principally at Schofield Barracks." Committee record, pp. 119, 120.

The situation with respect to artillery ammunition was testified to by General Burgin as follows: "They were all ready to go into action immediately, with the exception that the mobile batteries did not have the ammunition. The fixed batteries along the seacoast, those batteries bolted down to concrete, had the ammunition nearby. I had insisted on that with General Short in person and had gotten his permission to take this antiaircraft ammunition, move it into the seacoast gun battery positions, and have it nearby the antiaircraft guns. It was, however, boxed up in wooden boxes and had to be taken out. The ammunition for the mobile guns and batteries was in Aliamanu Crater, which, you may know or may not, is about a mile from Fort Shafter, up in the old volcano. The mobile batteries had to send there to get ammunition. In addition to that, the mobile batteries had to move out from the various posts to their field positions; They were not in field positions." Roberts Commission Record, pp. 2604–2605.

[45] See committee record, pp. 71, 72.

[46] Admiral Bellinger stated that of 62 patrol planes at Oahu, 2 were on 15-minute notice, 8 on 30-minute notice, 9 were undergoing repairs, and 42 were on 4 hours' notice. Committee record, p. 9303.

[47] See committee exhibit No. 5.

and following the attack, to locate the Japanese carrier force but to no avail. The attacking planes withdrew and were recovered by the fleet units without the latter being detected.

While it appears some planes under Navy direction were assigned to search the sector to the north of Oahu, generally regarded as the dangerous sector from the standpoint of an air attack, they were diverted to the southwest by reason of a false report that the Japanese carriers were in that direction.[48]

The deplorable feature of the action following the attack was the failure of the Navy and Army to coordinate their efforts through intelligence at hand. The same Army radar unit that had tracked the Japanese force in, plotted it back out to the north.[49] Yet this vital information, which would have made possible an effective search, was employed by neither service.[50]

DEFENSIVE FORCES AND FACILITIES OF THE NAVY AT HAWAII

The principal vessels in Pearl Harbor at the time of the attack were 8 battleships, 8 cruisers, and 29 destroyers. Inasmuch as there were no naval antiaircraft shore batteries in or around Pearl Harbor at the time of the Japanese attack, these warships provided the chief antiaircraft defense. The ship-based antiaircraft batteries totaled 780 guns, 427 of which had an effective range of from 500 to 2,500 yards and the remainder from 5,000 to 12,000 yards.[51]

The Navy is indicated to have had a total of 169 planes at Hawaii prior to the attack, 71 of which were patrol bombers and 15 fighter planes.[52] It is to be noted, however, that Admiral Bellinger in a report to Admiral Kimmel on December 19, 1941, concerning the availability and disposition of patrol planes on the morning of December 7 indicated 69 patrol planes as being at Hawaii. His tabulation was as follows: [53]

	In commission	Top available for flight	Under repair	Ready at base	In air
At Kaneohe	36	33	3	30	3
At Pearl	33	28	5	24	4
At Midway	12	11	1	4	7
Total	81	72	9	58	14

It thus appears that a total of 61 patrol planes were available for flight as of December 7. Fifty-four of the patrol planes were new PBY-5's that had been recently ferried to Hawaii between October 28 and November 23, 1941. Admiral Bellinger indicated that the new

[48] Admiral Smith, Chief of Staff to Admiral Kimmel, said he did not get the information as to the probable location from which the Japanese carriers launched the attack for some 2 days. There was a great deal of confusion including false civilian reports of troop parachute landings and a false report from one of our own planes concerning an enemy carrier to the south. A chart showing the position of the Japanese carriers was taken from a Japanese plane by the Army on December 7 but was not shown the Navy until the afternoon. See Navy Court of Inquiry record, p. 564.

With further respect to the confusion that prevailed, Captain Rochefort stated that when the attack began his communications unit at Pearl Harbor lost all contact with the "direction finder" stations, located at Lualualei and Aiea, and that in consequence no bearings on the attacking Japanese force were received by his unit. He commented that the failure of communications was the result of an accident, caused by Army personnel setting up new circuits. See Hewitt inquiry record, pp. 63, 64.

[49] See committee exhibit No. 155 for original radar plot of Opana station, December 7, 1941.

[50] Admiral Kitts said that on December 8 while in conference with General Davidson he was shown a plot showing planes coming in to Oahu and going out again. This plot was not reported to the Navy until Kitts saw it on December 8. See Hewitt inquiry record, p. 520.

[51] See testimony of Admiral Inglis, committee record, p. 122.

[52] See committee exhibit No. 6.

[53] See committee exhibit No. 120.

PBY-5's were experiencing the usual shake-down difficulties and were hampered in maintenance by an absence of spare parts. He pointed out that 12 of the patrol planes indicated as available for flight had returned from Midway on December 5 after an arduous tour of duty at Midway and Wake since October 17, and were in relatively poor material condition because of the extended operations.[54]

While radar equipment was available on three of the battleships and on one seaplane tender, it was not being manned inasmuch as the height of the land surrounding Pearl Harbor rendered ships' radar ineffective.[55]

DEFENSIVE FORCES AND FACILITIES OF THE ARMY IN HAWAII

As of December 6, 1941, General Short had a total of 42,959 officers and men under his command. The principal elements of the Hawaiian Department were 2 infantry divisions and supporting ground troops composing the beach and land defense forces; the Coast Artillery Command, consisting of the seacoast and antiaircraft defense forces; and the Hawaiian Air Force.[56]

The Hawaiian Coast Artillery Command had a total of 213 antiaircraft guns.[57] Eighty-six were 3-inch antiaircraft guns (70 percent mobile); 20, 37-millimeter; and 107 caliber .50.

The Army on December 7, prior to the attack, had a total of 227 planes [58] located principally at Hickam, Wheeler, and Bellows Fields. They consisted of 12 heavy bombers; 36 medium bombers (obsolescent); 14 light bombers (2 obsolescent); 152 pursuit planes (53 obsolescent); and 13 observation planes.[59] Eighty-seven of these planes for one reason or another were not available for flight, including 6 of the heavy bombers and 58 of the pursuit planes. Ninety-four pursuit planes (including 30 of the obsolescent craft) were available for flight.

In addition, the Army had six mobile radar units which were available and in operating condition.[60]

COMPARISON OF STRENGTH AND LOSSES: JAPANESE ATTACKING FORCE AND HAWAIIAN DEFENSIVE FORCES

The Japanese attacking force brought to bear 360 planes incident to the attack; whereas the Army and Navy together had a total of 402 planes of all types, not taking into account those not available for flight on the morning of December 7. The operating strength of the opposing forces by comparison follows:

---

[54] Id.

[55] The only ships in Pearl Harbor equipped with ship search radar on December 7 were the battleships *Pennsylvania*, *California*, and *West Virginia* and the seaplane tender *Curtiss*. The radar equipment on these ships was not manned since the height of the land around Pearl Harbor would have made it ineffective. The equipment of the *Curtiss* was put into operation at the beginning of the first attack and that on the *Pennsylvania* began to operate 15 minutes later, both with negative results. There were no naval radar stations on shore in Hawaii. See testimony of Admiral Inglis, committee record, p. 82.

[56] See testimony of Colonel Thielen, committee record, p. 64; also committee exhibit No. 5.

[57] The principal weapons of the Hawaiian Coast Artillery Command included: 4 16-inch guns, 2 14-inch guns (obsolescent), 4 12-inch guns (2 obsolescent), 4 3-inch seacoast guns, 36 155-millimeter guns, 86 3-inch antiaircraft guns (70 percent mobile), 20 37-millimeter antiaircraft guns, and 107 caliber .50 antiaircraft guns. Committee exhibit No. 5.

[58] The statement of General Short of events and conditions leading up to the Japanese attack, Roberts (Army) exhibit No. 7, reflected the status of planes as follows: Pursuit planes in commission, 80; pursuit planes out of commission, 69; reconnaissance planes in commission, 6; reconnaissance planes out of commission, 7; bombers in commission, 39; bombers out of commission, 33.

[59] See committee exhibit No. 5.

[60] Three additional radar units calling for permanent installation were not as yet in operating condition.

Japanese attacking force

Fighters	[61] 81
Dive bombers	135
Horizontal bombers	104
Torpedo planes	40

Defending forces		Available for flight	Not available for flight
Fighters	(30 obsolescent)	108	59
Army bombers	(21 obsolescent)	35	27
Navy patrol bombers		61	8
Navy scout bombers		36	1
Army observation planes		11	2
Miscellaneous Navy planes		45	1
(Planes from carrier *Enterprise* which joined the defense)		8	
Army-Navy antiaircraft			993 guns

A comparison of losses or severe damage in summary form is as follows:

Japanese attacking force		*Defending force* [62]	
Personnel (less than)	100		3, 435
Planes	29		188
Ships	0		a 18
Submarines (midget)	5		0

Facilities. (Extensive damage to Army and Navy installations on Oahu.)

a 8 battleships, 3 light cruisers, 3 destroyers, and 4 miscellaneous vessels.

The extreme disproportion of Army and Navy losses to equipment and facilities at hand is traceable to the complete surprise of the commanders in Hawaii when the Japanese struck on the morning of December 7. The Japanese employed, it is true, a powerful attacking force, much more powerful than they had been thought capable of utilizing in a single tactical venture. They executed the attack with a skill, daring, and military know-how of which we thought them incapable. However, as reflected by the comparison of relative strength, the Hawaiian commanders had formidable defensive forces which if properly coordinated and brought into play should have been capable of inflicting severe damage on the Japanese raiders and repelling the attack to a degree. How great the losses that might have been inflicted on the attacking force and the extent to which the attack might have been repulsed will forever remain a matter of conjecture— the real power of the defenses of Hawaii was not brought into the fight.[62a]

There can be no question that some damage would have been inflicted irrespective of the state of alertness that might have prevailed; for as a military proposition it is agreed that some attacking planes will invariably get through the screen of defense and carry home the attack. This is largely true no matter how fully equipped and how alert a garrison may be.[63] But this fact does not draw forth the con-

[61] It is reported that of the Japanese fighter planes, 39 were kept around the carriers as interceptors in case the American planes got in the air and made an attack. Committee Exhibit No. 8D (Enclosure 1, p. 2).

[62] It is interesting to note that Admiral Bloch testified that had the Japanese attacked the oil supply at Oahu, the drydocks, repair shops, barracks and other facilities instead of the airfields and ships of the fleet, the United States would have been hurt more so far as the prosecution of the war was concerned even though we did have a terrific loss of life. He pointed out that *the oil storage was in tanks above the ground or visible from the air.* See Hart Inquiry Record, p. 94.

[62a] It is interesting to note that the Japanese had estimated the air strength in Hawaii at roughly twice the actual strength and had expected to lose one-third of the striking force, including two of the aircraft carriers. See discussion "The Role of Espionage in the Attack", Part III, infra.

[63] It appears agreed as a military proposition that carrier-borne planes must be caught before they are launched in order to repel successfully a carrier attack. See, for example, testimony of Admiral Bellinger, Navy Court of Inquiry Record, p. 686; also Admiral Stark, Id., pp. 1023, 1024.

As stated by the Navy Court of Inquiry: "An attack by carrier aircraft can be prevented only by intercepting and destroying the carrier prior to the launching of planes. Once launched, attacking planes can be prevented from inflicting damage only by other planes or antiaircraft gunfire or both. Even when a determined air attack is intercepted, engaged by aircraft, and opposed by gunfire, some of the attacking planes rarely fail to get through and inflict damage." See Navy Court of Inquiry Report, committee exhibits Nos. 157 and 181.

clusion that the attackers cannot and must not be made to pay and pay heavily.

The disaster of Pearl Harbor lies in the failure of the Army and Navy in Hawaii to make their fight with the equipment at hand— it was not that they had no equipment, for they did, but that they did not utilize what they had. This failure is attributable to the complete surprise with which the attack came. It is proper, therefore, to inquire at this point to determine whether the Hawaiian commanders should thus have been surprised and, more particularly, whether they were justified in employing their defensive facilities in a manner least calculated to meet the Japanese on the morning of December 7.

(*The responsibilities relating to the disaster affecting both Hawaii and Washington will be found treated in Parts III and IV, respectively, infra.*)

PART III

RESPONSIBILITIES IN HAWAII

PART III. RESPONSIBILITIES IN HAWAII

Consciousness of Danger From Air Attack

ADMIRAL KIMMEL'S AWARENESS OF DANGER FROM AIR ATTACK

The Japanese raiding force approached the island of Oahu with virtually no danger of detection and executed its treacherous attack at a time when only a minimum state of readiness prevailed to meet it.[1] One of the causes of the disaster in consequence must lie in the failure to employ facilities available to detect the attacking force in sufficient time to effect a state of readiness best designed to repel or minimize the attack. That the attack on Pearl Harbor surprised the defending Army and Navy establishments is indisputable. The question therefore becomes, as previously indicated: Under all of the circumstances should the responsible commanders at Hawaii have been surprised or, more particularly, were they justified in failing to employ adequately the defensive facilities available to them on the morning of December 7, 1941?[2]

The estimate of both Admirals Richardson[3] and Kimmel[4] in a letter which they jointly prepared and dispatched to the Chief of Naval Operations on January 25, 1941, pointed out that if Japan entered the war or committed an overt act against the United States our position would be primarily defensive in the Pacific.[5] There were outlined in the letter certain assumptions upon which the action of the Pacific Fleet would be predicated, including:

(a) United States is at war with Germany and Italy; (b) war with Japan imminent; (c) Japan may attack without warning, and these attacks may take any form—even to attacks by Japanese ships flying German or Italian flags or by submarines, under a doubtful presumption that they may be considered German or Italian; and (d) Japanese attacks may be expected against shipping, outlying positions, or naval units. Surprise raids on Pearl Harbor, or attempts to block the channel are possible.

It was pointed out that the tasks to be undertaken by the fleet with respect to these assumptions included the taking of full security

[1] See section "State of Readiness," Part II. supra.

[2] The Army Pearl Harbor Board said: "Therefore, the situation on December 7 can be summed up as follows: No distant reconnaissance was being conducted by the Navy; the usual four or five PBY's were not out; the antiaircraft artillery was not out on its usual Sunday maneuvers with the Fleet air arm; the naval carriers with their planes were at a distance from Oahu on that Sunday; the aircraft were on the ground, were parked, both Army and Navy, closely adjacent to one another; the Fleet was in the harbor with the exception of Task Forces 9 and 12, which included some cruisers, destroyers, and the two carriers *Lexington* and *Enterprise*. Ammunition for the Army was, with the exception of that near the fixed antiaircraft guns, in ordnance storehouses, and the two combat divisions as well as the antiaircraft artillery were in their permanent quarters and not in battle positions. Everything was concentrated in close confines by reason of antisabotage Alert No. 1. This made of them easy targets for an air attack. *In short, everything that was done made the situation perfect for an air attack and the Japanese took full advantage of it."* See Report of Army Pearl Harbor Board, Committee Exhibit No. 157.

[3] Admiral James O. Richardson, who preceded Admiral Kimmel as commander in chief of the Pacific Fleet.

[4] Admiral Husband E. Kimmel assumed command of the United States Pacific Fleet on February 1, 1941, and served in that capacity until December 17, 1941. The evidence clearly indicates that while Admiral Kimmel was promoted over several other officers with more seniority, his selection was made because he was regarded as preeminently qualified for the position of commander in chief.

[5] See Navy Court of Inquiry exhibit No. 70.

measures for the protection of the fleet in port and at sea. Thereafter there were set forth observations concerning the existing deficiencies in the defenses of Oahu.

Under date of January 24, 1941, the Secretary of Navy addressed a communication to the Secretary of War, with copies designated for the commander in chief of the Pacific Fleet and the commandant of the Fourteenth Naval District, observing among other things: [6]

The security of the U. S. Pacific Fleet while in Pearl Harbor, and of the Pearl Harbor Naval Base itself, has been under renewed study by the Navy Department and forces afloat for the past several weeks. This reexamination has been, in part, prompted by the increased gravity of the situation with respect to Japan, and by reports from abroad of successful bombing and torpedo plane attacks on ships while in bases. *If war eventuates with Japan, it is believed easily possible that hostilities would be initiated by a surprise attack upon the Fleet or the Naval Base at Pearl Harbor.*

In my opinion, the inherent possibilities of a major disaster to the Fleet or naval base warrant taking every step, as rapidly as can be done, that will increase the joint readiness of the Army and Navy to withstand a raid of the character mentioned above.

The dangers envisaged *in their order of importance and probability* are considered to be:

(1) Air bombing attack.
(2) Air torpedo plane attack.
(3) Sabotage.
(4) Submarine attack.
(5) Mining.
(6) Bombardment by gun fire.

Defense against all but the first two of these dangers appears to have been provided for satisfactorily. The following paragraphs are devoted principally to a discussion of the problems encompassed in (1) and (2) above, the solution of which I consider to be of primary importance.

Both types of air attack are possible. They may be carried out successively, simultaneously, or in combination with any of the other operations enumerated. The maximum probable enemy effort may be put at twelve aircraft squadrons, and the minimum at two. Attacks would be launched from a striking force of carriers and their supporting vessels.

The counter measures to be considered are:

(a) Location and engagement of enemy carriers and supporting vessels before air attack can be launched;
(b) Location and engagement of enemy aircraft before they reach their objectives;
(c) Repulse of enemy aircraft by antiaircraft fire;
(d) Concealment of vital installations by artificial smoke;
(e) Protection of vital installations by balloon barrages.

The operations set forth in (a) are largely functions of the Fleet but, quite possibly, might not be carried out in case of an air attack initiated without warning prior to a declaration of war. Pursuit aircraft in large numbers and an effective warning net are required for the operations in (b). It is understood that only thirty-six Army pursuit aircraft are at present in Oahu, and that, while the organization and equipping of an Anti-Air Information Service supported by modern fire control equipment is in progress, the present system relies wholly on visual observation and sound locators which are only effective up to four miles. * * *

The foregoing communication was seen by Admiral Kimmel shortly after he assumed command. [7]

The Secretary of War on February 7, 1941, replied to the letter of the Secretary of Navy in the following terms: [8]

1. In replying to your letter of January 24, regarding the possibility of surprise attacks upon the Fleet or the Naval Base at Pearl Harbor, I wish to express complete concurrence as to the importance of this matter and the urgency of our making every possible preparation to meet such a hostile effort. The Hawaiian

[6] Committee Exhibit No. 10.
[7] Admiral Kimmel testified: "* * * I saw the letter of the Secretary of the Navy to the Secretary of War dated January 24, 1941, early in February 1941." Navy Court of Inquiry Record, p. 286.
[8] Navy Court of Inquiry exhibit No. 24.

Department is the best equipped of all our overseas departments, and continues to hold a high priority for the completion of its projected defenses because of the importance of giving full protection to the Fleet.

2. The Hawaiian Project provides for one hundred and forty-eight pursuit planes. There are now in Hawaii thirty-six pursuit planes; nineteen of these are P-36's and seventeen are of somewhat less efficiency. I am arranging to have thirty-one P-36 pursuit planes assembled at San Diego for shipment to Hawaii within the next ten days, as agreed to with the Navy Department. This will bring the Army pursuit group in Hawaii up to fifty of the P-36 type and seventeen of a somewhat less efficient type. In addition, fifty of the new P-40-B pursuit planes, with their guns, leakproof tanks and modern armor will be assembled at San Diego about March 15 for shipment by carrier to Hawaii.

3. There are at present in the Hawaiian Islands eighty-two 3-inch AA guns, twenty 37 mm AA guns (en route), and one hundred and nine caliber .50 AA machine guns. The total project calls for ninety-eight 3-inch guns, one hundred and twenty 37 mm AA guns, and three hundred and eight caliber .50 AA machine guns.

4. With reference to the Aircraft Warning Service, the equipment therefor has been ordered and will be delivered in Hawaii in June. All arrangements for installation will have been made by the time the equipment is delivered. Inquiry develops the information that delivery of the necessary equipment cannot be made at an earlier date.

5. The Commanding General, Hawaiian Department, is being directed to give immediate consideration to the question of the employment of balloon barrages and the use of smoke in protecting the Fleet and base facilities. Barrage balloons are not available at the present time for installation, and cannot be made available prior to the summer of 1941. At present there are three on hand and eighty-four being manufactured—forty for delivery by June 30, 1941, and the remainder by September. The Budget now has under consideration funds for two thousand nine hundred and fifty balloons. The value of smoke for screening vital areas on Oahu is a controversial subject. Qualified opinion is that atmospheric and geographic conditions in Oahu render the employment of smoke impracticable for large-scale screening operations. However, the Commanding General will look into this matter again.

6. With reference to your other proposals for joint defense, I am forwarding a copy of your letter and this reply to the Commanding General, Hawaiian Department, and am directing him to cooperate with the local naval authorities in making those measures effective."

In a letter to the Chief of Naval Operations dated January 27, 1941,[9] Admiral Kimmel stated he thought the supply of an adequate number of Army planes and guns for the defense of Pearl Harbor should be given the highest priority.

It should be noted at this point in considering the letter of the Secretary of Navy dated January 24, 1941, that the following dispatch dated February 1, 1941, was sent the commander in chief of the Pacific Fleet from the Chief of Naval Operations concerning the subject "Rumored Japanese attack on Pearl Harbor": [10]

1. The following is forwarded for your information. Under date of 27 January the American Ambassador at Tokyo telegraphed the State Department to the following effect:

"The Peruvian Minister has informed a member of my staff that he has heard from many sources, including a Japanese source, that in the event of trouble breaking out between the United States and Japan, the Japanese intend to make a surprise attack against Pearl Harbor with all of their strength and employing all of their equipment. The Peruvian Minister considered the rumors fantastic. Nevertheless he considered them of sufficient importance to convey this information to a member of my staff."

2. The Division of Naval Intelligence places no credence in these rumors. Furthermore, based on known data regarding the present disposition and employment of Japanese Naval and Army forces, no move against Pearl Harbor appears imminent or planned for in the foreseeable future.

---

[9] Committee exhibit No. 106.
[10] This dispatch is indicated to have been dictated by Lt. Comdr. (now Captain) A. H. McCollum on January 31, 1941. See committee exhibit No. 15.

The estimate made concerning the information supplied by the Peruvian Minister with respect to a rumored Japanese surprise attack on Pearl Harbor and a copy of the Secretary of the Navy's letter of January 24 were received by Admiral Kimmel at approximately the same time and are in apparent conflict. However, the dispatch of February 1 was an estimate of the rumor concerning the Japanese plan to make a surprise attack on Pearl Harbor based on the then present disposition and employment of Japanese forces, whereas the Secretary's letter relates to the dangers of the Pearl Harbor situation in contemplation of future conflict with Japan. The communications apparently were so interpreted by Admiral Kimmel for in a letter dated February 18, 1941, to the Chief of Naval Operations he said: [11]

I feel that a surprise attack (submarine, air, or combined) on Pearl Harbor is a possibility. We are taking immediate practical steps to minimize the damage inflicted and to ensure that the attacking force will pay.

In a letter of February 15, 1941 [12] the Chief of Naval Operations wrote Admiral Kimmel concerning antitorpedo baffles for protection against air-torpedo attack on Pearl Harbor. He stated that the congestion in the harbor and the necessity for maneuverability limited the practicability of the then present type of baffles. Further, the letter indicated that the shallow depth of water in Pearl Harbor limited the need for torpedo nets; that a minimum depth of water of 75 feet might be assumed necessary to drop torpedoes successfully from planes and that the desirable height for dropping is 60 feet or less. A similar communication was sent Admiral Bloch, the commandant of the Fourteenth Naval District, among others, requesting his recommendations and comments concerning the matter. [13]

In a letter of March 20, [14] Admiral Bloch replied, stating that the depth of water at Pearl Harbor was 45 feet and for this reason among others he did not recommend antitorpedo baffles. Admiral Kimmel was in agreement with this recommendation until such time as a light efficient net was developed. [15]

However, in June of 1941, the Chief of Naval Operations directed a communication to the commandants of naval districts as follows: [16]

1. * * * Commandants were requested to consider the employment of, and to make recommendations concerning, antitorpedo baffles especially for the protection of large and valuable units of the fleet in their respective harbors and especially at the major fleet bases. In paragraph 3 were itemized certain limitations to consider in the use of A/T baffles among which the following was stated:
"A minimum depth of water of 75 feet may be assumed necessary to successfully drop torpedoes from planes. About two hundred yards of torpedo run is necessary before the exploding device is armed, but this may be altered."
2. Recent developments have shown that United States and British torpedoes may be dropped from planes at heights of as much as three hundred feet, and in some cases make initial dives of considerably less than 75 feet, and make excellent runs. Hence, it may be stated that it cannot be assumed that any capital ship or other valuable vessel is safe when at anchor from this type of attack if surrounded by water at a sufficient run to arm the torpedo.
3. While no minimum depth of water in which naval vessels may be anchored can arbitrarily be assumed as providing safety from torpedo-plane attack, it may

[11] Committee exhibit No. 106.
[12] Id., No. 116.
[13] Letter from Chief of Naval Operations dated February 17, 1941. Committee exhibit No. 116.
[14] Committee exhibit No. 116.
[15] Letter to the Chief of Naval Operations dated March 12, 1941. Committee exhibit No. 116.
[16] Letter dated June 13, 1941, from Chief of Naval Operations to commandants of all naval districts. Committee exhibit No. 116. This communication made reference to the observations set forth in the letter of February 17, 1941 (committee exhibit No. 116), pointing out certain limitations with respect to air torpedo attack. Note 13, supra.

be assumed that depth of water will be one of the factors considered by any attacking force, and an attack launched in relatively deep water (10 fathoms [16a] or more) is much more likely.

4. As a matter of information the torpedoes launched by the British at Taranto were, in general, in thirteen to fifteen fathoms of water, although several torpedoes may have been launched in eleven or twelve fathoms.[17]

The foregoing communication clearly indicated that preconceived views concerning the invulnerability of Pearl Harbor to air-torpedo attack were in error.

Admiral Kimmel himself stated that during his visit to Washington in June of 1941 he told the President and Admiral Stark of certain dangers to the fleet at Pearl Harbor including air attack, blocking of the harbor, and similar matters.[18]

GENERAL SHORT'S AWARENESS OF DANGER FROM AIR ATTACK

On February 7, 1941, General Short [19] assumed command of the Hawaiian Department of the Army. Upon his arrival he had the benefit of conversations with General Herron,[20] his predecessor, with respect to problems prevailing in the Department. Significantly, General Herron had been directed by the War Department on June 17, 1940, to institute an alert against a possible trans-Pacific raid.[21] This alert was an all-out endeavor with full equipment and ammunition and lasted 6 weeks. It was suspended after the 6-week period and thereafter resumed for some time. Planes had been dispersed and gun crews alerted with the ammunition available. The Commanding General had the benefit of all the plans and operations incicent to the so-called "Herron alert" as a guide in estimating the steps to be taken on the occasion of a threat of enemy attack.

General Short saw both the letter from the Secretary of Navy dated January 24 and the reply of the Secretary of War dated February 7, set forth in the preceding section, concerning the danger of attack from the air.[22]

Under date of February 7, 1941, General Marshall directed a letter to General Short relating in utmost clarity the problems and responsibility of General Short in his new command.[23] This letter, which referred to a conversation with Admiral Stark, pointed out that there was need for additional planes and antiaircraft guns; that the fullest protection for the Pacific Fleet was *the* rather than *a* major consideration of the Army; that the risk of sabotage and the risk involved in a surprise raid by air and by submarine constituted the real perils of the situation; and, again, that they were keeping clearly in mind that the first concern is to protect the fleet.

On February 19, 1941, General Short wrote General Marshall [24] pointing out, among other things, the great importance of (1) cooperation with the Navy; (2) dispersion and protection of aircraft and of the repair, maintenarce, and servicing of aircraft; (3) improvement of the

[16a] A fathom is 6 feet.
[17] The evidence reflects repeated efforts by the Chief of Naval Operations to secure from the Bureau of Ordnance more efficient light-weight baffles. See committee exhibit No. 116.
[18] Navy Court of Inquiry record, p. 367.
[19] Lt. Gen. Walter C. Short served as commanding general of the Hawaiian Department from February 7, 1941, to December 17, 1941.
[20] Maj. Gen. Charles D. Herron.
[21] See Army Pearl Harbor Board record, pp. 213–215.
[22] Navy Court of Inquiry record, p. 237.
[23] Committee exhibit No. 53, pp. 1–3.
[24] Id., at pp. 4–9.

antiaircraft defense; (4) improvement of the situation with reference to searchlights; and (5) bombproofing of vital installations such as command posts and communication centers. General Short advised the Chief of Staff that he was taking the necessary steps in line with the important needs of the Department.

On March 5, 1941, the Chief of Staff wrote General short: [25]

I would appreciate your early review of the situation in the Hawaiian Department with regard to *defense from air attack*. The establishment of a satisfactory system of coordinating all means available to this end is a matter of first priority.

In a letter to the Chief of Staff dated March 6, 1941,[26] General Short observed that the Aircraft Warning Service was vital to the defense of the Hawaiian Islands and referred to delays in construction and establishment of sites. In a subsequent letter [27] General Short again referred to the necessity for the dispersion and protection of aircraft as well as to the matter of coordinating antiaircraft defense. A letter dated March 28, 1941,[28] from General Marshall made reference to General Short's proposal for relieving congestion by the construction of an additional airfield and by the dispersion of grounded aircraft in protected bunkers at existing airfields with the observation that the proposal was undoubtedly sound. He also indicated his hopefulness of arranging for the early augmentation of the antiaircraft garrison.

On April 14, 1941, General Short wrote the Chief of Staff, as follows: [29]

Knowing that you are very much interested in the progress that we are making in cooperating with the Navy, I am enclosing the following agreements made with them: [30]
    1. Joint Coastal Frontier Defense Plan, Hawaiian Department, and Fourteenth Naval District, Annex No. VII, Section VI, Joint Security Measure.
    2. Agreement signed by the Commander of the Hawaiian Air Force and Commander, Naval Base Defense Air Force, to implement the above agreement.
    3. Field Orders No. 1 NS (Naval Security) putting into effect for the Army the provisions of the joint agreement.

I have found both Admiral Kimmel and Admiral Bloch very cooperative and we all feel steps have been taken which make it possible for the Army and Navy air forces to act together and with the unity of command as the situation requires.

We still have some detail work to do with reference to coordinating the air force and the antiaircraft defense. I hope we shall arrive at something on that in the near future. The more I go into the details the more I am becoming convinced that it will be necessary for us to set up an air defense command. Some months before my arrival this matter was considered and at that time the conclusion was reached that it was not necessary. On this account I am anxious that both General Martin and General Gardner attend the West Coast Air Defense Exercise in the Fall.

Everything is going along extremely well although there is a great deal to be done as rapidly as possible. The Navy has felt very much encouraged by the increase in our Air and Antiaircraft defense. I shall write you from time to time as matters come up which I think will interest you.

In a letter to the Chief of Staff dated May 29, 1941, General Short made the following comments concerning the first phase of their recent maneuvers: [31]

The maneuver was divided into three phases. The first phase consisted of the air action and the actual issue of one day's fire and of Engineer Supplies for Field

[25] Id., at p. 10.
[26] Id., at pp. 11, 12.
[27] Letter dated March 15, 1941. Committee exhibit No. 53, pp. 15–17.
[28] Committee exhibit No. 53, p. 18.
[29] Id., at pp. 19, 20.
[30] See section "Plans for Defense of Hawaiian Coastal Frontier", infra.
[31] Committee exhibit No. 53, pp. 35, 36.

Fortifications and of Engineer tools. During the air phase our bombers acted under navy command in cooperation with the Naval Patrol Squadrons and actually located and bombed airplane carriers 250 miles out at sea. The movement of the carrier was entirely free so that the navy patrol planes had the mission of locating the ship and notifying our bombers and they then made the attack. Pursuit attacked enemy bombers represented by naval planes and our own bombers when they came in to attack ground defenses. Upon receipt of the warning for this phase our bombers were sent to fields on outlying islands and pursuit planes were dispersed. The Navy cooperated very fully during this phase and I believe we learned more about the coordination of Army Air Force, Navy Air Force, and Antiaircraft than we had during any previous exercise.

On August 19, 1941, General Marshall addressed a letter to General Short setting forth his reasons for deciding to establish an airfield base for the Fifteenth Pursuit Group at Kahuku Point and stated:

I feel sure that the Naval authorities comprehend fully the importance of adequate air defense of the Oahu Naval installation and accordingly, will entertain favorably any proposal which will implement the efficiency of such defense.[32]

The Chief of Staff on October 10, 1941, sent the following letter to General Short: [33]

The mimeographed standard operating procedure for the Hawaiian Department, dated July 14, has just come to my attention and I am particularly concerned with missions assigned to air units. For instance, the Hawaiian Air Force, among other things, is assigned the mission of defending Schofield Barracks and all air fields on Oahu against sabotage and ground attacks; and with providing a provisional battalion of 500 men for military police duty.

This seems inconsistent with the emphasis we are placing on air strength in Hawaii, particularly in view of the fact that only minimum operating and maintenance personnel have been provided. As a matter of fact, we are now in process of testing the organization of air-base defense battalions, consisting tentatively of a rifle company and two antiaircraft batteries, designed for the specific purpose of relieving the air maintenance people from ground missions of this kind at locations where there are no large garrisons for ground defense, as there are in Hawaii.

On October 28, 1941, General Marshall wrote General Short stating that he appreciated the reasons General Short had assigned for giving ground defense training to Air Corps personnel [34] but that it appeared the best policy would be to allow them to concentrate on technical Air Corps training until they have completed their expansion program and have their feet on the ground as far as their primary mission is concerned.[35]

From the foregoing correspondence there can be no doubt that General Short was adequately apprised of his responsibility to defend the fleet from attack and that he was conscious of the necessity of building up the defense against air attack.

PLANS FOR THE DEFENSE OF HAWAIIAN COASTAL FRONTIER

There is nowhere, however, a better expression of the keen understanding of the danger of a surprise air attack upon Oahu than is manifested in the plans which the Army and Navy jointly effected for the defense of the Hawaiian coastal frontier.

[32] Id., at pp. 40, 41.
[33] Id., at p. 42.
[34] In this connection General Short had written General Marshall on October 14, 1941, in part: "At the time our tentative Standing Operating Procedure was put out the Air Corps had 7,229 men. Full Combat details and all overhead required only 3,885 men for the planes and organizations actually on hand. This left a surplus of 3,344 men with no assigned duties during Maneuvers. One of the main reasons for the assignment was to give these men something to do during the Maneuvers. Another reason was the belief that any serious threat of an enemy ground attack of Oahu could come only after destruction of our Air Forces." See committee exhibit No. 53.
[35] Committee exhibit No. 53, pp. 44, 45.

The Hawaiian coastal frontier was listed in defense category D. This category covered *coastal frontiers that may be subject to major attack.* The war plans "Joint Action of the Army and Navy, 1935," the basic document controlling the relationship of the Army and Navy in the formulation of defense plans for the Hawaiian Islands, contains the following with respect to category D: [36]

Coastal frontiers that may be subject to major attack. Under this category, the coastal defense areas should, in general, be provided with the means of defense, both Army and Navy, required to meet enemy naval operations preliminary to joint operations. All available means of defense will generally find application, and a stronger outpost and a more extensive patrol, inshore and offshore, than for Category C (coastal frontiers that in all probabliity will be subject to minor attack) will be required. Under this category certain defensive sea areas will be established. In addition, an antiaircraft gun and machine-gun defense of important areas outside of harbor defenses should be organized; general reserves should be strategically located so as to facilitate prompt reinforcement of the frontiers; and plans should be developed for the defense of specific areas likely to become theaters of operations. Long-range air reconnaissance will be provided and plans made for use of the GHQ air force.

As a basic responsibility ("Joint Action Army and Navy 1935") under contemplation of normal circumstances responsibility for the defense of Pearl Harbor was that of the Army.[37] It was recognized that— [38]

* * * The strategic freedom of action of the Fleet must be assured. This requires that coastal frontier defense be so effectively conducted as to remove any anxiety of the Fleet in regard to the security of its bases * * *.

The basic allocation of Army and Navy responsibility for coastal defense was not possible under conditions prevailing in Hawaii during 1941. Fundamental deficiencies in equipment, particularly shortage of sufficient Army patrol planes, confronted the responsible commanders. As Admiral Kimmel stated shortly after assuming command at Pearl Harbor— [39]

There is a definite line of demarcation between this objective and longer range planning. The latter has its proper sphere and must be continued as an essential basis for determining and stressing improved readiness requirements. This planning will naturally include the more effective schemes of employment that improved readiness, when attained, will permit.
Current readiness plans, however, cannot be based on any recommendation for, or expectation of, improved conditions or facilities. *Such plans must be based only on hard fact.* They must be so developed as to provide for *immediate* action, based on facilities and materials that are *now* available.
A subject emphatically calling for attention in line with the foregoing is maximum readiness in the Hawaiian area, particularly for Pearl Harbor defense, of all available aviation components. As is well known, much remains to be done for adequate *future* effectiveness in this respect. Much, however, can *now* be done with means now available, to make arrangements for local employment of aviation more effective than they now are.

In realistic recognition of this situation, plans were conceived early in 1941 known as "The Joint Coastal Frontier Defense Plan, Hawaiian Coastal Frontier".[40] This plan was signed and placed in effect on April 11, 1941, by General Short and Admiral Bloch, commandant of the Fourteenth Naval District. The plan was based on the joint

[36] "Joint Action of the Army and Navy, 1935", Navy Court of Inquiry exhibit No. 6.
[37] Id.
[38] Id., at p. 42.
[39] Letter of February 4, 1941, from Admiral Kimmel to Pacific Fleet personnel. See committee record, pp. 14511, 14512.
[40] See committee exhibit No. 44; also Navy Court of Inquiry exhibit No. 7.

Army and Navy basic war plans [41] and was to constitute the basis on which all subsidiary peace and war projects, joint operating plans, and mobilization plans would be based. The method of coordination under the plan was by *mutual cooperation* which was to apply to all activities wherein the Army and the Navy would cooperate in coordination until and if the method of unity of command were invoked.

Under the Joint Coastal Frontier Defense Plan the following tasks of the Army and Navy were recognized:

a. JOINT TASK. To hold OAHU as a main outlying naval base, and to control and protect shipping in the Coastal Zone.

b. ARMY TASK. To hold OAHU against attacks by sea, land, and air forces, and against hostile sympathizers; to support the naval forces.

c. NAVY TASK. To patrol the Coastal Zone and to contol and protect shipping therein; to support the Army forces.

One of the most significant features of the plan was the assumption of responsibility by the Navy for distant reconnaissance, a normal task of the Army. In this regard, the plan provided: "The Commandant, Fourteenth Naval District, shall provide for: * * * i. *Distant Reconnaissance.*"

On March 28, 1941, an agreement, incorporated as an annex to the Joint Coastal Frontier Defense Plan,[42] was prepared and approved by General Short and Admiral Bloch on April 2 dealing with joint security measures and protection of the fleet and the Pearl Harbor base. This agreement was entered into—

in order to coordinate joint defensive measures for the security of the Fleet and for the Pearl Harbor Naval Base for defense against hostile raids or air attacks delivered prior to a declaration of war and before a general mobilization for war.

It was recognized that—

when the Commanding General of the Hawaiian Department and the Naval Base Defense Officer (the Commandant of the Fourteenth Naval District) *agree that the threat of a hostile raid or attack is sufficiently imminent* to warrant such action, each commander will take such preliminary steps as are necessary to make available without delay to the other commander such proportion of the air forces at his disposal as the circumstances warrant in order that joint operations may be conducted * * *

Joint air attacks upon hostile surface vessels were to be executed under the tactical command of the Navy. When naval forces were insufficient for long-distance patrol and search operations and Army aircraft were made available, these aircraft were to be under the tactical control of the Navy. It was contemplated that the Army would expedite the installation and operation of an Aircraft Warning Service through use of radar.

On March 31, 1941, Admiral Bellinger, as commander, Naval Base Defense Air Force, and General Martin, commanding Hawaiian Air Force, prepared a joint estimate covering joint Army and Navy air action in the event of sudden hostile action against Oahu or fleet units in the Hawaiian area. The situation was summarized in the following terms: [43]

(1) Relations between the United States and Japan are strained, uncertain, and varying.

(2) In the past Japan has never preceded hostile actions by a declaration of war.

---

[41] See Navy Court of Inquiry exhibits Nos. 4 and 5.
[42] Annex VII, sec. VI. See committee exhibit No. 44.
[43] See committee exhibit No. 44.

(3) A successful, sudden raid against our ships and naval installations on Oahu might prevent effective offensive action by our forces in the Western Pacific for a long period.

(4) A strong part of our fleet is now constantly at sea in the operating areas organized to take prompt offensive action against any surface or submarine force which initiates hostile action.

(5) It appears possible that Japanese submarines and/or a Japanese fast raiding force might arrive in Hawaiian waters with no prior warning from our intelligence service.

The estimate embracing a "Survey of Opposing Strength" indicated, among other things, that Japan might send into the Hawaiian area one or more submarines and one or more fast raiding forces composed of carriers supported by fast cruisers; that the most difficult situation to meet would be when several of the above elements were present and closely coordinating their actions; and that the aircraft available in Hawaii were inadequate to maintain for any extended period from bases on Oahu a patrol extensive enough to insure that an air attack from a Japanese carrier could not arrive over Oahu as a complete surprise. It was elsewhere observed in the estimate that it would be desirable to run daily patrols as far as possible to seaward through 360° but that this could only be effectively maintained with "present personnel and material" for a very short period, and as a practical measure could not therefore be undertaken unless other intelligence indicated that a surface raid was probable within narrow limits of time.[44]

The outline of possible enemy action as set forth in the Martin-Bellinger estimate is a startling harbinger of what actually occurred:[45]

(a) A declaration of war might be preceded by:
    1. A surprise submarine attack on ships in the operating area.
    2. A surprise attack on OAHU including ships and installations in Pearl Harbor.
    3. A combination of these two.
(b) It appears that *the most likely and dangerous form of attack on OAHU would be an air attack.* It is believed that at present such an attack would most likely be launched from one or more carriers which would probably approach inside of 300 miles.
(c) A single attack might or might not indicate the presence of more submarines or more planes awaiting to attack after defending aircraft have been drawn away by the original thrust.
(d) Any single submarine attack might indicate the presence of a considerable undiscovered surface force *probably* composed of fast ships accompanied by a carrier.
(e) In a dawn air attack there is a high probability that it could be delivered as a complete surprise in spite of any patrols we might be using and that it might find us in a condition of readiness under which pursuit would be slow to start, also it might be successful as a diversion to draw attention away from a second attacking force. The major disadvantage would be that we could have all day to find and attack the carrier. A dusk attack would have the advantage that the carrier could use the night for escape

---

[44] In a statement submitted to the Navy Court of Inquiry, Admiral Kimmel referred to this portion of the estimate and stated: "This plan was on file with the Departments in Washington. They knew of this decision. *They had done nothing to change or alter the basic deficiencies in personnel and material which required that decision.*"

This statement, it should be noted, is not strictly accurate. The number of Navy patrol bombers adaptable for distant reconnaissance was increased appreciably after the Martin-Bellinger estimate was prepared. As will subsequently appear, there were sufficient patrol planes at Oahu to conduct a distant reconnaissance for a considerable period of time after receipt of the November 27 "war warning" (detailed reference will be made to this warning, infra). The estimate made by Admiral Bellinger and General Martin was prepared in March of 1941 and was necessarily in contemplation of patrol planes then available. As indicated, the number of Navy planes available for this purpose was substantially increased before December 7. See committee exhibit No. 120.

[45] Committee exhibit No. 44.

and might not be located the next day near enough for us to make a successful air attack. The disadvantage would be that it would spend the day of the attack approaching the islands and might be observed. Under the existing conditions this might not be a serious disadvantage for until an overt act has been committed we probably will take no offensive action and the only thing that would be lost would be complete surprise. Midday attacks have all the disadvantages and none of the advantages of the above. After hostilities have commenced, a night attack would offer certain advantages but as an initial crippling blow a dawn or dusk attack would probably be no more hazardous and would have a better chance for accomplishing a large success. Submarine attacks could be coordinated with any air attack.

Pacific Fleet Confidential Letter No. 2CL–41 from Admiral Kimmel to the Pacific Fleet, concerning the security of the fleet at base and in operating areas, was issued in February 1941 and reissued in revised form on October 14, 1941.[46] This fleet order was predicated on two assumptions, one being—[47]

That a declaration of war may be preceded by—
> (1) A surprise attack on ships at Pearl Harbor.
> (2) A surprise submarine attack on ships in operating area.
> (3) A combination of these two.

Among the provisions of this letter concerning action to be taken if a submarine attacked in the operating area it was pointed out—

It must be remembered that a single attack may or may not indicate the presence of more submarines waiting to attack—

that—

it must be remembered too, that a single submarine attack may indicate the presence of a considerable surface force probably composed of fast ships accompanied by a carrier. The Task Force Commander must, therefore, assemble his task groups as quickly as the situation and daylight conditions warrant in order to be prepared to pursue or meet enemy ships that may be located by air search or other means.

A letter dated August 20, 1941, to the commanding general, Army Air Forces, Washington, prepared by General Martin, and transmitted through General Short, submitted as an enclosure a plan for the employment of long-range bombardment aviation in the defense of Oahu. Several observations set forth in this plan are of particular pertinence: [48]

The Hawaiian Air Force is primarily concerned with the destruction of hostile carriers in this vicinity before the approach within range of Oahu where they can launch their bombardment aircraft for a raid or an attack on Oahu.

*　　　*　　　*　　　*　　　*　　　*　　　*

Our most likely enemy, Orange (Japan), can probably employ a maximum of six carriers against Oahu.

*　　　*　　　*　　　*　　　*　　　*　　　*

* * * *The early morning attack is, therefore, the best plan of action open to the enemy.*

*　　　*　　　*　　　*　　　*　　　*　　　*

---

[46] Id.
[47] Referring to Admiral Kimmel's letter of October 14, 1941, to the fleet 2CL–41 (revised) wherein it was stated that a declaration of war may be preceded by a surprise attack on ships in Pearl Harbor (see committee exhibit No. 44), he was asked what form of surprise attack on ships in Pearl Harbor he contemplated by this statement. Admiral Kimmel replied:
"*An airplane attack. This was an assumption upon which to base our training. The probability of an air attack on Pearl Harbor was sufficient to justify complete training for this purpose.* I felt, as the situation developed, the Fleet might move away from Pearl Harbor, and in such a contingency the possibility of a quick raid on the installations at Pearl Harbor might be attempted. I thought it was much more probable that the Japs would attempt a raid on Pearl Harbor if the Fleet were away than if it were there. However, at no time did I consider it more than a possibility, and one which ordinary prudence would make us guard against." See Navy Court of Inquiry record, p. 287.
[48] See committee exhibit No. 13.

It is the opinion of some individuals that a late afternoon attack is highly probable since it permits an enemy carrier to *escape* under cover of darkness. This presupposes that search operations are impracticable. This headquarters cannot subscribe to this opinion for the following reasons:

(1) A minor surprise raid such as a single carrier is not a logical method of attack to reduce the defenses of Oahu.
(2) It permits us to operate against him for a long period on D-Day at close range.
(3) The enemy will be more concerned with deliverying a successful attack than he will be with escaping after the attack. He will have carefully considered the cost of the enterprise, will probably make a determined attack with maximum force and will willingly accept his losses if his attack is successful.

   *   *   *   *   *   *   *

The most favorable plan of action open to the enemy, and the action upon which we should *base our plans* of operation is the *early morning attack* in which the enemy must make good the following time schedule:

(1) Cross circle 881 nautical miles from Oahu at dawn of the day before the attack.
(2) Cross circle 530 nautical miles from Oahu at dusk of the day before the attack.
(3) Launch his planes 233 nautical miles from Oahu at dawn the day of the attack.
(4) Recover his planes 167 nautical miles from Oahu 2:30 after dawn the day of the attack.

   *   *   *   *   *   *   *

He (Japan) will not have unlimited avenues of approach for his attack.
a. He must avoid the shipping lanes to negate detection.
b. Any approach to Oahu which is made from east of the 158th meridian materially increases his cruising distance and the probability of detection by friendly surface vessels. *It seems that his most probable avenue of approach is the hemisphere from 0° (due north) counterclockwise to 180° around Oahu; the next probable*, the quadrant 180° counterclockwise to 90°; the least probable, 90° to 0°.

Admiral Kimmel and General Short were both fully familiar with all the provisions of the Joint Coastal Frontier Defense Plan. The plans effected for the defense of the Hawaiian coastal frontier viewed in their entirety were fully adequate under the circumstances and represent a commendable recognition by the Hawaiian commanders of the realities of their situation.[49] The unfortunate fact is that features of the plan designed to meet an air attack were not invoked prior to the actual attack in view of the imminence of hostile Japanese action. It is clear that the plans with respect to joint air operations was to be operative when the commanding general of the Hawaiian Department and the naval base defense officer "agree that the threat of a hostile raid or attack is sufficiently imminent to warrant such action."[50] It is equally clear that the joint security measures for the protection of the fleet and the Pearl Harbor base were designed in order to coordinate joint defensive measures for defense against hostile raids or air attacks delivered *prior to a declaration of war* and *before a general mobilization for war*. The plan against air attack was prepared in Hawaii; it was designed to meet the peculiar problems existing in

[49] Before the Army Pearl Harbor Board, Admiral Kimmel stated that "he (Admiral Bloch) accepted responsibility for distant reconnaissance, because he couldn't do anything else and be sensible." See Army Pearl Harbor Board Record, p. 1753.
He commented: "There weren't any general headquarters Army aircraft available in Hawaii, and we knew that there weren't going to be any." Id.
[50] Committee exhibit No. 44.

Hawaii; its invocation, implementation, and execution was essentially a responsibility resting in Hawaii.[51]

From a review of the defense plans prepared in Hawaii the conclusion is inescapable that the Army and Navy commanders there not only appreciated the dangers of an air attack on Pearl Harbor but had also prepared detailed arrangements to meet this threat.

CONCEPT OF THE WAR IN THE PACIFIC

It is to be recalled that from January 29 to March 27, 1941, staff conversations were held in Washington between Army and Navy officials of Great Britain and the United States to determine the best methods by which the armed forces of the United States and the British Commonwealth, with its allies, could defeat Germany and the powers allied with her *should the United States be compelled to resort to war.*[52] The report of these conversations, dated March 27, 1941, and referred to by the short title "ABC-1," reflected certain principles governing contemplated action, including: [53]

Since Germany is the predominant member of the Axis Powers, the Atlantic and European area is considered to be the decisive theater. The principal United States military effort will be exerted in that theater, and operations of United States forces in other theaters will be conducted in such a manner as to facilitate that effort.

In recognition of the foregoing principle that the Atlantic and European area was to be considered the decisive theater, the concept of military operations as respecting Japan was expressed as follows:[54]

Even if Japan were not initially to enter the war on the side of the Axis Powers, it would still be necessary for the Associated Powers to deploy their forces in a manner to guard against eventual Japanese intervention. If Japan does enter the war, *the military strategy in the Far East will be defensive.* The United States does not intend to add to its present military strength in the Far East but will employ the United States Pacific Fleet offensively in the manner best calculated to weaken Japanese economic power, and to support the defense of the Malay barrier by diverting Japanese strength away from Malaysia. The United States intends so to augment its forces in the Atlantic and Mediterranean areas that the British Commonwealth will be in a position to release the necessary forces for the Far East.

Pursuant to the principles and plans visualized in ABC-1, the Army and Navy prepared "Joint Army and Navy Basic War Plan— Rainbow No. 5," which was approved by the Secretary of the Navy on May 28, 1941, and by the Secretary of War on June 2, 1941.[55] On July 21, 1941, United States Pacific Fleet Operating Plan Rainbow Five was distributed to the Pacific Fleet by Admiral Kimmel. This

---

[51] The Secretary of War, Mr. Stimson, expressed this thought in the following terms: "* * * each theater commander is charged with the preparation of his own local defense plan, including the working out of any defense operations with the local naval authorities. Such plans are submitted to the appropriate division of the General Staff in Washington and are subject to any changes or modifications that might emanate from that source. *The primary responsibility for such plans and their execution, however, rests on the commanding officer familiar with the local situation and conditions.* Before December 7, 1941, detailed plans for the defense of the Hawaiian Department had been devised and worked out by General Short as well as a joint agreement with the local naval authorities for joint action in the event of an emergency, and *he and the Navy commanding officer had the primary responsibility of putting into effect these plans or such portions thereof as the occasion demanded.*" See statement of Secretary of War with respect to the report of the Army Pearl Harbor Board; committee exhibit No. 157.

[52] Committee exhibit No. 49. See section "ABCD Understanding?", Part IV, infra, this report.

[53] Committee exhibit No. 49, p. 5.

[54] Id., at pp. 5, 6.

[55] See Navy Court of Inquiry exhibit No. 4. This plan is also referred to as "WPL-46."

plan was designed to implement the Navy basic war plan (Rainbow Five) insofar as the tasks assigned the United States Pacific Fleet were concerned and was approved by the Chief of Naval Operations on September 9, 1941.[56] It assumed, consistent with "ABC-1" and the United States Pacific Fleet Operating Plan Rainbow Five, that the principal military efforts of the Associated Powers would be in the Atlantic and European areas, and that operations in other areas would be so conducted as to facilitate that effort.

In estimating the likely enemy (Japanese) action it was observed, among other things, that it was believed Japan's initial action would be toward "possibly raids or stronger attacks on Wake, Midway, and other outlying United States positions" and "raiding and observation forces widely distributed in the Pacific, and submarines in the Hawaiian Area." One of the tasks formulated to accomplish assigned missions contemplated by the plan under phase I (Japan not in the war) was to "guard against surprise attack by Japan."

Under phase IA (initial tasks—Japan in the war) the Pacific Fleet, among other things was to "make reconnaissance and raid in force on the Marshall Islands." Among the tasks under phase II (succeeding tasks) was "to capture and establish a protected fleet base anchorage in the Marshall Island area."

From the Army standpoint, as stated by General Marshall, the fullest protection for the Pacific Fleet was *the* rather than *a* major consideration.[57] The function of the Army, therefore, was primarily that of protecting Hawaii because it was the sea and air base of the fleet and to render protection to the fleet proper when it was in harbor.[58] Aside from these purposes, the protection of the Hawaiian Islands was secondary and necessary only to the extent of making it possible for the Army to execute its primary mission.

CONCLUSIONS WITH RESPECT TO CONSCIOUSNESS OF DANGER FROM AIR ATTACK

Considering all of the information made available to the commanding officers of the Army and Navy in Hawaii from the time of their assuming command until December 7, 1941, it must be concluded that both General Short and Admiral Kimmel knew that if Pearl Harbor was to be attacked the danger of a Japanese air attack upon that base was the greatest peril of their situation and that the necessity of taking steps to provide the best possible defense to this most dangerous form of attack was clearly indicated. It is further concluded that both responsible officers appreciated the fact that Japan might strike before a formal declaration of war.

It is clear that the function of both the Army and the Navy in the Pacific was essentially a defensive one, particularly in the early stages of the war. While diversionary and sporadic raids were envisaged for the fleet, naval operations were to be fundamentally defensive in character. Pending imminence of war against Japan both services were engaged in preparation and training for this eventuality.

---

[56] Id., exhibit No. 5. This plan is referred to as "U. S. Pacific Fleet Operating Plan, Rainbow 5, Navy Plan O-1, Rainbow Five (WPPac-46)."

[57] Committee exhibit No. 53, pp. 1-3.

[58] As stated by the Navy Court of Inquiry: "The defense of a permanent naval base is the direct responsibility of the Army. The Navy is expected to assist with the means provided the naval district within whose limits the permanent naval base is located and the defense of the base is a joint operation only to that extent." See Navy Court of Inquiry report, committee exhibit No. 157.

The next point of inquiry is to determine whether Admiral Kimmel and General Short, through information available to them, were adequately informed concerning the imminence of war in such manner as reasonably to contemplate they would employ every facility at their command in defense of the fleet and the fleet base.

INFORMATION SUPPLIED ADMIRAL KIMMEL BY WASHINGTON INDICATING THE IMMINENCE OF WAR

In a letter to Admiral Stark dated February 18, 1941, Admiral Kimmel set forth the following comments in a postscript: [59]

I have recently been told by an officer fresh from Washington that ONI considers it the function of Operations to furnish the Commander-in-Chief with information of a secret nature. I have heard also that Operations considers the responsibility for furnishing the same type of information to be that of ONI. I do not know that we have missed anything, but if there is any doubt as to whose responsibility it is to keep the Commander-in-Chief fully informed with pertinent reports on subjects that should be of interest to the Fleet, will you kindly fix that responsibility so that there will be no misunderstanding?

In reply the Chief of Naval Operations advised that the Office of Naval Intelligence was fully aware of its responsibility to keep the commander in chief of the Pacific Fleet adequately informed concerning foreign nations, activities of these nations, and disloyal elements within the United States; that information concerning the location of Japanese merchant vessels was forwarded by air mail weekly and if desired could be issued more frequently.

On February 25 Admiral Stark wrote Admiral Kimmel, forwarding a copy of a memorandum for the President, dated February 11, 1941, discussing the possibility of sending a detachment to the Philippines by way of the "southern route." [60] Also enclosed was a copy of another memorandum for the President of February 5, 1941, setting forth an analysis of the situation in Indochina, prepared by Admiral Stark. This expressed Admiral Stark's view that Japan had some fear that the British and the United States would intervene if Japan moved into southern Indochina and Thailand; and that the size of Japanese land forces in Formosa and Hainan was insufficient for occupying Indochina and Thailand, for attacking Singapore, and for keeping an expeditionary force ready to use against the Philippines. It observed that insofar as Admiral Stark could tell, an insufficient number of transports was assembled for a major move; that, as he saw the situation, Japan desired to move against the British, the Dutch, and the United States in succession, and not to take on more than one at a time; and that at present she desired not to go to war with the United States at all.

The following significant dispatch was sent on April 1, 1941, from the Chief of Naval Operations addressed to the commandants of all naval districts: [61]

PERSONNEL OF YOUR NAVAL INTELLIGENCE SERVICE SHOULD BE ADVISED THAT BECAUSE OF THE FACT THAT FROM PAST EXPERIENCE SHOWS THE AXIS POWERS OFTEN BEGIN ACTIVITIES

[59] Committee exhibit No. 106.
[60] Id.
[61] Committee exhibit No. 37, p. 1.

IN A PARTICULAR FIELD ON SATURDAYS AND SUNDAYS OR ON NATIONAL HOLIDAYS OF THE COUNTRY CONCERNED, THEY SHOULD TAKE STEPS ON SUCH DAYS TO SEE THAT PROPER WATCHES AND PRECAUTIONS ARE IN EFFECT.

In a letter of April 3, 1941,[62] Admiral Stark expressed his observations on the international situation to the commanders in chief, Pacific Fleet, Asiatic Fleet, and Atlantic Fleet, including a discussion of the preparation of Navy Basic War Plan Rainbow No. 5. Admiral Stark stated that the basic idea of this plan contemplated that the United States would draw forces from the Pacific Fleet to reenforce the Atlantic Fleet; that the British, if necessary, would transfer naval forces to the Far East to attempt to hold the Japanese north of the Malay barrier; and that the United States Asiatic Fleet would be supported through offensive operations of the United States Pacific Fleet. He then discussed the dangers facing Britain and stated that the Japanese attitude would continue to have an extremely important bearing on the future of the war in the Atlantic. He observed that for some time Japan had been showing less inclination to attack the British, Dutch, and the United States in the Far East. Admiral Stark instructed the addressees to watch this situation closely. He expressed the feeling that beyond question the presence of the Pacific Fleet in Hawaii had a stabilizing effect in the Far East but that the question was *when* and not *whether* we would enter the war. Admiral Stark's personal view was that we might be in the war against Germany and Italy within about 2 months, but there was a reasonable possibility that Japan might remain out altogether. However, he added, we could not act on that possibility. In the meantime, he suggested that as much time as available be devoted to training.

Under date of April 18, 1941, instructions were given various naval observers to include the commander in chief of the Pacific Fleet as an information addressee in all dispatch reports and to furnish one copy of all intelligence reports directly to him.[63]

In a memorandum dated May 26 to the Chief of Naval Operations the commander in chief of the Pacific Fleet suggested that he be guided by broad policy and objectives rather than by categorical instructions; and that it be made a cardinal principle that he be immediately informed of all important developments as soon as they occur and by the quickest secure means possible.[64]

---

[62] Committee exhibit No. 106.
[63] Committee exhibit No. 37, p. 3.
[64] Admiral Kimmel said:

"The Commander-in-Chief, Pacific Fleet, is in a very difficult position. He is far removed from the seat of government, in a complex and rapidly changing situation. He is, as a rule, not informed as to the policy, or change of policy, reflected in current events and naval movements and, as a result, is unable to evaluate the possible effect upon his own situation. He is not even sure of what force will be available to him and has little voice in matters radically affecting his ability to carry out his assigned tasks. The lack of information is disturbing and tends to create uncertainty, a condition which directly contravenes that singleness of purpose and confidence is one's own course of action so necessary to the conduct of military operations.

"It is realized that, on occasion, the rapid developments in the international picture, both diplomatic and military, and, perhaps, even the lack of knowledge of the military authorities themselves, may militate against the furnishing of timely information, but certainly the present situation is susceptible to marked improvement. Full and authoritative knowledge of current policies and objectives, even though necessarily late at times, would enable the Commander-in-Chief, Pacific Fleet, to modify, adapt or even reorient his possible courses of action to conform to current concepts. This is particularly applicable to the current Pacific situation, where the necessities for intensive training of a partially trained Fleet must be carefully balanced against the desirability of interruption of this training by strategic dispositions, or otherwise, to meet impending eventualities. Moreover, due to this same factor of distance and time, the Department itself is not too well informed as to the local situation, particularly with regard to the status of current outlying island development, *thus making it even more necessary that the Commander-in-Chief, Pacific Fleet, be guided by broad policy and objectives rather than by categorical instructions.*

"*It is suggested that it be made a cardinal principle that the Commander-in-Chief, Pacific Fleet, be immediately informed of all important developments as they occur and by the quickest secure means available.*" See committee exhibit No. 106.

In June of 1941 Admiral Kimmel visited Washington at which time matters of naval policy were reviewed with him.[65]

On July 3, 1941, Admiral Kimmel, among others, was advised "for action" by the Chief of Naval Operations,[66] that the unmistakable deduction from information obtained from numerous sources was that the Japanese Government had determined upon its future policy, supported by all principal Japanese political and military groups; that this policy probably involved war in the near future. It was pointed out that an advance by Japan against the British and Dutch could not be entirely ruled out but that the Chief of Naval Operations held to the opinion that Japanese activity in "the south" would be confined for the present to seizure and development of naval, army, and air bases in Indochina. The dispatch stated that the Japanese neutrality pact with Russia would be abrogated and the major military effort on the part of Japan against Russia would be toward the latter's maritime provinces probably toward the end of July, although the attack might be deferred until after the collapse of European Russia. It was pointed out that all Japanese vessels in United States Atlantic ports had been ordered to be west of the Panama Canal by August 1; that the movement of Japanese "flag shipping" from Japan had been suspended and additional merchant vessels were being requisitioned. With an admonition to secrecy, instructions were issued to inform the principal army commanders and the commander in chief's own immediate subordinates.

In another dispatch of July 3,[67] Admiral Kimmel was advised for action that definite information had been received indicating that between July 16 and 22 the Japanese Government had issued an order for 7 of the 11 Japanese vessels then in the North Atlantic and Caribbean areas to pass through the Panama Canal to the Pacific, and that under routine schedules three of the remaining ships were to move to the Pacific during the same period. It was suggested that in Japanese business communities strong rumors were current that Russia would be attacked by Japan on July 20, and that a definite move by the Japanese might be expected during the period July 20 to August 1, 1941.

On July 7 the commander in chief of the Pacific Fleet was advised for information of the substance of three intercepted dispatches, including one of July 2 from Tokyo to Berlin, stating: [68]

JAPAN IS PREPARING FOR ALL POSSIBLE EVENTUALITIES REGARDING SOVIET IN ORDER (TO) JOIN FORCES WITH GERMANY IN |ACTIVELY COMBATTING COMMUNIST (SIC) AND DESTROYING COMMUNIST SYSTEM IN EASTERN SIBERIA. AT SAME TIME JAPAN CANNOT AND WILL NOT RELAX EFFORTS |IN THE |SOUTH TO RESTRAIN BRITAIN AND THE UNITED |STATES. NEW INDOCHINA BASES WILL INTENSIFY RESTRAINT |AND BE VITAL CONTRIBUTION TO AXIS VICTORY.

And another of July 2 from Berlin to Tokyo: [69]

OSHIMA DELIVERS ABOVE NOTE AND TELLS RIBBENTROP IN PART, "MATSUOKA WILL SOON SUBMIT A DECISION. IF YOU GERMANS HAD ONLY LET US KNOW YOU WERE GOING TO FIGHT

[65] See Navy Court of Inquiry record, page 113.
[66] Committee exhibit No. 37, p. 4.
[67] Id., at p. 5.
[68] Id., at p. 6.
[69] Id. This dispatch and that indicated, note 68, supra, were based on the so-called Magic. For a discussion of Magic, see Part IV, this report.

RUSSIA SO SOON WE MIGHT HAVE BEEN READY. WE WERE PLAN-
NING TO SETTLE SOUTH SEAS QUESTIONS AND CHINA INCIDENT
HENCE DECISION CANNOT BE REACHED IMMEDIATELY, BUT
JAPAN WILL NOT SIT ON FENCE WHILE GERMANY FIGHTS."

The Chief of Naval Operations in a dispatch of July 15,[70] sent
Admiral Kimmel for information, supplied intelligence received to the
effect that within "the next day or two," Japan would begin commercial negotiations with Vichy France at which time she would
propose "in the name of mutual defense" Japan's taking over southern
French Indochina naval and air bases; and that at the same time
Japan would attempt to station army and navy air forces peacefully
with French agreement, if possible. It was pointed out that if Vichy
objected Japan had decided to use force; and that Japan did not intend
to move farther south or interfere with colonial government. On the
basis of the information received it was observed that the Japanese
move was necessary to guarantee supplies from "Colony and Thailand"
and to prevent "Syrian type British action"; and that while Tokyo
wished to avoid friction with Britain and particularly the United
States, if possible, the risk was regarded as necessary.

In a dispatch sent Admiral Kimmel on July 17 for his information,
he was advised of a six-point ultimatum sent by Tokyo to Vichy requiring an answer by July 20.[71] The six points were specified as:

(1) Japan to send necessary Army and Navy air forces to
southern French Indochina;

(2) Vichy to turn over certain naval and air bases;

(3) Japanese expeditionary force to have right to maneuver
and move about freely;

(4) Vichy to withdraw forces at landing points to avoid possible clashes;

(5) Vichy to authorize French Indochina military to arrange
details with Japanese either before or after landing;

(6) Colony to pay Japan 23,000,000 piastres annually to meet
cost of occupation.

This same dispatch advised of intelligence received on July 14 that
the Japanese Army was planning its advance on or about July 20 and,
of intelligence received on July 14, that Japan intended to carry out
its plans by force if opposed or if Britain or the United States interfered.

On July 19 Admiral Kimmel was advised for his information concerning the substance of an intercepted Japanese dispatch from
Canton to Tokyo, as follows: [72]

THE RECENT GENERAL MOBILIZATION ORDER EXPRESSES
JAPAN'S IRREVOCABLE RESOLUTION TO END ANGLO-AMERICAN
ASSISTANCE IN THWARTING JAPAN'S NATURAL EXPANSION AND
HER INDOMITABLE INTENTION TO CARRY THIS OUT WITH THE
BACKING OF THE AXIS IF POSSIBLE BUT ALONE IF NECESSARY.
FORMALITIES SUCH AS DINING THE EXPEDITIONARY FORCES
AND SAYING FAREWELL TO THEM WERE DISPENSED WITH TO
AVOID ALARM AND BECAUSE WE WISHED TO FACE THIS NEW
WAR WITH A CALM AND COOL ATTITUDE. * * * IMMEDIATE
OBJECT WILL BE TO ATTEMPT PEACEFUL FRENCH INDOCHINA
OCCUPATION BUT WILL CRUSH RESISTANCE IF OFFERED AND

---

[70] Committee exhibit No. 37, p. 8. This dispatch was based on Magic.
[71] Id., at page 9. This dispatch was also based on Magic.
[72] Id., at p. 10. This dispatch was likewise based on Magic, see committee exhibit No. 1, p. 2.

SET UP MARTIAL LAW. SECONDLY OUR PURPOSE IS TO LAUNCH THEREFROM A RAPID ATTACK WHEN THE INTERNATIONAL SITUATION IS SUITABLE. AFTER OCCUPATION NEXT ON OUR SCHEDULE IS SENDING ULTIMATUM TO NETHERLANDS INDIES. IN THE SEIZING OF SINGAPORE THE NAVY WILL PLAY THE PRINCIPAL PART. ARMY WILL NEED ONLY ONE DIVISION TO SEIZE SINGAPORE AND TWO DIVISIONS TO SEIZE NETHERLANDS INDIES. WITH AIR FORCES BASED ON CANTON, SPRATLEY, PALAU, SINGORA IN THAILAND, PORTUGUESE TIMOR AND INDOCHINA AND WITH SUBMARINE FLEET IN MANDATES, HAINAN, AND INDOCHINA WE WILL CRUSH BRITISH AMERICAN MILITARY POWER AND ABILITY TO ASSIST IN SCHEMES AGAINST US.

On July 19 Admiral Kimmel was advised of an intercepted dispatch from Tokyo informing that although the Japanese Cabinet had changed there would be no departure from the principle that the Tripartite Pact formed the keystone of Japan's national policy and that the new Cabinet would also pursue the policy of the former Cabinet in all other matters.[73] In another dispatch, supplying information concerning an intercepted Tokyo message to Vichy, Admiral Kimmel was advised on July 20, that the Japanese Army had made all preparations and had decided to advance regardless of whether Vichy France accepted her demands.[74]

Admiral Stark wrote to Admiral Hart on July 24, 1941,[75] sending a copy of the letter to Admiral Kimmel, concerning among other things, a 2-hour conversation between Admiral Stark and Ambassador Nomura. Admiral Stark expressed the thought that Nomura was sincere in his desire that the United States and Japan avoid open rupture; stated they had a very plain talk; and observed that he, Admiral Stark, liked Nomura. He advised that Nomura discussed at length Japan's need for the rice and minerals of Indochina. Admiral Stark said his guess was that with the establishment of bases in Indochina, Japan would stop for the time being, consolidate her positions and await world reaction; that no doubt the Japanese would use their Indochina bases from which to take early action against the Burma Road. He said that, of course, there was the possibility that Japan would strike at Borneo, but that he doubted this in the near future *unless* we were to embargo oil shipments to them. Admiral Stark also said that he talked with the President and hoped no open rupture would come but that conditions were not getting better.

On July 25, 1941, Admiral Kimmel was advised that beginning July 26 the United States would impose economic sanctions against Japan and that it was expected these sanctions would embargo all trade between Japan and the United States, subject to modification through a licensing system for certain material.[76] It was further pointed out that funds in the United States would be frozen except as they may be moved under licensing. In estimating the situation it was observed:

Do not anticipate immediate hostile reaction by Japan through the use of military means but you are furnished this information in order that you may take appropriate precautionary measures against hostile eventualities.

[73] Committee exhibit No. 37, p. 11.
[74] Id., at p. 12.
[75] Committee exhibit No. 106.
[76] Committee exhibit No. 37, p. 14.

In a letter to Admiral Kimmel dated July 31, 1941,[77] Admiral Stark discussed the over-all international situation, and stated that "after the Russian situation broke" he proposed to the President that they should start escorting immediately and that we should consider, along with the British, a joint protectorate over the Dutch East Indies. He stated he thought it fairly safe to say that the opinion was generally held that Japan would not go into the N. E. I.[78] but that Admiral Turner thought Japan would go into the maritime provinces in August. He commented that Turner might be right and usually was. Admiral Stark said his thought had been that while Japan would ultimately go into Siberia she would delay doing so until she had the Indochina-Thailand situation more or less to her liking and until there was some clarification of the Russian-German clash. He also said that we would give aid to Russia. A postscript to this letter stated, among other things, that—

obviously, the situation in the Far East continues to deteriorate; this is one thing that is factual.

Admiral Kimmel was advised on August 14 that the Japanese were rapidly completing withdrawal from world shipping routes, that scheduled sailings were canceled, and that the majority of ships in other than China and Japan Sea areas were homeward bound.[79]

The following dispatch of August 28 was sent to Admiral Kimmel, among others, for action: [80]

CERTAIN OPERATIONS PRESCRIBED FOR THE ATLANTIC BY WPL 51 ARE HEREBY EXTENDED TO AREAS OF THE PACIFIC OCEAN AS DESCRIBED HEREIN IN VIEW OF THE DESTRUCTION BY RAIDERS OF MERCHANT VESSELS IN THE PACIFIC OCEAN WITHIN THE WESTERN HEMISPHERE NEUTRALITY ZONE AS DEFINED IN THE DECLARATION OF PANAMA OF OCTOBER 3, 1939. FORMAL CHANGES IN WPL 51 WILL BE ISSUED, BUT MEANWHILE ACTION ADDRESSES WILL EXECUTE IMMEDIATELY THE FOLLOWING INSTRUCTIONS. CINCPAC CONSTITUTE THE SOUTHEAST PACIFIC FORCE CONSISTING OF TWO 7,500-TON LIGHT CRUISERS AND DISPATCH IT TO BALBOA. FOR TASK PURPOSES THIS FORCE WILL OPERATE DIRECTLY UNDER CNO [81] AFTER ENTERING THE SOUTHEAST PACIFIC SUB AREA AS DEFINED IN WPL 46 PAR. 3222 EXCEPT WESTERN LIMIT IS LONGITUDE 100° WEST. WITHIN THE PACIFIC SECTOR OF THE PANAMA NAVAL COASTAL FRONTIER AND WITHIN THE SOUTHEAST PACIFIC SUB AREA THE COMMANDER PANAMA NAVAL COASTAL FRONTIER AND COMMANDER SOUTHEAST PACIFIC FORCE WILL IN COOPERATION AND ACTING UNDER THE STRATEGIC DIRECTION OF THE CHIEF OF NAVAL OPERATIONS EXECUTE THE FOLLOWING TASK: DESTROY SURFACE RAIDERS WHICH ATTACK OR THREATEN UNITED STATES FLAG SHIPPING. INTERPRET AN APPROACH OF SURFACE RAIDERS WITHIN THE PACIFIC SECTOR OF THE PANAMA NAVAL COASTAL FRONTIER OR THE PACIFIC SOUTHEAST SUB AREA AS A THREAT TO UNITED STATES FLAG SHIPPING. FOR THE PRESENT THE FORCES CONCERNED WILL BASE BALBOA, BUT CNO WILL ENDEAVOR TO MAKE ARRANGEMENTS FOR BASING ON SOUTH AMERICAN PORTS AS

[77] Committee exhibit No. 106.
[78] Netherlands East Indies.
[79] Committee exhibit No. 37, p. 15.
[80] Id., at p. 16.
[81] Chief of Naval Operations.

MAY BE REQUIRED. ACTION ADEES [82] AND COMMANDER SOUTH-
EAST PACIFIC FORCE INFORM CNO WHEN THESE INSTRUCTIONS
HAVE BEEN PLACED IN EFFECT.

In a letter to Admiral Kimmel, also on August 28, 1941.[83] Admiral
Stark discussed, among other things, the status of the Japanese
situation and observed that the Japanese seemed to have arrived at
another one of their indecisive periods; that some very strong messages had been sent to them, but just what they were going to do he
did not know. He said he had told one of Japan's statesmen that
another move, such as the one into Thailand, would go a long way
toward destroying before the American public what good will still
remained. Admiral Stark said he had not given up hope of continuing
peace in the Pacific, but he wished the thread by which it continued to
hang were not so slender.

Admiral Kimmel raised specific questions in a letter to Admiral
Stark of September 12, 1941 [84] such as whether he should not issue
shooting orders to the escorts for ships proceeding to the Far East.
Admiral Kimmel also raised the question of what to do about submarine contacts off Pearl Harbor and vicinity. He said:

As you know, our present orders are to trail all contacts, but not to bomb
unless they are in the defensive sea areas. Should we now bomb contacts, without
waiting to be attacked?

Admiral Stark answered on September 23, 1941,[85] and stated, among
other things, that at the time the President had issued shooting orders
only for the Atlantic and Southeast Pacific submarine area; that the
longer they could keep the situation in the Pacific in *status quo*, the
better for all concerned. He said that no orders should be given to
shoot, at that time, other than those set forth in article 723 of the
Navy Regulations.[86] The letter also stated, in connection with the
question of submarine contacts, that they had no definite information
that Japanese submarines had ever operated in close vicinity to the
Hawaiian Islands, Alaska, or our Pacific coast; that existing orders,
i. e., not to bomb suspected submarines except in the defensive sea
areas, were appropriate, and continued:

If conclusive, and I repeat conclusive, evidence is obtained that Japanese submarines are actually in or near United States territory, then a strong warning and
a threat of hostile action against such submarines would appear to be our next
step. Keep us informed.

Going on, Admiral Stark said that he might be mistaken, but he did
not believe that the major portion of the Japanese Fleet was likely
to be sent to the Marshalls or the Caroline Islands under the circumstances that then seemed possible; and that in all probability the
Pacific Fleet could operate successfully and effectively even though
decidedly weaker than the entire Japanese Fleet, which certainly
could be concentrated in one area only with the greatest difficulty.
In this letter, Admiral Stark inquired:

* * * would it not be possible for your force to "carefully" get some pictures
of the Mandated Islands?

In a postscript to this letter, Admiral Stark stated that Secretary Hull
had informed him that the conversations with the Japanese had

[82] Addressees.
[83] Committee exhibit No. 106.
[84] Id.
[85] Id.
[86] These regulations provide for the use of force in self-preservation, in the sound judgment of responsible
officers, as a last resort.

practically reached an impasse.   He said that, as he saw it, we could
get nowhere toward a settlement and peace in the Far East until there
was some agreement between Japan and China, which seemed to be
remote.   A second postscript to the letter, in making reference to a
conversation between Admiral Stark and Nomura, said that Ambassador Nomura usually came in when he began to feel near the end of
his rope, and that there was not much to spare at that end then.
Admiral Stark observed that conversations without results could not
last forever and that if the conversations fell through, which looked
likely, the situation could only grow more tense.   Admiral Stark
said he had again talked to Secretary Hull and thought the Secretary
would make one more try.   He said that Secretary Hull kept him,
Admiral Stark, pretty fully informed; and, if there was anything of
moment, he would of course hasten to let Kimmel know.

With this letter there was enclosed a copy of a memorandum from
General Marshall to Admiral Stark setting forth what was being done
to strengthen the Philippines.   The memorandum indicated, among
other things, that on September 30, 26 Flying Fortresses would leave
San Francisco for Hawaii en route to the Philippines.

The following dispatch of October 16, 1941, was sent to the commander in chief, Pacific Fleet, for action: [87]

THE RESIGNATION OF THE JAPANESE CABINET HAS CREATED A
GRAVE SITUATION.   IF A NEW CABINET IS FORMED IT WILL PROB-
ABLY BE STRONGLY NATIONALISTIC AND ANTI-AMERICAN.   IF
THE KONOYE CABINET REMAINS THE EFFECT WILL BE THAT IT
WILL OPERATE UNDER A NEW MANDATE WHICH WILL NOT IN-
CLUDE RAPPROCHEMENT WITH THE U. S.   IN EITHER CASE HOS-
TILITIES BETWEEN JAPAN AND RUSSIA ARE A STRONG POSSI-
BILITY.   SINCE THE U. S. AND BRITAIN ARE HELD RESPONSIBLE
BY JAPAN FOR HER PRESENT DESPERATE SITUATION THERE IS
ALSO A POSSIBILITY THAT JAPAN MAY ATTACK THESE TWO
POWERS.   IN VIEW OF THESE POSSIBILITIES YOU WILL TAKE DUE
PRECAUTIONS INCLUDING SUCH PREPARATORY DEPLOYMENTS
AS WILL NOT DISCLOSE STRATEGIC INTENTION NOR CONSTITUTE
PROVOCATIVE ACTIONS AGAINST JAPAN.   SECOND AND THIRD
ADEES INFORM APPROPRIATE ARMY AND NAVAL DISTRICT
AUTHORITIES.   ACKNOWLEDGE.

Referring to the dispatch of October 16 concerning the resignation
of the Japanese Cabinet, Admiral Stark stated in a letter of October
17 to Admiral Kimmel: [88]

Personally I do not believe the Japs are going to sail into us and the message
I sent you merely stated the "possibility"; in fact I tempered the message handed
to me considerably.   Perhaps I am wrong, but I hope not.   In any case after
long pow-wows in the White House it was felt we should be on guard, at least
until something indicates the trend.

In a postscript to this letter Admiral Stark said:

Marshall just called up and was anxious that we make some sort of a reconnaissance so that he could feel assured that on arrival at Wake, a Japanese raider
attack may not be in order on his bombers.   I told him that we could not assure
against any such contingency, but that I felt it extremely improbable and that,
while we keep track of Japanese ships so far as we can, a carefully planned raid

_____
[87] Committee exhibit No. 37, p. 18.
[88] Committee exhibit No. 106.

on any of these Island carriers in the Pacific might be difficult to detect. However, we are on guard to the best of our ability, and my advice to him was not to worry.[89]

On October 17, 1941, Admiral Kimmel was advised for his information that, effective immediately, all trans-Pacific United States flag shipping to and from the Far East, India, and East India area was to be routed through the Torres Straits, keeping to the southward and well clear of the Japanese Mandates.[90] On the same day he was advised for action that—

BECAUSE OF THE GREAT IMPORTANCE OF CONTINUING TO RE-ENFORCE THE PHILIPPINES WITH LONG-RANGE ARMY BOMBERS YOU ARE REQUESTED TO TAKE ALL PRACTICAL PRECAUTIONS FOR THE SAFETY OF THE AIRFIELDS AT WAKE AND MIDWAY.[91]

Admiral Kimmel was advised, among other things, on October 23 that until further orders all Army and Navy "trans-Pacific troop transports, ammunition ships and such others with sufficiently important military cargo" would be escorted both ways between Honolulu and Manila.[92]

On November 4, 1941, Admiral Kimmel was informed that complete withdrawal from Western Hemisphere waters of Japanese merchant vessels appeared in progress.[93]

A letter to Admiral Kimmel from Admiral Stark on November 7 commented, among other things: [94]

Things seem to be moving steadily towards a crisis in the Pacific. Just when it will break, no one can tell. The principle reaction I have to it all is what I have written you before; it continually gets "worser and worser!" A month may see, literally, most anything. Two irreconcilable policies cannot go on forever—particularly if one party cannot live with the set-up. It doesn't look good.

On November 14, Admiral Stark wrote Admiral Kimmel, stating among other things:[95]

The next few days hold much for us. Kurusu's arrival in Washington has been delayed. I am not hopeful that anything in the way of better understanding between the United States and Japan will come of his visit. I note this morning in the press despatches a listing of a number of points by the Japan Times and

---

[89] Transmitted as an enclosure to this letter was an estimate dated October 17 prepared by Admiral Schuirmann with respect to the change in the Japanese Cabinet, stating:

"I believe we are inclined to overestimate the importance of changes in the Japanese Cabinet as indicative of great changes in Japanese political thought or action.

"The plain fact is that Japanese politics has been ultimately controlled for years by the military. Wheth-er or not a policy of peace or a policy of further military adventuring is pursued is determined by the military based on their estimate as to whether the time is opportune and what they are able to do, not by what cabinet is in power or on diplomatic maneuvering, diplomatic notes or diplomatic treaties."

After recounting that Konoye cabinets had time and again expressed disapproval of the acts committed by the Japanese military but remedial action had not been taken; that Konoye himself had declared Japan's policy was to beat China to her knees; that while the Konoye cabinet may have restrained the *extremists* among the military it had not opposed Japan's program of expansion by force; that when opportunities arise during the "coming months" which seemed favorable to the military for further advance, they would be seized; and that the same "bill of goods," regarding the necessity of making some concession to the "moderates" in order to enable them to cope with the "extremists" had been offered to the United States since the days when Mr. Stimson was Secretary of State and Debuchi Ambassador, Admiral Schuirmann concluded:

"Present reports are that the new cabinet to be formed will be no better and no worse than the one which has just fallen. Japan may attack Russia, or may move southward, but *in the final analysis this will be determined by the military on the basis of opportunity, and what they can get away with, not by what cabinet is in power*" (Committee exhibit No. 106).

[90] Committee exhibit No. 37, p. 21.

[91] Id., at p. 22.

[92] Id., at p. 23.

[93] Id., at p. 24.

[94] Committee exhibit No. 106.

[95] Id. As an enclosure to this letter, Admiral Stark forwarded a copy of a joint memorandum for the President which he and General Marshall had prepared dated November 5 and bearing caption "Estimate concerning Far Eastern Situation." This memorandum was prepared with respect to dispatches received indicating it to be Generalissimo Chiang Kai-shek's belief that a Japanese attack on Kunming was imminent and that military support from outside sources, particularly by the use of United States and British air units, was the sole hope for defeat of this threat. The Chief of Staff and Chief of Naval Operations opposed dispatching American military assistance to meet this supposed threat. For a discussion of this memorandum, see Part IV, infra, this report.

Advertiser upon which concessions by the United States are necessary for the·
"solution of the Pacific Crisis". Complete capitulation by the United States on
every point of difference between the Japanese and this country was indicated as
a satisfactory solution. It will be impossible to reconcile such divergent points
of view.

On November 24, 1941, Admiral Kimmel received the following
message marked for action: [96]

CHANCES OF FAVORABLE OUTCOME OF NEGOTIATIONS WITH
JAPAN VERY DOUBTFUL. THIS SITUATION COUPLED WITH STATE-
MENTS OF JAPANESE GOVERNMENT AND MOVEMENTS THEIR
NAVAL AND MILITARY FORCES INDICATE IN OUR OPINION
THAT *A SURPRISE AGGRESSIVE MOVEMENT IN ANY DIRECTION
INCLUDING ATTACK ON PHILIPPINES OR GUAM IS A POSSIBILITY.*
CHIEF OF STAFF HAS SEEN THIS DESPATCH CONCURS AND RE-
QUESTS ACTION ADEES TO INFORM SENIOR ARMY OFFICERS
THEIR AREAS. UTMOST SECRECY NECESSARY IN ORDER NOT
TO COMPLICATE AN ALREADY TENSE SITUATION OR PRECIPI-
TATE JAPANESE ACTION. GUAM WILL BE INFORMED SEPA-
RATELY.

The postscript of a personal letter dated November 25 from Admiral
Stark to Admiral Kimmel read: [97]

I held this up pending a meeting with the President and Mr. Hull today. I
have been in constant touch with Mr. Hull and it was only after a long talk with
him that I sent the message to you a day or two ago showing the gravity of the
situation. He confirmed it all in today's meeting, as did the President. Neither
would be surprised over a Japanese surprise attack. From many angles an attack
on the Philippines would be the most embarrassing thing that could happen to us.
There are some here who think it likely to occur. I do not give it the weight
others do, but I included it because of the strong feeling among some people.
You know I have generally held that it was not time for the Japanese to proceed
against Russia. I still do. Also I still rather look for an advance into Thailand,
Indo-China, Burma Road areas as the most likely.

I won't go into the pros or cons of what the United States may do. I will
be damned if I know. I wish I did. The only thing I do know is that we may
do most anything and that's the only thing I know to be prepared for; or we may
do nothing—I think it is more likely to be "anything."

On November 27, 1941, the following dispatch was sent Admiral
Kimmel for action: [98]

THIS DESPATCH IS TO BE CONSIDERED A WAR WARNING. NEGO-
TIATIONS WITH JAPAN LOOKING TOWARD STABILIZATION OF
CONDITIONS IN THE PACIFIC *HAVE CEASED* AND AN AGGRESSIVE
MOVE BY JAPAN IS EXPECTED WITHIN THE NEXT FEW DAYS.
THE NUMBER AND EQUIPMENT OF JAPANESE TROOPS AND THE
ORGANIZATION OF NAVAL TASK FORCES INDICATES AN AMPHIBI-
OUS EXPEDITION AGAINST EITHER THE PHILIPPINES THAI OR KRA
PENINSULA OR POSSIBLY BORNEO. *EXECUTE AN APPROPRIATE
DEFENSIVE DEPLOYMENT PREPARATORY TO CARRYING OUT THE
TASKS ASSIGNED IN WPL46.* INFORM DISTRICT AND ARMY
AUTHORITIES. A SIMILAR WARNING IS BEING SENT BY WAR
DEPARTMENT. SPENAVO [99] INFORM BRITISH. CONTINENTAL
DISTRICTS GUAM SAMOA DIRECTED TAKE APPROPRIATE MEA-
SURES AGAINST SABOTAGE.

---

[96] Committee exhibit No. 37, p. 32. This dispatch was also sent for action to commander in chief Asiatic
Fleet and commandants of the Twelfth, Thirteenth, and Fourteenth Naval Districts.
[97] Committee exhibit No. 106.
[98] Committee exhibit No. 37, p. 36. This dispatch was also sent for action to the commander in chief of
the Asiatic Fleet. It has been referred to throughout the proceedings as the "War Warning."
[99] Special naval observer.

The following dispatch dated November 28, 1941, referring to the November 27 warning, was supplied Admiral Kimmel for his information: [100]

* * * ARMY HAS SENT FOLLOWING TO COMMANDER WESTERN DEFENSE COMMAND "NEGOTIATIONS WITH JAPAN APPEAR TO BE TERMINATED TO ALL PRACTICAL PURPOSES WITH ONLY THE BAREST POSSIBILITIES THAT THE JAPANESE GOVERNMENT MIGHT COME BACK AND OFFER TO CONTINUE. JAPANESE FUTURE ACTION UNPREDICTABLE BUT HOSTILE ACTION POSSIBLE AT ANY MOMENT. IF HOSTILITIES CANNOT REPEAT NOT BE AVOIDED THE UNITED STATES DESIRES THAT JAPAN COMMIT THE FIRST OVERT ACT. THIS POLICY SHOULD NOT REPEAT NOT BE CONSTRUED AS RESTRICTING YOU TO A COURSE OF ACTION THAT MIGHT JEOPARDIZE YOUR DEFENSE. PRIOR TO HOSTILE JAPANESE ACTION YOU ARE DIRECTED TO UNDERTAKE SUCH RECONNAISSANCE AND OTHER MEASURES AS YOU DEEM NECESSARY BUT THESE MEASURES SHOULD BE CARRIED OUT SO AS NOT REPEAT NOT TO ALARM CIVIL POPULATION OR DISCLOSE INTENT. REPORT MEASURES TAKEN. A SEPARATE MESSAGE IS BEING SENT TO G TWO NINTH CORPS AREA RE SUBVERSIVE ACTIVITIES IN UNITED STATES. SHOULD HOSTILITIES OCCUR THEY WILL CARRY OUT THE TASKS ASSIGNED IN RAINBOW FIVE SO FAR AS THEY PERTAIN TO JAPAN. LIMIT DISSEMINATION OF THIS HIGHLY SECRET INFORMATION TO MINIMUM ESSENTIAL OFFICERS." WPL 52 IS NOT APPLICABLE TO PACIFIC AREA AND WILL NOT BE PLACED IN EFFECT IN THAT AREA EXCEPT AS NOW IN FORCE IN SOUTHEAST PACIFIC SUB AREA AND PANAMA NAVAL COASTAL FRONTIER. UNDERTAKE NO OFFENSIVE ACTION UNTIL JAPAN HAS COMMITTED AN OVERT ACT. BE PREPARED TO CARRY OUT TASKS ASSIGNED IN WPL 46 SO FAR AS THEY APPLY TO JAPAN IN CASE HOSTILITIES OCCUR.

On December 1 the Chief of Naval Operations sent Admiral Kimmel a dispatch for information describing a Japanese intrigue in Malaya. The dispatch indicated that Japan planned a landing at Khota Baru in Malaya in order to entice the British to cross the frontier from Malay into Thailand. Thailand would then brand Britain an aggressor and call upon Japan for aid, thereby facilitating the Japanese entry into Thailand as a full-fledged ally and give Japan air bases on the Kra Peninsula and a position to carry out any further operations along Malaya. [100a]

---

[100] Committee exhibit No. 37, p. 38. This dispatch was sent for action to the naval commanders on the west coast.

[100a] This dispatch, No. 011400 which was addressed to the commander in chief of the Asiatic Fleet for action, read: "AMBASSADOR TSUBOKAMI IN BANGKOK ON TWENTY NINTH SENT TO TOKYO AS NUMBER EIGHT SEVEN TWO THE FOLLOWING QUOTE CONFERENCES NOW IN PROGRESS IN BANGKOK CONSIDERING PLANS AIMED AT FORCING BRITISH TO ATTACK THAI AT PADANG BESSA NEAR SINGORA AS COUNTER MOVE TO JAPANESE LANDING AT KOTA BHARU. SINCE THAI INTENDS TO CONSIDER FIRST INVADER AS HER ENEMY, ORANGE BELIEVES THIS LANDING IN MALAY WOULD FORCE BRITISH TO INVADE THAI AT PADANG BESSA. THAI WOULD THEN DECLARE WAR AND REQUEST ORANGE HELP. THIS PLAN APPEARS TO HAVE APPROVAL OF THAI CHIEF OF STAFF BIJITTO. THAI GOVERNMENT CIRCLES HAVE BEEN SHARPLY DIVIDED BETWEEN PROBRITISH AND PROORANGE UNTIL TWENTY FIVE NOVEMBER BUT NOW WANITTO AND SHIN WHO FAVOR JOINT MILITARY ACTION WITH ORANGE HAVE SILENCED ANTI ORANGE GROUP AND INTEND TO FORCE PREMIUR PIBUL TO MAKE A DECISION. EARLY AND FAVORABLE DEVELOPMENTS ARE POSSIBLE UNQUOTE." See committee exhibit No. 112, p. 67.

On December 3, 1941, Admiral Kimmel was supplied the following information for action: [101]

HIGHLY RELIABLE INFORMATION HAS BEEN RECEIVED THAT CATEGORIC AND URGENT INSTRUCTIONS WERE SENT YESTERDAY TO JAPANESE DIPLOMATIC AND CONSULAR POSTS AT HONGKONG, SINGAPORE, BATAVIA, MANILA, WASHINGTON AND LONDON TO DESTROY MOST OF THEIR CODES AND CIPHERS AT ONCE AND TO BURN ALL OTHER IMPORTANT CONFIDENTIAL AND SECRET DOCUMENTS.

And, again, on December 3, 1941, he received the following message for his information: [102]

CIRCULAR TWENTY FOUR FORTY FOUR FROM TOKYO ONE DECEMBER ORDERED LONDON, HONGKONG, SINGAPORE AND MANILA TO DESTROY MACHINE. BATAVIA MACHINE ALREADY SENT TO TOKYO. DECEMBER SECOND WASHINGTON ALSO DIRECTED DESTROY, ALL BUT ONE COPY OF OTHER SYSTEMS, AND ALL SECRET DOCUMENTS. BRITISH ADMIRALTY LONDON TODAY REPORTS EMBASSY LONDON HAS COMPLIED.

On December 4, 1941, a dispatch [103] was supplied the commander in chief of the Pacific Fleet, for his information, instructing Guam to destroy all secret and confidential publications and other classified matter except that essential for current purposes, and to be prepared to destroy instantly, in event of emergency, all classified matter.

A dispatch to Admiral Kimmel of December 6 [104] for action stated that "in view of the international situation and the exposed position of our outlying Pacific islands" he was authorized to order the destruction in such outlying islands secret and confidential documents "now or under later conditions of greater emergency." It was pointed out that means of communication to support "our current operations and special intelligence" should be maintained until the last moment.

From a review of dispatches and correspondence sent Admiral Kimmel it is concluded that he was fully informed concerning the progressive deterioration of relations with Japan and was amply warned of the imminence of war with that nation.

Information Supplied General Short by Washington Indicating the Imminence of War

The accepted practice in the Navy whereby the Chief of Naval Operations supplemented official dispatches by personal correspondence does not appear to have been followed by the War Department. The letters sent by the Chief of Staff to General Short, heretofore discussed, related largely to the latter's responsibility, steps necessary to improve the Army defenses in Hawaii, and suggestions and comments with respect thereto. It does not appear that such correspondence was employed to acquaint the commanding general of the Hawaiian Department with the international situation generally nor to convey the personal estimates and impressions of the Chief of Staff. The

---

[101] Committee exhibit No. 37, p. 40. This dispatch was also sent for action to the commander in chief of the Pacific Fleet and the commandants of the Fourteenth and Sixteenth Naval Districts.

[102] Committee exhibit No. 37, p. 41. This dispatch was sent for action to the commander in chief Asiatic Fleet and the commandant of the Sixteenth Naval District.

[103] Committee exhibit No. 37, p. 44.

[104] Id., at p. 45.

evidence indicates that the Army did not forward the substance of any intercepted Japanese dispatches to field commanders because of the feeling that the Army codes were generally not so secure as those of the Navy.[105]   General Short, however, was supplied either directly from the War Department or by reference from his naval opposites in Hawaii adequate information concerning the critical international situation and the impending likelihood of war with Japan.

The dispatch of July 3, 1941, to Admiral Kimmel, advising among other things that the unmistakable deduction from information received from numerous sources was to the effect that Japan was agreed on a policy involving war in the near future, carried instructions to advise General Short.[106]

Admiral Kimmel was instructed to supply General Short the information contained in the dispatch of July 25 advising of economic sanctions against Japan and possible Japanese reaction.[107]

The following Navy message of October 16, 1941, was received by General Short through reference from Admiral Kimmel: [108]

THE FOLLOWING IS A PARAPHRASE OF A DISPATCH FROM THE C. N. O. WHICH I HAVE BEEN DIRECTED TO PASS TO YOU.   QUOTE: "JAPANESE CABINET RESIGNATION CREATES A GRAVE SITUATION.   IF A NEW CABINET IS FORMED IT WILL PROBABLY BE ANTI-AMERICAN AND EXTREMELY NATIONALISTIC.   IF THE KONOYE CABINET REMAINS IT WILL OPERATE UNDER A NEW MANDATE WHICH WILL NOT INCLUDE RAPPROACHMENT WITH THE UNITED STATES.   EITHER WAY HOSTILITIES BETWEEN JAPAN AND RUSSIA ARE STRONGLY POSSIBLE.   SINCE BRITAIN AND THE UNITED STATES ARE HELD RESPONSIBLE BY JAPAN FOR HER PRESENT SITUATION THERE IS ALSO A POSSIBILITY THAT JAPAN MAY ATTACK THESE TWO POWERS.   IN VIEW OF THESE POSSIBILITIES YOU WILL TAKE DUE PRECAUTIONS INCLUDING SUCH PREPARATORY DEPLOYMENTS AS WILL NOT DISCLOSE STRATEGIC INTENTION NOR CONSTITUTE PROVOCATIVE ACTION AGAINST JAPAN."

In a radiogram of October 20 signed "Adams" [109] the War Department advised the commanding general of the Hawaiian Department of its estimate of the situation in the following terms:

TENSION BETWEEN THE UNITED STATES AND JAPAN REMAINS STRAINED BUT NO ABRUPT CHANGE IN JAPANESE FOREIGN POLICY APPEARS IMMINENT.[110]

Admiral Kimmel was instructed to advise General Short concerning the dispatch of November 24 from the Chief of Naval Operations [111] advising, among other things, that "chances of favorable outcome of negotiations with Japan very doubtful" and movements of Japanese forces "indicate in our opinion that a surprise aggressive movement in any direction including attack on Philippines or Guam is a possibility."   General Short expressed the belief that he had seen this dispatch.[112]

[105] See committee record, pp. 2220–2222.
[106] Committee exhibit No. 37, p. 4; also, No. 32, p. 1.
[107] Committee exhibit No. 37, p. 14; also No. 32, p. 2.
[108] Committee exhibit No. 37, p. 18; also, No. 32, p. 3.   See Army Pearl Harbor board record, p. 279.
[109] Maj. Gen. Emory S. Adams, Adjutant General.
[110] Committee exhibit No. 32, p. 4.   See also Army Pearl Harbor board record, p. 4258.
[111] Committee exhibit No. 32, p. 5.
[112] See Army Pearl Harbor board record, p. 4258.

A dispatch of November 26 signed "Adams" was sent General Short reading in part as follows: [113]

* * * IT IS DESIRED THAT THE PILOTS BE INSTRUCTED TO PHOTOGRAPH TRUK ISLAND IN THE CAROLINE GROUP JALUIT IN THE MARSHALL GROUP. VISUAL RECONNAISSANCE SHOULD BE MADE SIMULTANEOUSLY. INFORMATION DESIRED AS TO THE NUMBER AND LOCATION OF NAVAL VESSELS INCLUDING SUB-MARINES * * * INSURE THAT BOTH B–TWENTY FOUR AIR-PLANES ARE FULLY EQUIPPED WITH GUN AMMUNITION UPON DEPARTURE FROM HONOLULU.[114]

The November 27 dispatch from the Chief of Naval Operations to Admiral Kimmel beginning "This despatch is to be considered a war warning" [115] contained instructions that General Short be informed and he did in fact see this warning.

On November 27 the following dispatch signed "Marshall" [116] was sent General Short by the War Department: [117]

NEGOTIATIONS WITH JAPAN APPEAR TO BE TERMINATED TO ALL PRACTICAL PURPOSES WITH ONLY THE BAREST POSSIBILITIES THAT THE JAPANESE GOVERNMENT MIGHT COME BACK AND OFFER TO CONTINUE. JAPANESE FUTURE ACTION UNPREDICT-ABLE BUT *HOSTILE ACTION POSSIBLE AT ANY MOMENT.* IF HOSTILITIES CANNOT, REPEAT CANNOT, BE AVOIDED THE *UNITED STATES DESIRES THAT JAPAN COMMIT THE FIRST OVERT ACT.* THIS POLICY SHOULD NOT, REPEAT NOT, BE CONSTRUED AS RE-STRICTING YOU TO A COURSE OF ACTION THAT MIGHT JEOPARD-IZE YOUR DEFENSE. PRIOR TO HOSTILE JAPANESE ACTION *YOU ARE DIRECTED TO UNDERTAKE SUCH RECONNAISSANCE AND OTHER MEASURES AS YOU DEEM NECESSARY* BUT THESE MEAS-URES SHOULD BE CARRIED OUT SO AS NOT, REPEAT NOT, TO ALARM CIVIL POPULATION OR DISCLOSE INTENT. REPORT MEASURES TAKEN. SHOULD HOSTILITIES OCCUR YOU WILL CARRY OUT THE TASKS ASSIGNED IN RAINBOW FIVE SO FAR AS THEY PERTAIN TO JAPAN. LIMIT DISSEMINATION OF THIS HIGHLY SECRET INFORMATION TO MINIMUM ESSENTIAL OFFICERS.

The following dispatch signed "Miles",[118] and also dated November 27, was sent the commanding general, Hawaiian Department:[119]

JAPANESE NEGOTIATIONS HAVE COME TO PRACTICAL STALE-MATE *HOSTILITIES MAY ENSUE.* SUBVERSIVE ACTIVITIES MAY BE EXPECTED. INFORM COMMANDING GENERAL AND CHIEF OF STAFF ONLY.

On November 28 a dispatch signed "Adams" was directed to General Short, as follows:[120]

CRITICAL SITUATION DEMANDS THAT ALL PRECAUTIONS BE TAKEN IMMEDIATELY AGAINST SUBVERSIVE ACTIVITIES WITHIN FIELD OF INVESTIGATIVE RESPONSIBILITY OF WAR DEPARTMENT (SEE PARAGRAPH THREE MID SC THIRTY—FORTY FIVE). ALSO

[113] Committee exhibit No. 32, p. 6.
[114] This reconnaissance was not flown inasmuch as the Army planes were not made ready prior to the December 7 attack.
[115] Committee exhibit No. 37, p. 36.
[116] Gen. George C. Marshall, Army Chief of Staff.
[117] Committee exhibit No. 32, p. 7.
[118] Brig. Gen. Sherman Miles, Chief of G-2, Army Intelligence.
[119] Committee exhibit No. 32, p. 10.
[120] Id., at p. 13.

DESIRED THAT YOU INITIATE FORTHWITH ALL ADDITIONAL MEASURES NECESSARY TO PROVIDE FOR PROTECTION OF YOUR ESTABLISHMENTS, PROPERTY, AND EQUIPMENT AGAINST SABOTAGE, PROTECTION OF YOUR PERSONNEL AGAINST SUBVERSIVE PROPAGANDA AND PROTECTION OF ALL ACTIVITIES AGAINST ESPIONAGE. THIS DOES NOT REPEAT NOT MEAN THAT ANY ILLEGAL MEASURES ARE AUTHORIZED. PROTECTIVE MEASURES SHOULD BE CONFINED TO THOSE ESSENTIAL TO SECURITY, AVOIDING UNNECESSARY PUBLICITY AND ALARM. TO INSURE SPEED OF TRANSMISSION IDENTICAL TELEGRAMS ARE BEING SENT TO ALL AIR STATIONS BUT THIS DOES NOT REPEAT NOT AFFECT YOUR RESPONSIBILITY UNDER EXISTING INSTRUCTIONS.[120a]

Again on November 28 another dispatch from the War Department was sent the commanding general, Hawaiian Department, as follows:[121]

ATTENTION COMMANDING GENERAL HAWAIIAN AIR FORCE. THAT INSTRUCTIONS SUBSTANTIALLY AS FOLLOWS BE ISSUED TO ALL ESTABLISHMENTS AND UNITS UNDER YOUR CONTROL AND COMMAND IS DESIRED: AGAINST THOSE SUBVERSIVE ACTIVITIES WITHIN THE FIELD OF INVESTIGATIVE RESPONSIBILITY OF THE WAR DEPARTMENT (SEE PARAGRAPH THREE MID SR 30—45) THE PRESENT CRITICAL SITUATION DEMANDS THAT ALL PRECAUTIONS BE TAKEN AT ONCE. IT IS DESIRED ALSO THAT ALL ADDITIONAL MEASURES NECESSARY BE INITIATED BY YOU IMMEDIATELY TO PROVIDE THE FOLLOWING: PROTECTION OF YOUR PERSONNEL AGAINST SUBVERSIVE PROPAGANDA, PROTECTION OF ALL ACTIVITIES AGAINST ESPIONAGE, AND PROTECTION AGAINST SABOTAGE OF YOUR EQUIPMENT, PROPERTY AND ESTABLISHMENTS. THIS DOES NOT REPEAT NOT AUTHORIZE ANY ILLEGAL MEASURES. AVOIDING UNNECESSARY ALARM AND PUBLICITY PROTECTIVE MEASURES SHOULD BE CONFINED TO THOSE ESSENTIAL TO SECURITY.

IT IS ALSO DESIRED THAT ON OR BEFORE DECEMBER FIVE THIS YEAR REPORTS BE SUBMITTED TO THE CHIEF ARMY AIR FORCES OF ALL STEPS INITIATED BY YOU TO COMPLY WITH THESE INSTRUCTIONS. SIGNED ARNOLD.

A dispatch dated December 5 and signed "Miles",[122] was sent the assistant chief of staff headquarters, G–2, Hawaiian Department, to—

CONTACT COMMANDER ROCHEFORT IMMEDIATELY THROUGH COMMANDANT FOURTEENTH NAVAL DISTRICT REGARDING BROADCASTS FROM TOKYO REFERENCE WEATHER.[123]

Action Taken by Admiral Kimmel Pursuant to Warnings and Orders from Washington

DISPATCH OF OCTOBER 16 FROM CHIEF OF NAVAL OPERATIONS

In the dispatch of October 16 [124] Admiral Kimmel was advised that the resignation of the Japanese Cabinet had created a grave situation;

[120a] For the reply of General Short to this message from the Adjutant General, see committee exhibit No. 32, p. 17.
[121] Id., at p. 14. This message was also signed "Adams."
[122] Committee exhibit No. 32, p. 20.
[123] This dispatch refers to the so-called winds code which will be found discussed in detail in Part IV, infra, this report.
[124] Committee exhibit No. 37, p. 18.

that there was a strong possibility of hostilities between Japan and Russia and there also was a possibility Japan might attack the United States and Great Britain; and that he should—

take due precautions including such *preparatory deployments* [125] as will not disclose strategic intention nor constitute provocative actions against Japan.

Pursuant to the order Admiral Kimmel ordered submarines to assume a "war patrol" off both Wake and Midway; he reinforced Johnston and Wake with additional marines, ammunition, and stores and also sent additional marines to Palmyra Island; he ordered the commandant of the Fourteenth Naval District to direct an alert status in the outlying islands; he placed on 12 hours' notice certain vessels of the fleet which were in west-coast ports, held 6 submarines in readiness to depart for Japan, and delayed the sailing of 1 battleship which was scheduled to visit a west-coast navy yard; he dispatched 12 patrol planes to Midway with orders to carry out daily patrols within 100 miles of the island and placed in effect additional security measures in the fleet operating areas.[126]

On October 22, Admiral Kimmel reported by letter [127] these dispositions to the Chief of Naval Operations, Admiral Stark. By letter dated November 7 Admiral Stark wrote the commander in chief of the Pacific Fleet: [128]

OK on the disposition which you made in connection with the recent change in the Japanese Cabinet. The big question is—what next?

DISPATCH OF NOVEMBER 24 FROM CHIEF OF NAVAL OPERATIONS

In the dispatch of November 24 [129] Admiral Kimmel was advised that the chances of a favorable outcome of negotiations with Japan were very doubtful and that the movements of Japanese naval and military forces—

indicate in our opinion that a surprise aggressive movement in any direction including attack on Philippines or Guam is a possibility.

This dispatch carried no orders for the commander in chief of the Pacific Fleet [130] and would appear designed to acquaint him with the mounting tenseness of the situation as well as to supply him with an estimate of probable Japanese action.[131] No action appears to have been taken by Admiral Kimmel pursuant to this dispatch and he has stated that he felt the message required no action other than that which he had already taken.[132]

"WAR WARNING" DISPATCH OF NOVEMBER 27

The dispatch of November 27 began with the words:[133] "This dispatch is to be considered a war warning." [134] It stated that negotiations with Japan looking toward stabilization of conditions in the

---

[125] Admiral Kimmel said: "The term 'preparatory deployments' used in this dispatch is nontechnical. It has no especial significance other than its natural meaning." Committee record, pp. 6708, 6709.
[126] See testimony of Admiral Kimmel, committee record, p. 6709.
[127] Committee exhibit No. 106.
[128] Id.
[129] Committee exhibit No. 37, p. 32.
[130] See Navy court of inquiry record, pp 50–53.
[131] Admiral Turner testified: "*The dispatch of the 24th we did not consider required any immediate action, except to get ready plans for putting into effect when we gave them another warning.*" Committee record, p. 5159
[132] See Navy court of inquiry record, pp. 298, 299.
[133] Committee exhibit No. 37, p. 36.
[134] Admiral Kimmel observed: "The phrase 'war warning' cannot be made a catch-all for all the contingencies hindsight may suggest. It is a characterization of the specific information which the dispatch contained." Committee record, p. 6717.

Pacific had ceased and "an aggressive move by Japan is expected within the next few days," and that "the number and equipment of Japanese troops and the oganization of naval task forces indicates an amphibious expedition against either the Philippines, Thai or Kra Peninsula, or possibly Borneo." Admiral Kimmel was ordered "to execute an appropriate defensive deployment preparatory to carrying out the tasks assigned in WPL–46."

After receiving this warning Admiral Kimmel made the deliberate decision not to institute long-range reconnaissance from Pearl Harbor against possible air attacks for reasons which will subsequently appear.[135] Between the warning and the attack on December 7 the following deployments were made and action taken:

1. On November 28, Admiral Halsey left Pearl Harbor en route to Wake in command of Task Force 8, consisting of the carrier *Enterprise*, three heavy cruisers and nine destroyers. He carried out morning and afternoon searches to 300 miles for any sign of hostile shipping.[136] The sending of this force to Wake was pursuant to a dispatch dated November 26 to Admiral Kimmel stating, in part—

in order to keep the planes of the 2nd marine aircraft wing available for expeditionary use OpNav [137] has requested and Army has agreed to station 25 Army pursuit planes at Midway and a similar number at Wake provided you consider this feasible and desirable. It will be necessary for you to transport these planes and ground crews from Oahu to these stations on an aircraft carrier.[138]

Admiral Halsey knew of the war warning dispatch and held a lengthy conference with Admiral Kimmel and other officers on November 27. He stated that when he prepared to depart with the task force for Wake Island, he asked Admiral Kimmel how far the latter wanted him to go; that Admiral Kimmel replied "Use your common sense." [139] Admiral Smith said that before Admiral Halsey left in the *Enterprise*, he asked Admiral Kimmel what he should do in case he met Japanese forces, to which Admiral Kimmel replied he should use his own discretion. Admiral Smith stated that Admiral Halsey commented these were the best orders he had received and that if he found even a Japanese sampan he would sink it.[140]

2. On December 5, Admiral Newton left Pearl Harbor en route to Midway in command of Task Force 2, consisting of the carrier *Lexington*, three heavy cruisers, and five destroyers. Like Halsey, Newton conducted scouting flights with his planes to cover his advance.[141] Despite the fact, however, that Admiral Newton was leaving Pearl Harbor with some of the most powerful and valuable units of the Pacific fleet he was not even shown the war warning, had no knowledge of it, and indeed had no knowledge of the dispatches of October

---

[135] The Navy court of inquiry found: "It was the duty of Rear Admiral Bloch, when and if ordered by the commander in chief, Pacific Fleet, to conduct long-range reconnaissance. The commander in chief, Pacific Fleet, for definite and sound reasons and after making provision for such reconnaissance in case of emergency, specifically ordered that no routine long-range reconnaissance be undertaken and assumed full responsibility for this action. The omission of this reconnaissance was not due to oversight or neglect. *It was the result of a military decision, reached after much deliberation and consultation with experienced officers, and after weighing the information at hand and all the factors involved.*" Navy court of inquiry report, committee exhibit No. 157.

[136] Testimony of Admiral Kimmel, committee record, p. 6750. See also testimony of Admiral Halsey, Hart inquiry record, p. 299.

[137] Office of Naval Operations.

[138] Dispatch from Chief of Naval Operations to commander in chief of the Pacific Fleet, No. 270038, dated November 26, 1941. Committee exhibit No. 112. See also committee record, pp. 1614, 1615; also Hart inquiry record, p. 299.

[139] Hart inquiry record, pp. 297, 298.

[140] Id., at p. 43.

[141] Testimony of Admiral Kimmel, committee record, p. 6750; see also testimony of Admiral Newton, Hart inquiry record, p. 318.

16 and November 24 or the December 3 dispatch concerning the destruction of codes to which reference will hereafter be made. Except for what he read in the press, Admiral Newton received no information concerning the increasing danger of our relations with Japan. He was given no special orders and regarded his departure from Hawaii as a mission with no special significance other than to proceed to Midway for the purpose of flying off the *Lexington* a squadron of planes for the reinforcement of the island. In consequence, no special orders were given for the arming of planes or making preparation for war apart from ordinary routine.[142] The failure to supply Admiral Newton any orders or information is in marked contrast with the "free hand" orders given Admiral Halsey. In his testimony Admiral Kimmel stated that Admiral Newton's orders and information would have come through Admiral Brown, who was Newton's superior.[142a]

3. Admiral Wilson Brown on December 5 left Pearl Harbor en route to Johnston Island with Task Force 3 to conduct landing exercises.[143]

4. On November 28, orders were issued to bomb unidentified submarines found in the operating sea areas around Oahu. Full security was invoked for the ships at sea, which were ordered to bomb submarine contacts.[144] However, no change was made in the condition of readiness in port except that a Coast Guard patrol was started off Pearl Harbor and they began sweeping the harbor channel and approaches.[145]

5. Upon receipt of the war warning Admiral Kimmel ordered a squadron of patrol planes to proceed from Midway to Wake and search the ocean areas en route. While at Wake and Midway on December 2 and 3 they searched to a distance of 525 miles.[146]

6. A squadron of patrol planes from Pearl Harbor was ordered to replace the squadron which went from Midway to Wake. This squadron of patrol planes left Pearl Harbor on November 30. It proceeded from Johnston to Midway, making another reconnaissance sweep on the way. Upon reaching Midway, this squadron of patrol planes conducted distant searches of not less than 500 miles of varying sectors from that island on December 3, 4, 5, and 6. On December 7, five of these Midway based patrol planes were searching the sector 120° to 170° from Midway, to a distance of 450 miles. An additional two patrol planes of the Midway squadron left at the same time to rendezvous with the *Lexington* at a point 400 miles from Midway. Four of the remaining patrol planes at Midway, each loaded with bombs, were on 10-minute notice as a ready striking force.[147]

Admiral McMorris, Director of War Plans under Admiral Kimmel, testified before the Hewitt inquiry with respect to what defensive deployment was executed, stating—

there was no material change in the disposition and deployment of the fleet forces at that time other than the movement of certain aircraft to Midway and

---

[142] See Hart inquiry record, pp. 316–318.

[142a] In this regard, the testimony of Admiral Brown indicates that he was not shown the "war warning" See testimony of Rear Admiral Brown before the Roberts Commission, Committee exhibit No. 143.

[143] Testimony of Admiral Kimmel, committee record, p. 6751.

[144] See Navy Court of Inquiry record, pp. 299, 300; see also committee exhibit No. 112, p. 96.

[145] See Navy Court of Inquiry record, p. 395.

[146] Testimony of Admiral Kimmel, committee record, p. 6751.

[147] See testimony of Admiral Kimmel, committee record, page 6752; also testimony of Admiral Bellinger, Navy Court of Inquiry record, p. 684.

It should be noted that Admiral Inglis stated, "*There is no written record available of any searches having been made on December 6, either from the Hawaiian area or from Midway.*" For further testimony of Admiral Inglis concerning the matter of reconnaissance see committee record, pp. 70–73.

Wake and of the carriers with their attendant cruisers and destroyers, to those locations to deliver aircraft.[148]

While the dispatch of the three task forces does not appear to have been primarily made by Admiral Kimmel as a result of the implications of the war warning,[149] this action combined with the other steps above-mentioned had the effect of providing reconnaissance sweeps of the patrol-plane squadrons moving from Midway to Wake; from Pearl Harbor to Johnston and from Johnston to Midway; from Wake to Midway and Midway to Pearl Harbor covering a distance of nearly 5,000 miles. Each squadron as it proceeded would cover a 400-mile strand of ocean along its path, bring under the coverage of air search about 2,000,000 square miles of ocean area. In addition, submarines of the Fleet on and after November 27 were on war patrols from Midway and Wake Islands continuously.[150] The southwest approaches to Hawaii were thereby to a degree effectively screened by reconnaissance from a raiding force bent on attacking Pearl Harbor by surprise.[151] *Nothing was done, however, to detect an approaching hostile force coming from the north and northwest, recognized as the most dangerous sector, and it is into the justification for this nonaction that we shall inquire.*[152]

EVALUATION OF THE "WAR WARNING" DISPATCH OF NOVEMBER 27

ON WHERE THE ATTACK MIGHT COME

Admiral Kimmel stated that the war warning dispatch of November 27 did not warn the Pacific Fleet of an attack in the Hawaiian area nor did it state expressly or by implication that an attack in the Hawaiian area was imminent or probable.[153]

The warning dispatch did not, it is true, mention Pearl Harbor as a specific point of attack, and gave the estimate that the number and equipment of Japanese troops and the organization of naval task forces indicated an amphibious expedition against either the Philippines, Thailand or the Kra Peninsula or possibly Borneo.[153a] It is to be recalled in this connection, however, that the November 24 dispatch [153b] to Admiral Kimmel warned of *"a surprise aggressive movement in any direction including attack on Philippines or Guam is a possibility"*. The latter dispatch while indicating that an attack would possibly come in the vicinity of the Philippines or Guam did nevertheless indicate, by use of the words *"in any direction,"* that just where the attack might come could not be predicted.[154]

---

[148] Hewitt inquiry record, pp. 321, 322.
[149] See committee record, pp. 9312, 9313.
[150] Testimony of Admiral Kimmel, committee record, p. 6752.
[151] In this connection, see testimony of Admiral Bellinger, committee record, pp. 9321, 9324.
[152] See testimony of Admiral Bellinger, committee record, pp. 9324, 9325; also 9436, 9437.
[153] Admiral Kimmel testified: "The so-called 'war warning' dispatch of November 27 did not warn the Pacific Fleet of an attack in the Hawaiian area. It did not state expressly or by implication that an attack in the Hawaiian area was imminent or probable." Committee record, p. 6715. For a detailed statement by Admiral Kimmel concerning where the attack might come based on the "war warning," see Navy Court of Inquiry record, p. 301.
[153a] For the full text of the "war warning" dispatch, see p. 98, supra.
[153b] For the full text of the November 24 dispatch, see p. 98, supra.
[154] Admiral Kimmel stated that in the November 24 dispatch the words "in any direction" did include, so far as his estimate was concerned, a possible submarine attack on the Hawaiian Islands but not an air attack. See Navy Court of Inquiry record, p. 299.
It has been pointed out that the estimate of enemy action referred to in the "war warning"—*an amphibious operation to the South*—is to be distinguished from *a surprise aggressive movement in any direction* mentioned in the November 24 warning; that the distinction between an amphibious expedition and a surprise aggressive movement is such that a war warning in making reference to such an expedition in no way superseded the estimate of surprise aggressive action mentioned in the November 24 dispatch. See in this regard the testimony of Admiral Turner, Navy Court of Inquiry record, pp. 997, 1020.

The fact that Admiral Kimmel was ordered to take "an appropriate *defensive deployment* preparatory to carrying out the tasks assigned in WPL-46" indicated that his situation was subject to possible danger requiring such action.[155]   It was Washington's responsibility to give Admiral Kimmel its best estimate of where the major strategic enemy effort would come.[156]   It was Admiral Kimmel's responsibility as commander in chief of the Pacific Fleet to be prepared for the worst contingency, and when he was warned of war and ordered to execute a defensive deployment it was necessarily in contemplation that such action would be against all possible dangers with which the Hawaiian situation was fraught.[157]

OTHER DISPATCHES RECEIVED ON NOVEMBER 27

Admiral Kimmel stated that two other dispatches which he received on November 27 were affirmative evidence that the War or Navy Departments did not consider hostile action on Pearl Harbor imminent or probable.[158]   The first of these dispatches read:[159]

Army has offered to make available some units of infantry for reenforcing defence battalions now on station if you consider this desirable.   Army also proposes to prepare in Hawaii garrison troops for advance bases which you may occupy but is unable at this time to provide any antiaircraft units.   Take this into consideration in your plans and advise when practicable number of troops desired and recommended armament.

The second read:[160]

In order to keep the planes of the second marine aircraft wing available for expedition-ary use Op Nav has requested and Army has agreed to station 25 Army pursuit planes at Midway and a similar number at Wake provided you consider this feasible and desir-able.   It will be |necessary for you to transport these planes and ground crews from Oahu to these stations on an aircraft carrier.   Planes will be flown off at destination and ground personnel landed in boats; essential spare parts, tools, and ammunition will be taken in the carrier or on later trips of regular Navy supply vessels.   Army understands these forces must be quartered in tents.   Navy must be responsible for supplying water and subsistence and transporting other Army supplies. Stationing these planes must not be allowed to interfere with planned movements of Army bombers to Philippines.   Additional parking areas should be laid prompt-ly if necessary.   Can Navy bombs now at outlying positions be carried by Army bombers which may fly to those positions for supporting Navy operations? Confer with commanding general and advise as soon as practicable.

Both of these dispatches, however, were dated November 26, the day before the war warning dispatch.   The latter dispatch was not to be controlled by messages which antedated it.   The reinforcing of Wake and Midway was left up entirely to Admiral Kimmel both as to feasibility and desirability.[161]   The fact that other outposts needed reinforcements and steps were outlined in that direction did not elim-

---

[155] In this connection it is to be noted that the "war warning" dispatch was directed *for action* to the commander in chief of the Asiatic Fleet and the commander in chief of the Pacific Fleet (committee exhibit No. 37, p. 36).   This would appear to be an indication to Admiral Kimmel that the same defensive action was expected of him as of Admiral Hart in the Philippine area who was located in the path of the Japanese move to the south; that the message of November 27 placed in the same category—exposed to the same perils and requiring the same action—the Asiatic and the Pacific Fleets.

[156] See testimony of Admiral Ingersoll, Navy Court of Inquiry record, pp. 839–842.

[157] See discussion regarding "Admiral Kimmel's awareness of danger from air attack," Part III, p. 75 et seq, supra.

[158] Testimony of Admiral Kimmel, committee record, pp. 6716, 6717.

[159] Committee exhibit No. 112, p. 54.

[160] Id., at p. 55.

[161] Admiral Kimmel testified before the Nay Court of Inquiry that he regarded the proposal from the Chief of Naval Operations to transfer Army pursuit planes to Midway and Wake in order to conserve the marine planes for expeditionary duty as a suggestion and not a directive.   See Navy Court of Inquiry record, p. 307.

inate the necessity for the defense of Hawaii, the best-equipped outpost the United States possessed, nor remove it as a possible point of attack. The same is true with respect to the use of Hawaii as a crossroads for dispositions going to the Philippines or elsewhere; Hawaii was the only point we controlled in the Pacific which had adequate facilities to be such a crossroads.

"PSYCHOLOGICAL HANDICAPS" INDICATED BY ADMIRAL KIMMEL

In his testimony Admiral Kimmel has suggested that one can appreciate the "psychological handicaps" that dispatches he received placed upon the Navy in Hawaii. He stated:

> In effect, I was told:
> "Do take precautions" [162]
> "Do not alarm civilians" [163]
> "Do take a preparatory deployment" [164]
> "Do not disclose intent" [165]
> "Do take a defensive deployment" [166]
> "Do not commit the first overt act." [167]

In this connection, however, it is to be noted that the only cautions mentioned, which were contained largely in Army messages, were not to alarm civilians, not to disclose intent, and not to commit the first overt act. To have deployed the fleet; to have instituted distant reconnaissance; to have effected a higher degree of readiness, on a maneuver basis if necessary—none of these steps would have alarmed the civilian population of Hawaii, [168] have disclosed intent, or have constituted an overt act against Japan.

Admiral Kimmel's contention must be judged in light of the fact that on November 28 on his own responsibility, [169] he instructed the fleet to depth bomb all submarine contacts expected to be hostile in the fleet operating areas. [170] The Office of Naval Operations acquiesced in this order to depth bomb submarine contacts.

Admiral Halsey, prior to departing for Wake Island on November 28, received orders from Admiral Kimmel which he interpreted as permitting him to sink "even a Japanese sampan" if he found it. [171] Asked by Admiral Halsey as to how far he "should go" Admiral Kimmel replied, "Use your common sense." [172]

---

[162] Referring to the dispatch of October 16 advising of the resignation of the Japanese Cabinet and stating in part, "You will take due precautions including such preparatory deployments as will not disclose strategic intention nor constitute provocative action against Japan." See committee exhibit No. 37.

[163] Referring to a portion of the dispatch of November 28 sent Admiral Kimmel for information and incorporating a portion of an Army message sent the commanding general of the Western Defense Command, which latter message stated in part, "The United States desires that Japan commit the first overt act * * * . Measures should be carried out so as not to alarm civil population or disclose intent." See committee exhibit No. 37.

[164] Referring to the dispatch of October 16, note 162, supra.

[165] Referring to the dispatches of October 16 and November 28, notes 162 and 163, supra.

[166] Referring to the "war warning" dispatch of November 27. Committee exhibit No. 37.

[167] Referring to the dispatch of November 28, note 163, supra.

[168] There had been air raid drills at Pearl Harbor on April 24, May 12, 13; June 19; July 10, 26; August 1, 20; September 5, 27; October 13, 27; and November 12, 1941. Committee exhibit No. 120.

[169] As stated by the Navy court of inquiry: " * * * he (Admiral Kimmel) has issued, on his own responsibility, orders that all unidentified submarines discovered in Hawaiian waters were to be depthcharged and sunk. In so doing he exceeded his orders from higher authority and *ran the risk of committing an overt act against Japan,* but did so feeling that it is best to follow the rule 'shoot first and explain afterwards'." See Navy Court of Inquiry report, committee exhibit No. 157.

[170] See dispatch No. 280355 from Admiral Kimmel to the Pacific Fleet with a copy for information to the Office of Naval Operations; committee exhibit No. 112, p. 96. For a description of the fleet operating sea areas, see committee exhibit No. 6, Item 3.

[171] See Hart inquiry record, p. 43.

[172] Id., at pp. 297, 298.

The "war warning" dispatch of November 27 to the commander in chief of the Pacific Fleet contained no cautions, admonitions, or restraints whatever.[173]

THE "WAR WARNING" AND TRAINING

It has been pointed out by Admiral Kimmel that had he effected all-out security measures upon receiving each alarming dispatch from Washington, the training program would have been curtailed so drastically that the fleet could not have been prepared for war.[174] To appraise the merit of this observation it is necessary to consider the nature of instructions with respect to training under which the fleet operated. Admiral Kimmel has stated he was under a specific injunction to continue the training program, referring in this connection to a letter from the Chief of Naval Operations dated April 3, 1941.[175]

In this letter, however, the Chief of Naval Operations had stated the question was *when* and not *whether* we would enter the war and that in the meantime he would advise that Admiral Kimmel devote as much time as may be available to training his forces in the particular duties which the various units might be called upon to perform under the Pacific Fleet operating plans. Clearly the suggestion that training be conducted was made pending a more critical turn indicating the imminence of war. The dispatch of November 27 with vivid poignance warned of war with Japan. It stated that negotiations with Japan looking to stabilization of conditions in the Pacific had *ceased* and that an *aggressive move* by Japan was expected *within the next few days*. The time for training for a prospective eventuality was past—the eventuality, war, was at hand.[176] In none other of the dispatches had the commander in chief been so emphatically advised that war was imminent. Indeed the November 27 dispatch used the words "war warning," an expression which Admiral Kimmel testified he had never before seen employed in an official dispatch in all of his 40 years in the Navy. Manifestly the commander in chief of the United States Fleet and the Pacific Fleet would not expect that it would be necessary for the Navy Department to advise him to put aside his training now that war was imminent. The "war warning" provided adequate indication that the *primary function* thereafter was not training but *defense* against a treacherous foe who had invariably struck without a declaration of war.

THE TERM "DEFENSIVE DEPLOYMENT" AND FAILURE TO INSTITUTE DISTANT RECONNAISSANCE

Admiral Kimmel has made particular reference to the fact that the term "defensive deployment" was nontechnical and that it was to be

---

[173] Referring to the November 27 warning, Admiral Stark said: "This message begins with the words 'This dispatch is to be considered a war warning.' These words were carefully weighed and chosen after considerable thought and discussion with my principal advisors and with the Secretary of the Navy. The words 'war warning' had never before been used in any of my dispatches to the commander in chief, Pacific Fleet. They were put at the beginning of the message to accentuate the extreme gravity of the situation. We considered the picture as we saw it and we felt that there was grave danger of Japan striking anywhere. We wanted our people in the Pacific to know it, and we used language which we thought would convey what we felt." Committee record, pp. 5650, 5651.

[174] Committee record, p. 6703; see also testimony of Admiral Bellinger, Committee record, p. 9350.

[175] Committee record, p. 6702. For letter see committee exhibit No. 106.

[176] Before the Navy Court of Inquiry, Admiral Kimmel stated, after outlining the circumstances attending the decision, testified: "* * * I made the decision on the 27th of November not to stop training in the Fleet but to continue until further developments." Navy Court of Inquiry record, p. 285.

effected "preparatory to carrying out the tasks assigned in WPL–46." This plan called for a raid upon the Marshall Islands by the Pacific Fleet very shortly after hostilities with Japan should begin. Admiral Kimmel has pointed out that the prime purpose of the raids was to divert Japanese strength from the Malay Barrier. He has observed that the only patrol planes of consequence at Pearl Harbor were assigned to the fleet and that these planes would be required in the raid on the Marshalls. He further pointed out that he had only 49 patrol planes in flying condition, an insufficient number to conduct each day a 360° distant reconnaissance from Oahu. In this connection he observed that to insure an island base against a surprise attack from fast carrier-based planes, it was necessary to patrol the evening before to a distance of 800 miles and that this required 84 planes on one flight of 16 hours to cover the 360° perimeter. He testified that, of course, the same planes and the same crews cannot make a 16-hour flight every day and therefore for searches of this character over a protracted period 250 patrol planes would be required. He observed that a search of all sectors of approach to an island base is the only type of search that deserves the name and that he manifestly had an insufficient number of planes for this purpose.[177] In consequence of this situation, Admiral Kimmel decided to undertake no distant reconnaissance whatever from Pearl Harbor and regarded the deployment of the task forces and other measures already indicated as an adequate defensive deployment within the terms of the order contained in the war warning.[178]

In this connection, as heretofore pointed out, Admiral McMorris, Director of War Plans under Admiral Kimmel, testified before the Hewitt Inquiry with respect to what defensive deployment was executed, stating—

there was no material change in the disposition and deployment of the fleet forces at that time other than the movement of certain aircraft to Midway and Wake and of the carriers with their attendant cruisers and destroyers, to those locations to deliver aircraft.[179]

He further stated that the language with respect to a defensive deployment in the war warning was a "direction" and that he considered the action taken constituted an appropriate defensive deployment; that it was a major action in line with the measure to execute an appropriate defensive deployment; and that the major portion of the fleet was disposed in Hawaiian waters and reinforcements were sent to Midway and Wake. He said, however, that the establishing of an air patrol from Oahu to guard against a surprise attack by Japan would have been an appropriate act but that—

no one act nor no one disposition can be examined independent of other requirements.[180]

Admiral Smith, Chief of Staff to Admiral Kimmel, said that following the war warning of November 27 the establishment of aircraft patrols from Oahu would have been an appropriate defensive deployment to carry out the initial tasks assigned by the Pacific Fleet war plans.[181]

---

[177] See testimony of Admiral Kimmel, committee record, pp. 6752–6759.
[178] See committee record, pp. 6759–6761; also Navy Court of Inquiry record, pp. 1144, 1145.
[179] Hewitt Inquiry record, pp. 321, 322.
[180] Id., at pp. 323, 324.
[181] Hewitt Inquiry record, pp. 372, 373.

Admiral Turner, Director of War Plans, who had a principal part in preparing the November 27 war warning, testified as follows with respect to the term *defensive deployment:*[182]

Before coming to the meat of the answer, I invite attention to the fact that this dispatch has a multiple address. It goes to the commander in chief of the Asiatic Fleet for action and it goes to the commander in chief of the Pacific Fleet for action. It is as if it were the Army practice, with two dispatches, one addressed to each, but both in identical terms.

A "deployment" is a spreading out of forces. A naval deployment means to spread out and make ready for hostilities. To get into the best positions from which to execute the operating plans against the enemy. The defensive deployment as applied to Hawaii, which is of chief interest, was for the defense of Hawaii and of the west coast of the United States, because one of the tasks of WPL46 is to defend the territory and coastal zones, our own territory and coastal zones, and to defend our shipping.

Instead of being in a concentrated place, or instead of being off in some distant region holding exercises and drills, it meant that the forces under the command of the commander in chief of the Pacific Fleet could take station for the most probable attack against them or against the Hawaiian Islands, keeping in mind their responsibilities for covering the United States and Panama.

The deployment in the vicinity of Hawaii, if wide enough, would in itself constitute a formidable barrier against any attempt further east, and we definitely did not expect an attack, that is, the Navy did not, an attack on the west coast or in Panama, as is indicated by a dispatch going out the same day to the commandants of districts to take precautions against subversive activities, but we did not tell them to make any defensive deployment.

The deployment from Hawaii might have been made in a number of different ways. Certainly I would expect that in accordance with the plans that should have been drawn up, and they were, that airplanes would have been sent to Midway, if not already there, to Wake, to Johnston Island, to Palmyra, the reconnaissance planes as well as defensive planes, and that a reconnaissance would have been undertaken. The movement of those planes and forces to those positions constituted part of the defensive deployment.

The battleships, of course, were of no use whatsoever against undamaged fast ships. Naturally, it was not to be expected that the Japanese would bring over slow ships unless they were making their full and complete effort against Hawaii, so that a proper deployment for the battleships would have been in the best position to do what was within their power, which was only to defend Hawaii against actual landings. In other words, if they had been at sea and in a retired position even, such that if actual landings were attempted on the Hawaiian Islands and at such a distance that they could arrive prior to or during the landings, they would have been most useful indeed to have interfered with and defeated the landings.

Since, as has been pointed out previously, the danger zone, the danger position of Hawaii was to the north, because there were not little outlying islands there from which observation could have been made, since there was no possibility of detecting raiders from the north except by airplanes and ships, an appropriate deployment would have been to have sent some fast ships, possibly with small seaplanes, up to the north to assist and possibly to cover certain sectors against approach, which the long-range reconnaissance could not have done. Of course, these ships would naturally have been in considerable danger, but that was what they were there for, because fighting ships are of no use unless they are in a dangerous position so that they can engage the enemy and inflict loss on them.

Another part of a deployment, even where airplanes would not be moved, would have been to put them on operating air fields scattered throughout the islands so that they could be in a mutual supporting position with respect to other fields and to cover a somewhat wider arc.

Another part of the deployment would have been to have sent submarines, as many as were available, out into a position from which they could exercise either surveillance or could make attacks against approaching vessels.

It is to be noted that there was no offensive action ordered for submarines. The offensive action, of course, would have been to send them into Japanese waters.

[182] Committee record, pp. 5168–5172.

With respect to the same matter, Admiral Stark said that he had anticipated that full security measures would be taken, that the Army would set a condition of readiness for aircraft and the aircraft warning service, that Admiral Kimmel would invoke full readiness measures, distant reconnaissance and anti-submarine measures, and that the plans previously agreed on with the Army would be implemented.[183]

In considering the validity of Admiral Kimmel's position that the order to execute an appropriate defensive deployment is inseparable from the language "preparatory to carrying out the task assigned in WPL–46" it is necessary to consider what the purport of the message would have been without the words "execute an appropriate defensive deployment." In such case Admiral Kimmel might conceivably have been partially justified in making all preparations with a view to carrying out the tasks assigned after war began. But under the terms of the dispatch as received by him he was to do something else. He was to execute a defensive deployment preparatory to carrying out these tasks—a defensive deployment before war broke.

Furthermore, Admiral Kimmel received for his information the message of November 28 directed for action to the naval commanders on the west coast.[184] After quoting the Army dispatch of November 27 to the commander of the Army Western Defense Command, this message stated: "* * * Be prepared to carry out tasks assigned in WPL–46 so far as they apply to Japan in case hostilities occur." The west coast commanders were not ordered to effect a defensive deployment, only to *be prepared to carry out the tasks assigned in WPL-46.* Here was a clear indication to the Commander of the Pacific Fleet that he was to do something significantly more than merely getting prepared to carry out war tasks. He was to execute a *defensive deployment* preparatory to carrying out such tasks.

And among Admiral Kimmel's tasks under the war plans, prior to outbreak of war, were the maintenance of fleet security and guarding "against a surprise attack by Japan." As has already been seen in the plans for the defense of the Hawaiian coastal frontier it was recognized that a declaration of war might be preceded by a surprise submarine attack on ships in the operating areas and a surprise attack on Oahu including ships and installations in Pearl Harbor; that it appeared "the most likely and dangerous form of attack on Oahu would be an air attack." [185]

---

[183] See Navy Court of Inquiry record, pp. 54–62, 84. Asked what was meant by the "defensive deployment" in the message of November 27, Admiral Stark said: "My thought in that message about the defensive deployment was clear all-out security measures. Certainly, having been directed to take a defensive deployment, the Army having been directed to make reconnaissance, but regardless of the Army, our message to Admiral Kimmel, that the natural thing—and perhaps he did to it—was to take up with the Army right away in the gravity of the situation, the plans that they had made, and then make dispositions as best he could against surprise for the safety not only of the ships which he decided to keep in port but also for the safety of the ships which he had at sea. He had certain material which he could use for that and we naturally expected he would use it."

"* * * a defensive deployment would be to spread and to use his forces to the maximum extent to avoid surprise and, if he could, to hit the other fellow and in conjunction with the Army, to implement the arrangements which had previously been made for just this sort of thing." Committee record, pp. 5705, 5706.

[184] Committee exhibit No. 37, p. 38.

[185] See committee exhibit No. 44.

Admiral Bellinger testified that in his opinion an air attack was the most likely form of attack on Pearl Harbor. Committee record, p. 9355. He further testified that the Martin-Bellinger estimate was not an estimate of the strategy that the Japanese would employ in starting the war but rather an estimate covering the event of sudden hostile action against Oahu; in other words, that it was not an estimate which indic ted that Japan was going to strike against Oahu as part of their national strategy but rather if they were going to strike Oahu this was the estimate of how it would be done. Committee record, p. 9382.

With the clear recognition that Japan might attack before a declaration of war and with a war warning carrying an order to execute an appropriate defensive deployment preparatory to performing tasks during war, it is difficult to understand why Admiral Kimmel should have concluded that no distant air reconnaissance should be conducted, *particularly in the dangerous sector to the north*. Apart from radio intelligence which will be later discussed, distant reconnaissance admittedly was the only adequate means of detecting an approaching raiding force in sufficient time to avoid a surprise attack. Certainly the sector from the west to the south was covered, partially at least, by the three task forces. And yet the most dangerous sector the 90° counterclockwise from due north to due west, the sector through which the Japanese striking force approached, was given no attention whatever.[186] Admiral Bellinger testified that had distant reconnaissance been conducted it would have been to the north[187] and, although he was responsible for Navy patrol planes, Admiral Bellinger was not even shown the war warning.[188]

Admiral Kimmel has suggested that under the Joint Coastal Frontier Defense Plan Admiral Bloch was responsible for distant reconnaissance and had the latter desired planes he could have called upon the commander in chief of the Pacific Fleet.[189] This suggestion, apart from being incompatible with Admiral Kimmel's stating he made the decision not to conduct distant reconnaissance, is not tenable. Admiral Bloch had no planes with which to conduct distant patrols and Admiral Kimmel knew it.[190] While he was on the ground, it was the responsibility of the commander in chief of the Pacific Fleet to take all necessary steps in line with a defensive deployment and in recognition of the realities at Hawaii to protect the fleet.[191]

Admiral Kimmel's assertion that only a 360°-distant reconnaissance is worthy of the name ignores the fact that a 90° arc to the southwest was being partially covered, a fact concerning which he has made a point in testifying before the committee. Manifestly, to have conducted reconnaissance to any extent would have been more effective than no reconnaissance at all.[192] And Admiral Kimmel had adequate

---

[186] See testimony of Admiral Bellinger, Committee record, pp. 9369, 9370; also section "Plans for the Defense of the Hawaiian Coastal Frontier," Part III, this report.

[187] Committee record, pp. 9324, 9325; also Hewitt Inquiry record, pp. 506, 507.
In testifying before the Navy Court of Inquiry Admiral Kimmel was asked what he could consider the most probable areas of approach for a surprise attack launched from carriers against Pearl Harbor. He replied: "I testified before the so-called Roberts Commission that I thought the northern sec'or was the most probable. I thought at the time that the aircraft had come from the north—the time I testified I mean—and I didn't wish to make alibis. However, I feel that there is no sector around Oahu which is much more dangerous than any other sector. We have an island which can be approached from any direction. There is no outlying land which prevents this, and you have got a 360° arc, minus the very small line which runs up along the Hawaiian chain. From the southern, we have observation stations, Johnston and Palmyra, and the closest Japanese possession is to the southwestward in the Marshalls, and these Japanese carriers were fuel eaters and short-legged. I would say that while all sectors are important, if I were restricted, I would probably search the western 180° sector first." Navy Court of Inquiry record, p. 305.

[188] Committee record, pp. 9305, 9306; also 9362, 9363.

[189] Navy Court of Inquiry record, p. 1125.

[190] See Navy Court of Inquiry record, p. 1125.
The Navy Court of Inquiry found: "The Naval Base Defense Officer (Admiral Bloch) was entirely without aircraft, either fighters or patrol planes, assigned permanently to him. He was compelled to rely upon Fleet aircraft for joint effort in conjunction with Army air units." See Navy Court of Inquiry report, committee exhibit No. 157.

[191] Admiral Bellinger testified that in the absence of definite information as to the probability of an attack, it was the responsibility of Admiral Kimmel to order long-range reconnaissance. Hart Inquiry record, p. 125.

[192] Admiral Bellinger testified that covering certain selected sectors was a possible and feasible operation. Hewitt inquiry record, p. 477.
Admiral Kimmel admitted that "Of course, any patrol run has some value. I will admit that as far as surface ship." Navy Court of Inquiry record, p. 1125.
Admiral Stark testified: "When you haven't got enough planes to search the entire area which you would like to search, whether it is planes or what not, you narrow down to where you think is the most likely area of travel, and your next study is how can you cover that or how much of it can you cover." Committee record, p. 5702.

patrol planes to conduct distant reconnaissance for an extended period throughout the most dangerous sectors. The evidence reflects that there were 81 planes available to the commander in chief of the Pacific Fleet which were capable of performing distant reconnaissance.[193] Estimates of the number which can properly be regarded as in a state of readiness to conduct reconnaissance flights from Oahu as of December 7 range from 48 to 69. In addition the Army had six long-range bombers [194] which were available to the Navy under the plans for joint air operations at Hawaii. Even with the minimum estimate of 48 and the conservative basis of employing each plane only once every 3 days,[195] a sector of 128° could have been covered daily for several weeks.[196] This fact, when considered with the reconnaissance sweeps from Midway and by the task forces, leaves clear that the most dangerous sectors could have been fully covered.[197] In all events it would have been entirely possible and proper to have employed aircraft to any extent available for distant reconnaissance in the more dangerous sectors, using submarines, destroyers, or other vessels in the less dangerous approaches to Oahu.[198] That substantial and effective distant reconnaissance could have been conducted is demonstrated by the fact that it was instituted immediately after the attack despite the fact that over half the available planes were rendered inoperative by the attack.[199]

Yet Admiral Kimmel contends that use of all his available planes would have unduly impaired his ability to carry out the offensive measures assigned the Pacific Fleet in the event of war.[200] The evidence establishes, however, that his plans for the conduct of

---

[193] See committee exhibit No. 120.
[194] Admiral Bellinger stated, however, that the Army reported 8 B-17's available for December 6, 1941. Committee record, p. 9307.
[195] See testimony of Admiral Bellinger, committee record, pp. 9328, 9329.
[196] Id., Hewitt inquiry record, pp. 480–507. See also committee record, p. 9330 where Bellinger stated the patrol could be maintained for 11 days to 2 weeks, perhaps longer. Admiral Bellinger testified that 1 patrol plane could cover 8° to 700 miles. Committee record, p. 9325.
[197] Admiral Davis, fleet aviation officer, said that the entire 360° circumference was not of equal importance; that a considerable arc to the north and west and another arc to the south and west were the most important. He said that although there were not enough planes and pilots to have established and maintained a long-range 360° search indefinitely, there were enough to have made searches using relatively short-range planes in the least dangerous sectors and by obtaining some assistance from available Army aircraft. Hart Inquiry record, pp. 98, 99; 240, 241.
[198] The evidence before the committee contradicts the following conclusion of the Navy Court of Inquiry: "Neither surface ships nor submarines properly may be employed to perform this duty (reconnaissance), even if the necessary number be available. The resulting dispersion of strength not only renders the fleet incapable of performing its proper function, but exposes the units to destruction in detail. A defensive deployment of surface ships and submarines over an extensive sea area as a means of continuously guarding against a possible attack from an unknown quarter and at an unknown time, is not sound military procedure either in peace or in war." *The committee regards the employment of surface vessels for the purpose of reconnaissance as sound military procedure where reconnaissance is imperative and the more adaptable facilities, patrol planes, are not sufficiently available.* See also note 192, *supra.*
It is highly significant that the Commandant of the *15th Naval District (Panama)* was taking the following action, as reported by General Andrews to the War Department under date of November 29, 1941: "In the Panama Sector, the *Commandant of the 15th Naval District is conducting continuous surface patrol of the area included within the Panama Coastal Frontier, supplemented, within the limits of the aircraft at his disposal, by an air patrol.* In my opinion, the Commandant of the 15th Naval District, does not have sufficient aircraft or vessels within his control for adequate reconnaissance." See Committee Exhibit No. 32, p. 18.
[199] See testimony of Admiral Bellinger, committee record, pp. 9371, 9372.
[200] In his statement submitted to the Navy Court of Inquiry, Admiral Kimmel said: "Having covered the operating areas by air patrols it was not prudent in my judgment and that of my staff to fritter away our slim resources in patrol planes in token searches and thus seriously impair their required availability to carry out their functions with the Fleet under approved War Plans."
When questioned concerning the time that Admiral Kimmel would be expected to start a raid against the Marshall Islands after war began, Admiral Ingersoll stated that Admiral Kimmel "*could have chosen any date, and we did not expect him to move on any particular date, we expected him to move to carry out that task when he was ready.*" If I can digress a little bit on that, I do not know that Admiral Kimmel, or anybody, knew what was the state of the Japanese fortifications and defenses in the Marshall Islands. Any movement of that kind I have no doubt would have been preceded by reconnaissance, possibly from carrier planes or possibly from some of the long-range Army planes which were fixed up for photographic purposes, and they would undoubtedly have made a reconnaissance to determine where the Japanese strength was, what islands were fortified, and so forth, and upon the receipt of that intelligence base their plans. As a matter of fact, I think we were trying to get out of the Army a reconnaissance of those islands in connections with the flight of Army planes from Hawaii to Australia. I believe it did not take place until after Pearl Harbor." Committee record, p. 11457.

offensive operations, after outbreak of war, contemplated the use of a maximum of 24 patrol planes.[201]   Even if this number were deducted from those available, there were still sufficient planes to have covered at least the entire dangerous northwest sector.   The offensive tasks of the future did not justify disregarding the danger that the Pacific Fleet might be caught by surprise while still in port and before offensive operations could begin.

In making the decision not to conduct distant reconnaissance, Admiral Kimmel erred.[202]   In determining whether making the decision that he did evinced poor judgment consideration must be given his responsibility as commander in chief and the realities of his situation. It was essentially his duty to protect the Pacific Fleet from all dangers to the utmost of his ability.   He knew that the primary function of the Pacific Fleet in the early stages of the war was a defensive one, save for sporadic raids and limited offensive operations, in recognition of the fact that our Pacific Fleet was inferior to that of Japan.   He was ordered to effect an appropriate defensive deployment.   This was a general directive consistent with his specific suggestion that the commander in chief of the Pacific Fleet be guided by broad policy and objectives rather than by categorical instructions.[203]   He was given free rein to effect defensive security, in line with his more intimate knowledge of the detailed and peculiar problems affecting the Pacific Fleet, prior to carrying out the tasks assigned in the Pacific war plans.   He knew that one of the tasks before the outbreak of war was guarding against a possible surprise attack by Japan.   He knew that the only effective means of detecting a surprise raiding force in adequate time to combat it was by distant reconnaissance.   He knew the Japanese reputation for deceit and treachery.   He knew the greatest danger to the Fleet at Pearl Harbor was the possibility of an air raid.   He knew that the maintenance and protection of the Fleet while in its base constituted a fundamental element in making military dispositions at Pearl Harbor.   He had been categorically warned of war.   He knew or must have known that the necessity of Japan's striking the first blow required of him greater vigilance consistent with his fundamental duty as commander in chief to prepare for the worst contingency.   He had adequate facilities to patrol the most dangerous approaches to Pearl Harbor.   The decision was not a simple one, but, failing to resolve his dilemma by seeking advice from the Navy Department,[204] Admiral Kimmel displayed poor judgment in failing to

[201] See committee record, p. 9316 et seq.
    As to the use of long-distance patrol planes by Admiral Kimmel in prospective raids on the Marshall Islands under the war plans, Admiral Ingersoll stated: "The radius of patrol planes out there was about 600 miles, or somewhere in the neighborhood of a 1,200-mile flight.   They could not have been used in that operation to cover actual operations in the Marshalls area, unless he was able to establish a base in the Marshalls from which the planes could operate.   They could, however, cover the movement of vessels to the westward of Johnston and Palmyra and Wake to the extent that their radius could take them; that is, 600 miles from those positions." Committee record, p. 11450.
    [202] There is no substantial evidence of any specific discussions between Admiral Kimmel and members of his staff on or after the receipt of the "war warning" concerning the advisability or practicability of distant reconnaissance from Oahu.   Admiral McMorris, war plans officer, thought that the subject must have been discussed, but could recall no specific discussion.   The commander of the fleet patrol planes, Admiral Bellinger, who had not been informed of any of the significant warning messages, testified that Admiral Kimmel had no discussion with him concerning the matter.
    [203] See memorandum from Admiral Kimmel to the Chief of Naval Operations, dated May 26, 1941, committee exhibit No. 106.
    Admiral Stark testified that the handling of the Pacific Fleet was up to the commander in chief: "* * * it was then up to the Commander in Chief on the spot.   I would not have presumed, sitting at a desk in Washington, to tell him what to do with his fleet.   There were many factors involved, of which he was the only person who had the knowledge, and once I had started, if I had started, to give him directives, I would have been handling the fleet.   That was not my job." Committee record, p. 5705.
    [204] Referring to the order to execute an appropriate "defensive deployment," Admiral Kimmel stated: "This appropriate defensive deployment was a new term to me.   I decided that what was meant was something similar to the disposition I had made on October 16, which had been approved by the originator of both these dispatches (Chief of Naval Operations), and I therefore made the dispositions which I have outlined." See Navy Court of Inquiry record, p. 305.

employ every instrumentality at his command to defend the fleet.[205]

Conceding for purposes of discussion that Admiral Kimmel's decision to employ none of the fleet patrol planes for distant reconnaissance was a reasonable military decision under the circumstances, the very fact of having made such decision placed upon him the affirmative responsibility of determining that every other available means for reconnaissance was being employed to protect the fleet. His determination not to conduct long-range reconnaissance is of itself a recognition by him that it was his obligation to provide such reconnaissance. He knew that the Army was depending upon him for certain defensive measures.[206] Further, the fact that there was an agreement with the Army at Hawaii whereby the Navy was to perform distant reconnaissance placed upon Admiral Kimmel the obligation of advising General Short that he had decided not to conduct such reconnaissance. Indeed, General Short, who saw the war warning, testified that in his opinion the "defensive deployment" which the Navy was directed to execute "would necessarily include distant reconnaissance." [207] Admiral Kimmel's clear duty, therefore, in the absence of Navy reconnaissance was to confer with General Short to insure that Army radar, antiaircraft, and planes were fully utilized and alerted. None of these things were done. And there appears to be no substantial reason for failure to call upon the Army, consistent with the joint plans, for the six long-range bombers which were admittedly available to the Navy at Hawaii for the asking.[208]

ACTION WHICH WAS NOT TAKEN UPON RECEIPT OF THE "WAR WARNING"

As has been seen, following the warning dispatch of November 27 no distant reconnaissance as such was instituted.[208a] This meant that there was no adequate means whatever taken by the Navy to detect

[205] The Navy Court of Inquiry found: "It is a fact that the use of fleet patrol planes for daily long-range, all-around reconnaissance was not justified in the absence of information indicating that an attack was to be expected within narrow limits of time." The committee is in essential disagreement with this conclusion. Admiral Kimmel was warned in categorical fashion of war on November 27, 2 days *after* the Japanese Task Force had left Hitokappu Bay and while on the way to Pearl Harbor. *It is difficult to imagine how it would have been possible from Washington to have narrowed the limits of time in which Japan might strike in any more timely fashion, particularly inasmuch as Radio Intelligence had lost track completely of substantial carrier units of the Japanese Fleet.* This being true, distant reconnaissance was the only possible means of detecting the striking force within adequate time to prepare to meet the attack. There was no other channel for *indicating* that an attack was to be expected within narrow limits of time or otherwise.

Going on, the Navy Court of Inquiry stated: "It is a further fact that, even if justified, this was not possible with the inadequate number of fleet planes available." The court is here of course referring to all-around reconnaissance from Oahu. *As has been clearly indicated, there were adequate facilities for patrolling the more dangerous sectors, a procedure that was practical, feasible, and desirable.*

[206] As stated by the commander in chief, United States Fleet and Chief of Naval Operations Admiral King: "In the case of Pearl Harbor, where local defenses were inadequate, the commander in chief of the Pacific Fleet could not, and did not, evade responsibility for assisting in the defense, merely because, in principle, this is not normally a fleet task. It appears from the record that Admiral Kimmel appreciated properly this phase of the situation. His contention appears to be that Pearl Harbor *should* have been strong enough for self-defense. The fact that it *was not* strong enough for self-defense hampered his arrangements for the employment of the fleet, but, nevertheless, he was aware of, and accepted the necessity for, employing the fleet in the defensive measures." See "Second Endorsement" to report of Navy Court of Inquiry, committee exhibit No. 157.

Admiral King also observed, "I think * * * that Admiral Kimmel was fully aware that, in view of the weakness of local defenses, the fleet had to be employed to protect Pearl Harbor and the Hawaiian Islands in general." Id.

[207] Committee record, pp. 7926, 7927.

[208] See in this connection testimony of Admiral Bellinger, committee record, p. 9310.

[208a] When questioned as to any reason why Admiral Kimmel should not have had long-range reconnaissance operating from November 27 on through to the time Japan struck, with whatever planes we had even if it were only "three," Admiral Ingersoll replied: "I had every reason to expect that he would do that, and I was surprised that he had not done it. As I stated the other day, I was very much surprised that the attack had gotten in undetected * * * I expected that it would be done not only because the planes were there, but because this (WPL-46) plan inferred that it was going to be done. It never occurred to me that it was not being done." Committee record, p. 11420.

the approach of a raiding force in sufficient time to repel it or effectively minimize the force of an attack. The Pacific Fleet patrol planes which were under the control of Admiral Kimmel were operating in accordance with schedules prepared as of November 22, 1941, stressing training operations. These schedules were not changed prior to the attack.

No effort was made to secure the available long-range bombers of the Army for reconnaissance.

No change was made in the condition of readiness of vessels in Pearl Harbor which had been in effect for a considerable period of time preceding November 27.[209] This condition of readiness has been referred to as "an augmented Navy No. 3," the No. 3 condition being the lowest state of readiness.[210] The three conditions of readiness established for the Navy were:

No. 1. Entire crew, officers and men at battle stations. Action imminent.

No. 2. Provides the means of opening fire immediately with one-half the armament. Enemy believed to be in vicinity.

No. 3. Provides a means of opening fire with a portion of the secondary and antiaircraft batteries in case of surprise encounter.

While it appears that condition No. 3 prevailed subsequently during wartime at Pearl Harbor and is the condition normally maintained in port, there nevertheless was an extensive distant reconnaissance designed to alert the fleet to a higher condition of readiness prior to possible attack and to afford a considerable measure of protection. This means of protection was not available to the fleet on the morning of December 7.[211]

[209] In testifying before the Navy Court of Inquiry, Admiral Kimmel was asked: "On the morning of 7 December 1941, preceding the attack, can you tell the court what the material condition of readiness was in effect on ships of the Pacific Fleet in Pearl Harbor?" Admiral Kimmel replied: "The condition of readiness No. 3, as laid down in 2CL-41 had been prescribed some time before by Vice Admiral Pye, and that was in effect on the day of the attack. In addition to that, the Commander of Battleships, Battle Force, had issued an order requiring two 5-inch guns and two 50-calibre guns on each battleship to be manned at all times. These were, to the best of my knowledge and belief, manned on the date in question." p. 278.

The three conditions of readiness with respect to naval base defense, as set forth in 2CL-41 follow:

Condition I. General quarters in all ships. Condition of aircraft as prescribed by naval base defense officer.

Condition II. One-half of antiaircraft battery of all ships in each sector manned and ready. Condition of aircraft as prescribed by naval base defense officer.

Condition III. Antiaircraft battery (guns which bear in assigned sector) of at least one ship in each sector manned and ready (minimum of four guns required for each sector). Condition of aircraft as prescribed by naval base defense officer.

See committee exhibit No. 44.

Admiral Kimmel was asked whether, upon receipt of the November 27 war warning, he consulted with the commandant of the Fourteenth Naval District on any measures of security to be adopted in the Fourteenth Naval District that were different from any then in effect. He replied that he discussed the message with the commandant of the Fourteenth Naval District but no additional measures of security were deemed advisable as a result of the conversation. See Navy Court of Inquiry record, p. 303.

[210] While virtually all antiaircraft guns aboard ship were firing within 10 minutes, only about one-fourth were "ready machine guns" available to fire immediately. Inasmuch as by far the greatest damage was effected by the torpedo planes in the first wave, a higher degree of readiness would have reduced beyond question the effectiveness of this initial thrust. Admiral Kimmel said: "*Had it not been for the torpedoes I think the damage would have been enormously less.*" Roberts record, p. 547.

For the indicated reason the conclusion of Navy Court of Inquiry that "a higher condition of readiness could have added little, if anything to the defense" is in error. See Navy Court of Inquiry report, committee exhibit No. 157.

[211] In its report, the Navy Court of Inquiry has observed: "It has been suggested, that each day all naval planes should have been in the air, all naval personnel at their stations, and all antiaircraft guns manned. The Court is of the opinion that the wisdom of this is questionable when it is considered that it would not be known when an attack would take place and that, to make sure, it would have been necessary to impose a state of tension on the personnel day after day, and to disrupt the maintenance and operating schedules of ships and planes beginning at an indefinite date between 16 October and 7 December.

This statement contains within itself the certain proof of its invalidity. It was for the very reason that it could not be known *when* an attack would take place that it was essential a higher degree of readiness prevail. If it were possible to know with definitiveness when the attack would come the necessity for a higher state of readiness would be obviated until the time for the attack had approached. Furthermore, the extreme state of readiness suggested by the court is a far cry from the lowest conditions of readiness which prevailed at the time of the attack in both the Army and Navy Commands.

No change was effected in the state of readiness of naval aircraft. The aircraft on the ground and the patrol planes moored on the water were not in condition to take to the air promptly. Approximately 50 percent of the planes on December 7 were on 4 hours' notice.

Having elected to institute no distant reconnaissance by aircraft, no effort was made to inaugurate patrols by surface or subsurface craft to compensate and partially serve in lieu of distant reconnaissance by planes.[212] The evidence shows there were 29 destroyers and 5 submarines in Pearl Harbor on the morning of December 7.[213] While the employment of surface craft or submarines in lieu of distant air reconnaissance is not altogether satisfactory or fully effective, it nonetheless would have provided a measure of protection more to be desired than no reconnaissance whatever.

No effort was made to maintain a striking force at sea in readiness to intercept possible raiding forces approaching through the dangerous northern sector.[214]

No change was made in the schedules of ships proceeding to Pearl Harbor with a view to maintenance of a minimum force at harbor with provision for entry into port at irregular intervals.

After the decision to institute no distant reconnaissance, the Navy did not check or otherwise maintain effective liaison with the Army as to the readiness of Army antiaircraft defense and aircraft warning installations.

Estimate and Action Taken by General Short With Respect to the Warning Dispatch of November 27

The commanding general of the Hawaiian Department does not appear to have taken any appreciable action, apart from his normal training operations, on the basis of any information received by him with respect to our critical relations with Japan prior to the warning of November 27 from the Chief of Staff, General Marshall.

This dispatch, No. 472,[215] advised that negotiations with Japan appeared terminated to all practical purposes with only the barest possibilities that the Japanese Government might come back and offer to continue; that Japanese future action was unpredictable but hostile action was possible at any moment. It stated that if hostilities could not be avoided the United States desired that Japan commit the first overt act. It pointed out, however, that this policy should not be construed as restricting General Short to a course of action that might jeopardize his defense. It ordered the commanding general, prior to hostile Japanese action, to undertake such reconnaissance and other measures as he deemed necessary but admonished that these measures should be carried out so as not to alarm the civil population or disclose intent. It instructed that should hostilities occur, General Short should carry out the tasks assigned in the war plans insofar as they applied to Japan. He was to limit the dissemination of "this highly secret information to minimum essential officers" and to report measures taken.

---

[212] See note 192, *supra*.
[213] Committee exhibit No. 6.
[214] Id.
[215] Committee exhibit No. 32, p. 7.

Within 30 minutes of receiving this dispatch and after consulting only with his chief of staff, Colonel Phillips,[216] General Short replied to the War Department as follows: [217]

Reurad four seven two 27th. Report Department alerted to prevent sabotage. Liaison with the Navy.

SHORT.

As a result of the November 27 dispatch General Short decided to institute alert No. 1, the lowest of three alerts provided for the Hawaiian Department. The three alerts were: [218]

No. 1. Defense against sabotage and uprisings. *No threat from without.*

No. 2. Security against attacks from hostile subsurface, surface, and aircraft, in addition to No. 1.

No. 3. Requires occupation of all field positions by all units, prepared for maximum defense of Oahu and the Army installations on outlying islands.

At the same time that he ordered alert No. 1, the commanding general directed that the Interceptor Command, including the Aircraft Warning Service (Radar) and Information Center, should operate from 4 a. m. to 7 a. m. daily. In addition, it should be noted that the six mobile radar stations operated daily except Sunday from 7 a. m. to 11 a. m. for routine training and daily, except Saturday and Sunday, from 12 noon until 4 p. m. for training and maintenance work.[219] In explaining his reasons and the considerations responsible for his instituting an alert against sabotage only, General Short has stated: (1) That the message of November 27 contained nothing directing him to be prepared to meet an air raid or an all-out attack on Hawaii; [220] (2) that he received other messages after the November 27 dispatch emphasizing measures against sabotage and subversive activities; [221] (3) that the dispatch was a "do-don't" message which conveyed to him the impression that the avoidance of war was paramount and the greatest fear of the War Department was that some international incident might occur in Hawaii which Japan would regard as an overt act; [222] (4) that he was looking to the Navy to provide him adequate warning of the approach of a hostile force, particularly through distant reconnaissance which was a Navy responsibility; [223] and (5) that instituting alerts 2 or 3 would have seriously interfered with the training mission of the Hawaiian Department.[224]

NO WARNING OF ATTACK ON HAWAII

The first statement by General Short that there was nothing directing him to be prepared to meet an air raid or an all-out attack on Hawaii will be considered. Implicit in this contention is the assumption that, despite the known imminence of war between the United States and Japan and the fact that he commanded a Pacific outpost,

[216] Colonel Walter C. Phillips. See committee record, pp. 7945, 7946.
[217] Committee exhibit No. 32, p. 12.
[218] See committee exhibit No. 44. See also testimony of General Short, committee record pp. 7944, 7945.
[219] Testimony of General Short, committee record, p. 7946.
[220] General Short said, "There was nothing in the message directing me to be prepared to meet an air raid or an all-out attack." Committee record, p. 7929.
[221] Committee record, p. 7929.
[222] Id., at p. 7927.
[223] Id., at p. 7946 *et seq.*
[224] Id., at pp. 7948–7951.

it was not his duty to be on the alert against a threat from without. This assumption does not appear to be supported by military doctrine or the logic of the Hawaiian situation prior to the attack.[225]

The wording of the November 27 dispatch indicated the possibility of an attack from without in ordering General Short to undertake reconnaissance. The only conceivable reconnaissance which could have been undertaken by the Army was through employment of aircraft or radar, either or both of which would be in contemplation of an attack from without. General Marshall had told the commanding general of the Hawaiian Department much earlier, with emphasis and clarity, that *the* function of the Army in Hawaii was to defend the fleet base. Despite this fact, when warned that Japan's future action was unpredictable but hostile action was possible at any moment and when his attention was called to the necessity for reconnaissance, General Short proceeded to institute an alert against sabotage only. This was done although there had not been one single act of sabotage on the islands up to that time; for that matter, there were no acts of sabotage thereafter, although this danger in Hawaii had been recognized by both the Hawaiian Department and Washington.[225a] However, in all of General Short's correspondence with General Marshall the subject of sabotage was not emphasized and scarcely discussed. Quite to the contrary, the letters referred repeatedly to aircraft and antiaircraft defense.

DISPATCHES INDICATING THREAT OF SABOTAGE

We will now consider the contention made by General Short that he received other messages emphasizing measures against sabotage and subversive activities, which to his mind confirmed the accuracy of his judgment in instituting an alert against sabotage only. All of these messages, however, were received after the warning dispatch of November 27 and *after* he had replied thereto.[226] They could not, therefore, have influenced in any way his decision to institute an alert against sabotage only.

The first of the messages concerning possible subversive activities was signed by General Miles and was dated November 27. It pointed out that hostilities may ensue and that subversive activities may be expected. This message made definitely clear that subversive activities and sabotage were not all that might be expected but hostilities as well. In this connection, however, General Short has referred to the fact that sabotage was a form of hostile action.[227]

On November 28 the Hawaiian Department received two dispatches from the War Department specifically warning of the danger of sabotage and subversive activities.[228] To the first of these dispatches which was signed by General Adams, the Adjutant General, the

---

[225] As expressed by Secretary Stimson in his statement submitted for the committee's consideration: "The outpost commander is like a sentinel on duty in the face of the enemy. His fundamental duties are clear and precise. He must assume that the enemy will attack at his particular post; and that the enemy will attack at the time and in the way in which it will be most difficult to defeat him. It is not the duty of the outpost commander to speculate or rely on the possibilities of the enemy attacking at some other outpost instead of his own. It is his duty to meet him at his post at any time and to make the best possible fight that can be made against him with the weapons with which he has been supplied." Committee record, pp. 14405, 14406.

[225a] See in this connection an aide memoire concerning "Defense of Hawaii" prepared by the War Department and presented to the President by General Marshall in May of 1941. Part IV, Note 42, infra.

[226] Committee exhibit No. 32, pp. 10, 13, and 34.

[227] General Short said: " 'Hostile action at any moment' meant to me that as far as Hawaii was concerned the War Department was predicting sabotage. Sabotage is a form of hostile action." Committee record, p. 7929.

[228] For the full text of these two dispatches see pages 102 and 103, supra.

following reply (directed to the Adjutant General) was made on November 29: [229]

Re your secret radio four eight two twenty eighth, full precautions are being taken against subversive activities within the field of investigative responsibility of War Department (paragraph three MID SC thirty dash forty five) and military establishments including personnel and equipment. As regards protection of vital installations outside of miltary reservations such as power plants, telephone exchanges and highway bridges, this headquarters by confidential letter dated June nineteen nineteen forty one requested the Governor of the Territory to use the broad powers vested in him by section sixty seven of the organic act which provides, in effect, that the Governor may call upon the commanders of military and naval forces of the United States in the territory of Hawaii to prevent or suppress lawless violence, invasion, insurrection, etc. Pursuant to the authority stated the Governor on June twentieth confidentially made a formal written demand on this headquarters to furnish him and to continue to furnish such adequate protection as may be necessary to prevent sabotage, and lawless violence in connection therewith, being committed against vital installations and structures in the Territory. Pursuant to the foregoing request appropriate military protection is now being afforded vital civilian installations. In this connection, at the instigation of this headquarters the City and County of Honolulu on June thirtieth nineteen forty one enacted an ordnance which permits the commanding general Hawaiian Department, to close, or restrict the use of and travel upon, any highway within the City and County of Honolulu, whenever the commanding general deems such action necessary in the interest of national defense. The authority thus given has not yet been exercised. Relations with FBI and all other federal and territorial officials are and have been cordial and mutual cooperation has been given on all pertinent matters.

The reply (directed to General Arnold) to the second dispatch was not received in the War Department until December 10, 1941.[230]

General Short, as heretofore indicated, has referred to the two dispatches from the War Department of November 28 warning of the danger of sabotage and subversive activities as confirming his original decision to institute an alert against sabotage only. It is significant, however, that the army commanders at Panama, on the West Coast, and in the Philippines received these same dispatches warning of subversive activities that were received by the Hawaiian commander.[230a] They did not deter the commanders at these other places from taking full and complete measures to alert their commands or convey to their minds that defense against sabotage was the only action required.[230b]

The November 27 warning to General Short concerning possible hostile action at any moment was signed by General Marshall—a command directive—whereas the dispatches relating to sabotage and subversive activities were signed by subordinate officials of the War Department. Inasmuch as General Marshall's message contained no reference to sabotage whatever, it would seem fair to suggest that upon receiving subsequent dispatches from subordinate War Department officials warnings of this danger there should have been aroused in the Commanding General's mind the thought that perhaps he had misjudged the purport of the original warning. The evidence reflects that any reference to sabotage or subversive activities was deliberately omitted from the warning message sent General Short (and the commanders at Panama, on the West Coast, and in the Philippines) on November 27 in order *"that this message could be interpreted only as*

[229] Committee exhibit No. 32, pp. 17, 18.
[230] Id., at pp. 19, 20.
[230a] See Committee exhibit No. 35, p. 2.
[230b] For dispatches reflecting the full and complete measures taken by these commanders (Panama, West Coast, the Philippines) see Committee exhibit No. 32 pp. 11, 15, 15a, 16, 18, 18a, and 18b.

warning the commanding general in Hawaii against an attack from without." [230c]

General Short stated that he assumed the Navy would conduct distant reconnaissance [230d] and that he was relying on the Navy to give him timely warning of an attack, indicating thereby that he realized the warning messages required precautionary measures against all possible contingencies. It naturally follows that his failure to take the action required by the November 27 warning was not due to the subsequent emphasis on the specific danger of subversive activities but rather by reason of his failure to institute liaison with the Navy— failure to determine what the Navy was really doing—as he advised the War Department he had done, and his unwarranted assumption that even though he did not himself institute precautionary measures against the danger of an air attacк, the Navy would do so.

"DO-DON'T" CHARACTER OF THE NOVEMBER 27 DISPATCH AND "AVOIDANCE OF WAR"

As earlier indicated, General Short has referred to the November 27 dispatch as a "do-don't" message which conveyed to him the impression that the avoidance of war was paramount and the greatest fear of the War Department was that some international incident might occur in Hawaii which Japan would regard as an overt act. To test the merits of this contention it is necessary to aline the directives and intelligence beside the prohibitions and admonitions:

Negotiations with the Japanese appear to be terminated to all practical purposes with only the barest possibilities that the Japanese Government might come back and offer to continue. Japanese future action unpredictable but hostile action possible at any moment.	If hostilities cannot be avoided the United States desires that Japan commit the first overt act.
This policy should not be construed as restricting you to a course of action that might joepardize your defense. Prior to hostile Japanese action, you are directed to undertake such reconnaissance and other measures as you deem necessary	but these measures should be carried out so as not to alarm the civil population or disclose intent.
Report measures taken. Should hostilities occur, you will carry out the tasks assigned in Rainbow Five so far as they pertain to Japan.	Limit the dissemination of this highly secret information to minimum essential officers.

The first admonition appearing in the foregoing dispatch is a statement of traditional American policy against the initiation of war— *if hostilities cannot be avoided the United States desires the prospective enemy to commit the first overt act.* This General Short already knew. Certainly he did not have in mind committing an overt act against Japan. There was nothing here to restrict the commanding general's

---

²³⁰ᶜ See testimony of General Gerow, Committee record, pp. 2696–2698.
²³⁰ᵈ See committee record, p. 7927.

contemplated plan of action. Indeed, the dispatch itself clearly pointed out that the policy should not be construed as restricting General Short to a course of action that might jeopardize his defense.[231] The very fact that Japan must commit the first overt act emphasized the need for greater vigilance and defenseive effort.

The prohibition in the dispatch was that reconnaissance and "other measures" should not be carried out so as to alarm the civil population or disclose intent. This was incorporated in the message because of the large number of Japanese inhabitants and it was felt that nothing should be done, unless necessary to defense, to alarm the civil population and thus possibly precipitate an incident which would give Japan an excuse to go to war saying we had committed the first overt act.[232] No one appreciated more than General Short the abnormally large percentage of Japanese among the population of Hawaii. He knew that 37 percent or approximately 160,000 of the population were of Japanese descent, some 35,000 being aliens. This was one of the principal reasons for the alert against sabotage.[233]

The civil population was inured to Army and Navy maneuvers which were going on continuously.[234] To have taken any of the logical steps to defend Oahu—reconnaissance, 24 hour operation of radar, effecting a high state of aircraft and anti-aircraft readiness—would not have alarmed a population accustomed to simulated conditions of warfare.[235] In this respect the November 27 dispatch from the War Department interjected no deterrent to full and adequate defensive measures.

The admonition to limit dissemination of the information in the dispatch to *minimum essential* officers was within the complete discretion of the Commanding General. Dissemination of the information was to *follow* and not *precede* the selection of the proper alert; and there were no restrictions in the November 27 warning which should have precluded General Short's instituting an alert commen-

---

[231] Mr. Stimson stated: "When General Short was informed on November 27 that 'Japanese action unpredictable' and that 'hostile action possible at any moment,' and that the policy directed 'should not comma repeat not comma be construed as restricting you to a course of action that might jeopardize your defense,' we had a right to assume that he would competently perform this paramount duty entrusted to him." Mr. Stimson's statement, committee record, pp. 14397, 14398.

[232] See statement of Mr. Stimson, committee record, p. 14397. This admonition was not included in the message to General MacArthur but was contained in the message to the Commanding General, Western Defense Command. See committee exhibit No. 32, pp. 8, 9.

[233] It is to be noted that one of the best criterions that General Short possessed to determine what might alarm the civil population was the so-called Herron Alert during the summer of 1940. This was an all-out alert with complete dispersal of planes and troops with ammunition at the guns and reconnaissance being conducted. There was no disturbance of the civil population resulting from this action. See in this connection Army Pearl Harbor Board record, pp. 1398, 2025, 2720, 2738, 2772, 2772, 3096, 3097.

[234] *General Maxwell Murray testified that the action required by Alert No. 1—taking over water, lights, gas and oil utilities, patrols all over, all important bridges guarded—was just as much of an alarm to the people that something was anticipated "as if they had gone to the beaches"—all out alert.* See Army Pearl Harbor Board Record, p. 3096, 3097.

[235] Before the Navy Court of Inquiry, Admiral Kimmel testified: "I discussed the question of air attack on Pearl Harbor with the commanding general on various occasions. We simulated such attack; we sent planes in to attack Pearl Harbor, I don't know how many times, but several times, during the year I was out there, and we put the defending planes or other elements into operation." Navy Court of Inquiry record, p. 1131.

Testifying before the Navy Court of Inquiry, Admiral Kimmel was asked whether there were any drills furthering joint Army-Navy exercises. He replied: "Yes. Air raid drills for several months were conducted each week. For about 2 to 3 months prior to December 7, 1941, we conducted the drills once every 2 weeks. This was in order to insure the participation of all elements in each drill as held, and when the drills were held weekly there were too many people excused due to overhauling a plane or some work that they considered essential and more important than taking part in drills." Navy Court of Inquiry Record, p. 296.

surate with the warning and orders contained therein.[236] Perhaps, after the event the warning message could be improved upon. It nevertheless was adequate and its orders should have been carried out with an appreciation of the implications of the warning it conveyed.

COMMANDING GENERAL'S RELIANCE ON THE NAVY

It is apparent from the evidence that General Short was depending on the Navy to give him timely and adequate warning of any enemy force approaching Hawaii. He stated that from repeated conversations with the Navy he knew that the Japanese naval vessels were supposed to be either in their home ports or proceeding south; that he knew the Navy had task forces at sea with reconnaissance from Midway, Wake, Palmyra, and Johnston Islands, which would render an air attack highly improbable; that the War Plans Officer on Admiral Kimmel's staff, Admiral McMorris, had stated that there was no chance of a surprise attack on Oahu; that it was only through the Navy that he could obtain information concerning the movement of Japanese vessels; and that distant reconnaissance was a Navy responsibility.[237]

General Short's unfortunate predicament on the morning of December 7 was occasioned to a degree by reason of his reliance on the Navy to provide him timely warning. However, the fact that he was relying on the Navy does not excuse General Short for his failure to determine whether his assumptions with respect to what the Navy was doing were correct. He assumed operations of the task forces rendered an air attack highly improbable; he assumed the Navy was conducting distant reconnaissance from Oahu; he assumed the Navy would advise him of the location and movement of Japanese warships. Yet a simple inquiry by General Short would have revealed that the task forces effected no coverage of the dangerous northern approaches to Oahu; that the Navy was not conducting distant reconnaissance; and that the Navy did not know where the Japanese carrier strength was for over a week prior to December 7. We can understand General Short's dependence on the Navy, but we cannot overlook the fact that he made these assumptions with no attempt to verify their correctness.

INTERFERENCE WITH TRAINING

General Short has pointed out that the factor of training was considered in selecting Alert No. 1; that the use of Alerts 2 or 3 would

---

[236] In commenting concerning the November 27 warning sent General Short, Secretary Stimson said: "This message has been characterized as ambiguous and described as a 'do-don't' message. The fact is that it presented with the utmost precision the situation with which we were all confronted and in the light of which all our commanding officers, as well as we ourselves in Washington, had to govern our conduct. The situation was admittedly delicate and critical. On the one hand, in view of the fact that we wanted more time, we did not want to precipitate war at this moment if it could be avoided. If there was to be war, moreover, we wanted the Japanese to commit the first overt act. On the other hand, the matter of defense against an attack by Japan was the first consideration. In Hawaii, because of the large numbers of Japanese inhabitants, it was felt desirable to issue a special warning so that nothing would be done, unless necessary to the defense, to alarm the civil population and thus possibly to precipitate an incident and give the Japanese an excuse to go to war and the chance to say that we had committed the first overt act." Further: *"All these considerations were placed before the commanding officers of their respective areas, and it was because they were thought competent to act in a situation of delicacy requiring judgment and skill that they had been placed in these high posts of command."* Mr. Stimson's statement, committee record, pp. 14396, 14397.

[237] Committee record, page 7946 *et seq.*

have seriously interfered with his training mission. He observed that the soldiers and officers of his command were in large part relatively new to the Army and to their specialized tasks and that regular training was essential. He stated that the War Department dispatch of November 27 "had not indicated in any way that our training mission was modified, suspended or abolished, and that all troops were to go immediately into tactical status." [238]

General Short has pointed out that the Hawaiian Air Force had the particular mission of training combat crews and ferrying B-17's to the Philippine Islands. He recalled that on September 8, 1941, 9 trained combat teams were sent to the Philippines; that before November 27, 18 trained combat teams had been sent to the mainland and 17 more teams were ready to go to the mainland for ferrying purposes; and that 12 more combat crews had to be trained for planes expected to arrive at an early date. He observed that only 6 of his 12 Flying Fortresses were in condition and available for the training and that it was imperative General Martin make maximum use of these planes for training. He felt that if war were momentarily expected in the Hawaiian coastal frontier, the training considerations would give way but that every indication was that the War Department expected the war to break out, if at all, only in the far Pacific and not at Hawaii.[239]

As has been earlier indicated, however, the very fact of having suggested to General Short that he undertake reconnaissance was an indication of the possibility of an attack on Hawaii from without. This committee believes that the warning dispatch of November 27 was ample notice to a general in the field that his training was now secondary—that his primary mission had become execution of the orders contained in the dispatch and the effecting of maximum defensive security.

The Order to Undertake Reconnaissance

The very fact that General Short noted the order with respect to undertaking reconnaissance contained in the dispatch of November 27 and thereafter instituted an alert against sabotage only demonstrates a failure to grasp the serious circumstances confronting his command. It is to be recalled in this connection that Army commanders in the Philippines, at Panama, and on the West Coast, upon receiving the dispatch of November 27 in substantially the same terms as General Short, instituted full measures adequately to alert their commands.[240]

The observation has been made by General Short that he presumed the man who prepared the message of November 27 ordering him to undertake reconnaissance was unfamiliar with the fact that the Navy

[238] Id., at pp. 7948, 7949.
[239] Id.
[240] See Committee Exhibit No. 32, pp. 11, 15, 16 and 18 for replies, pursuant to the warning messages of November 27, from General MacArthur in the Philippines, General DeWitt on the West Coast, and General Andrews at Panama.
General MacArthur replied under date of November 28: "Pursuant to instructions contained in your radio six two four, air reconnaissance has been extended and intensified in conjunction with the Navy. Ground security measures have been taken. Within the limitations imposed by present state of development of this theatre of operations everything is in readiness for the conduct of a successful defense. Intimate liaison and cooperation and cordial relations exist between Army and Navy."
A significant portion of the reply from General Andrews follows: "In the Panama Sector, the Commandant of the 15th Naval District is conducting continuous surface patrol of the area included within the Panama Coastal Frontier, supplemented, within the limits of the aircraft at his disposal, by an air patrol. In my opinion, the Commandant of the 15th Naval District, does not have sufficient aircraft or vessels within his control for adequate reconnaissance."

was responsible for distant reconnaissance.[241] It is inconceivable, however, that in the face of a specific directive with respect to reconnaissance General Short should not have requested clarification from the War Department in the event he felt the latter did not mean what it had unequivocally said and had failed to take into consideration the Navy's responsibility for reconnaissance. This fact takes on added importance when it is realized that the November 27 dispatch was the first and only dispatch General Short had received signed by General Marshall, the Chief of Staff, since becoming commanding general of the Hawaiian Department. It was a *command directive* which should have received the closest scrutiny and consideration by the Hawaiian general.

Certainly the least that General Short could have done was to advise Admiral Kimmel or Admiral Bloch and consult with them at once concerning the fact that he had been directed to undertake reconnaissance if he presumed the Navy was to perform this function. The Joint Coastal Frontier Defense Plan, the very document wherein the Navy assumed responsibility for distant reconnaissance, contained in an annex thereto provision for joint operations *when the Commanding General of the Hawaiian Department and the Naval Base Defense Officer agree that a threat of a hostile raid or attack is sufficiently imminent.* The failure to appreciate the necessity for following through on an order to undertake reconnaissance is not in keeping with the good judgment expected from the commanding general of the Hawaiian Department.

It is further to be borne in mind that General Short had six mobile radar units which were available for reconnaissance use. He ordered their operations from 4 a. m. to 7 a. m., in addition to the normal training operation of radar during the day, but failed to provide the necessary officers handling the equipment with the knowledge that war was at hand in order that they would intelligently attach significance to information which the radar might develop. In testifying before the committee concerning the operation of radar, General Short said: [241a] "That (the radar) was put into alert during what I considered the most dangerous hours of the day for an air attack, from 4 o'clock to 7 o'clock a. m. daily." The very fact that radar was ordered operated at all was in recognition of the danger of a threat from without; indeed it was only in contemplation of such a threat that General Short would have been supplied radar at all.[242]

---

[241] Army Pearl Harbor Board record, pp. 4436, 4437.
[241a] Committee record, p. 8054.
[242] In a statement submitted for the committee's consideration, Mr. Stimson said: "You will notice that this message of November 27th specifically mentions that reconnaissance is to be undertaken. This to my mind was a very important part of the message, not only because of its obvious desirability but also because we had provided the Hawaiian Department with what I regarded as a most effective means of reconnaissance against air attack and one to which I had personally devoted a great deal of attention during the preceding months. I refer to the radar equipment with which the Hawaiian Department was then provided. This equipment permitted approaching planes to be seen at distances of approximately 100 miles; and to do so in darkness and storm as well as in clear daylight. In the early part of 1941 I had taken up earnestly the matter of securing such radar equipment for aircraft protection. I knew, although it was not then generally known, that radar had proved of the utmost importance to the British in the Battle of Britain, and I felt in the beginning of 1941 that we were not getting this into production and to the troops as quickly as we should, and put on all the pressure I could to speed up its acquisition. By the autumn of 1941 we had got some of this equipment out to Hawaii, and only a few days before this I had received a report of the tests which had been made of this equipment in Hawaii on November 19th, which indicated very satisfactory results in detecting approaching airplanes. I testified at considerable length with regard to this before the Army Pearl Harbor Board (A. P. H. B. 4064, et seq.). When we specifically directed the commanding officer at Hawaii, who had been warned that war was likely at any moment, to make reconnaissance, I assumed *that all means of reconnaissance available to both the Army and Navy would be employed.* On the same day a war warning was dispatched to the Commander-in-Chief of the Pacific Fleet by the Chief of Naval Operations. The standing instructions to the theatre commanders were that all messages of this character were to be exchanged between the Army and Navy commands." Committee record, pp. 14398, 14399.

THE SHORT REPLY

It is recalled that the dispatch of November 27, No. 472, carried instructions to report measures taken and that General Short, referring to the dispatch by number, advised that the Hawaiian Department was "alerted to prevent sabotage. Liaison with Navy." As paraphrased and reviewed in the War Department, this reply read: "Report Department alerted to prevent sabotage. Liaison with Navy reurad four seven two twenty seven." [243] No action was taken by the War Department following receipt of this reply.

General Short has stated that the silence and failure of the War Department to reply to his report of measures taken constituted reasonable grounds for his belief that his action was exactly what the War Department desired. He has pointed out that if the action taken by him was not consistent with the desires of the War Department it should have informed him of that fact. [244]

The question at this point, however, is not whether Washington should have replied to General Short's dispatch but whether the commanding general was entitled to believe that his reply had adequately informed Washington that he had or had not carried out the orders contained in General Marshall's warning of November 27. [245] General Gerow has already assumed full responsibility for failure to follow up to insure that the alert to prevent sabotage was not the only step taken by the Hawaiian Department under the circumstances. No one in Washington appears to have been impressed with or caught the fact that General Short's report of measures taken was inadequate and not sufficiently responsive to the directive. This failure of supervision cannot be condoned.

However, a reasonable inference from the statement "liaison with Navy" was that through liaison with the Navy he had taken the necessary steps to implement the War Department warning, including the undertaking of reconnaissance. This was clearly recognized by General Short. In testifying before the Army Pearl Harbor Board he was asked the question: [246] "In your message of November 27, you say, 'Liaison with the Navy.' Just what did you mean by that? How did that cover anything required by that particular message?"

General SHORT. To my mind it meant very definitely keeping in touch with the Navy, knowing what information they had and what they were doing."

Question. Did it indicate in any way that you expected the Navy to carry out its part of that agreement for long-distance reconnaissance?

General SHORT. Yes. Without any question, whether I had sent that or not, it would have affected it, because they signed a definite agreement which was approved by the Navy as well as our Chief of Staff.

---

[243] See committee exhibit No. 32, p. 12.
[244] Committee record, p. 7965 et seq.
[245] Referring to General Short's reply, Secretary Stimson said: "* * * he then sent a reply message to Washington which gave no adequate notice of what he had failed to do and which was susceptible of being taken, and was taken, as a general compliance with the main warning from Washington. My initials show that this message crossed my desk, and in spite of my keen interest in the situation it certainly gave me no intimation that the alert order against an enemy attack was not being carried out. Although it advised me that General Short was alert against sabotage, I had no idea that being 'alerted to prevent sabotage' was in any way an express or implied denial of being alert against an attack by Japan's armed forces. The very purpose of a fortress such as Hawaii is to repel such an attack, and Short was the commander of that fortress. Furthermore, Short's statement in his message that 'liaison' was being carried out with the Navy, coupled with the fact that our message of November 27th had specifically directed reconnaissance, naturally gave the impression that the various reconnaissance and other defensive measures in which the cooperation of the Army and the Navy is necessary, were under way and a proper alert was in effect." Committee record, pp. 14408, 11409.
[246] Army Pearl Harbor Board record, p. 380.

General Short was not entitled to presume that his responsibilities as Commander of the Hawaiian Department had been discharged or shifted to the War Department through dispatch of his reply.[247] This conclusion is most fully appreciated when he admittedly was not clear concerning the order to undertake reconnaissance.[248] The War Department was entitled to expect the commanding general had carried out the order to effect reconnaissance or in the alternative that he would have requested clarifying instructions. Conceding that General Short presumed the War Department would correct him if he was in error, the fact that supplemental instructions were not issued does not serve to remove that error. Had he made no report whatever the situation in Hawaii on the morning of December 7 would have been the same.

Although General Short specifically advised the War Department on November 27 that he was maintaining "liaison with Navy" the evidence is unmistakably clear, as will subsequently appear, that he did not establish liaison with the Navy concerning the action to be taken pursuant to the Department's warning message.

ACTION WHICH WAS NOT TAKEN UPON RECEIPT OF THE NOVEMBER 27 DISPATCH

Apart from instituting an alert against sabotage and ordering the operation of radar from 4 to 7 a. m. no other appreciable steps were taken by the commanding general to prepare his command for defense against possible hostilities.[249]

No change was made in the state of readiness of aircraft which were on four hours' notice. There was therefore no integration of aircraft and radar, even in the latter's limited operation from 4 to 7 a. m. The maximum distance radar could pick up approaching planes was approximately 130 miles. With the Army aircraft on 4 hours' notice a warning from the radar information center would have been of little avail.

Operation of radar was not instituted on a 24-hour basis. It was so operated immediately after the attack, although as a matter of fact it was not until December 17 that the aircraft warning service was placed under complete control of the Air Corps and the Signal Corps, handling the training phases, removed from the picture.[250]

No action was taken with a view to tightening up the antiaircraft defenses.[251] The ammunition for the 60 mobile antiaircraft guns was

---

[247] See committee record, pp. 4420, 4421.

[248] Referring to the testimony of General Gerow to the effect that the commanding general's report would have been perfectly clear if he had indicated he was alerted against sabotage *only* (see note 247, supra) General Short commented that General Gerow "was unwilling to read my message and admit it meant what it said, no more and no less." Yet General Short failed to accord the War Department the same privilege he was taking; that is, that the order to undertake reconnaissance *meant what it said, no more and no less*. See committee record, pp. 7967, 7968.

[249] Referring to the action taken by General Short, Secretary Stimson stated: " * * * to cluster his airplanes in such groups and positions that in an emergency they could not take the air for several hours, and to keep his antiaircraft ammunition so stored that it could not be promptly and immediately available, and to use his best reconnaissance system, the radar, only for a very small fraction of the day and night, in my opinion betrayed a misconception of his real duty which was almost beyond belief." See statement of Secretary Stimson submitted for the committee's consideration; committee record, p. 14408.

[250] Committee record, p. 8379.

[251] In testifying before the Navy Court of Inquiry, Admiral Kimmel was asked which service was charged with repulsing enemy aircraft by antiaircraft fire on December 7, 1941. He replied: "The Army, I should say, had the prime responsibility. The plans that we had provided for the Navy rendering every possible assistance to the Army. It provided for the use of all guns, including 30 calibers and even shoulder rifles by the marines in the navy yard, and by the crews of the flying field. In addition, it provided that the batteries of all ships should take part in shooting down the planes." Navy Court of Inquiry record, p. 295.

located in Aliamanu Crater, between 2 and 3 miles from Fort Shafter.[252] The crews of the antiaircraft guns were not alerted in such manner as to provide effective defense even with maximum warning from the radar information center.

As in the case of Admiral Kimmel, no effective action was taken with a view to integration and coordination of Army-Navy facilities for defense.

The "Code Destruction" Intelligence

As has been seen, Admiral Kimmel was advised "for action" on December 3 of information received that categoric and urgent instructions were sent on December 2 to Japanese diplomatic and consular posts at Hongkong, Singapore, Batavia, *Manila, Washington*, and London to destroy most of their codes and ciphers at once and to burn all other important confidential and secret documents.[253]

Testifying with respect to the foregoing intelligence, Admiral Kimmel stated that both he and his staff noted that *most* of the codes and ciphers—*not all*—were to be destroyed and that this information appeared to fit in with the information "we had received about a Japanese movement in South East Asia." He commented that Japan would naturally take precautions to prevent the compromise of her communication system in the event her action in southeast Asia caused Britain and the United States to declare war, and take over diplomatic residences.[254]

Admiral Kimmel did not supply General Short the information he had received concerning the orders from Tokyo to destroy codes, ciphers, and confidential documents. He testified: "I didn't consider that of any vital importance when I received it   *   *   * ."[255]

General Short, on the other hand, has complained that he was not provided this intelligence and has indicated it would have been of the greatest significance to him. Referring to the intelligence concerning the fact that Washington had been ordered to destroy its code machine [256] General Short said: "The one thing that would have affected me more than the other matter was the fact they had ordered their code machines destroyed, because to us that means just one thing: that they are going into an entirely new phase and that they want to be perfectly sure that the code will not be broken for a minimum time, say of three or four days   *   *   *."[257] He further testified that had the Navy given him any of the dispatches received concerning the destruction of codes he would have gone into a more serious alert.[258]

In strange contrast with the view of the code burning intelligence taken by Admiral Kimmel, virtually all witnesses have agreed that this was the most significant information received between November 27 and December 6 with respect to the imminence of war. Indeed, the overwhelming weight of the testimony is to effect that orders to

---

[252] See Army Pearl Harbor Board record, pp. 2604–2607.
[253] Committee exhibit No. 37, p. 40.
On the same day Admiral Kimmel was advised for his information of the substance of an intercepted Tokyo dispatch of December 1 ordering London, Hongkong, Singapore, and Manila to destroy (their code) machine.   It was stated that the Batavia (code) machine had already been sent to Tokyo and on December 2 Washington was also directed to destroy all but one copy of other systems and all secret documents; that the British Admiralty had reported London Embassy had complied.   Committee exhibit No. 37, p. 41.
[254] Committee record, p. 6723.
[255] Id., at p. 7477.
[256] This advice was contained in a December 7 dispatch from the War Department which was not received by General Short until after the attack.   This dispatch will be found discussed in detail, Part IV, infra.
[257] Roberts Commission record, p. 1620.
[258] Committee record, p. 8397.

destroy codes mean from a military standpoint only one thing—war within a very few days.[259]

It is concluded that the failure of Admiral Kimmel to supply this intelligence to General Short was inexcusable and that the purport of this information was to advise the commander in chief within reasonably narrow limits of time as to when Japan might be expected to strike. While orders to burn codes may not always mean war in the diplomatic sense, it very definitely meant war—and soon—in a military sense after the "war warning" of November 27. Admiral Kimmel received this intelligence less than 4 days before the attack; it gave him an opportunity to correct his mistake in failing to institute distant reconnaissance and effect a state of readiness commensurate with the likelihood of hostilities after the November 27 war warning. Nothing was done—General Short was not even informed.

On December 4 the commander in chief of the Pacific Fleet was advised for information of orders instructing Guam to destroy all secret and confidential publications and other classified matter except that essential for current purposes, and to be prepared to destroy instantly, in event of emergency, all classified matter.[260] This intelligence was of the greatest significance. It meant that not only was war almost immediately at hand but that a landing operation by Japan against Guam was regarded as a possibility. Nothing was done.

On December 6 the Chief of Naval Operations sent a dispatch to Admiral Kimmel advising, for action, that in view of the international situation and the exposed position of our outlying Pacific Islands he was authorized to order destruction in such outlying islands secret and confidential documents "now or under later conditions of greater emergency." [261] This dispatch suggested the possibility of landing operations against our outlying islands including Wake and Midway.

GENERAL SHORT'S KNOWLEDGE OF DESTRUCTION OF CONFIDENTIAL MATTER BY JAPANESE CONSULATE

The evidence reflects that although Admiral Kimmel received significant information on four different occasions between December 3 and 6 concerning the destruction of codes and confidential documents in Japanese diplomatic establishments as well as in our own outlying possessions, he failed to convey this information to General Short. Despite this fact it appears that the commanding general obtained adequate information concerning the destruction of confidential matter by Japanese diplomatic establishments.

Col. George W. Bicknell, assistant G–2 of the Hawaiian Department, stated that he learned from Navy sources in Hawaii about December 3 that diplomatic representatives of Japan in Washington,

---

[259] See Part IV, infra, re code destruction.
[260] Committee exhibit No. 37, p. 44.
[261] Committee exhibit No. 37, p. 45.
A memordandum submitted by the Navy Department, concerning this dispatch, under date of January 29, 1946 stated: "Opnav dispatch 061743 was transmitted to Radio Honolulu at 5:54 p. m. December 6 1941, Washington local time" (Committee record, p. 11441).
It is to be noted that during committee examination Admiral Kimmel was asked whether he had testified as to when he had received the message of December 6, 1941, authorizing the destruction of confidential papers referred to in the preceding paragraph. Admiral Kimmel said: "I will look at it. I couldn't tell you when that was received, but to the best of my recollection I never saw it until after the attack. It is an even bet as to whether I saw it before or after the attack. I think I didn't get it until after the attack. * * * I have no record upon which I can definitely state that. I can only state my recollection."
Going on, Admiral Kimmel said: "*At any rate, if I did receive this before the attack, it was no more than I would have expected under the circumstances. * * * And that (referring to the message) was not particularly alarming.*" See committee record, pp. 7649, 7650.

London, Hongkong, Singapore, Manila, and elsewhere were destroying their codes and papers. He further stated that about the same time he learned from the Special Agent in Charge of the FBI that the latter had intercepted a telephone "message from the Japanese consulate, Honolulu, which disclosed that the Japanese consul general was burning and destroying all his important papers." Colonel Bicknell said: [262]

> In the morning of 6 December 1941, at the usual staff conference conducted by the Chief of Staff for General Short I told those assembled, which included the Chief of Staff, what I had learned concerning the destruction of their important papers by Japanese consuls, and stated that because of this and concurrent information which I had from proved reliable sources that the destruction of such papers had a very serious intent and that something warlike by Japan was about to happen somewhere.

General Fielder stated that he was present at the staff conference and that on December 6 he gave to General Short the information that the Japanese consul at Honolulu had destroyed his codes and papers.[263] Colonel Phillips also stated that this information was given by him to General Short.

The Special Agent in Charge of the FBI stated that on December 3 the district intelligence officer of the Navy asked him if he could verify information that the Japanese consul general in Honolulu was burning his codes and papers; that about 2 hours later the FBI intercepted a telephone conversation between the cook of the Japanese consulate and a Japanese in Honolulu in the course of which the cook stated that the consul general was "burning and destroying all his important papers." He stated that he immediately gave this information to the district intelligence officer of the Navy and the assistant G-2 of the Army; and thereupon sent a dispatch to Director J. Edgar Hoover in Washington: "Japanese Consul General Honolulu is burning and destroying all important papers." [264]

In testifying before the Roberts Commission General Short stated that he received no information from his intelligence officer until after the attack that the consular records were being burned. He stated: [265]

> As a matter of fact, I didn't know that they had really burned anything until the time that the FBI arrested them on the 7th; they interrupted the burning. I wasn't cognizant of the fact that they had burned the previous day.

Before the committee, however, General Short corrected his former testimony, stating that he had been advised on the morning of December 6 that the Honolulu consul was burning his papers.[266]

While the evidence would indicate that General Short was advised on December 6 that the Japanese consul was burning his *codes* and *papers*, a point has been made by the commanding general that his information was limited to the fact that the consul was burning his papers without reference to *codes*. Even conceding this to be true, the fact that the consul was burning his papers after General Short had been informed hostilities were possible at any moment was of adequate import to impress the commanding general with the fact that our relations with Japan were extraordinarily critical. It is

---

[262] See affidavit dated February 25, 1945, of Colonel Bicknell before Major Clausen. Committee exhibit No. 148.

[263] See affidavit of Colonel (now General) Kendall J. Fielder dated May 11, 1945, before Major Clausen. Committee exhibit No. 148.

[264] See affidavit of Robert L. Shivers dated April 10, 1945, before Major Clausen.

[265] Roberts Commission record, p. 1620.

[266] Committee record, pp. 8398, 8399.

concluded that General Short received prior to the attack substantially the intelligence concerning the destruction of codes and confidential papers *by Japanese diplomatic representatives*, although he was not informed by Admiral Kimmel of the very significant fact that the Navy Department had issued orders for the destruction of codes *in certain of our own outlying possessions.*

THE "LOST" JAPANESE CARRIERS—RADIO INTELLIGENCE AT HAWAII

Perhaps the most vital intelligence available to the commander in chief of the Pacific Fleet indicating Pearl Harbor as a possible point of attack was that gathered from his own Radio Intelligence Unit at Hawaii. This unit was engaged in "traffic analyses"; that is, identifying, locating, and determining the movements of Japanese warships through their call signals. The location of vessels was effected through radio-direction methods.[267]

Information of a similar type was contained in dispatches from the Radio Intelligence Unit in the Philippines and from the Far Eastern Section of Naval Intelligence in Washington. Fortnightly intelligence bulletins incorporating information received from the radio intelligence units in the Philippines and at Pearl Harbor were issued by the Office of Naval Intelligence. These bulletins were made available to Admiral Kimmel.

Because of conflicting reports that had been received concerning Japanese naval movements and the further fact that reports received from the commandant of the Sixteenth Naval District (Philippines) were considered the most reliable, the Chief of Naval Operations on November 24 advised the commanders in chief of the Asiatic and Pacific Fleets, among others, that other reports should be carefully evaluated and sent to the commandant of the Sixteenth Naval District for action and to the Office of Naval Operations for information. After combining all incoming reports the commandant of the Sixteenth Naval District was to direct dispatches to the Office of Naval Operations with copies to Admiral Kimmel for information setting forth his evaluation and best possible continuity.

The commandant of the Fourteenth Naval District on November 26 advised the Office of Naval Operations and the commandant of the Sixteenth Naval District in summary form of information with respect to Japanese naval movements obtained by the Radio Intelligence Unit at Pearl Harbor during the preceding month. This dispatch expressed the belief that a strong concentration of Japanese submarines and air groups, including at least one carrier division unit (not necessarily a carrier) and probably one-third of the submarine fleet, were located in the vicinity of the Marshall Islands. The estimate of the situation was to the effect that a strong force might be preparing to operate in southeastern Asia, while some units might operate from Paleo and the Marshalls. On the same day, the Radio Intelligence Unit in the Philippines advised, among others, the commander in chief of the Pacific Fleet and the Office of Naval Operations, in commenting on the November 26 dispatch from Hawaii, that traffic analysis for the past few days indicated that the commander in chief of the Second Fleet (Japanese) was directing various fleet units in a loose-knit task force that apparently would be divided into two

[267] See testimony of Capt. Edwin T. Layton, Hewitt Inquiry record, pp. 182-292.

sections, the first of which was expected to operate in the south China area, the second, in the Mandates. It was estimated that the second section included Carrier Division 3 "*Ryujo*, and one *Maru*." This dispatch further pointed out that the commandant of the Sixteenth Naval District *could not confirm* the supposition that carriers and submarines in force were in the Mandated Islands and that his best indications were that all known carriers were still in the Sasebo-Kure area. The opinion was expressed that this evaluation was regarded as reliable.

Periodically after November 27, 1941, there were sighting reports from the Asiatic Fleet as well as from other observers confirming the movement of important Japanese naval forces southward from Japan. These reports, however, copies of which were received by Admiral Kimmel, did not indicate the movement of any Japanese carriers.

The Radio Intelligence Unit at Pearl Harbor continued the practice after November 27 of preparing daily summaries of the information received through its traffic analyses of Japanese naval communications.[268] These summaries were submitted each day to the Fleet Intelligence Officer, Captain Layton, for transmittal to Admiral Kimmel on the following morning. On November 28, an intelligence summary, reviewed by Admiral Kimmel, stated there was no further information concerning the presence of a carrier division in the Mandates and that "carriers were still located in home waters." The next day he received the November 28 summary which indicated, among other things, the view that the Japanese radio intelligence net was operating at full strength upon United States Naval Communications and "is getting results." There was no information set forth in the summary with respect to carriers. On the following day, Admiral Kimmel received the summary dated November 29, indicating that Carrier Division 3 was under the immediate command of the commander in chief, Second Fleet. On December 1, Admiral Kimmel received the previous day's summary which stated with respect to carriers that the presence of a unit of "plane guard" destroyers indicated the presence of at least one carrier in the Mandates, although this had not been confirmed.

The Fortnightly Intelligence Summary dated December 1 [269] received by Admiral Kimmel from the Office of Naval Intelligence in Washington stated, among other things, with respect to the Japanese naval situation that " * * * the major capital ship strength remains in home waters, as well as the greatest portion of the carriers." This summary related to information obtained during the 2 weeks preceding its date of December 1 and the Washington estimate of the situation was necessarily based on radio intelligence information received largely from the Philippines and Hawaii before the sudden and unexplained change in the call signals of Japanese vessels on December 1.

The December 1 summary, which Admiral Kimmel received from Captain Layton stated that all Japanese service radio calls of forces afloat had changed promptly at 0000 on December 1; that previously service calls had been changed after a period of 6 months or more and that calls had been last changed on 1 November 1941. This summary stated:

The fact that service calls lasted only one month indicates an additional progressive step in preparing for operations on a large scale.

[268] For these summaries, see committee exhibits Nos. 115 and 115A.
[269] Committee exhibit No. 80.

This statement was underlined by Admiral Kimmel. The summary also stated, among other things, that a large number of submarines were believed to be east of Yokosuka-Chichijima and Saipan, and that as to carriers there was "no change."

On December 2, 1941, Admiral Kimmel examined a memorandum which Layton had prepared on December 1 at his request. This contained Layton's estimate, on the basis of all available information, concerning the location of Japanese naval forces. This estimate placed in the Bako-Takao area Carrier Division 3 and Carrier Division 4, which included four carriers, and the *Kasuga Maru* (believed to have been a converted carrier). The estimate placed one carrier "*Koryu* (?) plus plane guards" in the Marshalls area.

Layton's written estimate made no mention of Japanese Carrier Divisions 1 and 2, consisting of four carriers. This omission was deliberate, the reason being that Layton considered the information as to the location of those carriers was not sufficient to warrant a reliable estimate of their whereabouts.[270]

On December 2, 1941, according to Captain Layton, he and Admiral Kimmel had the following conversation:[271]

Captain LAYTON. As best I recall it, Admiral Kimmel said "What! You don't know where Carrier Division 1 and Carrier Division 2 are?" and I replied, "No, sir, I do not. I think they are in home waters, but I do not know where they are. The rest of these units, I feel pretty confident of their location." Then Admiral Kimmel looked at me, as sometimes he would, with somewhat a stern countenance and yet partially with a twinkle in his eye and said, "Do you mean to say that they could be rounding Diamond Head and you wouldn't know it?" or words to that effect. My reply was that, "I hope they would be sighted before now," or words to that effect.

Captain Layton observed that the incident was impressed on his mind and that Admiral Kimmel was pointing out to him his complete ignorance as to the location of the Japanese carrier divisions. However, the very reference by Admiral Kimmel to the carriers rounding "Diamond Head" was recognition by him of this possibility and his complete lack of knowledge as to where they might be. Admiral Kimmel and Captain Layton discussed—

radio intelligence, its faults and its promises, its inexactities and yet the over-all picture that it will produce. *Whether then or at other times, we discussed the fact that a force can take sealed orders, proceed under radio silence and never be detected by visual or other sighting.*[272]

The December 2 radio intelligence summary, which was delivered to Admiral Kimmel on December 3, read as follows:

Almost a complete blank of information on the carriers today. Lack of identification has somewhat promoted this lack of information. However, since over 200 service calls have been partially identified since the change on the 1st of December and not one carrier call has been recovered, it is evident that carrier traffic is at a low ebb.

The Radio Intelligence summary delivered to Admiral Kimmel on December 4 stated, in part, "No information on submarines or carriers." The summary delivered on December 5 contained no mention of carriers. The summary delivered on December 6 stated "No traffic from the Commander Carriers or Submarine Force has been seen either."

Other than radio intelligence and sighting reports from other sources, the only way by which Admiral Kimmel would have obtained in-

[270] See Hewitt Inquiry record, p. 212.
[271] Hewitt Inquiry record, pp. 212, 213.
[272] Testimony of Captain Layton, Hewitt Inquiry record, p. 215.

formation as to the location or movements of Japanese naval forces from 27 November to 7 December 1941 was by distant air reconnaissance. Knowledge of the location of Japanese carriers was vital to the commander in chief of the Pacific Fleet. Two carrier divisions very definitely could not be located. The service calls of Japanese vessels were changed on December 1, a most unusual procedure inasmuch as they had been changed only a month previously on November 1. Admiral Kimmel fully appreciated the significance of this change and actually underscored the statement submitted to him: "*The fact that service calls lasted only one month indicates an additional progressive step in preparing for operations on a large scale.*" It would appear Admiral Kimmel regarded the preparation to be in anticipation of a Japanese movement to South East Asia.

The presumption was made that inasmuch as the Japanese carriers could not be located they were in home waters. It was fully known, however, that the missing carriers of Japan were not engaged in a movement to the south since such an operation would be open to visual observation by our forces in the Philippines as well as by friendly powers. In consequence, only two reasonable alternatives remained—either the carriers were in home waters or they were engaged in an operation under radio silence in some direction other than to the south. It was Admiral Kimmel's duty to be prepared for the alternative most dangerous to him. Had he concluded that the unusual change in service signals on December 1 clothed a Japanese major operation, perhaps to the eastward at Hawaii, he could have predicted within reasonably narrow limits of time as to when such an attack would come.[273]

Admiral Kimmel has referred to the lack of exactitude of radio intelligence and the fact that this was not the first instance in which his staff had been unable to get a line on the location of Japanese vessels.[273a] Recognizing all of the vagaries of radio intelligence analysis, however, it was still not in keeping with his responsibility as commander in chief of the Fleet for Admiral Kimmel to ignore the sinister implications of the information supplied through the Radio Intelligence Unit after he had been warned of war. In many respects the picture presented by radio intelligence was among the most significant information relating to *when* and, to a degree, *where* the Japanese would possibly attack.

[273] Secretary of the Navy Forrestal observed: "I am of the view that the information as to the location and movements of the Japanese naval forces which was received by Admiral Kimmel during the week preceding the attack, coupled with all the other information which he had received, including the 'war warning' and other messages from the Chief of Naval Operations, should have been interpreted as indicating that an attack on Hawaii was not unlikely and that the time of such an attack could be predicted within fairly narrow limits." See "Fourth Endorsement" to report of Navy Court of Inquiry, committee exhibit No. 157.

And again: "The absence of positive information as to the location of the Japanese carriers, a study of the movement which was possible to them, under radio silence, through the unguarded areas of the Pacific and a due appreciation of the possible effects of an air attack should have induced Admiral Kimmel to take all practicable precautions to reduce the effectiveness of such an attack." Id.

[273a] In this regard, Admiral Kimmel stated, among other things: "The failure to identify Japanese carrier traffic, on and after December first when the call signs changed, was not an unusual condition. During the six months preceding Pearl Harbor, there were seven periods of eight to fourteen days each, in which there was a similar uncertainty about the location of the Japanese battleships. During the six months preceding Pearl Harbor, there was an almost continual absence of positive indications of the locations of the cruisers of the Japanese First Fleet, and eight periods of ten to twenty days each, in which the location of the greater number of cruisers of the Japanese Second Fleet was uncertain. As to the Japanese carriers, during the six months preceding Pearl Harbor, there existed a total of one hundred and thirty-four days— in twelve separate periods—each ranging from nine to twenty-two days, when the location of the Japanese carriers from radio traffic analysis was uncertain." Committee record, pp. 6727, 6728.

THE "MORI CALL"

The Federal Bureau of Investigation on December 6 delivered to responsible Army and Navy intelligence officers at Hawaii a transcript of an intercepted trans-Pacific radiotelephone conversation [274] between a person in Honolulu named "Mori" [275] and an individual in Japan. The transcript of this conversation indicated, among other things, that the individual in Japan was interested in the daily flights of airplanes, particularly large planes, from Honolulu; whether searchlights were being used; and the number of ships present at Pearl Harbor. Reference was made during the conversation to various flowers,[276] the significance of which was not known, but which conceivably could have been an open code employed to convey information concerning the presence or absence of fleet vessels to the approaching Japanese attack force, which could have listened in on the conversation.

Instead of taking action on the basis of the conversation, the office of the District Intelligence Officer of the Navy decided that it should be studied further by a Japanese linguist. This was not done until after the attack and in consequence the transcript of the conversation was not seen by Admiral Kimmel before December 7. The transcript was delivered to General Short and his G-2 on the evening of December 6 by Colonel Bicknell, his assistant G-2, the latter attaching great significance to the matters discussed. Colonel Bicknell stated that the special agent in charge of the FBI was alarmed at what he considered the military implications of the Mori conversation with respect to Pearl Harbor and that he, Bicknell, concurred in this view, considering the conversation as very irregular and highly suspicious. He stated, however, that "both Colonel Fielder and General Short indicated that I was perhaps too 'intelligence conscious' and that to them the message seemed to be quite in order, and that it was nothing to be excited about." [277] No action whatever was taken by General Short.

Regardless of what use the Japanese made of the "Mori call," the conversation should have been, on its very face, of the greatest significance to the responsible commanders in Hawaii. Members of the Mori family were the subject of investigation by the FBI, a fact known to the intelligence offices of both the Army and Navy. An interest by Japan in the daily flights of "large airplanes" and whether searchlights were employed could have but one meaning to alert Commanders who were properly vigilant and should have been prepared for the worst in the knowledge that hostilities were imminent—a desire to know whether air reconnaissance was being conducted and whether searchlights were employed for defense against air attack. The undecipherable and suspicious reference to flowers should have intensified alertness by reason of the very fact that the true meaning could not be gathered. *The Mori call pointed directly at Hawaii.*

The decision of the District Intelligence Office of the Navy to place the matter aside for further study was inexcusable and reflects the apathetic state of alertness throughout the Navy command.

[274] See committee exhibit No. 84 for complete transcript of the conversation.
[275] The Mori family included Dr. Motokazu Mori, his wife Mrs. Ishiko Mori, his father Dr. Iga Mori, and his son Victor Motojiro Mori. The family was the subject of security investigations in Hawaii.
[276] In the course of the conversation the question was asked, "What kind of flowers are in bloom in Hawaii at present?" The reply was: "Presently, the flowers in bloom are fewest out of the whole year. However, *the hibiscus and the poinsettia are in bloom now.*"
[277] See affidavit of Col. George W. Bicknell dated February 25, 1945, before Major Clausen. Committee exhibit No. 148.

DETECTION OF JAPANESE SUBMARINE ON MORNING OF DECEMBER 7

The U. S. S. *Condor*, a minesweeper, at 3:42 a. m. (Honolulu time), December 7, reported sighting a submarine periscope off the entrance buoys to Pearl Harbor in a defensive area where American submarines had been restricted from operating while submerged. The *Condor* by visual signal reported this sighting to the U. S. S. *Ward*, a destroyer of the Inshore Patrol between 3:50 and 3:58 a. m. After receiving this information the *Ward* searched for the submarine for approximately one and one-half hours without results. It thereupon contacted the *Condor*, inquiring as to the distance and course of the submarine that was sighted. At 5:20 a. m. the *Condor* replied but the *Ward* was unable to effect the submarine's location on the basis of this information. The commander of the *Ward* thought the *Condor* had been mistaken in concluding that it had seen a submarine and made no report to higher authority.[278] The radio conversation between the *Ward* and the *Condor* was overheard and transcribed in the log of the Section Base, Bishop's Point, Oahu, a radio station under the jurisdiction of the Inshore Patrol, Fourteenth Naval District. Inasmuch as the conversation was solely between the ships, was not addressed to the Section Base, and no request was made that it be relayed, the radio station did not report it to higher authority.

At 6:30 a. m. the U. S. S. *Antares*, arriving off Pearl Harbor with a barge in tow, sighted a suspicious object which appeared to be a small submarine. The *Antares* notified the *Ward*, asking it to investigate, and at approximately 6:33 a. m. observed a Navy patrol plane circle and drop two "smoke pots" near the object. At 6:40 the *Ward* sighted an unidentified submarine apparently following the *Antares*. The *Ward* opened fire at 6:45 and the *Antares*, observing the fire of the *Ward*, noted about the same time that a Navy patrol plane appeared to drop depth charges or bombs on the submarine. When the submarine keeled over and started to sink, the *Ward* ceased firing and then dropped depth charges.

At 6:51 the *Ward* radioed the Commandant, Fourteenth Naval District: "We have dropped depth charges upon subs operating in defensive sea area." The captain of the *Ward* followed this dispatch with a supplemental message at 6:53: "We have attacked, fired upon and dropped depth charges upon submarine operating in defensive sea area." This information was received by the Chief of Staff to Admiral Bloch at 7:12 and by the Duty Officer of Admiral Kimmel at 7:15. Admiral Kimmel stated he received this information between 7:30 and 7:40 a. m.

Admiral Bloch, according to his testimony, was informed by his Chief of Staff, but in view of numerous previous reports of submarine contacts, their reaction was that the *Ward* had probably been mistaken, but that if it were not a mistake, the *Ward* and the relief duty destroyer could take care of the situation; that Admiral Kimmel to whom the information had been referred had the power to take any action which might be desired.[279] Admiral Kimmel testified:[280]

Between 7:30 and 7:40, I received information from the Staff Duty Officer of the *Ward's* report, the dispatch of the ready-duty destroyer to assist the *Ward*,

[278] See Hewitt inquiry record, pp. 87–92; 428, 429.
[279] Id., at pages 414–416; 452–469. For further details concerning this incident, see Hewitt inquiry exhibits Nos. 18, 73, 75, and 76.
[280] Committee record, p. 6760–6770.

and the efforts then underway to obtain a verification of the *Ward's* report. I was awaiting such verification at the time of the attack. In my judgment, the effort to obtain confirmation of the reported submarine attack off Pearl Harbor was a proper preliminary to more drastic action in view of the number of such contacts which had not been verified in the past.

It is to be noted, however, that in Admiral Kimmel's own statement he refers to only two reports concerning possible submarine contacts after November 3 in addition to the *Ward* incident. He stated: [281]

* * * On November 28, 1941, the U. S. S. *Helena* reported that a radar operator without knowledge of my orders directing an alert against submarines was positive that a submarine was in a restricted area. A search by a task group with three destroyers of the suspected area produced no contacts. During the night of December 2, 1941, the U. S. S. *Gamble* reported a clear metallic echo in latitude 20–30, longitude 158–23. An investigation directed by Destroyer Division Four produced no conclusive evidence of the presence of a submarine.

The reported sighting of a submarine periscope at 3:42 a. m. on the morning of December 7, in close proximity to Pearl Harbor, even though not verified, should have put the entire Navy command on the *qui vive* and when at 6:40 a. m. the presence of a submarine was definitely established, the entire Navy command should have been on a full alert. In the Martin-Bellinger estimate annexed to the Joint Coastal Frontier Defense Plan it was pointed out that a single submarine attack may indicate the presence of a considerable surface force probably composed of fast ships accompanied by a carrier. Admiral Kimmel in his letter to the Fleet, 2CL–41 (Revised), *dated October 14, 1941*, made this identical statement and followed it with the words: [282] "The Task Force Commander must, therefore, assemble his task groups as quickly as the situation and daylight conditions warrant *in order to be prepared to pursue or meet enemy ships that may be located by air search or other means.*"

The evidence does not reflect that the sighting and sinking of a submarine, particularly in close proximity to Pearl Harbor, was of such frequent occurrence as to justify the failure to attach significance to the events of the morning of December 7. This is especially true when it is realized that a war warning had been received and Admiral Kimmel's own estimates indicated the extreme significance of submarine activity. As a matter of fact the *Condor* and *Ward* incidents appear to be the *first* instance of reported sighting and sinking of a submarine since the critical turn in our negotiations with Japan.

The reported sighting was at 3:42 a. m., *over 4 hours before the Japanese air force struck.* Appearing before the Roberts Commission, General Short commented as follows with respect to the *Ward* incident: [283]

That would, under the conditions, have indicated to me that there was danger. The Navy did not visualize it as anything but a submarine attack. They considered that and sabotage their greatest danger; and it was Admiral Bloch's duty as Commander of the District to get that information to me right away. He stated to me in the presence of Secretary Knox that at the time he visualized it only as a submarine attack and was busy with that phase of it and just failed to notify me; that he could see then, after the fact, that he had been absolutely wrong, but that at the time the urgent necessity of getting the information to me had not—at any rate, I did not get the information until after the attack.

[281] Id., at p. 6769.
[282] Hewitt inquiry exhibit No. 8; committee exhibit No. 44.
[283] Roberts Commission record, p. 311.

The supposed sighting of a submarine at 3:42 a. m. and the attack upon a submarine at 6:45 a. m., December 7, should have been recognized as immediate basis for an all-out alert to meet all military contingencies.[284]

RADAR DETECTION OF JAPANESE RAIDING FORCE

The army radar was scheduled for operation on Sunday morning, December 7 from 4 a. m. to 7 a. m.[284a] The normal operation for training purposes after 7 a. m. was discontinued for this particular Sunday by reason of special authorization obtained from the control officer.

At one of the more remote aircraft warning stations, Opana, Privates Joseph Lockard and George Elliott had been on duty from 4 to 7 a. m. Inasmuch as they were waiting for the army truck to return them to quarters for breakfast, it was decided to operate the radar after 7 a. m. in order that Private Lockard, who was skilled in the operation of the radar detector, might afford his partner additional instruction. As the machine was being adjusted, Private Lockard saw on the radar screen an unusual formation he had not previously seen in the machine. Inasmuch as the indicator reflected a large number of planes coming in and he was confident there was nothing like it in the air, he felt that the machine must be at fault. After additional checking he found, however, that the machine was operating properly and concluded at 7:02 a. m. that there was a large number of planes approaching Oahu at a distance of 132 miles from 3° east of north.[285]

After some discussion concerning the advisability of informing the information center, Private Lockard called the center at 7:20 a. m. advising that a large number of planes were heading toward Oahu from the direction indicated. It is to be noted that, as General Short stated, "At 7 a. m. all the men at the information center except the telephone operator had folded up their equipment and left."[286] The switchboard operator was unable to do anything about the call and accordingly, since the information center personnel had departed, referred it to Lt. Kermit A. Tyler, a pursuit officer of the Air Corps whose tour of duty at the center was until 8 a. m. He was there solely for training and observation.

Lieutenant Tyler, upon being advised of the approach of a large number of planes, told Private Lockard in substance and effect to "forget it." He assumed that the flight indicated was either a naval patrol, a flight of Hickam Field bombers, or possibly some B–17's from the mainland that were scheduled to arrive on December 7.

---

[284] In the light of the known and declared significance to be attached to the presence of a Japanese submarine in the vicinity of Pearl Harbor, this committee does not concur in the implications of the conclusion made by the Navy Court of Inquiry that: "There was nothing, however, in the presence of a single submarine in the vicinity of Oahu to indicate that an air attack on Pearl Harbor was imminent." See Navy Court of Inquiry report, committee exhibit No. 157.

[284a] In the course of examination by Counsel, General Short was asked if radar was put on the alert after the warning of November 27. General Short replied: "*That was put into alert during what I considered the most dangerous hours of the day for an air attack, from 4 o'clock to 7 o'clock a. m. daily.*"

Asked if just putting the radar into operation was effective without an Information Center that worked with it, General Short said: "*The information center was working with it.*" Committee record, page 8054.

The evidence reflects that installation of three permanent radar stations had not been completed. The mobile sets had been in operation, however, for some time prior to December 7 with very satisfactory results. See in this regard Note 287, infra.

[285] For complete discussion, see testimony of Joseph L. Lockard, Army Pearl Harbor Board record, pp. 1014–1034; Navy Court of Inquiry record, p. 628–643; testimony of George E. Elliott, Army Pearl Harbor Board record, pp. 994–1014; Navy Court of Inquiry record, pages 644–659; and committee record, p. 13380–13499.

[286] Committee record, p. 7976.

General Short stated:[287]

If he (Tyler) had alerted the interceptor command there would have been time, if the pursuit squadrons had been alerted, to disperse the planes. There would not have been time to get them in the air. * * *. It would have made a great difference in the loss * * *. It would have been a question of split seconds instead of minutes in getting into action.

In testifying before the joint committee, General Short said:[288]

If Lieutenant Tyler had realized that the incoming flight was Japanese, there would have been time to disperse the planes but not to warm up the engines and get them into the air. Lieutenant Tyler made no report of this matter to me and as far as I know did not report the incident to the control officer, Major Tyndall, after the information center was manned about 8:30 a. m. This matter was not brought to my attention until the next day when it was too late to be of value. Had this incident been reported to the control officer at 8:30 a. m. on the 7th, he would have informed the Navy and it might have enabled them to locate the carriers.

If the Army command at Hawaii had been adequately alerted, Lieutenant Tyler's position would be indefensible. He was at the information center for training and observation, had no knowledge on which to predicate any action, and accordingly should have consulted higher authority. His fatal estimate—"Forget it"—was empty assumption. The fact that Lieutenant Tyler took the step that he did, merely tends to demonstrate how thoroughly unprepared and how completely lacking in readiness the Army command really was on the morning of December 7.

Further, the evidence reflects that Privates Lockard and Elliott debated the advisability of informing the Information Center concerning the approach of a large number of planes. It would appear that this unusual information concerning a large number of planes—so unusual in fact that Private Lockard stated he had never before seen such a formation—should have provided immediate and compelling reason for advising the Information Center had the necessary alert been ordered after the November 27 warning and the proper alertness pervaded the Army command.

While it was not possible with the then state of radar development to distinguish friendly planes from hostile planes, this fact is of no application to the situation in Hawaii; for in a command adequately alerted to war any presumptions of the friendly or enemy character of approaching forces must be that they are enemy forces. It is to be noted General Short has stated that if Lieutenant Tyler had alerted the interceptor command there would have been time to disperse the planes and to have reduced the losses.

The real reason, however, that the information developed by the radar was of no avail was the failure of the commanding general to

---

[287] Roberts Commission record, pp. 312, 313. However, in a memorandum dated November 14, 1941, Lt. Col. C. A. Powell, Signal Corps, Hawaiian Department, stated: "In recent exercises held in the Hawaiian Department, the operation of the radio set SCR–270 was found to be very satisfactory. The exercise was started approximately 4:30 in the morning and with three radio sets in operation. We noted when the planes took off from the airplane carrier in the oscilloscope. We determined this distance to be approximately 80 miles, due to the fact the planes would circle around waiting the assemblage of the remainder from the carrier.

"As soon as the planes were assembled, they proceeded toward Hawaii. *This was very easily determined and within six minutes, the pursuit aircraft were notified and they took off and intercepted the incoming bombers at approximately 30 miles from Pearl Harbor . . .*"

A copy of this memorandum was forwarded under date of November 19, 1941, to Mr. Harvey H. Bundy, special assistant to the Secretary of War. See committee exhibit No. 136.

[288] Committee record, p. 7977.

order an alert commensurate with the warning he had been given by the War Department that hostilities were possible at any moment.[288a]

OTHER INTELLIGENCE RECEIVED BY ARMY AND NAVY IN HAWAII

CHANNELS OF INTELLIGENCE

Both the Army and Navy commanders in Hawaii had responsible intelligence officers whose duty it was to coordinate and evaluate information from all sources and of all pertinent types for their superiors.   The record reflects full exploitation of all sources for this purpose including the interview of passengers transiting Hawaii. The record also reflects that the Federal Bureau of Investigation and other agencies in Hawaii were supplying Army and Navy intelligence officers with data available.[289]

The Special Agent in Charge of the FBI at Honolulu, for example, stated that on or about November 28, 1941, he received a radio communication from Director J. Edgar Hoover to the effect "that peace negotiations between the United States and Japan were breaking down and to be on the alert at all times as anything could happen" and that, on the same day, he delivered this information to responsible Army and Navy intelligence officers in Hawaii.[290]

THE "MANILA MESSAGE"

Both the Army and Navy intelligence offices received about December 3, 1941, the following dispatch from a British source in Manila through a British representative in Honolulu: [291]

We have received considerable intelligence confirming following developments in Indo-China:
A. 1. Accelerated Japanese preparation of airfields and railways.
  2. Arrival since Nov. 10 of additional 100,000 repeat 100,000 troops and considerable quantities fighters, medium bombers, tanks, and guns (75 mm).
B. Estimates of specific quantities have already been telegraphed Washington Nov. 21 by American Military Intelligence here.
C. *Our considered opinion concludes that Japan envisages early hostilities with Britain and U. S. Japan does not repeat not intend to attack Russia at present but will act in South.*
You may inform Chiefs of American Military and Naval Intelligence Honolulu.

The assistant G-2 of the Hawaiian Department stated he gave the foregoing intelligence to General Short.[292]

THE HONOLULU PRESS

The information available in the Hawaiian Islands from the press and the attendant state of the public mind in the days before Pearl Harbor can to a great extent be gathered from a recitation of the headlines appearing in Honolulu newspapers.   Among the headlines were the following: [293]

[288a] Illustrative of the insufficiency of the radar alert is the fact that although the charts plotting the Japanese force in and plotting the force as it retired were turned over to higher authority during the course of the attack, this information was not employed to assist in locating the Japanese task force and it appears no inquiries were made concerning it for a considerable period of time after the attack.
[289] See testimony of Col. George W. Bicknell before the joint committee, committee record, pp. 13536–13620.
[290] See affidavit of Robert L. Shivers, dated April 10, 1945, before Major Clausen; Clausen investigation, pp. 88–91.
[291] See exhibits, Clausen investigation.
[292] See supplemental affidavit of Col. George W. Bicknell, dated August 14, 1945, before Clausen.
[293] Committee record, p. 13622–13627.

Honolulu Advertiser

November 7, 1941

"Kurusu Carrying Special Note to F. D. R. From Premier Tojo—Japan Ready to Act Unless Tension Eases."

"Japan Waits Before Move in Far East—Aggression in Pacific Appears Shelved Until Kurusu's Mission has been Completed in U. S."

"Invasion Held too Difficult by Officials—Offensive May Start in Middle East Soon; Invasion of Continent Impracticable at Present."

November 13, 1941

"Tokyo Radio Asserts War is Already on—Any Military Moves Only Logical Result of Encirclement Policy, Japanese Staff Says."

"Envoy Undismayed—Carries Broad Powers to Act—Kurusu Denies Taking Message, Implies Errand of Bigger Scope."

November 14, 1941

"Japanese Confident of Naval Victory."

November 26, 1941

"Americans Get Warning to Leave Japan, China."
"Hull Reply to Japan Ready."

November 27, 1941

"U. S.-Japan Talks Broken Off as Hull Rejects Appeasement—Full Surrender Demanded in U. S. Statement."
"Evacuation Speeded as Peace Fades."

November 28, 1941

"Parris Island, S. C.—This is the tail assembly of the captive barrage balloon at Parris Island, S. C., looking for all the world like an air monster. The wench controlling it is in the sandbagged structure protected there from bomb splinters. The helium sausage may be used to protect beachheads, bridgeheads and other strong points, thereby differing from the British technique which keeps them flying over London. The marines encamped on Parris Island, S. C., have a special training school on these balloons."

November 29, 1941

"U. S. Rejects Compromise in Far East—Washington Insists on Maintenance of Status Quo, Withdrawal from China by Japan Army."

"U. S. Warplanes May Protect Burma Road—Protective Force of 200 Planes, 500 Pilots Held Sufficient to Ward Off Attack by Japanese."

November 30, 1941

"Kurusu Bluntly Warned Nation Ready for Battle—Foreign Affairs Expert Attacks Tokyo Madness."

"Leaders Call Troops Back in Singapore—Hope Wanes as Nations Fail at Parleys; Nightly Blackouts Held in P. I.; Hawaii Troops Alerted."

December 1, 1941

"Japanese Press Warns Thailand."
"Burma Troops Are Reinforced—British, Indian Units Arrive at Rangoon."
"F. D. R. Hurries to Parleys on Orient Crisis."

December 2, 1941

"Japan Called Still Hopeful of Making Peace with U. S.—Thailand Now in Allied Bloc, Press Charges."
"Japan Gives Two Weeks More to Negotiations—Prepares for Action in Event of Failure."
"Malaya Forces Called to Full Mobilization."
"Quezon Held to Blame in P. I. Defense Delay."

December 3, 1941

"Huge Pincer attack on U. S. by Japan, France Predicted—Pepper Visions Nations Acting as Nazi Pawns."
"U. S. Demands Explanation of Japan Moves—Americans Prepare for Any Emergency; Navy Declared Ready."

December 4, 1941

"Hawaii Martial Law Measure Killed for Present Session."
"Japanese Pin Blame on U. S.—Army Paper Charges Violation by F. D. R."

December 5, 1941

"Probe of Japanese Activities Here Will Be Made by Senate—Spy Inquiry Rapidly Gets Tentative O. K. by State Department."
"Pacific Zero Hour Near; Japan Answers U. S. Today."
"Japan Calls in Nationals."
"Japan Has Secret Shanghai Agents."

December 6, 1941

"America Expected to Reject Japan's Reply on Indo China—Hull May Ask Proof, Suggest Troop's Recall."
"Japan Troops Concentrated on Thai Front—Military Observers Say Few Units Have Been Posted in North."

December 7, 1941

"F. D. R. Will Send Message to Emperor on War Crisis—Japanese Deny Massing Troops for Thai War."
"British Fear Tientsin Row, Call Up Guards—May Isolate Concession to 'Prevent' Agitation over U. S.-Japan Rumors."
"Hirohito Holds Power to Stop Japanese Army."

Honolulu Star Bulletin

November 10, 1941

"Navy Control for Honolulu Harbor."

December 1, 1941

"U. S. Army Alerted in Manila—Singapore Mobilizing as War Tension Grows."
"Japan Envoys Resume Talks Amid Tension."

December 4, 1941

"Japan Spurns U. S. Program—Press Holds Acceptance Not Possible."

December 5, 1941

"Japan Parries Open U. S. Break."
"Further Peace Efforts Urged—Tokyo Claims Policy 'Misunderstood' in Washington as One of Force and Conquest."

December 6, 1941

"Singapore on War Footing—Sudden Order Calls Troops to Positions—State of Readiness is Completed; No Explanation Given."
"New Peace Effort Urged in Tokyo—Joint Commission to Iron Out Deadlock with U. S. Proposed."
It would seem difficult to imagine how anyone—upon reading the newspapers alone [294]—could have failed to appreciate the increasing tenseness of the international situation and the unmistakable signs of war.[295]

THE ROLE OF ESPIONAGE IN THE ATTACK

It has been suggested that Admiral Kimmel and General Short should be charged with knowledge that the Japanese were conducting extensive espionage activity in Hawaii and by reason thereof they should have exercised greater vigilance commensurate with the realization that Japan knew everything concerning the fleet, the fleet base and the defenses available thereto. Implicit in this suggestion is the assumption that superior intelligence possessed by Japan concerning Pearl Harbor conditioned her decision to strike there or,

[294] Referring to the commanding general of the Hawaiian Department, Secretary Stimson expressed this idea in the following terms:
"Even without any such message (the War Department dispatch of November 27) the outpost commander should have been on the alert. If he did not know that the relations between Japan and the United States were strained and might be broken at any time, he must have been almost the only man in Hawaii who did not know it, for the radio and the newspapers were blazoning out those facts daily, and he had a chief of staff and an intelligence officer to tell him so. And if he did not know that the Japanese were likely to strike without warning, he could not have read his history of Japan or known the lessons taught in the Army schools in respect to such matters." Statement of Mr. Stimson, committee record, p. 14408.
[295] Both Admiral Kimmel and General Short have made a point of the fact that after the warnings of November 27 they were dependent on the newspapers for information concerning the state of negotiations and from the press, gathered that the conversations were still continuing. It is to be recalled, however, that the "code destruction" intelligence was made available after November 27 and indicated with unmistakable clarity that effective negotiations were at an end. In any event it would appear anomalous that the commanding general of the Hawaiian Department and the commander in chief of the Pacific Fleet would permit unofficial newspaper accounts to take precedence over official War and Navy Department dispatches, setting forth the break-down in negotiations. Admiral Kimmel, himself, admitted that he did not act on newspaper information in preference to official information supplied him by the Navy Department, after having previously observed that he obtained a major portion of his "diplomatic information from the newspapers." See Navy Court of Inquiry record, pp. 306, 307.

otherwise stated, that Japan would not have attacked Pearl Harbor on the morning of December 7 if she had not the benefit of unusual and superior intelligence. Virtually every report that has been heretofore prepared concerning the disaster has referred to the probability of supposed extensive espionage activity in Hawaii and the peculiar vulnerability of the fleet base to such activity by reason of the surrounding mountainous terrain.[296]

There is evidence before the committee, however, which reveals several salient considerations indicating that Japanese Hawaiian espionage was not particularly effective and that from this standpoint there was nothing unusual about the Hawaiian situation. It is clear beyond reasonable doubt that superior Japanese intelligence had nothing whatever to do with the decision to attack Pearl Harbor. Among the considerations giving rise to this conclusion are the following:

1. Radar equipment was available on Oahu for use in detecting approaching planes. That Japan knew of radar and its capabilities would seem clear if for no other reason than on November 22 her consul in Panama advised her that the United States had set up airplane detector bases and "some of these detectors are said to be able to discover a plane 200 miles away." [297] The attacking force was actually detected through radar over 130 miles from Oahu. Had Japanese espionage developed the fact that radar was in use at Hawaii and so advised Tokyo of that fact, it would seem unlikely that the attacking planes would have come in for the raid at high altitude but, on the other hand, would have flown a few feet above the water in order to take advantage of the radar electrical horizon—presupposing of course that Japan possessed at least an elementary working knowledge of radar and its potentialities.

2. Perhaps the greatest single item of damage which the attacking force could have inflicted on Oahu and our potential for effectively prosecuting the war would have been to bomb the oil-storage tanks around Pearl Harbor.[298] These tanks were exposed and visible from the air. Had they been hit, inexplicable damage would have resulted. Considering the nature of installations that were struck during the attack, it is questionable whether Japanese espionage had developed fully the extraordinary vulnerability of the oil storage to bombing and its peculiar and indispensable importance to the fleet.

3. The evidence before the Committee reflects that other Japanese consulates were supplying Tokyo as much information as the Honolulu consulate.[299] Information supplied by the Manila and Panama consuls was detailed in character and related meticulously to defenses available and those in process of development. It appears that it was not until a few days before December 7 that the Honolulu consul supplied his Japanese superiors any significant information concerning the defenses of Oahu, and

---

[296] See reports of Army Pearl Harbor Board and Navy Court of Inquiry, committee exhibit No. 157.
[297] Committee exhibit No. 2, p. 49.
[298] Admiral Bloch pointed out that, had the Japanese attacked the oil supply at Oahu, the drydocks, repair shop, barracks, and other facilities instead of the airfields and the ships of the fleet, the United States would have suffered more insofar as the prosecution of the war was concerned. See Hart inquiry record, p. 94. It is, of course, known that the Japanese knew generally as to the location of the oil-storage tanks as reflected by a map recovered after the attack. See Hewitt inquiry, exhibit No. 30.
[299] From evidence before the Committee it appears that the Manila and Panama consuls were supplying Tokyo more information and of a type far more indicative of an attack than that received concerning Hawaii. See section "Ships in Harbor Reports," Part IV, infra, this report.

at a time when the attacking force was already on its way to Pearl Harbor.[300]

4. The Japanese task force left Hitokappu Bay on November 25 with December 7 set as the time for the attack. This departure, it would seem clear, was in anticipation of the failure to secure concessions from the United States through further negotiations. The date December 7 had been recognized as suitable for the attack in discussions prior to November 7. It is hardly credible that superior intelligence should have precipitated or otherwise conditioned the attack when the decision to strike on December 7 was made many days earlier and, manifestly, in the interim between the decision and the attack date the entire defensive situation at Hawaii could have changed.[301] As a matter of fact two of our task forces left Pearl Harbor while the raiders were en route for the attack.

5. It is apparent from the evidence obtained through Japanese sources since VJ-day that the decision to attack on December 7 was made on the basis of the general assumption that units of the fleet ordinarily came into Pearl Harbor on Friday and remained over the week end.[302] With this realization providing adequate odds that substantial units of the Pacific Fleet would be in Pearl Harbor on Sunday, December 7, that date was selected.

6. In February of 1941 Admiral Yamamoto is reported to have stated,

If we have war with the United States we will have no hope of winning unless the U. S. Fleet in Hawaiian waters can be destroyed.[303]

This statement is clearly in line with the premise laid down by several witnesses before the committee that Japan would open her attack on us by hitting our Pacific Fleet wherever it might be—whether at Pearl Harbor, Manila, Panama, or on the west coast—in order to immobolize it as a threat to Japanese moves to the south.[304] The fleet happened to be based at Pearl Harbor and in consequence that was where Japan struck.

7. The "Mori call," to which reference has heretofore been made, was on the evening of December 5. It would appear doubtful that Japan should have been seeking information just before the attack in the rather inexpert manner displayed in the call if she possessed any wealth of intelligence gleaned through espionage agents in Hawaii.

8. Investigation conducted in Japan since VJ-day indicates, as a matter of fact, that espionage agents, apart from the consul and his staff, played no role whatever in the attack.[305] The sources of information employed, according to Japanese interviewed, were naval attaches to the Japanese Embassy in Washington, public newspapers in the United States, American radio broadcasts (public), crews and passengers on ships which put in at Honolulu, and general information.[306]

[300] See committee exhibit No. 2.
[301] Committee exhibit No. 8.
[302] Id.
[303] Committee exhibit No. 8D.
[304] See testimony of Capt. Arthur McCollum, committee record, pp. 9115–9288; testimony of Capt. Ellis Zacharias, committee record, pp. 8709–8778, 8909–9044.
[305] See committee exhibit No. 8. Also note 6, Part II, this report.
[306] Id.

9. As late as December 2, Tokyo was solicitously asking its Honolulu consul—

whether or not there are any observation balloons above Pearl Harbor or if there are any indications they will be sent up. Also advise me whether the warships are provided with antimine nets.[307]

On December 6, the Honolulu Consul advised Tokyo:

In my opinion the battleships do not have torpedo nets. The details are not known. I will report the results of my investigation.[308]

The foregoing is hardly indicative of any superior sources or facilities for obtaining intelligence.

It is reported that the decision to employ a horizontal-bombing attack on Pearl Harbor in conjunction with an air-torpedo attack was for the reason that Tokyo could not determine whether ships at Pearl Harbor were equipped with torpedo nets and the horizontal bombing could be depended upon to inflict some damage if the torpedo attack failed.[309]

10. In planning for the attack, Japan made elaborate precautions to protect the raiding task force which was of itself very formidable, probably more so as a striking force than the entire fleet based at Pearl Harber. A large striking force was held in readiness in the Inland Sea to proceed to assist the raiding force if the latter were detected or attacked.[310] It is proper to suggest that such precautions would seem unlikely and misplaced if Japan had known through superior espionage information that there was no air or other reconnaissance from Oahu and the defenses were not properly alerted.

The evidence reflects that the raiding task force probably determined the extent of reconnaissance through plotting in our plane positions with radio bearings. Further, the Japanese force followed the broadcasts from Honolulu commercial radio stations on the theory that if the stations were going along in their normal manner, the Hawaiian forces were still oblivious to developments.[311]

11. In moving in for the attack on December 7, the Japanese ran the risk of tipping over the apple cart by sending out scouting planes a considerable period of time ahead of the bombers.[312] They took the further risk of having several submarines in the operating sea areas around Pearl Harbor. If Japan had possessed extraordinary intelligence concerning the state of Hawaiian defenses or lack thereof, it would seem improbable that she would have invited disaster by taking such risks.

12. Reference has been made to the large number of semi-official consular agents that were stationed in Hawaii, the implication being they were engaged in widespread espionage activity Yet the facts before the committee reflect no evidence that these agents committed a single act of espionage, except as it may be inferred from the information sent by the Honolulu consul to Tokyo, which as will be indicated was no more extensive than was being received from other consulates.

[307] See committee exhibit No. 2, p. 21.
[308] Id., at pp. 27, 28.
[309] See committee exhibit No. 8.
[310] Id.
[311] See committee exhibit No. 8D.
[312] Id.

13. It would seem likely that Japan expected some of the most effective striking units of the Pacific Fleet, particularly the carriers, to be in Pearl Harbor at the time of the attack. The raiders, for example, as testified by Admiral Kimmel, bombed a vessel with lumber on its upper deck, apparently thinking it was a carrier. In the light of retrospection and the experiences of the war, it is suggested that Japan would not have indulged the Pyrrhic victory of destroying our lumbering battleships if she had not also hoped to find the fast striking units of the fleet.

14. Japanese estimates in the late fall of 1941 as to the disposition of United States air strength in the Pacific were, with respect to Hawaii, as follows: Fighter planes, 200; small attack planes, 150; 4-engine planes, 40; 2-engine planes, 100; reconnaissance and patrol planes, 35; and flying boats, 110, for a total of 635 planes.[312a] This estimate is roughly twice that of the actual number of planes at Hawaii and reflects a thoroughly erroneous impression as to the ratio of planes in a particular category. The inability to make an approximation of enemy strength within more narrow limits of exactitude can hardly be credited as superior intelligence.

15. In the last analysis it is difficult to believe that Japanese espionage was actually able to develop satisfactorily the real strength of our Pacific Fleet. In December of 1941 the Japanese fleet was superior to our fleet in the Pacific. The latter would have been unable, based on the testimony of witnesses questioned on the subject, to have proceeded, for example, to the aid of General MacArthur in the Philippines even had Pearl Harbor not been attacked. Our war plan in the Pacific, particularly in the early stages, was essentially defensive in character, save for sporadic tactical raids.

If the Japanese really knew the weakness of the Pacific Fleet they must also have known that it did not present a formidable deterrent to anything Japan desired to do in the Far East. As already suggested, the question presents itself: *Why, if Japanese espionage in Hawaii was superior, would Japan invite the unqualified wrath of the American people, weld disunited American public opinion, and render certain a declaration of war by the Congress through a sneak attack on Pearl Harbor when the only real weapon we had, our Pacific Fleet, presented itself no substantial obstacle to what Japan had in mind?* A logical answer would seem to be that Japan had not been able to determine and, in consequence, was not cognizant of our real naval weakness in the Pacific.[312b] The extremely large raiding force and the excessive number of attacking planes would appear to be further confirmation of this conclusion.

[312a] See War Department memorandum dated May 21, 1946, transmitting a letter of the same date from Commander Walter Wilds, Office of the Chairman of the United States Strategic Bombing Survey. Committee record, p. 14626.
[312b] When questioned as to the deterring effect the Pacific Fleet based at Pearl Harbor in December 1941 might have on Japanese aggressive action in the Far East, Admiral Ingersoll declared: "The Pacific Fleet had no train, it had no trainsports, it did not have sufficient oilers to leave the Hawaiian Islands on an offensive campaign and *Japan knew it* just as well as we did and she knew that she could make an attack in the area in which she did, that is, Southeast Asia and the Philippines, with impunity." Committee record, p. 11370.
It appears that the statement by Admiral Ingersoll concerning his estimate of Japanese knowledge concerning the capacity of the Pacific Fleet is illogical and completely incompatible with the risks entailed by Japan in attacking Pearl Harbor.
During the war games carried on at the Naval War College, Tokyo, from September 2 to 13, 1941, *it was assumed that the Pearl Harbor Striking Force would suffer the loss of one-third of its participating units; it was specifically assumed that one AKAGI class carrier, and one SORYU class carrier would be lost.* See committee record, p. 457.

From the foregoing considerations it is proper to suggest that the role played by espionage in the Pearl Harbor attack may have been magnified all out of proportion to the realities of the situation.

The Japanese diplomatic establishments and others did, however, have uncensored channels of communication with Tokyo as a result of statutory restrictions imposed upon our own counterespionage agencies by the Communications Act of 1934. The position assumed in 1941 by the Federal Communications Commission was expressed in a memorandum dated September 29, 1944, by the Chairman, James Lawrence Fly, as follows: [312c]

> The United States was at peace with Japan prior to the attack on Pearl Harbor on December 7, 1941, and the Communications Act of 1934, under which the Federal Communications Commission was organized and from which it derives its powers, prohibited the tapping of wires or other interception of messages transmitted between points in the United States, including its territories, and a foreign country (sec. 605). Since that prohibition upon the Commission had not been in any way superseded, the Commission did not intercept any messages over the radio-telegraph, cable telegraph, or radiotelephone circuits between the United States (including Hawaii) and Japan prior to Dec. 7, 1941.

The situation should never again be permitted whereby the efforts of our Government to combat forces inimical to our national security are hamstrung by restrictions of our own imposition which aid the enemy.

Liaison Between Admiral Kimmel and General Short

Consistent with instructions from the Chief of Staff,[313] General Short set about immediately upon assuming command of the Hawaiian Department to establish a cordial and cooperative relationship with Admiral Kimmel and his staff. That he was successful is undisputed and there can be no doubt that a bond of personal friendship developed between the commanders of the Army and the Navy in Hawaii. They addressed themselves to the task of preparing for war and set about to perfect plans for defense resulting in the Joint Coastal Frontier Defense Plan. As has been seen, this plan was thorough, despite the recognized limitations of equipment, well conceived and if timely invoked using all of the facilities at hand was adequate to effect maximum defensive security. The evidence reflects, however, that personal friendship was obviously confused with effective liaison at a time when the latter was indispensable to the security of the Hawaiian Coastal Frontier.[314]

They exchanged the warning messages of November 27 and discussed their import. They did not, however, in the face of these warnings sit down with one another to determine what they *together* had and what they could *jointly* do to defend the fleet and the fleet base. This action and this alone could have demonstrated effective liaison in a command by mutual cooperation. After reading the "war warning" sent Admiral Kimmel, General Short assumed the

---

[312c] See report of the Army Pearl Harbor Board, committee exhibit No. 157.

[313] General Short testified: "The one thing that that letter (letter of February 7, 1941, from General Marshall) emphasized to me, I think, more than anything else, was the necessity for the closest cooperation with the Navy. I think that that part of the letter impressed me more than anything else." Army Pearl Harbor Board Record, p. 355.

[314] The Army Pearl Harbor Board, it should be noted, said: "General Short accomplished what he set out to do, to establish a cordial and friendly relationship with the Navy. His instructions from the Chief of Staff to do this were not for the purpose of social intercourse, but for more effectively accomplishing the objective of a sound and complete detail working agreement with the Navy to get results. He successfully accomplished fully only the cordial relationship with his opposite numbers in the Navy, i. e., the top rank of the Navy; he did not accomplish fully the detailed working relationship necessary for his own full information, the complete execution of his own job and the performance of his mission. The claim of a satisfactory relationship for practical purposes is not substantiated." See Report of Army Pearl Harbor Board, committee exhibit No. 157.

Navy would be conducting distant reconnaissance when ordered to effect a defensive deployment preparatory to carrying out war tasks.[315] Admiral Kimmel assumed, on the other hand, that the Army in the face of the warnings would be on an all-out alert.[316] In fact, he testified he didn't know the Army was alerted to prevent sabotage only; that he thought they were on an all-out alert; and that he didn't know they had any other kind of alert. He also assumed the Army radar would be in full operation. Even though General Short testified that he conferred with Admiral Kimmel on December 1, 2, and 3 and they talked over every phase of what they were doing [317] these fatal assumptions still persisted. In short, when the time came for really effective liaison it was entirely absent.

The Navy failed to advise General Short of information received on four different occasions between December 3 and 6 concerning the destruction of codes and confidential documents in Japanese diplomatic establishments and in our own outlying islands.[318] General Short testified that had he known of these messages he would have ordered a more "serious alert." [319]

On November 26 the commandant of the Fourteenth Naval District expressed to the Chief of Naval Operations the belief, based on radio intelligence, that a strong Japanese concentration of submarines and air groups, including at least one carrier division unit (not necessarily a carrier) and probably one-third of the submarine fleet, were located in the vicinity of the Marshall Islands. In spite of the believed dangerous proximity to Hawaii of possible Japanese carrier units, the commanding general was not advised of this highly significant information.[320] While this information was questioned the same day by the radio intelligence unit in the Philippines, it nevertheless displays the futility of General Short's assumption that the Navy would keep him informed of the location of Japanese warships.

On November 28, 1941, the commander in chief of the Asiatic Fleet directed a dispatch to the Chief of Naval Operations with a copy to Admiral Kimmel for information concerning the establishment by Japan of the celebrated "winds code" to be employed in "ordinary Tokyo news broadcasts" to advise when "diplomatic relations are on the verge of being severed." [321] Certain Japanese phrases were set up to indicate a break of relations with the United States, England and the Netherlands, and Russia. Efforts were made by the Navy at Hawaii to monitor for a broadcast employing this code. On December 1 the Chief of Naval Operations sent a dispatch to the commander in chief of the Asiatic Fleet, with a copy to Admiral Kimmel, advising of Japanese broadcast frequencies.[322] Despite the importance which was attached to the winds code at the time, General Short has testified this information was not supplied him by the Navy in Hawaii.[323]

---

[315] Committee record, pp. 7926, 7927.
[316] Yet it is difficult to understand why he should have expected such an alert when in his statement submitted to the Navy Court of Inquiry, Admiral Kimmel said: "On November 28th the messages from the War and Navy Departments were discussed (with General Short). We arrived at the conclusion at this and succeeding conferences that probable Japanese actions would be confined to the Far East with Thailand most probably and Malaya, the Netherlands East Indies and the Philippines the next most probable objectives in the order named. *In general, we arrived at the conclusion that no immediate activity beyond possible sabotage was to be expected in Hawaii*" (p. 31 of statement). See committee exhibit No. 146.
[317] See Navy Court of Inquiry record, pp. 242, 251.
[318] See committee record, pp. 8366–8368.
[319] Id., at p. 8397.
[320] Id., at p. 8261.
[321] Committee exhibit No. 142. See discussion of "Winds Code," Part. IV, infra.
[322] Committee record, p. 8374.
[323] Id., at p. 8374.

Beginning November 30, Admiral Kimmel made a daily memorandum entitled: "Steps to be taken in case of American-Japanese war within the next twenty-four hours," the last of these memoranda being reviewed and approved by him on the morning of December 6. Although conferences were held with Admiral Kimmel subsequent to the initiation of these memoranda, General Short has testified he did not know of these steps being taken by the Navy.[324] There is some indication that Admiral Kimmel acted as arbiter of what information General Short received.[325]

Admiral Bellinger, who was not shown the war warning, has stated that between November 27 and December 7 he did not confer with the Army Air Force commander, General Martin, regarding long-range reconnaissance.[326] In other words, there were no discussions during this critical period between the two officers responsible for the air arms of the Army and Navy in Hawaii. It is to be recalled that Admiral Bellinger and General Martin prepared the estimate of possible Japanese action against Hawaii which reflected in such startling detail what did occur on the morning of December 7.

At 3:42 a. m. on December 7 (Honolulu time) a Navy mine sweeper reported the sighting of a submarine periscope off the entrance buoys to Pearl Harbor in the defensive sea area where American submarines had been restricted from operating submerged. Between 6:30 and 6:45 a. m. a submarine was sunk in naval action. Both Admiral Kimmel and Admiral Bloch knew of this prior to the attack. Although the Martin-Bellinger estimate of possible enemy action had stated that any single submarine attack might indicate the presence of a considerable undiscovered surface force probably composed of fast ships accompanied by a carrier, General Short was not advised of the fact that the submarine had been sighted and sunk.

The Army radar at 7:02 a. m. December 7 detected a large contingent of airplanes which turned out to be the attacking force approaching Oahu at a distance of 132 miles away. This information was not supplied the Navy until after the attack.

Although the Army radar plotted the withdrawal to the north of the Japanese force after the attack, this vital information was not employed following the raid in searches for the raiders.[327] This situation is traceable to faulty liaison and a complete failure in integration of Army-Navy effort.

The Navy maintained a liaison officer in the Army operations section for purposes of informing the Fourteenth Naval District concerning action being taken by the Army. No liaison officer, however, was maintained in the Navy operations section by the Army, although an

---

[324] Id., at pp. 8375–8378.

[325] Before the Navy Court of Inquiry Admiral Kimmel was asked: "Did your organization exchange intelligence with the Commanding General of the Hawaiian Department?" Admiral Kimmel replied: "We did, to this extent: The Commanding General of the Hawaiian Department had his interests restricted to the defense of Hawaii and to such of the outlying islands as he had his forces and the ones to which he expected to send his forces. He was primarily interested in the probability of attack where his forces were stationed, and in general the information I gave to him bore upon his interests, or was confined to his interests. My own interests covered a much greater geographical area and many more factors. I tried to keep the Commanding General informed of everything that I thought would be useful to him. I did not inform the Commanding General of my proposed plans and what I expected to do in the Marshalls and other places distant from Hawaii. I saw no reason for taking the additional chance of having such information divulged by giving it to any agency who would have no part in the execution of the plan." See Navy Court of Inquiry record, p. 282.

[326] Navy Court of Inquiry record, p. 672.

[327] Committee record, pp. 9343–9346.

officer was assigned on an 8-hour shift to the harbor patrol.[328] That Admiral Kimmel was completely oblivious of what the Army was really doing evinces the ineffectiveness of the liaison that was maintained by the Navy in the Army operations section.

No conferences were held by Admiral Kimmel and General Short between December 3 and the attack.[329]

General Short said: [330] "I would say frankly that I imagine that as a senior admiral, Kimmel would have *resented it* if I tried to have him report every time a ship went in or out. * * *"

The considerations which apparently occasioned Admiral Kimmel's failure to acquaint himself with what the Army was doing were voiced by him as follows: [331]

* * * when you have a responsible officer in charge of the Army and responsible commanders in the Navy, *it does not sit very well to be constantly checking up on them.*

And yet when asked whether, in the method of mutual cooperation, it was necessary for one commander to know what the other commander was doing and what his plans were, Admiral Kimmel admitted that this knowledge was necessary.[332]

While such concern for the sensibilities of another may have social propriety, it is completely out of place when designed to control the relationship of two outpost commanders whose very existence is dependent upon full exchange of information and coordination of effort.[333] It defeats the purpose of command by mutual cooperation and is worse than no liaison at all. At least, without the pretense of liaison, each commander would not be blindly relying on what the other was doing.

It can fairly be concluded that there was a complete failure in Hawaii of effective Army-Navy liaison during the critical period November 27 to December 7.[334] There was but little coordination and no integration of Army and Navy facilities and efforts for defense. Neither of the responsible commanders really knew what the other was doing with respect to essential military activities.[335]

Estimate of the Situation

The consideration overshadowing all others in the minds of the Hawaiian commanders was the belief and conviction that Pearl Har-

---

[328] Id., at pp. 8205, 8206.
[329] See committee record, p. 8204.
[330] Army Pearl Harbor Board record, p. 363.
[331] Roberts Commission record, p. 631.
[332] Id.
[333] The Army Pearl Harbor Board, for example, commented: "Apparently Short was afraid that if he went much beyond social contacts and really got down to business with the Navy to get what he had a right to know in order to do his job, he would give offense to the Navy and lose the good will of the Navy which he was charged with securing." See Report of Army Pearl Harbor Board, committee exhibit No. 157.
[334] Admiral McMorris, Chief of War Plans to Admiral Kimmel, admitted that he had no knowledge as to whether the Army antiaircraft defenses were actually alerted nor as to their condition of readiness, but he assumed they were in a state of readiness. "* * * Perhaps I was remiss in not acquainting myself more fully as to what they were doing. We knew that our own establishment was fairly good. Actually they proved not to be as good as I felt. *We were a bit too complacent there.* I had been around all of the aircraft defenses of Hawaii; I knew their general location. I had witnessed a number of their antiaircraft practices and knew the quantity and general disposition of their aircraft. I knew that they were parked closely together as a more ready protection against sabotage rather than dispersed. *Nonetheless, I was not directly acquainted or indirectly acquainted with the actual state of readiness being maintained or of the watches being kept.*" Hewitt Inquiry record, pp. 330–332.
[335] See committee record, p. 8205.
During the course of examination Admiral Kimmel was asked: "In other words, neither you nor any member of your staff made any attempt to verify or find out what the condition of alertness was with respect to the antiaircraft guns operated by the Army?" He replied: "And neither did General Short make any attempt to find out the details of an alert that the Fleet had in effect at that time." Committee record, p. 7053.

bor would not be attacked.[336]   It explains the reason for no effective
steps being taken to meet the Japanese raiders on the morning of
December 7.   This was not occasioned through disregard of obligations or indifference to responsibilities but rather because of unfortunate errors of judgment.   The commander in chief of the Pacific
Fleet and the commanding general of the Hawaiian Department
failed to appreciate the demands of their situation and the necessities
of their responsibility in the light of the information and warnings
they had received.   More than anyone else it cannot be doubted that
Admiral Kimmel and General Short would have desired to avoid the
disaster of December 7.   But unfortunately they were blinded by
the self-evident; they felt that Japan would attack to the south and
Hawaii was safe.   Their errors of judgment were honest mistakes—
yet errors they were.

The evidence reflects that both General Short and Admiral Kimmel
addressed themselves assiduously to the task of training and otherwise preparing the outpost of Hawaii and the Pacific Fleet for war.
Throughout their respective tenures as commanding general of the
Hawaiian Department and commander in chief of the Pacific Fleet
they manifested a keen awareness of the imperative necessity that
personnel and material be increased commensurate with the realities
and responsibilities in the Pacific.   From the time of assuming command throughout the year 1941 their correspondence with the War
and Navy Departments is replete with clear statements concerning
shortages in equipment and expressions of the need for improving
Hawaiian defenses.   As will subsequently appear, they were successful in effecting marked improvement in the situation generally and
the potential capacity of Hawaii to defend itself particularly.   General
Short and Admiral Kimmel were conscientious and indefatigable commanders.   They were relentless in what they regarded as the consuming need in their commands—training and preparation for war.

One of the major responsibilities of Admiral Kimmel and the major
responsibility of General Short was defense of the Hawaiian coastal
frontier and the Pacific Fleet.   They knew that an air attack on
Hawaii was a possibility; they knew this to be the most dangerous
form of attack to Oahu; they knew that extensive efforts had been
made to improve Hawaiian defenses against air attack; they had been
warned of war; they knew of the unfailing practice of Japan to launch
an attack with dramatic and treacherous suddenness without a declaration of war; they had been given orders calling for defensive action
against an attack from without; they were the commanders of the
Hawaii outpost.   In the face of this knowledge it is difficult to understand that the withering Japanese attack should have come without
any substantial effort having been made to detect a possible hostile
force and with a state of readiness least designed to meet the onslaught.   That the responsible commanders were surprised that Japan

[336] During the course of counsel's examination of Admiral Kimmel, he was asked this question: "The
fact is, is it not, Admiral, that as you approached December 7 you very definitely gave the Navy program
for action in event of the declaration of war precedence over the establishment of the defense of Pearl Harbor?" and Admiral Kimmel replied; *"If I had believed in those days preceding Pearl Harbor that there was a
50-50 chance or anything approaching that of an attack on Pearl Harbor, it would have changed my viewpoint
entirely.*   I didn't believe it.   And in that I was of the same opinion as that of the members of my staff, my
advisers, my senior advisers."   Committee record, p. 7054.

struck Hawaii is understandable; that they should have failed to prepare their defenses against such a surprise is not understandable.[337]

The estimate of the situation made by Admiral Kimmel and General Short is not altogether incredible in the light of the inevitable lassitude born of over 20 years of peace.[338] But the fact that their inaction is to a degree understandable does not mean that it can be condoned. The people are entitled to greater vigilance and greater resourcefulness from those charged with the duty of defending the Nation from an aggressor.

Hawaii is properly chargeable with possessing highly significant information and intelligence in the days before Pearl Harbor, including: Correspondence with Washington and plans revealing the possible dangers of air attack, the warning dispatches, the code-destruction intelligence, radio intelligence concerning the "lost" Japanese carriers, the Mori call, the report of sighting and subsequent attack on a Japanese submarine in close proximity to Pearl Harbor, and radar detection of the Japanese raiding force over 130 miles from Oahu on the morning of December 7. Despite the foregoing, the estimate was made and persisted that Hawaii was safe from an air attack, although the very assumptions made by the Army and Navy commanders are implicit with the contemplation of an attack from without. General Short assumed the Navy was conducting distant reconnaissance. Admiral Kimmel assumed, on the other hand, that the Army would alert its aircraft warning service, antiaircraft guns, and fighter planes.[339]

Both Admiral Kimmel and General Short have insisted they received no information that Hawaii was to be attacked. Yet commanders in the field cannot presume to expect that they will be advised of the exact time and place an enemy will attack or indeed that their particular post will be attacked. As outpost commanders it was their responsibility to be prepared against surprise and the worst possible contingency.[340] They have suggested that the War

---

[337] This distinction was clearly recognized by Admiral Ingersoll when he was asked if he was surprised when the Japanese attacked Pearl Harbor on December 7, 1941. He replied: "*I was surprised that Pearl Harbor was attacked but I was more surprised that the attack was not detected, that was my first reaction, and if I express it in the words which I used at the time, it was, 'How in the hell did they get in there without somebody finding it out?'*" Committee record. p. 11310.

[338] Admiral Kimmel stated: " * * * and what is so often overlooked in connection with this Pearl Harbor affair is that we were still at peace and still conducting conversations, and there were limits that I could take with planes and aviators. We were still in the peace psychology, and I myself was affected by it just like everybody else." Navy Court of Inquiry Record, page 1126, 1127.

[339] See note 336, supra.

[340] Incident to proceedings of the Army Pearl Harbor Board, the following interrogation occurred:
Question. "In estimating the situation with which a military commander is confronted, our teachings in the military establishment generally have been along the lines of taking all information that is available, evaluating it and using it as a guide. Is that correct?"
General SHORT. "Yes."
Question. "That is in accordance with our Leavenworth teaching, our war college teaching and our actual practice in the organization. Now in coming to a decision on military disposition and general practice in the Army, Army teachings, as perhaps Army tradition, indicate that a commander should prepare for enemy action of what character?"
General SHORT. "The worst." See Army Pearl Harbor Board record, pp. 436 and 437.
The Report of the Army Pearl Harbor Board stated: "It is a familiar premise of military procedure in estimating a situation *to select the most dangerous and disastrous type of attack the enemy may make and devote your primary efforts to meeting this most serious of the attacks.*" (Citing Army Pearl Harbor Board record, pp. 1121, 2662.) See committee exhibit 157 for APHB Report.
Mr. Stimson said, "One of the basic policies of the Army command, which has been adhered to throughout the entire war, and in most instances with complete success, has been to give the local commander his objective and mission but not to interfere with him in the performance of it." Stimson's statement, committee record, p. 14397.
Testifying before the Army Pearl Harbor Board, General Herron, General Short's predecessor, was asked the question: "I have one more question on alerts. The fact that you received a directive from the War Department to alert the command (General Herron on June 17, 1940, had been directed by Washington to institute an alert): Did that leave the impression in your mind that if anything serious happened in the future the War Department would direct you to go on the alert, or leave it up to your judgment?" He replied: "I always felt that I was entirely responsible out there and I had better protect the island." See Army Pearl Harbor Board record, p. 228; also pp. 213–215.

and Navy Departments possessed additional information which they were not given. But the fact that additional information may have been available alsewhere did not alter fundamental military responsibilities in the field. Admiral Kimmel and General Short were the responsible military commanders at Hawaii. They were officers of vast experience and exemplary records in their respective services. That Admiral Kimmel and General Short were supplied enough information as reasonably to justify the expectation that Hawaiian defenses would be alerted to any military contingency is irrefutable.[341] That there may have been other information which could have been supplied them cannot becloud or modify this conclusion. It is into the nature of this further information that we shall hereafter inquire.

[341] And yet Admiral Kimmel has indicated he felt he was entitled to more warning. In a statement submitted to the Navy Court of Inquiry, he said: "I had many difficult decisions to make but none which required more accurate timing than the decision as to when to drastically curtail training and to utilize all my forces in the highest form of alert status. The warnings I received prior to 7 December 1941, were of such a nature that I felt training could still continue. *I felt that I was entitled and would receive further warnings before the actual outbreak of war.* I am convinced now that my estimate based on the intelligence received was correct." (P. 38 of statement.) See committee exhibit No. 146.

PART IV

RESPONSIBILITIES IN WASHINGTON

PART IV. RESPONSIBILITIES IN WASHINGTON

BASING THE PACIFIC FLEET AT HAWAII

Beginning in May of 1940 the entire American Pacific Fleet operated in the Hawaiian theater with Pearl Harbor as its base.[1] Prior to that time the fleet had been based on the west coast with certain contingents operating from time to time in the Hawaiian area. Admiral James O. Richardson, who was commander in chief of the Pacific Fleet in 1940, stated that while the fleet was in Hawaii incident to exercises during the summer of 1940 he received instructions to announce to the press that "at his request" the fleet would continue at Hawaii for the purpose of carrying out further exercises.[2] It was his understanding that the decision to base the Pacific Fleet at Pearl Harbor was with a view to its providing a restraining influence on Japan.[3]

At the time of original contemplation it appears that the fleet was to remain at Hawaii on a relatively temporary basis.[4] Admiral Richardson did not concur in the decision to station the fleet there and so informed the Chief of Naval Operations.[5] He testified with respect to his objections as follows:[6]

My objections for remaining there were, primarily, that you only had one port, secure port, and very crowded, no recreation facilities for the men, a long distance from Pearl Harbor to the city of Honolulu, inadequate transportation, inadequate airfields.

A carrier cannot conduct all training for her planes from the carrier deck. In order to launch her planes she must be underway at substantial speed, using up large amounts of fuel. So that wherever carriers are training their squadrons there must be flying fields available, so that while the ship herself is undergoing overhaul, or repair, or upkeep, the planes may conduct training, flying from the flying fields.

There were inadequate and restricted areas for anchorages of the fleet; to take them in and out of Pearl Harbor wasted time.

Another reason, which was a substantial one: Americans are perfectly willing to go anywhere, stay anywhere, do anything when there is a job to be done and they can see the reason for their being there, but to keep the fleet, during what the men considered normal peacetimes, away from the coast and away from their families, away from recreation, rendered it difficult to maintain a high state of morale that is essential to successful training.

For those reasons, and because I believed that the fleet could be better prepared for war on a normal basis on the west coast, I wanted to return to the west coast.

As a result of a visit to Washington in July of 1940, Admiral Richardson stated he gained three distinct impressions:[7]

First. That the Fleet was retained in the Hawaiian area solely to support diplomatic representations and as a deterrent to Japanese aggressive action;

Second. That there was no intention of embarking on actual hostilities against Japan;

Third. That the immediate mission of the Fleet was accelerated training and absorption of new personnel and the attainment of a maximum condition of

---

[1] See committee exhibit No. 9 for file of correspondence between Admirals Stark and Richardson concerning, among other things, the matter of basing the fleet at Hawaii. For a description of the base at Pearl Harbor, see appendix F to this report.

[2] Committee record, p. 669.

[3] See committee record, p. 682; also Navy Court of Inquiry, pp. 1057, 1058.

[4] Committee record, p. 668.

[5] See committee exhibit No. 9.

[6] Committee record, pp. 674, 675.

[7] See memorandum dated October 22, 1940, from Admiral Richardson to the Chief of Naval Operations. Committee exhibit No. 9.

material and personnel readiness consistent with its retention in the Hawaiian area.

In a memorandum for the Secretary of Navy dated September 12, 1940, Admiral Richardson pointed out several disadvantages from a Navy point of view of retaining the fleet in the Hawaiian area and stated:[8]

If factors other than purely naval ones are to influence the decision as to where the fleet should be based at this time, the naval factors should be fully presented and carefully considered, as well as the probable effect of the decision on the readiness of the Fleet. In other words, is it more important to lend strength to diplomatic representations in the Pacific by basing the Fleet in the Hawaiian Area, than to facilitate its preparation for active service in any area by basing the major part of it on normal Pacific coast bases?

During October of 1940 while in Washington he talked with President Roosevelt at which time the President informed him that the Pacific Fleet was retained in the Hawaiian area in order to exercise a restraining influence on the actions of Japan. Admiral Richardson testified:[9]

I stated that in my opinion the presence of the fleet in Hawaii might influence a civilian political government, but that Japan had a military government which knew that the fleet was undermanned, unprepared for war, and had no training or auxiliary ships without which it could not undertake active operations. Therefore, the presence of the Fleet in Hawaii could not exercise a restraining influence on Japanese action. I further stated we were more likely to make the Japanese feel that we meant business if a train were assembled and the fleet returned to the Pacific coast, the complements filled, the ships docked, and fully supplied with ammunition, provisions, stores, and fuel, and then stripped for war operations.

He stated that the President's comment to the foregoing was in effect, "Despite what you believe, I know that the presence of the fleet in the Hawaiian area, has had, and is now having a restraining influence on the actions of Japan." [10]

Admiral Richardson testified that he replied that he still did not believe this to be the case and that he knew the Pacific Fleet was disadvantageously disposed to prepare for or to initiate war operations, whereupon the President said: [11] "I can be convinced of the desirability of returning the battleships to the west coast if I can be given a good statement which will convince the American people and the Japanese Government that in bringing the battleships to the west coast we are not stepping backward."

It is clear from consideration of the evidence that Admiral Richardson's position was based on the feeling that the fleet could be better prepared for war if based on the west coast and not because he feared for the security of the fleet at Pearl Harbor.[12] In a letter to Admiral Stark on November 28 concerning the matter of the security of the Pacific Fleet in the Hawaiian area he said:[13] *"This feature of the problem*

---

[8] Committee exhibit No. 9.
[9] Committee record, pp. 682, 683.
[10] Committee record, p. 683.
[11] Id.
[12] See, however, in this connection the testimony of Mr. Sumner Welles, committee record, pp. 1124, 1125.
[13] Committee exhibit No. 9. This comment was made by Admiral Richardson pursuant to a letter from Admiral Stark dated November 22, 1940, in which the latter had stated, among other things: "Since the Taranto incident my concern for the safety of the Fleet in Pearl Harbor, already great, has become even greater. This concern has to do both with possible activities on the part of the Japanese residents of Hawaii and with the possibilities of attack coming from overseas. By far the most profitable object of sudden attack in Hawaiian waters would be the Fleet units based in that area. Without question the safety of these units is paramount and imposes on the Commander-in-Chief and the forces afloat a responsibility in which he must receive the complete support of Commandant Fourteen, and of the Army. I realize most fully that you are giving this problem comprehensive thought. My object in writing you is to find out what steps the Navy Department and the War Department should be taking to provide additional equipment and additional protective measures."

does not give me a great deal of concern and, I think, can be easily provided for." Admiral Stark testified that Admiral Richardson did not raise any question concerning the safety of the fleet at Pearl Harbor as a reason for bringing it back to the west coast.[14]

Referring to the decision to base the fleet at Hawaii Admiral Kimmel stated:[15]

When I assumed command, the decision to base the Fleet in the Hawaiian area was an historical fact. The target and base facilities required to train the Fleet for war were in the process of being moved from the West Coast to Hawaii. The Fleet had been practically without gunnery practice for nearly a year due to the previous uncertainty as to the location of its base. Any further uncertainty would have delayed the availability of the mobile facilities to maintain, repair, and train the Fleet. The resulting loss of time in starting intensive training would have been disastrous. This was my view when I took command. My appointment was in no wise contingent upon any acquiescence on my part in a decision already made months before to keep the Fleet in Hawaiian waters.

Admiral Kimmel stated that during his visit to Washington in June of 1941, he told the President and Admiral Stark of certain dangers to the fleet at Pearl Harbor, including air attack, blocking of the harbor, and similar matters. He said that generally he felt the fleet should not remain at Pearl Harbor but he made no protests and submitted no recommendation for withdrawal of any of the battleships or carriers.[16]

Regardless of the position taken by the commander in chief of the Pacific Fleet during 1940 with respect to basing the fleet at Pearl Harbor, extensive measures were taken thereafter and long before the outbreak of war to improve the fleet's security at Hawaii.[17] The Secretary of State, as well as our Ambassador to Japan, were satisfied that the presence of the Pacific Fleet at Pearl Harbor did in fact prove a deterrent to Japanese action as did the Chief of Naval Operations.[18] Referring to the presence of our fleet at Hawaii, the Japanese Foreign Minister in June of 1940 stated to Ambassador Grew that "the continued stay of our fleet in those waters (Hawaiian) constitutes an implied suspicion of the intentions of Japan *vis-a-vis* the Netherlands East Indies and the South Seas * * *."[19] As Secretary Hull stated,[20] "The worst bandit * * * doesn't like for the most innocent citizen to point an unloaded pistol or an unloaded gun at him * * *. They will take cognizance of naval establishments, somewhere on the high seas, whether fully equipped or not." The degree to which the presence of the Pacific Fleet in Hawaiian waters influenced Japanese action necessarily cannot be precisely determined but the fact is the Japanese did not strike at the Netherlands East Indies and the Malay barrier for more than a year and a half after it was contemplated she would make such a move.

The wisdom and merit of the decision to base the Pacific Fleet at Hawaii cannot be divorced from the high Government policy of which that decision was a part. As has elsewhere been observed, the traditional interest of the United States in the Pacific and our determination

[14] Committee record, p. 5687.
[15] Committee record, pp. 6661, 6662.
[16] Navy Court of Inquiry record, p. 367.
[17] See section, infra, "Defensive Facilities Available in Hawaii."
[18] See testimony of Secretary Hull, committee record, pp. 1203–1205, 1452, 1464, 1603, 1608; testimony of Mr. Grew, committee record, pp. 1570, 1738, 1919, 1969.
In a letter of April 3, 1941, to the commanders in chief, Pacific Fleet, Asiatic Fleet, and Atlantic Fleet, Admiral Stark expressed the feeling that beyond question the presence of the Pacific Fleet in Hawaii had a stabilizing effect in the Far East. See committee exhibit No. 106.
[19] See "Foreign Relations," vol. II, p. 69.
[20] Committee record, p. 1603.

to aid the valiant Chinese fighting under insuperable odds the Juggernaut of Japanese aggression made imperative our taking every reasonable step which would assist in deterring the insatiable Japanese ambition for conquest and at the same time bolster flagging Chinese morale. Basing of the fleet at Pearl Harbor was but one of the steps taken in this direction.[21]

The fact that it had been decided to make Hawaii the base of the fleet did not require that all of the battleships and other substantial fleet units should be *in* Pearl Harbor on the morning of December 7 after the responsible commander had been warned of war and ordered to execute an appropriate defensive deployment.[22] The very words *defensive deployment* could have meant nothing if not that the fleet should be moved and stationed in such manner as to afford maximum defensive security not only to the fleet itself but to the Hawaiian Islands, the west coast, and the Panama Canal as well. This order required the deploying of vessels in the Hawaiian waters, which afforded the commander in chief a vast scope of operations, and it was left to his judgment and discretion as to what specific action was required consistent with his responsibilities. It has certainly never been suggested that because a particular harbor has been designated as the base for a fleet its vessels are thereby restricted to that harbor, particularly after an order has been issued for their deployment.

It remains a debatable question as to whether the Pacific Fleet was exposed to any greater danger by reason of the fact that it was based at Hawaii. The 360° perimeter of the islands afforded unlimited avenues for operations and the maximum channels for escape in the event of attack by a hostile superior force. The west coast, on the other hand, afforded only a 180° scope of operation with no avenues for escape from a superior attacking force and left only the alternative of proceeding into the teeth of such a force. Nor does it appear that the fleet was exposed to any greater danger from the standpoint of espionage by reason of its being at Hawaii.[23] The evidence before this Committee reflects that Tokyo was receiving as much information, if not more information, from its diplomatic establishments which operated outside the restraining counterespionage efforts of our own Government, located in Panama, on the west coast, and in Manila as from the Honolulu consulate.[24] There is a strong possibility that Japan would have taken the Hawaiian Islands by amphibious operations as she did in the case of so many other outlying Pacific Islands had the fleet not been based at Pearl Harbor.[25] Fur-

[21] See Part I, supra, "Diplomatic Background of the Pearl Harbor Attack."
[22] In the course of counsel's examination, Admiral Turner was asked: "During this time after around November 27 to December 7, in all your discussions around the Navy with those in authority was any consideration given to the question of whether the fleet should be moved out of Pearl Harbor and sent to sea?"
   Admiral TURNER. "No; there was not that I recall. I assumed that most or all of it would be at sea."
   Question. "Well, why did you assume that?"
   Admiral TURNER. "Well, that was the place for them under Admiral Kimmel's operating plan for their deployment." Committee record, pp 5224, 5225.
   The evidence reflects that the Office of Naval Operations in Washington did not know the exact location of the various units of the Pacific Fleet. See committee record, p 13956.
[23] See section "The Role of Espionage in the Attack," Part III, this report.
[24] In referring to Japanese espionage activity, Admiral Stark said: "We had felt that *not only in Hawaii* but at practically all our given posts the Japs knew everything we were doing." Committee record, p 5707.
[25] In the course of his testimony before the committee, General Short was asked whether he believed, assuming that the fleet had been withdrawn to the west coast and conditions at Pearl Harbor were otherwise the same, the Japanese could have made a landing with the striking air forces that they had and brought the planes down as they did. He replied: "It would have been thoroughly possible. If they had sent as large a force as they sent against the Philippines they could have made the landing." Committee record, pp. 8293, 8294.

thermore, had the fleet been based on the west coast a raid on our west coast cities and the Panama Canal could not have been entirely repulsed. For it is agreed as a military proposition that even with the most effective resistance to an enemy air attack some units will inevitably get through the screen of defense and carry home the attack.

In this connection, the opinion has been expressed by several naval witnesses that it was their belief Japan would attack our Pacific Fleet *wherever it might be* at the very outset of hostilities with a view to immobilizing it, temporarily at least, as a restraining and deterring influence on Japanese sea-borne operations in Pacific Far Eastern waters.[26] Under this view, which has the weight of logic and the experience of December 7, the fact the fleet was based at Hawaii bore no conclusive relationship to nor conditioned the Japanese decision to attack our Pacific Fleet.

As has been indicated, the basing of the fleet at Hawaii is inseparable from the global plan of operations in which the Pacific Fleet was to perform only one phase. It was an integral part of our policy and action in the Atlantic and can only be questioned save as one presumes to challenge the policies of the United States Government from 1937 to 1941 and our determination to aid the impoverished free peoples of the world striving in desperation to stem the overpowering tide of Axis aggression and world conquest.

Defensive Facilities Available in Hawaii

There can be no question that Hawaii was regarded as the best equipped of our outposts and possessed the greatest potential for its own defense.[27] In this connection General Marshall testified:[28]

I will say as to the attack on Pearl Harbor, we felt that was a vital installation, but *we also felt that that was the only installation we had anywhere that was reasonably well equipped. Therefore, we were not worried about it. In our opinion, the commanders had been alerted. In our opinion, there was nothing more we could give them at the time for the purpose of defense. In our opinion, that was one place that had enough within itself to put up a reasonable defense.*

MacArthur, in the Philippines, was just beginning to get something. His position was pitiable, and it was still in a state of complete flux, with the ships on the ocean en route out there and the planes half delivered and half still to go.

The Panama Canal was quite inadequate at that period, seriously inadequate in planes, and, of course, of vast importance to anything in the Pacific.

The only place we had any assurance about was Hawaii, and for that reason we had less concern about Hawaii because we had worked on it very industriously, we had a tremendous amount of correspondence about it, and we felt reasonably secure at that one point.

Therefore we felt that it would be a great hazard for the Japanese to attack it.

The correspondence between the Chief of Staff and General Short during 1941,[29] as well as that between the Chief of Naval Operations and Admiral Kimmel,[30] manifest clearly the mutual desire to improve

[26] See section, supra, Part III, "The Role of Espionage in the Attack."

[27] In the course of committee examination Admiral Turner was asked: "Did you consider the fleet in Hawaii prepared for that attack at the time it did come?"
Admiral Turner. "Yes, sir, within the limits of the material improvements program, I felt that the fleet was efficient and was ready for war."
Question. "You felt confident that the Pacific Fleet based at Pearl Harbor was ready for war on December 7, 1941?"
Admiral Turner. "Yes, sir, and further that the district was ready for war within the limits of the material that we had been able to provide. *We all had the utmost confidence in the command of the fleet and the command ashore.*" Committee record, pp. 5253, 5254.

[28] Committee record, pp. 13792, 13793.

[29] See committee exhibit No. 53.

[30] Id., No. 106.

to the utmost the defensive facilities available to the Hawaiian commanders. But both General Marshall and Admiral Stark, in addition to their interest in Hawaii, had the enormous task and responsibility of allocating to many places, consistent with an ever-expanding global conflict, the military and naval equipment that was produced during the year 1941.[31] They had the obligation to spread the results of our productive efforts in those quarters where the needs and exigencies appeared in their best judgment to be most pressing. Our defensive facilities on the mainland were in great need of improvement; Panama and the Philippines were in woeful need of additional equipment; the Nation had committed itself to aiding the Chinese who had been fighting Japanese aggression for 4 years with little more than sheer courage and the will to exist as a nation; we were determined that supplies being shipped under lend-lease should not be destroyed by German and Italian raiders before they reached their destination, necessitating thereby the building up of our naval power in the Atlantic; we were determined to aid Britain and Russia to the extent of our capacity for our own self-protection before the overpowering might of the German war machine had destroyed the last vestige of resistance on the continent of Europe and we were left alone to stem the Axis thrust for world conquest—all of these considerations were a part of the problem posed for the Chief of Staff and the Chief of Naval Operations in making allocations of the matériel at hand. It should be noted that most of the lend-lease transfers effected prior to December 7, 1941, were in a category in which, by the terms of the Lend-Lease Act, it was provided that transfers to foreign governments could be made only after consultation with the Chief of Staff of the Army or the Chief of Naval Operations of the Navy. The Chief of Staff or the Chief of Naval Operations personally approved these transfers.[32]

The only justifiable allegation concerning the shortage of equipment at Hawaii relating to the failure to detect the Japanese task force was the fact that insufficient long-range patrol planes were available to conduct a 360° distant search from Oahu. As has been seen, however, adequate patrol planes were on hand to cover the vital and more dangerous sectors.[33] Referring to the lack of long-range planes, it is in order to determine the extent to which such planes were available and conceivably might have been sent to Hawaii.

In the case of 210 B-17's and B-24's, Army heavy bombers adaptable for distant reconnaissance, delivered between February 1 and November 30, 1941, none were shipped under lend-lease and a total

---

[31] In a letter of November 7, 1941, Admiral Stark pointed out to Admiral Kimmel the difficulties experienced through shortage of material needs: "I note the great desirability of *many* things for the Pacific Fleet—particularly destroyers and cruisers. We *just* haven't *any* destroyers or cruisers to give you at the moment, nor is the prospect bright for getting any for you in the near future. I fully appreciate your need for them. We could profitably employ twice the number we now have if they were available. I will not burden you with a recital of King's troubles but he is up against it for DDs for escort—and defense against raiders." (Admiral King at the time was commander in chief of the Atlantic Fleet.) Committee record, p. 5575.

[32] See letter from Chester T. Lane, Deputy Commissioner, Office of Foreign Liquidation Commissioner, Department of State, concerning the organization of Lend-Lease. Committee record, p. 14095 et seq.

[33] See Part III, supra.

of 113 were sold for cash to foreign countries; 12 B–17's were shipped to Hawaii and 35 to the Philippines.[34]

With respect to Navy planes, there were no lend-lease transfers of long-range patrol bombers or scout bombers during the same period. Of a total of 835 Navy planes of all types delivered during this period, February 1 to November 30, 582 were delivered to the Navy and 253 to foreign countries (Britain, Canada, Australia, the Netherlands, and Norway) under cash transactions. Of the 582 planes delivered to the Navy, 218 were sent to the Hawaiian area, 146 of the planes being assigned to carriers.[35]

It appears that of 3,128 Army and Navy planes of various types delivered between February 1 and November 30, 1941, only 177 were shipped under lend-lease to foreign countries and none of these were capable of performing distant reconnaissance. The record is clear, therefore, that the Chief of Staff and the Chief of Naval Operations did not prejudice our own defenses in approving excessive allocations to foreign governments. A brief review of the improvement effected in the Hawaiian situation during the year 1941 will serve to demonstrate the manner in which the exigencies and problems prevailing in the Pacific were recognized.

The total number of Army planes in the Hawaiian Department was virtually doubled between January 31 and December 7, 1941, having been increased from 124 to 227 planes. The number of B–17 four-motored bombers was increased from none on January 31 to 21 as of May 31, 1941, this number subsequently being reduced to 12 by reason of the transfer of 9 B–17's to the Philippines in September. As of September 1, 1941, the United States possessed 109 B–17's

[34] See enclosure to War Department memorandum to committee counsel dated March 20, 1946, committee exhibit No. 172. In response to a request of the general counsel of the Committee, the War Department on March 20, 1946, transmitted a tabulation supplied by the Army Air Forces reflecting, among other things, the total deliveries and types of American-produced planes delivered between February 1 and November 30, 1941, without any break-down as to months. This tabulation reflects a total of 579 planes delivered having a maximum range *without bombs* in excess of 1,600 miles. In addition to this figure, the tabulation shows 836 planes delivered having ranges of 2,000 and 1,120 miles with no break-down indicating how many planes were produced in a particular range category. The tabulation of plane deliveries was not introduced as an exhibit by the general counsel until May 23, 1946. General Marshall appeared before the committee for the second time on April 9, 1946, but he was asked no questions concerning the dispositions of these planes, it being noted that General Marshall had earlier testified that Hawaii had received priority consideration in the disposition of equipment. Although the tabulation delivered by the War Department on March 20 was available to the Committee counsel it was not available to the members of the committee for consideration and examination at the time General Marshall appeared on April 9.

The committee has thus been placed in the position of not having inquired concerning the adaptability, design, and potentialities of these planes with ranges exceeding 1,600 miles; of not having determined where they may otherwise have been disposed and the exigencies requiring such dispositions; of not having determined whether there were crews available to man these planes; of not having determined whether ferrying facilities were available had they been directed to Hawaii; of not having determined exactly when the planes were delivered to determine whether they could have been sent to Hawaii before December 7, 1941; and of not having determined whether they would satisfy the distant reconnaissance requirements in Hawaii, among other things.

In the latter connection, however, it is to be noted that General Martin, commanding general of the Hawaiian Air Forces, under date of August 20, 1941, recommended the War Department give consideration to the allotment of "B–17D type airplanes or *other four-engine* bombers with equal or better performance and operating range" for reconnaissance purposes, committee exhibit No. 13. It would appear that in the making of aircraft dispositions the indicated needs of the Hawaiian Department would be a controlling consideration.

It appears from the evidence before the committee that only 210 of the Army-type planes delivered between February 1 and November 30, 1941, were four-engine bombers of a type adaptable to the type of long distance reconnaissance required by the plans and requirements of the Hawaiian commanders. It is to be noted that a tabulation of factory deliveries of bombers to foreign countries appearing on page 12991 of the Committee record is superseded by Committee exhibit No. 172.

[35] See enclosure to Navy Department memorandum to committee counsel dated April 12, 1946, committee exhibit No. 172.

disposed: 21 in Hawaii, 7 in Panama, and 81 in the continental United States.[36]   The number of P–40 pursuit planes was increased from none in January to 99 as of November 30; and the number of P–36's from 19 to 39.[37]

In the case of the Navy at Hawaii, during January of 1941 a squadron of 12 PBY–3's left the west coast for the Hawaiian area. In April a second squadron equipped with 12 PBY–3's also moved to Hawaii. In October and November of 1941, 3 squadrons of 12 planes each and 1 squadron of 6 planes, then in the Hawaiian area, returned to the west coast and exchanged their PBY–3's for PBY–5's after which they returned to Hawaii. During this same period the third squadron of Patrol Wing 1, equipped with 12 new PBY–5's left the west coast for Hawaii. This represents an over-all increase of 36 in the number of patrol planes between January 1 and November 30, 1941.[38] During the period February 1 to November 30, 1941, 146 planes were assigned to carriers in the Pacific; and on May 13, 1941, 18 planes arrived at Ewa Field, Hawaii, being assigned to a marine scout bomber squadron.[39]

The Committee did not inquire into the matter of allocations, generally, of Army and Navy planes or other equipment to points other than to Hawaii. There is no evidence before us that General Marshall and Admiral Stark made dispositions of the matériel available [40] inconsistent with their best judgment in the light of the situation as it could be viewed in the days before Pearl Harbor.[41]

The question of whether Japan would have struck Hawaii had additional equipment been available there must be considered in light of the fact that in their estimates made in the fall of 1941, the Japanese placed the number of aircraft in Hawaii at roughly twice that of the actual air strength. Further, during the war games carried on at the Naval War College, Tokyo, from September 2 to 13, 1941, it was assumed that the Pearl Harbor striking force would suffer the loss of one-third of its participating units.[41a] It was specifically assumed that one *Akagi*-class carrier and one *Soryu*-class carrier would be lost.

It is clear that immediately after December 7 every effort was made to increase the matériel facilities in Hawaii as much as possible,

---

[36] Memorandum from War Department dated December 13, 1945. See committee record p. 14595.
A study contemplating 360° long-distance reconnaissance and attacks, submitted by the commander of the Army Air Forces in Hawaii on August 20, 1941, and endorsed by the Army commander, called for 180 Army 4-engine bombers, the B–17's. Committee exhibit No. 13. As of December 7, there were only 148 B–17's in the entire Army: 35 of these were in the Philippines, 12 at Hawaii, 8 in the Caribbean area, 6 at Atlantic bases, and 87 in the continental United States. Committee record, pp. 2865, 2866.
[37] Army aircraft in Hawaiian Department as reflected by AAF monthly inventories. See also committee exhibit No. 5.
[38] See enclosure to Navy memorandum for committee counsel dated April 12, 1946. Committee exhibit No. 172.
[39] Id.
[40] As expressed by Mr. Stimson: "During those days in November 1941 we at the War Department had been informed and believed that Hawaii had been more generously equipped from the Nation's inadequate supplies of men and munitions than either of the other three important Pacific outposts, and we believed that with the fleet at hand there it was more capable of defense." Statement of Mr. Stimson to the committee. Committee record, p. 14,407.
[41] Admiral Stark testified that he gave to Admiral Kimmel all that he could of what he had. Committee record, pp. 5701–5704.
He said: "We were not able to give the Commander in Chief, Pacific Fleet, all the ships and men he wanted but neither were we able to put in the Atlantic or in the Asiatic Fleet the strength we knew they wanted." Committee record, p. 5575.
On November 25, Admiral Stark wrote Admiral Kimmel, in part: "We have sweat blood in the endeavor to divide adequately our forces for a two-ocean war; but you cannot take inadequate forces and divide them into two or three parts and get adequate forces anywhere. It was for this reason that almost as soon as I got here I started working on increasing the Navy." Committee record, p. 5578.
[41a] See War Department memorandum dated May 21, 1946, transmitting a letter of the same date from Commander Walter Wilds, Office of the Chairman of the United States Strategic Bombing Survey, Committee record, p. 14626. See further, committee record, p. 457.

necessarily at the expense of sacrificing the needs of other installations. The evidence reflects, however, that it was a very considerable period of time after the attack before the Nation's production of war materials was sufficient to approach satisfaction of all the Hawaiian requirements.

Both Admiral Kimmel and General Short had repeatedly requested more equipment, and that their needs and requests were not ignored [42] is made clear by the improved situation effected during 1941.[43] The same requests made by the Hawaiian commanders were coming from many other commanders and many other quarters. As virtually all witnesses have testified, alert commanders are always striving to improve and increase their equipment, facilities, and personnel; and it is doutful if at any time even during the war any commander ever had all he wanted or thought he needed.[44]

It is necessarily speculative as to how additional equipment in Hawaii might have altered the situation on December 7 inasmuch as the facilities which were available were not brought into the fight.[45]

Transfer of Pacific Fleet Units to the Atlantic

In May of 1941 three battleships, one aircraft carrier, four cruisers, and nine destroyers were detached from the Pacific Fleet and transferred to the Atlantic. This shift was contemplated by the Navy basic war plan, WPL–46.[46] In a letter to Admiral Stark dated September 12, 1941, Admiral Kimmel expressed concern regarding possible further transfers from the Pacific to the Atlantic:[47]

The emphasis, in the President's speech, on the Atlantic also brings up the question of a possible further weakening of this Fleet. A strong Pacific Fleet is unquestionably a deterrent to Japan—a weaker one may be an invitation. I cannot escape the conclusion that the maintenance of the status quo out here is almost entirely a matter of the strength of this Fleet. It must not be réduced, and, in event of hostilities, must be increased if we are to undertake a bold offensive.[48]

---

[42] In an aiae memoir concerning "Defense of Hawaii" submitted by the War Department to the President in May of 1941, the following observations were made:

"*The Island of Oahu*, due to its fortification, its garrison, and its physical characteristics, is believed to be the strongest fortress in the world.

"To reduce Oahu the enemy must transport overseas an expeditionary force capable of executing a forced landing against a garrison of approximately 35,000 men, manning 127 fixed coast defense guns, 211 anti-aircraft weapons, and more than 3,000 artillery pieces and automatic weapons available for beach defense. Without air superiority this is an impossible task.

"*Air Defense.* With adequate air defense, enemy carriers, naval escorts and transports will begin to come under air attack at a distance of approximately 750 miles. This attack will increase in intensity until when within 200 miles of the objective the enemy forces will be subject to attack by all types of bombardment closely supported by our most modern pursuit.

"Hawaiian Air Defense. Including the movement of aviation now in progress Hawaii will be defended by 35 of our most modern flying fortresses, 35 medium range bombers, 13 light bombers, 150 pursuit of which 105 are of our most modern type. In addition Hawaii is capable of reinforcement by heavy bombers from the mainland by air. With this force available a major attack against Oahu is considered impracticable.

"In point of sequence, sabotage is first to be expected and may, within a very limited time, cause great damage. On this account, it would be highly desirable to set up a military control of the islands prior to the likelihood of our involvement in the Far East." Committee exhibit No. 59.

[43] As pointed out by Admiral Stark, "During 1940 and 1941, many of the shortcomings of Pearl Harbor as a base, disclosed by the long stay of the Pacific Fleet, were remedied." Committee record, p. 5587. See in this connection the Annual Report of the Commander in Chief, United States Pacific Fleet, for the year ending June 30, 1941. Committee record, pp. 5587–5589.

[44] See testimony of Admiral Turner, committee record, p. 5254, concerning the insatiable desire of field commanders for matériel. He said: " * * * you never have enough, you always want more and you want things to be better."

[45] Admiral Turner testified he believed that the Pacific Fleet at Hawaii was sufficient on December 7, 1941, to have defeated or greatly reduced the effect of the Japanese raid on Hawaii if it had been fully alerted. Committee record, pp. 5258, 5259.

[46] See statement of Admiral Stark, committee record, p. 5591.

[47] Committee exhibit No. 106. See testimony of Admiral Stark, committee record, p. 5591.

[48] Admiral Kimmel commented in his prepared statement to the committee: "When I was in Washington in June 1941, it was seriously proposed to transfer from the Pacific to the Atlantic an additional detachment to consist of three battleships, four cruisers, two squadrons of destroyers, and a carrier. I opposed this strenuously. The transfer was not made." Committee record, p. 6680.

Replying on September 23, Admiral Stark wrote the commander in chief of the Pacific Fleet:[49]

We have no intention of further reducing the Pacific Fleet except that prescribed in Rainbow 5, that is the withdrawal of four cruisers about one month after Japan and the United States are at war. The existing force in the Pacific is all that can be spared for the tasks assigned your fleet, and new construction will not make itself felt until next year.

The transfer of the Pacific Fleet units in May of 1941, it would appear, had as its immediate objective the possibility of their engaging in an expedition to take the Azores,[50] in order that these vital Portuguese possessions might not fall into German hands. The occasion for taking the Azores, however, did not materialize and, as stated by Admiral Stark, "it just went on diplomatically there".[51] The fleet units, formerly attached to the Pacific Fleet, were not returned to Pearl Harbor but were employed further to augment the Atlantic Fleet, particularly in the vicinity of Iceland.

The record reflects that the transfer of a portion of the Pacific Fleet to the Atlantic in May of 1941 was in line with the basic war plans which recognized the Atlantic as the principal theater of operations and was designed to forestall the possibility of an indispensable strategic area falling into German hands. The transfer was an inextricable part of the over-all military policies prepared to meet the Axis threat.[52]

"ABCD" UNDERSTANDING?

A great deal of inquiry was made during the course of proceedings to determine whether the Government of the United States had entered into an agreement with Great Britain and the Netherlands committing this Nation to war upon Japan in the event British or Dutch possessions were attacked by the Japanese.[52a] It is clear from evidence before the Committee that no agreement was entered into in this regard. The President and his Cabinet, while momentarily expecting an attack by Japan, recognized and observed the constitutional mandate that this Government could only be committed to war by a declaration of the Congress.

Recognizing the inevitable consequences of the Tripartite Pact, representatives of the War and Navy Departments participated during 1941 in a series of staff conversations with military and naval experts

---

[49] Committee exhibit No. 106.

[50] In a letter to Admiral Kimmel of May 24, 1941, Admiral Stark stated, among other things, "Day before yesterday afternoon the President gave me an overall limit of 30 days to prepare and have ready an expedition of 25,000 men to sail for, and to take the Azores. Whether or not there would be opposition I do not know but we have to be fully prepared for strenuous opposition. You can visualize the job particularly when I tell you that the Azores recently have been greatly reinforced. The Army, of course, will be in on this but the Navy and the Marines will bear the brunt." Committee record, pp. 5607, 5608.

[51] Committee record, pp. 13977, 13978.
In the course of committee examination, Admiral Stark was asked: "How would you attack and take the Azores without a declaration of war on Portugal? She owned them."
He replied: "I can tell you one way. Suppose the Germans had taken Portugal. Would we have to declare war on Portugal to take the Azores? I don't think we would have.* * * I always construed that situation, with regard to the Azores, as to have plans ready, and be ready if an emergency arose there." Committee record, p. 13979.

[52] See Part I, pp. 10–13, supra, this report. It does not appear from the evidence that additional Fleet units would have assisted in detecting the approaching Japanese striking force, in view of the dispositions made by the commander in chief of the Pacific Fleet, or otherwise have materially aided in the defense against an air attack. As previously suggested, had the major Fleet units transferred to the Atlantic in May of 1941 been in Pearl Harbor on December 7 they, too, would in all probability have been destroyed. See in the latter connection, Part II, pp. 69–72, this report.

[52a] This inquiry appears to have been largely precipitated by a remark attributed to Prime Minister Churchill during an address before the House of Commons on January 27, 1942. He is quoted as having stated: "On the other hand, the probability, since the Atlantic Conference at which I discussed these matters with President Roosevelt, that the United States, even if not herself attacked, would come into the war in the Far East and thus make the final victory sure, seems to allay some of these anxieties, and that expectations had not been falsified by the events." See Committee record, p. 1286.

of Great Britain, Canada, and the Netherlands.[53]   The first of these meetings, initiated by the Chief of Naval Operations [54] and limited to American and British representatives, was held in Washington from January 29 to March 27, 1941.   The official report of the conversations, referred to as "ABC-1," points out specifically that the discussions were held with a view "to determine the best methods by which the armed forces of the United States and British Commonwealth, with its present allies, could defeat Germany and the powers allied with her, *should the United States be compelled to resort to war.*" [55] The report states clearly that the plans to accomplish this purpose, as embodied in the report, were subject to confirmation by the highest military authorities in the United States and Great Britain and by the governments of both countries as well.[56]   This was in accord with the joint statement of the position the American representatives would take, made by the Chief of Naval Operations and the Chief of Staff on January 27 at the outset of the conversations.[57]

"ABC-1" was approved by the Chief of Naval Operations and the Secretary of the Navy and by the Chief of Staff and the Secretary of War,[58] thereafter being submitted to the President on June 2, 1941. On June 7 the President returned "ABC-1" without formal approval, pointing out that since the plan had not been finally approved by the British Government, he would not approve it at that time but that in case of war the report should be returned to him for approval.[59]

Shortly after the staff conversations in Washington military and naval representatives of the United States, Great Britain, and the Netherlands conferred in April of 1941 at Singapore in order to draft a plan for the conduct of operations in the Far East based on "ABC-1."   In the instructions sent the commander in chief of our Asiatic Fleet [60] prior to the Singapore conversations it was emphatically pointed out that the results of such conversations were likewise subject to ratification by the governments concerned and were to involve no political commitment by the United States.[61] The report of the conversations,[62] referred to as "ADB", explicitly recognized that no political commitments were implied.[63]   Nevertheless, the Chief of Naval Operations and the Chief of Staff withheld their approval feeling that

[53] Admiral Stark said: "In our planning, we assumed that if the United States was drawn into war, it would be alined with Great Britain and against the Axis Powers. We also knew that while our most immediate concern was with the war then in progress in the Atlantic and in Europe, we might also be faced—perhaps concurrently—with a war in the Pacific. With these thoughts in mind, we held extensive staff conversations with the British and Canadians early in 1941 and the report of these conversations was embodied in a document known as ABC-1, dated March 27,.1941." Committee record, p. 5572.

[54] Admiral Stark was asked: "* * * it was in 1940, the fall of 1940 that you communicated with Admiral Sir Dudley Pound of the British Navy, requesting that he send his naval experts to the United States to discuss collaboration between the two navies?"
Admiral STARK: "That is correct, in case of war."
Question: "Upon whose responsibility was that message sent?"
Admiral STARK: "My own."
Question: "Did you discuss the subject with the President?"
Admiral STARK: "I sent that on my own, and I did not notify the President until after I had done it."
Committee record, p. 13927.

[55] See committee exhibit No. 49 for a full report of the staff conversations.
[56] Committee exhibit No. 49.
[57] Id.
[58] See committee record, p. 2617.
[59] Id., at pp. 2619, 2620.
[60] Id., at p. 6320.
[61] Id., at p. 5123.
[62] For the report of the Singapore conversations, see committee exhibit No. 50.
[63] In testifying concerning the Singapore conversations, Admiral Turner said: "In none of these papers was there ever a political commitment, or a definite military commitment.   This was a plan of action, or these were plans of action based on assumptions that should the United States enter the war, then these papers would be effective, provided they were approved by the proper authorities.
"None of the ADB papers were ever presented to either the Secretary of the Navy or the Secretary of War or the President, although all of those officers as well as the Secretary of State were aware that these conversations were being held from time to time." Committee record, p. 5122.

some of the statements in the report had political implications.[64] One of the proposals of the Singapore conference, however, was subsequently incorporated *as a recommendation* in the joint memoranda of November 5 and 27 which the Chief of Staff and the Chief of Naval Operations submitted to the President; i. e., that military counteraction should be undertaken in the event Japan attacked or directly threatened the territory or mandated territory of the United States, the British Commonwealth, or the Netherlands East Indies, or if the Japanese moved forces into Thailand west of 100° east or south of 10° north, Portuguese Timor, New Caledonia, or the Loyalty Islands.[65]

As elsewhere pointed out, it was mutually understood at the Atlantic Conference in August of 1941 by President Roosevelt and Prime Minister Churchill that the Governments of both the United States and Great Britain needed more time to prepare for resistance against possible Japanese attack in the Far East.[66]   It was agreed, however, that steps should be taken to make clear to Japan that further aggressive action by her against neighboring countries would result in each country being compelled to take all necessary measures to safeguard the legitimate rights of its country and nationals and to insure its country's safety and security.[67]   Accordingly, upon returning to Washington the President on August 17, 1941 informed the Japanese Ambassador that if the Japanese Government took any further steps in line with a program of military domination by force or threat of force of neighboring countries, the Government of the United States would be compelled to take any and all steps necessary toward safeguarding its legitimate rights and interests and toward insuring the security of the United States.[68]

During the latter half of 1941 negotiations to meet the American objections to the "ADB" report proceeded slowly until discussions were opened in the Far East in November between Admiral Hart, commander in chief of our Asiatic Fleet, and Admiral Phillips, the British Far Eastern naval commander.   Soon after the out-break of war, the two commanders completed arrangements for initial American and British naval dispositions to meet probable Japanese action in the Far East.   Admiral Hart's report of his conversations with Admiral Phillips was received in the Navy Department about 11 p. m., December 6, 1941, and was approved in a dispatch sent out by the Chief of Naval Operations on December 7 after the attack on Pearl Harbor.[69]

On December 6, 1941, Admiral Hart cabled the Chief of Naval Operations concerning a report received from Singapore that the United States had "assured British armed support under three or four eventualities".[70]   None of the witnesses who were questioned on this

[64] See committee exhibit No. 65.   Also testimony of Admiral Turner, committee record, pp. 5118, 5119.
[65] See section, infra, Avoidance of War.
[66] See Part I, this report.
[67] Id.
[68] Id.
[69] See testimony of Admiral Stark before the joint committee.
[70] Admiral Hart's dispatch was based on a communication which he had received on December 6, 1941, from Capt. John M. Creighton, who was a naval attaché in Singapore, as follows: "Brooke Popham received Saturday from War Department London Quote We have now received assurance of American armed support in cases as follows: Afirm we are obliged execute our plans to forestall Japs landing Isthmus of Kra or take action in reply to Nips invasion any other part of Siam; Baker if Dutch Indies are attacked and we go to their defense; Cast if Japs attack us the British.   Therefore without reference to London put plan in action if first you have good info Jap expedition advancing with the apparent intention of landing in Kra, second if the Nips violate any part of Thailand Para if NEI are attacked put into operation plans agreed upon between British and Dutch.   Unquote." Committee record, pp. 13520, 13521.
In the course of his testimony before the committee Captain Creighton stated he had no knowledge of an agreement between the United States and Great Britain or the Dutch and that the report transmitted to Admiral Hart must have come to him second-hand.   Committee record, pp. 13515-13537.

point, including Admiral Hart,[71] was aware of any evidence to substantiate the report. In his testimony, the Chief of Naval Operations suggested that the report may have been based on a misconception as to the state of negotiations following the Singapore conference.[72] There is no evidence to indicate that Japanese knowledge of the "ABC" and "ADB" conversations was an inducing factor to Japan's decision to attack the United States coincident with her thrust to the south. Indeed, the idea of attacking us at Pearl Harbor was conceived before these conversations were initiated.[73] Manifestly any estimate which the Japanese made of American probable action was based on this country's long-standing Far Eastern policy and the course of diplomatic negotiations, and not on nonpolitical, technical discussions on a staff level.[74]

It should be noted that on November 7 the President took an informal vote of his Cabinet as to whether it was thought the American people would support a strike against Japan in the event she should attack England in Malaya or the Dutch in the East Indies. The Cabinet was unanimous in the feeling that the country would support such a move. The following significant statement appears in the diary of Secretary Stimson for December 2:

> The President is still deliberating the possibility of a message to the Emperor, although all the rest of us are rather against it, but in addition to that he is quite settled, I think, that he will make a Message to the Congress and will perhaps back that up with a speech to the country.[75]

From all of the evidence, as earlier indicated, there is no basis for the conclusion that an agreement had been effected committing the United States to war against Japan in the event of an attack by her upon the British or the Dutch. It is indisputable that the President and his Cabinet contemplated presenting the problem to the Congress should our position in the Far East become intolerable.[76] Further, the reports of the 1941 staff conversations contain clear disclaimers of any political commitments and the voluminous records relating to these conversations will be searched in vain for any suggestion that an agreement binding the United States to go to war was made. Additionally, all the witnesses who were questioned on the point [77]—including the ranking military and naval leaders of the country at the time—testified that *in these meetings the constitutional prerogative of the Congress to declare war was scrupulously re-*

[71] Committee record, pp. 12785–12875.

[72] Id., at p. 6317.

[73] See Part II. this report re Japanese plans for the attack.

[74] Before the committee, General Marshall was asked: "Let us assume first that they (the Japanese) knew that we were going to go to war if they attacked Malaya or any portion of that land there. Let us assume on the other hand that they knew we were not going to participate unless we were directly attacked ourselves. To what extent would their decisions as to action be affected by that knowledge?"
He replied: "Japanese psychology being what it is and the Japanese Army domination being what it was their general scheme for the assumption of power throughout the Far East, particularly the Southwest Pacific, being known now, I don't think that would have had any particular effect one way or the other." Committee record, p. 13786.

[75] See statement of Mr. Stimson. Committee record, p. 14427.

[76] Admiral Stark said: "Under our Constitution the Congress had to declare war, and we could not take any independent action, so far as hostilities were concerned." Committee record, p. 13875.
Again, " * * * as to our striking after declaration of war on our part, if the situation became intolerable to us, and our national safety, if the Japs had not struck and we thought then that our safety was imperiled, if we did not fight, I think it would have been done in a constitutional manner." Committee record, pp. 13892–13893.
Further, " * * * I do again make the statement, and I want it clear on the record, so far as my thoughts were concerned, that if Japan had not attacked and if conditions had become intolerable to our national safety because of what she was doing, and that would have been through the Congress." Committee record, p. 13895.

[77] See testimony of Secretary Hull, Sumner Welles, General Marshall, Admiral Stark, Admiral Turner, Admiral Ingersoll, General Gerow before the committee.

spected.[78] The preliminary planning done at these conferences manifested commendable foresight and indeed our military leaders would have been inexcusably negligent had they not participated in these conversations in the face of the clear pattern of conquest mapped out by the Axis.[79] This planning saved precious time and lives once Japan struck.

While no binding agreement existed, it would appear from the record that the Japanese were inclined to the belief that the United States, Britain and the Netherlands would act in concert. An intercepted November 30 dispatch from Tokyo to Berlin stated in pertinent part: [80]

* * * it is clear that the United States is now in collusion with those nations (England, Australia, the Netherlands, and China) and has decided to regard Japan, along with Germany and Italy, as an enemy.

A message of December 3 which was intercepted from the Washington Embassy to Tokyo related:[81]

Judging from all indications, we feel that some joint military action between Great Britain and the United States, with or without a declaration of war is a definite certainty, in the event of an occupation of Thailand.

There is nothing, however, in the foregoing intelligence having any relationship to the Hawaiian situation;—to have advised the commanders there that the Japanese regarded an attack upon the British or Dutch as tantamount to an attack upon the United States would have added nothing—they had already been categorically warned that hostile action by Japan against the United States itself was possible at any moment.

Avoidance of War

As has been seen in considering the diplomatic background of the Pearl Harbor attack, every effort was made compatible with national honor to forestall the inevitable conflict with Japan. The policy of the United States *condemned aggression;* the policy of Japan was *predicated on aggression.* It was only a question of time, therefore, before these two irreconcilable principles would engender war.[82] Officials of our Government were faced with the problem of effecting a delicate balance between gaining time to improve our military preparedness on the one hand and not forsaking our principles, national honor, and Allies on the other.

[78] That the certain prerogative of the Congress to declare war was recognized in discussions with other governments is revealed by the following dispatch from Ambassador Winant to the State Department dated November 30, 1941, transmitting a message from Prime Minister Churchill to President Roosevelt:
"It seems to me that one important method remains unused in averting war between Japan and our two countries, namely a plain declaration, secret or public as may be thought best, that any further act of aggression by Japan will lead immediately to the gravest consequences. *I realize your constitutional difficulties* but it would be tragic if Japan drifted into war by encroachment without having before her fairly and squarely the dire character of a further aggressive step. I beg you to consider whether, at the moment which you judge right which may be very near, you should not *say that 'any further Japanese aggression would compel you to place the gravest issues before Congress'* or words to that effect. We would, of course, make a similar declaration or share in a joint declaration, and in any case arrangements are being made to synchronize our action with yours. Forgive me, my dear friend, for presuming to press such a course upon you, but I am convinced that it might make all the difference and prevent a melancholy extension of the war." Committee exhibit No. 24. See also testimony of General Marshall, committee record, pp. 2785, 2786.
[79] In the course of counsel's examination, General Gerow was asked: " * * * has it been the practice of the War Plans Division from time immemorial to make all sorts of plans about war operations on the contingency that some day or other we might be involved in hostilities with other nations?"
He replied: "Oh, yes, sir. We had at all times kept current plans for operations against any major power or combination of major powers, sir * * * at one time I think we had plans against almost everybody, sir, and I think that is the practice of every general staff of every nation." Committee record, pp. 2673, 2674.
As stated by Admiral Stark, "It is our business to draw up plans for any contingency." Committee record, p. 13977.
[80] Committee exhibit No. 1 p. 205.
[81] Id., at p. 227. For a full treatment of the matter, however, indicating that no agreement whatever existed for military action on our part in the event of a Japanese invasion of Thailand, see committee exhibit No. 169.
[82] See Part I, *supra,* this report.

In summing up the salient features of the situation as they appeared to him in November of 1941, Mr. Stimson said:[83]

1. War with Germany and Japan would ultimately be inevitable.
2. It was vitally important that none of the nations who were then desperately fighting Germany—England, Russia, or China—should be knocked out of the war before the time came when we would be required to go in.
3. While we very much wanted more time in which to prepare, nevertheless we felt we had a fair chance to make an effective fight against Japan for the Philippines even if we had to enter the war at that time, in view of the air power that we were building up in the Philippines.
4. If war did come, it was important, both from the point of view of unified support of our own people as well as for the record of history, that we should not be placed in the position of firing the first shot, if this could be done without sacrificing our safety, but Japan should appear in her true role as the real aggressor.

It should be noted that in October of 1940 the President advised Admiral Richardson that if the Japanese attacked Thailand, or the Kra Peninsula, or the Dutch East Indies the United States would not enter the war—

that if they even attacked the Philippines he doubted whether we would enter the war, but that they (the Japanese) could not always avoid making mistakes and that as the war continued and the area of operations expanded sooner or later they would make a mistake and we would enter the war.[84]

On October 30, 1941, a message was received from Generalissimo Chiang Kai-shek indicating his belief that a Japanese attack on Kunming (Yunnan), located on the Burma Road, was imminent, and that military support from outside sources, particularly by the use of United States and British air units, was the sole hope for defeat of this threat.[85] The Secretary of State requested the advice of the Chief of Staff and the Chief of Naval Operations as to the attitude which this Government should assume toward a Japanese offensive against Kunming and the Burma Road. In a joint memorandum for the President dated November 5 they set forth the following conclusions and recommendations, after reviewing the situation in China:[86]

The Chief of Naval Operations and the Chief of Staff are in accord in the following conclusions:

(a) The basic military policies and strategy agreed to in the United States-British Staff conversations remain sound. The primary objective of the two nations is the defeat of Germany. If Japan be defeated and Germany remain undefeated, decision will still have not been reached. In any case, an unlimited offensive war should not be undertaken against Japan, since such a war would greatly weaken the combined effort in the Atlantic against Germany, the most dangerous enemy.

(b) War between the United States and Japan should be avoided while building up defensive forces in the Far East, until such time as Japan attacks or directly threatens territories whose security to the United States is of very great importance. Military action against Japan should be undertaken only in one or more of the following contingencies:

(1) *A direct act of war by Japanese armed forces against the territory or mandated territory of the United States, the British Commonwealth, or the Netherlands East Indies;*

(2) *The movement of Japanese forces into Thailand to the west of 100 degrees East or south of 10 degrees North; or into Portuguese Timor, New Caledonia, or the Loyalty Islands.*

(c) If war with Japan cannot be avoided, it should follow the strategic lines of existing war plans; i. e., military operations should be primarily defensive, with the object of holding territory, and weakening Japan's economic position.

---

[83] See statement of Mr. Stimson, committee record, p. 14385.
[84] Testimony of Admiral Richardson, committee record, pp. 683, 684.
[85] See committee exhibit No. 16A. Similar messages were received through the American ambassador in Chungking, the Magruder Mission and the United States naval attache. Exhibits Nos. 16, 16A.
[86] Committee exhibit No. 16.

(d) Considering world strategy, a Japanese advance against Kunming, into Thailand except as previously indicated, or an attack on Russia, would not justify intervention by the United States against Japan.

(e) All possible aid short of actual war against Japan should be extended to the Chinese Central Government.

(f) In case it is decided to undertake war against Japan, complete coordinated action in the diplomatic, economic, and military fields, should be undertaken in common by the United States, the British Commonwealth, and the Netherlands East Indies.

The Chief of Naval Operations and the Chief of Staff recommend that the United States policy in the Far East be based on the above conclusions.

Specifically, they recommend:

That the dispatch of United States armed forces for intervention against Japan in China be disapproved.

That material aid to China be accelerated consonant with the needs of Russia, Great Britain, and our own forces.

That aid to the American Volunteer Group be continued and accelerated to the maximum practicable extent.

That no ultimatum be delivered to Japan.

The reply of the President to Chiang Kai-shek's message was handed to the Chinese Ambassador on November 14 and followed the recommendations of General Marshall and Admiral Stark. It pointed out that it did not appear preparations by Japan for a land campaign against Kunming had advanced to a point which would indicate probable immediate imminence of an attack and observed, among other things:[87]

* * * Under existing circumstances, taking into consideration the world situation in its political, military, and economic aspects, we feel that the most effective contribution which we can make at this moment is along the line of speeding up the flow to China of our lend-lease materials and facilitating the building up of the American volunteer air force, both in personnel and in equipment. We are subjected at present, as you know, to demands from many quarters and in many connections. We are sending materials not only to China and Great Britain, but to the Dutch, the Soviet Union, and some twenty other countries that are calling urgently for equipment for self-defense. In addition, our program for our own defense, especially the needs of our rapidly expanding Navy and Army, calls for equipment in large amount and with great promptness. Nevertheless, I shall do my utmost toward achieving expedition of increasing amounts of material for your use. Meanwhile we are exchanging views with the British Government in regard to the entire situation and the tremendous problems which are presented, with a view to effective coordinating of efforts in the most practicable ways possible.

In a joint memorandum for the President, prepared under date of November 27, 1941, General Marshall and Admiral Stark pointed out that "if the current negotiations end without agreement, Japan may attack: the Burma Road; Thailand; Malaya; the Netherlands East Indies; the Philippines; the Russian Maritime Provinces."[88] They observed that:

The most essential thing now, from the United States viewpoint, is to gain time. Considerable Navy and Army reinforcements have been rushed to the Philippines but the desirable strength has not yet been reached. The process of reinforcement is being continued. Of great and immediate concern is the safety of the Army convoy now near Guam, and the Marine Corps' convoy just leaving Shanghai. Ground forces to a total of 21,000 are due to sail from the United States by December 8, 1941, and it is important that this troop reinforcement reach the Philippines before hostilities commence. Precipitance of military action on our part should be avoided so long as consistent with national policy. The longer the delay, the more positive becomes the assurance of retention of these islands as a naval and air base.

---

[87] Id.
[88] Committee exhibit No. 17.

Japanese action to the south of Formosa will be hindered and perhaps seriously blocked as long as we hold the Philippine Islands. War with Japan certainly will interrupt our transport of supplies to Siberia, and probably will interrupt the process of aiding China.

After consultation with each other, United States, British, and Dutch military authorities in the Far East agreed that joint military counteraction against Japan should be undertaken *only in case Japan attacks or directly threatens the territory or mandated territory of the United States, the British Commonwealth, or the Netherlands East Indies, or should the Japanese move forces into Thailand west of 100 degrees East or south of 10 degrees North, Portuguese Timor, New Caledonia, or the Loyalty Islands.*[89]

Japanese involvement in Yunnan or Thailand up to a certain extent is advantageous, since it leads to further dispersion, longer lines of communication, and an additional burden on communications. However, a Japanese advance to the west of 100 degrees East or south of 10 degrees North, immediately becomes a threat to Burma and Singapore. Until it is patent that Japan intends to advance beyond these lines, no action which might lead to immediate hostilities should be taken.

It is recommended that:

> Prior to the completion of the Philippine reinforcement, military counteraction be considered only if Japan attacks or directly threatens United States, British, or Dutch territory, as above outlined;
>
> In case of a Japanese advance into Thailand, Japan be warned by the United States, the British, and the Dutch Governments that advance beyond the lines indicated may lead to war; prior to such warning no joint military opposition be undertaken;
>
> Steps be taken at once to consummate agreements with the British and Dutch for the issuance of such warning.[90]

It is to be noted that the foregoing memorandum was dated November 27, 1941, the day after the Secretary of State had delivered our Government's reply to the Japanese ultimatum of November 20. The evidence shows, however, that the memorandum was considered at an Army-Navy Joint Board meeting on the morning of November 26, following the meeting of the War Council on the preceding day at which Secretary Hull had stated that there was practically no possibility of an agreement being achieved with Japan.[91] The memorandum of the Chief of Staff and the Chief of Naval Operations conveys two cardinal thoughts governing the approach of the military to the negotiations; i. e., *the most essential thing was to gain time, and the precipitance of military action should be avoided so long as consistent with national policy.* In this connection General Marshall referred to the reaction of the Army and Navy to the dropping of the thought of a *modus vivendi* in the following terms: [92]

My recollection is, and I have a fairly clear recollection of our disappointment that from the military point of view, meaning Army and Navy, that we would not gain any more time; our relationship to these discussions was on the one side the desire to gain as much time as we possibly could and on the other to see that commitments were not made that endangered us from a military point of view.

---

[89] General Marshall testified that this paragraph referred to the conference of military leaders held in Singapore in April of 1941. He was asked: "When you say that the Dutch, British, and the United States military authorities had *agreed* to that action did you mean that they had made an agreement on behalf of the United States, or agreed to recommend it to their governments?"

General Marshall replied: *"Agreed to recommend it.* They had no power whatever to agree for our government and it was so stipulated * * *." Committee record, pp 2784, 2785.

[90] See note 78, supra, and note 111, infra.

[91] With reference to the Marshall-Stark memorandum for the President dated November 27, 1941 (exhibit No. 17), Admiral Ingersoll recalled that he "* * * presented at a Joint Board Meeting on apparently the day before this memorandum was sent, I presented at that meeting the arguments why we should not precipitate a war, and when I came back here to Washington 4 years later, I had forgotten completely that I had ever presented such a memorandum at the Joint Board Meeting. The only satisfaction I had was that it didn't sound silly after 4 years. And this was based on that." Committee record, p. 11366.

[92] Committee record, p. 13775.

In pointing out the distinction between his approach and that of Secretary Stimson,[93] General Marshall said: [94]

He [Secretary Stimson] was very much afraid—he feared that we would find ourselves involved in the developing situation where our disadvantages would be so great that it would be quite fatal to us when the Japanese actually broke peace.

He also felt very keenly that, and thought about this part a great deal more than I did, because it was his particular phase of the matter, that we must not go so far in delaying actions of a diplomatic nature as to sacrifice the honor of the country. He was deeply concerned about that.

My approach to the matter, of course, was much more materialistic. I was hunting for time. Hunting for time, so that whatever did happen we would be better prepared than we were at that time, that particular time.

So it was a question of resolving his views as to the honor, we will say, of the United States, and his views of a diplomatic procedure which allowed the Japanese to continue movements until we would be in a hopeless situation before the peace was broken, and mine, which as I say, were much more materialistic, as I think they should have been, that we should get as much time as we could in order to make good the terrible deficiencies in our defensive arrangements.

It is apparent from the memorandum of November 27 that the Chief of Staff and the Chief of Naval Operations desired more time insofar as consistent with national policy and not at the expense of forsaking the honor of the Nation. As General Marshall testified: [95]

Mine was, in a sense, a technical job. I was struggling with the means to fight. * * * *I wanted time, and the question was how much time could be given to us and still maintain the honor of the United States and not get ourselves in a hopeless position.*

Further, the memorandum relates to the matter of precipitance of war by the United States; that is, no affirmative steps should be taken by the United States to bring about war with Japan—"precipitance of military action on our part should be avoided so long as consistent with national policy."

As observed in reviewing the diplomatic background of the Pearl Harbor attack, the November 26 note of our Government to Japan was not a precipitant of war—it was merely a laudable restatement of the principles for which we had stood for many years in the Orient. There can, therefore, be no question that the delivery to Japan of the American note of November 26 was not in any way in contravention of the expressed position of our own military. Furthermore, Tokyo advised her emissaries in Washington on November 20 that a *modus vivendi* would not be acceptable to Japan,[96] and in consequence had our Government submitted a *modus vivendi* to the Japanese, no more time would have been afforded the Army and Navy. *General Marshall and Admiral Stark had themselves recommended that we take military counter-action should Japan attack the very territory which she was already poised to attack in the event she failed to secure the demands contained in the Japanese ultimatum of November 20.*[97]

Indeed, at the very time Japan's ambassadors were discussing a temporary truce, her military was continuing its move to the South. Secretary Stimson's diary for November 26, 1941, reflects the following comments, among others: [98]

---

[93] In this diary for November 27, Mr. Stimson commented: "Knox and Admiral Stark came over and conferred with me and General Gerow. Marshall is down at the maneuvers today and I feel his absence very much. There was a tendency, not unnatural, on the part of Stark and Gerow to seek for more time. I said that I was glad to have time but I didn't want it at any cost of humility on the part of the United States or of reopening the thing which would show a weakness on our part." Committee record, p. 14422.

[94] Committee record, p. 13821.

[95] Id., at p. 13822.

[96] Committee exhibit No. 1, p. 160.

[97] Id., No. 17.

[98] Committee record, p. 14420.

. . . I talked to the President over the telephone and I asked him whether he had received the paper which I had sent him over last night about the Japanese having started a new expedition from Shanghai down towards Indo-China. He fairly blew up—jumped up into the air, so to speak, and said he hadn't seen it and that that changed the whole situation because it was an evidence of bad faith on the part of the Japanese that while they were negotiating for an entire truce—an entire withdrawal (from China)—they should be sending this expedition down there to Indo-China. I told him that it was a fact that had come to me through G-2 and through the Navy Secret Service and I at once got another copy of the paper I had sent last night and sent it over to him by special messenger.

It is to be noted that Mr. Stimson's diary for November 25, 1941, describes a meeting at the White House attended by the President; Secretaries Hull, Knox, and Stimson; General Marshall; and Admiral Stark. It states, in part:[99] "There the President, instead of bringing up the Victory Parade [100] brought up entirely the relations with the Japanese. He brought up the event that we were likely to be attacked (as soon as) next Monday without warning, and the question was what we should do. *The question was how we should maneuver them into the position of firing the first shot without allowing too much danger to ourselves.* It was a difficult proposition."[101]

In referring to Mr. Stimson's comment concerning maneuvering the Japanese into the position of firing the first shot without too much danger to ourselves,[102] General Marshall testified: [103]

"* * * they were trying to arrange a diplomatic procedure, rather than firing off a gun, that would not only protect our interests, by arranging matters so that the Japanese couldn't intrude any further in a dangerous way, but also anything they did do, they would be forced to take the offensive action, and what we were to do had to be prepared for the President by Mr. Hull. It was not a military order. It was not a military arrangement."

The Chief of Staff stated that Secretary Stimson was referring to what the *diplomatic* procedure was to be; not the *military* procedure.[104]

On November 28 Secretary Stimson called upon the President inasmuch as Military Intelligence had supplied him a summary of the information in regard to the movements of the Japanese in the Far East and "it amounted to such a statement of dangerous possibilities that I decided to take it to the President before he got up." Referring to his conversation with the President on this occasion, Mr. Stimson wrote in his diary: [105]

He (the President) branched into an analysis of the situation himself as he sat there on his bed, saying there were three alternatives and only three that he could see before us. I told him I could see two. His alternatives were—first,

---

[99] Id., at p. 14418.
[100] This was an office nickname for the General Staff strategic plan of national action in case of war in Europe.
[101] Mr. Stimson pointed out in this connection that our military and naval advisers had warned us that we could not safely allow the Japanese to move against British Malaysia or the Dutch East Indies without attempting to prevent it. Committee record, p. 14418.
[102] In the course of committee examination, Admiral Stark was asked: "Now, I want to know why, if you know, there was a distinction between the Atlantic and the Pacific about the firing of the first shot."
He replied: "Germany had attacked and sunk one of our ships in June. She had attacked three destroyers in the Atlantic, sinking one of them—I think it was in October or November, along in there, between September and October. And certainly the 1st of December she had attacked and wounded badly one tanker, the *Salinas*, I believe it was, which got back to the Canadian coast. The Congress of the United States had voted billions for material to go to Britain. We considered it our job to get that material through not simply to use this money for material and let it be sunk without taking any action on it. There were certain waters defined, and limits established, which, I believe, we called our waters. The President's speech shows it very plainly, in which he stated, if the Germans came within that area they would do so at their peril. They came in and attacked us. As a result, we got together what we called the hemispheric defense plans, which I have outlined previously and which provided for shooting at any German combatant ships which came within that area, and we did do it * * * I think that that situation is not comparable to what was going on in the Pacific, where the Japs had not attacked our ships, unless you go back to the *Panay* incident." Committee record, pp. 13981, 13982.
[103] Committee record, p. 13801.
[104] Id., at p. 13799.
[105] Id., at p. 14423.

to do nothing; second, to make something in the nature of an ultimatum again, stating a point beyond which we would fight; third, to fight at once. I told him my only two were the last two, because I did not think anyone would do nothing in this situation, and he agreed with me. I said of the other two my choice was the latter one.

Mr. Stimson set forth the following observations concerning the War Council meeting on November 28: [106]

It was the consensus that the present move (by the Japanese)—that there was an Expeditionary Force on the sea of about 25,000 Japanese troops aimed for a landing somewhere—completely changed the situation when we last discussed whether or not we could address an ultimatum to Japan about moving the troops which she already had on land in Indochina. It was now the opinion of everyone that if this expedition was allowed to get around the southern point of Indochina and to go off and land in the Gulf of Siam, either at Bangkok or further west, it would be a terrific blow at all of the three Powers, Britain at Singapore, the Netherlands, and ourselves in the Philippines. *It was the consensus of everybody that this must not be allowed.* Then we discussed how to prevent it. It was agreed that if the Japanese got into the Isthmus of Kra, the British would fight. It was also agreed that if the British fought, we would have to fight. And it now seems clear that if this expedition was allowed to round the southern point of Indochina, this whole chain of disastrous events would be set on foot of going.

It further became a consensus of views that rather than strike at the force as it went by without any warning on the one hand, which we didn't think we could do; or sitting still and allowing it to go on, on the other, which we didn't think we could—that the only thing for us to do was to address it a warning that if it reached a certain place, or a certin line, or a certain point, we should have to fight. The President's mind evidently was running towards a special telegram from himself to the Emperor of Japan. This he had done with good results at the time of the *Panay* incident, but for many reasons this did not seem to me to be the right thing now and I pointed them out to the President. In the first place, a letter to the Emperor of Japan could not be couched in terms which contained an explicit warning. One does not warn an Emperor. In the second place it would not indicate to the people of the United States what the real nature of the danger was. Consequently I said there ought to be a message by the President to the people of the United States and I thought that the best form of a message would be an address to Congress reporting the danger, reporting what we would have to do if the danger happened. The President accepted this idea of a message but he first thought of incorporating in it the terms of his letter to the Emperor. But again I pointed out that he could not publicize a letter to an Emperor in such a way; that he had better send his letter to the Emperor separate as one thing and a secret thing, and then make his speech to the Congress as a separate and a more understandable thing to the people of the United States. This was the final decision at that time and the President asked Hull, and Knox and myself to try to draft such papers.

Mr. Stimson's diary for December 2, 1941, contains the following comments concerning a meeting at the White House: [107]

The President went step by step over the situation and I think has made up his mind to go ahead. He has asked the Japanese through Sumner Welles what they intend by this new occupation of southern Indo-China—just what they are going to do—and has demanded a quick reply. The President is still deliberating the possibility of a message to the Emperor, although all the rest of us are rather against it, but in addition to that *he is quite settled, I think, that he will make a Message to the Congress and will perhaps back that up with a speech to the country. He said that he was going to take the matters right up when he left us.*

On December 6 President Roosevelt dispatched his appeal to the Emperor; and, after the bombs had already fallen on Hawaii, our Ambassador in Tokyo was informed that it was desired the Japanese Memorandum of December 7, which was keyed for delivery to the United States coincident with the attack on Pearl Harbor, be regarded as the Emperor's reply to the President. [108]

[106] Id., at pp. 14424, 14425.
[107] Id., at p. 14427.
[108] See Part I, supra, this report.

It is clear from the evidence that the feeling of the President and his advisers that the United States must fight if the British and Dutch were attacked was predicated on the necessities of our own security and not occasioned by reason of any formal commitment or agreement requiring such action on the part of the United States.[109] That our Government was hoping to avoid war long after any real hope existed[110] is made manifest by the fact that the President contemplated sending a warning to Japan on "Tuesday afternoon or evening" (December 9) if no answer was received from the Emperor by Monday (December 8).[111] In referring to the appeal to the Emperor, Mr. Hull said:[112]

The President was now making an additional last-minute appeal. He, of course, knew that the huge Japanese armada had already left the jumping-off place in Indochina which from our viewpoint meant that the danger of attack could not have been more imminent. Nevertheless, *the President believed that he should not neglect even the slim chance that an additional last-minute appeal might save the situation. It also served to make clear to the American people and to the world our interest in maintaining peace up to the very last minute.*

Intelligence Available in Washington

The "Magic"

With the exercise of the greatest ingenuity and utmost resourcefulness, regarded by the committee as meriting the highest commendation, the War and Navy Departments collaborated in breaking the Japanese diplomatic codes. Through the exploitation of intercepted and decoded messages between Japan and her diplomatic establishments, the so-called Magic, a wealth of intelligence concerning the purposes of the Japanese was available in Washington.[113]

Both the Army and Navy maintained several stations throughout the United States and in the Pacific for the purpose of intercepting Japanese radio communications. These stations operated under instructions emanating from Washington and forwarded the intercepted traffic to Washington without themselves endeavoring to decode or translate the material. The only exception to this procedure was in the case of the Corregidor station which had been provided with facilities for exploiting many of the Japanese diplomatic messages in view of its advantageous location from the standpoint of intercepting Tokyo traffic.[114]

Insofar as the commanding officers in Hawaii were concerned they received none of the Magic save as it was supplied them by the War and Navy Departments in the original, paraphrased, or captioned form or, operationally, through instructions predicated on this source of intelligence. While the highest military officials in Washington did not know the precise nature of radio intelligence activities in Hawaii, it is clear that those charged with handling the Magic did not

---

[109] See statement of Mr. Stimson, committee record, p. 14418. Also committee exhibits Nos. 16, 17.
[110] Admiral Stark was asked: "Was not that our intention (of doing anything possible to prevent war with the Japanese) right up to December 7, if it could be done without sacrificing American honor and principles?"
He replied: "Yes, sir; and we had been working for months on that, and the record is complete in that regard." Committee record, p. 13915.
[111] See committee record, pp. 13741, 13742.
[112] See Secretary Hull's replies to committee interrogatories, committee record, p. 14266.
[113] See committee exhibits Nos. 1 and 2. For a discussion of Magic and its great significance to the prosecution of the war see letters dated September 25 and 27, 1944, from General Marshall to Governor Dewey. Committee record, pp. 2979-2989.
[114] For a discussion of the mechanics of the Magic, see testimony of Admiral Noyes and Capts. L. F. Safford and A. D. Kramer of the Navy, and Cols. Otis K. Sadtler and Rufus Bratton of the Army before the committee.

rely upon either the Army or Navy in Hawaii being able to decode the diplomatic messages which were decoded in Washington. However, both Admirals Stark and Turner testified that they were under the impression that Japanese diplomatic messages were being decoded by the Navy in Hawaii.[115] No justification for this impression existed in fact apart from the failure of these officers to inform themselves adequately concerning Navy establishments.[116] Under arrangements existing during 1941 between the Army and the Navy in Washington the decoding and translating of Magic was divided between the Army Signal Intelligence Service under the direction of the Chief Signal Officer and a unit in the Navy, known as OP–20–G, under the control of the Director of Naval Communications. The responsibility for decoding and translating messages was allocated between the two services on the basis of the dates of the messages with each service ordinarily handling all messages originated on alternate days, the Army being responsible for even dates and the Navy, for odd dates. This procedure was flexible in that it was departed from in order to expedite the handling of material as the occasion demanded or in the case of any unusual situation that might prevail in one or the other of the services.

POLICY WITH RESPECT TO DISSEMINATION OF MAGIC

The Magic intelligence was regarded as preeminently confidential and the policy with respect to its restricted distribution was dictated by a desire to safeguard the secret that the Japanese diplomatic codes were being broken.[117] Delivery of the English texts of the intercepted messages was limited, within the War Department, to the Secretary of War, the Chief of Staff, the Chief of the War Plans Division, and the Chief of the Military Intelligence Division; within the Navy, to the Secretary of Navy, the Chief of Naval Operations, the Chief of the War Plans Division, and the Director of Naval Intelligence; to the State Department; and to the President's naval aide for transmittal to the President. By agreement between the Army and Navy in Washington, the Army was responsible for distribution of Magic within the War Department and to the State Department; the Navy, for distribution within the Navy Department and to the White House. Any disclosure of the fact that the Japanese messages were being decoded or any disclosure of information obtainable only from that source would inevitably have resulted in Japan's changing her codes with attendant loss completely of the vital Magic. This fact was responsible for the translated material being closely held among a

---

[115] See committee record, p. 5095.

[116] Admiral Stark testified: "I inquired on two or three occasions as to whether or not Kimmel could read certain dispatches when they came up and which we were interpreting and sending our own messages and I was told that he could. However, *I want to make it plain that that did not influence me in the slightest regarding what I sent.* I felt it my responsibility to keep the commanders in the field and to see to it that they were kept informed of the main trends and of information which (would) be of high interest to them. Regardless of what dispatches I might have seen, they may have formed background for me but I saw that affirmative action was taken from the Chief of Naval Operations to the commanders in the field on matters which I thought they should have." Committee record, p. 5793.

[117] During the course of his testimony, General Miles was asked: "Who made the decision that these messages should not be sent to Hawaii as they were intercepted and translated as far as the Army is concerned?"

He replied: "That followed from the general policy laid down by the Chief of Staff that these messages and the fact of the existence of these messages or our ability to decode them should be confined to the least possible number of persons; no distribution should be made outside of Washington. * * *

"The value of that secret, the secret that we could and did decode Japanese messages, in their best code, was of incalculable value to us, both in the period when war threatened and most definitely during our waging of that war. That was the basic reason for the limitation on the distribution of those messages and of the constantly increasing closing in, as I might express it, on any possible leaks in that secret." Committee record, pp. 2092, 2093.

few key individuals, in addition necessarily to those who processed the messages.

The policy generally prevailed in the days before Pearl Harbor that the Magic materials were not ordinarily to be disseminated to field commanders.[118] This policy was prescribed for the reason that (1) the Japanese might conceivably intercept the relayed Magic intelligence and learn of our success in decrypting Japanese codes:[119] (2) the volume of intercepted traffic was so great that its transmission, particularly during the critical period of diplomatic negotiations, would have overtaxed communication facilities; and (3) responsibility for evaluation of this material which was largely diplomatic in nature was properly in Washington, where the Magic could be considered along with other pertinent diplomatic information obtained from the State Department and other sources. There was no inflexible rule, however, which precluded sending to theater commanders in proper instances, either in its original form as paraphrased or in the form of estimates, conclusions, or orders based wholly or in part upon Magic. Important information derived therefrom was from time to time sent to the Hawaiian commanders by the Navy Department in paraphrased form or in the form of estimates.[120] The War Department, on the other hand, did not send the Magic to the field, for the reason that the Army code was not believed to be as secure as that of the Navy.[121]

For purposes of the investigation Magic fell generally into two categories: first, messages relating to diplomatic matters of the Japanese Government;[122] and second, messages relating to espionage activities by Japanese diplomatic representatives, particularly with respect to American military installations and establishments.[123]

The decision not to endeavor to supply field commanders all of the Magic intelligence as such was a reasonable one under the circumstances. However, *it is incumbent to determine whether responsible commanding officers were otherwise supplied the equivalent of intelligence obtained from the Magic materials.*

"SHIPS IN HARBOR" REPORTS

NATURE OF CONSULAR ESPIONAGE

In addition to the Magic materials relating strictly to diplomatic negotiations, a great many messages between Japan and her diplomatic establishments were intercepted reflecting espionage activities by the consular staffs.[124] These intercepts related in the main to instructions sent by Tokyo and replies pursuant thereto concerning the movement and location of American ships and the nature of military and defensive installations.

[118] For a discussion concerning this matter, see letter dated April 22, 1941, from Capt. Arthur N. McCollum in Washington to Capt. Edwin T. Layton, Pacific Fleet intelligence officer. Committee record, pp. 12917–12923.

[119] This factor applied principally to the Army. See testimony of General Miles. Note 121, infra.

[120] See committee exhibit No. 37, pp. 4–12, 40, 41.

[121] In testifying concerning the matter of distributing Magic to field commanders General Miles was asked: "Do I understand from your answer that these messages intercepted and translated were not sent to Hawaii by the Army?"

He replied: "They were not. In some cases the substance of some messages were sent to Hawaii, and almost always in naval code, I think always in naval code, because the naval code was considered;to be more secure than the Army code." Committee record, pp. 2091, 2092.

[122] Committee exhibit No. 1.

[123] Id., No. 2.

[124] Id.

The Hawaiian commanders have strongly insisted that messages to and from the Japanese Consulate in Honolulu clearly indicated Japan's intention to attack the fleet at Pearl Harbor. They contend they were wrongfully deprived of this information, basing this contention to a great extent on an intercepted dispatch from Tokyo of September 24, 1941 [125] issuing the following instructions to its Honolulu Consultate: [126]

Strictly secret.

Henceforth, we would like to have you make reports concerning vessels along the following lines insofar as possible:

1. The waters (of Pearl Harbor) are to be divided roughly into five subareas. (We have no objections to your abbreviating as much as you like.)

Area A. Waters between Ford Island and the Arsenal.

Area B. Waters adjacent to the Island south and west of Ford Island. (This area is on the opposite side of the Island from Area A.)

Area C. East Loch.

Area D. Middle Loch.

Area E. West Loch and the communication water routes.

2. With regard to warships and aircraft carriers, we would like to have you report on those at anchor (these are not so important) tied up at wharves, buoys, and in docks. (Designate types and classes briefly. If possible we would like to have you make mention of the fact when there are two or more vessels along side the same wharf.) [127]

The foregoing message, No. 83, has been gratuitously characterized throughout the proceedings as the "bomb plot message", the "harbor berthing plan", and by similar terms. Three other intercepted messages relate in a pertinent manner to the September 24 dispatch and to Tokyo's interest in the fleet at Pearl Harbor:

(1) In a message from Tokyo to the Honolulu Consul, dated November 15, 1941 (translated December 3, 1941) it was stated:[128]

As relations between Japan and the United States are most critical, make your "ships in harbor report" irregular, but at a rate of twice a week. Although you already are no doubt aware, please take extra care to maintain secrecy.

(2) An intercept from Tokyo dated November 20, 1941 (translated December 4) read:[129]

Please investigate comprehensively the fleet—bases in the neighborhood of the Hawaiian military reservation.

(3) An intercept of November 29 (translated December 5) stated:[130]

We have been receiving reports from you on ship movements, but in future will you also report even when there are no movements?

Referring to the indicated messages, Admiral Kimmel testified: [131]

In no other area was the Japanese Government seeking information as to whether two or more vessels were alongside the same wharf. Prior to the dispatch of September 24, the information which the Japanese sought and obtained about Pearl Harbor followed the general pattern of their interest in American Fleet movements in other localities. One might suspect this type of conventional espionage. With the dispatch of September 24, 1941, and those which followed, there was a significant and ominous change in the character of the information

[125] Translated October 9.
[126] Committee exhibit No. 2, p. 12.
[127] Some of the subsequent reports from the Japanese Consulate in Honolulu were made pursuant to the instructions contained in the September 24 dispatch from Tokyo. See committee exhibit No. 2 pp. 13 and 14.
[128] Committee exhibit No. 2, p. 13.
[129] Id., at p. 15.
Captain Kramer testified with respect to the blank, a garble, in this message between the words "fleet" and "bases" that he believed the original Japanese version in ungarbled form if it were available would read: "Please investigate comprehensively the fleet air bases." Committee record, pp. 1162-1163.
[130] Committee exhibit No. 2, 15 r.
[131] Committee record, pp. 6779, 6780.

which the Japanese Government sought and obtained. The espionage then directed was of an unusual character and outside the realm of reasonable suspicion. It was no longer merely directed to ascertaining the general whereabouts of ships of the fleet. It was directed to the presence of particular ships in particular areas; to such minute detail as what ships were double-docked at the same wharf. In the period immediately preceding the attack, the Jap Consul General in Hawaii was directed by Tokyo to report even when there were no movements of ships in and out of Pearl Harbor. *These Japanese instructions and reports pointed to an attack by Japan upon the ships in Pearl Harbor.* The information sought and obtained, with such painstaking detail had no other conceivable usefulness from a military viewpoint. Its utility was in planning and executing an attack upon the ships in port. Its effective value was lost completely when the ships left their reported berthings in Pearl Harbor.

In the same connection General Short testified: [132]

> While the War Department G-2 may not have felt bound to let me know about the routine operations of the Japanese in keeping track of our naval ships, they should certainly have let me know that the Japanese were getting reports of the exact location of the ships in Pearl Harbor, which might indicate more than just keeping track, *because such details would be useful only for sabotage, or for air or submarine attack in Hawaii.* As early as October 9, 1941, G-2 in Washington knew of this Japanese espionage. *This message, analyzed critically, is really a bombing plan for Pearl Harbor.*

In endeavoring to evaluate the intercepted dispatch of September 24 and related dispatches, it is to be borne in mind that the Japanese were insistent in their desire to secure information concerning the location and movements of American vessels everywhere and not merely at Pearl Harbor. There are no other dispatches before the Committee, however, in which *Tokyo* manifested an interest concerning the disposition of ships *within* a harbor, as in the case of the "berthing plan," as distinguished from the desire to know whether a vessel was *at* a particular harbor. Viewing the September 24 instructions to her Honolulu consul in this light, it would appear that Tokyo was manifesting an unusual interest in the presence of our Pacific Fleet and the detailed location thereof in Pearl Harbor.

The evidence reflects, however, that no one in Washington attached the significance to the "berthing plan" which it is now possible to read into it. To determine whether failure to appreciate the plan represents a lack of imagination and a dereliction of duty, we consider now the contentions of the officers who saw this intelligence before December 7, 1941, and the circumstances under which it was received in Washington.

At the time the "berthing plan" was translated, the practice was being followed by Captain Kramer of preparing a gist of intercepted messages to expedite consideration of them by recipients.[133] Asterisks were employed along with the gist to provide an indication of the significance of messages—one asterisk meant "interesting messages"; two asterisks, "especially important or urgent messages."[134] The gist relating to the berthing plan read:[135] "Tokyo directs special reports on ships with(in) Pearl Harbor which is divided into five areas for the purpose of showing exact location" and was indicated by one asterisk

---

[132] Id., at p. 7989.
[133] The practice of preparing gists is indicated to have been discontinued during the month of November 1941, for the reason that the President insisted on seeing the original messages "because he was afraid when they tried to condense them, someone would change the meaning." See testimony of Captain Safford, Hewitt Inquiry Record, p. 408; also Clarke Inquiry Exhibit No. 23.
[134] Committee record, pp. 11206, 11207.
[135] Id., at pp. 11207, 11208.

as being an "interesting message". In explaining his estimate of the message, Captain Kramer testified:[136]

* * * Your interpretation, Senator, that this was a bombing map, I do not believe, from conversations I had at the time in showing and going over days' traffic with various recipients; I do not believe it was interpreted by any of those persons as being materially different than other messages concerning ship movements being reported by the Japanese diplomatic service.

I recollect that this was interpreted. I am uncertain of the precise wording of the interpretation. This was considered, and *I believe it was, approximately, my consideration at the time as being an attempt on the part of the Japanese diplomatic service to simplify communications.*

That view is substantiated by many factors.

One is that the Japanese were repeatedly and continually directing their diplomatic service to cut down traffic. They were repeatedly preparing and sending out abbreviations to be used with codes already in existence. Diplomatic codes were frequently asking for additional funds for quarterly allotments, and so forth, to cover telegraphic expenses. Those expenses were usually paid and furnished in part when so requested by Tokyo. Those and other considerations I think explain, probably, the handling of this particular message, sir.

Upon being asked what evaluation he placed on the harbor berthing plan and related intercepts, Admiral Wilkinson testified: [137]

The Japanese for many years had the reputation, and the facts bore out that reputation, of being meticulous seekers for every scrap of information, whether by photography or by written report or otherwise.

We had recently, as reported to me, apprehended two and I think three Japanese naval officers on the west coast making investigations of Seattle, Bremerton, Long Beach, and San Diego. In the reports that we had gotten from them there had been indications of movements and locations of ships; in the papers that they had there were instructions for them to find out the movements and locations of ships except in Hawaii and the Philippines, the inference being that these fellows that were planted in America, these naval officers, were not to be responsible for movements in Hawaii and the Philippines because there were agencies finding that information there.

My general impression of adding all this reputation and this fact and these data together was that these dispatches were part of the general information system established by the Japanese. We knew also that certain information had been sought in Panama and again in Manila. I did not, I regret now, of course attribute to them the bombing target significance which now appears.

And again: [138]

* * * the location of the ship, whether it was alongside of a dock or elsewhere, did give an inference of work going on aboard her which would be of value to the question of when she might be moved, what her state of readiness was and the inference that we drew from this was that they wanted to know everything they could not only about the movement of the ships and those that were present and, therefore, accounted for and not a threat to them in some other waters, but also with reference to those that were present where they were located with reference to state of repair. For instance, the ships that were particularly in Pearl Harbor might be in repair and not ready to go to sea, whereas those at anchor in the stream would be ready, or would be so on short notice. Those at double-banked piers might not be, particularly the inside one might take some time to go out.

Admiral Wilkinson thought he had mentioned to one or more officers that the Japanese seemed curious as to the lay-out in Pearl Harbor and testified "at the time I thought that that was an evidence of their nicety of intelligence." [139]

On the other hand, Admiral Stark, who stated he had no recollection of having seen the berthing plan and accompanying messages prior to the attack, testified: [140]

---

[136] Id., at p. 1160.
[137] Id., at pp. 4620, 4621.
[138] Id., at pp. 4622, 4623.
[139] Id., at p. 4624.
[140] Id., at pp. 5788, 5789.

These messages are of a class of message which gives positions of ships in harbor, gives locations. The message, however, is distinctly different from the usual type of ship report, which simply would say, "So many ships" or give their names, in Pearl Harbor. This dispatch is different in that it calls for the location of a ship in the harbor in her particular berth.

I recall no such request from Tokyo to the field; that is, to the Japanese people, to report like that except for Pearl Harbor. There might have been. We did not see it. I believe there are one or two places were ships were reported like in Puget Sound, in a certain berth or a dock, alongside of a dock, but this dispatch while of a class is of a character which is different.

In the light of hindsight it stands out very clearly, with what we can read into it now, as indicating the possibility or at least the ground work for a Japanese raid on Pearl Harbor. That significance which we now have in the light of hindsight was not pointed out to me by anyone, nor do I have the slightest recollection of anybody ever having given that significance at the time.

Asked if he felt significance should have been attached to the plan at the time it was received, Admiral Stark said: [141]

It is very difficult to separate hindsight from foresight. I can only say that it went through our people, it went through the Army, who were likewise vitally interested in the defense of Pearl Harbor, and I do not recollect anyone having pointed it out. There was literally a mass of material coming in. We knew the Japanese appetite was almost insatiable for detail in all respects. The dispatch might have been put down as just another example of their great attention to detail.

If I had seen it myself I do not know what I would have done. I might have said, "Well, my goodness, look at this detail," or I might have read into it because it is different, I might have said, "Well, this is unusual. I wonder why they want it?" I might have gone on, and diagnosed it or I might not. I simply do not know. We read it now in the light of what has happened.

Captain McCollum,[142] who was not in Washington at the time the harbor berthing plan was intercepted or translated, suggested certain reasons why the plan would not have been interpreted as a "bombing plot."[143] He observed that beginning in 1935 the Japanese Navy was apparently not satisfied with the type of intelligence forwarded by the consular agents and in consequence undertook to set up an observation net of its own, particularly on the west coast of the United States, but that it was his feeling the Japanese had been unable to put naval observers into the consulate at Honolulu. Therefore, as he testified: [144]

As we estimated it, the consul general at Honolulu was receiving, through the Foreign Office at the instance of the Japanese Naval Department, explicit directions of the type of intelligence that was needed, much more in detail than any of the other key consulates on the west coast, because he did not have the benefit of the services of a Japanese Naval Intelligence officer within his consulate.

Therefore this thing here, if I saw it, I am quite certain I would have felt it was just another move to get explicit information, to cut down the frequently voluble type of reports made by consular officials which the Jap Navy did not like.

Captain McCollum further pointed out that the matter of how ships were anchored and where they were anchored was designed to indicate the facility with which the fleet was prepared to *sortie*, considering that the anchorage at Pearl Harbor is "chopped up" into a number of more or less independent locks. He testified: [145]

To give a general statement of where the ships were, the stuff they are requiring here, would require a rather long-winded dispatch, where the same device such as breaking it up into areas A, B, and C, such a simple device could be used. With

[141] Id., at pp. 5790, 5791.
[142] Capt. Arthur N. McCollum, Chief of the Far Eastern Section of Naval Intelligence.
[143] Captain McCollum left Washington on September 24 and did not return until October 11. Committee record, p. 9195.
[144] Committee record, pp. 9140, 9141.
[145] Id., at pp. 9178, 9179.

this area discovered, a rather simple and short dispatch would suffice to give the essential information as to the location of the fleet and also an indication of their readiness for sortie. I would suggest that that is a reasonable, tenable hypothesis as to why they wished information, apparently, in this detail.

In summary, Captain McCollum stated he would not now necessarily regard the harbor berthing plan as a "bombing plan" *unless* "I had known Pearl Harbor had been bombed." [146]

It appears clear that there were many other messages between Tokyo and her consulates, received in Washington, indicating a likely Japanese purpose to attack at points other than at Hawaii.[147] These messages indicate a definite interest in the state of defenses at many points. A dispatch from Tokyo on October 16 to its Seattle consul instructed "Should patrolling be inaugurated by naval planes, report it at once." [148] In the same message the Consulate was instructed to report on the movement and basing of warships at least once every 10 days, "As long as there is no great change," but a report was to be submitted "Should more than 10 vessels of any type arrive or depart from port at one time." A June 23, 1941 dispatch from Tokyo to Mexico instructed:[149] "Regarding the plans for procuring maps of the Panama Canal and vicinity, please have career attaché Kihara make an official trip to Panama * * *. Have the maps taken out by plane, and then have Sato, the naval attaché, bring them to Tokyo with him when he returns." While no instructions from Tokyo to Panama are available subsequent to August 2, 1941, the reports to Tokyo contain detailed information concerning the location of airfields, air strength, ammunition, location and camouflage of petroleum supply tanks, location and strength of artillery patrols, radar detectors and their range, map procurement and other matters which would obviously be of interest only if an attack on the Panama Canal were contemplated.[150] While some of these messages were translated after December 7, they have a distinct bearing on whether, before the event, the harbor berthing plan was reasonably designed to be a harbinger of the December 7 attack.[151]

With respect to other messages concerning defenses, Tokyo on August 1 requested Manila to obtain information "regarding the camouflage and distinguishing marks of the American naval and military aeroplanes in Manila".[152] On October 4 Tokyo instructed Manila "to make a reconnaissance of the new defense works along the east, west, and southern coasts of the Island of Luzon, reporting on their progress, strength, etc." [153] Tokyo instructed Manila on November 5, pursuant to a request of the "Naval General Staff", to obtain information with respect to each port of call concerning "(1) conditions at airports on land", "(2) types of planes at each, and number of planes", "(3) warships; also machinery belonging to land forces", and "(4) state or progress being made on all equipment and establishments." [154] On November 15 Tokyo requested Manila to "make investigations again" as to the number of large bombers in

[146] Id., at p. 9141.
[147] See committee exhibit No. 2.
[148] Id., at p. 111.
[149] Id., at p. 122.
[150] Id., at pp. 31–52.
[151] General Marshall stated he was always in fear of a surprise attack on United States territory but the probabilities pointed to the Panama Canal and to the Philippines before Hawaii. Navy Court of Inquiry record, p. 863.
[152] Committee exhibit No. 2, p. 54.
[153] Id., at p. 72.
[154] Id., at p. 82.

the Philippines.[155] Some 50 messages between Manila and Tokyo during the period August 1 to December 1, 1941, contained detailed information concerning airfields, air strength and activity, strength and activity of land forces, location of antiaircraft guns, and other items of defense.[156]

Seattle advised Tokyo on September 20 that a warship under repair at Bremerton, Wash. had "the upper part of the bridge and left side of the bow spotted here and there with red paint".[157] A message of September 6 from Tokyo to Singapore and Batavia requested detailed information concerning various types of fishing vessels should Japan "require the use of these fishing vessels".[158] On October 22 a message from Tokyo to Singapore reflected a specific request, on behalf of the vice chief of the Japanese General Staff, for information concerning the air forces stationed in the Federated Malay States.[159] Another dispatch from Tokyo to Batavia on the same day stated that the Assistant Chief of Staff desired an inspection and report "on the air force in the Dutch Indies" in regard to training, formation, and aerial combat methods; organization, types, number, and location of planes; and types and number of planes being sent from England and the United States.[160]

The exhibits are replete with evidence of the interest of Tokyo not only in the state of defenses but in ships as well, at many different points. For example, an intercepted dispatch from Tokyo to San Francisco of November 29 read:[161] "Make full report beginning December 1 on the following: Ship's nationality, ship's name, port from which it departed (or at which it arrived), and port of destination (or from where it started), date of departure, etc., in detail of all foreign commercial and war ships now in the Pacific, Indian Ocean, and South China Sea." Nor was the Honolulu consul the only one reporting the exact location of ships in harbor. Manila advised Tokyo on November 12 that on the morning of the 12th, an American cruiser of the *Chester* class entered port—"She is tied up at dock No. 7 * * *." [162] And again on November 22, Manila advised Tokyo, among other things, that a camouflaged British cruiser entered port on the "morning of the 21st and anchored at pier No. 7 * * *." [163] Other examples of such reports will be hereinafter set forth.

Even today, of course, we do not know as a matter of fact that the "berthing plan" was a bomb plot. On the basis of testimony before the committee, the desire to know or the supplying of information with respect to the location of vessels *within* a harbor is not of itself conclusive that its only purpose was in contemplation of an attack inasmuch as such information also has the value of indicating what ships are under repair and the readiness of vessels for sortie.[164] For example, Seattle advised Tokyo on September 20, "*Saratoga* class aircraft carrier, 1 ship (*tied up alongside the pier*)" at Bremerton.[165] San Francisco advised Tokyo on October 2, "One *Oklahoma* class battle-

[155] Id., at p. 91.
[156] Id., at pp. 54–98.
[157] Id., at p. 109.
[158] Id., at p. 101.
[159] Id., at p. 102.
[160] Id., at p. 102.
[161] Id., at p. 115.
[162] Id., at p. 87.
[163] Id., at p. 94.
[164] See Committee record, pp. 4622, 4623, 9178, and 9179.
[165] Committee exhibit No. 2, p. 109.

ship has arrived in port and is *moored in front ot the Bethlehem ship-building yard.*[166] It may be argued that if obtaining information concerning the location of ships within a harbor should be construed as definitely indicating a purpose to attack the ships at harbor then these messages would logically appear to indicate a purpose to attack at Bremerton and at San Francisco.

In seeking to determine whether the harbor berthing plan was in reality a "bomb plot" it is noted that in making his report of December 5 [167] and his last report of December 6 [168] to Tokyo concerning vessels at Pearl Harbor, the Honolulu consul did not employ the system established in the plan for indicating the location of ships *within* the harbor. In the report of December 5, he said:

* * * the following ships were in port on the afternoon of the 5th: 8 battle-ships, 3 light cruisers, 16 destroyers * * *.

In the last report, the consul said:

On the evening of the 5th, among the battleships which entered port were (garble) and one submarine tender.   The following ships were observed at anchor on the 6th: 9 battleships, 3 light cruisers, 3 submarine tenders, 17 destroyers and in addition there were 4 light cruisers, 2 destroyers lying at docks (the heavy cruisers and airplane carriers have all left) * * *.

Failure to use the plan for indicating the location of ships within the harbor at the only time when it could have materially assisted the attacking force in locating ships as targets for bombing, that is on December 5 and 6 immediately before the attack, raises a serious question as to whether the berthing plan was in reality a bomb plot at all.

Japanese interviewed since VJ-day have asserted that intelligence obtained from the consulates was regarded as of little importance. They did not include the intelligence under discussion in listing the information which the Task Force employed in planning and executing the attack on December 7.[168a]

The record reflects that no one in Washington interpreted the harbor berthing plan of September 24 and related dispatches as indicative of an attack on the fleet at Pearl Harbor or was in any way conscious of the significance of the messages which it is now possible to read into them.   There was in consequence no conscious or deliberate with-holding of this intelligence from the Hawaiian commanders.   General Marshall, and Admirals Stark, Turner, and Ingersoll testified they had no recollection of having seen these dispatches.[169]

The peculiar division of Pearl Harbor into many lochs, the insatiable desire of Japan for meticulous information concerning vessels of other governments everywhere, the manner in which the berthing plan lent itself to convenience of communications, the fact that Tokyo was repeatedly instructing its consulates to cut down on traffic, the feeling in Washington that Tokyo had no naval observer in Honolulu and in consequence more detailed instructions to its consulate there were required, Japan's natural interest in full information concerning our Pacific Fleet base, the many intercepted dispatches indicating a likely

---

[166] Id., at p. 110.
[167] Id., at p. 26.
[168] Id., at p. 29.
[168a] See Part II, this report concerning Japanese plans for the attack; also section "The Role of Espionage in the Attack", Part III, this report.
[169] Committee record, pp. 2912, 5788, 5108, and 11311. Admiral Stark said: "We have been over this bomb plot thing from start to finish, all of us in the front office, and I still not only have no recollection of having seen it, it is my honest opinion that I did not see it."   Committee record, p. 13969.

Japanese attack at points other than at Pearl Harbor—all of these considerations necessarily entered into the appraisal of the berthing plan.   It may be contended that under such circumstances it would be manifestly unfair to criticize an officer with many other responsibilities [170] for failure to interpret properly a message, considered before the critical turn in our negotiations with Japan, which we single out after the event for minute analysis and conclude may have been designed to assist the Japanese in the bombing of Pearl Harbor.[171]

Similarly, it may be argued that the absence of apparent interest by Japan in the defenses at Hawaii when compared with the avid interest manifested in the defense facilities in the Philippines, Panama, Singapore, Batavia, and on the west coast is indicative, in the days before December 7, of the fact that Hawaii was a much less likely point of attack than these other places; and that in this light, Tokyo's detailed interest in our ship locations and movements was subject to the reasonable construction that Japan desired to be warned in advance of any contemplated action by our fleet and was not seeking information with a view to an attack upon it or, otherwise stated, that she desired information with a view to the fleet's availability for distant operations rather than its susceptibility as a target.[172]   Further, that Pearl Harbor was the base of the Pacific Fleet, the only substantial deterrent to complete freedom of action by the Japanese Navy in Pacific waters and that in consequence thereof an unusual interest by Japan in the location of our fleet units would appear quite understandable.   It may be proper to insist that since Pearl Harbor was the fleet base, Japan could be reasonably sure that substantial fleet units would be located there at virtually all times; [173] and that, with this in mind, failure to manifest an interest in the defenses of Hawaii when compared with such an interest shown at other points has a distinct bearing on whether the information exchanged between Tokyo and Honolulu concerning ship locations and movements could have pointed in any way to likelihood of an attack at Pearl Harbor. In this connection, the evidence does reflect that none of the intercepted messages translated before the attack, between Tokyo and Honolulu for over a year prior to December 7, contain any reference to the defenses of the Army or Navy in Hawaii as distinguished from locations of fleet units.

From these considerations it may be contended that a careful comparison and evaluation of messages relating to espionage activities by Japan's diplomatic establishments would not have reasonably indicated in the days before December 7 any greater likelihood of an attack on Pearl Harbor than was warned against in the dispatches sent the Hawaiian commanders on November 27.[174]

CONCLUSIONS WITH RESPECT TO SHIPS IN HARBOR REPORTS

Despite the foregoing observations, we think there are certain circumstances which distinguish the request for detailed information on

---

[170] See committee record, pp. 2131-2138.

[171] General Miles observed: "* * * this message taken alone would have been of great military significance but it was not taken alone unless you look at it by hindsight, which focuses all light on the event which did happen.   It was one of a great number of messages being sent by the Japanese to various parts of the world in their attempt to follow the movements of our naval vessels, a matter which we knew perfectly well they were doing, and which we ourselves were doing in regard to the Japanese."   Committee record, p. 2100.

[172] See Hewitt Inquiry record, p. 407.

[173] This appears to be the premise assumed by the Japanese in planning and launching the attack.   See Part II, this report.

[174] Committee exhibits Nos. 32 and 37, pp. 9 and 36, respectively.

the berthings of ships in Pearl Harbor from similar or other requests for information concerning other points. War with Japan was admittedly probable for months before it actually occurred. Many of our highest military and naval authorities considered it all but inevitable. As the imminence of war increased so increased the importance of our Pacific Fleet, the home base of which was Pearl Harbor, for in the broad picture of the Pacific, the fleet was our strong arm of defense. Safety and fitness of the Pacific Fleet was of prime importance, and any communication or information bearing thereon should have been given prompt and full consideration by competent authority. We realize the exceedingly great demands upon the intelligence divisions of the War and Navy Departments occasioned by reason of the great flood of intelligence coming in from all parts of the world in the days before Pearl Harbor. Nor do we overlook the Japanese policy of acquiring detailed information of every kind from many points. It may be fair to attribute to this and other considerations the failure to see anything of unusual significance in the request of September 24 for detailed information as to the berthing of ships in Pearl Harbor; but it is difficult to escape the feeling that, when the message of November 15 was translated on December 3 referring to the critical relations between Japan and the United States and requesting that the "ships in harbor report" be made irregularly but at least twice a week and directing that extra care be taken to maintain secrecy, it should have raised in someone's mind the thought that this intelligence was highly important because it dealt with that which was most vital to our safety in the Pacific—the Pacific Fleet. The message of November 20, translated December 4, directing a comprehensive investigation of "the fleet (garble) bases" in the neighborhood of the Hawaiian military reservation should not have lessened such interest.[175]

It cannot be forgotten that a surprise attack by air on Pearl Harbor had been listed and understood, both in Washington and Hawaii, as the greatest danger to that base. We must assume that military men realized that in order to execute successfully such an attack the Japanese would necessarily need detailed information as to dispositions at the point of attack. It would seem to be a natural consequence that if Japan undertook an attack on Pearl Harbor she would seek to acquire such detailed information and in point of time as nearly as possible to the hour of such attempt.

We are unable to conclude that the berthing plan and related dispatches pointed directly to an attack on Pearl Harbor, nor are we able to conclude that the plan was a "bomb plot" in view of the evidence indicating it was not such.[176] We are of the opinion, however, that the berthing plan and related dispatches should have received careful consideration and created a serious question as to their significance. Since they indicated a particular interest in the Pacific Fleet's base this intelligence should have been appreciated and supplied the commander in chief of the Pacific Fleet and the commanding general of the Hawaiian Department for their assistance, along with other information and intelligence available to them, in making their estimate of the situation.

---

[175] It may be argued that the fact that a "war warning" had been sent the Fleet on November 27 along with the code destruction intelligence before these latter messages were translated had a bearing on or possibly conditioned the failure to attach significance to them.

[176] Admiral Kimmel said: "These Japanese instructions and reports pointed to an attack by Japan upon the ships in Pearl Harbor." Committee record, pp. 6779, 6780.

General Short said: "* * * such details would be useful only for sabotage, or for air or submarine attack on Hawaii." Committee record, p. 7989.

The "Winds Code" [177]

On November 19, 1941, Tokyo set up a code designed to be employed in daily Japanese language short-wave news broadcasts or general intelligence broadcasts in the event ordinary commercial channels of communication were no longer available. Two circular [178] dispatches Nos. 2353 and 2354 were translated by the Navy Department: [179]

From: Tokyo
To: Washington
19 November 1941
Circular #2353
  "Regarding the broadcast of a special message in an emergency.
  In case of emergency (danger of cutting off our diplomatic relations), and the cutting off of international communications, the following warnings will be added in the middle of the daily Japanese language short-wave news broadcast.
  (1) In case of a Japan–U. S. relations in danger: *HIGASHI NO KAZEAME.*[1]
  (2) Japan–U. S. S. R. relations: *KITA NO KAZE KUMORI.*[2]
  (3) Japan-British relations: *NISHI NO KAZE HARE.*[3]
  This signal will be given in the middle and at the end as a weather forecast and each sentence will be repeated twice.   When this is heard destroy all code papers, etc.   This is as yet to be a completely secret arrangement.
  Forward as urgent intelligence.

[1] East wind rain.
[2] North wind cloudy.
[3] West wind clear.

From: Tokyo
To: Washington
19 November 1941
Circular #2354
  When our diplomatic relations are becoming dangerous, we will add the following at the beginning and end of our general intelligence broadcasts:
  (1) If it is Japan-U. S. relations, "HIGASHI".
  (2) Japan-Russia relations, "KITA".
  (3) Japan-British relations (including Thai, Malaya, and N. E. I.), "NISHI".
  The above will be repeated five times and included at beginning and end.
  Relay to Rio de Janeiro, Buenos Aires, Mexico City, San Francisco.

These intercepts were confirmed by a dispatch from the commander in chief of the Asiatic Fleet to the Office of Naval Operations dated November 28, 1941; [180] a message directed to the State Department from its diplomatic representative in Batavia dated December 4, 1941; [181] and a dispatch from the Army's military representative in Batavia, reading as follows: [182]

  Japan will notify her consuls of war decision in her foreign broadcasts as weather report at end.   East wind rain, United States.   North wind cloudy, Russia. West wind clear, England with attack on Thailand Malay and Dutch East Indies.   Will be repeated twice or may use compass directions only.   In this case words will be introduced five times in general text.

The foregoing message was sent "deferred" by naval communications for General Miles of the War Department and was not decoded until the morning of December 5, 1941.

Both the War and Navy Departments extended themselves in an effort to monitor for a message in execution of the winds code.   Exten-

[177] A detailed record study of the winds code will be found set forth as Appendix E to this report.
[178] The circular dispatches were designed for Japanese diplomatic establishments generally.
[179] Committee exhibit No. 1, pp. 154, 155.
[180] Id., No. 142.
[181] Id.
[182] Id.

sive evidence has been taken concerning the matter, the preponderate weight of which indicates that no genuine execute message was intercepted by or received.in the War and Navy Departments prior to the attack on Pearl Harbor. Investigation conducted in Japan strongly indicates no execute message was dispatched before the attack and the British and Dutch, who were also monitoring for an execute message, have advised that no such message was intercepted.[183] A reasonable construction of the code is that it was designed for use in the event ordinary commercial channels of communication were no longer available to Japan, a contemplation which did not materialize prior to Pearl Harbor. The fact that a message "West wind clear," applying to England, was broadcast after the attack tends to confirm this conclusion.[184] Inasmuch as the question of the winds code has been one of the few disputed factual issues in the Pearl Harbor case, there has been set forth in Appendix E to this report a detailed study of the matter.

Based on the evidence it is concluded that no genuine "winds" message in execution of the code and applying to the United States was received by the War or Navy Departments prior to the attack on December 7, 1941. It appears, however, that messages were received which were initially thought possibly to be in execution of the code but were determined not to be execute messages.

Granting for purposes of discussion that a genuine execute message applying to the winds code was intercepted before December 7, we believe that such fact would have added nothing to what was already known concerning the critical character of our relations with the Empire of Japan.

"Hidden Word" Code

In addition to the winds code the Japanese in a dispatch on November 27 established another emergency system of communications that has been familiarly referred to as the "hidden word" code.[185] The dispatch establishing this code, which was sent as a circular to all diplomatic establishments, stated: "With international relations becoming more strained, the following system of despatches, using *INGO DENPO* (hidden word, or misleading language telegrams) is placed in effect" and further "in order to distinguish these cables from others, the English word *STOP* will be added at the end as an indicator." Thereafter, a number of code words, apparently arbitrarily chosen, were set forth with the meaning of each word placed opposite thereto. Among the code words were: *HATTORI* meaning "Relations between Japan and * * * (blank) are not in accordance with expectation"; *KOYANAGI* meaning "England"; and *MINAMI* meaning "U. S. A."

On the morning of December 7 a circular telegram from Tokyo was intercepted reading:[186]

URGENT 92494 *KOYANAGI* RIJIYORI SEIRINOTUGOO ARUNITUKI *HATTORI MINAMI* KINENBUNKO SETURITU KIKINO KYOKAIN-GAKU SIKYUU DENPOO ARITASS STOP—TOGO.

---

[183] Id.
[184] Id.
[185] Committee exhibit No. 1, pp. 186–188. The original code was supplemented by a dispatch of December 2 from Tokyo to Singapore which was translated after the attack. Committee exhibit No. 1, pp. 216–219.
[186] Committee exhibit No. 142-B.

The translation as made by the Navy of the foregoing hidden-word message was distributed in Washington to authorized recipients of, Magic at 11 a. m. on December 7 in the following form:[187]

Relations between Japan and England are not in accordance with expectation.

This was not the complete message, which should have been translated: "Relations between Japan and the following countries are not in accordance with expectation: England, United States."[188]

The reason for the message having been distributed on the morning of December 7 with the words *United States* omitted is explained by the fact that Captain Kramer in his haste occasioned by the necessity of delivering other messages, including the "one o'clock message", overlooked the code word relating to the United States and translated the message as meaning only that "relations between Japan and England are not in accordance with expectation." He indicated that he later discovered the error and telephoned at "a quarter of one or 1 o'clock" the correction to his superior and an officer of Military Intelligence.[189]

It is clear that the hidden-word message as literally translated [190] contained no information of any import not already greatly overshadowed, as will hereinafter appear, by other intelligence available on the morning of December 7 even had the words *United States* been included at the time of distribution.

The "Deadline Messages"

The following message, No. 736, from Tokyo to the Japanese Embassy in Washington, relating to the then current Japanese United States negotiations, was intercepted on November 5, 1941: [191]

Because of various circumstances, *it is absolutely necessary that all arrangements for the signing of this agreement be completed by the 25th of this month.* I realize that this is a difficult order, but under the circumstances it is an unavoidable one. Please understand this thoroughly and tackle the problem of saving the Japanese-U. S. relations from falling into a chaotic condition. Do so with great determination and with unstinted effort, I beg' of you.

This information is to be kept strictly to yourself only.

On November 11, 1941 another message from Tokyo to Washington, No. 762, was intercepted, referring to the deadline set in the message of November 5: [192]

Judging from the progress of the conversations, there seem to be indications that the United States is still not fully aware of the exceedingly criticalness of the situation here. *The fact remains that the date set forth in my message #736**is absolutely immovable under present conditions. It is a definite dead line and therefore it is essential that a settlement be reached by about that time.* The session of Parliament opens on the 15th (work will start on [the following day?]) according to the schedule. The government must have a clear picture of things to come, in presenting its case at the session. You can see, therefore, that the situation is nearing a climax, and that time is indeed becoming short.

I appreciate the fact that you are making strenuous efforts, but in view of the above mentioned situation, will you redouble them. When talking to the Secretary of State and others, drive the points home to them. Do everything in your power

---

[187] Id.
[188] The Army translation of the message supplied in March 1944 read as follows: "Relations between Japan and _____ are approaching a crisis (on the verge of danger): England, United States." Committee exhibit No. 142-B.
[189] Hewitt Inquiry record, pp. 133–136.
[190] Id., at pp. 579–581.
[191] Committee exhibit No. 1, p. 100.
[192] Id., at pp. 116, 117.

to get a clear picture of the U. S. attitude in the minimum amount of time. *At the same time do everything in your power to have them give their speedy approval to our final proposal.*

We would appreciate being advised of your opinion on whether or not they will accept our final proposal A.

The deadline was again referred to in a dispatch of November 15 from Tokyo to Washington, stating: [193]

It is true that the United States may try to say that since we made no particular mention of the changed status of the talks, they were under the impression that they were still of a preliminary nature.

Whatever the case may be, *the fact remains that the date set forth in my message #736 is an absolutely immovable one.* Please, therefore, make the United States see the light, so as to make possible the signing of the agreement by that date.

Referring to a dispatch from its Washington Ambassador, the following message from Tokyo was intercepted on November 16:[194]

I have read your #1090,[195] and you may be sure that you have all my gratitude for the efforts you have put forth, but *the fate of our Empire hangs by the slender thread of a few days,* so please fight harder than you ever did before.

What you say in the last paragraph of your message is, of course, so and I have given it already the fullest consideration, but I have only to refer you to the fundamental policy laid down in my #725.[196] Will you please try to realize what that means. In your opinion we ought to wait and see what turn the war takes and remain patient. However, I am awfully sorry to say that the situation renders this out of the question. I set the dead line for the solution of these negotiations in my #736, and there will be no change. Please try to understand that. You see how short the time is; therefore, do not allow the United States to sidetrack us and delay the negotiations any further. Press them for a solution on the basis of our proposals, and do your best to bring about an immediate solution.

Responding to requests of its Ambassadors,[197] in an intercepted message of November 22, 1941, Tokyo extended the deadline date from November 25 to November 29 in the following terms: [198]

To both you Ambassadors.

It is awfully hard for us to consider changing the date we set in my #736. You should know this, however, I know you are working hard. Stick to our fixed policy and do your very best. Spare no efforts and try to bring about the solution we desire. There are reasons beyond your ability to guess why we wanted to settle Japanese-American relations by the 25th, but if within the next three or four days you can finish your conversations with the Americans; *if the signing can be completed by the 29th,* (let me write it out for you—twenty-ninth); if the pertinent notes can be exchanged; if we can get an understanding with Great Britain and the Netherlands; and in short if everything can be finished, *we have decided to wait until that date.* This time we mean it, that the dead line absolutely cannot be changed. *After that things are automatically going to happen.* Please take this into your careful consideration and work harder than you ever have before. This for the present, is for the information of you two Ambassadors alone.

As a follow-up to the foregoing message, Tokyo on November 24, 1941, advised its Ambassadors that the time limit set in the message of November 22 was in Tokyo time.[199]

It is clear from the foregoing messages that "things are automatically going to happen" after November 29, Tokyo time. It is equally clear from information now available that the happening was to be the contemplated departure of the Japanese task force to attack

[193] Id., at p. 130.
[194] Id., at pp. 137, 138.
[195] See committee exhibit No. 1, pp. 127–129.
[196] Id., at pp. 92–94.
[197] Id., at p. 159.
[198] Id., at p. 165.
[199] Id., at p. 173.

Pearl Harbor. But the question is not what the deadline messages are seen now to mean but what they reasonably conveyed to officials in Washington in the days before December 7.

Tokyo had indicated the extreme importance of time as the dead line approached:[200] "The fate of our Empire hangs by the slender thread of a few days." But does this importance and the fact of the deadline indicate an attack at Pearl Harbor or, for that matter, an attack upon the United States elsewhere? It must be recalled that on August 17, following the Atlantic Conference, President Roosevelt advised the Government of Japan that if she took any further steps in pursuance of a program of domination by force or threat of force of neighboring countries, the Government of the United States would be compelled to take any and all steps necessary toward insuring the security of the United States.[201] It is not unreasonable to conclude that, failing to secure a satisfaction of her demands by November 29, Japan had determined to launch a program of aggression which she felt would involve her in war against the United States. The extensive deployment of her forces to the south after November 29, it would reasonably appear, was regarded as the action to be taken upon expiration of the deadline date. Washington had expressed this estimate to Admiral Kimmel on November 27:[202]

> The number and equipment of Japanese troops and the organization of naval task forces indicates an amphibious expedition against either the Philippines, Thai, or Kra Peninsula or possibly Borneo.

One of the factors considered in dispatching the "war warning" to Admiral Kimmel on November 27 was that of alerting the Fleet before the cut-off date of November 29.[203] We believe that the dispatch of November 27 to Admiral Kimmel beginning, "This dispatch is to be considered a war warning" and the dispatch to General Short of the same date advising that "hostile action possible at any moment" was the equivalent of and in fact was of greater significance than the so-called "deadline messages" merely informing that things would automatically happen after November 29.

Based on what is now known concerning the plan of the Japanese attack, it is believed that in contemplation of the future intelligence such as the deadline messages could well be supplied field commanders as an item of information for their assistance along with dispatches designed to alert and to supply them with an estimate of the situation.

DISPATCHES INDICATING FRAUDULENT NATURE OF NEGOTIATIONS AFTER NOVEMBER 28, 1941

The following message (No. 844) from Tokyo to the Japanese Embassy in Washington, intercepted on November 28, 1941, indicated that negotiations thereafter were to be a sham and fraud: [204]

> Well, you two Ambassadors have exerted superhuman efforts, but in spite of this, the United States has gone ahead and presented this humiliating proposal. This was quite unexpected and extremely regrettable. The Imperial Government can by no means use it as a basis for negotiations. *Therefore, with a report of the views of the Imperial Government on this American proposal which I will send*

---

[200] Id., at p. 137.
[201] See Part I, *supra*, "Diplomatic Background of the Pearl Harbor Attack".
[202] Committee exhibit No. 37, p. 36.
[203] See testimony of Admiral Turner. It also appears that the November 24 warning to the commander in chief of the Pacific Fleet was sent with a view to the deadline date of November 25.
[204] Committee exhibit No. 1, p. 195.

*you in two or three days, the negotiations will be de facto ruptured.   This is inevitable.
However, I do not wish you to give the impression that the negotiations are broken off.*
Merely say to them that you are awaiting instructions and that, although the
opinions of your Government are not yet clear to you, to your own way of thinking
the Imperial Government has always made just claims and has borne great sacrifices for the sake of peace in the Pacific.   Say that we have always demonstrated
a long-suffering and conciliatory attitude, but that, on the other hand, the United
States has been unbending, making it impossible for Japan to establish negotiations.   Since things have come to this pass, I contacted the man you told me
to in your #1180 and he said that under the present circumstances that you
suggest is entirely unsuitable.   From now on do the best you can.

In the light of hindsight, an intercepted dispatch of November 29
(translated November 30) portrayed the extent of Japanese guile
in perpetrating the fraud: [205]

Re my #844.
We wish you would make one more attempt verbally along the following lines:
The United States government has (always?) taken a fair and judicial position
and has formulated its policies after full consideration of the claims of both sides.
However, the Imperial Government is at a loss to understand why it has now
taken the attitude that the new proposals we have made cannot be made the basis
of discussion, but instead has made new proposals which ignore actual conditions
in East Asia and would greatly injure the prestige of the Imperial Government.
With such a change of front in their attitude toward the China problem, what
has become of the basic objectives that the U. S. government has made the basis
of our negotiations during these seven months?   On these points we would request
careful self-reflection on the part of the United States government.
(In carrying out this instruction, please be careful that this does not lead to
anything like a breaking off of negotiations.)

It is to be noted in passing that the foregoing dispatch, without
benefit of retrospection, conceivably sugested at the time of its
interception, the possibility that Japan was putting out a "feeler"
with a view to our withdrawing from the position assumed in Secretary
Hull's note of November 26.

In an intercepted dispatch from Tokyo to its Washington Ambassador on December 1 it was observed that the deadline date of November
29 had come and gone with the situation continuing to be increasingly
critical, however, "to prevent the United States from becoming unduly
suspicious we have been advising the press and others that though
there are some wide differences between Japan and the United States,
the negotiations are continuing.   (The above is for only your information.)" [206]

During a trans-Pacific telephone conversation between Yamamoto
in Tokyo and Kurusu on November 27 (translated November 28)
instructions were issued to Kurusu: "Regarding negotiations, don't
break them off." [207]

The following significant trans-Pacific conversation was had between
Kurusu and Yamamoto on November 30: [208]

Kurusu. It is all arranged for us to meet Hull tomorrow.   We received a short
one from you, didn't we?   Well, we will meet him in regard to that.   There is a
longer one coming isn't there?   In any case we are going to see him about the
short one (i. e., telegram.   The longer one is probably Tokyo's reply to Mr.
Hull's proposals.)
YAMAMOTO. Yes.   I see.
KURUSU. The President is returning tomorrow.   He is hurrying home.
Y. Is there any special significance to this?
K. The newspapers have made much of the Premier's speech, and it is having
strong repercussions here.

---

[205] Id., at p. 199.
[206] Id., at p. 208.
[207] Id., at pp. 188–191.
[208] Id., at pp. 206–207.

Y. Is that so.

K. Yes. It was a drastic statement he made. The newspapers carried large headlines over it; and the President seems to be returning because of it. There no doubt are other reasons, but this is the reason the newspapers are giving.

(Pause.)

Unless greater caution is exercised in speeches by the Premier and others, it puts us in a very difficult position. All of you over there must watch out about these ill-advised statements. Please tell Mr. Tani.

Y. We are being careful.

K. We here are doing our best, but these reports are seized upon by the correspondents and the worst features enlarged up. Please caution the Premier, the Foreign Minister, and others. Tell the Foreign Minister that we had expected to hear something different, some good word, but instead we get this. (i. e. Premier's speech.)

(After a pause, Kurusu continues, using voice code.)

K. What about the internal situation? (In Japan.)

Y. No particular _ _ _ _ (one or two words faded out) _ _ _ _.

K. Are the Japanese-American negotiations to continue?

Y. Yes.

K. *You were very urgent about them before, weren't you; but now you want them to stretch out. We will need your help. Both the Premier and the Foreign Minister will need to change the tone of their speeches!*—Do you understand? Please all use more discretion.

Y. When will you see them. The 2nd?

K. Let's see—this is Sunday midnight here. Tomorrow morning at ten. That will be Monday morning here.

(Pause.)

Actually the real problem we are up against is the effects of happenings in the South. You understand don't you?

Y. Yes. Yes. How long will it be before the President gets back?

K. I don't know exactly. According to news reports he started at 4:00 this afternoon. He should be here tomorrow morning sometime.

Y. Well then—Goodbye.

Admiral Kimmel in testifying before the joint committee said: [209]

The intercepted Japanese diplomatic dispatches show that on and after November 29, a Japanese plan of action automatically went into effect; that the plan was of such importance that it involved the fate of the empire; and that Japan urgently wanted the United States to believe that negotiations were continuing after the deadline date to prevent suspicion as to the nature of the plan.

What was this plan? Why such elaborate instructions to stretch out negotiations as a pretext to hide the operation of this plan? Anyone reading the Japanese intercepted messages would face this question.

Certainly the concealed Japanese plans which automatically went into effect on November 29 would hardly be the Japanese movement in Indo-China * * * "No effort was made to mask the movements or presence of the naval forces moving southward, because physical observations of that movement were unavoidable and the radio activity of these forces would provide a desirable semblance of normalcy". (Testimony of Admiral Inglis, Committee Transcript, page 453.) The troop movements to southern Indo-China were the subject of formal diplomatic exchanges between the two governments of Japan and the United States.

* * * * * * *

Thus, it was apparent to the Japanese government from this formal representation of the United States that our government was aware of the movement in Indo-China. The United States expressed its concern about potential Japanese action against the Philippines, the East Indies, Malaya, or Thailand. There was, therefore, very little reason for Japan to keep up a pretext of negotiations for the purpose of disguising these objectives.

Consequently, as time went on after November 29, and as Japan insisted to her envoys upon the continuance of negotiations as a pretext to divert the suspicion of the United States, it must have been apparent to a careful student of the intercepted dispatches that Japan on a deadline date of November 29 had put into effect an operation, which was to consume a substantial time interval before its results were apparent to this government, and which appeared susceptible of effective concealment in its initial phases.

[209] Committee record, pp. 6791–6793.

The observations of Admiral Kimmel are well taken, however, they are colored by knowledge of subsequent events. He has stated that on or after November 29 "A Japanese *plan* of action automatically went into effect" whereas the Japanese had stated that after that date "things are automatically going to happen." He comments that "negotiations were continuing after the deadline date to prevent suspicion as to the nature of the plan" whereas it is only after the event that this ruse could be apparent. He refers to the "concealed Japanese plans" and observes that Japan's open move to the South could not be the "automatic move." This premise presupposes that the "automatic move" was to be concealed, a fact which was not and could not be known until after the attack.

Admiral Kimmel makes reference to the intensification of Japanese activity to the South about November 29 [210] but fails to consider that this activity was subject to the reasonable construction that the "automatic move" was the move to the South and the desire to "stretch out" negotiations was a natural step in seeking to prevent a thwarting of Japanese plans in that direction before she was fully poised for attack. That the Japanese movement to the South effectively diverted attention from other points and effectively disguised the strike against Pearl Harbor is indisputable. But this is known only after the attack.

With the benefit of hindsight it is possible to attach to the fraudulent character of Japanese negotiations after November 28 the greatest significance—to see that it clothed a Japanese action fraught with typical treachery. But it is clear from the evidence that the salient questions in the minds of responsible officials in Washington in the few days before Pearl Harbor was not—*Would* the Japanese attack?—but *when* and *where* would she attack? The fact that an attack would come was the considered judgment of our military. The Tokyo dispatch of November 28 did not supply the highly essential information which was desired. Neither the intercepted dispatches from Tokyo indicating the fraudulent nature of negotiations after November 28 nor the deadline messages supplied the *when* or *where* of the attack. We do not believe that this intelligence, if taken together, would have predicted Pearl Harbor as a likely place of attack.

To have advised Admiral Kimmel and General Short on November 28 that negotiations thereafter were a Japanese fraud could not have suggested itself strongly to officials in Washington who had only the day before told these commanders: "This dispatch is to be considered a war warning. Negotiations with Japan looking toward stabilization of conditions in the Pacific have ceased and an aggressive move by Japan is expected within the next few days"; and "Japanese future action unpredictable but hostile action possible at any moment."

STATUS OF DIPLOMATIC NEGOTIATIONS AND THE ARMY DISPATCH OF NOVEMBER 27

It is to be recalled that the "war warning" dispatch of November 27 from the Chief of Naval Operations to Admiral Kimmel related, with respect to the status of our diplomatic relations with the Japanese, "Negotiations with Japan looking toward stabilization of condi-

---

[210] Id.

tions in the Pacific *have ceased* * * *." The message from the War Department to General Short, on the other hand, stated "Negotiations with Japan appear to be terminated to *all practical purposes* with only the *barest possibilities* that the Japanese might come back and offer·to continue."

The statement has been made that the estimate of the diplomatic situation given General Short was not accurate and left the impression there was still a possibility of the negotiations continuing whereas we were in reality at "sword's point" with Japan.[211]

The message stated negotiations appeared to be terminated to *all practical purposes* with *only the barest possibilities* that the Japanese might offer to continue. To be sure Secretary Hull had advised the Secretary of War on the morning of November 27 that he had "broken the whole matter off"—had abandoned the idea of a *modus vivendi*—and that he had washed his hands of it and "it is now in the hands of you and Knox, the Army and Navy." [212] But this was precisely the duty of the Secretary of State—*to advise the Army and Navy when the probabilities were that negotiations had passed beyond the diplomatic stage and were in the hands of the military.* Secretary Hull was indicating that he had given up the idea of a temporary diplomatic truce with Japan and was expressing his personal and official feeling that the Japanese Government would not respond to our Government's note of November 26 in such manner as to permit further negotiations. Mr. Hull did not *know* that Japan would not possibly reply with a counter proposal nor did anyone in our Government in Washington at the time the November 27 dispatch was prepared.

In 'recounting the circumstances attending the November 27 dispatch to the Commanding General of the Hawaiian Department (as well as to Panama, the Western Defense Command, and the Philippines) Secretary Stimson stated that he telephoned the President on the morning of November 27 suggesting that a final alert be sent pointing out that commanders be on the *qui vive* for any attack and explaining the exact situation. He stated the President approved this idea. As related by Mr. Stimson:[213] "Ordinarily, of course, there would be no reason for me to participate in the sending of any such message which was the normal function of the military staff.[214] As the President himself, however, had now actually directed the sending of the message, and as I wanted the message clearly to apprise the commanding officers in the various areas as to exactly what the diplomatic situation was, I undertook to participate in the forming of this message myself. In order that it should be strictly accurate, I called up Mr. Hull myself on the telephone and got his exact statement as to the status of the negotiations, which was then incorporated in the first sentence of the messages."

[211]See committee exhibit No. 157. The comment of the Army Pearl Harbor Board was: "This statement on Japanese information is inadequate. It did not convey to·Short the full import of the information concerning the American-Japanese relations which was in the hands of the War Department. It was misleading in that it stated that there was a bare possibility of the resumption of negotiations, which carried with it the implication that such resumption would influence the Japanese-American relations, i. e., that war might not come. The War Department was convinced that war would come."

[212] See Part I, *supra*. section "Diplomatic and Military Liaison in Washington."

[213] See statement of Mr. Stimson, committee record, p. 14395.

[214] General Marshall who ordinarily would have prepared such a dispatch was in North Carolina on November 27 incident to troop maneuvers. It appears that prior to his departure from Washington he had discussed generally with General Gerow the matter of sending a warning message to our outpost commanders. The message was finally prepared by Secretary Stimson in collaboration with General Gerow, among others. See statement of Mr. Stimson, committee record, pp. 14394, 14395.

It is to be noted that, according to Mr. Stimson's diary, after Secretary Hull had told him the matter was now in the hands of the Army and Navy, he called the President who gave him a little different view—"He said they had ended up, but they ended up with a magnificent statement prepared by Hull. I found out afterwards that this was not a reopening of the thing but a statement of our constant and regular position." [215] It was later during the day, while in conference with the Secretary of Navy and General Gerow incident to preparing the warning dispatch, that Mr. Stimson called Mr. Hull [216] and "got the exact statement from him of what the situation was." [217] And from information available on November 27 there was *only the barest possibility*, precisely the statement in the warning, that Japan would accept or respond with a counter proposal to the note of November 26.

It is to be noted that it was not until November 28 that a dispatch from Tokyo to Washington was intercepted stating in part: [218]

* * * with a report of the views of the Imperial Government on this American proposal which I will send you in two or three days, the negotiations will be *de facto* ruptured. This is inevitable. However, I do not wish you to give the impression that the negotiations are broken off.

While this message would indicate at the time and we now know it to be a fact that Japanese negotiations were thereafter a fraud, on the very next day, November 29, a dispatch from Tokyo to Washington was intercepted stating,[219] "We wish you would make *one more attempt* verbally along the following lines," thereafter suggesting a line of approach in the discussions and concluding, "In carrying out this instruction, please be careful that this does not lead to anything like a breaking off of negotiations." Here there is manifested more than a "bare possibility" that the Japanese would continue the negotiations and had this *Magic* message been supplied General Short there is no doubt he would have concluded the same thing even after November 27. Indeed, had Admiral Kimmel and General Short been supplied all of the diplomatic messages reviewed by this Committee it is concluded that their estimate of the diplomatic situation would not have gone beyond a belief that there was only the barest possibility that Japan would continue the negotiations; for the messages indicate throughout a conflicting and variable disposition by Japan with respect to pursuance of the negotiations and her desire for peace.[220]

The message to General Short is regarded as more accurately stating the status of the diplomatic negotiations than did the Navy message advising flatly that negotiations had ceased. The action taken by the Navy was with a view to making clear beyond question the seriousness [221] of the situation whereas the Army message, as stated by Secretary Stimson, sought to give General Short the *exact* diplomatic situation. It is to be noted that General Short had available the

[215] Committee record, p. 14422.
[216] See testimony of Mr. Hull, committee record, p. 1188.
[217] See Mr. Stimson's diary, committee record, p. 14423; see also pp. 2686, 2687.
[218] Committee exhibit No. 1, p. 195.
[219] Id., at p. 199.
[220] See in this connection the testimony of Admiral Leigh Noyes, committee record, pp. 12720–12722. It should be noted that Captain McCollum said: "I discounted anything which showed that they were not going to jump on us. Everything I tried to say is that I felt that they were going to jump on us, that I was convinced that the situation between us and Japan was intensely acute. Had I not felt that way I certainly should not have put my office on a 24-hour basis early in November." Committee record, p. 9268.
[221] See testimony of Admiral Turner, committee record, p. 5163.

Navy estimate of the situation inasmuch as he saw the "war warning" of November 27 just as Admiral Kimmel, in turn, saw the War Department warning of the same date.

Even conceding for purposes of discussion that the dispatch to General Short should have contained the same statement as did the Navy message; that is, "negotiations * * * have ceased", such does not in any way alter the responsibilities in the case. Certainly in any situation no commanding officer will determine his course of action on the basis of the bare possibility that negotiations may be continued. How much more is this true when in the same message he is told that hostilities are possible at any moment and is given orders indicating the necessity for defense against an attack from without!

It is in fact believed that had the message been otherwise worded, stating only that there was a *possibility the negotiations would be ruptured* and carrying the same orders, it was the duty of the Commanding General of the Hawaiian Department to gird his defense against the implications of that possibility. General Short was advised there was only the barest possibility that negotiations were *not already ruptured.*

FAILURE TO FOLLOW-UP ON THE SHORT REPLY OF NOVEMBER 28

It is to be recalled that General Short's reply to the warning message of November 27 signed "Marshall," [222] read: [223]

Report Department alerted to prevent sabotage. Liaison with Navy reurad four seven two twenty seventh.

The evidence reflects that it was the responsibility of the War Plans Division of the War Department to prepare the warning and the orders it contained for approval by the Chief of Staff or the Secretary of War.[224] Having instructed the commanding general in Hawaii to report measures taken, it was the responsibility of the War Plans Division to review the report and to advise the Hawaiian commander in the event the action taken by him was not in keeping with the desires of the War Department. The brief report of action taken, as sent by General Short, was initialed by General Gerow, Chief of the War Plans Division and by the Secretary of War.[225] The evidence is not clear as to whether the report was seen by General Marshall inasmuch as it was not initialed by him although he did initial other reports from overseas garrisons to which the Short report may have been attached.[226]

---

[222] For reference convenience, this dispatch was as follows:

"Negotiations with Japan appear to be terminated to all practical purposes with only the barest possibilities that the Japanese Government might come back and offer to continue. Japanese future action unpredictable but hostile action possible at any moment. If hostilities cannot be avoided the United States desires that Japan commit the first overt act. This policy should not, repeat not, be construed as restricting you to a course of action that might jeopardize your defense. Prior to hostile Japanese action you are directed to undertake such reconnaissance and other measures as you deem necessary but these measures should be carried out so as not, repeat not, to alarm civil population or disclose intent. Report measures taken. Should hostilities occur you will carry out the tasks assigned in rainbow five so far as they pertain to Japan. Limit dissemination of this highly secret information to minimum essential officers." (Committee exhibit No. 32, p. 7.)

[223] See exhibit No. 32, p. 12. This is the form of the message as paraphrased and reviewed in the War Department. The message as sent read: "Reurad four seven two 27th. Report Department alerted to prevent sabotage. Liaison with the Navy. Short." It was addressed to   *Chief of Staff.*

[224] See testimony of General Gerow, committee record, p. 2687 *et seq.*

[225] Id.

[226] Id.

General Marshall testified: [227]

I do not remember whether or not I saw General Short's reply, but the presumption must be that I did. In any event that was my opportunity to intervene which I did not do.

General Gerow testified that when the reply from General Short came through he assumed it was in answer to the G–2 message that was sent by General Miles to the Hawaiian Department [228] concerning the likelihood of subversive activities.[229] He stated that after seeing the reply he sent it to Colonel Bundy (now deceased) [229a] who headed the "plans group" and that "it is reasonable to assume that he may possibly have interpreted the message to mean, or the part of the message which said 'liaison with the Navy,' that the commanding general out there had instituted protective measures against sabotage and was working with the Navy to arrange for other defensive measures, including reconnaissance." [230] It should be noted that General Gerow did not discuss the matter with Colonel Bundy but merely suggested this as a reasonable assumption from the way the message was worded. General Gerow said: "I think my executive officer; or the chief of my plans group, might possibly have interpreted the message that way, and that is why it was not brought back to me and my attention invited to the fact that it did not explicitly cover the operation." [231] He observed that the reference to a "No. 472" meant nothing to him at the time since this number was put on the outgoing message by the Signal Corps and was not the number assigned the document by the War Plans Division.[232]

General Gerow admitted that no inquiry was sent to General Short with respect to his report of action taken and that in the light of subsequent events he felt "it might have been desirable to send such an inquiry, and had such an inquiry been sent it would probably have developed the fact that the commanding general in Hawaii was not at that time carrying out the directive in the message signed 'Marshall'." [233] He remarked that "if that had been done, there would have been an opportunity to correct the situation" but that he did not believe "the message could necessarily be interpreted as meaning that sabotage measures only were being taken." [234] After stating that he interpreted the report of General Short to be in reply to the Miles message concerning subversive activities and noting that such an interpretation left him without any reply whatever from the Hawaiian Department with respect to the November 27 warning,

[227] Committee record, p. 3010. See also in this connection, Committee Record, pp. 2899 and 3088.
[228] This message, addressed to G–2 Hawaiian Department, read: "Japanese negotiations have come to practical stalemate. Hostilities may ensue. Subversive activities may be expected. Inform Commanding General and Chief of Staff only." Committee exhibit No. 32, p. 10.
[229] Committee record, p. 2714.
[229a] Col. Charles W. Bundy was killed in a plane crash shortly after the attack while en route to Pearl Harbor.
[230] Id., at pp. 2713, 2714. In this connection Secretary Stimson said: "* * * he (General Short) then sent a reply message to Washington which gave no adequate notice of what he had failed to do and which was susceptible of being taken, and was taken, as a general compliance with the main warning from Washington. My initials show that this message crossed my desk, and in spite of my keen interest in the situation it certainly gave me no intimation that the alert order against an enemy attack was not being carried out. Although it advised me that General Short was alert against sabotage, I had no idea that being 'alerted to prevent sabotage' was in any way an express or implied denial of being alert against an attack by Japan's armed forces. The very purpose of a fortress such as Hawaii is to repel such an attack, and Short was the commander of that fortress. Furthermore, Short's statement in his message that 'liaison' was being carried out with the Navy, coupled with the fact that our message of November 27 had specifically directed reconnaissance, naturally gave the impression that the various reconnaissance and other defensive measures in which the cooperation of the Army and the Navy is necessary, were under way and a proper alert was in effect." See statement of Mr. Stimson, committee record, pp. 14408, 14409.
[231] Committee record, pp. 2716, 2717.
[232] Id., at p. 2715.
[233] Id., at p. 2716.
[234] Id.

General Gerow explained: "I was handling a great many papers at that time, and it was the responsibility of the officers in my division to check the messages and correspondence and bring to my attention anything of importance that required action on my part." [235] He further observed that it did not occur to him that General Short would not take some reconnaissance and other defensive measures after receiving the November 27 message—"he was an experienced commander and it never entered my mind that he would not take such action." [236] In the course of Counsel's examination reference was made to the following comments by Secretary Stimson with respect to the investigation conducted by the Army of the Pearl Harbor disaster: [237]

Again, as I have pointed out, General Short, in response to a message which had been sent out containing a warning of possible hostilities and a request for a report of actions, had sent a message to the War Department which was susceptible of the interpretation that he was on the alert against sabotage only, and not on the alert against an air raid or other hostile action.

While this interpretation was not necessarily to be had from the wording of his message, nevertheless, a keener sense of analysis and a more incisive comparison of the messages exchanged, would have invited further inquiry by the War Plans Division of General Short and his failure to go on the necessary alert might well have been discovered.

The Chief of this division and certain of his subordinates knew that a report of the measures taken by General Short had been asked for. General Short's reply was brought to the attention of the chief of the division. A clear and satisfactory reply should have been required. This was not done, and a more efficient functioning of the division would have demanded that careful inquiry as to the meaning of General Short's message be made and no room for ambiguity permitted.

General Gerow was asked if he felt the foregoing was a fair statement of the situation. He replied: [238]

Yes, sir; I do, and if there was any responsibility to be attached to the War Department for any failure to send an inquiry to General Short, the responsibility must rest on War Plans Division, and *I accept that responsibility as Chief of War Plans Division.*

Upon being asked if it were not the function of the Chief of Staff and the Secretary of War to follow up on General Short's report, General Gerow stated: [239]

No, sir; I was a staff adviser to the Chief of Staff, and I had a group of 48 officers to assist me. It was my responsibility to see that those messages were checked, and if an inquiry was necessary, the War Plans Division should have drafted such an inquiry and presented it to the Chief of Staff for approval. As I said, I was chief of that division, and it was my responsibility.

---

[235] Committee record, p. 2717.
[236] Id., at pp. 2719, 2720.
[237] Id., at pp. 2727, 2728. See also committee exhibit No. 157.
[238] Committee record, pp. 2726–2729. In the course of Committee examination of General Marshall the following questions were propounded and answers given:
Question: "Well, a large number of people saw it (the Short reply)? General Gerow saw it and General Gerow testified here that when he saw it he thought first that it was in response to a telegram sent out by G–2 relating to sabotage and when his attention was called to the fact, when I asked counsel to ask hom some further questions and his attention was called to the fact that this was a direct response to your telegram No. 472 of the 27th and was addressed to the Chief of Staff, he then changed his position and said, 'I as Chief of Operations or Chief of War Plans assume full responsibility.'
"Now, I think it is only fair, General Marshall, in the conduct of this examination in ascertaining the facts to find out whether or not, just as General Gerow testified here, whether you assume the same responsibility that he did?"
Answer: "I said earlier in this hearing, Mr. Keefe, in relation to the very thing you are talking about, when I was questioned in regard to General Gerow's statement, that I thought there was a difference; that he had a direct responsibility and I had the full responsibility. Is that an answer to your question?"
Question: "He had a direct responsibility?"
Answer: "And I had the full responsibility."
Question: "And you had the full responsibility. Well, just what do you mean by that?"
Answer: "His was in concern to the handling of the details of the matter and he had a responsibility there. I am responsible for what the General Staff did or did not do."
See Committee Record, pp. 3727, 3728.
[239] Id., at p. 2729.

As earlier pointed out, the War Plans Division had the duty of issuing operational orders and directives; it directed an order to General Short on November 27, instructing him to report measures taken; it failed properly to supervise the report submitted by the commanding general pursuant to direction. General Gerow, the head of the War Plans Division, saw the report of measures taken in the Hawaiian Department and presumed it was in response to a dispatch from Military Intelligence warning of the likelihood of subversive activities. This is not a tenable premise, however, inasmuch as the report by General Short was addressed to the Chief of Staff and was therefore a reply to the warning of November 27, signed "Marshall"; a reply to the message concerning subversive activities would not have been addressed to the Chief of Staff unless the latter had signed the message, which was not the case.[240] Furthermore, the reference by General Short to the number of the message to which he was replying necessarily entailed calling from file the original outgoing dispatch in the event there was any doubt or presumptions necessary in gauging to what the commanding general's report was responsive. Knowing that a reply from General Short had been called for, it was incumbent upon the War Plans Division to follow closely the receipt of such reply and to insure that the action taken was in accordance with that desired. While the reply from General Short was ambiguous and misleading, it was nevertheless the duty of War Plans to require a clear and unequivocal response. By its sheer brevity and lack of detail alone, the report should have suggested the possibility that the official mandate had not been adequately implemented.

The supervision by the War Plans Division in this instance was slipshod. General Gerow, as head of the Division, must bear his share of responsibility for this serious error, a responsibility which he has unhesitatingly assumed. The primary responsibility, however, rests with the appropriate subordinates of General Gerow who had the duty and responsibility for supervision of details.[241]

THE "BERLIN MESSAGE"

An intercepted message from Tokyo to Berlin dated November 30, 1941 (translated December 1) follows: [242]

The conversations begun between Tokyo and Washington last April during the administration of the former cabinet, in spite of the sincere efforts of the Imperial Government, now stand ruptured—broken. (I am sending you an outline of developments in separate message #986) In the face of this, our Empire faces a grave situation and must act with determination. Will Your Honor, therefore, immediately interview Chancellor HITLER and Foreign Minister RIBBENTROP and confidentially communicate to them a summary of the developments. Say to them that lately England and the United States have taken a provocative attitude, both of them. Say that they are planning to move military forces into various places in East Asia and that we will inevitably have to counter by also moving troops. *Say very secretly to them that there is extreme danger that war may suddenly break out between the Anglo-Saxon nations and Japan through some clash of arms and add that the time of the breaking out of this war may come quicker than anyone dreams.*

---

[240] Id., at pp. 2721–2724.
[241] See section "Nature of Responsibilities," *infra*.
[242] Dispatch No. 985, committee exhibit No. 1, p. 204.

Another message of the same date from Tokyo to Berlin read, in part:[243]

Judging from the course of the negotiations that have been going on, we first came to loggerheads when the United States, in keeping with its traditional ideological tendency of managing international relations, re-emphasized her fundamental reliance upon this traditional policy in the conversations carried on between the United States and England in the Atlantic Ocean. The motive of the United States in all this was brought out by her desire to prevent the establishment of a new order by Japan, Germany, and Italy in Europe and in the Far East (that is to say, the aims of the Tri-Partite Alliance). As long as the Empire of Japan was in alliance with Germany and Italy, there could be no maintenance of friendly relations between Japan and the United States was the stand they took. From this point of view, they began to demonstrate a tendency to demand the divorce of the Imperial Government from the Tri-Partite Alliance. This was brought out at the last meeting. *That is to say that it has only been in the negotiations of the last few days that it has become gradually more and more clear that the Imperial Government could no longer continue negotiations with the United States. It became clear, too, that a continuation of negotiations would inevitably be detrimental to our cause.*

And again: [244]

The proposal presented by the United States on the 26th made this attitude of theirs clearer than ever. In it there is one insulting clause which says that no matter what treaty either party enters into with a third power it will not be interpreted as having any bearing upon the basic object of this treaty, namely the maintenance of peace in the Pacific. This means specifically the Three-Power Pact. It means that in case the United States enters the European war at any time the Japanese Empire will not be allowed to give assistance to Germany and Italy. It is clearly a trick. *This clause alone, let alone others, makes it impossible to find any basis in the American proposal for negotiations.* What is more, before the United States brought forth this plan, they conferred with England, Australia, the Netherlands, and China—they did so repeatedly. *Therefore, it is clear that the United States is now in collusion with those nations and has decided to regard Japan, along with Germany and Italy, as an enemy.*

This valuable intelligence added to the total of information pointing to the mounting tenseness of relations but does not materially add to that which was supplied our Hawaiian outpost in the warnings of November 27, insofar as the prime duties of the commanders there were concerned. These messages merely confirmed the conclusions already voiced three days earlier to the outpost commanders that war was imminent; that negotiations had ceased to all practical purposes; that hostile action was possible at any moment.

CODE DESTRUCTION INTELLIGENCE

As has already been observed, Admiral Kimmel was advised by the Navy Department concerning the intercepted messages relating to the destruction of codes in various Japanese diplomatic establishments.[245] While Admiral Kimmel failed to supply General Short this intelligence it is apparent that the commanding general otherwise obtained substantially the equivalent of this information. He was not, however, supplied such information directly by the War Department.

In explaining the reason for the Army's not sending the code-destruction intelligence to Hawaii, General Miles testified:[246]

The main reason was that the code experts apparently agreed, at least the Navy was particularly strong on the point, that their code was much more secure

---

[243] Dispatch No. 986, committee exhibit No. 1, p.p 205-206.
[244] Id., at p. 206.
[245] See Part III, *supra;* also committee exhibit No. 37. For the original intercepted messages concerning the destruction of codes see committee exhibit No. 1, pp. 209, 215, 216, 236, 249, among others.
[246] Committee record, p. 2221.

than ours. It was obviously, of course, of great importance in security that a message be sent in only one code and not two and we had every reason to believe, or thought we did, that a Navy message to Hawaii would be promptly transmitted to the Army authorities there.

The reason advanced by General Miles is consistent with the general practice of the Army not to distribute Magic to field commanders for security reasons.[247] While it appears that in some instances the Navy in Hawaii was specifically advised to inform the Army of messages received, the failure to instruct Admiral Kimmel to so inform General Short concerning the Japanese destruction of codes did not by inference or otherwise indicate that this intelligence should not be supplied the Army. Considering that Hawaii was a command by *mutual cooperation*, the War Department was properly privileged to take for granted that there was a full exchange of information between the Army and Navy commanders,[248] particularly after General Short had specifically stated in his reply to the Department's warning of November 27 that he had established *liaison with the Navy*.

The overwhelming preponderance of testimony by Army and Navy experts is to the effect that the destruction of codes and confidential documents under the circumstances prevailing in early December of 1941 meant war from a military standpoint.[249] It is clear that Washington adequately discharged its responsibility in transmitting this information to Hawaii. With the failure, however, of Admiral Kimmel to read into this intelligence what it is agreed should have been self-evident to him, it is believed that in contemplation of the future the intelligence as well as the departmental appraisal and estimate thereof should be supplied field commanders.[250]

THE MCCOLLUM DISPATCH

The Navy Department in Washington had available substantially the information which was in the possession of Admiral Kimmel with respect to radio intelligence concerning the location and movements of Japanese vessels. It knew, as did Admiral Kimmel, that substantial carrier units of the Japanese Fleet could not be located. This information was carefully considered by the Office of Naval Intelligence.[251] Capt. Arthur McCollum, Chief of the Far Eastern Section of Naval Intelligence, was particularly charged with handling radio intelligence material and it was he who drafted the dispatch of November 24,

---

[247] See section "The 'Magic' ", *supra*.

[248] See committee record, pp. 2220–2224. Secretary Stimson stated: "It was the rule that all such information should be exchanged between the Army and Navy at Pearl Harbor, and the War Department had a right to believe that this information communicated to Admiral Kimmel was also available to General Short." See statement of Secretary Stimson with respect to Army Pearl Harbor Board's report, committee exhibit No. 157.

[249] Admiral Turner, for example, stated: " * * * the destruction of codes in that manner and in those places in my mind and experience is a definite and sure indication of war with the nations in whose capitals or other places those codes are destroyed. * * * It indicates war within two or three days." Committee record, pp. 5294, 5295.

It is to be noted that Washington did not minimize the significance of the code destruction intelligence, despite the fact there were indications this move by Tokyo might be in anticipation of the possibility that the United States would close down her consulates. The following intercepted dispatch of December 3, 1941, from Washington to Tokyo is of pertinence in this regard: "*If we continue to increase our forces in French Indo-China, it is expected that the United States will close up our Consulates, therefore consideration should be given to steps to be taken in connection with the evacuation of the Consuls.*" Committee exhibit No. 1, p. 227.

[250] Before the Roberts Commission, Admiral Kimmel said: " * * * the Department sent me a message that these codes were being burned, and I feel, while that was good information, that they might very well have enlarged somewhat on what they believed it meant. I didn't draw the proper answer. I admit that. I admit that I was wrong. Nobody can gainsay the fact that if I had drawn different conclusions from what I got we might have changed things. Nevertheless, such a dispatch as that, with no amplification, was not near as valuable as it would have been if they had amplified and drawn the conclusions." See Roberts Commission record, p. 589.

[251] See committee record, pp. 9119, 9120.

1941,[252] to the commander in chief of the Asiatic Fleet, a copy of which was sent Admiral Kimmel for information, instructing that the commandant of the Sixteenth Naval District serve in effect as a clearinghouse for data concerning Japanese naval movements inasmuch as the information obtainable in the Philippine area was considered most reliable.

Captain McCollum prepared a memorandum dated December 1, 1941, pointing out that Japanese "service radio calls for units afloat were changed at 0000, 1 December 1941".[253] He also prepared another memorandum bearing the same date summarizing the generally critical situation with respect to Japan.[254] At a meeting attended by Admirals Stark, Ingersoll, Turner and Wilkinson, among others, in the Navy Department on the morning of December 1, Captain McCollum personally read his memorandum last-mentioned, pointing out the imminence of war or rupture of diplomatic relations. He requested information as to whether the fleets in the Pacific had been adequately alerted and testified: "I was given a categorical assurance by both Admiral Stark and Admiral Turner that dispatches fully alerting the fleets and placing them on a war basis had been sent." It is significant that at this time neither Admiral Wilkinson nor Captain McCollum had knowledge of the "war warning" message to Admiral Kimmel.[255]

About December 4, 1941, Captain McCollum prepared a dispatch designed to alert naval outposts, based in part on his memorandum of December 1 outlining the critical situation in the Far East. He testified:[256]

Captain McCollum. * * * I was put in the rather difficult position of not personally knowing what had been sent out to the fleet. Possibly it was none of my business. As I pointed out to you, the basis of this memorandum—the information it was based on—was actually as of about the 28th of November. As time went on we had sent out dispatches to our naval attachés in Tokyo, Pieping, Bangkok, and Shanghai to destroy all of their codes, and to report by the use of a code word, and those codes were destroyed.

We were getting reports from our observers of the Japanese task force which was moving down the Kra Peninsula. Our planes were sighting forces moving; our submarines were trailing them. We had some little information in addition. I still did not know what had been sent to the fleet.

I drafted a rather brief dispatch, outlining the information pretty much as is in this memorandum, but greatly condensed. I went further and stated that we felt everything pointed to an imminent outbreak of hostilities between Japan and the United States. That dispatch was taken by me to my Chief, Captain Hurd, and together we went in to see Admiral Wilkinson. We did it in view of the fact that the function of evaluation of intelligence; that is, the drawing of inferences therefrom, had been transferred over to be a function of the War Plans Division.

I was directed to take that dispatch and present it for the consideration of Admiral Turner, the Director of the War Plans Division, which I did.

Admiral Turner read the dispatch over. He then made a number of corrections in it, striking out all except the information parts of it, more or less, and then showed me for the first time the dispatch which he had sent on the 27th, which I believe is referred to as the "war warning" dispatch, and the one which was sent, I believe, on the 24th—wasn't it?

Counsel. That is right.

Captain McCollum (continuing). Which preceded that dispatch, and said did not I think that was enough. I said, "Well, good gosh, you put in the words 'war warning'. I do not know what could be plainer than that, but, nevertheless I would like to see mine go too."

[252] Dispatch No. 242239, committee exhibit No. 37, p. 33.
[253] Committee exhibit No. 85.
[254] Id., No. 81.
[255] See testimony of Captain McCollum, committee record, p. 9112–9123; also testimony of Admiral Wilkinson.
[256] Committee record, pp. 9130–9134.

He said, "Well, if you want to send it, you either send it the way I corrected it, or take it back to Wilkinson and we will argue about it"—or words to that effect. I cannot presume to remember precisely.

I took it back to Admiral Wilkinson and discussed it with him, and he said, "Leave it here with me for a while," and that is all.

Now, I would like it understood that merely because this was prepared on a dispatch blank in no sense means it was an official dispatch. It was merely my recommendation to my superiors which they were privileged to throw in the wastebasket, I imagine. It was in no sense a part of the official file. It is nothing other than a recommendation for the dispatch officer. I have written dozens of dispatches for the admiral, and he could either throw them away, or use them. There is no record kept of that sort of thing.

Admiral Turner's testimony with respect to the foregoing incident is as follows:[257]

COUNSEL. There is some evidence here that Captain McCollum sometime between the 1st of December and the 7th of December indicated or showed a view that some further warning ought to be sent to Pearl Harbor. Do you know anything about that?

Admiral TURNER. Yes, sir; and I was here yesterday when Senator Ferguson read my testimony from the Navy Court of Inquiry, and I was a little confused in that. I had nothing to refer to, I had not received any warning of more than 2 or 3 days about the proceedings and since that time in going over it myself and thinking about it I arrived at what I believe is a correct statement on that subject.

From time to time Captain McCollum would come to me with drafts of memoranda to the CNO concerning the situation and we would discuss them. I think that he had such a memorandum about the 1st of December but I do not believe that it was intended to go out as a dispatch but merely for the information of the Chief of Naval Operations. Now, I have not seen such a memorandum but I have a recollection of that.

Now, about the 1st or 2d of December—and this is sure, I am completely sure of this, I remember it very distinctly—about the 1st or 2d of December Commander McCollum came into my office and handed me a proposed dispatch written on one sheet of paper and approximately the length of the dispatch of November 27 which he proposed that the Chief of Naval Operations send out to the fleets concerning the imminence of war. It covered the same ground approximately as the CNO dispatches of the 24th and 27th.

Now, I know that Admiral Wilkinson and some other officers in ONI had seen those two dispatches and I asked McCollum if he had seen them.

COUNSEL. You mean seen the officers or seen the dispatches?

Admiral TURNER. If he had seen the two dispatches of the 24th and 27th, and he said, "No." So I pulled the two dispatches out and handed them to him and said, "Well, read these over and then see if you think your dispatch ought to go."

He sat down and read them over and handed them back to me and he said, "No" and tore up his proposed dispatch. It had the same general coverage but was not as specific as these two messages."

COUNSEL. Not as specific as those two that were sent?

Admiral TURNER. Not quite; no, sir.

COUNSEL. Can you give us any information from your recollection as to what his proposed dispatch contained?

Admiral TURNER. I agreed with it entirely, he and I agreed on the situation and he was afraid that a warning had not been sent out and he had prepared himself a dispatch which he wanted to send out to the commander in chief. I did not ask him not to send it but I just merely said, "See if you think it ought to go after you read these dispatches" and he read the two dispatches and he said, "No." He said, "That is enough."

Admiral Wilkinson had no independent recollection of the events attending the McCollum dispatch.[258]

It is regarded as extremely regrettable that the proposed dispatch of Captain McCollum is not in existence in order that an objective estimate of its contents might be made. Captain Safford in testifying before Admiral Hart, stated: [259]

[257] Id., at pp. 5217–5219.
[258] Id., at pp. 4655–4658.
[259] Hart inquiry record, p. 360.

* * * On the 4th of December 1941, Commander McCollum drafted a long warning message to the Commanders in Chief of the Asiatic and Pacific Fleets, summarizing significant events up to that date, quoting the "Winds Message," and ending with the positive warning that war was imminent. Admiral Wilkinson approved this message and discussed it with Admiral Noyes in my presence. I was given the message to read after Admiral Noyes read it, and saw it at about three p. m., Washington time, on December 4, 1941. Admiral Wilkinson asked, "What do you think of the message?" Admiral Noyes replied, "I think it is an insult to the intelligence of the Commander in Chief." Admiral Wilkinson stated, "I do not agree with you. Admiral Kimmel is a very busy man with a lot of things on his mind, and he may not see the picture as clearly as you and I do. I think it only fair to the Commander in Chief that he be given this warning and I intend to see it if I can get it released by the front office." Admiral Wilkinson then left and I left, a few minutes later. At the time of the Japanese attack on Pearl Harbor, I thought that this warning message had been sent, and did not realize until two years later, when I studied the Roberts report very carefully, that McCollum's message had not been sent.

The statement by Captain Safford that the proposed dispatch referred to an implementation of the "winds code" was contradicted by Captain McCollum who categorically testified that his dispatch contained no reference to a winds execut message and that, in fact, to his knowledge no such message had been received.[260] As elsewhere pointed out, the conclusion is made from all of the evidence that no execution message based on the "winds code" was ever received in the War or Navy Departments prior to December 7.

The fact that Admiral Kimmel already possessed the vital intelligence with respect to the "lost" Japanese carriers and the unusual change in service calls on December 1 would necessarily have conditioned any consideration of an additional warning to him based thereon. However, considering all of the significant intelligence available around December 1, Captain McCollum, not knowing of the warning dispatches, prepared at sometime between December 1 and 4 an alerting message which he felt should have been dispatched. Admiral Turner looked with disfavor on this message for the reason that he felt it added nothing to what had already been supplied the fleet and the further fact that he regarded responsible commanders as adequately alerted, an attitude which prevailed throughout the War and Navy Departments. Captain McCollum, too, regarded the "war warning" of November 27 as fully adequate but testified he would also "like" to see his warning transmitted. There is no evidence before the Committee indicating with any degree of accuracy the contents of the so-called McCollum dispatch to assist in determining whether it may have added anything to the warning dispatches of November 27 to the Hawaiian commanders.[261]

EVENTS OF DECEMBER 6 AND 7, 1941

An extensive amount of testimony has been taken concerning the events of December 6 and 7, 1941, attending the interception, distribution, and action taken with respect to four diplomatic dispatches from Japan to her Washington ambassadors. These four dispatches, each of which will elsewhere be discussed fully, were:

(1) The so-called "Pilot Message," No. 901, on December 6 advising that a long 14-part memorandum for the United States

---

[260] Committee record, p. 9134.

[261] This same observation would apply with respect to a warning dispatch said to have been prepared in the War Department by Colonel Otis K. Sadtler which allegedly was not sent for the reason that military outposts were regarded as adequately alerted. The facts concerning the "Sadtler message" are seriously in doubt.

was to be sent as a result of the American proposal of November 26 and that instructions concerning the time of presentation to the United States would be provided in a separate message.[262]

(2) The 14-part memorandum, message No. 902 (transmitted in English) to be presented to the Government of the United States. The first thirteen parts were intercepted on December 6 and the fourteenth part on the morning of December 7.[263]

(3) The message, No. 907, intercepted on December 7, directing the Japanese Ambassador to submit the 14-part memorandum to the United States at 1 p. m., December 7, Washington time.[264]

(4) Message No. 910, intercepted on December 7, directing that the remaining cipher machine (in the Japanese Washington Embassy) be destroyed along with all code machines and that similar disposition be made of secret documents.[265]

Considering the time that has elapsed there has been an understandable amount of discrepancy with respect to the recollection of the participants as to the exact time of handling the foregoing messages in Washington. However, as subsequently will appear, composite consideration of all the testimony tends to present a reasonably satisfactory picture. It is to be recalled that in December of 1941 the Army and Navy cryptographic units were dividing the work incident to decoding and translating Japanese diplomatic messages, the Magic, with the Army generally assuming responsibility for messages bearing even dates of the month and the Navy, the odd dates.[266] Immediately upon decoding and translating messages both the War and Navy Departments each received copies. It was the responsibility of the Army to make distribution of Magic within the War Department and to the Secretary of State, while the Navy was responsible for distribution within the Navy Department and to the White House.

THE "PILOT MESSAGE"

At 6:56 a. m. on December 6 there was filed in Tokyo and between 7:15 and 7:20 a. m. intercepted by a Navy monitoring station[267] a dispatch that has come to be known as the "Pilot Message":[268]

1. The Government has deliberated deeply on the American proposal of the 26th of November and as a result we have drawn up a memorandum for the United States contained in my separate message #902 (in English).

2. This separate message is a very long one. *I will send it in fourteen parts and I imagine you will receive it tomorrow. However, I am not sure. The situation is extremely delicate, and when you receive it I want you to please keep it secret for the time being.*

3. Concerning the time of presenting this memorandum to the United States, I will wire you in a separate message. However, I want you in the meantime to put in nicely drafted form and make every preparation to present it to the Americans just as soon as you receive instructions.

A teletype sheet containing this message in Japanese code was received by the Army from the Navy at 12:05 p. m., December 6.[269] There is no documentary evidence available as to the exact time of decoding, translating, and typing of the pilot message by the Army

[262] Committee exhibit No. 1, pp. 238, 239.
[263] Id., at pp. 239–245.
[264] Id., at p. 248.
[265] Id., at p. 249.
[266] See Army Pearl Harbor Board record, p. 122.
[267] See committee exhibit No. 41.
[268] Committee exhibit No. 1, pp. 238, 239.
[269] Id., No. 41.

apart from the fact that these operations were completed on December 6. Capt. Alwyn D. Kramer was primarily responsible for distribution of Magic on behalf of the Navy. He initially testified before the committee that he was quite certain the pilot message was contained in the folder also containing the first 13 parts of the 14-part memorandum which were distributed by him during the evening of December 6.[270] Captain Kramer subsequently modified this testimony, based on a study of records available in the Navy Department relating to the Magic materials. He testified:[271]

Yesterday afternoon when being questioned concerning this so-called pilot message I made the statement that I believed that the pilot message had arrived sometime late Saturday afternoon, 6 December 1941, or Saturday evening, and that I believed it was distributed Saturday evening with the Japanese note and other papers. I find as a result of my study last night that *the pilot message was not disseminated, at least in the Navy, until Sunday morning subsequent to 10 o'clock,* at the time when the so-called hidden-word message and a number of other short messages, including the 1 o'clock message, were disseminated.

It would seem in consequence, from the best testimony available, that no distribution was made of the pilot message in the Navy Department or to the White House until the morning of December 7. However, it is to be noted that Admiral Wilkinson testified he saw the pilot message before leaving the Navy Department on December 6.[272]

It appears on the other hand that distribution of the message in the War Department and to the State Department was made during the afternoon of December 6. Col. Rufus Bratton, who was responsible for distribution of Magic by the Army, testified:[273]

Distribution of the so-called pilot message was made that afternoon (December 6) about 3 o'clock. I do not now recall whether I did it in person or whether one of my assistants did it, but I do recall discussing the subject both with General Miles and General Gerow Saturday afternoon.[273a]

The military significance of the pilot message will be treated in connection with the discussion of the first 13 parts of the 14-part memorandum.

THE 14-PART MEMORANDUM

First 13 Parts

The first 13 parts of the 14-part memorandum were received in the Navy Department between 11:49 a. m. and 2:51 p. m. on December 6.[274] They had been decoded and typed in the Navy Department and were ready for distribution by approximately 9 p. m. on that date. Copies were thereupon delivered to the War Department.[275] Captain Kramer in making distribution of this material on behalf of the Navy arrived at the White House between 9:30 and 10 p. m., delivering the first 13 parts to Commander Schulz,[276] an assistant to Admiral Beardall,[277] the President's naval aide, with the request they be given the President at the earliest possible moment. Commander Schulz did thereafter deliver the messages to the President who along

---

[270] Committee record, p. 10677.
[271] Id., at p. 10739.
[272] Id., at p. 4659.
[273] Id., pp. 12049, 12050.
[273a] The evidence tends to indicate some doubt, however, as to whether the "Pilot Message" was seen by General Marshall on December 6. See Committee record, p. 3472.
[274] Committee exhibit No. 41.
[275] See Army Pearl Harbor Board (top secret) record, pp. 152–171.
[276] Lt. (now Commander) Lester Robert Schulz.
[277] Admiral John R. Beardall.

with Mr. Harry Hopkins read their contents. Kramer then proceeded to the Wardman Park Hotel where delivery was made to Secretary Knox, who read the dispatches. He then went to the home of Admiral Wilkinson where a dinner party was in progress attended by Admiral Beardall, General Miles, and of course, Admiral Wilkinson, among others. The first 13 parts were read by these officers.[278] Kramer returned to the Navy Department at approximately 1 a. m. and thereafter retired upon seeing that the fourteenth part of the Japanese memorandum had not been received.[279] Copies of the first 13 parts were delivered on the evening of December 6 by an unidentified representative or representatives of the Navy Department to Admirals Ingersoll and Turner at their homes.[280]

The testimony with respect to distribution of the 13 parts by the Army is conflicting, the weight of the evidence indicating, however, that no distribution was made to authorized recipients in the War Department on December 6. The evidence is in dispute as to whether they were delivered to a watch officer at the State Department on the evening of that date.[280a]

The evidence indicates that the first 13 parts were read on the evening of December 6, by, particularly, the President, Mr. Harry Hopkins, Secretary Knox, Admiral Ingersoll, Admiral Turner, Admiral Wilkinson, Admiral Beardall, General Miles, Captain Kramer, and Colonel Bratton.[281] It is concluded from the evidence of record that the message was not seen by Secretary Hull, Secretary Stimson, General Marshall, Admiral Stark, or General Gerow [282] prior to the morning of December 7.

Analysis and Significance of First 13 Parts Proper

In view of the conflicting interpretations that have been placed on the first 13 parts of the 14-part memorandum, they are being set forth in their entirety: [283]

---

[278] Committee record, pp. 4663–4666.
[279] Id., at pp. 10451 et seq.
[280] Id., at pp. 5097; 11295.
[280a] Colonel Bratton testified that the last of the 13 parts came into his office some time between 9 and 10 o'clock that night, and that he was in his office when the last of the 13 parts came in (committee record 12049). He further testified that he personally delivered the 13 parts to the night duty officer at the State Department some time after 10 o'clock that night, telling the duty officer that it was a "highly important message as far as the Secretary of State was concerned" and that it should be sent out to Secretary Hull's quarters, which he was assured would be done (committee record 12052–12053). This testimony is directly contrary to the affidavit of Col. Clyde Dusenbury, then Colonel Bratton's chief assistant, in the Clausen investigation. In his affidavit, Colonel Dusenbury stated that he specifically recalled the intercepted message in question and that "it started coming in the night of 6 December 1941 when I was on duty. Colonel Bratton was also on duty then and saw the message coming in and he remained until about half of it had been received. Thereupon he left and went home at about 9 p. m. I stayed so he could go home and sleep. I waited for the remainder. The fourteenth part, being the final part of the message, was received about 12 that night. Thereupon I left and went home. I returned the next morning *to begin the distribution of this intercept consisting of the fourteen parts* and *I began the distribution of the fourteen parts comprising this intercept* about 9 a. m. on 7 December 1941 and finished with the delivery to the State Department *as Kurusu and Nomura were meeting with the Secretary of State.* When I delivered the copy for OPD that morning I handed it to then Col. Thomas D. Handy, who, upon reading it, said to me: "This means war," or words to that effect. *None of these parts comprising this intercept was delivered before the morning of 7 December 1941* because the first half had been received while Colonel Bratton was on duty and he had seen this and had not had it delivered that night" (Clausen Investigation, committee exhibit No. 148, p. 50).
Colonel Dusenbury's statements in his affidavit are in accord with the testimony of Gen. Sherman Miles, then Chief of the Military Intelligence Division and the superior officer of Colonel Bratton and Colonel Dusenbury, who stated that Secretary Hull, Secretary Stimson, and the others on the War Department's "magic" distribution list received on December 6 all intercepted Japanese messages that were translated that day up to midnight *"except the first 13 parts of the 14-part message"* (committee record 4123–4124).
[281] Captain McCollum is indicated to have seen the first 6 or 7 parts before leaving his office on December 6. Committee record, pp. 9232, 9233.
[282] See committee record, p. 2741.
[283] Committee exhibit No. 1, pp. 239–245.

MEMORANDUM

(Part 1 of 14)

1. The Government of Japan, prompted by a genuine desire to come to an amicable understanding with the Government of the United States in order that the two countries by their joint efforts may secure the peace of the Pacific area and thereby contribute toward the realization of world peace, has continued negotiations with the utmost sincerity since April last with the Government of the United States regarding the adjustment and advancement of Japanese-American relations and the stabilization of the Pacific area.

The Japanese Government has the honor to state frankly its views, concerning the claims the American Government has persistently maintained as well as the measures the United States and Great Britain have taken toward Japan during these eight months.

2. It is the immutable policy of the Japanese Government to insure the stability of east Asia and to promote world peace, and thereby to enable all nations to find each its proper place in the world.

Ever since the China affair broke out owing to the failure on the part of China to comprehend Japan's true intentions, the Japanese Government has striven for the restoration of peace and it has consistently exerted its best efforts to prevent the extension of warlike disturbances. It was also to that end that in September last year Japan concluded the tripartite pact with Germany and Italy.

(Part 2 of 14)

However, both the United States and Great Britain have resorted to every possible measure to assist the Chungking regime so as to obstruct the establishment of a general peace between Japan and China, interfering with Japan's constructive endeavors toward the stabilization of east Asia, exerting pressure on the Netherlands East Indies or menacing French Indochina, they have attempted to frustrate Japan's aspiration to realize the ideal of common prosperity in cooperation with these regions. Furthermore, when Japan in accordance with its protocol with France took measures of joint defense of French Indochina, both American and British Governments, willfully misinterpreted it as a threat to their own possessions and inducing the Netherlands Government to follow suit, they enforced the assets freezing order, thus severing economic relations with Japan. While manifesting thus an obviously hostile attitude, these countries have strengthened their military preparations perfecting an encirclement of Japan, and have brought about a situation which endangers the very existence of the empire.

(Part 3 of 14)

Nevertheless, facilitate a speedy settlement, the Premier of Japan proposed, in August last, to meet the President of the United States for a discussion of important problems between the two countries covering the entire Pacific area. However, while accepting in principle the Japanese proposal, insisted that the meeting should take place after an agreement of view had been reached on fundamental—(75 letters garbled)—The Japanese Government submitted a proposal based on the formula proposed by the American Government, taking fully into consideration past American claims and also incorporating Japanese views. Repeated discussions proved of no avail in producing readily an agreement of view. The present cabinet, therefore, submitted a revised proposal, moderating still further the Japanese claims regarding the principal points of difficulty in the negotiation and endeavored strenuously to reach a settlement. But the American Government, adhering steadfastly to its original proposal, failed to display in the slightest degree a spirit of conciliation. The negotiation made no progress.

(Part 4 of 14)

Thereupon, the Japanese Government, with a view to doing its utmost for averting a crisis in Japanese-American relations, submitted on November 20 still another proposal in order to arrive at an equitable solution of the more essential and urgent questions which, simplifying its previous proposal, stipulated the following points:

(1) The Governments of Japan and the United States undertake not to dispatch armed forces into any of the regions, excepting French Indochina, in the southeastern Asia and Southern Pacific area.

(2) Both Governments shall cooperate with a view to securing the acquisition in the Netherlands East Indies of those goods and commodities of which the two countries are in need.

(3) Both Governments mutually undertake to restore commercial relations to those prevailing prior to the freezing of assets.

The Government of the United States shall supply Japan the required quantity of oil.

(4) The Government of the United States undertakes not to resort to measures and actions prejudicial to the endeavors for the restoration of general peace between Japan and China.

(5) The Japanese Government undertakes to withdraw troops now stationed in French Indochina upon either the restoration of peace between Japan and China or the establishment of an equitable peace in the Pacific area and it is prepared to remove the Japanese troops in the southern part of French Indochina to the northern part upon the conclusion of the present agreement.

(Part 5 of 14)

As regards China, the Japanese Government, while expressing its readiness to accept the offer of the President of the United States to act as "introducer" of peace between Japan and China as was previously suggested, asked for an undertaking on the part of the United States to do nothing prejudicial to the restoration of Sino-Japanese peace when the two parties have commenced direct negotiations.

The American Government not only rejected the above-mentioned new proposal, but made known its intention to continue its aid to Chiang Kai-Shek; and in spite of its suggestion mentioned above, withdrew the offer of the President to act as the so-called "introducer" of peace between Japan and China, pleading that time was not yet ripe for it. Finally, on November 26, in an attitude to impose upon the Japanese Government those principles it has persistently maintained, the American Government made a proposal totally ignoring Japanese claims, which is a source of profound regret to the Japanese Government.

(Part 6 of 14)

4. From the beginning of the present negotiation the Japanese Government has always maintained an attitude of fairness and moderation, and did its best to reach a settlement, for which it made all possible concessions often in spite of great difficulties.

As for the China question which constituted an important subject of the negotiation, the Japanese Government showed a most conciliatory attitude. As for the principle of nondiscrimination in international commerce, advocated by the American Government, the Japanese Government expressed its desire to see the said principle applied throughout the world, and declared that along with the actual practice of this principle in the world, the Japanese Government would endeavor to apply the same in the Pacific area, including China, and made it clear that Japan had no intention of excluding from China economic activities of third powers pursued on an equitable basis.

Furthermore, as regards the question of withdrawing troops from French Indochina, the Japanese Government even volunteered, as mentioned above, to carry out an immediate evacuation of troops from southern French Indochina as a measure of easing the situation.

(Part 7 of 14)

It is presumed that the spirit of conciliation exhibited to the utmost degree by the Japanese Government in all these matters is fully appreciated by the American Government.

On the other hand, the American Government, always holding fast to theories in disregard of realities, and refusing to yield an inch on its impractical principles, caused undue delays in the negotiation. It is difficult to understand this attitude of the American Government and the Japanese Government desires to call the attention of the American Government especially to the following points:

1. The American Government advocates in the name of world peace those principles favorable to it and urges upon the Japanese Government the acceptance thereof. The peace of the world may be brought about only by discovering a mutually acceptable formula through recognition of the reality of the situation and mutual appreciation of one another's position. An attitude such as ignores realities and imposes one's selfish views upon others will scarcely serve the purpose of facilitating the consummation of negotiations.

(Part 8 of 14)

Of the various principles put forward by the American Government as a basis of the Japanese-American agreement, there are some which the Japanese Government is ready to accept in principle, but in view of the world's actual conditions, it seems only a Utopian ideal, on the part of the American Goverment, to attempt to force their immediate adoption.

Again, the proposal to conclude a multilateral nonaggression pact between Japan, the United States, Great Britain, China, the Soviet Union, The Netherlands, and Thailand, which is patterned after the old concept of collective security, is far removed from the realities of east Asia.

The American proposal contains a stipulation which states: "Both governments will agree that no agreement, which either has concluded with any third powers, shall be interpreted by it in such a way as to conflict with the fundamental purpose of this agreement, the establishment and preservation of peace throughout the Pacific area." It is presumed that the above provision has been proposed with a view to restrain Japan from fulfilling its obligations under the tripartite pact when the United States participates in the war in Europe, and, as such, it cannot be accepted by the Japanese Government.

(Part 9 of 14)

The American Government, obsessed with its own views and opinions, may be said to be scheming for the extension of the war. While it seeks, on the one hand, to secure its rear by stabilizing the Pacific area, it is engaged, on the other hand, in aiding Great Britain and preparing to attack, in the name of self-defense, Germany and Italy, two powers that are striving to establish a new order in Europe. Such a policy is totally at variance with the many principles upon which the American Government proposes to found the stability of the Pacific area through peaceful means.

3. Whereas the American Government, under the principles it rigidly upholds, objects to settling international issues through military pressure, it is exercising in conjunction with Great Britain and other nations pressure by economic power. Recourse to such pressure as a means of dealing with international relations should be condemned as it is at times more inhuman than military pressure.

(Part 10 of 14)

4. It is impossible not to reach the conclusion that the American Government desires to maintain and strengthen, in collusion with Great Britain and other powers, its dominant position it has hitherto occupied not only in China but in other areas of east Asia. It is a fact of history that one countr—(45 letters garbled or missing)—been compelled to observe the status quo under the Anglo-American policy of imperialistic exploitation and to sacrifice the —es to the prosperity of the two nations. The Japanese Government cannot tolerate the perpetuation of such a situation since it directly runs counter to Japan's fundamental policy to enable all nations to enjoy each its proper place in the world.

(Part 11 of 14)

The stipulation proposed by the American Government relative to French Indochina is a good exemplification of the above-mentioned American policy. That the six countries—Japan, the United States, Great Britain, The Netherlands, China, and Thailand—excepting France, should undertake among themselves to respect the territorial integrity and sovereignty of French Indochina and equality of treatment in trade and commerce would be tantamount to placing that territory under the joint guarantee of the Governments of those six countries. Apart from the fact that such a proposal totally ignores the position of France, it is unacceptable to the Japanese Government in that such an arrangement cannot but be considered as an extension to French Indochina of a system similar to the n—(50 letters missed)—sible for the present predicament of east Asia.

(Part 12 of 14)

5. All the items demanded of Japan by the American Government regarding China such as wholesale evacuation of troops or unconditional application of the principle of nondiscrimination in international commerce ignore the actual conditions of China, and are calculated to destroy Japan's position as the stabilizing factor of east Asia. The attitude of the American Government in demanding

Japan not to support militarily, politically, or economically any regime other than the regime at Chungking, disregarding thereby the existence of the Nanking government, shatters the very basis of the present negotiation. This demand of the American Government falling, as it does, in line with its above-mentioned refusal to cease from aiding the Chungking regime, demonstrates clearly the intention of the American Government to obstruct the restoration of normal relations between Japan and China and the return of peace to east Asia.

(Part 13 of 14)

5. In brief, the American proposal contains certain acceptable items such as those concerning commerce, including the conclusion of a trade agreement, mutual removal of the freezing restrictions, and stabilization of the yen and dollar exchange, or the abolition of extraterritorial rights in China. On the other hand, however, the proposal in question ignores Japan's sacrifices in the 4 years of the China affair, menaces the empire's existence itself and disparages its honour and prestige. *Therefore, viewed in its entirety, the Japanese Government regrets that it cannot accept the proposal as a basis of negotiations.*

6. The Japanese Government, in its desire for an early conclusion of the negotiation, proposed that simultaneously with the conclusion of the Japanese-American negotiation, agreements be signed with Great Britain and other interested countries. The proposal was accepted by the American Government. However, since the American Government has made the proposal of November 26 as a result of frequent consultations with Great Britain, Australia, The Netherlands and Chungking, andnd (probably "and as") presumably by catering to the wishes of the Chungking regime on the questions of Chtual ylokmmtt (probably "China, can but") be concluded that all these countries are at one with the United States in ignoring Japan's position.

The foregoing message is a long and argumentative rehash of the Japanese-American negotiations. The motives and proposals of the Japanese Empire are clothed in language of the most flattering terms whereas the purposes of the United States are assigned a base character. The language employed in the first 13 parts is much stronger than had theretofore been employed by Japan in her proposals. In the thirteenth part it is stated, "Therefore, viewed in its entirety, the Japanese Government regrets that it cannot accept the proposal as a basis of negotiation." Taken from its context this statement would indicate that Japan is rejecting the November 26 note of our Government and would possibly suggest that the current negotiations were to be broken off at some time in the near future. But as pointed out by Admiral Wilkinson, "It is one thing to break off negotiations and another thing to break off diplomatic relations. The same negotiations, I believe, had been broken off earlier and then resumed." [284]

Commander Schulz, who delivered the first 13 parts of the Japanese reply to the President, testified that the President read the message and "Mr. Hopkins then read the papers and handed them back to the President. The President then turned toward Mr. Hopkins and said in substance—I am not sure of the exact words, but in substance, *'This means war'.*[285] Mr. Hopkins agreed and they discussed then for perhaps 5 minutes the situation of the Japanese forces, that is, their deployment." [286]

[284] Committee record, p. 4668.
[285] Asked what his action would have been had he known of the President's remark, General Marshall said: "I can't say. *I doubt if I would have sent anything on that statement of the President at that time.*" Committee record, p. 13804.
Admiral Stark was asked: "* * * if you had known that the President did say something in substance 'This means war,' about the 13-part message, was there anything you would have done that night except to read the message? Is there anything you could now tell us you would have done, in the way of backsight or hindsight that you would have done that you did not do?"
He replied: "It would not be backsight or hindsight, because when I read it on Sunday morning *I saw nothing in it to cause me to take any further action on it.*" Committee record, pp. 13912, 13913.
[286] Committee record, p. 12441.

To the query as to whether he could recall what either the President or Mr. Hopkins said, Commander Schulz testified as follows:[287]

Commander SCHULZ. In substance I can. There are only a few words that I can definitely say I am sure of, but the substance of it was that—I believe Mr. Hopkins mentioned it first, that since war was imminent, that the Japanese intended to strike when they were ready, at a moment when all was most opportune for them—when all was most opportune for that. That is, when their forces were most properly deployed for their advantage. Indochina in particular was mentioned, because the Japanese forces had already landed there and there were implications of where they should move next.

The President mentioned a message that he had sent to the Japanese Emperor concerning the presence of Japanese troops in Indochina, in effect requesting their withdrawal.

Mr. Hopkins then expressed a view that since war was undoubtedly going to come at the convenience of the Japanese it was too bad that we could not strike the first blow and prevent any sort of surprise. The President nodded and said, in effect, "No, we can't do that. We are a democracy and a peaceful people." Then he raised his voice, and this much I remember definitely. He said, "But we have a good record."

The impression that I got was that we would have to stand on that record, we could not make the first overt move. We would have to wait until it came.

During this discussion there was no mention of Pearl Harbor. The only geographic name I recall was Indochina. The time at which war might begin was not discussed, but from the manner of the discussion there was no indication that tomorrow was necessarily the day. I carried that impression away because it contributed to my personal surprise when the news did come.

COUNSEL. Was there anything said, Commander, with reference to the subject of notice or notification as a result of the papers that were being read?

Commander SCHULZ. There was no mention made of sending any further warning or alert. However, having concluded this discussion about the war going to begin at the Japanese convenience, then the President said that he believed he would talk to Admiral Stark. He started to get Admiral Stark on the telephone. It was then determined—I do not recall exactly, but I believe the White House operator told the President that Admiral Stark could be reached at the National Theater.

COUNSEL. Now, that was from what was said there that you draw the conclusion that that was what the White House operator reported?

Commander SCHULZ. Yes, sir. I did not hear what the operator said, but the National Theater was mentioned in my presence and the President went on to state, in substance, that he would reach the Admiral later, that he did not want to cause public alarm by having the Admiral paged or otherwise when in the theater where I believe the fact that he had a box reserved was mentioned and that if he had left suddenly he would surely have been seen because of the position which he held and undue alarm might be caused and the President did not wish that to happen because he could get him within perhaps another half an hour in any case.[287a]

In considering the remark [288] by the President to Mr. Hopkins that the first 13 parts meant war it is significant that there was no indication as to *when* or *where* war might be expected.[288a] The testimony of Commander Schulz should be considered with that of Admiral Beardall, to which reference will hereafter be made, in seeking to determine the reaction of the President to the full Japanese 14-part memorandum.

[287] Id., at pp. 12441–12444.
[287a] The evidence tends to indicate that following his return home after the theater, Admiral Stark was advised that the White House had called, and that he did thereupon call the White House. See testimony of Capt. H. D. Krick, U. S. Navy, before the committee.
[288] Referring to the comment made by the President, General Marshall testified: "He didn't tell me, and he didn't tell the Secretary of War. So he made a statement offhand on reading the thing" (13 parts). Committee record, p. 13803.
[288a] In connection with the remark attributed to the President it is to be noted that at a meeting of the War Council on November 25, President Roosevelt warned that we were likely to be attacked, perhaps as soon as the following Monday, for the "Japanese are notorious for making an attack without warning." See statement of Mr. Stimson, committee record, p. 14390.

The estimate given the first 13 parts by witnesses before the committee who reviewed them on the night of December 6 follows: [289]

Admiral TURNER. However, when I saw the 13 parts, which I believe was about 11:30 on the night of December 6, I inquired from the officer who showed it to me and brought it to my house as to who had seen that dispatch, and he informed me that Admiral Wilkinson and Admiral Ingersoll and Secretary Knox had all seen it before it had been shown to me. I considered the dispatch very important, but as long as those officers had seen it, I did not believe it was my function to take any action.

Admiral INGERSOLL.[290] * * * when I read the 13 parts there was nothing on which the Navy Department as such could that night take-action. The gist of the 13 parts was a restatement of the Japanese position we had known, of course, all along.

Admiral WILKINSON.[291]. * * * both General Miles and myself, and to some extent Captain Kramer, felt that this was a diplomatic message; it was a message that indicated, or that resembled the diplomatic white papers, of which we had often seen examples, that it was a justification of the Japanese position.

The strain was largely in the 14th part which we discussed the next morning.

Admiral Wilkinson agreed that he, General Miles, and Admiral Beardall discussed the first 13 parts and referred to it as more or less a "white paper" or diplomatic communication—"A justification for the Japanese position".[292]

General MILES.[293] I called him for the purpose of finding out what had been done, what was going to be done with these first 13 parts, but I wish to call your attention, Senator, to the fact that the first 13 parts as such was not of great military significance. We had already discounted through many days the fact that in all probability the Japanese reply to our note of November 26 would be unfavorable and that was all that the first 13 parts told us. When we got the fourteenth part we saw quite a different picture, when we got the 1 p. m. message we saw quite a different picture, but there was no reason for alerting or waking up the Chief of Staff, we will say, or certainly Secretary Hull, on the night of December 6 that I could see.

Captain KRAMER.[294] I have stated that the first part I recollect seeing is part 8. If you will refer to that you will see that there is nothing in that part—in fact, the last half of that part quotes the United States note—that was materially different than the general tenor of previous notes back and forth between the United States and Japan.

When the first 13 parts were complete I did, however, have that distinct impression, that this note was far and appreciably stronger language than earlier notes had been and that it indicated a strong probability that the Japanese were concluding any further negotiations.

Colonel BRATTON [295] * * * I considered the presence of the 13 parts in Washington relatively unimportant militarily that evening.

I did so consider it upon their receipt and I still consider it now. They contributed no information, they contributed no additional information to the matters that we already had from magic and other sources as to the impending crisis with Japan.

The message was incomplete. It ended on the note, in the thirteenth part: "Therefore, viewed in its entirety, the Japanese government regrets that it cannot accept the proposal as a basis of negotiation."

This was primarily of interest, immediate interest to the Secretary of State, not to the Secretary of War or the Chief of General Staff for it was not an ulti-

[289] Committee record, p. 5097.
[290] Id., at p. 11377.
[291] Id., at p. 4665.
[292] Id., at p. 4667.
[293] Id., at pp. 2482, 2483.
[294] Id., at pp. 10445, 10446.
[295] Id., at pp. 12057, 12058.

matum, it was not a declaration of war, nor was it a severance of diplomatic relations.

The committee has noted the emphasis, publicity and speculation concerning the whereabouts of General Marshall, the Chief of Staff, and Admiral Stark, the Chief of Naval Operations, on the evening of December 6. General Marshall has testified that while he could not recall his whereabouts with certainty he presumed he was at home. Admiral Stark could not recall his whereabouts, but the evidence establishes that he was at the National Theater seeing *The Student Prince*.[295a] Similar emphasis has been placed on the fact that the Chief of Staff was horseback riding on the morning of December 7, as was his Sunday-morning custom. The first 13 parts were neither delivered to nor read by either General Marshall or Admiral Stark on the evening of December 6. In any event, the question of their whereabouts on Saturday evening, December 6, is by any construction unimportant inasmuch as both officers saw nothing in the first 13 parts to serve as basis for additional warnings to our outposts when they read them on the morning of December 7.[295b] In this connection, it is to be noted that the evidence conclusively establishes that no conferences were held at the White House or elsewhere with respect to the Pacific situation by ranking military and executive officials on the evening of December 6, 1941.

The consensus of testimony by officers of the War and Navy Departments is to the effect that the first 13 parts, as such, of the 14-part message bore little or no military significance.[296] While they revealed a position assumed by Japan to which our Government could not subscribe there was no statement that negotiations were to be ruptured and certainly no intimation of the treacherous attack to be delivered at Pearl Harbor the following morning. From the "pilot message" it was clear that a fourteenth part was to be transmitted and that it would probably be received on December 7. Considering this fact and the further fact that the first 13 parts gave no indication of immediate military action by Japan, there was no occasion on the evening of December 6 to dispatch additional warnings to outposts, already regarded as alerted, on the basis of a message that was manifestly not complete. It is clear there was no intelligence contained in the message itself which had not been known for some time.

Military Significance of "Pilot" and 13-Part Messages Apart from Messages Proper

An intercepted dispatch of November 28, 1941, from Tokyo to its Washington ambassadors had stated, referring to Mr. Hull's note of November 26: [297]

Well, you two Ambassadors have exerted superhuman efforts but, in spite of this, the United States has gone ahead and presented this humiliating proposal. This was quite unexpected and extremely regrettable. The Imperial Govern-

---

[295a] See note 287a, supra.

[295b] General Marshall said: "* * * the first 13 parts were not of the nature of a vital threat as the 14th part. That was a message of direct importance to the Secretary of State and of related importance, of course, to the Secretary of War and the Secretary of Navy who had been collaborating with him in his relationship in the dealings with Japan." Committee record, p. 3095.

For Admiral Stark's estimate of the first 13 parts, see Note 296, infra.

[296] Admiral Stark stated that he regarded the first 13 parts, when he saw them on the morning of December 7, as routine, a rehashing of the attitude of the Japanese towards the situation which had been accumulating over a period of weeks or months. In other words, that the 13 parts by themselves carried no implication other than indicated; that it was a rehashing, a restatement of their attitude. Committee record, p. 13722.

[297] Committee exhibit No. 1, p. 195.

ment can by no means use it as a basis for negotiations. *Therefore, with a report of the views of the Imperial Government on this American proposal which I will send you in two or three days, the negotiations will be de facto ruptured.* This is inevitable.

In the foregoing dispatch the Japanese Government stated it would send a reply to Nomura and Kurusu within 2 or 3 days. This presupposes the presence and *availability* in Washington of these ambassadors to receive the reply. Clearly, therefore, war between Japan and the United States was not to eventuate *until* the reply had been received in Washington, otherwise the Japanese ambassadors would not be available for the purpose of receiving such reply. By the same token war would not eventuate until the ambassadors had an opportunity to *deliver* the reply, otherwise little or no purpose would be served in sending it whatever.

Knowledge of this fact should have intensified alertness in the War and Navy Departments to such a point that from the moment the 14-part reply started coming in, all hands should have been on the *qui vive* and additionally an adequate number of responsible officers should have been actually at their stations with full authority to act in any emergency throughout the night of December 6–7. This statement is of course subject to the observation that Japan had indicated in the pilot message that the full reply would not be received until the following day, Sunday, December 7, and even that was not certain; that instructions would be sent in a separate dispatch with respect to the time of presentation and "the situation is extremely delicate, and when you receive it (the reply) I want you to please *keep it secret for the time being.*" Further, it is clear from the evidence that the receipt of the pilot message and portions of the first 13 parts of the 14-part memorandum served as basis for special measures taken by the War and Navy Departments to insure prompt handling, decoding, and distribution of this magic material on the evening of December 6. The naval officers who received the first 13 parts on the evening of December 6 appear to have regarded them as requiring no action during the evening. Within the Army the first 13 parts were seen by the Chief of the Military Intelligence Division, who in view of the fact that the fourteenth part had not been received and the further fact that the message appeared to him to be of interest primarily to the State Department, decided that it required no further distribution within the Army that evening but should be delivered to the State Department.[297a] But the fact that the message was being received removed the last *known* barrier to Japan's taking military action.[298]

In consequence, it is not believed the War and Navy establishments in Washington were sufficiently alerted on the evening of December 6

[297a] As has been indicated, the evidence is in dispute as to whether the first 13 parts were in reality delivered to a watch officer at the State Department on the evening of December 6. See Note 280a, supra.

[298] However, it should be noted that Ambassador Nomura in a dispatch to Tokyo of November 26, 1941, stated: "The United States is using the excuse that she is at present negotiating with the various competent countries. In view of the fact that she will propagandize that we are continuing these negotiations only with the view of preparing for our expected moves, should we, during the course of these conversations, deliberately enter into our scheduled operations, there is great danger that the responsibility for the rupture of negotiations will be cast upon us. There have been times in the past when she could have considered discontinuing conversations because of our invasion of French Indo-China. Now, should we, without clarifying our intentions, force a rupture in our negotiations and suddenly enter upon independent operations, there is great fear that she may use such a thing as that as counter-propaganda against us. They might consider doing the same thing insofar as our plans for Thai are concerned. Nevertheless, such a thing as the clarification of our intention is a strict military secret; consequently, *I think that it might be the better plan, dependent of course on the opinions of the Government, that the current negotiations be clearly and irrevocably concluded either through an announcement to the American Embassy in Tokyo or by declaration for internal and external consumption.* I would like, if such a course is followed, to make representations here at the same time." Committee exhibit No. 1, p. 183.

with a view to receiving the Japanese reply. As events turned out, however, there was nothing contained in the first 13-parts to have served as basis for additional warnings to outposts already regarded as adequately alerted. The information contained in the first 13-parts of the 14-part message did not add to the sum total of information already supplied the commanders in Hawaii who had been warned of war and advised "hostile action possible at any moment." It did not point to Hawaii. It did not provide the essential *where* or, with any degree of definitiveness, the *when* of the attack. There is no intelligence contained in the first 13-parts which this Committee can conclude could reasonably be expected to have changed the decisions already made in Hawaii.

The Fourteenth Part

At 2:38 a. m., December 7, there was filed in Tokyo and intercepted by a Navy monitoring station between 3:05 and 3:10 a. m. the fourteenth and final part of Japan's reply to Secretary Hull's note of November 26.[299] This message as subsequently decoded by the Navy read as follows: [300]

(Part 14 of 14)

7. Obviously it is the intention of the American Government to conspire with Great Britain and other countries to obstruct Japan's efforts toward the establishment of peace through the creation of a New Order in East Asia, and especially to preserve Anglo-American rights and interests by keeping Japan and China at war. This intention has been revealed clearly during the course of the present negotiations. Thus, the earnest hope of the Japanese Government to adjust Japanese-American relations and to preserve and promote the peace of the Pacific through cooperation with the American Government has finally been lost.

The Japanese Government regrets to have to notify hereby the American Government that in view of the attitude of the American Government it cannot but consider that it is impossible to reach an agreement through further negotiations.

The fourteenth part was available in the Navy Department for distribution at some time between 7:30 and 8:00 a. m.[301] Captain Kramer made delivery within the Navy Department shortly after 8 a. m. The delivery to the White House and to Secretary Knox, who was at the State Department for a 10 a. m. meeting with Secretaries Hull and Stimson, was made shortly before 10 a. m. Distribution of the fourteenth part within the War Department was begun at 9 a. m. with subsequent delivery to the State Department.

It is to be noted there is no statement that Japan intended to declare war on the United States nor, indeed, that formal diplomatic relations were to be broken—merely that the current negotiations cannot produce an agreement. The fourteenth part is much less severe than the strongly worded first 13 parts would have indicated. Admiral Beardall testified as follows with respect to delivery of the fourteenth part to the President: [302]

As I recollect it, I went into his room, early, about 10:00 o'clock on Sunday morning, with a message or messages, which I presume, to the best of my recollection, was the 14th part of this 13-part message that came in the night before, which I delivered to him.

---

[299] Committee exhibit No. 41.
[300] Id., No. 1, p. 245. As forwarding instructions to the radio station handling the fourteenth part there appeared at the beginning the plain English phrase "VERY IMPORTANT".
[301] Committee record, pp. 10461–10463.
[302] Id., at pp. 14010, 14011.

Asked if there was any discussion or conversation with the President when he made the delivery, Admiral Beardall testified: [303]

No discussion. We never discussed magic. I do recollect him saying though, which marks this in my mind, that *it looked as though the Japs are going to sever negotiations, break off negotiations.*

Admiral Beardall further testified that at the time of delivering the fourteenth part to the President there was nothing in the manner of the President which would indicate he was expecting an attack within a period of hours; that there "was no alarm, or no mention of this, mention of war, or of any actions on his part that would indicate that he was expecting an attack." [304]

As to the question whether termination of negotiations would indicate certain war it is significant to note that the Japanese Ambassadors themselves stated in a message to Tokyo dated November 26, 1941: [305]

We suppose that *the rupture of the present negotiations does not necessarily mean war between Japan and the United States,* but after we break off, as we said, the military occupation of Netherlands India is to be expected of England and the United States. Then we would attack them and a clash with them would be inevitable * * *.

From a review of the fourteenth part it is clear that nothing is added to what was already known with respect to Japan's reaction to Secretary Hull's note. To be sure it is observed that the "hope * * * to preserve and promote the peace of the Pacific through cooperation with the American Government has finally been lost" and "in view of the attitude of the American Government it cannot but consider that it is impossible to reach an agreement through further negotiations." But these facts had already been known for several days and the only paramount considerations at this time were *when* and *where* Japan would strike. A thorough consideration of the fourteen-part message, when viewed in the light of all other intelligence already available in Washington, reflects no added information, particularly of a military character, which would serve further to alert outpost commanders who had already been supplied a "war warning" and informed that "hostile action possible at any moment." [306] This conclusion is partially modified to the extent that actual delivery of the fourteen part message to the American Government might be construed as removing the last diplomatic obstacle, in the minds of the Japanese, to launching an attack.

"ONE O'CLOCK" AND FINAL CODE DESTRUCTION MESSAGES

Two messages intercepted on the morning of December 7 have received paramount consideration—the celebrated "one o'clock" message specifying the time for delivery of the Japanese 14-part memorandum to the Government of the United States and the message setting forth final instructions to the Japanese Embassy concerning

---

[303] Id.

[304] Committee record, p. 14047.

[305] Committee exhibit No. 1, p. 181.

[306] General Marshall stated: "* * * the particular part which affected me and caused me to act was not the 14 parts. It was the one o'clock, which, unfortunately, they put on the bottom of the pile and I read through everything before I came to that." Committee record, p. 13805.

Referring to the Japanese 14-part memorandum, Admiral Turner said: "I did not consider that that message and the fact that it appeared to be an ultimatum changed the over-all situation in the least degree, because I was certain in my mind that there was going to be war immediately between the United States and Japan, and this was merely confirmatory. The full orders, and what I felt was the full picture of the situation had been given to the fleet commanders in the dispatch of November 27, and confirmed definitely by the later dispatches regarding the destruction of the Japanese codes and the Navy Department's orders for our people to destroy codes in exposed positions." Committee record, p. 5099.

the destruction of codes and secret papers. The latter was as follows: [307]

> After deciphering part 14 of my #902 and also #907,[308] #908,[309] and #909,[310] please destroy at once the remaining cipher machine and all machine codes. Dispose in like manner also secret documents.

This message was intercepted shortly after the one o'clock message but from the evidence it appears that both these intercepts were distributed at approximately the same time. The "one o'clock" message read as follows: [311]

> Will the Ambassador please submit to the United States Government (if possible to the Secretary of State) our reply to the United States at 1:00 p. m. on the 7th, your time.

This dispatch was filed by the Japanese at 4:18 a. m. December 7, and intercepted by a Navy monitoring station at 4:37 a. m.[312] It was decrypted and available in the Navy Department at approximately 7 a. m. thereupon being sent to the Army for translation inasmuch as there was no translator on duty in the Navy Department at that time. Translated copies of the "one o'clock" message appear to have been returned to the Navy at approximately 9 a. m. Captain Kramer testified[313] that upon his return to the Navy Department at 10:20 a. m. he found the "one o'clock" message and thereafter, between 10:30 and 10:35 a. m., delivered it to the office of the Chief of Naval Operations, where a meeting was in progress. Delivery was then made within approximately 10 minutes to an aide to Secretary Hull at the State Department and thereafter within roughly another 10 minutes, to a Presidential aide at the White House. In the course of delivery to the office of the Chief of Naval Operations and to· Secretary Hull's aide mention was made of the fact that 1 p. m., Washington time, was about dawn at Honolulu and about the middle of the night in the Far East. *No mention was made that the time indicated an attack at Pearl Harbor.*[314]

Delivery of the "one o'clock" message within the War Department was made at some time between 9 and 10 a. m. General Marshall, after being advised at his quarters that an important message had been received, arrived at his office at some time between 11:15 and 11:30 a. m. where he saw for the first time the 14-part memorandum, General Gerow, General Miles, and Colonel Bratton, among others, being present. After completion of his reading of the memorandum, General Marshall came to the "one o'clock" message and appears to have attached immediate significance to it. He testified that he and the officers present in his office were certain the hour fixed in the "one o'clock" message had "some definite significance;" that "something was going to happen at 1 o'clock;" that "when they specified a day,

[307] Committee exhibit No. 1, p. 249.
[308] The dispatch set forth, infra, concerning delivery at 1 p. m., December 7, of the 14-part memorandum.
[309] No. 908, dated December 7, read: "All concerned regret very much that due to failure in adjusting Japanese-American relations, matters have come to what they are now, despite all the efforts you two Ambassadors have been making. I wish to take this opportunity to offer my deepest thanks to you both for your endeavors and hard work as well as for what all the members of the Embassy have done." Committee exhibit No. 1, p. 248.
[310] No. 909, dated December 7, read: "(From Bureau Chief Yamamoto to Commercial Attache Iguchi and his staff as well as to Secretary Yuki) I, together with the members of the Bureau, deeply appreciate and heartily thank you for your great effort which you have been making for many months in behalf of our country despite all difficulties in coping with the unprecedented crisis. We pray that you will continue to be in good health." Committee exhibit No. 1, p. 248.
[311] Committee exhibit No. 1, p. 248.
[312] Id., No. 41.
[313] Committee record, pp. 10470–10479.
[314] See testimony of Captain Kramer before the committee; also Captain McCollum, committee record, p. 9275.

that of course had significance, but not comparable to an hour;" and, again, that it was "a new item of information of a peculiar character." [315]   At 11:30 or 11:40 a. m. General Marshall telephoned Admiral Stark [316] and, upon learning the latter had read the message, proposed that a warning be sent immediately to all theaters concerned. It should be noted that the exact time of Admiral Stark's arrival at the Navy Department is not definitely established although it is known that he was there by 10:30 a. m. on the morning of December 7, at the very latest.[317]   Admiral Stark hesitated because he regarded the theater commanders as already alerted and he was afraid of confusing them further.[318]   General Marshall nevertheless wrote in longhand the draft of a warning message to the Western Defense Command, the Panama Command, the Hawaiian Command, and the Philippine Command, as follows: [319]

The Japanese are presenting at 1 P. M. Eastern Standard Time, today, what amounts to an ultimatum. Also they are under orders to destroy their code machine immediately. Just what significance the hour set may have we do not know, but be on alert accordingly.

He instructed Colonel Bratton to take the foregoing message immediately to the message center to be dispatched by radio but as Colonel Bratton was leaving the room, Admiral Stark called to request that there be placed on the dispatch the "usual expression to inform the naval officer". The following was therefore added in handwriting by General Marshall, "Inform naval authorities of this communication".[320]

EVENTS ATTENDING TRANSMITTAL OF THE DECEMBER 7 DISPATCH

By 11:50 a. m. the handwritten warning had been delivered by Colonel Bratton to Colonel French,[321] in charge of the message center. When Colonel Bratton returned, General Marshall inquired as to how much time would be required to encipher and dispatch the message. Not understanding the explanation, he instructed both Colonels Bratton and Bundy to obtain a clearer picture from the message center. These two officers upon returning advised that the message would be in the hands of the recipients within thirty minutes. Still not being satisfied, General Marshall is indicated to have sent the

[315] Army Pearl Harbor Board (top secret) Report, pp. 7, 8; committee record, p. 13806.
[316] See committee exhibit No. 58.
[317] See committee record, p. 5813. The testimony of some witnesses indicates Admiral Stark arrived at the Navy Department as early as 9 a. m.
[318] See Army Pearl Harbor Board (top secret) record, pp. 7, 8. Admiral Stark said: "During the morning of Sunday, 7 December 1941, we had information to the effect that the Japanese Ambassador was to present his Government's reply to the 10-point note to the Secretary of State at 1 p. m. that same day. I was discussing this note and the time of its presentation with the head of the Central Division (Captain Schuirmann) when General Marshall called me on the phone to ask if I knew of it. I told him I did, and he asked me what I thought about sending the information concerning the time of presentation on to the various commanders in the Pacific. *My first answer to him was that we had sent them so much already that I hesitated to send more.* I hung up the phone, and not more than a minute or two later I called him back, stating that there might be some peculiar significance in the Japanese Ambassador calling on Mr. Hull at 1 p. m. and that I would go along with him in sending the information to the Pacific. I asked him if his communications were such that he could get it out quickly because our comunications were quite rapid when the occasion demanded it. He replied that he felt they could get it through very quickly. I then asked him to include in the dispatch instructions to his people to inform their naval opposites." Committee record, p. 5676.
[319] Committee exhibit No. 32, p. 21.
[320] Id.
[321] Col. Edward F. French.

two officers back again and their report upon returning was regarded as satisfactory; that is, he felt assured from what he was told that the warning would be received by the pertinent commanders before 1:00 p. m.[322]

After receiving the message Colonel French personally took charge of its dispatch. Learning that the War Department radio had been out of contact with Honolulu since approximately 10:20 a. m. he thereupon immediately decided that the most expeditious manner of getting the message to Hawaii was by commercial facilities; that is, Western Union to San Francisco, thence by commercial radio to Honolulu. The message was filed at the Army signal center at 12:01 p. m. (6:31 a. m., Hawaii); teletype transmission to Western Union completed at 12:17 p. m. (6:47 a. m., Hawaii); received by RCA Honolulu 1:03 p. m. (7:33 a. m., Hawaii); received by signal office, Fort Shafter, Hawaii, at approximately 5:15 p. m. (11:45 a. m., Hawaii) after the attack. It appears that the teletype arrangement between RCA in Honolulu and Fort Shafter was not operating at the particular hour the message was received with the result that it was dispatched by a messenger on a bicycle who was diverted from completing delivery by the first bombing.

CHOICE OF FACILITIES

Colonel French testified that important messages to be transmitted immediately had previously been sent by commercial means when there was interference on the Army circuit between Honolulu and the War Department; that on the morning of December 7 Honolulu appeared to be in touch with San Francisco; that he had a teletype connection from his office to the Western Union office in Washington and knew Western Union had a tube connecting with RCA across the street in San Francisco; that RCA had 40 kilowatts of power whereas his set had 10 kilowatts; and that he concluded the fastest means of transmission would be via Western Union and RCA. He stated that he acted within his authority in deciding to send the message by commercial means and did not tell General Marshall how the message was going.[323]

Colonel French stated further that he had not considered using the telephone; that the telephone was never used by the signal center; that it was unsuitable for a classified message; and that, in any event, "if they wanted to use the telephone that was up to the individuals themselves, Chief of Staff, or whoever the individual concerned." [324]

According to General Marshall, the telephone was not considered as a means of transmission, or that it may have been considered but would not have been used, he was quite certain, certainly not to Hawaii first; that if he had thought he could put a telephone call through, he would have called General MacArthur first, and then would have called

---

[322] Army Pearl Harbor Board Record, pp. 8–10, 14. There is some testimony indicating only two trips were made by Colonel Bratton to the message center.
[323] Army Pearl Harbor Board Record, pp. 188, 195; Roberts Commission Record, pp. 1843, 1844, 1846.
[324] Army Pearl Harbor Board (top secret) record, pp. 189–205.

the Panama Canal. He observed that it was important to send the message in code because it was not known what "one o'clock meant" and that it might have meant only a termination of diplomatic relations or some action in southeast Asia. General Marshall pointed out that there was no secrecy in the telephone and that he was trying to gain time and yet had to be careful not to "precipitate the whole business" or do anything which could be construed as an act of war; that it was important not to disclose to the Japanese our reading of their codes.[325]

With respect to the matter of using Navy radio facilities, Colonel French stated that the Navy used more power than did the Army and occasionally the Army asked the Navy to communicate messages but that in practice they did not use the Navy for expediting traffic to Honolulu. He considered the possible use of Navy transmission of the warning message but decided against it since it would have required time to determine whether the Navy was also having trouble getting through to Hawaii and the message would have had to be delivered from the Navy at Pearl Harbor to Fort Shafter.[326]

General Marshall had no knowledge on the morning of December 7 that the Army radio could not establish contact with Hawaii nor that the Navy had a more powerful radio to Honolulu.[327] It is to be noted that the message got through to addressees other than Hawaii prior to the attack.

After the event it is easy to find other means of communication which General Marshall might have employed. This will always be the case. It is clear from the record, however, that he selected a secure means dictated by the contents of the message and was assured after two or three requests for verification that the message would get through in adequate time. It did not reach Hawaii because of a failure in communications concerning which he could not have known and concerning which he was not advised. It was the failure of communications and not the selection of an improper channel that occasioned the delay.

While it is not regarded as contributing to the disaster, for reasons hereinafter to appear, it is considered extremely regrettable that Colonel French did not advise the Chief of Staff upon his inability to employ the Army's radio, the anticipated means of communication, particularly when he realized the great importance of the message and the personal concern of the Chief of Staff for its expeditious transmittal.

SIGNIFICANCE OF THE "ONE O'CLOCK" AND CODE DESTRUCTION MESSAGES

No one knew or presumed to know definitely just what the time "one o'clock" meant.[328] Indeed, the warning sent by the Chief of

---

[325] Army Pearl Harbor Board (top secret) Record, pp. 10–14. See also Roberts Commission record, p. 1803.
[326] Army Pearl Harbor Board record, pp. 203, 204. Roberts Commission record, p. 1844.
[327] Roberts Commission record, p. 1801.
[328] Admiral Stark observed: "My first reaction was that we had sent so much out that—and as there was no deduction from the message, as to what it meant, at least we had made none at that time, that it would be just as well not to send it. A few days previous, when we had a discussion whether to send out anything more, the question came up, be careful not to send too much, it might create the story of 'wolf'." Committee Record, page 5815. In this regard it is to be noted that Admiral Smith, Chief of Staff to Admiral Kimmel, said that he thought there had been too much "crying wolf" and that such warnings had been received not only during Admiral Kimmel's administration but also previously by Admiral Richardson. See Hart Inquiry Record, page 64.

Staff stated *"just what significance the hour set may have we do not know."* Despite this fact the Hawaiian commanders have asserted or implied that if they had received this information at the earliest possible moment on the morning of December 7, they would have anticipated a surprise air attack upon Pearl Harbor and have instituted appropriate defensive measures accordingly.[329] It is to be noted, however, that one of the asserted justifications by Admiral Kimmel and General Short for their not having taken the necessary defensive measures prior to December 7 was the fact that the warnings they had received, while indicating that war was imminent, pointed to southeast Asia and not to Hawaii as the likely point of attack.

There was nothing in the fact that the Japanese ambassadors were to present their Government's reply to the American note of November 26 at 1 p. m., December 7, pointing any more to an attack on Hawaii than to any other point to which General Marshall directed his dispatch: Panama, the west coast, the Philippines. The intelligence contained in the "one o'clock" intercept indicated no more than the distinct possibility that *some* Japanese military action would take place *somewhere* at 1 p. m.

What Admiral Kimmel and General Short would have done upon receiving this intelligence or the Marshall dispatch before the attack is necessarily speculative.

Testifying before the Roberts Commission concerning that portion of the December 7 warning pointing out that instructions had been issued for the Japanese Embassy to destroy its code machine immediately, General Short was asked whether his dispositions would have been changed if the message had reached him, say three hours before the attack. He replied:[330]

General SHORT. Yes. Oh, yes. I would have gone immediately to either—to at least an alert against an air attack, and I probably would have gone against a complete attack, because it looked so significant.

The CHAIRMAN. Well, can you tell me what was in that message that would have stirred you up?

General SHORT. The thing that would have affected me more than the other matter was the fact that they had ordered the code machines destroyed, because to us that means just one thing; that they are going into an entirely new phase, and that they want to be perfectly sure that the code will not be broken for a minimum time, say of 3 or 4 days. That would have been extremely significant to me, the code machine, much more significant than just the ultimatum.

It is to be noted that when appearing before the Roberts Commission, General Short insisted he had no knowledge concerning the destruction by Japanese diplomatic representatives of codes and confidential papers, prior to December 7. As has been seen, the evidence before this committee reflects that he received substantially this information on December 6.

Admiral Kimmel has likewise suggested that the fact the Japanese Washington Embassy had been ordered to destroy its code machine would have been of greater significance to him than information received on December 3 that the Embassy, among others, had been ordered to destroy *"most* of its codes." [331] With respect to the latter

---

[329] General Short said: "This message (the one o'clock message) definitely pointed to an attack on Pearl Harbor at 1 p. m., Washington time." Committee Record, page 7992.
[330] Roberts Commission record, pp. 1619, 1620.
[331] Committee record, pp. 7476, 7477.

intelligence Admiral Kimmel has testified: [332] "I didn't consider that of any vital importance when I received it * * *" Significantly, however, on December 6 the commandant of the Fourteenth Naval District advised the Navy Department: "believe local consul has destroyed all but one system * * *" [333]

It is concluded that the information contained in the Japanese intercept of December 7 instructing the Washington Embassy to destroy its remaining code machine, added little if any information to that already possessed by Admiral Kimmel concerning Japanese destruction of codes and confidential matter; and that if the intelligence supplied him in this regard on December 3 did not serve to warn of the immediate imminence of war the information concerning the destruction of the Japanese code machine on the morning of December 7 would not have effectively modified the situation. In the case of General Short, as elsewhere pointed out, it appears that while Admiral Kimmel did not supply him with the intelligence he had received concerning the destruction of codes, the Commanding General none-the-less received information of an equivalent character.

We believe, however, that the "one o'clock" intercept should have been recognized as indicating the distinct possibility that some Japanese military action would occur somewhere at 1 p. m., December 7, Washington time. If properly appreciated, this intercept should have suggested a dispatch to *all* Pacific outpost commanders supplying this information, as General Marshall attempted to do immediately upon seeing it.

SIGNIFICANT MESSAGES TRANSLATED AFTER THE ATTACK

INTELLIGENCE CONCERNING HAWAIIAN DEFENSES

One of the most unfortunate circumstances attending the handling of Magic is the fact that several very significant messages were not translated until after the attack. After December 7, 13 messages [334] between Tokyo and Honolulu from November 24 to December 6 were translated, several of these differing markedly from any of the messages between these points translated prior to December 7. Three of the 13 messages were from Tokyo, two of which related to instructions and interest concerning fleet locations and movements [335] with the third, however, containing for the first time an inquiry from Tokyo concern-

---

[332] Id., at p. 7477.
[333] The extreme importance of codes being destroyed in the consulates was expressed by Admiral Ingersoll in his testimony:

"I considered that the information which we received regarding the destruction of the codes and which was sent out to the fleets as one of the two most important messages that were sent out by the Chief of Naval Operations during the entire period before Pearl Harbor, the other one being the dispatch stating that, 'This is a war warning' in effect and that all hope of negotiations had broken off . . .

"The importance of the messages regarding the destruction of the codes is this: If you rupture diplomatic negotiations you do not necessarily have to burn your codes. The diplomats go home and they can pack up their codes with their dolls and take them home. Also, when you rupture diplomatic negotiations you do not rupture consular relations. The consuls stay on.

"Now in this particular set of dispatches they not only told their diplomats in Washington and London to burn their codes but they told their consuls in Manila, in Hongkong, Singapore, and Batavia to burn their codes and that did not mean a rupture of diplomatic negotiations, *it meant war, and that information was sent out to the fleet as soon as we got it* * * *" Committee record, pp. 11286, 11287.
[334] Committee exhibit No. 2, pp. 16–29.
[335] Id., at pp. 18, 26.

ing the defenses of the fleet in port. The latter message dated December 2 (translated December 30) read:[336]

In view of the present situation, the presence in port of warships, airplane carriers, and cruisers is of utmost importance. Hereafter, to the utmost of your ability, let me know day by day. Wire me in each case whether or not there are any observation balloons above Pearl Harbor or if there are any indications that they will be sent up. Also advise me whether or not the warships are provided with antimine nets.

The messages translated after December 7 from Honolulu to Tokyo also reflect for the first time that information relating to the defenses at Pearl Harbor was being collected and supplied to Japan. In a message of November 24, Tokyo was advised that on the preceding night five mine layers had conducted mine-laying operations outside the harbor.[337] A November 28 message reported, "there are eight 'B-17' planes at Midway and the altitude range of their anti-aircraft guns is (5,000 feet?)"; that "12,000 men (mostly marines) are expected to reinforce the troops in Honolulu during December or January"; and that "there has usually been one cruiser in the waters about (15,000 feet?) south of Pearl Harbor and one or two destroyers at the entrance to the harbor." [338]

Of extreme significance are two messages of December 6 (both translated December 8) one of which reads as follows: [339]

Re the last part of your #123.[340]

1. On the American Continent in October the Army began training barrage balloon troops at Camp Davis, North Carolina. Not only have they ordered four or five hundred balloons, but it is understood that they are considering the use of these balloons in the defense of Hawaii and Panama. Insofar as Hawaii is concerned, though investigations have been made in the neighborhood of Pearl Harbor, they have not set up mooring equipment, nor have they selected the troops to man them. Furthermore, there is no indication that any training for the maintenance of balloons is being undertaken. At the present time there are no signs of barrage balloon equipment. In addition, it is difficult to imagine that they have actually any. However, even though they have actually made preparations, because they must control the air over the water and land runways of the airports in the vicinity of Pearl Harbor, Hickam, Ford, and Ewa, there are limits in the balloon defense of Pearl Harbor. *I imagine that in all probability there is considerable opportunity left to take advantage for a surprise attack against these places.*

2. In my opinion the battleships do not have torpedo nets. The details are not known. I will report the results of my investigation.

The other message of December 6 from Honolulu to Tokyo reported, among other things, "it appears that no air reconnaissance is being conducted by the fleet air arm." [341]

Also of particular interest is a message from Honolulu on December 3 [342] establishing a "number code" to indicate whether warships of a given category were preparing to sortie or had departed. A system

[336] Id., at p. 21. This message was transmitted from Hawaii and was translated by the Army in Washington, the translation bearing the notation, "This message was received on December 23."

[337] Translated December 16, 1941, by the Army. Committee exhibit No. 2, p. 17.

[338] Translated December 8, 1941, by the Army. Committee exhibit No. 2, p. 19.

[339] Committee exhibit No. 2, pp. 27, 28. Army translation. *The record indicates that this information was taken from material published in newspapers.*

[340] See committee exhibit No. 2, p. 21.

[341] Id., p. 29. Army translation.

of houselights, newspaper want ads and bonfires, in addition to the use of a sail boat, was designed to indicate the code numbers. While this system of communication did not relate to the defenses of Hawaii, it was clearly in anticipation that the normal channels for transmitting information regarding the movements of the fleet might be cut off and that a visual means of communication, probably to submarines offshore, was desired. It is also to be noted that no provision was made in the code for transmitting information concerning the departure of ships after December 6.

This message was decrypted and translated in rough form on December 6 by a civilian translator in the Navy Department, it having been received from a radio intercept station of the Army at Fort Hunt, Va. While Captain Kramer testified he had no positive recollection of having seen the translation prior to the attack, the evidence tends to indicate that the rough translation was shown to him on the afternoon of December 6 but that on account of the pressure of work on other important diplomatic messages, including the first 13 parts of the Japanese 14-part memorandum, no action was taken on the translation until December 8.[343] It is to be noted that this intercept of December 3 was in a code system referred to as "PA-K2" whereas the important Japanese 14-part reply which started coming in on the afternoon of December 6 was in the so-called Purple code system. The Purple was afforded first priority which, it appears, explains Captain Kramer's not giving undivided attention to the PA-K2 dispatch of December 3 together with the fact that this message was badly garbled and the civilian translator who handled it, while proficient in Japanese, had not as yet had adequate experience concerning the handling of the intercepted dispatches.[344]

CONSIDERATIONS RESPONSIBLE FOR DELAY IN TRANSLATIONS

Of the 13 messages between Tokyo and Honolulu intercepted before December 7 but not translated until after the attack, 5 were transmitted on or after December 4. The evidence shows that because of technical difficulties a delay of 3 days in transmitting, decoding, and translating such messages was not unusual or unreasonable.[345]

---

[342] Id., pp. 22–24.
[343] See Hewitt Inquiry Record, pp. 588, 589; also pp. 511–515.
Captain Safford stated that on the week end of December 6, 1941, his unit handled three times the normal traffic on a busy day. Navy Court of Inquiry record, p. 756.
[344] See testimony of Captain McCollum, committee record, pp. 9283, 9284. The December 3 dispatch from the Honolulu consul was obtained by the district intelligence officer of the Navy in Hawaii and was turned over on December 5, 1941, to the Radio Intelligence Unit for decryption and translation. Being in the more simple PA-K2 system the unit in Hawaii while capable of breaking the message down did not decrypt and translate it until after the attack.
[345] In discussing the matter of delays in securing the translations of the Magic, General Miles stated:
"* * * it was not only a question of personnel and facilities here in Washington for the decoding and translation of those messages, but also very definitely out in the field. Those messages had to be picked out of the air by intercepting stations. They were not all picked up by the same station. There was no one station that could have picked them up.
"In fact, I understand now that the best intercepting station for the few messages emanating from Japan itself was Manila.
"Now, some of those intercepting stations had teletype facilities by which they could promptly transmit the message intercepted to Washington. Some did not. Some of the messages were received in Washington by air mail.
"So we had not only a question of personnel and facilities and a very rapidly growing traffic to handle it in Washington but also the actual intercepting of the message in the field and the transmission of those messages to Washington." Committee record, pp. 2111, 2112.

The same difficulty partially explains the delays ranging from 5 to 9 days in decoding and translating six of the eight messages transmitted prior to December 4.

Of the remaining two messages, one dated November 24 was not translated until 20 days after it had been received in Washington. The key in which this message was transmitted was not recovered until about December 16. The other is the message from Tokyo, dated December 2, requesting information as to observation balloons and antimine nets at Pearl Harbor. A transmission of this message was intercepted by a Navy station on the west coast on December 2 and was received by the Navy on December 6 by air mail. This version of the intercept text, however, was badly garbled and the actual decoding and translating was based on a copy obtained from the Honolulu office of a radio corporation after the attack on Pearl Harbor.

The two messages transmitted from Honolulu to Tokyo on December 6, reporting the absence of barrage balloons, torpedo nets, and air reconnaissance, were intercepted by an Army station on the west coast at 7:22 p. m. on December 6 and 12:42 a. m. on December 6, respectively (Washington time), but were not processed as rapidly as were the diplomatic messages transmitted from Tokyo to Washington on the same night. On the basis of experience as to the contents of messages over particular circuits and in particular codes, the very highest priority was given to messages between Tokyo and Washington transmitted in the most secure Japanese code, the so-called purple, and the "pilot message" of December 6 had alerted the services to what was coming on the Tokyo-Washington circuit.

The messages from Honolulu to Tokyo on December 6 were transmitted in the PA–K2 code system, a relatively insecure Japanese code and one past experience had shown was not ordinarily used for messages which Tokyo considered of the highest importance. The actual content of any message could not of course be known until it had been decoded and translated, and before the attack there was no reason to suspect that the two messages sent from Honolulu to Tokyo on December 6 would prove of unusual interest. It is to be noted, however, that the low-grade PA–K2 system was virtually the only code available to the Honolulu consul after he had destroyed his major codes pursuant to instructions from Tokyo on December 2.[346]

Despite the unfortunate fact that these messages were not processed prior to December 7, no basis exists for criticizing the system which was set up for decrypting and translating the intercepted Japanese messages and for determining the priorities in the processing of the various classes of messages. The evidence shows that throughout the period of tense relations between the United States and Japan in 1941, the important diplomatic messages were intercepted, transmitted to Washington, decoded and translated, and disseminated with utmost speed. Not infrequently they were in the hands of the authorized recipients of Magic in our Government as soon as they were in the

---

[346] See exhibit No. 1, pp. 215, 216.

hands of the Japanese addressees. Many of the civilian and military personnel engaged in handling the Magic worked long hours far in excess of those prescribed with no additional compensation nor special recognition. *The success achieved in reading the Japanese diplomatic codes merits the highest commendation and all witnesses familiar with Magic material throughout the war have testified that it contributed enormously to the defeat of the enemy, greatly shortened the war, and saved many thousands of lives.*[347]

Conclusions With Respect to Intelligence Available in Washington Which Was Not Supplied Hawaii

Both Admiral Kimmel and General Short have complained that they were wrongfully deprived of intelligence available to Washington through the Magic which would have altered completely their estimate of the situation and would have resulted, if it had been supplied them, in a proper alert and appropriate dispositions consistent with an adequate defense of the Hawaiian coastal frontier. In a prepared statement, read before the committee, Admiral Kimmel said: [348]

The question will arise in your minds, as it has in mine: Would the receipt of this information have made a difference in the events of December 7? No man can now state as a fact that he would have taken a certain course of action four years ago had he known facts which were then unknown to him. All he can give is his present conviction on the subject, divorcing himself from hindsight as far as humanly possible, and re-creating the atmosphere of the past and the factors which then influenced him. I give you my views, formed in this manner.

Had I learned these vital facts and the "ships in harbor" messages on November 28th, it is my present conviction that I would have rejected the Navy Department's suggestion to send carriers to Wake and Midway. I would have ordered the third carrier, the *Saratoga*, back from the West Coast. I would have gone to sea with the Fleet and endeavored to keep it in an intercepting position at sea. This would have permitted the disposal of the striking power of the Fleet to meet an attack in the Hawaiian area. The requirement of keeping the Fleet fuelled, however, would have made necessary the presence in Pearl Harbor from time to time of detachments of various units of the main body of the Fleet.

In the last analysis, however, there are only four messages or groups of messages which the commander in chief of the Pacific Fleet and the commanding general of the Hawaiian Department contend pointed to Pearl Harbor as a likely place of attack; i. e., the harbor berthing plan and related dispatches,[349] the deadline messages,[350] the dispatches which indicated the fraudulent nature of Japanese negotiations after November 28,[350a] and the dispatch specifying 1 p. m., December 7, as the time for delivery of the Japanese memorandum to the Secretary of State.[350b]

Referring to the berthing plan (and related dispatches) Admiral Kimmel said,[350c] "These Japanese instructions and reports pointed to

---

[347] See note 113, *supra*.
[348] See committee record, pp. 6805, 6806.
[349] See section " 'Ships in Harbor' Reports," supra.
[350] See section "The Deadline Messages," supra.
[350a] See section "Dispatches Indicating Fraudulent Nature of Negotiations after November 28, 1941," supra.
[350b] See section "Significance of the 'One o'clock and Code Destruction Messages," supra.
[350c] Committee record, pp. 6779, 6780.

an attack by Japan upon the ships in Pearl Harbor." Additionally, he has indicated that the dispatches concerning the deadlines and fraudulent negotiations [350d] pointed to Pearl Harbor.

During the course of committee examination General Short was asked whether, "outide of the message carving up Pearl Harbor into five divisions," there was any information among the Magic intelligence which pointed to an attack upon Pearl Harbor any more than upon any other place. He replied: [350e]

That was the most definite thing, and then the fact that the delivery of the message was at 1 p. m. Washington time, which would be shortly after dawn in Honolulu, which I think was an indication.

At another point, referring to the "harbor berthing plan" and the so-called "one o'clock" message, General Short said,[350f] "I think those two things are the really definite things that pointed to Pearl Harbor" and that the other intercepted messages related to the "more tense situation as it developed."

As heretofore pointed out, we are unable to conclude that the berthing plan and related dispatches pointed directly to an attack on Pearl Harbor, nor are we able to conclude that the plan was a "bomb plot" in view of the evidence indicating it was not such.[350g] We are of the opinion, however, that the berthing plan and related dispatches should have received careful consideration and created a serious question as to their significance. Since they indicated a particular interest in the Pacific Fleet's base this intelligence should have been appreciated and supplied the commander in chief of the Pacific Fleet and the commanding general of the Hawaiian Department for their assistance, along with other information and intelligence available to them, in making their estimate of the situation.

We believe that the deadline messages and the messages indicating fraudulent Japanese diplomacy after November 28 in themselves no more indicated Hawaii as a likely point of attack than any other point in the Pacific. The equivalent of this intelligence was supplied Admiral Kimmel in the dispatch of November 27 beginning, "This dispatch is to be considered a war warning" and advising, "negotiations with Japan looking toward stabilization of conditions in the Pacific have ceased and an aggressive move by Japan is expected within the next few days." It was supplied General Short in the November 27 warning, stating, "Japanese future action unpredictable but hostile action possible at any moment."

The "one o'clock intercept", as previously indicated, was an unusual piece of intelligence suggesting the distinct possibility that *some-*

[350d] See committee record, pp. 6791–6793.

[350e] Committee record, pp. 8126, 8127. At another point, when asked if his thought was that the Magic messages that were not sent Hawaii would have been more important than the messages he did receive, General Short said: "There were two that could hardly fail. The intercept which was the bombing plan of Pearl Harbor and the message stating that the ultimatum would be delivered at 1 p. m. which could have been sent to me 4 hours before the attack, and reached me 7 hours after the attack. These two messages would have meant something to me." Committee record, p. 8201.

[350f] Id., at pp. 8126–8128.

[350g] See section " 'Ships in Harbor' Reports," supra.

Japanese military action would take place *somewhere* at 1 p. m. but it did not reasonably point to Pearl Harbor any more than to any other place in the Pacific. This intelligence indicated the need for particular alertness at 1 p. m. to meet the dangers contemplated on the basis of estimates already made as to where a Japanese attack might come.

The burden of the statements of both Admiral Kimmel and General Short to the committee is that Washington withheld vital information from them. In fact, Admiral Kimmel has charged that the Navy Department's handling of Magic constituted an affirmative misrepresentation. On the basis of the evidence before the committee, this charge is without foundation in fact.

Both Hawaiian commanders all but ignore the fact that they are properly chargeable with possessing far more vital intelligence indicating an attack on Hawaii than was in the hands of anyone in the War or Navy Departments. They had, among other things, correspondence with Washington and plans revealing the possible dangers of air attack, the warning dispatches, the code-destruction intelligence, radio intelligence concerning the "lost" Japanese carriers, the Mori call, the report of sighting and subsequent attack on a Japanese submarine in close proximity to Pearl Harbor, and radar detection of the Japanese raiding force over 130 miles from Oahu on the morning of December 7. General Short assumed the Navy was conducting distant reconnaissance. Admiral Kimmel assumed that the Army would alert its aircraft warning service, antiaircraft guns, and fighter planes. From these assumptions and the estimate and action taken on the basis of information available to them, it is problematical as to what steps would have been taken by the Hawaiian commanders had they received all of the intelligence which they contend was withheld from them.

Estimate of the Situation in Washington

The evidence reflects that virtually everyone in Washington was surprised Japan struck Pearl Harbor at the time she did. Among the reasons for this conclusion was the apparent Japanese purpose to move toward the south—the Philippines, Thailand, the Kra Peninsula; and the feeling that Hawaii was a near-impregnable fortress that Japan would not incur the dangers of attacking. The latter consideration necessarily contemplated that Hawaii was alert and that the enemy would be met with the full weight of Army and Navy power provided for defense. It is apparent, however, that an attack on the fleet by Japan at some time was regarded as a distinct possibility. The warning messages sent the Hawaiian commanders contained orders requiring defensive measures against this possibility. Admiral Turner, Director of War Plans in the Navy Department, is the only officer in Washington in the higher echelons who indicated a strong belief that Hawaii would be attacked—he testified that he regarded such an attack as a "50–50 chance." [351]   Asked if he had gained this impression around December 1 as a result of the Japanese ship-location reports,[352] he testified:[353]

No. That had been the opinion all along, expressed by the Navy Department, expressed in Hawaii, expressed by the War Department, expressed by everybody else, that there was a strong possibility that there would be an attack, a raid, that is, against Hawaii. That was merely following along the line the Navy officers and Army officers had been thinking about for 25 years or more. There was no change.

When asked why, around November 27, if the Navy felt in this way about the chances of an air raid on the fleet in Pearl Harbor, some further message was not sent suggesting this possibility, Admiral Turner stated: [354]

That had been in correspondence right along. The dispatch of November 27 fully covers it, in my opinion. I think on the 5th, the afternoon of the 5th of December, after convassing the situation with officers in my Division, I went into Admiral Ingersoll's office and we talked for an hour as to what more the Navy Department could do to warn the forces in the field, the fleets, what ought to be done, should we send any more dispatches, or what. We came, both, to the conclusion that everything had been done covering the entire situation that ought to be done and we then proceeded into Admiral Stark's office, discussed the same question with him for 15 minutes, and *it was the unanimous decision that the orders that we had sent out for Admiral Kimmel to take a defensive deployment there were sufficient.*
What was he going to take a defensive deployment against? Just one thing. That is the meat of that dispatch. It is all in there.

The foregoing thoughts expressed by Admiral Turner characterized the feelings of all the ranking officers of the War and Navy Departments: *that the Hawaiian commanders had been adequately alerted to all contingencies.* Admiral Stark stated, "We considered we had fully alerted them (referring to the 'war warning' of November 27) with the directives which were given both by the Army and by ourselves * * * We felt we were fully alerted. Our plans were ready, if

---

[351] It is to be noted that the record clearly indicates that Admiral Turner's estimate of a possible attack at Hawaii was not based on any intelligence which he possessed indicating such an attack but rather on his personal appraisal of possible Japanese action.
In this connection Captain McCollum said: "I was not surprised at the Japanese attack, sir. I was astonished at the success attained by that attack, sir. * * * I do not mean by that statement to imply that I had any knowledge that the Japanese were going to attack Pearl Harbor, and I wish to state categorically that there was no bit of intelligence that I had at my disposal that definitely to my mind indicated that the Japanese would attack Pearl Harbor, but I had * * * for many years felt that in the event of an outbreak of hostilities between the United States and Japan that the Japanese would make a very definite attempt to strike the fleet at or near the commencement time of those hostilities." Committee record, pp. 9259, 9260.
The following committee examination reflects the feeling of Captain McCollum with respect to a possible Japanese attack on our fleet:
Question: "And you always felt that if the Japs were going to strike with her fleets the place to start was by attacking our fleet?"
Captain McCollum: "That is correct."
Question: "The place they would start would be by attacking the fleet."
Captain McCollum: "They not only would do that, but that there was historical precedent, if the Japanese wished to start a war with us. Their war with China in 1895 was started that way; their war with Russia in 1907 was started that way; their war against Germany in Tsingtao in 1914 was started in that way. * * * Attacking their fleet and timing a declaration of war on presentation of the final notes." Committee record, pp. 9275, 9276.
[352] Radio Intelligence concerning the "lost" Japanese carriers.
[353] Committee record, p. 5200.
[354] Id., at p. 5201.

war broke, in all theaters." [355]   General Marshall said, "In our opinion, the commanders had been alerted." [356]   As expressed by Mr. Stimson: [357]

> We assumed that when he (General Short) had been warned that hostile action was possible at any moment, it would not be necessary to repeat that warning over and over again during the ensuing days. The fact was of course that General Short did receive, not only from Washington but from other sources, repeated intelligence of the impending crisis.

Captain McCollum, who had suggested (not knowing the "war warning" had been sent) an additional warning dispatch, stated in referring to the dispatch sent Admiral Kimmel on November 27: [358]

> It does not come in the life of most naval officers to receive or see a message containing such words and my personal feeling is that a message containing the information "This is a war warning," indicated clearly that the Department expected a war to break out there at any moment from then on.
> * * * I think that a commander to whom such a message as that is addressed must assume that war is going to break out over his forces and take the steps necessary to cover it.

The consummate confidence that field commanders were adequately alert on the basis of dispatches sent them is manifested by the reluctance of Admiral Stark to dispatch a message based on the "one o'clock intercept." As stated by General Marshall: "I asked him if he had read the final message referring to one o'clock. He stated that he had, and I proposed an immediate message to all theaters concerned. *Admiral Stark hesitated, because he said (he) had alerted them all and he was afraid of confusing them further.*" [359]

As indicated, the record reflects the judgment of responsible officers in both the War and Navy Departments that they had fully and adequately alerted our military outposts before December 7. [360]   We believe that Admiral Kimmel and General Short received sufficient information to justify the expectation that they would be fully alert to the implications of their military responsibilities in Hawaii.   In this connection it is to be noted that all other outpost commanders, receiving the warning messages of November 27 in substantially the same form as did Admiral Kimmel and General Short, took full and ample measures to effect a state of readiness commensurate with the fact that war was imminent.   Hawaii was the *only* outpost that failed to institute a proper alert.

---

[355] Id., at pp. 13733, 13747.
[356] Id., at pp. 13792, 13793.
[357] See Mr. Stimson's statement, committee record, p. 14398.
[358] Committee record, pp. 9194, 9195, 9281, 9282. McCollum said: "I had been given to understand that they (the Fleet) had been thoroughly alerted * * * and on their toes." Committee record, p. 9156.
[359] Army Pearl Harbor Board (top secret) record, pages 7, 8.
[360] General Miles said: "G-2 was charged with the dissemination of information. The essential information contained in the Chief of Staff's November 27 message, that hostilities might occur at any time on the initiative of the Japanese, held good right up to December 7. The information emphasized the increasing tension of the crisis.
"But these things were known in Hawaii. *That Fortress, like a sentinel on post, had been warned of the danger which was its sole reason for being. Anything else was considered to be redundant.*" Committee record, p. 2216.

Nature of Responsibilities

In seeking to make an assessment of responsibilities for the Pearl Harbor disaster, apart from that which is forever Japan's, it is imperative that the duties and obligations existing in Hawaii be placed in the proper perspective with respect to those attaching to Washington. The responsibility of the commander in the field with his well-defined scope of activity is manifestly to be distinguished from that of the officer in Washington who is charged with directing the over-all operations of the military on a global basis.

DUTIES IN HAWAII

It has been a cardinal principle of military theory to select capable commanders for our outposts, give them broad directives,[361] and leave to their discretion and good judgment the implementation of the Departmental mandate consonant with their more intimate and detailed familiarity with the peculiar problems existing in their particular commands.[362] Admiral Kimmel and General Short were selected because of their impeccable records for two of the most important field commands of the Navy and Army—Commander in Chief of the Pacific Fleet and Commanding General of the Hawaiian Department. These two officers were primarily and fundamentally responsible— they were the men to whom Washington and the Nation were properly entitled to look—for the defense of the Hawaiian Coastal Frontier.

With respect to Hawaii and the fleet, theirs were the obligations to plan for war, to train for war, and to be alerted for war when it came. The first two of these obligations they discharged in an exemplary manner but in the case of the third, alertness for war, they failed.[363] All of the intelligence, thought, and energies of the field commander are to be devoted to his command. He is to apply all information and intelligence received to his particular situation. He is not privileged to think or contemplate that he will not be attacked. On the contrary, he is to assume and to expect that his particular post will be attacked. He cannot wholly assume that others will inform him

---

[361] It is to be recalled, as heretofore pointed out, that Admiral Kimmel said: "* * * the Department itself is not too well informed as to the local situation, particularly with regard to the status of current outlying island development, thus making it even more necessary that the Commander-in-Chief, Pacific Fleet, be guided by *broad policy and objectives rather than by categorical instructions.*" Letter from Admiral Kimmel to Admiral Stark, dated May 26, 1941. See committee exhibit No. 106.

[362] Referring to the plans for the defense of the Hawaiian Coastal Frontier, Admiral Turner said: "After reading these splendid plans that had been sent in by the Commander in Chief, and by the Fourteenth Naval District, why, my feeling was that these people knew their business. They knew what to do about it, probably a lot more than I did, or the rest of us here, because they were the ones that were on the firing line." Committee record, p. 5211. See also testimony of General Gerow, committee record, p. 2719.

[363] In striking contrast with the failure to effect adequate readiness in Hawaii is the manner in which the Russians prepared to meet in June and July of 1941 the possibility of a Japanese thrust against the Soviet Union. An intercepted dispatch from Vladivostok to Tokyo on July 3, 1941, stated: "Since the beginning of the German-Soviet war the naval authorities here have tightened up on watch and are engaged in naval preparations by enforcing various exercises to meet *any eventuality.* However, naval exercises are limited to only one section of the force for there are many ships which are undergoing repairs. *Evidently the preparations are intended for* defense against Japan." Committee exhibit No. 2, p. 125. See also committee record, pp. 7509–7512.

when and where the foe will strike. He is "like a sentinel on duty in the face of the enemy. His fundamental duties are clear and precise. It is not the duty of the outpost commander to speculate or rely on the possibilities of the enemy attacking at some other outpost instead of his own. It is his duty to meet him at his post at any time and to make the best possible fight that can be made against him with the weapons with which he has been supplied." [364]

The commanders in Hawaii were clearly and unmistakably warned of war with Japan. They were given orders and possessed information that the entire Pacific area was fraught with danger. They failed to carry out these orders and to discharge their basic and ultimate responsibilities. They failed to defend the fortress they commanded— their citadel was taken by surprise. Aside from any responsibilities that may appear to rest in Washington, the ultimate and direct responsibility for failure to engage the Japanese on the morning of December 7 with every weapon at their disposal rests essentially and properly with the Army and Navy commands in Hawaii whose duty it was to meet the enemy against which they had been warned.

DUTIES IN WASHINGTON

The Chief of Staff of the Army and the Chief of Naval Operations of the Navy had the over-all responsibility for supervision of our military and naval operations and establishments everywhere, including Hawaii. Theirs was the obligation of determining that all of the equipment available was supplied the field commander which would assist him in discharging his responsibilities.[365] In supplying equipment it was their duty to consider the demands for material from many quarters in the light of the commitments and interests of the United States—to estimate where the most dangerous and likely point of enemy attack might be—and then to effect dispositions which in their best judgment most nearly satisfied the exigencies of the hour. They discharged this duty to the best of their ability.

They had the duty of alerting our outposts in view of the critical situation in our relations with Japan in the days before December 7 and of informing them of probable enemy action.[366] In the dispatch of November 27, sent Admiral Kimmel and Admiral Hart, the commander in chief of the Asiatic Fleet, there was outlined what at the time was regarded and appeared to be the major strategic effort of the enemy. The Japanese major effort did follow the course outlined in the dispatch. Pearl Harbor was not known to be a point of Japanese attack but it was known that such an attack was a possibility and both responsible commanders in Hawaii were accordingly ordered to take action contemplated to meet this possibility.

[364] See statement of Mr. Stimson, committee record, p. 14406.
[365] See committee record, pp. 2764–2771; 5594, 5595. Also see committee exhibit No. 42.
[366] Admiral Turner said: "My function was to give the major strategic over-all picture for the use of my superiors and disseminate that." Committee record, p. 5074.

The officers in the intelligence and war plans divisions of the War and Navy Departments handling matters in the Pacific had a *particular* responsibility with respect to the magic intelligence just as the Hawaiian commanders had a *particular* responsibility for the defense of the fleet and the Hawaiian coastal frontier. It was the duty of these officers to evaluate and disseminate the magic in the form of estimates, as originally obtained, or otherwise. This responsibility they failed to discharge with that high degree of skill and imagination which this intelligence warranted.[367]

In the case of the War Plans Division of the War Department, once it had warned General Short of hostilities, issued order in contemplation of this contingency, and directed him *to report measures taken*, it thereby assumed responsibility for reviewing the report of action and advising the commanding general in the event the measures taken by him were not in accordance with those desired.

While the report submitted by General Short was ambiguous and disarmingly terse, it was the duty of the War Plans Division through the exercise of proper supervision to require a reply reflecting with clarity that there had been satisfactory compliance with the departmental orders.[368]

Hawaii was but one of many points of concern to General Marshall, the Chief of Staff, and Admiral Stark, the Chief of Naval Operations. As stated by the Chief of Staff, "the only place we had any assurance about was Hawaii, and for that reason we had less concern about Hawaii because we had worked on it very industriously, we had a tremendous amount of correspondence about it, and we felt reasonably secure at that one point." [369]   Theirs was the obligation of mapping the strategy of global war, of advising and counseling the President and others on military and naval matters, of following and encouraging the progress of preparation for defense in the event of war, of outlining and justifying to the Congress the manifold needs of the Army and Navy, of over-all responsibility for many military and naval outposts and interests, of disposing and allocating the scanty

---

[367] As expressed by Mr. Stimson: "A keener and more imaginative appreciation on the part of some of the officers in the War and Navy Departments of the significance of some of the information might have led to a suspicion of an attack specifically on Pearl Harbor. I do not think that certain officers in the War Department functioned in these respects with sufficient skill. At all times it must be borne in mind, however, that it is easy to criticize individuals in the light of hindsight, and very difficult to recreate fairly the entire situation and information with which the officers were required to deal at the time of the event." See statement of the Secretary of War with respect to the report of the Army Pearl Harbor Board, committee exhibit No. 157.

[368] In this connection, however, the marked distinction between the character of the responsibility resting on the War Plans Division and that reposing in General Short was expressed by Mr. Stimson:
"It must clearly be borne in mind that in November and December 1941 the responsibilities of the War Plans Division covered many fields and many theaters. Their preoccupation with the theaters most likely to be threatened, such as the Philippines toward which the Japanese activities then appeared to be pointed, may be subject to criticism in the light of the subsequent disaster, but it is understandable. All signs pointed to an attack in that direction, and they were exercising particular care with respect to that theater. Their conduct must be viewed in an entirely different light from that of the theater commander, such as General Short, who was like a sentinel on post and whose attention and vigilance must be entirely concentrated on the single position which he has been chosen to defend and whose alertness must not be allowed to be distracted by consideration of other contingencies in respect to which he is not responsible." See statement of the Secretary of War with respect to the report of the Army Pearl Harbor Board Committee exhibit No. 157.

[369] Committee record, p. 13793.

materials of war consistent with the overwhelming demands and requirements from many quarters, and of performing the innumerable functions of the Chief of Staff and Chief of Naval Operations in a democracy that was all too slowly preparing itself against the inevitable day of war.[370] Such diversity and magnitude of responsibilities is to be distinguished from that of the outpost commander with his singleness of purpose and well-defined sphere of activity. It was the duty of General Marshall and Admiral Stark to alert our military and naval garrisons which they attempted to do and felt assured they had done. To superimpose the administrative burden of supervising details would be to enmesh them in such a confusing and bewildering network of detail as to defeat the very purpose for which the positions of Chief of Staff and Chief of Naval Operations were created.

UNITY OF COMMAND

The evidence adduced in the course of the various Pearl Harbor investigations reveals the complete inadequacy of command by *mutual cooperation* where decisive action is of the essence. Both the Army and Navy commanders in Hawaii failed to coordinate and integrate their combined facilities for defense in the crucial days between November 27 and December 7, 1941. While they had been able over a period of time to conceive admirable plans for the defense of the Hawaiian Coastal Frontier consistent with the system of mutual cooperation, when the time came for the implementation of these plans they remained hollow and empty contracts that were never executed. Had the responsible commanders conferred together in such manner as to reach joint decisions consonant with their plans, the system of mutual cooperation would have proved adequate. It is clear, however, that this system presents unnecessary and inevitable opportunities for personal failures and shortcomings. The ubiquitous tendency to "let George do it," to assume the other fellow will take care of the situation, is an inseparable part of command by mutual cooperation.

The tragic assumptions made by Admiral Kimmel and General Short concerning what the other was doing are a manifestation of this fact. Each was the victim of the natural human reluctance to pry into what is regarded as another's business.[370a] The commander in chief assumed that the Army would be on a full alert—the antiaircraft, the aircraft warning service, and the interceptor command—yet he

---

[370] Mr. Stimson said: "Our General Staff officers were working under a terrific pressure in the face of a global war which they felt was probably imminent. Yet they were surrounded, outside of the offices and almost throughout the country, by a spirit of isolationism and disbelief in danger which now seems incredible. * * * The officers of the Army were then trying to do their duty in the deadening, if not actually hostile, atmosphere of a nation that was not awake to its danger. We are now engaged in passing judgment upon their actions in the wholly different atmosphere of a nation which has suffered some of the horrors of the greatest and most malignant war in history. In my opinion, it would be highly unjust to them if this complete difference of atmosphere was not given the weight which it deserves." Statement of Mr. Stimson to the Committee. Committee record, pp. 14410, 14411.

[370a] See testimony of General Short, Committee record, pp. 8122, 8123.

did not inquire to determine whether this was the case, apparently because it might not "sit very well" with General Short.[371] The commanding general assumed that the Navy would be conducting reconnaissance which would afford him adequate warning in order properly to alert his command. Yet he did not inquire as to whether the Navy was conducting the reconnaissance upon which he was relying for his protection, presumably because he felt such an inquiry might be "resented" by Admiral Kimmel.[372]

The conduct of operations in this state of joint oblivion was possible in a command by *mutual cooperation;* but none of these false and unwarranted assumptions could have obtained under *unity of command.* Under the latter system a single commander would have been charged with complete responsibility; all of the warnings, intelligence, and orders would have been his to interpret, estimate, and implement; it would have been his duty only to effect a state of readiness commensurate with the realities of the situation. Conceivably, a single commander might have arrived at the same estimate as did Admiral Kimmel and General Short; namely, that Hawaii would not be attacked. But such a decision would have been clear-cut and devoid of all the anomalous and incompatible assumptions that are in strange contradiction of the estimate made by the Hawaiian commanders that their outpost was safe. He would not have arrived at a conclusion concerning the defensive measures required on a fallacious assumption with respect to the decisions and defensive measures of someone else, nor could he have interpreted the same order at once in two different and inconsistent ways.

Furthermore, in a command by mutual cooperation there is the unfailing likelihood of conflicting and overlapping prerogatives. In the case of the plans for the defense of the Hawaiian Coastal Frontier, it was the joint mission of the Army and Navy to hold Oahu as a main outlying naval base, each being specifically charged with supporting the other. It was necessary that the local commanders jointly agree upon the existence of the appropriate emergency as a condition precedent to the detailed allocation of specific missions as between the two services. The Navy was primarily responsible for distant reconnaissance and long-range attacks against hostile vessels, while the Army was charged with short-range defense. In the case of each of these defensive measures, one service was charged with supporting the forces of the other service having primary responsibility; and particularly, in the case of air operations, the service having the primary responsibility was to control the available planes of the other service. This was a sliding and shifting arrangement with respect to primary responsibility depending on the nature of the attack. The mutual agreement required by such operations would necessarily be forth-

[371] See Roberts Commission record, p. 631.
[372] See Army Pearl Harbor Board record, p. 363.

coming only when a particular type of attack was sufficiently imminent as to suggest the advisability of the Army or the Navy, as the case might be, assuming primary responsibility to meet the attack.[373]

The completely ineffective liaison between the Army and the Navy in Hawaii at a time when the fullest exchange of intelligence was absolutely imperative dictates that military and naval intelligence, particularly, must be consolidated.[374] The extraordinarily anomalous situation of the one hand not knowing what the other hand knew or was doing should never be permitted to exist again.

Invocation of unity of command was within the scope of the authority of the responsible commanders in Hawaii, upon agreement as to the service that should exercise command,[374a] or of the Secretaries of War and Navy, acting jointly.[375] Inasmuch as there was a complete failure of the system of mutual cooperation on December 7, 1941, and unity of command had not been effected by or imposed upon the Hawaiian commanders, it is proper to inquire as to the reason for unity of command not having been invoked at least as soon as it was known that hostilities were possible at any moment.

The evidence reflects that during the period from November 27 to December 7 the leading subject of conferences between Admiral Kimmel and General Short was the question and near-dispute as to whether the Army or the Navy should exercise command over the islands of Wake and Midway after the Marines on these islands were relieved by Army troops.[376] No agreement was concluded in this regard before the outbreak of war. If neither would agree to the

---

[373] See section, *supra*, concerning plans for the defense of the Hawaiian Coastal Frontier, Part III, this report.

[374] *General Marshall said he thought unity of consolidation (sic) or centralization of military and naval intelligence was very necessary.* Committee record, p. 2966.

[374a] Admiral Kimmel testified that he never had any discussions with the commanding general of the Hawaiian Department on the desirability of putting unity of command into effect. He said he would not have effected unity of command, or accepted responsibility for the Army actions, without reference to the Navy Department. See Navy Court of Inquiry record, pp. 296, 297.

[375] See committee exhibit No. 44. General Gerow said: "A fact frequently lost sight of in consideration of the method of coordination under the principle of mutual cooperation is that although the major operation is being conducted under that principle, *joint operations subordinate thereto may still be conducted under the principle of unity of command if so agreed to by the Army and Navy commanders concerned.* This method is particularly applicable to joint operations by forces having similar combat characteristics, such as the air forces of the two services." See memorandum prepared by General Gerow for Chief of Staff dated November 17, 1941. Committee exhibit No. 48.

[376] Admiral W. W. Smith testified: "He (Admiral Kimmel) had a shock, though, in the week preceding Pearl Harbor, when we had orders from the Navy Department, and General Short had orders from the War Department, to prepare a plan immediately for bringing all the marines off the outlying islands, and replacing them with soldiers and with Army planes, and, as I remember it, practically the entire week before Pearl Harbor was spent with the two Staffs together. The Army was undecided whether to put P-39's or P-40's on these islands. We told them that any planes they put on Wake would remain their for the duration, in case of war, because they would have to be taken off from a carrier and could not come back, and we had no means of putting a ship in there to bring them off, and during the discussion of this with General Short and his staff, the Commanding General of the Army Air Force (General Martin) and Admiral Pye were present, and also Admiral Wilson Brown, the War Plans officer, the Operations Officers and I believe Admiral Bloch. Admiral Kimmel said, 'What can I expect of Army fighters on Wake?' And General Martin replied, 'We do not allow them to go more than fifteen miles off shore.' That was a shock to all of us and Admiral Kimmel's reply was, 'Then, they will be no damn good to me.' The exchange was never made because the war broke before-hand. *The only dispute between the Army and Navy over that exchange was that General Short said, 'If I have the man these islands, I shall have to command them.' Admiral Kimmel replied, 'No, that won't do. If the Army commanded one of the islands, I wouldn't be able to get a ship into one of the ports,' or words to that effect, and General Short said, 'Mind you, I do not want to man these islands, I think they are better manned by Marines, but if I man them, I must command them.' That was as near to a dispute between General Short and Admiral Kimmel as I ever saw, but the plan was made and submitted but never carried out,"* Hart inquiry record, pp. 40, 41.

other's commanding Wake or Midway, it is not in the least surprising or unexpected that neither one of the commanders would have agreed to subordinate himself and his entire command to the other.

In the case of Washington, the matter of establishing unity of command at our outposts was under consideration and discussion by the War and Navy Departments throughout the year 1941 and especially during the few weeks prior to December 7.[377] No decision, however, was reached concerning unity of command at Hawaii or at any of our outposts until the responsible officials were confronted by war with powerful adversaries on two fronts and the barrier of departmental prerogative had been severely jolted by the Pearl Harbor disaster. The Joint Board of the Army and Navy during 1941 had considered specific proposals for unity of command as made by each of the services but prior to December 7 no effective agreement was reached as to which service should exercise command at a particular outpost. It generally appears, however, that it was agreed the system of mutual cooperation in the Caribbean, at Panama, and at Hawaii should be replaced by unity of command. The Navy proposed that command in the Caribbean be vested in the Navy; at Panama in the Army, except when major naval forces were based there; and at Hawaii in the Navy, except when no major naval forces were based there.[378] The Army, on the other hand, proposed unity of command in all coastal frontiers, command to rest in the Army except when a major portion of the fleet was operating against comparable hostile forces within the range of possible support by Army aviation and when the Army and Navy commanders should agree to transfer command from one to the other.[379]

In view of these conflicting proposals following virtually a year of discussion, General Gerow, chief of War Plans in the War Department, recommended to the Chief of Staff on November 17, 1941, that the system of command in the outposts remain by mutual cooperation, thereby suggesting abandonment of the idea of unity of command.[380] In testifying before the committee, General Gerow explained his action by stating he thought the only way to have effective unity of command was for the heads of the Army and Navy to say that "So and so is in command, and he is in command from now on." He observed that—[381] "You cannot vary that command

[377] See committee record, pp. 2749–2761; also 2963 et seq.
[378] Committee record, pp. 2750–2757. See also committee exhibit No. 48.
[379] Id.
[380] Id. General Gerow recommended: "That coordination of joint operations in the Caribbean, Panama and Hawaiian Coastal Frontiers continue to be effected by mutual cooperation. If this recommendation is approved, such a proposal will be discussed with the Navy section of the Joint Planning Committee." See memorandum prepared by General Gerow for Chief of Staff dated November 17, 1941. Committee exhibit No. 48.
Referring to this memorandum, General Marshall stated in a memorandum for General Gerow dated December 5, 1941: "I would like this matter of Coordination of Command discussed with the Naval Section of the Joint Planning Committee. However, I think it is important that a general policy, or what might be called an explanation, should first be decided on, expressed in carefully considered sentences, as to the *application* of unity of command.
"A discussion of this runs through a series of paragraphs on your memorandum and you have covered it orally to me, but no where is it presented in a concise form." Committee exhibit No. 48A.
[381] Committee record, p. 2757.

from day to day depending on what the operation is. One man must be responsible for preparing that place for operation, and he must be responsible for commanding it after he has prepared it." He pointed out that the joint Army-Navy planning committee had contemplated an arrangement whereby command would shift back and forth from the Army to the Navy and from the Navy to the Army depending on the nature of attack or defense.[382] General Gerow said that he thought the system of mutual cooperation would be better than such a continual switching of command.[383] He commented:

"I did not think either the Army or Navy Planning Group would agree to say wholeheartedly 'You take everything and it will be agreeable to us.' Neither would agree to that." [384] He agreed that it would be necessary that "somebody at the top had to knock their heads together and tell them what to do." [385] General Marshall epitomized the essentially human proclivities characterizing the situation: [386]

I have said this before; I will repeat it again. *It is a very simple thing to have unity of command if you give it to the other man.* But that also applied in all of our dealings with the British and among ourselves and always will continue to be so.

The ultimate result was that no agreement was reached between the War and Navy Departments before Pearl Harbor for the establishment of unity of command in our military and naval outposts. The factors and considerations attending eventual invocation of unity of command were expressed by the Chief of Staff in a letter dated December 20, 1941, to General Short's successor, Gen. Delos C. Emmons: [387]

Instructions to the Army and Navy were issued a few days ago assigning unity of command to the Navy in Hawaii. At the same time unity of command was assigned to the Army in Panama.

For your confidential information, this action was taken in the following circumstances: In the first place, the Secretary of War and the Secretary of the Navy were determined that there should be no question of future confusion as to responsibility. Further, the efforts I have been making for more than a year to secure unity of command in various critical regions have been unavailing. *All sorts of Naval details, such as the operations of ships and submarines, the coordination of efforts to locate purely Naval objectives and similar matters had been raised in objection to Army control wherever that was proposed. I must say at the same time that some of the Army staff brought up somewhat similar objections to Naval control.* Both Stark and I were struggling to the same end, but until this crash of December 7th the difficulties seemed, at least under peacetime conditions, almost insurmountable. However, the two decisions I have just referred to have been made and further ones are in process of being made, all of which I feel will add immeasurably to our security, whatever the local embarrassments. Also, I regard these as merely stepping stones to larger decisions involved in our relations with Allies.

I am giving you this information in order that you may better appreciate the problem and, therefore, be better prepared to assist me by endeavoring to work with Nimitz in complete understanding.

[382] Id.
[383] Id., at p. 2758.
[384] Id.
[385] Id.
[386] Committee record, pp. 2962, 2963.
[387] See committee exhibit No. 48; also committee record, pp. 2759–2761.

Whatever difficulties arise that cannot be adjusted locally, should be brought to our attention here for consideration by Admiral Stark and myself. *These days are too perilous for personal feelings in any way to affect efficiency.*

This is a very hasty note, but I want General McCoy to take it off with him this morning.

You have my complete confidence and I will do everything possible to support you.

The foregoing considerations evince more than mere reluctance and procrastination toward effecting action by command rather than by joint agreement; they reveal that inherent in our system of separate services there exists the basic deficiency of conflicting interests which precipitate serious and unnecessary obstacles to the solution of pressing military problems. It is to be necessarily noted, however, that while considering the advisability of unity of command, Washington was assuming that the system of mutual cooperation was working within its limitations and that local commanders were fully discharging their responsibilities. It was only in the wake of the Pearl Harbor disaster that the inherent and intolerable weaknesses of command by mutual cooperation were exposed.[388]

As earlier indicated, the failure to integrate and coordinate Army-Navy efforts in Hawaii appears to have been attributable to a feeling on the part of each commander that he would intrude upon the prerogatives of the other and thereby invite similar intrusion if he inquired as to what the sister service was doing. In Washington, the failure to impose unity of command was occasioned by the inability of the Army and the Navy as entities to agree upon a basis for unified command.

GENERAL OBSERVATIONS

THE "WYMAN MATTER"

The Committee has carefully reviewed the investigation conducted by the Army Pearl Harbor Board with respect to the activities of Col. Theodore Wyman, Jr., while district engineer in the Hawaiian Department, insofar as his activities may have relationship to the Pearl Harbor disaster.[389] The Army Pearl Harbor Board concluded from the evidence that Wyman performed the duties of district engineer in a wholly unsatisfactory manner. Under his administration, engineering and construction work in the Hawaiian Department was defective and was characterized by delays.

The activities of Wyman and his associates were not fully inquired into by the Committee inasmuch as they did not appear to have contributed in any material or proximate manner to the disaster for

---

[388] In the course of counsel's examination, General Marshall was asked: "Without asking you any questions about the unity of command, complete unity of command generally in the Army and Navy Departments, limiting it to the question of posts like Hawaii, or Panama, for instance, do you want to express any views as to the wisdom of maintaining such unity of command in peacetime as compared with war?" The Chief of Staff replied: "*I think it is an imperative necessity.*'

[389] See in this regard the report of the Army Pearl Harbor Board, Committee Exhibit No. 157.

reasons heretofore set forth.[390] It is recommended, however, that the Wyman matter be investigated by an appropriate committee of the Senate or the House of Representatives.

THE PHILIPPINE ATTACK

The Committee has considered in the course of its proceedings the Japanese attack on the Philippines on December 7, 1941, and has concluded that this attack bears no relevant relationship to the disaster at Pearl Harbor. In consequence, the Philippine attack was not made the subject of detailed inquiry although the reader will find an account of this attack in the committee's record.[391]

PRIOR INQUIRIES CONCERNING THE PEARL HARBOR ATTACK

We have not presumed to pass judgment on the nature of or charges of unfairness [392] with respect to seven prior inquiries and investigations of the Pearl Harbor attack, feeling that by conducting a full and impartial hearing our report to the Congress along with the Committee's record would present to the American people the material and relevant facts of the disaster. The Committee does desire to observe, however, that charges to the effect that the original report of the Roberts Commission was abridged, modified, or amended, or portions deleted were found to be without foundation in fact.[393] Prior investigations were conducted during the course of the most devasta-

[390] As has been seen the disaster was the failure, with attendant increase in personnel and material losses, of the Army and Navy in Hawaii to institute measures designed to detect an approaching enemy force, to effect a state of readiness commensurate with the realization that war was at hand, and to employ every facility at their command in repelling the Japanese.
[391] See in this regard, Committee record, pp. 14133–14173.
[392] In referring to the inquiry conducted by the Roberts Commission, Admiral Kimmel has stated (Committee record, pp. 6809–6811):
(1) That he was told he was not on trial (Roberts Commission record, p. 581);
(2) That he was not permitted to be present at the testimony of other witnesses or to examine or cross-examine them;
(3) That the Roberts Commission was informed of or impressed with the fact that Hawaii was given all of the information available to the Navy Department (referring in this regard to committee record, pp. 4893–5022);
(4) That it appeared the so-called Magic was freely discussed before the Commission and in consequence the latter likely received the impression that the intercepted Japanese diplomatic messages were either forwarded to Washington by Admiral Kimmel or available to him in Hawaii.
Testifying before the committee, Justice Roberts stated:
(1) That the Commission's investigation was not intended to be a trial. "This seemed to me a preliminary investigation, like a grand jury investigation, and I did not think, for our report, that was to be taken as precluding every one of the men mentioned in it from a defense before his peers. In other words, you would not conduct a proceeding without cross-examination and without publicity and call it a trial. *It was not a trial * * * It was an investigation and it was the formation of a judgment to be handed the President.*" (Committee record, pp. 8801, 8802).
(2) That, as indicated, one would not conduct a proceeding without cross-examination and without publicity and call it a trial. He observed the proceedings were closed and every witness asked to observe secrecy for the reason "that there were questions of broken codes. We were informed that the Army and Navy were getting invaluable information every day; that the Japanese did not realize that their codes were broken, and indeed the Navy was rather chary about even telling us about the thing for fear there might be some leak from our Commission. Of course, if we held open hearings there was a chance we might do a great damage to our forces, our military program" (id., at pp. 8788, 8789).
(3) That the Roberts Commission knew outposts were *not* getting the Magic. "We knew the commanders weren't given what was taken off the breaking of the code" (id., at p. 8813).
(4) That "*We were never shown one of the Magic messages*" nor the substance thereof (id., at pp. 8828, 8829) although the Commission did know codes were being broken and generally what was obtained from the traffic (id., at p. 8829; also pp. 8836, 8846).
[393] See testimony of Mr. Justice Roberts before the Committee. Committee record, pp. 8779–8908.

ting war in history and within the necessary limitations of secrecy imposed by war and the national security. Public hearings concerning the disaster were properly deferred until the cessation of hostilities; to have done otherwise would have been to imperil the entire war effort. Parties in interest during previous inquiries, who for necessary security reasons did not have the full and ready access to information throughout the war that may have been desired, did have such information available for consideration before the Committee. Admiral Kimmel and General Short, as well as others, have attested to the full, fair, and impartial hearing which they were afforded by the Committee.

It is believed that with the additional evidence developed since VJ-Day and the greater accessibility of witnesses, together with the greater scope of inquiry conducted, we are in a much better position to form proper estimates and conclusions concerning responsibilities relating to the disaster than has heretofore been possible because of the proper and necessary restrictions within which other inquiries and investigations were conducted during wartime.

Shortly after the disaster both Admiral Kimmel and General Short were retired from active duty. Consideration was thereafter given by the War and Navy Departments to the question of whether the errors made in Hawaii justified proceedings by court martial. Admiral Kimmel and General Short were requested in the interest of the Nation's war effort to waive their rights to plead the statute of limitations in bar of trial by general court martial for the duration of the war and 6 months thereafter.[394] Both these officers properly and commendably did so waive their rights. It was the duty of the Offices of the Judge Advocate General of the Army and the Navy to consider the facts of the disaster as relating to the responsibilities of the Hawaiian commanders, even though after inquiry and deliberation it was determined that the errors were errors of judgment and not derelictions of duty.

On the morning of December 7, 1941, Admiral Kimmel and General Short were catapulted by the Empire of Japan into the principal roles in one of the most publicized tragedies of all time. That improper and incorrect deductions were drawn by some members of the public, with consequent suffering and mental anguish to both officers, cannot be questioned, just as erroneous conclusions were made by others with respect to the extent and nature of responsibility in Washington. But this is the result of the magnitude of public interest and speculation inspired by the disaster and not the result of mistreatment of anyone. The situation prevailing at Pearl Harbor on the morning of December 7 in the wake of the Japanese attack cast everyone, whether immediately or remotely concerned, beneath the white light of world scrutiny.

---

[394] See Committee exhibits Nos. 170, 171.

PART V

CONCLUSIONS AND RECOMMENDATIONS

PART V. CONCLUSIONS AND RECOMMENDATIONS

CONCLUSIONS WITH RESPECT TO RESPONSIBILITIES

1. The December 7, 1941, attack on Pearl Harbor was an unprovoked act of aggression by the Empire of Japan. The treacherous attack was planned and launched while Japanese ambassadors, instructed with characteristic duplicity, were carrying on the pretense of negotiations with the Government of the United States with a view to an amicable settlement of differences in the Pacific.

2. The ultimate responsibility for the attack and its results rests upon Japan, an attack that was well planned and skillfully executed. Contributing to the effectiveness of the attack was a powerful striking force, much more powerful than it had been thought the Japanese were able to employ in a single tactical venture at such distance and under such circumstances.

3. The diplomatic policies and actions of the United States provided no justifiable provocation whatever for the attack by Japan on this Nation. The Secretary of State fully informed both the War and Navy Departments of diplomatic developments and, in a timely and forceful manner, clearly pointed out to these Departments that relations between the United States and Japan had passed beyond the stage of diplomacy and were in the hands of the military.

4. The committee has found no evidence to support the charges, made before and during the hearings, that the President, the Secretary of State, the Secretary of War, or the Secretary of Navy tricked, provoked, incited, cajoled, or coerced Japan into attacking this Nation in order that a declaration of war might be more easily obtained from the Congress. On the contrary, all evidence conclusively points to the fact that they discharged their responsibilities with distinction, ability, and foresight and in keeping with the highest traditions of our fundamental foreign policy.

5. The President, the Secretary of State, and high Government officials made every possible effort, without sacrificing our national honor and endangering our security, to avert war with Japan.

6. The disaster of Pearl Harbor was the failure, with attendant increase in personnel and material losses, of the Army and the Navy to institute measures designed to detect an approaching hostile force, to effect a state of readiness commensurate with the realization that war was at hand, and to employ every facility at their command in repelling the Japanese.

7. Virtually everyone was surprised that Japan struck the Fleet at Pearl Harbor at the time that she did. Yet officers, both in Washington and Hawaii, were fully conscious of the danger from air attack; they realized this form of attack on Pearl Harbor by Japan was at least a possibility; and they were adequately informed of the imminence of war.

8. Specifically, the Hawaiian commands failed—

(a) To discharge their responsibilities in the light of the warnings received from Washington, other information possessed by them, and the principle of command by mutual cooperation.

(b) To integrate and coordinate their facilities for defense and to alert properly the Army and Navy establishments in Hawaii, particularly in the light of the warnings and intelligence available to them during the period November 27 to December 7, 1941.

(c) To effect liaison on a basis designed to acquaint each of them with the operations of the other, which was necessary to their joint security, and to exchange fully all significant intelligence.

(d) To maintain a more effective reconnaissance within the limits of their equipment.

(e) To effect a state of readiness throughout the Army and Navy establishments designed to meet all possible attacks.

(f) To employ the facilities, matériel, and personnel at their command, which were adequate at least to have greatly minimized the effects of the attack, in repelling the Japanese raiders.

(g) To appreciate the significance of intelligence and other information available to them.

9. The errors made by the Hawaiian commands were errors of judgment and not derelictions of duty.

10. The War Plans Division of the War Department failed to discharge its direct responsibility to advise the commanding general he had not properly alerted the Hawaiian Department when the latter, pursuant to instructions, had reported action taken in a message that was not satisfactorily responsive to the original directive.

11. The Intelligence and War Plans Divisions of the War and Navy Departments failed:

(a) To give careful and thoughtful consideration to the intercepted messages from Tokyo to Honolulu of September 24, November 15, and November 20 (the harbor berthing plan and related dispatches) and to raise a question as to their significance. Since they indicated a particular interest in the Pacific Fleet's base this intelligence should have been appreciated and supplied the Hawaiian commanders for their assistance, along with other information available to them, in making their estimate of the situation.

(b) To be properly on the *qui vive* to receive the "one o'clock" intercept and to recognize in the message the fact that some Japanese military action would very possibly occur somewhere at 1 p. m., December 7. If properly appreciated, this intelligence should have suggested a dispatch to all Pacific outpost commanders supplying this information, as General Marshall attempted to do immediately upon seeing it.

12. Notwithstanding the fact that there were officers on twenty-four hour watch, the Committee believes that under all of the evidence the War and Navy Departments were not sufficiently alerted on December 6 and 7, 1941, in view of the imminence of war.

RECOMMENDATIONS

Based on the evidence in the Committee's record, the following recommendations are respectfully submitted:

That immediate action be taken to insure that unity of command is imposed at all military and naval outposts.

That there be a complete integration of Army and Navy intelligence agencies in order to avoid the pitfalls of divided responsibility which experience has made so abundantly apparent; that upon effecting a unified intelligence, officers be selected for intelligence work who possess the background, penchant, and capacity for such work; and that they be maintained in the work for an extended period of time in order that they may become steeped in the ramifications and refinements of their field and employ this reservoir of knowledge in evaluating material received. The assignment of an officer having an aptitude for such work should not impede his progress nor affect his promotions. Efficient intelligence services are just as essential in time of peace as in war, and this branch of our armed services must always be accorded the important role which it deserves.

That effective steps be taken to insure that statutory or other restrictions do not operate to the benefit of an enemy or other forces inimical to the Nation's security and to the handicap of our own intelligence agencies. With this in mind, the Congress should give serious study to, among other things, the Communications Act of 1934; to suspension in proper instances of the statute of limitations during war (it was impossible during the war to prosecute violations relating to the "Magic" without giving the secret to the enemy); to legislation designed to prevent unauthorized sketching, photographing, and mapping of military and naval reservations in peacetime; and to legislation fully protecting the security of classified matter.

That the activities of Col. Theodore Wyman, Jr., while district engineer in the Hawaiian Department, as developed by the Army Pearl Harbor Board, be investigated by an appropriate committee of the Senate or the House of Representatives.

That the military and naval branches of our Government give serious consideration to the 25 supervisory, administrative, and organizational principles hereafter set forth.

SUPERVISORY, ADMINISTRATIVE, AND ORGANIZATIONAL DEFICIENCIES IN OUR MILITARY AND NAVAL ESTABLISHMENTS REVEALED BY THE PEARL HARBOR INVESTIGATION

The Committee has been intrigued throughout the Pearl Harbor proceedings by one enigmatical and paramount question: *Why, with some of the finest intelligence available in our history, with the almost certain knowledge that war was at hand, with plans that contemplated the precise type of attack that was executed by Japan on the morning of December 7—Why was it possible for a Pearl Harbor to occur?* The answer to this question and the causative considerations regarded as having any reasonably proximate bearing on the disaster have been set forth in the body of this report. Fundamentally, these considerations reflect supervisory, administrative, and organizational deficiencies which existed in our Military and Naval establishments in the days before Pearl Harbor. *In the course of the Committee's investigation still other deficiencies, not regarded as having a direct bearing on the disaster, have presented themselves.* Otherwise stated, all of these deficiencies reduce themselves to principles which are set forth, not for their novelty or profundity but for the reason that, by their very self-evident simplicity, it is difficult to believe they were ignored.

It is recognized that many of the deficiencies revealed by our investigation may very probably have already been corrected as a result of the experiences of the war. We desire, however, to submit these principles, which are grounded in the evidence adduced by the Committee, for the consideration of our Army and Navy establishments in the earnest hope that something constructive may be accomplished that will aid our national defense and preclude a repetition of the disaster of December 7, 1941. We do this after careful and long consideration of the evidence developed through one of the most important investigations in the history of the Congress.

1. Operational and intelligence work requires centralization of authority and clear-cut allocation of responsibility

Reviewing the testimony of the Director of War Plans and the Director of Naval Intelligence, the conclusion is inescapable that the proper demarcation of responsibility between these two divisions of the Navy Department did not exist. War Plans appears to have insisted that since it had the duty of issuing operational orders it must arrogate the prerogative of evaluating intelligence; Naval Intelligence, on the other hand, seems to have regarded the matter of evaluation as properly its function. It is clear that this intradepartmental misunderstanding and near conflict was not resolved before December 7 and beyond question it prejudiced the effectiveness of Naval Intelligence.

In Hawaii, there was such a marked failure to allocate responsibility in the case of the Fourteenth Naval District that Admiral Bloch testified he did not know whom the commander in chief would hold responsible in the event of shortcomings with respect to the condition and readiness of aircraft.[1] The position of Admiral Bellinger was a wholly anomalous one. He appears to have been responsible to everyone and to no one. The pyramiding of superstructures of organization cannot be conducive to efficiency and endangers the very function of our military and naval services.

2. Supervisory officials cannot safely take anything for granted in the alerting of subordinates

The testimony of many crucial witnesses in the Pearl Harbor investigation contains an identical note: "I thought he was alerted"; "I took for granted he would understand"; "I thought he would be doing that." It is the same story—each responsible official seeking to justify his position by reliance upon the fallacious premise that he was entitled to rely upon the assumption that a certain task was being performed or to take for granted that subordinates would be properly vigilant. This tragic theme was particularly marked in Hawaii.

The foregoing was well illustrated in Admiral Kimmel's failure to appreciate the significance of dispatches between December 3 and 6, advising him that Japanese embassies and consulates, including the

---

[1] See Army Pearl Harbor Board record, p. 1522.

Embassy in Washington, were destroying their codes. Navy Department officials have almost unanimously testified that instructions to burn codes mean "war in any man's language" and that in supplying Admiral Kimmel this information they were entitled to believe he would attach the proper significance to this intelligence. Yet the commander in chief of the Pacific Fleet testified that he did not interpret these dispatches to mean that Japan contemplated immediate war on the United States. That the Navy Department was entitled to rely upon the feeling that Admiral Kimmel, as a responsible intelligent commander, should have known what the burning of codes meant appears reasonable; but this is beside the point in determining standards for the future. The simple fact is that the dispatches were not properly interpreted. Had the Navy Department not taken for granted that Kimmel would be alerted by them but instead have given him the benefit of its interpretation, there could now be no argument as to what the state of alertness should have been based on such dispatches. With Pearl Harbor as a sad experience, crucial intelligence should in the future be supplied commanders accompanied by the best estimate of its significance.

3. Any doubt as to whether outposts should be given information should always be resolved in favor of supplying the information

Admiral Stark hesitated about sending the "one o'clock" intelligence to the Pacific outposts for the reason that he regarded them as adequately alerted and he did not want to confuse them. As has been seen, he was properly entitled to believe that naval establishments were adequately alert, but the fact is that one—Hawaii—was not in a state of readiness. This one exception is proof of the principle that any question as to whether information should be supplied the field should always be resolved in favor of transmitting it.

4. The delegation of authority or the issuance of orders entails the duty of inspection to determine that the official mandate is properly exercised

Perhaps the most signal shortcoming of administration, both at Washington and in Hawaii, was the failure to follow up orders and instructions to insure that they were carried out. The record of all Pearl Harbor proceedings is replete with evidence of this fundamental deficiency in administration. A few illustrations should clearly demonstrate this fact.

In the dispatch of November 27, 1941, which was to be considered a "war warning," Admiral Kimmel was instructed to "execute an appropriate defensive deployment preparatory to carrying out the tasks assigned in WPL–46." Very little was done pursuant to this order with a view to a *defensive* deployment; the Navy Department did nothing to determine what had been done in execution of the order. Yet virtually every responsible Navy Department official has testified as to what he "assumed" Kimmel would do upon receipt of this dispatch. While it appears to have been the policy to leave the implementation of orders to the local commander, as a matter of future practice it would seem a safer policy to recognize as implicit in the delegation of authority or the issuance of orders the responsibility of inspecting and supervising to determine that the delegated authority is properly administered and the orders carried out.

The story of Admiral Kimmel's administration of the Pacific Fleet and supervision of the Fourteenth Naval District as well as General Short's administration of the Hawaiian Department in the critical days before December 7 is the epitome of worthy plans and purposes which were never implemented. The job of an administrator is only half completed upon the issuance of an order; it is discharged when he determines the order has been executed.

5. *The implementation of official orders must be followed with closest supervision*

In the November 27 warning sent General Short he was ordered "to undertake such reconnaissance and other measures as you deem necessary" and to "report measures taken." The commanding general reported: "Re your 472. Department alerted to prevent sabotage. Liaison with Navy." This message from General Short was not clearly responsive to the order. Yet during the 9 days before Pearl Harbor not one responsible officer in the War Plans Division of the War Department pointed out to the commanding general his failure to alert the Hawaiian Department consistent with instructions. As a matter of fact, it does not affirmatively appear that anyone upon receipt of General Short's reply "burdened" himself sufficiently to call for message No. 472 in order to determine to what the report was responsive.

6. *The maintenance of alertness to responsibility must be insured through repetition*

It has been suggested, in explaining why additional warnings were not sent to Admiral Kimmel and General Short, that it was desired to avoid crying "wolf" too often lest the department commanders become impervious to the significance of messages designed to alert them. The McCollum message, for example, was not dispatched for the reason that overseas garrisons were regarded as fully alerted. Admiral Noyes is alleged to have referred to the proposed dispatch as an insult to the intelligence of the commander in chief inasmuch as he felt Admiral Kimmel had received adequate information. Although the exact provisions of the McCollum dispatch are unknown, it would seem to have been a safer practice to have sent this additional warning to intensify and insure alertness over a period of time through repetition, particularly under the critical circumstances prevailing between November 27 and December 7, 1941.

No consideration appears to have been given to the thought that since nothing occurred for 9 days after the warnings of November 27 there would be a lessening of vigilance by reason of the simple fact that *nothing did occur for several days* following such warnings. Of course, this observation has little or no application to the Hawaiian situation; for had Japan struck on November 28, the next day after the warnings, the same lack of readiness would substantially have prevailed as existed on the morning of December 7. There could have been no lessening of alertness there for the reason that the Hawaiian commands were at no time properly alert.

7. Complacency and procrastination are out of place where sudden and decisive action are of the essence

Beyond serious question Army and Navy officials both in Hawaii and in Washington were beset by a lassitude born of 20 years of peace. Admiral Kimmel admitted he was affected by the "peace psychology" just like "everybody else." As expressed by Admiral McMorris, "We were a bit too complacent there." The manner in which capable officers were affected is to a degree understandable, but the Army and the Navy are the watchdogs of the Nation's security and they must be on the alert at all times, no matter how many the years of peace.

As indicated in the body of this report, there was a failure in the War and Navy Departments during the night of December 6–7 to be properly on the *qui vive* consistent with the knowledge that the Japanese reply to our Government's note of November 26 was being received. The failure of subordinate officials to contact the Chief of Staff and Chief of Naval Operations on the evening of December 6 concerning the first 13 parts of the 14-part memorandum is indicative of the "business as usual" attitude. Some prominent military and naval officials were entertaining and, along with other officers, apparently failed to read into the 13 parts the importance of and necessity for greater alertness.

Of a similar tenor is the remark of Admiral Kimmel with respect to the "lost" Japanese carriers—"Do you mean to say that they could be rounding Diamond Head   *   *   *?"   Or the observation attributed to General Short with respect to the transcript of the "Mori" conversation—that it looked quite in order and was nothing to be excited about.

The people are entitled to expect greater vigilance and alertness from their Army and Navy—whether in war or in peace.

8. The coordination and proper evaluation of intelligence in times of stress must be insured by continuity of service and centralization of responsibility in competent officials

On occasion witnesses have echoed the sentiment that the Pearl Harbor debacle was made possible, not by the egregious errors or poor judgment of any individual or individuals but rather by reason of the imperfection and deficiencies of the *system* whereby Army and Navy intelligence was coordinated and evaluated. Only partial credence, however, can be extended this conclusion inasmuch as no amount of coordination and no system could be effected to compensate for lack of alertness and imagination. Nevertheless, there is substantial basis, from a review of the Pearl Harbor investigation in its entirety, to conclude that the system of handling intelligence was seriously at fault and that the security of the Nation can be insured only through continuity of service and centralization of responsibility in those charged with handling intelligence. *And the assignment of an officer having an aptitude for such work over an extended period of time should not impede his progress nor affect his promotions.*

The professional character of intelligence work does not appear to have been properly appreciated in either the War or Navy Departments. It seems to have been regarded as just another tour of duty, as reflected by limitations imposed on the period of assignment to such work, among other things. The committee has received the distinct impression that there was a tendency, whether realized or not, to relegate intelligence to a role of secondary importance.

As an integrated picture, the Pearl Harbor investigations graphically portray the imperative necessity, in the War and Navy Departments, (1) for selection of men for intelligence work who possess the background, capacity, and penchant for such work; (2) for maintaining them in the work over an extended period of time in order that they may become steeped in the ramifications and refinements of their field and employ this reservoir of knowledge in evaluating data received; and (3) for the centralization of responsibility for handling intelligence to avoid all of the pitfalls of divided responsibility which experience has made so abundantly apparent.

9. The unapproachable or superior attitude of officials is fatal; there should never be any hesitancy in asking for clarification of instructions or in seeking advice on matters that are in doubt

Despite the fact that the record of testimony in the Pearl Harbor proceedings is filled with various interpretations as to what War and Navy Department dispatches meant, in not one instance does it appear that a subordinate requested a clarification. General Short was ordered to undertake reconnaissance, yet he apparently ignored the order assuming that the man who prepared it did not know of his special agreement with the Navy in Hawaii whereby the latter was to conduct distant reconnaissance. He chose to implement an order which manifestly he did not understand, without the presumption that the man who prepared it did not know what he was doing, rather than request clarifying instructions. On November 27 Admiral Kimmel received a message beginning with the words: "This dispatch is to be considered a war warning." Every naval officer who has testified on the subject has stated that never before in his naval experience had he ever seen a dispatch containing the words "war warning"; Admiral Kimmel testified that never before in his some 40 years as a naval officer had he seen these words employed in an official dispatch. In the same message there was another term, "defensive deployment," which the commander in chief manifestly did not clearly understand. In spite of his apparent uncertainty as to the meaning of the message, Admiral Kimmel, it can be presumed, chose to endeavor to implement it without seeking advice from the Navy Department.

While there is an understandable disposition of a subordinate to avoid consulting his superior for advice except where absolutely necessary in order that he may demonstrate his self-reliance, the persistent failure without exception of Army and Navy officers, as revealed by the investigation, to seek amplifying and clarifying instructions from their superiors is strongly suggestive of just one thing: That the military and naval services failed to instill in their personnel the wholesome disposition to consult freely with their superiors for the mutual good and success of both superior and subordinate. One witness, upon being asked why an explanation was not requested replied, in effect: "Well, I have found the asking is usually the other way"; that is, the superior asking the subordinate. Such a situation is not desirable, and the services should not be prejudiced by walls of "brass."

10. There is no substitute for imagination and resourcefulness on the part of supervisory and intelligence officials

As reflected by an examination of the situation in Hawaii, there was a failure to employ the necessary imagination with respect to the intelligence which was at hand.

Washington, like Hawaii, possessed unusually significant and vital intelligence. Had greater imagination and a keener awareness of the significance of intelligence existed, concentrating and applying it to particular situations, it is proper to suggest that someone should have concluded that Pearl Harbor was a likely point of Japanese attack.

The committee feels that the failure to demonstrate the highest imagination with respect to the intelligence which was available in Hawaii and in Washington is traceable, at least in part, to the failure to accord to intelligence work the important and significant role which it deserves.

11. Communications must be characterized by clarity, forthrightness, and appropriateness

The evidence before the Committee reflects an unusual number of instances where military officers in high positions of responsibility interpreted orders, intelligence, and other information and arrived at opposite conclusions at a time when it was imperative for them to estimate the situation and to arrive at identical conclusions.

Admiral Kimmel was ordered to execute an *appropriate defensive deployment*. Everyone in Washington in testifying before the committee seems reasonably certain as to just what this meant; Admiral Kimmel did not feel that it required his doing anything greatly beyond what he had already done, even though he knew that Washington knew what he had previously done. In using the words "this dispatch is to be considered a war warning" everyone in Washington felt the commander in chief would be sharply, incisively, and emphatically warned of war; Admiral Kimmel said he had construed all the messages he had received previously as *war warnings*. Everyone in Washington felt that upon advising Hawaii the Japanese were destroying their codes it would be understood as meaning "war in any man's language"; Admiral Kimmel said that he did not consider this intelligence of any vital importance when he received it.

The War Department warned General Short that hostilities were possible at any moment, meaning armed hostilities; General Short felt that sabotage was one form of hostilities and instituted an alert against sabotage only. Washington ordered the commanding general to undertake reconnaissance; the latter took for granted that the War Department had made a mistake and proceeded in effect to ignore the order on the basis of this assumption. General Short was instructed to report the measures taken by him pursuant to departmental orders. He replied that his department was alerted against sabotage and that he had effected liaison with the Navy; the Director of War Plans saw the reply and took for granted the commanding general was replying to a different warning concerning subversive activities, at the same time suggesting that some of his subordinates may have interpreted the reply to mean that, in effecting liaison with the Navy, General Short had necessarily carried out the order to conduct reconnaissance.

General Short said he thought the order given Admiral Kimmel to execute a defensive deployment necessarily required distant reconnaissance; the commander in chief did not so interpret the order. Admiral Kimmel saw the warning General Short received and took for granted the Army would be on a full alert designed to protect the fleet base.

As has been seen, an objective consideration of the warnings received by the Hawaiian commanders indicates they were adequate. But on the basis of the disaster, in the future *adequacy* cannot be regarded as sufficient. Dispatches must be unmistakably clear, forthright, and devoid of any conceivable ambiguity.

The committee feels that the practice, indulged by the Navy, of sending to several commanders an identical dispatch for action, even though the addressees may be located in decidedly different situations, is distinctly dangerous. In the preparation of messages to outposts the dispatch to a particular officer should be applicable to his peculiar situation. What may well be characterized as the "lazy" practice of preparing a single dispatch should be replaced by a more industrious and effective system whereby a separate "individualized" dispatch is sent to each commander whose particular situation varies greatly from that of another commander or there may be reason for him because of distance or other factors to believe so.

It is believed that brevity of messages was carried to the point of being a fetish rather than a virtue. Dispatches must be characterized by sufficient amplitude to be meaningful not only to the sender but, beyond reasonable doubt, to the addressee as well.

12. There is great danger in careless paraphrase of information received and every effort should be made to insure that the paraphrased material reflects the true meaning and significance of the original

To preserve the security of their own codes the War and Navy Departments followed the natural and proper practice of paraphrasing messages received. From a review of several messages as paraphrased the committee is of the opinion that the utmost caution and care should be employed in preserving the original meaning of material. One classic example will serve to illustrate this point.

In replying to the War Department's directive of November 27, 1941, General Short said:

Re your 472. Department alerted to prevent sabotage. *Liaison with Navy.*

As paraphrased upon receipt at the War Department, this message read:

Department alerted to prevent sabotage. *Liaison with Navy re your 472.*

It is to be recalled that the Army and Navy had entered into a special agreement at Hawaii whereby the Navy assumed responsibility for long-range reconnaissance. Therefore, having ordered General Short to undertake reconnaissance, a reasonable construction of his message as paraphrased would be that the commanding general, through liaison with the Navy, had made the necessary arrangements for reconnaissance as instructed in the War Department's warning of November 27. The message which Short actually sent, however, cannot so easily be afforded this construction. The seriousness of this matter lies in the fact that failure to conduct long-range reconnaissance at Hawaii was the prime factor responsible for the Army and Navy having been caught flat-footed. Conceivably, had the message as paraphrased not been misleading, the War Department might well have followed up on General Short's message, pointing out that he had failed to take the necessary action to alert his command.

13. Procedures must be sufficiently flexible to meet the exigencies of unusual situations

Reviewing the Pearl Harbor evidence there are, in both the War and Navy establishments, several illustrations of inflexible procedures that could not be or at least were not subjected to sufficient alteration to satisfy the exigencies of the situation. Everything seems perforce to have followed a grooved pattern regardless of the demands for distinctive action. The idea of proceeding "through channels" was carried to an extreme.

Among the best illustrations of this fact was the failure of Admiral Kimmel to advise Admiral Newton that the "war warning" had been received. Admiral Newton was departing from Pearl Harbor with some of the most vital units of the Pacific Fleet, yet because the table of organization indicated Admiral Brown to be Newton's superior, the commander in chief did not take it upon himself to insure that Newton was fully informed as to the critical situation between the United States and Japan, and relied upon the usual procedure whereby Brown would keep Newton advised of developments.

14. Restriction of highly confidential information to a minimum number of officials, while often necessary, should not be carried to the point of prejudicing the work of the organization

The Magic intelligence was preeminently important and the necessity for keeping it confidential cannot be overemphasized. However, so closely held and top secret was this intelligence that it appears the *fact* the Japanese codes had been broken was regarded as of more importance than the *information* obtained from decoded traffic. The result of this rather specious premise was to leave large numbers of policy-making and enforcement officials in Washington completely oblivious of the most pertinent information concerning Japan.

The Federal Bureau of Investigation, for example, was charged with combating espionage, sabotage, and un-American activities within the United States. On February 15, 1941, Tokyo dispatched to Washington a detailed outline as to the type of espionage information desired from this country.[2] The FBI was never informed of this vital information necessary to the success of its work, despite the fact that the closest liaison was supposed to exist among the FBI, Naval Intelligence, and Military Intelligence.

Gen. Hayes A. Kroner, who was in charge of the intelligence branch of G-2, has testified that he at no time was permitted to avail himself of the Magic. And this despite the fact that to effectively perform

[2] Committee exhibit No. 2, pp. 117, 118.

his work he should have known of this intelligence and one of his subordinates, Colonel Bratton, was "loaned" to General Miles to distribute magic materials to authorized recipients.

While, as previously indicated, it is appreciated that promiscuous distribution of highly confidential material is dangerous, it nevertheless should be made available to all those whose responsibility cannot adequately and intelligently be discharged without knowledge of such confidential data. It would seem that through sufficient paraphrase of the original material the source of the information could have been adequately protected. Certainly as great confidence could be placed in ranking officials of various departments and bureaus of the Government as in the numerous technicians, cryptographers, translators, and clerks required for the interception and processing of the Magic.

15. *There is great danger of being blinded by the self-evident*

Virtually every witness has testified he was surprised at the Japanese attack on Pearl Harbor. This was essentially the result of the fact that just about everybody was blinded or rendered myopic by what seemed to be the self-evident purpose of Japan to attack toward the south—Thailand, Malaysia, the Kra Peninsula, and perhaps the Philippines and Guam. Japan had massed ships and amphibious forces, had deployed them to the south, and had conducted reconnaissance in that direction. So completely did everything point to the south that it appears everyone was blinded to significant, albeit somewhat disguised, handwriting on the wall suggesting an attack on us elsewhere.

The advice of the Army lieutenant to the radar operators to "forget it" when they informed him of the approach of a large number of planes appears to have been based on the self-evident assumption that the planes were Army or Navy craft on patrol or the expected B–17's due to arrive from the west coast.

16. *Officials should at all times give subordinates the benefit of significant information*

Before the committee Admiral Turner testified that he regarded an attack on Pearl Harbor as a 50–50 possibility. Assuming this to be correct, there can be little doubt, considering the position he held as Director of War Plans in the Navy Department, that he could have given the commander in chief of the Pacific Fleet the benefit of his conclusion had he been disposed to do so. As a matter of fact Admiral Turner had the principal hand in preparing the November 27 "war warning."

As has been seen, the orders contained in the war warning necessarily carried the implication of an attack from without; however, the dispatch did not reflect the likelihood of an attack upon the fleet with the degree of likelihood manifested by Admiral Turner in indicating to the committee his estimate of the situation. Admiral Turner's position would be indefensible were his estimate based on any information or intelligence he may have possessed. It appears, on the other hand, that his conclusion was predicated on a rather long-standing impression in the Navy that an attack on our Pacific Fleet by Japan could be expected at one time or another. It is regarded as unfortunate, however, that Admiral Turner did not see fit to give to the Pacific Fleet the benefit of his conclusions outlined, with benefit of retrospection, in such detail before the committee.

17. An official who neglects to familiarize himself in detail with his organization should forfeit his responsibility

It would seem that War and Navy Department officials both in Washington and Hawaii were so obsessed by an executive complex that they could not besmirch their dignities by "stooping" to determine what was going on, or more especially what was not going on, in their organizations. Examples should illustrate this observation.

Admirals Stark and Turner both have testified they "thought" the commander in chief of the Pacific Fleet was receiving the Magic intelligence. Yet in a period of over 6 months, with relations between the United States and Japan mounting in tenseness and approaching a crisis, neither of these ranking officers determined for a fact whether the fleet was receiving this information.

In the case of Hawaii, the evidence indicates failures on the part of the commanding general and the commander in chief to actually determine what was going on in their organizations. Additionally, in a command by mutual cooperation it was as important that Admiral Kimmel know what General Short was doing, and *vice versa*, as that he know what the fleet itself was doing. But, as has been heretofore pointed out, neither of these officers really verified whether his assumptions concerning what the other was doing were correct.

18. Failure can be avoided in the long run only by preparation for any eventuality

The record tends to indicate that appraisal of likely enemy movements was divided into *probabilities* and *possibilities*. Everyone has admitted that an attack by Japan on Pearl Harbor was regarded as at least a possibility. It was felt, however, that a Japanese movement toward the south was a probability. The over-all result was to look for the probable move and to take little or no effective precautions to guard against the contingency of the possible action.

While it appears satisfactorily established that it is the basic responsibility of an outpost commander to prepare for the worst contingency, it is believed that this premise has been applied more in theory than in practice. The military and naval branches of the Government must be continuously impressed by, and imbue their personnel with, the realization that failure can be avoided over an extended period of time only by preparation for any eventuality, at least when hostilities are expected.

19. Officials, on a personal basis, should never countermand an official instruction

On October 16, 1941, the Chief of Naval Operations sent to the commander in chief of the Pacific Fleet a dispatch concerning the resignation of the Japanese Cabinet, pointing out, among other things, that "since the U. S. and Britain are held responsible by Japan for her present desperate situation there is also a possibility that Japan may attack these two powers." But on October 17, referring to this dispatch, Admiral Stark, in a letter to Admiral Kimmel, said: "Things have been popping here for the last twenty-four hours but from our dispatches you know about all that we do. *Personally I do not believe the Japs are going to sail into us and the message I sent you merely stated the 'possibility'; in fact, I tempered the message handed to me considerably.*"

It appears to have been a generally accepted practice in the Navy for the Chief of Naval Operations to supplement official dispatches by correspondence of a quasi-personal nature.[3] Despite this fact, it is regarded as an extremely dangerous practice for the Chief of Naval Operations to express an opinion on a personal basis to an outpost commander which has the inevitable effect of tempering the import of an official dispatch. Were it not for the fact that Admiral Stark supplied the commander in chief of the Pacific Fleet highly pertinent and significant information after his letter of October 17 and before December 7, the manner in which he emasculated the October 16 dispatch would be inexcusable. However, as has been seen in this report, some of the most vital intelligence and orders relating to Japan were supplied Hawaii during November and December of 1941.

20. *Personal or official jealousy will wreck any organization*

This principle is the result of the general impression obtained by the committee concerning the relationship between the Army and the Navy as well as concerning certain intraorganizational situations which existed. The relationship, understanding, and coordination between the War Plans Division and the Office of Naval Intelligence were wholly unsatisfactory. The War Plans Division, particularly, appears to have had an overzealous disposition to preserve and enhance its prerogatives.

The whole story of discussions during 1941 with respect to unity of command is a picture of jealous adherence to departmental prerogatives and unwillingness to make concessions in the interest of both the Army and Navy. The same comment is applicable to the near dispute between Admiral Kimmel and General Short as to which of them should command Wake and Midway when the marines were replaced by soldiers. It is proper to suggest that, had both the commanding officers in Hawaii been less concerned between November 27 and December 7 about preserving their individual prerogatives with respect to Wake and Midway and more concerned about working together to defend the Hawaiian Coastal Frontier in the light of the warnings they had received, the defensive situation confronting the Japanese on the morning of December 7 might well have been entirely different.

21. *Personal friendship, without more, should never be accepted in lieu of liaison or confused therewith where the latter is necessary to the proper functioning of two or more agencies*

One of the more "human" aspects of the testimony of both Admiral Kimmel and General Short is the manner in which each sought to bring out their personal friendship for the purpose of demonstrating

---

[3] Admiral Stark said: "I might point out, in passing, that there was nothing unusual in this so-called 'personal' correspondence between the Chief of Naval Operations and the Commanders in Chief—it was a long-established custom when I took office." Committee record, p. 5594.

the close relationship that existed between them. They played golf together; they dined together—but they did not get together on official business in such manner as to insure that each possessed the same knowledge of the situation as the other and to effect coordination and integration of their efforts.

22. No considerations should be permitted as excuse for failure to perform a fundamental task

Both the commanding officers in Hawaii have offered as explanation and excuse for failure to perform various supervisory and administrative responsibilities in their commands the fact that they had countless and manifold duties in their respective positions as commander in chief of the Pacific Fleet and commanding general of the Hawaiian Department. Additionally, Admiral Kimmel has referred to the extraordinarily competent staff which he had in Hawaii. The most fundamental responsibility that both commanders had under the circumstances, however, was to make certain beyond any reasonable doubt that there was an integrated and coordinated employment of defensive facilities consistent with the principle of command by mutual cooperation. No excuse or explanation can justify or temper the failure to discharge this responsibility which superseded and surpassed all others.

23. Superiors must at all times keep their subordinates adequately informed and, conversely, subordinates should keep their superiors informed

In Washington, Admiral Wilkinson, Director of Naval Intelligence, and Captain McCollum, Chief of the Far Eastern Section of that Division, were not adequately and currently informed as to the nature of the dispatches being sent to our outposts emanating from the War Plans Division. Subordinate officials in both the War and Navy Departments failed to appreciate the importance and necessity of getting to both General Marshall and Admiral Stark the first 13 parts of the Japanese 14-part memorandum immediately on the evening of December 6. Colonel French did not inform the Chief of Staff that he had been unable to raise the Army radio in Hawaii on the morning of December 7.

In Hawaii, Admiral Kimmel failed to insure that Admiral Bellinger, who was responsible for Navy patrol planes, knew of the war warning of November 27. Admiral Newton, as previously pointed out, was permitted to leave Pearl Harbor with a task force completely oblivious of any of the warning messages. General Short, construing the caution to disseminate the information in the warning of November 27 to "minimum essential officers" in a too-narrow manner, failed to inform the essential and necessary officers of his command of the acute situation in order that the proper alertness might pervade the Hawaiian Department.

does not appear that any record system was established for initialing the messages or otherwise fixing responsibility. The system existing left subordinate officers charged with the duty of disseminating the Magic at the complete mercy of superior officers with respect to any question as to whether a particular message had been delivered to or seen by them.

25. In a well-balanced organization there is close correlation of responsibility and authority

Witnesses have testified rather fully as to what their responsibilities were, both in Washington and at Hawaii. However, it does not appear that any of them, except the highest ranking officers, possessed any real authority to act in order decisively to discharge their responsibilities. It cannot be presumed that it will be possible to meet the exigencies of an emergency if the officer charged with the duty of acting at the time the emergency arises does not possess the necessary authority to follow through on the situation. There should be a close correlation between responsibility and authority; to vest a man with responsibility with no corresponding authority is an unfair, ineffective, and unsatisfactory arrangement.

> ALBEN W. BARKLEY, *Chairman.*
> JERE COOPER, *Vice Chairman.*
> WALTER F. GEORGE.
> SCOTT W. LUCAS.
> J. BAYARD CLARK.
> JOHN W. MURPHY.
> BERTRAND W. GEARHART.
> FRANK B. KEEFE (with additional views)
> (Senators Brewster and Ferguson are filing
>   minority views.)

ADDITIONAL VIEWS OF MR. KEEFE

INTRODUCTION

The committee report is divided into five parts. Part I deals with the diplomatic background of the Pearl Harbor attack. Part II describes the actual attack and its aftermath. Part III discusses responsibilities in Hawaii. Part IV discusses responsibilities in Washington, and Part V includes certain recommendations of the committee. Scattered throughout the entire five sections of the committee report are conclusions with respect to individuals in charge of carrying out our diplomatic, military, and naval obligations prior to the attack on Pearl Harbor. I find myself in agreement with most of these conclusions and recommendations. The voluminous facts contained in the committee report have been accurately assembled from the enormous record compiled by the committee. Any criticism which I may have toward the marshaling of facts in the committee report is directed to the manner in which such facts have been used to sustain the various arguments and conclusions indulged in in the committee report.

It correctly states that both Washington and Hawaii were surprised at the attack upon Pearl Harbor. It is apparently agreed that both Washington and Hawaii expected the initial attack to come in the Asiatic area. What was done in Washington as well as what was done in Hawaii was admittedly done in the light of the universal military belief that Hawaii was not in danger from an initial attack by Japan. If this belief was unjustified, as I believe it was, then the mistake lies on the Washington doorstep just as much as it does upon that of Hawaii. Throughout the long and arduous sessions of the committee in the preparation of the committee report, I continuously insisted that whatever "yardstick" was agreed upon as a basis for determining responsibilities in Hawaii should be applied to the high command at Washington. This indicates in a general way my fundamental objection to the committee report. I feel that facts have been martialed, perhaps unintentionally, with the idea of conferring blame upon Hawaii and minimizing the blame that should properly be assessed at Washington.

A careful reading of the committee report would indicate that the analysis of orders and dispatches is so made as to permit criticism of our commands in Hawaii while at the same time proposing a construction which would minimize the possibility of criticism of those in charge at Washington.

I think it is true that none of the military chiefs at Washington or Hawaii thought the attack would come at Pearl Harbor. I conclude that they all thought it would come first in the Far East. Obviously this was a fatal mistake, and I agree that the mistake was without proper justification and that neither Hawaii nor Washington should be excused from criticism for having made it. I think that the facts in this record clearly demonstrate that Hawaii was always the No. 1 point of danger and that both Washington and Hawaii should have known it at all times and acted accordingly. Consequently I agree that the high command in Hawaii was subject to criticism for concluding that Hawaii was not in danger. However, I must insist that the same criticism with the same force and scope should apply to the high command in Washington. It is in this respect that I think the tenor of the committee report may be subject to some criticism.

I fully agree with the doctrine relating to the placing of responsibility on military officers in the field and their resulting duty under such responsibilities. I agree that they must properly sustain this burden in line with the high and peculiar abilities which originally gave them their assignments.

In the execution of their vitally important duties, however, the officers at the front in the field are fairly entitled to all aids and help and all information which can reasonably be sent to them from the all-powerful high staff command in Washington. If both commands are in error, both should be blamed for what each should have done and what each failed to do respectively. The committee report, I feel, does not with exactitude apply the same yardstick in measuring responsibilities at Washington as has been applied to the Hawaiian commanders. I cannot supress the feeling that the committee report endeavors to throw as soft a light as possible on the Washington scene.

In order to clearly appraise the contentions herein expressed, I feel compelled to restate some of the basic military aspects of the Pearl Harbor disaster as shown by the evidence.

MILITARY ASPECTS OF THE PEARL HARBOR DISASTER

During the year 1941 the United States Pacific Fleet was based in Pearl Harbor in the Hawaiian island of Oahu. It had proceeded to the Hawaiian area for Fleet exercises in the spring of 1940. Its scheduled return to its regular bases on the west coast was delayed from time to time. From these delays there gradually emerged evidence of the President's decision to retain the Fleet in the Hawaiian area, to deter Japan from aggression in the Far East. The Commander in Chief of the Fleet, Admiral J. O. Richardson, protested this decision with a vigor which caused him to be relieved of command. He believed that the readiness of men and ships of the Fleet for war operations would impress Japan rather than its presence in Hawaii, where facilities to render it ready for war were greatly inferior to those available on the west coast. Richardson was succeeded in command by Admiral H. E. Kimmel in February 1941. The appointment of Kimmel was made on his record as a capable officer. There was no political or other favoritism involved. At this time the decision to base the Fleet in Hawaii was an established fact. Pearl Harbor was the only anchorage in the Hawaiian area offering any security. It was then, however, an extremely deficient Fleet base. Its exposed position rendered concealment of Fleet movements practically impossible in an area filled with Japanese agents. The Army's equipment for antiaircraft defense was meager. The local Army-Navy defense forces did not have sufficient long-range patrol planes to perform effective distant reconnaissance, even if the patrol planes of the fleet were made available to augment the handful of Army reconnaissance planes.

Under these circumstances, the position of the Fleet in the Hawaiian area was inherently untenable and dangerous. The Fleet would sacrifice its preparations for war, and its potential mobility in war, if it concentrated its resources on the defense of its base. Moreover, with only four tankers suitable for fueling ships at sea, ships of the Fleet had to come into Pearl Harbor for refueling, to say nothing of maintenance and repair, and the necessary rest and relaxation of crews. Once the ships were in Pearl Harbor, with its single channel, they were a target for any successfully launched air attack from carrier-borne planes. The severity of the attack might be mitigated, but damage to the ships found in port was inevitable. To prevent a hostile carrier from successfully launching planes required that it be first discovered and attacked. Discovery, other than by lucky accident, required air reconnaissance of the perimeter of a circle of 800-mile radius from Oahu. The Fleet did not at any time have patrol planes sufficient in number to carry out such reconnaissance. The Japanese task force which raided Oahu on December 7, 1941, was composed of six carriers. The Pacific Fleet had on that date three carriers, one of which was on the Pacific coast for repair, leaving only two immediately available in the area of a prospective sea engagement. An engagement at sea would have found the preponderant strength with Japan.

Although the Fleet was placed by the President in the Hawaiian area in 1940 as an implement of diplomacy and as a deterrent to Japan, its strength was appreciably reduced in April and May of 1941. At that time, one aircraft carrier, three battleships, four cruisers and eighteen destroyers were detached from the Pacific Fleet and transferred to the Atlantic. The President directed the Chief of Naval Operations to consult the British Chiefs of Staff on the proposal to effect this transfer. They gave their opinion "that the consequential reduction in the strength of the United States Pacific Fleet would not unduly encourage Japan" (exhibit 158, letter from Admiral Danckwerts to Admiral Turner, April 28, 1941). The transfer to the Atlantic was then carried out. The Commander in Chief of the United States Pacific Fleet was not asked for his opinion. The Chief of Naval Operations wrote him about the proposed transfer stating "I am telling you, not arguing with you" (exhibit 106, letter from Admiral Stark to Admiral Kimmel, dated April 19, 1941).

The primary mission assigned the Pacific Fleet under existing Navy War Plans was the making of raids on the Marshalls. These were to divert Japanese strength from the so-called Malay barrier. No existing War Plan of the United States in 1941 contemplated that the Pacific Fleet would go to the rescue of the Philippines or resist Japanese naval forces attacking the Philippines. The Pacific Fleet was so inferior to the Japanese Navy in every category of fighting ship that such a mission was considered too suicidal to attempt. The American public in 1941 was deluded about the fighting strength of our Fleet in the Pacific, by irresponsible utterances from men in authority. Japan was under no such misconception. Her consular agents in the Hawaiian islands needed only their eyesight, and possibly binoculars, to appraise correctly the strength of the Fleet.

An inferior Fleet, under enemy surveillance in an exposed naval base without resources to protect it could only avert disaster by receiving the best possible evidence of the intentions of its potential enemy. The Commander-in-Chief of the Fleet in 1941 recognized that information was essential to his making appropriate disposition to meet any crisis. He formally requested the Chief of Naval Operations that he "be immediately informed of all important developments as they occur and by the quickest secure means available" (exhibit 106, Official Letter CINCPAC to CNO, dated May 26, 1941).

The best evidence of Japanese intentions in the year 1941, available to the United States Government, were messages exchanged between the Government of Japan and her diplomatic consular agents abroad. These were intercepted by the Army and Navy. They were decoded and translated in Washington. The President, the Secretaries of State, War and Navy, the Chief of Staff, and Chief of Naval Operations regularly received these intercepted messages.

The President and the other officials receiving the intercepted messages in Washington prior to December 7, 1941, considered it likely that Japan would attack the United States. At a meeting of the President and his so-called War Council on November 25, 1941, according to Mr. Stimson's notes the President stated: "that we were likely to be attacked perhaps (as soon as) next Monday" (Stimson Statement, page 47). There was abundant evidence in the intercepted messages that Japan intended to attack the United States. Japan had fixed a deadline date of November 25, extended to November 29, for reaching a diplomatic agreement with the United States. There were at least six Japanese messages emphasizing this deadline. If the deadline date passed without agreement, the Japanese government advised her Ambassadors in Washington: "Things are automatically going to happen." The necessity for agreement by the deadline date was stressed by Japan in these terms: "The fate of our Empire hangs by the slender thread of a few days"; "We gambled the fate of our land on the throw of this die" (exhibit 1, page 137, 93). On November 26, 1941, prior to the advanced "deadline" date, the United States government delivered to Japan a diplomatic note, which the intercepted messages revealed Japan considered to be a "humiliating proposal", impossible of acceptance (exhibit 1, p. 195). The intercepted diplomatic messages further revealed that Japan expected to "rupture" negotiations with the United States when she replied to the American note of November 26 (exhibit 1, p. 195). To prevent the United States from becoming unduly suspicious Japan instructed her envoys in Washington to keep up a pretext of continuing negotiations until this Japanese reply was ready for delivery (exhibit 1, p. 208). A message from the Japanese government to its Ambassador in Berlin, sent on November 30, was intercepted and translated by the Navy in Washington on December 1 (exhibit 1, p. 204). In this message the Japanese Ambassador was instructed to—

immediately interview Chancellor Hitler and Foreign Minister Ribbentrop and confidentially communicate to them a summary of developments. * * * *Say very secretly to them that there is extreme danger that war may suddenly break out between the Anglo-Saxon nations and Japan through some clash of arms and add the time of the breaking out of this war may come quicker than anyone dreams.* [Italics supplied.]

The President regarded this message as of such interest that he retained a copy of it, contrary to the usual practice in handling the intercepted messages (R. 10887). On December 2, 1941 elaborate instructions from Japan were intercepted dealing in precise detail with the method of internment of American and British nationals in Asia "on the outbreak of war with England and the United States" (exhibit 1, p. 198).

In the "bomb plot" or "ships in harbor" message of September 24 the Japanese government gave detailed instructions to its Consul-General in Hawaii as to the character of report it required concerning vessels in Pearl Harbor. Pearl Harbor was to be divided into five sub areas. An alphabetical symbol was given each area. The Japanese government instructed the consul:

With regard to warships and aircraft carriers, we would like to have you report on those at anchor (these are not so important) tied up at wharves, buoys, and in docks. (Designate types and classes briefly.) If possible we would like to have you make mention of the fact when there are two or more vessels alongside the same wharf.

This despatch was decoded and translated in Washington on October 9, 1941 (exhibit 2, p. 12).

On September 29, 1941, the Japanese Consul in Hawaii replied to his government. He established a system of symbols to be used in designating the location of vessels at key points in Pearl Harbor. This despatch was decoded and translated in Washington on October 10, 1941.

On November 15, 18, 20, and 29 the Japanese government urgently called for information about the location of ships in Pearl Harbor (exhibit 2, pp. 13 and 15). On November 15 the Japanese Consul in Honolulu was directed to make his "ships in harbor report" irregular but at the rate of twice a week (exhibit 2, p. 13). The reports were to give vessel locations in specific areas of the harbor, using the symbols established in September (exhibit 2, p. 15). The greatest secrecy was enjoined, because relations between Japan and the United States were described as "most critical." On November 18, the Japanese Consul General reported to Tokyo the locations of the ships in the various sub areas of Pearl Harbor, giving minute descriptions of the courses, speed and distances apart of destroyers entering the harbor (exhibit 2, p. 15). On November 29 reports were requested even though there were no movements of ships. These despatches were intercepted, decoded and translated in Washington on December 3, 4, 5, and 6, 1941.

The "bomb plot" or "ships in harbor" message, and those messages relating to Pearl Harbor which followed it, meant that the ships of the Pacific Fleet in Pearl Harbor were marked for a Japanese attack. No other American harbor was divided into sub areas by Japan. In no other area did Japan seek information as to whether two or more vessels were alongside the same wharf. Prior to this message Japanese espionage in Hawaii was directed to ascertain the general whereabouts of the American Fleet, whether at sea or in port. With this message Japan inaugurated a new policy directed to Pearl Harbor and to no other place, in which information was no longer sought merely as to the general whereabouts of the Fleet, but as to the presence of particular ships in particular areas of the harbor. In the period immediately preceding the attack Japan required such reports even when there was no movement of ships in and out of Pearl Harbor. The reports which Japan thus sought and received had a useful purpose only in planning and executing an attack upon the ships in port. These reports were not just the work of enthusiastic local spies gathering meticulous details in an excess of zeal. They were the product of instructions emanating from the government of Japan in Tokyo. Officers of the high command in Washington have admitted before us that this message, if correctly evaluated, meant an attack on ships of the Pacific Fleet in Pearl Harbor (R. 3036, 4014; 4874; 2100-2102; 11313-11314; 6390, 6394; 5378).

Lt. Commander Kramer of Naval Intelligence in Washington promptly distributed the Pearl Harbor "bomb plot" message to the President, the Secretary of the Navy, the Chief of Naval Operations, Admiral Stark, the Director of Naval Communications, the Director of War Plans, and the Director of Naval Intelligence (R. 11209). It bore the notation "interesting message" (R. 11207). It was accompanied by a summary of its contents as follows:

Tokyo directs special reports on ships in Pearl Harbor which is divided into five areas for the purpose of showing exact locations (R. 11207).

Military Intelligence through Colonel Bratton delivered the "bomb plot" message to the Secretary of War, the Chief of Staff, and the Chief of the War Plans Division (R. 12083). The message was discussed several times by Colonel Bratton, Chief of the Far Eastern Section, Military Intelligence Division, War Department General Staff, with his opposite numbers in the Navy Department (R. 12105). They discussed possible significance of the message, as indicating a plan for an air attack on ships in Pearl Harbor (R. 12105). In the course of these discussions Officers in Naval Intelligence stated that the Japanese were wasting their time in getting such meticulous detail about the location of ships in Pearl Harbor because the Fleet would not be in Pearl Harbor when the emergency arose (R. 12105). Despite the fact that the "bomb plot" message and related intercepts dealing with the berthing of ships in Pearl Harbor were delivered to General Marshall and Admiral Stark, they testified before the Committee that they have no recollection of ever seeing them (R. 2911–2912; 5787–5792). No intimation of these messages was given to General Short or Admiral Kimmel in Hawaii. On the contrary, Admiral Kimmel had been advised by the Navy Department on February 1, 1941:

* * * no move against Pearl Harbor appears imminent or planned for in the foreseeable future (exhibit 15).

In the days immediately preceding Pearl Harbor, Japan made no effort to conceal the movements or presence of her naval forces in Southeast Asia (R. 453). The movements of her troops in Indo-China at that time were the subject of diplomatic exchanges between the United States and Japan (Foreign Relations of the United States, Japan, 1931–41, vol. II, p. 779). Yet, the intercepts showed that some Japanese plan went into effect automatically on November 29, from which Japan hoped to divert American suspicion by a pretext of continued negotiations. What was its nature? Only the President and his top advisers in Washington had this information.

Despite the elaborate and labored arguments in the report and despite the statements of high ranking military and naval officers to the contrary, I must conclude that the intercepted messages received and distributed in Washington on the afternoon and evening of December 6 and the early hours of December 7, pointed to an attack on Pearl Harbor:

1. The "Pilot Message". This was a message from Japan to her Ambassadors in Washington advising them that the Japanese reply to the American note of November 26 was ready and being sent to them in fourteen parts; that it was to be treated with great secrecy pending instructions as to the time of its delivery; and that the time for its delivery was to be fixed in a separate message (exhibit 1, p. 238).

2. The first thirteen parts of the Japanese reply. This included all but the last paragraph of the Japanese note handed to the Secretary of State on December 7 (exhibit 1, pp. 239–244).

3. The fourteenth and last paragraph of the Japanese reply, and the message to the Japanese Ambassadors which fixed the time for delivery of the Japanese note as 1 p. m., Washington time, December 7 (exhibit 1, p. 248).

The "Pilot Message" was filed in Tokyo at 6:56 A. M. Washington time December 6; it was intercepted by the Navy by 7:20 A. M. Washington time December 6 and forwarded to the Navy Department. It was sent by the Navy to the Army for decryption and translation about noon, Washington time, on December 6 (exhibit 41). It was decrypted, translated, and distributed about 3 P. M. Washington time by the Army to Mr. Hull, Mr. Stimson, General Marshall, the Chief of the War Plans Division, General Gerow, and the Chief of Military Intelligence, General Miles (R. 12050). In the Navy Department the Director of Naval Intelligence, Admiral Wilkinson, received the so-called Pilot Message prior to 6 P. M. Washington time on December 6 (R. 4658). He had previously told his subordinates to be on the lookout for the Japanese reply and felt sure that he gave instructions that the Pilot Message was to be delivered to Admiral Stark (R. 4661–4662). Admiral Turner, Chief of the War Plans Division in the office of the Chief of Naval Operations, received the "Pilot Message" in the evening of December 6 (R. 5440–5442). Admiral Stark and General Marshall each deny that on December 6 he had knowledge of the Pilot Message (R. 3473; 5813). We find on the testimony of General Miles and Colonel Bratton that the "Pilot Message" was delivered to General Marshall during the afternoon of December 6, 1941 (R. 3589–3590; 12049–12050). This Pilot Message said that Japan's reply to the American note of November 26 was about to be sent from Tokyo to Washington, and indicated that a rupture of diplomatic relations or war was a matter of hours.

On the evening of December 6, between 9 P. M. and midnight, Washington time, the first thirteen parts of the Japanese reply to the United States were delivered to the President, Mr. Knox, the office of the Secretary of State and the Chiefs of Army and Navy Intelligence (R. 10453–10455; 12052–12054). After reading this message the President stated "This means war" (R. 12441). He later telephoned Admiral Stark about the critical turn of events (R. 14757–14759). When Mr. Knox received the message he called Mr. Stimson and Mr. Hull and arranged a conference with them for Sunday morning (R. 10675–10681).

Mr. Stimson asked the Navy Department on Saturday evening to furnish him by 9 A. M. Sunday morning the following information:

Compilation of men of war in Far East; British, American, Japanese, Dutch, Russian; *also compilation of American men of war in the Pacific Fleet, with locations*, and a list of American men of war in the Atlantic without locations [Italics supplied, R. 13988.]

Admirals Stark, Ingersoll and the Secretary of the Navy were consulted about this request. The Secretary of the Navy directed that the information be compiled and delivered prior to 10 o'clock Sunday, December 7 (R. 13988). This was done. The compilation showed that practically all the ships of the Pacific Fleet were in Pearl Harbor (exhibit 176).

In the early morning of December 7, 1941, about 5 A. M. Washington time, the message fixing the hour for delivery of the Japanese note as 1 P. M. Washington time was available in the Navy Department in Washington (R. 10694–10701). This was eight and one-half hours before the attack on Pearl Harbor. Admiral Stark and his principal subordinates have testified before us that they had knowledge of this message about 10:30 A. M. (R. 4675, 9146–9148, 10469). This was five and one-half hours after it had been received in the Navy Department. It was about three hours before the attack. The relation of 1 P. M. Washington time to early morning in Hawaii was pointed out to Admiral Stark. (R. 9146–9148; 9154–9156; 9236–9254; 4679; 4685). Admiral Stark was urged by the Director of Naval Intelligence to send a warning to the Fleet (R. 4673). The chief intelligence officers of the Army had the "1 pm message" by 9 A. M. Washington time, immediately appreciated its significance, but did not succeed in bringing it to General Marshall's attention until nearly several hours later (R. 12077–12078; 12079–12081). Marshall was horseback riding in Virginia. No action was taken by the Army until he saw and read the 1 P. M. message and related intercepts, at which time he sent a message to General Short which went over commercial facilities and was received after the Pearl Harbor attack (R. 2935–2939; 8396). Admiral Stark took no action on this information except to agree to the inclusion in the belated Army message of instructions to General Short to advise Admiral Kimmel of its contents (R. 5814–5816).

Mr. Hull, Mr. Stimson, and Mr. Knox had the 1 P. M. message at their conference about 10:30 A. M. Washington time December 7 (R. 10473). The relation of Washington time to time in Hawaii and the Philippines was brought to their attention (R. 10473–10475). Mr. Stimson's notes describing the Sunday morning conference state:

Today is the day that the Japanese are going to bring their answer to Hull, and everything in MAGIC indicated they had been keeping the time back until now in order to accomplish something hanging in the air. Knox and I arranged a conference with Hull at 10:30 and we talked the whole matter over. Hull is very certain that the Japs are planning some deviltry and we are all wondering where the blow will strike (Stimson statement, p. 59).

The 1 P. M. message was delivered to the President about 10:30 A. M. (R. 10476).

Why did the high command in Washington fail to disclose promptly to Admiral Kimmel, General Short, and other American commanders in the field the information available in Washington, Saturday night and early Sunday morning? In seeking the answer to this question we have encountered failures of memory and changes in sworn testimony. I am constrained to reach these conclusions:

As a result of his conversation with the President late Saturday night December 6, Admiral Stark, Chief of Naval Operations, did receive notice of a critical turn in Japanese-American relations (R. 14757–14759). Even if it be assumed that he had no inkling until that time of vital information which had been available to him for at least six hours, the call from the President should have provoked his active and immediate efforts to elicit from his subordinates the data which they possessed as to the immediacy of war. *He failed to make such efforts.* Sunday morning, when the Saturday messages are known to have come to his attention together with the 1 P. M. message, he again did not take action, despite the recommendations of the Chief of Naval Intelligence that a warning be sent to the Fleet. He failed to exercise the care and diligence which his position required.

General Marshall, Chief of Staff of the Army, had the "Pilot Message" available to him on the afternoon of Saturday, December 6. This placed on him an obligation to make sure he would promptly receive the subsequent information which the Pilot message indicated would be soon forthcoming. He did not do so. In placing himself outside of effective contact with his subordinates for several hours on Sunday morning, he failed to exercise the care and diligence which his position required.

The alleged failure of the chief subordinates of Admiral Stark and General Marshall to furnish them promptly with the intercepted messages on Saturday night was unusual for two reasons. First, it was a departure from the usual routine for the distribution of intercepts. Second, these two were the only usual recipients of intercepts who testified that the messages were not brought to their attention on Saturday night. Neither Admiral Stark nor General Marshall made any effort thereafter to ascertain why such a colossal breakdown should occur in the functioning of their staffs on the eve of war (R. 3490–3491; 6215).

I have pointed out that during the critical period prior to the attack, the Administration in Washington made certain over-all policy decisions as to how to deal with the Japanese crisis. One decision was that Japan should commit the first overt act against the United States and thus resolve the dilemma in which the Administration's secret diplomacy had placed it. The other was to be in instant readiness to strike at Japan to check her further aggression against the British and Dutch in Far East Asia. Certainly the information and orders sent to General Short and Admiral Kimmel prior to the attack reflected the policy adopted in Washington.

General Short and Admiral Kimmel were not informed about the most important diplomatic steps in 1941. They were not informed of the parallel action agreement at the Atlantic Conference or the warning to Japan which followed. They were not informed of the significant terms of the American note to Japan of November 26. They were not informed of the commitment made to Great Britain, as set forth in the Brooke-Popham telegram of December 6. They did not receive the vital intercepted Japanese messages or any condensation or summary of them. In response to Admiral Kimmel's request for information in his letter of May 26, 1941, he did receive in July 1941 from the Navy Department the actual text of seven intercepted Japanese diplomatic messages (exhibit 37, pp. 6–12). In the week before the attack he received the text of another intercepted message describing the Japanese intrigue in Thailand. Kimmel testified that he believed that he was getting all pertinent information affecting the Pacific Fleet. This was the assurance Admiral Stark had given in response to the definite request in the letter of May 26, 1941. The Intelligence Officer of the Pacific Fleet, Captain Layton, wrote to Captain McCollum, his opposite number in Naval Intelligence in Washington, on March 11, 1941, to urge that intercepted Japanese diplomatic traffic be sent to the Fleet. McCollum's reply satisfied Layton that the Fleet would receive diplomatic traffic which affected its actions (R. 12923). But the vital intercepts were not sent to Admiral Kimmel or General Short. The fact that a few intercepts were sent to Admiral Kimmel shows that the withholding of others was not attributable to fear of the security of Naval communications and consequent prejudice to the Secret of Magic. The "bomb plot" message and related intercepts would have been of incalculable value both to General Short and Admiral Kimmel. Yet they were given no intimation of their existence.

The message of November 27 to Admiral Kimmel warned him of the threatened Japanese move in southeast Asia, and ordered him to be ready to execute a Fleet offensive against the Marshalls required by War Plans. Readiness for an offensive at some distance from Hawaii precluded concentrating the limited resources of the Fleet upon the defense of its base, which no despatch from the Navy Department mentioned as a point of attack. The offensive missions prescribed by the War Plans required the full use of the patrol planes of the Fleet. These planes were recently acquired and required alterations and maintenance work to put them in shape for war. The planes were too few for full distant searches from Hawaii. Partial searches were properly considered of doubtful value and involved the risk of making the planes useless for the reconnaissance required in the raids on the Marshalls at the time when they would be needed. Task forces at sea and patrol planes going to and from outlying islands carried out such distant reconnaissance as was feasible. As suggested by the Navy Department on November 27, the two carriers of the Pacific Fleet were sent on missions to outlying islands. Lacking air protection the battleships appeared better disposed in port than at sea. The fuel limitations and other logistic deficiencies of the Pacific Fleet were so acute that it was physically impossible to keep the whole Fleet, or major portions of it, at sea for extended intervals. The disposition of the ships and the use of patrol planes on and after November 27 were logical and reasonable in view of the message of that date.

On the evening of December 6, in response to Secretary Stimson's request and at the direction of Secretary Knox, the Navy Department compiled from its records a summary showing that all the major ships of the Pacific Fleet were in Pearl Harbor. At this time the information available in Washington showed that war was only hours away. Yet the two Secretaries and the high command made no effort to direct any change in the dispositions of the Fleet as shown in the Navy Department summary. They took no steps to furnish Admiral Kimmel the information which they possessed as to the imminence of war. Consequently they deprived him of any chance to alter his dispositions in the light of that information. I conclude that Secretaries Stimson and Knox and the high command in Washington knew that the major units of the Fleet were in Pearl Harbor on December 6–7, 1941, and were satisfied with that situation.

The message of November 27 to Admiral Kimmel illustrates one feature of the pre-Pearl Harbor plan of action of the Administration. The Fleet was to be in readiness for offensive raids on the Marshalls to counter the Japanese advance in southeast Asia. The message sent to General Short by General Marshall on November 27, 1941 shows the other feature of the Administration's plan of action—to make sure that the Japanese would strike first so that the offensive by the Fleet would be approved by the American public. The message to General Short stated:

If hostilities cannot, repeat cannot be avoided the United States desires that Japan commit the first overt act. This policy should not, repeat not, be construed as restricting you to a course of action that might jeopardize your defense. Prior to hostile Japanese action you are directed to undertake such reconnaissance and other measures as you deem necessary but these measures should be carried out so as no, repeat not, to alarm the civil population or disclose intent (exhibit 32, p. 7).

General Marshall testified that instructions about the "overt act" were put into the message on the personal order of the President (R. 3443–3447). In addition the War Department sent three other messages to the Army and Army Air Forces in Hawaii, on November 27 and 28, all of which were directed to sabotage and subversive activities. One of these messages from the War Department on November 28 stated:

Protective measures should be confined to those essential to security, avoiding unnecessary publicity and alarm (exhibit 32, p. 13).

The Navy Department also cautioned Admiral Kimmel against committing the first overt act. On November 29 he received from the

Navy Department the substance of the Army's message to General Short with the additional directive—

Undertake no offensive action until Japan has committed an overt act (exhibit 37, p. 38).

On November 27, 1941, General Short reported to General Marshall the measures he had taken in response to General Marshall's message. His reply specifically referred to General Marshall's message by its number: It stated: "Report Department alerted to prevent sabotage Liaison with the Navy. Reurad four seven two twenty-seventh" (exhibit 32, p. 12). The Chief of the War Plans Division of the Army, General Leonard T. Gerow, saw General Short's reply, noted and initialled it (exhibit 46). This reply was routed by General Gerow to General Marshall, Chief of Staff. Some question has arisen as to whether General Marshall in fact actually saw General Short's reply. In order that the reader may have the exact facts, I desire to report the evidence, question and answer, beginning page 1420 of the printed record:

Mr. KEEFE. Now with the country on the brink of war, General Marshall, you having the then impression as you have stated it a few moments ago, that Japan was liable to precipitate war by attacking any time, any place, it would be highly important to the Chief of Staff to see to it that the orders which he had given were carried out, would it not?

General MARSHALL. That is correct, sir.

Mr. KEEFE. Now when General Short's message came back the evidence indicates, somewhat inconclusively perhaps, that it was part of three or four papers, the top one being the reply of MacArthur, then Short, then a route sheet, the MacArthur message being on top and that bears your endorsement with your initials.

General MARSHALL. Correct, sir.

Mr. KEEFE. Your initials do not appear on the Short message but they do show the initials of the Secretary of War and the War Plans Department, General Gerow. Now am I correct in the assumption from an understanding of your evidence on that point that you think you must have seen the Short message although you did not initial it, having initialed the top one?

General MARSHALL. That was my assumption, sir.

Mr. KEEFE. Well, is that a mere assumption or is it a fact?

General MARSHALL. I stated I did not recall, sir; that I must assume that I had seen it.

Mr. KEEFE. Well, if you saw that Short message, General Marshall, as Chief of Staff it imposed some responsibility upon you, did it not?

General MARSHALL. That is correct, sir.

Mr. KEEFE. It was addressed to you as Chief of Staff, was it not?

General MARSHALL. That is correct, sir.

Mr. KEEFE. And the very telegram itself indicates that it is in response to the command order which you had issued to him?

General MARSHALL. That is correct, sir.

Mr. KEEFE. And it was a message which attempted on the part of Short to convey to you as Chief of Staff the nature of the alert under which he was operating?

General MARSHALL. That is correct, sir.

Mr. KEEFE. That was his response to your order?

General MARSHALL. Yes, sir.

Mr. KEEFE. Now, I have read the various statements, General Marshall, that you have made at various times in connection with this matter. You recall that when you were before the Army board first you were somewhat confused about those things because you thought that at some time in November there had been a change in alert numbers. Do you remember that?

General MARSHALL. Yes, sir.

Mr. KEEFE. Now, it is perfectly clear now that a reading of this message indicates that there isn't any alert number specified in Short's wire.

General MARSHALL. That is correct, sir.

Mr. KEEFE. So that puts that out of the picture, doesn't it?

General MARSHALL. Yes, sir.

Mr. KEEFE. So we get down to the simple fact that here is a message from your commanding general in the bastion of defense in the Pacific to which all of our defenses, as you have testified, were tied, in which he tells you that he is alerted to prevent sabotage; liaison with Navy. Now in all fairness, General Marshall, in the exercise of ordinary care as Chief of Staff ought you not to have proceeded to investigate further and give further orders to General Short when it appeared that he was only alerted against sabotage?

General MARSHALL. As I stated earlier, that was my opportunity to intervene and I did not do it.

Mr. KEEFE. Well, now, you say that was your opportunity. That was your responsibility, was it not?

General MARSHALL. You can put it that way, sir.

Mr. KEEFE. Well, I don't want to put it that way. I am asking you. You used the words "that was your opportunity," I do not want an opportunity to arise in the future discussion of this matter to have a conflict of words and not to be able to understand just want you meant. Do I understand that your use of the word "opportunity" is synonymous with responsibility?

General MARSHALL. Mr. Keefe, I had an immense number of papers going over my desk every day informing me what was happening anywhere in the world. This was a matter of great importance. It had gone into the machine, it had been sent out, the acknowledgments had come back. They passed the important messages over my desk. I noted them and initialed them; those that I thought the Secretary of War ought specifically to see I put them out for him to see, to be sure that he would see it in case by any chance he did not see the same message.

I was not passing the responsibility on to the Secretary of War. I merely wanted him to know.

Now the same thing related to these orders of the War Department. I was responsible. I was responsible for the actions of the General Staff throughout on large matters and on the small matters. I was responsible for those, but I am not a bookkeeping machine and it is extremely difficult, it is an extremely difficult thing for me to take each thing in its turn and give it exactly the attention that it had merited.

Now in this particular case a very tragic thing occurred, there is no question about that, there is no question in regard to my responsibility as Chief of Staff. I am not attempting to evade that at all, but I do not think it is quite characterized in the manner that you have expressed yourself.

Mr. KEEFE. Well, now, let me put it in another way. You have now stated it was your responsibility as Chief of Staff to see to it that General Short out there in Hawaii, which you have described as being your bastion of defense, to see that he was alerted, and if he misinterpreted your order to see that that order was carried out.

General MARSHALL. That is my responsibility, sir.

Mr. KEEFE. Now, I have stated it correctly, haven't I?

General MARSHALL. Yes, sir, you have.

Subsequently, in the same examination (printed record pp. 1422–1423) General Marshall stated that General Gerow had a direct responsibility in this matter and that he had full responsibility as Chief of Staff. General Marshall was very fair. He admitted that a tragic mistake had been made, and while it was the direct responsibility of General Gerow, Chief of War Plans, to have "caught" General Short's reply and to have immediately advised his Chief of Staff, yet General Marshall as Chief of Staff did assume over-all responsibility for failure of the Washington headquarters to interpret and evaluate General Short's reply and to see to it that he was on an all-out alert in accordance with the command directive issued in the message from Marshall to Short on November 27. The Secretary of War saw, noted and initialled General Short's reply. (Exhibit 46). It was the responsibility of General Marshall to see that General Short was properly alerted (R. 3723). General Short, after being ordered to report his state of readiness to General Marshall, was entitled to assume that this state of readiness was satisfactory to the

Chief of Staff unless he heard to the contrary (R. 3443). Neither General Marshall, General Gerow nor Secretary of War Stimson made any criticism or suggestion to General Short about the condition of his alert in Hawaii in the ten-day period prior to the attack. Because of their silence General Short was led to believe that the Chief of Staff approved his alert against sabotage. I believe that Secretary Stimson, and Generals Marshall and Gerow, understood the nature of his alert which was plainly indicated in the reply itself. I further believe they were satisfied with General Short's alert until the blow fell on Hawaii.

On June 17, 1940, General Marshall had placed the Hawaiian Department on all-out war alert by the following message (exhibit 52):

Immediately alert complete defensive organization to deal with possible trans-Pacific raid comma to greatest extent possible without creating public hysteria or provoking undue curiosity of newspapers or alien agents. Suggest maneuver basis. Maintain alert until further orders. Instructions for secret communication direct with Chief of Staff will be furnished you shortly. Acknowledge.

General Marshall followed up this alert with great care and received considerable detailed information about it. (Exhibit 52.) He described the information which caused the alert in 1940 in a letter to the Commanding General in Hawaii, General Herron, as follows:

You have no doubt wondered as to the alert instructions sent to you on the 17th. Briefly, the combination of information from a number of sources led to the deduction that recent Japanese-Russian agreement to compose their differences in the Far East was arrived at and so timed as to permit Japan to undertake a trans-Pacific raid against Oahu, following the departure of the U. S. Fleet from Hawaii.

Presumably such a raid would be in the interest of Germany and Italy, to force the United States to pull the Fleet back to Hawaii.

Whether the information or deductions were correct, I cannot say. Even if they were, the precautions you have taken may keep us from knowing they were by discouraging any overt act (exhibit 52, p. 13).

On November 27, 1941, the information which General Marshall had showed a far more severe crisis in Japanese-American relations than existed in June of 1940. As his letter to General Herron shows, he felt that this all-out alert in Hawaii in 1940 may have discouraged the Japanese from attacking that area. Yet he did not repeat on November 27, 1941, his message of June 17, 1940, to Hawaii with its clear-cut order: *"Immediately alert complete defensive organization to deal with possible trans-Pacific raid."* He assigned as a reason for not doing so, the fact that in the message of November 27, 1941, "you had to include instructions of the President regarding overt acts" (R. 3975).

Mr. Stimson describes the preparation of the Army message of November 27 to General Short as follows:

If there was to be war, moreover, we wanted the Japanese to commit the first overt act. On the other hand, the matter of defense against an attack by Japan was first consideration. In Hawaii because of the large numbers of Japanese inhabitants, it was felt desirable to issue a special warning so that nothing would be done, unless necessary to defense, to alarm the civil population and thus possibly precipitate an incident and give the Japanese an excuse to go to war and the chance to say that we had committed the first overt act (Stimson statement, pp. 21-22).

Again on December 7, Mr. Stimson noted in his diary:

When the news first came that Japan had attacked us, my first feeling was of relief that the indecision was over and that a crisis had come in a way which would unite all our people. This continued to be my dominant feeling in spite of the news of catastrophies which quickly developed (Stimson statement, p. 62).

The same fear of publicity, alarm, or anything which might savor of a first overt act by the United States, rather than by Japan, is reflected in the President's message to High Commissioner Sayre in the Philippines on November 26, 1941. After describing the crisis in Japanese-American relations, the President directed Mr. Sayre to impress upon the President of the Philippines "the desirability of avoiding public pronouncement or action since that might make the situation more difficult" (R. 13861–13862).

On Saturday night December 6 the President read the first 13 parts of the final Japanese diplomatic note, remarked "This means war," and decided to get in touch with the Chief of Naval Operations (R. 12442, 12443). He learned that the Chief of Naval Operations was at the theater. He then stated that he would reach the Admiral later, that he did not want to cause public alarm by having the Admiral paged. The fact that the Admiral had a box reserved was mentioned. The President did not wish him to leave suddenly because he would surely be seen and undue alarm might be caused (R. 12444).

General Marshall failed to use the scrambler telephone on his desk to call General Short in Hawaii on Sunday morning December 7, nearly two hours before the attack, and give him the same information which he sent in the delayed telegram which reached General Short after the attack. General Marshall testified that among the possible factors which may have influenced him against using the scrambler telephone was the possibility that the Japanese could construe the fact that the Army was alerting its garrisons in Hawaii as a hostile act (R. 3390).

The Japanese would have grasped at most any straw to bring to such portions of our public that doubted our integrity of action that we were committing an act that forced action on their part (R. 3193).

The concept of an "incident" as a factor which would unify public opinion behind an all-out war effort either in the Atlantic or Pacific had influenced the thinking of officials in Washington for a long time. Many plans which might have produced an incident were from time to time discussed and considered. As early as October 10, 1940, Secretary Knox had advised Admiral Richardson, then Commander-in-Chief of the Pacific Fleet, of a plan the President was considering to shut off all trade between Japan and North and South America. This would be accomplished by means of a patrol of American ships in two lines extending from Hawaii westward to the Philippines, and from Samoa toward the Dutch East Indies (R. 792). This plan was to be instituted in the event Japan retaliated against Great Britain upon the reopening of the Burma Road scheduled for October 17, 1940 (R. 792). Admiral Richardson was amazed at this proposal and stated that the Fleet was not prepared to put such a plan into effect, nor for the war which would certainly result from such a course of action (R. 793).

On February 11, 1941, the Chief of Naval Operations in a Memorandum for the President, described the President as considering a plan to send a detachment of vessels to the Far East and perhaps to permit a "leak" that they were going out there (exhibit 106). He quoted the President in the same memorandum as stating that he would not mind losing one or two cruisers, but that he did not want to take a chance on losing five or six. Again, in a letter of April 19, 1941 the Chief of Naval Operations quoted the President as saying to him:

> Betty, just as soon as those ships come back from Australia and New Zealand, or perhaps a little before, I want to send some more out. I just want to keep them popping up here and there and keep the Japs guessing (exhibit 106).

On May 24, 1941, Admiral Stark wrote Admiral Kimmel—

> Day before yesterday the President gave me an overall limit of 30 days to prepare and have ready an expedition of 25,000 men to sail for and to take the Azores. Whether or not there would be opposition I do not know but we have to be fully prepared for strenuous opposition (exhibit 106).

On July 25, 1941 the Chief of Naval Operations wrote Admiral Kimmel to the effect that he might be called upon to send a carrier-load of planes to Russia via one of the Asiatic Russian ports (exhibit 106). "I don't know that you will, but the President has told me to be prepared for it, and I want you to have the thought." Admiral Kimmel replied to this suggestion as follows:

> I entertain no doubt that such an operation, if discovered (as is highly probable), will be tantamount to initiation of a Japanese-American war. If we are going to take the initiative in commencing such a war, I can think of more effective ways for gaining initial advantage. In short, it is my earnest conviction that use of a carrier to deliver aircraft to Asiatic Russian ports in the present period of strained relations is to invite war. If we have decided upon war it would be far better to take direct offensive action. If for reasons of political expediency, it has been determined to force Japan to fire the first shot, let us choose a method which will be more advantageous to ourselves (exhibit 106).

On July 31, 1941, Admiral Stark sent Admiral Kimmel a copy of a letter to Captain Charles M. Cooke as follows:

> Within 48 hours after the Russian situation broke I went to the President, with the Secretary's approval, and stated that on the assumption that the country's decision is not to let England fall, we should immediately seize the psychological opportunity presented by the Russian-German clash and announce and start escorting immediately, and protecting the Western Atlantic on a large scale; that such a declaration, followed by immediate action on our part, would almost certainly involve us in the war and that I considered every day of delay in our getting into the war as dangerous and that much more delay might be fatal to Britain's survival. I reminded him that I had been asking this for months in the State Department and elsewhere, etc., etc., etc. I have been maintaining that only a war psychology could or would speed things up the way they should be speeded up; that strive as we would it just is not in the nature of things to get the results in peace that we would, were we at war.
>
> The Iceland situation may produce an "incident". You are as familiar with that and the President's statements and answers at press conferences as I am. Whether or not we will get an "incident" because of the protection we are giving Iceland and the shipping which we must send in support of Iceland and our troops, I do not know—only Hitler can answer (exhibit 106).

Again Admiral Kelly Turner, War Plans Officer for the Chief of Naval Operations stated, in describing United States-British Staff conversations on War Plans in 1941:

> It was felt by the Naval Department that there might be a possibility of war with Japan without the involvement of Germany, but at some length and over a considerable period this matter was discussed and it was determined that in such a case the United States would, if possible, initiate *efforts to bring Germany into the war against us in order that we would be able to give strong support to the United Kingdom in Europe* (testimony of Admiral R. K. Turner before Admiral Hart, pp. 251, 252, question 10, exhibit 144). [Italics supplied.]

On November 29, 1941, the Chief of Naval Operations sent a despatch to the Commander in Chief of the Asiatic Fleet which commenced with this unusual statement:

President directs that the following be done as soon as possible and within two days if possible after receipt this despatch (exhibit 37, p. 39).

The President's directions were that the Commander in Chief of the Asiatic Fleet was to charter three small vessels to form a "defensive information patrol." The minimum requirements to establish these ships as United States men of war would suffice in manning them. These requirements were: command by a Naval officer and the mounting of a small gun and one machine gun. The employment of Filipino crews with the minimum number naval ratings was authorized. The ships were to observe and report by radio Japanese movement in the West China Sea and Gulf of Siam. The President prescribed the point at which each vessel was to be stationed. One vessel was to be stationed between Hainan and Hue; one between Camranh Bay and Cape St. Jaques; one off Pointe De Camau (exhibit 37, p. 39). All these points were clearly in the path of the Japanese advance down the coast of Indo-China, and towards the Gulf of Siam. The Navy Department did not originate this plan (R. 11351). The Navy Department would not have directed it to be done unless the President had specifically ordered it (R. 11351). Admiral Hart was already conducting reconnaissance off· that coast by planes from Manila (R. 11350). So far as the Navy Department was concerned, sufficient information was being received from this air reconnaissance (R. 11351). Had the Japanese fired upon any one of these three small vessels, it would have constituted an overt act on the part of Japan (R. 11352).

AFTERMATH OF THE PEARL HARBOR ATTACK

Eleven days after Pearl Harbor, the Roberts Commission was appointed by the President to find the facts about the Pearl Harbor attack. Its duty was:

to provide bases for sound decisions whether any derelictions of duty or errors of judgment on the part of United States Army or Navy personnel contributed to such successes as were achieved by the enemy * * * and, if so, what these derelictions or errors were, and who were responsible therefor.

General Marshall and Admiral Stark were witnesses at the first meeting of the Commission. Their testimony was not given under oath and was not recorded. Neither was that of their chief subordinates, Admiral Turner and General Gerow. The Commission examined General Short and Admiral Kimmel under oath in Hawaii. They were not permitted to be present during the testimony of other witnesses, to examine or cross-examine them, or to know what evidence had been presented.

The Commission knew that Japanese messages had been intercepted and were available, prior to the attack, to the high command in Washington. It did not inquire about what information these intercepts contained or who received them. Mr. Justice Roberts testified before this Committee: "I would not have bothered to read it (the intercepted Japanese traffic) if it had been shown to us" (R., vol. 47, p. 8836). Misleading statements made to the Roberts Commission by high ranking naval officers in Washington to the effect that

Admiral Kimmel had all the information available to the Navy Department (R. 4891–4900, 4893–4895, 5021–5022) went unchallenged.

The Roberts Commission's failure to inquire into the Japanese intercepts and their distribution and evaluation in Washington, prevented it from correctly assessing responsibility for the disaster. The facts were then fresh in the minds of key witnesses in Washington. They could not then have honestly forgotten their whereabouts at important times. When the Roberts Commission bypassed the facts about the intercepted messages, it nearly buried the truth about Pearl Harbor. Its report became the indictment of two officers based upon incomplete evidence.

The Roberts report was published January 25, 1942. General Short, reading it in the press, was dumbfounded and immediately called his friend General Marshall on the telephone to inquire whether he should retire. Marshall advised him to "stand pat," but told Short he would consider the telephone conversation "authority" for Short's retirement if it became necessary (R. 8446). On the same day, the Secretary of the Navy directed that Admiral Kimmel in San Francisco be informed that Short had submitted a request for retirement (exhibit 121). This information was immediately telephoned to Kimmel. Kimmel, who had not previously thought of retiring, construed the telephone message as a request that he do so, and submitted a formal request for retirement dated January 26, 1942. General Short, who thought it was not fair to General Marshall to have to act only on the basis of a telephone conversation, sent to Marshall a formal request for retirement in writing, addressed to the Adjutant General dated January 25, 1942. On January 26 General Marshall recommended to Secretary of War Stimson that General Short's application for retirement be accepted "today" but that it be done "quietly without any publicity at the moment" (R. 8459). Admiral Stark requested the Army to keep him advised about Short's retirement as he proposed to "communicate this fact to Admiral Kimmel in the hope Kimmel will likewise apply for retirement" (R. 8459). However, on January 28, 1942, he sent a telephone message to Kimmel to the effect that the previous telephone notification about Short's retirement was not intended to influence him. Thereupon Admiral Kimmel submitted his letter of January 28, 1942, to the Secretary of the Navy, in which he stated: "I desire my request for retirement to stand, subject only to determination by the Department as to what course of action will best serve the interests of the country and the good of the service" (exhibit 121).

The President personally directed the method of handling the requests for retirement of Kimmel and Short. On January 29, 1942, he instituted a three-point program for dealing with the matter. The Army and Navy were to act together. After a week's waiting they were to announce that Kimmel and Short had applied for retirement and that their applications were under consideration. After another week had passed, public announcement was to be made that the applications had been accepted with the condition that acceptance did not bar subsequent court-martial proceedings. Court-martial proceedings, however, were to be described as impossible without the disclosure of military secrets. The wording of the condition in the acceptance was troublesome to the Administration. The President, Secretary Stimson, Secretary Knox, and Attorney General Biddle labored over the language (R. 8462, 8464, exhibit 171). The Administration wanted to avoid public criticism for having barred court-martial proceedings. On the other hand, it did not wish to stimulate the public or the two officers to expect or demand court-martial proceedings (R. 8464, 8467). Finally language as suitable as possible was agreed upon. The phrase to be used in accepting the retirement applications was "without condonation of any offense or prejudice to future disciplinary action." Admiral Kimmel and General Short were each retired by letters so worded, dated respectively, February 16 and February 17, 1942. The Secretary of the Navy, in announcing the Navy's action, stated that he had directed the preparation of charges for court martial of Admiral Kimmel alleging dereliction of duty. The public were informed that a trial could not be held until such time as the public interest and safety would permit.

The public reaction was as planned. Kimmel and Short were considered solely responsible for Pearl Harbor. The Roberts report, considered by Justice Roberts as only an indictment, became, in effect, a conviction. The two officers were helpless. No court martial could be had. They had no way of defending themselves. They remained in ignorance of what evidence the Roberts Commission had heard. Admiral Stark wrote to Admiral Kimmel on February 21, 1942:

> Pending something definite, there is no reason why you should not settle yourself in a quiet nook somewhere and let Old Father Time help the entire situation, which I feel he will—if for no other reason than he always has (exhibit 121).

The high civilian and military officials in Washington who had skillfully maneuvered Kimmel and Short into the position of exclusive blame knew at the time all the hidden facts about Pearl Harbor, at least as much and probably more than this investigation has been able to uncover. As the two-year statutory period for instituting court-martial proceedings was about to expire, Kimmel and Short were requested by the Secretaries of War and Navy to waive the Statute of Limitations. Admiral Kimmel did so but with the provision that any court martial be held in "open court" (exhibit 171). General Short did likewise (R. 8496–8499). Similar requests were not made of other officers, not even of those who before this Committee publicly accepted responsibility for certain failures of the high command in Washington.

In June of 1944 the Congress directed the Secretaries of War and Navy to conduct investigations into the Pearl Harbor attack. The War Department denied the Army Board of Investigation access to the intercepted messages. General Miles, Director of Military Intelligence, at the time of Pearl Harbor, was ordered by General Marshall not to testify on the subject of the intercepts (R. 11843). For a considerable period the Navy Court of Inquiry was denied access to the same material (exhibit 195). After repeated demands by Admiral Kimmel, the Navy Department released this restriction upon its own Court. The War Department finally followed the same course. For the first time, late in the Board's proceedings, Army officers were permitted to testify before the Army Board as to all details regarding the intercepts (R. 12035). But many important Army witnesses had already testified under the limitations previously ordered.

In the fall of 1944 the Army Board and Navy Court made their reports to the Secretaries of the War and Navy. These reports were critical of the conduct of Admiral Stark and General Marshall. The findings were not made public. The Navy Court exonerated Admiral Kimmel. Admiral Kimmel's request to read its report was refused by the Secretary of the Navy (R. 6811). The Secretaries of War and Navy instituted further secret investigations dispensing with the services of the three-man Board and Court previously established, and each entrusting the conduct of proceedings to a single officer. Admiral Kimmel's request to be present at the further Navy investigation, to introduce evidence, to confront and cross-examine witnesses was denied by the Secretary of the Navy (R. 6812). The affidavits and testimony at the further investigations contain many instances where witnesses gave evidence materially different from that which they had previously sworn to before the Army Board and the Naval Court. These changes were especially marked in testimony of certain key witnesses on the subject of the dissemination and evaluation of the intercepted messages in Washington. Again, before this Committee these same witnesses further changed their testimony from that sworn to twice previously, or pleaded lapses of memory.

The record of the high military and civilian officials of the War and Navy Departments in dealing with the Pearl Harbor disaster from beginning to end does them no credit. It will have a permanent bad effect on the morale and integrity of the armed services. The Administration had ample opportunity to record and preserve all the facts about Pearl Harbor, even if their public disclosure needed to wait upon the war's end. This was not done. The policy adopted was to place the public responsibility for the disaster on the commanders in the field, to be left there for all time. The policy failed only because suppression created public suspicion, and the Congress was alert.

CONCLUSIONS AND RECOMMENDATIONS

This investigation has not brought to light all the facts about Pearl Harbor. We have been denied much vital information. Mr. Stimson did not answer certain important interrogations which, in consideration of the state of his health, were submitted to him in writing. He has also denied to the Committee his diary entries for the days December 2 to December 6, 1941. These were significantly omitted from his written statement. Mr. Hull's health permitted only a brief appearance before us and no examination by the minority members of the Committee. Written interrogatories were submitted as to when he first saw or obtained information as to the contents of certain vital intercepted messages, including the 1 P. M. message. Mr. Hull answered: "I do not recall the exact times that I first saw or learned of the contents of the messages you cite" (R. 14316). "I do not recall" was an answer frequently received from other important witnesses. Messrs. Maxwell Hamilton, Eugene Dooman and Stanley Hornbeck, State Department officials who played important roles in 1941 in our Far Eastern diplomacy, have not testified. We have been denied Ambassador Grew's diary. In December 1941 General Bedell Smith was secretary to the General Staff of the Army. He did not testify. His possible knowledge of the distribution of intercepted messages to General Marshall on Saturday evening, December 6, was not investigated. Admiral (then Captain) Glover was the duty officer in the office of the Chief of Naval Operations on December 6, 1941. His log for that night contained the vital information about Mr. Stimson's interest in precise locations of the ships of the Pacific Fleet. Admiral Glover sent the Committee a telegram but did not testify. Mr. Welles' memoranda of Atlantic Charter conferences was obtained from State Department only after his oral testimony before us had been completed.

On the evidence before us I concur in the findings of the committee with respect to responsibilities of our commanders in Hawaii. I believe that the "mistakes of judgment" referred to in the committee report are directly related to the failures of the high commands in Washington to have their organizations fully alerted and on a war footing and that those in command at the Washington level must bear their full share of the responsibility for the tragedy of Pearl Harbor.

I further conclude that secret diplomacy was at the root of the tragedy. The United States had warned Japan that an advance to Malaya or the Dutch East Indies would mean war with this nation. The President gave Great Britain assurances of our armed support in such event. What Japan and Britain knew, our commanders in the field and our own people did not know. Washington feared that national unity could not be attained unless Japan committed the first overt act. Accordingly, the Army in Hawaii was put on an anti-sabotage alert, a defensive posture containing the least possible risk of incident in Hawaii which Japan might claim was an overt act by the United States. The mobilization of American public opinion in support of an offensive by the Pacific Fleet against Japan was to be accomplished, if at all, by a message to Congress "at the last stage of our relations, relating to actual hostilities." This message was to be the prelude to hostilities by the United States if Japan attacked the British and the Dutch at the outset of the war and did not attack this nation. A direct attack by Japan against the United States at the outset of hostilities would make such a message unnecessary. Mr. Stimson's diary describes the plan succinctly: "The question was how we should maneuver them into the position of firing the first shot without allowing too much danger to ourselves." In formulating this plan undoubtedly Washington was influenced by public promises to keep us out of war unless attacked.

With full knowledge of Japan's intentions prior to the attack, Washington had one plain duty to the American people. That duty was to inform them of their peril. This was not done. Washington had a further duty to make sure that our forces were ready to meet the attack by furnishing their commanders afield and afloat with all available information, or by evaluating that information and giving them appropriate clear and categoric instructions.

Those who find in various instances of poor coordination between the services the causes of Pearl Harbor are satisfied with a superficial explanation. The state of readiness of our armed forces in the field was a reflection of over-all policy adopted on the highest level in Washington. The President had delivered to him the Japanese intercepted messages and possessed much more information about Japanese plans and intentions than any field commander. He gave most minute directions to commanders in the field, even as to the scouting positions of individual ships, when he thought such directions necessary. A merger of the armed forces and unity of command in Hawaii in November and December, 1941, could not have eliminated the dangers in the policy of maneuvering Japan into striking the first blow. That policy would still have shaped the orders given, as well as the information sent to a single commander in the field.

Those who find American public opinion responsible for Pearl Harbor accept an entirely false theory. Enlightened public opinion is based on accurate public information. The American people, if kept well informed of their real diplomatic position, do not need an incident to unite them. If foreign policy and diplomatic representations are treated as the exclusive, secret information of the President and his advisers, public opinion will not be enlightened. The very nature of the consequent public alarm places the armed forces of the Nation in effective readiness ar.d may even deter an enemy from executing its planned attack. The best deterrent to a predatory Japan in late 1941 was a thoroughly informed and obviously alerted America.

In this connection it will be noted that when the reports of the Army Board and the Navy Court of Inquiry were submitted to President Truman on August 30, 1945, he made the following statement:

> I have read it (the Pearl Harbor reports) very carefully, and I came to the conclusion that the whole thing is the result of the policy which the country itself pursued. The country was not ready for preparedness. Every time the President made an effort to get a preparedness program through the Congress, it was stifled. Whenever the President made a statement about the necessity of preparedness, he was vilified for doing it. I think the country is as much to blame as any individual in this final situation that developed in Pearl Harbor.

An examination of the facts ought to compel any person to reject this conclusion. The record clearly demonstrates how the Army and Navy get the funds needed for national defense. The Army and Navy are required to submit their respective estimates each year to the Bureau of the Budget. This Bureau acting for the President conducts hearings and finally makes recommendations to the President as to the amounts to be recommended to the Congress for appropriation. The Congress is in effect the people of America. The record discloses that in the fiscal years 1934 to 1941, inclusive, the Army and Navy jointly asked for $26,580,145,093. This is the combined total of Army and Navy requests made to the Bureau of the Budget. In the same period the President recommended to the Congress that it appropriate to the combined services $23,818,319,897. The Congress actually made available to the Army and Navy in this period $24,943,987,823. Thus it is apparent that the President himself recommended to the Congress in the fiscal years 1934 to 1941, inclusive, that it appropriate for the Army and Navy $2,761,826,033 less than had been requested by the Army and Navy. The people's representatives in the Congress gave to the Army and Navy in the form of appropriations and authorizations for expenditure $1,256,667,926 more than the President had recommended in his budget messages to the Congress.

The mere recital of these undisputed figures should dispose of the contention that "the country is as much to blame as any individual in this final situation that developed in Pearl Harbor." I am including herein for ready reference a complete statement:

	Asked	Budget	Congress
1934	$320, 900, 513	$280, 746, 841	$280, 066, 381
1935	305, 271, 321	288, 960, 155	283, 862, 094
1936	361, 351, 154	331, 799, 277	363, 224, 957
1937	467, 022, 915	391, 065, 510	401, 914, 645
1938	468, 204, 851	436, 495, 336	439, 872, 423
1939	630, 803, 130	598, 016, 016	611, 848, 391
1940	1, 019, 342, 730	995, 442, 760	970, 822, 098
1941	13, 612, 977, 763	13, 067, 553, 812	13, 487, 184, 058
Total	17, 185, 874, 377	16, 390, 079, 707	16, 828, 795, 047
Total both services	17, 185, 874, 377 9, 394, 271, 553	16, 390, 079, 707 7, 428, 240, 190	16, 828, 795, 047 8, 115, 192, 776
	26, 580, 145, 930	23, 818, 319, 897	24, 943, 987, 823

Roosevelt cut: $2,761,826,033.
Congress restored: *$1,256,667,926* of the Budget cut.

Another subject that has been bandied about the country for a number of years relates to what has been frequently referred to as the failure or refusal of Congress to fortify the island of Guam. The contention has been made that Congress refused to appropriate money to fortify the island of Guam and that as a result of such failure the entire war in the Pacific in its initial stages was lost to the Japanese.

The fact is that no proposal was ever submitted to the Congress involving the fortification of Guam. The Navy did request an appropriation of five million dollars for the purpose of dredging the harbor at Guam (Stark testimony, record pp. 6546–6547). The first request of the Navy was rejected by the Congress. Thereafter, the appropriation requested by the Navy was passed with only one vote against it. The dredging operation was being carried on when war broke out with Japan.

It is interesting to note that "Rainbow No. 5", which is the Joint Chiefs' of Staff worldwide war plan, placed the island of Guam in Category "F" (record p. 6535). The following questions and answers tell the story:

Mr. KEEFE. Now, I would like to ask a question which bothered me with respect to your Rainbow No. 5, which places the island of Guam in what is called Category F.

Admiral STARK. I have the category here.

Mr. KEEFE. Now will you state for the record what Category F means?

Admiral STARK. Yes, sir. We have that, I am sure. This is out of Joint Action, Army and Navy, and refers to degrees of preparation, and they are put in categories of defense, A, B, C, D, E, and F.

Mr. KEEFE. Well, take Guam to start with. That is in F. Now give us what Category F means.

Admiral STARK. Category F: "Positions beyond the continental limits of the United States which may be subject to either minor or major attack for the purpose of occupation but which cannot be provided with adequate defense forces. Under this category the employment of existing local forces and local facilities will be confined principally to the demolition of those things it is desirable to prevent falling into the hands of the enemy."

Mr. KEEFE. Then, so far as Guam was concerned, at the time this basic war plan was devised it was the considered opinion of both the Army and Navy that it could not be defended and it therefore was placed in Category F that required those on the island, through demolition or otherwise, to destroy anything of value to the enemy and to permit it to be taken?

Admiral STARK. Yes, sir.

Mr. KEEFE. And to surrender?

Admiral STARK. Yes, sir.

Mr. KEEFE. That is right, is it not?

Admiral STARK. That is correct, yes, sir (record, p. 6537).

Mr. KEEFE. Now, at the time of the attack on Guam and the capture of Guam by the Japs were improvements on the harbor being made at that time or had they been completed?

Admiral STARK. They had not been completed. Of course, I recall very clearly the legislation with regard to that. I do not know just what their status was at this moment. I had obtained from Congress the appropriation, I believe it was $6,000,000, for certain improvements to the harbor. You recall the first year I lost it by six votes, and the following year it went through almost unanimously, only one vote being opposed to it. Just how far we had gotten along with that I do not recall at the moment.

Mr. KEEFE. With those improvements completed, Guam would still be in Category F, would it not?

Admiral STARK. In the same category, Category F. The improvements were not such as improved the defense of Guam but very little.

Mr. KEEFE. Even with the improvements that were requested and contemplated the Island of Guam, in the opinion of the Joint Army and Navy Board, could not be successfully defended due to the power that Japan had in the mandated islands surrounding it, is that right?

Admiral STARK. That is correct (record, p. 6547).

These simple facts as disclosed to the public for the first time in these hearings should effectively dispose of the contention that "Congress refused to fortify the Island of Guam, and hence the United States suffered tremendous loss in the initial stages of the war with Japan."

In the future the people and their Congress must know how close American diplomacy is moving to war so that they may check its advance if imprudent and support its position if sound. A diplomacy which relies upon the enemy's first overt act to insure effective popular support for the nation's final war decision is both outmoded and dangerous in the atomic age. To prevent any future Pearl Harbor more tragic and damaging than that of December 7, 1941, there must be constant close coordination between American public opinion and American diplomacy.

APPENDIX A

PRIOR INVESTIGATIONS CONCERNING THE PEARL HARBOR ATTACK

PRIOR INVESTIGATIONS CONCERNING PEARL HARBOR ATTACK

The Roberts Commission

The Roberts Commission was organized under an Executive order, dated December 18, 1941, of President Franklin D. Roosevelt, which defined the duties of the Commission thus: "To ascertain and report the facts relating to the attack made by Japanese armed forces upon the Territory of Hawaii on December 7, 1941. The purposes of the required inquiry and report are to provide bases for sound decisions whether any derelictions of duty or errors of judgment on the part of United States Army or Navy personnel contributed to such successes as were achieved by the enemy on the occasion mentioned; and, if so, what these derelictions or errors were, and who were responsible therefor." This inquiry was commenced on December 18, 1941, and was concluded on January 23, 1942. The record of its proceedings and exhibits covers 2,173 printed pages. Members of the Commission were Mr. Justice Owen J. Roberts, United States Supreme Court, Chairman; Admiral William H. Standley, United States Navy, retired; Rear Adm. Joseph M. Reeves, United States Navy, retired; Maj. Gen. Frank R. McCoy, United States Army, retired; and Brig. Gen. Joseph T. McNarney, United States Army.

The Hart Inquiry

The inquiry conducted by Admiral Thomas C. Hart, United States Navy, retired, was initiated by precept dated February 12, 1944, from Secretary of the Navy Frank Knox to Admiral Hart "For an Examination of Witnesses and the Taking of Testimony Pertinent to the Japanese Attack on Pearl Harbor, Territory of Hawaii." The precept stated "* * * Whereas certain members of the naval forces, who have knowledge pertinent to the foregoing matters, are now or soon may be on dangerous assignments at great distances from the United States * * * it is now deemed necessary, in order to prevent evidence being lost by death or unavoidable absence of those certain members of the naval forces, that their testimony, pertinent to the aforesaid Japanese attack, be recorded and preserved, * * *"
This inquiry was commenced on February 12, 1944, and was concluded on June 15, 1944. The record of its proceedings and exhibits covers 565 printed pages.

The Army Pearl Harbor Board

The Army Pearl Harbor Board was appointed pursuant to the provisions of Public Law 339, Seventy-eighth Congress, approved June 13, 1944, and by order dated July 8, 1944, of The Adjutant General, War Department. The board was directed "to ascertain and report the facts relating to the attack made by Japanese armed forces upon the Territory of Hawaii on December 7, 1941, and to make such recommendations as it may deem proper." The board held sessions beginning July 20, 1944, and concluded its investigation on October 20, 1944. The record of its proceedings and exhibits covers 3,357 printed pages. Members of the board were Lt. Gen. George Grunert, president; Maj. Gen. Henry D. Russell and Maj. Gen. Walter A. Frank.

The Navy Court of Inquiry

The Navy Court of Inquiry was appointed pursuant to the provisions of Public Law 339, Seventy-eighth Congress, approved June 13, 1944, and by order dated July 13, 1944, of the Secretary of the Navy James Forrestal. The court was ordered to thoroughly "inquire into the attack made by Japanese armed forces on Pearl Harbor, Territory of Hawaii, on 7 December 1941 * * * and will include in its findings a full statement of the facts it may deem to be established. The court will further give its opinion as to whether any offenses have been committed or serious blame incurred on the part of any person or persons in the naval service, and in case its opinion be that offenses have been committed or serious blame incurred, will specifically recommend what further proceedings should be had." The court held sessions beginning July 24, 1944, and concluded its inquiry on October 19, 1944. The record of its proceedings and exhibits covers 1,397 printed pages. Members of the court were Admiral Orin G. Murfin, retired, president; Admiral Edward C. Kalbfus, retired, and Vice Adm. Adolphus Andrews, retired.

The Clarke Inquiry

The investigation conducted by Col. Carter W. Clarke "regarding the manner in which certain Top Secret communications were handled" was pursuant to oral instructions of Gen. George C. Marshall, Chief of Staff, United States Army. Colonel Clarke was appointed by Maj. Gen. Clayton Bissell, Chief of the Military Intelligence Division, War Department, under authority of a letter dated September 9, 1944, from The Adjutant General. This investigation was conducted from September 14 to 16, 1944, and from July 13 to August 4, 1945. Testimony was taken concerning the handling of intercepted Japanese messages known as Magic, the handling of intelligence material by the Military Intelligence Division, War Department, and the handling of the message sent by General Marshall to Lt. Gen. Walter C. Short at Hawaii on the morning of December 7, 1941. The record of the proceedings of this investigation, together with its exhibits, covers 225 printed pages.

The Clausen Investigation

Secretary of War Henry L. Stimson announced on December 1, 1944, that the report of the Army Pearl Harbor board had been submitted to him, and that: "In accordance with the opinion of the Judge Advocate General, I have decided that my own investigation should be further continued until all the facts are made as clear as possible, and until the testimony of every witness in possession of material facts can be obtained, and I have given the necessary directions to accomplish this result." By memorandum dated February 6, 1945, for Army personnel concerned, Secretary Stimson stated that "Pursuant to my directions and in accordance with my public statement of 1 December 1944, Major Henry C. Clausen, JAGD, is conducting for me the investigation supplementary to the proceedings of the Army Pearl Harbor Board." This investigation was commenced on November 23, 1944 and was concluded on September 12, 1945. The record of its proceedings and exhibits covers 695 printed pages.

THE HEWITT INQUIRY

The inquiry conducted by Admiral H. Kent Hewitt, United States Navy, was initiated under precept dated May 2, 1945, from Secretary of the Navy James Forrestal to conduct "Further investigation of facts pertinent to the Japanese attack on Pearl Harbor, Territory of Hawaii, on 7 December 1941." The precept stated that upon review of the evidence obtained by the examinations conducted by Admiral Thomas C. Hart and by the Navy Court of Inquiry, "the Secretary (of Navy) has found that there were errors of judgment on the part of certain officers in the Naval Service, both at Pearl Harbor and at Washington. The Secretary has further found that the previous investigations have not exhausted all possible evidence. Accordingly he has decided that the investigation directed by Public Law 339 of the 78th Congress should be further continued until the testimony of every witness in possession of material facts can be obtained and all possible evidence exhausted. * * * You are hereby detailed to make a study of the enclosures (Proceedings of Hart Inquiry and Navy Court of Inquiry) and then to conduct such further investigation, including the examination of any additional persons who may have knowledge of the facts pertinent to the said Japanese attack, and to reexamine any such person who has been previously examined, as may appear necessary, and to record the testimony given thereby." This inquiry commenced on May 14, 1945, and was concluded on July 11, 1945. The record of its proceedings and exhibits covers 1,342 printed pages.

NAMES AND POSITIONS OF PRINCIPAL ARMY
AND NAVY OFFICIALS IN WASHINGTON AND AT
HAWAII AT THE TIME OF THE ATTACK ALONG
WITH THE LEADING WITNESSES IN
THE VARIOUS PROCEEDINGS

NAMES AND POSITIONS OF PRINCIPAL ARMY AND NAVY OFFICIALS IN WASHINGTON AND AT HAWAII AT THE TIME OF THE ATTACK ALONG WITH THE LEADING WITNESSES IN THE VARIOUS PROCEEDINGS

ORGANIZATION AND PERSONNEL WAR DEPARTMENT DEC. 7, 1941

Secretary of War, Henry L. Stimson.
Chief of Staff, Gen. George C. Marshall.
Deputy Chiefs of Staff:
General Administration and Ground Forces, Maj. Gen. William Bryden.
Armed Forces and Supply, Maj. Gen. Richard C. Moore.
Air, Maj. Gen. Henry H. Arnold.
Secretary, General Staff, Col. Walter Bedell Smith.
Assistant Secretary, General Staff, Col. John R. Deane.
G–1 (Personnel Division), Brig. Gen. Wade H. Haislip.
G–2 (Intelligence Division), Brig. Gen. Sherman Miles.
Administrative Branch, Col. Ralph C. Smith.
Counterintelligence Branch, Lt. Col. John T. Bissell.
Intelligence Branch, Col. Hayes A. Kroner.
Administrative Section, Lt. Col. Moses W. Pettigrew.
Situation Section, Lt. Col. Thomas J. Betts.
Far Eastern Section, Col. Rufus S. Bratton.
Assistant, Col. Carlysle C. Dusenbury.
G–3 (Operations and Training Division), Brig. Gen. Harry L. Twaddle.
G–4 (Supply Division), Brig. Gen. Brehon B. Somervell.
War Plans Division, Brig. Gen. Leonard T. Gerow.
Executive officer, Maj. Charles K. Gailey, Jr.
Plans Group, Col. Charles W. Bundy.
Projects Group, Col. Robert W. Crawford.
Chief Signal Officer, Maj. Gen. Dawson Olmstead.
Operations Branch, Col. Otis K. Sadtler.
Traffic Division and Signal Center, Col. Edward T. French.
Signal Intelligence Service, Col. Rex W. Minckler.
Principal Cryptanalyst, William F. Friedman.
Communication Liaison Division, Lt. Col. W. T. Guest.

ARMY AIR FORCES

(Under over-all command of General Marshall)

Commanding General, Maj. Gen. Henry H. Arnold.
Chief of Air Staff, Brig. Gen. Martin F. Scanlon.
Air Forces Combat Command, Lt. Gen. Delos C. Emmons.
Air Corps, Maj. Gen. George Brett.

ORGANIZATION AND PERSONNEL, NAVY DEPARTMENT, DEC. 7, 1941

Secretary of the Navy, Frank Knox.
Chief of Naval Operations, Admiral Harold R. Stark.
 Administrative aide and flag secretary, Capt. Charles Wellborn, Jr.
 Aide, Capt. John L. McCrea.
Assistant Chief of Naval Operations, Rear Adm. Royal E. Ingersoll.
War Plans Division, Rear Adm. Richmond K. Turner.
 Pacific Ocean and Asiatic Areas Section, Capt. Robert O. Glover.
Central Division (State Department liaison), Capt. R. E. Schuirmann.
Ship Movements Division, Vice Adm. Roland M. Brainard.
 War Information Room, Rear Adm. F. T. Leighton.
Intelligence Division, Rear Adm. Theodore S. Wilkinson.
 Domestic Branch and Assistant, Rear Adm. Howard F. Kingman.
 Foreign Branch, Capt. William A. Heard.
  Far Eastern Section, Capt. Arthur H. McCollum.
Communications Division, Rear Adm. Leigh Noyes.
 Assistant, Capt. Joseph R. Redman.
 Security (Intelligence) Section, Capt. L. F. Safford.
 Translation Section, Lt. Comdr. A. D. Kramer (on loan from Far Eastern Section, Intelligence Division).
 Cryptographic Research:
  (Decrypting) Section:
   Senior watch officer, Lt. (jg) George W. Lynn.
   Watch officers, Lt. (jg) Alfred V. Pering, Lt. (jg) F. M. Brotherhood, Lt. (jg) Allan A. Murray.
 Correlating and Dissemination Section, Lt. Fredrick L. Freeman.

ORGANIZATION AND PERSONNEL, HAWAIIAN DEPARTMENT, DEC. 7, 1941

Commanding General, Lt. Gen. Walter C. Short.
Chief of Staff, Col. Walter C. Phillips.
G–1 (Personnel), Lt. Col. Russell C. Throckmorton.
G–2 (Intelligence), Lt. Col. Kendall J. Fielder.
 Assistant G–2, Lt. Col. George W. Bicknell.
G–3 (Operations and Training), Lt. Col. William E. Donegan.
G–4 (Supply), Col. Morrill W. Marston.
 Assistant G–4, Maj. Robert J. Fleming.
Adjutant General, Col. Robert H. Dunlop.
Chemical Warfare, Lt. Col. G. F. Unmacht.
Ordnance, Col. W. A. Capron.
Judge Advocate General, Col. T. H. Green.
Provost Marshal, Lt. Col. Melvin L. Craig.
Engineer, Col. A. K. B. Lyman.
Quartermaster, Col. William R. White.
Finance, Col. E. S. Ely.
Signal Corps, Lt. Col. Carrol A. Powell.
Inspector General, Col. Lathe B. Row.
Surgeon General, Col. Edgar King.
Twenty-fourth Infantry Division, Brig. Gen. Durward S. Wilson.
Twenty-fifth Infantry Division, Maj. Gen. Maxwell Murray.
Coast Artillery Command, Maj. Gen. Henry T. Burgin.

HAWAIIAN AIR FORCE

(Under over-all command of General Short)

Commanding General, Maj. Gen. Frederick L. Martin.
Chief of Staff, Col. James A. Mollison.
Intelligence, Col. Edward W. Raley.
Signal Officer, Lt. Col. Clay I. Hoppough.
Eighteenth Bombardment Wing, Brig. Gen. Jacob H. Rudolph.
Fourteenth Pursuit Wing, Brig. Gen. Howard C. Davidson.
Hickam Field, Col. W. E. Farthing.
Wheeler Field, Col. William J. Flood.
Bellows Field, Lt. Col. Leonard D. Weddington.

STAFF OF COMMANDER IN CHIEF, U. S. FLEET AND U. S. PACIFIC FLEET, DEC. 7, 1941

Commander in chief, Admiral Husband E. Kimmel.
Chief of Staff and personal aide, Capt. W. W. Smith.
Flag Secretary and personal aide, Lt. Comdr. P. C. Crosley.
Operations Officer and Assistant Chief of Staff, Capt. W. S. DeLany.
    First assistant operations officer, Commander R. F. Good.
    Second assistant operations officer, Lt. Comdr. H. L. Collins.
War Plans Officer, Capt. Charles H. McMorris.
    Assistants, Commander V. R. Murphy, Commander L. D. McCormick, Lt. F. R. DuBorg.
    Assistant War Plans and Marine Officer, Col. O. T. Pheifer, United States Marine Corps.
Communications officer, Commander M. E. Curts.
    Assistant, Lt. (jg) W. J. East, Jr.
Security officer, Lt. Allan Reed.
Radio officer, Lt. Comdr. D. C. Beard.
Public Relations officer, Lt. Comdr. W. W. Drake.
    Assistant, Lt. (jg) J. E. Bassett.
Maintenance officer, Commander H. D. Clark.
Medical officer, Capt. E. A. M. Gendreau, United States Marine Corps.
Gunnery officer, Commander W. A. Kitts III.
Aviation officer, Commander Howard C. Davis.
Aerologist and personnel officer, Lt. Comdr. R. B. Black.

Commander, Navy Pacific Fleet Air Wing, Rear Adm. P. N. L. Bellinger. Also commander Hawaiian Based Patrol Wings 1 and 2; commander, Fleet Air Detachment, Ford Island, Pearl Harbor; commander, Naval Base Defense Air Force (under commandant, Fourteenth Naval District as naval base defense officer, Pacific Fleet.)
Operations officer, Capt. Logan C. Ramsey.

Commander Battle Force (Task Force 1), Vice Adm. W. S. Pye.
Commander Aircraft, Battle Force (Task Force 2), Vice Adm. William F. Halsey.
Commander Scouting Force (Task Force 3), Vice Adm. Wilson Brown.
Commander Task Force 4, Rear Adm. Claude C. Bloch.

Commander Submarines Scouting Force (Task Force 7), Rear Adm. Thomas Withers.

Commander Task Force 9, Rear Adm. P. N. L. Bellinger.

Commander Base Force (Task Force 15), Rear Adm. W. L. Calhoun.

ORGANIZATION AND PERSONNEL, FOURTEENTH NAVAL DISTRICT, DEC. 7, 1941

Commandant (also commander, Hawaiian Naval Coastal Sea Frontier; commandant, Pearl Harbor Navy Yard; commander of local defense forces, and, as an officer of Pacific Fleet, the naval base defense officer; commander Task Force 4, United States Pacific Fleet), Rear Admiral Claude C. Bloch.

Chief of Staff, Capt. J. B. Earle.

Intelligence officer, Capt. Irving H. Mayfield.

Counterespionage Section, Lt. William B. Stephensen.

Communications Security (Intelligence) Unit, Commander Joseph J. Rochefort.

Translator, Col. Alva B. Lasswell, United States Marine Corps.

Cryptanalyst, Lt. (jg) F. C. Woodward, Commander Wesley A. Wright (on loan from staff of Admiral Kimmel, where he was assistant communications officer).

LIST OF WITNESSES APPEARING BEFORE THE JOINT COMMITTEE AND THEIR ASSIGNMENTS AS OF DECEMBER 7, 1941

Beardall, John R., rear admiral; naval aide to President Roosevelt.

Beatty, Frank E., rear admiral; aide to Secretary of the Navy Frank Knox.

Bellinger, P. N. L., vice admiral, commander Hawaiian Naval Base Air Force (commander Patrol Wing 2).

Bicknell, George W., colonel, assistant chief, Military Intelligence Service, Hawaiian Department.

Bratton, Rufus S., colonel, chief, Far Eastern Section, Military Intelligence Service, War Department.

Clausen, Henry C., lieutenant colonel,[1] Judge Advocate General's Office, assisting Army Pearl Harbor Board and conducting supplemental investigation for Secretary of War.

Creighton, John M., captain, U. S. N., naval observer, Singapore.

Dillon, John H., major, U. S. M. C., aide to Secretary Knox.

Elliott, George E., sergeant, A. U. S., operator at Opana radar detector station, Oahu, T. H.

Gerow, Leonard T., major general, Chief, War Plans Division, Army General Staff, War Department.

Grew, Joseph C., United States Ambassador to Japan.

Hart, Thomas C., admiral, commander in chief, Asiatic Fleet.

Hull, Cordell, Secretary of State.

Ingersoll, Royal E., admiral, Assistant Chief of Naval Operations, Navy Department.

Inglis, R. B., rear admiral,[1] presented to committee Navy summary of Pearl Harbor attack.

Kimmel, Husband E., rear admiral, commander in chief, United States Fleet; commander in chief, Pacific Fleet.

Kramer, A. D., commander, Section Chief, Division of Naval Communications, handling translations and recovery of intercepted Japanese codes.

Krick, Harold D., captain, U. S. N., former flag secretary to Admiral Stark.

Leahy, William D., admiral, Chief of Staff to the President.

Layton, Edwin T., captain, U. S. N., fleet intelligence officer, Pacific Fleet.

Marshall, George C., general, Chief of Staff, United States Army, War Department.

McCollum, Arthur N., captain, U. S. N., Chief, Far Eastern Section, Office of Naval Intelligence, Navy Department.

Miles, Sherman, major general, Chief, Military Intelligence Service, Army General Staff, War Department.

Noyes, Leigh, rear admiral, Chief, Office of Naval Communications, Navy Department.

Phillips, Walter C., colonel, Chief of Staff to General Short.

Richardson, J. O., admiral, former commander in chief, United States Fleet and Pacific Fleet.

Roberts, Owen J., Mr. Justice,[1] Chairman, Roberts Commission.

Rochefort, Joseph John, captain, U. S. N., communications intelligence officer, Pacific Fleet.

Sadtler, Otis K., colonel, Chief, Military Branch, Army Signal Corps, War Department.

Safford, L. F., captain, U. S. N., Chief, Radio Intelligence Unit, Office of Naval Communications, Navy Department.

Schukraft, Robert E., colonel, Chief, Radio Intercept Unit, Army Signal Corps, War Department.

Schulz, Lester Robert, commander, assistant to Admiral Beardall.

Short, Walter C., major general, commanding general, Hawaiian Department.

Smith, William W., rear admiral, Chief of Staff to Admiral Kimmel.

Sonnett, John F., lieutenant commander,[1] Special Assistant to the Secretary of the Navy, and assistant to Admiral H. K. Hewitt in his inquiry.

Stark, Harold R., admiral, Chief of Naval Operations, Navy Department.

Stimson, Henry L., Secretary of War (sworn statement and sworn replies to interrogatories only).

Thielen, Bernard, colonel,[1] presented to committee Army summary of Pearl Harbor attack.

Turner, Richmond K., rear admiral, Chief, War Plans Division, Navy, Department.

Welles, Sumner, Under Secretary of State.

Wilkinson, T. S., rear admiral, Chief, Office of Naval Intelligence, Navy Department.

Zacharias, Ellis M., captain, United States Navy, commanding officer, U. S. S. *Salt Lake City*, Pacific Fleet.

---

[1] Denotes witness whose connection with this investigation relates to his assignment after December 7, 1941.

List of Leading Witnesses in Prior Proceedings Who Did Not
Testify Before the Joint Committee, and Their Assignments
as of December 7, 1941

Arnold, H. H., general, commanding general, Army Air Forces, War
Department.

Bissell, John T., colonel, executive officer, Counter Intelligence
Group, Military Intelligence Division, War Department.

Bloch, Claude C., admiral, commandant, Fourteenth Naval District;
commander, Hawaiian Sea Frontier; Pearl Harbor Naval Base
defense officer.

Brotherhood, Francis M., lieutenant (junior grade), watch officer,
Security Section, Office of Naval Communications, Navy Department.

Brown, Wilson, rear admiral, commander, Scouting Force (Task
Force 3) Pacific Fleet.

Calhoun, W. L., vice admiral, commander Base Force, Pacific Fleet.

Crosley, Paul C., commander; flag secretary to Admiral Kimmel.

Curts, M. E., captain, U. S. N., communication officer, Pacific Fleet,
and liaison officer, Radio and Sound Division.

Davidson, Howard C., major general, commanding general, Fourteenth Pursuit Wing, Hawaiian Air Force.

Davis, Howard C., rear admiral, fleet aviation officer, Pacific Fleet.

DeLany, Walter S., rear admiral, Chief of Staff for Operations, staff
of commander in chief, Pacific Fleet.

Dusenbury, Carlisle Clyde, colonel, assistant to Col. R. S. Bratton,
Far Eastern Section, Military Intelligence Division, War Department.

Fielder, Kendall J., colonel, Chief, Military Intelligence Division,
Hawaiian Department.

French, Edward F., colonel, officer in charge, Traffic Division and
Signal Center, Signal Corps, War Department.

Friedman, William F., principal cryptanalyst, Signal Ingellitence
Service, Signal Corps, War Department.

Halsey, William F., admiral, commander Aircraft Battle Force
(Task Force 2), Pacific Fleet.

Hamilton, Maxwell M., Chief, Division of Far Eastern Affairs, State
Department.

Heard, William A., captain U. S. N., Chief, Foreign Branch, Office of
Naval Intelligence, Navy Department.

Herron, Charles D., major general, former commanding general,
Hawaiian Department.

Hornbeck, Stanley K., adviser on foreign relations, State Department.

Kitts, Willard A., III, rear admiral, fleet gunnery officer, staff of commander in chief, Pacific Fleet.

Kroner, Hayes A., brigadier general, Chief, Intelligence Branch, Military Intelligence Division, War Department.

Lockard, Joseph L., lieutenant A. U. S., operator OPAN radar detector station, Oahu, T. H.

Lynn, George W., lieutenant commander, senior watch officer, Security Section, Office of Naval Communications, Navy Department.

MacArthur, Douglas, general, commanding general, United States
Army Forces in the Far East.

Martin, F. L., major general, commanding general, Hawaiian Air Force.

Mayfield, Irving H., captain U. S N., Chief, Office of Naval Intelligence, Fourteenth Naval District.

McDonald, Joseph P., sergeant, Five Hundred and Eightieth Aircraft Warning Company, assigned as telephone switchboard operator, operations center, Aircraft Warning Service, Hawaiian Department.

McMorris, C. H., rear admiral, war plans officer, staff of commander in chief, Pacific Fleet.

Murray, Allan A., lieutenant commander, watch officer, Cryptographic (Decrypting) Unit, Security Section, Office of Naval Communications, Navy Department.

Newton, J. H., vice admiral, commander, Cruisers Scouting Force, Pacific Fleet.

Nimitz, C. W., admiral, Chief, Bureau of Navigation (now Personnel), Navy Department.

O'Dell, Robert H., lieutenant A. U. S., assistant military attaché, American Legation, Melbourne, Australia, under Col. Van S. Merle-Smith, military attaché.

Pering, Alfred V., lieutenant commander, watch officer, Security Section, Office of Naval Communications, Navy Department.

Pettigrew, Moses W., colonel, executive officer, Intelligence Group, Military Intelligence Division, War Department.

Poindexter, Joseph B., governor, Governor of the Territory of Hawaii.

Powell, C. A., colonel, chief signal officer, Hawaiian Department.

Pye, William S., vice admiral, commander Battle Force (Task Force 1), Pacific Fleet.

Ramsey, Logan C., captain U. S. N., operations officer, Commander Patrol Wing 2 (Admiral Bellinger), Pacific Fleet, and Commander Patrol Wings, Hawaiian Area.

Redman, Joseph R., rear admiral, Assistant Director, Office of Naval Communications, Navy Department.

Schuirmann, R. E., rear admiral, Director, Central Division, Office of Chief of Naval Operations, Navy Department.

Shivers, Robert L., special agent in charge, Federal Bureau of Investigation, Department of Justice, Honolulu, T. H.

Smith-Hutton, H. H., captain U. S. N., naval attaché, United States Embassy, Tokyo, Japan.

Stimson, Henry L., Secretary of War.

Sutherland, Richard K., lieutenant general, Chief of Staff to General MacArthur.

Taylor, William E. G., commander, temporary duty with Army Interceptor Command, Hawaiian Air Force, as adviser for establishment of aircraft warning service.

Tyler, Kermit A., lieutenant colonel, executive officer, Eighth Pursuit Squadron, Hawaiian Air Force, on duty December 7, 1941 at information center, Aircraft Warning Service, Hawaiian Department.

Willoughby, C. A., major general, Chief, Military Intelligence Division, staff of General MacArthur.

Wilson, Durward S., major general, commanding general, Twenty-fourth Division, Hawaiian Department.

Withers, Thomas, rear admiral, commander submarines, Pacific Fleet.

COMMUNICATIONS FROM THE PRESIDENT OF THE UNITED STATES RELATING TO THE PEARL HARBOR INVESTIGATION

COMMUNICATIONS FROM THE PRESIDENT OF THE
UNITED STATES RELATING TO THE PEARL HARBOR
INVESTIGATION

THE WHITE HOUSE,
Washington, October 13, 1945.

Hon. ALBEN W. BARKLEY,
United States Senate, Washington, D. C.

DEAR SENATOR BARKLEY: Replying to your letter of the 5th,
regarding the appointment of someone in the Executive Offices to
consult with the committee and its counsel, I am appointing Judge
Latta, who has been in charge of all the files in the White House for
the past 28 years.

Any information that you want will be cheerfully supplied by him.

For your information all the files of the previous administration
have been moved to the Archives Building and Hyde Park. If there
is any difficulty about your having access to them I'll be glad to issue
the necessary order so that you may have complete access.

Sincerely yours,

HARRY S. TRUMAN.

———

[Copy]

AUGUST 28, 1945.

Memorandum for—
    The Secretary of State.
    The Secretary of War.
    The Secretary of the Navy.
    The Attorney General.
    The Joint Chiefs of Staff.
    The Director of the Budget.
    The Director of the Office of War Information.

Appropriate departments of the Government and the Joint Chiefs
of Staff are hereby directed to take such steps as are necessary to
prevent release to the public, except with the specific approval of the
President in each case, of—

Information regarding the past or present status, technique or procedures, degree of success attained, or any specific results of any
cryptanalytic unit acting under the authority of the United States
Government or any Department thereof.

HARRY S. TRUMAN.

Restricted.

Memorandum for—

The Secretary of State.
The Secretary of War.
The Secretary of Navy.
The Joint Chiefs of Staff.

In order to assist the Joint Congressional Committee on the Investigation of the Pearl Harbor Attack in its desire to hold public hearings and make public pertinent evidence relating to the circumstances of that attack, a specific exception to my memorandum dated August 28, 1945, relating to the release of information concerning cryptanalytic activities, is hereby made as follows:

The State, War, and Navy Departments will make available to the Joint Committee on the Investigation of the Pearl Harbor Attack, for such use as the committee may determine, any information in their possession material to the investigation, and will respectively authorize any employee or member of the armed services whose testimony is desired by the committee to testify publicly before the committee concerning any matter pertinent to the investigation.

(Signed) Harry S. Truman,
HARRY S. TRUMAN.

Approved October 23, 1945.

———

THE WHITE HOUSE,
Washington, November 7, 1945.

MEMORANDUM FOR THE CHIEF EXECUTIVES OF ALL EXECUTIVE DEPARTMENTS, AGENCIES, COMMISSIONS, AND BUREAUS, INCLUDING THE JOINT CHIEFS OF STAFF

Section 3 of the concurrent resolution creating the Joint Congressional Committee on the Investigation of the Pearl Harbor Attack reads as follows:

SEC. 3. The testimony of any person in the armed services, and the fact that such person testified before the joint committee herein provided for, shall not be used against him in any court proceeding or held against him in examining his military status for credits in the service to which he belongs.

In order to assist the joint committee to make a full and complete investigation of the facts relating to the events leading up to or following the attack, you are requested to authorize every person in your respective departments or agencies, if they are interrogated by the committee or its counsel, to give any information of which they may have knowledge bearing on the subject of the committee's investigation.

You are further requested to authorize them whether or not they are interrogated by the committee or its counsel to come forward voluntarily and disclose to the committee or to its counsel any information they may have on the subject of the inquiry which they may have any reason to think may not already have been disclosed to the committee.

This directive is applicable to all persons in your departments or agencies, whether they are in the armed services or not and whether or not they are called to testify before the joint committee.

HARRY S. TRUMAN.

MEMORANDUM FOR THE CHIEF EXECUTIVES OF ALL EXECUTIVE DEPART-
MENTS, AGENCIES, COMMISSIONS, AND BUREAUS, INCLUDING THE
JOINT CHIEFS OF STAFF

With further reference to my letter of November 7, 1945, addressed
to the above executives, you are requested further to authorize every
person in your respective departments or agencies, whether or not
they are interrogated by the committee or its counsel, to come forward and disclose orally to any of the members of the Joint Congressional Committee on the Investigation of the Pearl Harbor Attack
any information they may have on the subject of the inquiry which
they may have any reason to think has not already been disclosed
to the committee.

This does not include any files or written material.

(Handwritten) O. K.
H. S. T.

REVIEW OF THE DIPLOMATIC CONVERSATIONS BETWEEN THE UNITED STATES AND JAPAN, AND RELATED MATTERS, FROM THE ATLANTIC CONFERENCE IN AUGUST 1941 THROUGH DECEMBER 8, 1941

Appendix D

REVIEW OF THE DIPLOMATIC CONVERSATIONS BETWEEN THE UNITED STATES AND JAPAN, AND RELATED MATTERS, FROM THE ATLANTIC CONFERENCE IN AUGUST, 1941 THROUGH DECEMBER 8, 1941

INTRODUCTORY STATEMENT

This appendix reviews, upon the basis of the record before the Committee and in greater detail than in Part I of the report to which it is annexed, the diplomatic conversations between the United States and Japan, and related matters, from the Atlantic Conference in August 1941 through December 8, 1941. While it is not to be regarded as including all of the material contained in the record before the Committee that touches upon those conversations during that period, it does attempt to set forth the material facts in connection therewith.

Prior to the Committee's investigation, nearly all of the information concerning the diplomatic conversations during 1941 between the United States and Japan that had been made public was contained in the official State Department publications, "Peace and War" (ex. 28)[1] and "Foreign Relations of the United States, Japan, 1931–1941" (ex. 29), together with former Ambassador Joseph C. Grew's book, "Ten Years in Japan" (ex. 30), which were published during the war and were subject to wartime restrictions. To the basic material contained in those publications, the Committee has added hundreds of documents, personal as well as official, from the files of the State Department and of the late President Franklin D. Roosevelt. In addition, the Committee has received in evidence hundreds of messages between the Japanese Foreign Office in Tokyo and the Japanese Ambassadors in Washington, as intercepted, translated, and available at the time to high officials in the United States Government in Washington, including President Roosevelt and Secretary of State Cordell Hull. There is also before the Committee testimony of former Secretary of State Hull and of former United States Ambassador in Japan Joseph C. Grew, a prepared statement and answers to interrogatories submitted by former Secretary of War Henry L. Stimson, and collateral (regarding diplomatic matters) testimony of Gen. George C. Marshall, Admiral Harold R. Stark, and other high-ranking officers of the Army and Navy. The record before the Committee also contains hundreds of captured Japanese documents, as well as reports of interrogations conducted in Japan for the supreme allied commander, Gen. Douglas MacArthur, at the request of the Committee, many of which are directly concerned with the diplomatic events immediately preceding Pearl Harbor, including an authoritative translation of the memoirs of Prince Fumimaro Konoye, Premier of Japan until October

---

[1] All references in this appendix indicated in this manner are to exhibits introduced at the hearings before the Committee.

16, 1941. This mass of testimony and documentary evidence, from so many different and independent sources, and including official documents of the Japanese and other governments, as well as of the United States Government, affords countless opportunities for verification by cross-checking.

By interweaving the diplomatic material contained in the documentary evidence and testimony before the Committee, this appendix attempts to reconstruct chronologically the significant events in the diplomatic conversations between the United States and Japan during the 4 months that immediately preceded the Japanese attack on Pearl Harbor. Only thus, for example, can the intercepted Japanese diplomatic messages between Tokyo and Washington be examined in the surrounding circumstances in which they were first seen by high officials in the United States Government, for those messages were the day-to-day instructions sent by the Japanese Foreign Office in Tokyo to the Japanese Ambassadors in Washington for the purpose of guiding them in their conversations with Secretary Hull and President Roosevelt, and the Ambassadors' reports and comments to the Japanese Foreign Office concerning those conversations. While in American hands the diplomatic messages between Tokyo and Washington not only provided Secretary Hull and President Roosevelt with advance knowledge of the Japanese plans for the conduct of the conversations but also were one of the most important and significant types of intelligence information available to the Army and Navy in Washington, they did not contain any information pointing toward Pearl Harbor as a possible target of Japanese attack.

Since the report to which this appendix is annexed discusses in detail the military aspects and implications of the diplomatic conversations between the United States and Japan and of the intercepted Japanese diplomatic messages between Tokyo and Washington, no attempt is made here to tie in the events on the "diplomatic front" with the various warning messages sent by the Army and Navy from Washington to the commanders in the Pacific, although the latter messages were to a considerable extent based upon the state of Japanese-American diplomatic relations at the time they were dispatched. Neither does this appendix attempt to describe the process of building up American military strength in the Pacific area which was underway during the period in question, although by taking up the Marshall-Stark joint memoranda of November 5 and November 27 in connection with the events that gave rise to each, it does indicate in general terms the over-all military and naval considerations that affected American policies in the Pacific during the latter part of 1941. Parenthetically, it may be noted here that the inherent relationship between diplomatic policies and military and naval power was succinctly stated by Secretary Hull when he testified before the Committee that soon after he came to the State Department he learned that the representatives of the aggressor nations with whom he talked "were looking over my shoulder at our Navy and our Army," and that the diplomatic strength of the United States went up or down with their estimate of what the United States Army and Navy "amounted to."

The record before the Committee shows that the United States Government participated in the conversations with Japan in an effort to dissuade the Japanese Government from its course of military aggression and its Axis ties with Germany and Italy. The fact that the United States was engaging in such conversations with Japan was believed to strengthen the position of the elements in that country who disapproved of the policies of those who dominated the Japanese Government; success in negotiations with Japan on the basis of the principles to which the United States Government adhered would have had many material and other advantages for both the United States and Japan. American participation in the conversations had the further purpose of giving the United States Army and Navy more time to prepare their defense of areas in the Pacific regarded as vital to the safety and security of the United States. Recognition of this dual purpose is the key to an understanding of the day-to-day course of the conversations. Every action taken, every move made, on the American side must be considered in the light of those objectives.

BRIEF RÉSUMÉ OF THE JAPANESE-AMERICAN CONVERSATIONS PRIOR TO THE ATLANTIC CONFERENCE

This narrative begins in August, 1941 with the President of the United States and the Prime Minister of Great Britain, in conference on a warship off the coast of Newfoundland, discussing how to prevent the outbreak of war with Japan. It ends on December 7–8, 1941, with Japanese bombs falling on ships of the United States Pacific Fleet in Pearl Harbor, with Japanese troops invading Thailand and British Malaya, and with other Japanese attacks on Singapore, Hong Kong, the Philippine Islands, Guam, Wake, and Midway.

Into the intervening 4 months were crowded events the causes of which lay deeper and were more fundamental than the Japanese occupation of southern French Indochina in July or the breaking off of the Japanese-American conversations and the freezing of Japanese assets in the United States which had immediately followed that Japanese move. By August 1941, there was but a slim chance that the Japanese Government would "reverse the engine," as Ambassador Grew expressed it, and abandon the course of aggression through force of arms to which it had been committed. Although it was true that the informal conversations in Washington between the new Japanese Ambassador, Admiral Kichisaburo Nomura, had revealed an apparent willingness on the part of the Japanese Government to go along with certain of the peaceful principles to which the United States was committed, *provided those principles were stated in sufficiently general terms to make their application in specific situations wholly unpredictable,* those conversations had disclosed three crucial points of difference between the two Governments: the question of nondiscrimination in international trade, the question of the withdrawal of Japanese troops from China, and the question of Japan's obligations under the Tripartite Pact.

During the latter part of January 1941, through private Japanese and American citizens, the suggestion had reached President Roosevelt and Secretary Hull that the Japanese Government would welcome an opportunity to alter its political alignments and modify its attitude toward the "China Incident" (ex. 29, vol. II, pp. 328–329; ex. 179). The initial reaction of the United States Government had been one of caution (ex. 29, vol. II, p. 330). Secretary Hull testified that—

In the light of Japan's past and current record and in view of the wide divergences between the policies which the United States and Japan had been pursuing in the Far East, I estimated from the outset that there was not 1 chance in 20 or 1 in 50 or even 1 in 100 of reaching a peaceful settlement. Existing treaties relating to the Far East were adequate, provided the signatory governments lived up to them. We were, therefore, not calling for new agreements. But if there was a chance that new agreements would contribute to peace in the Pacific, the President and I believed that we should not neglect that possibility, slim as it was.

We had in mind doing everything we could to bring about a peaceful, fair and stabilizing settlement of the situation throughout the Pacific area. Such a course was in accordance with the traditional attitudes and beliefs of the American people. Moreover, the President and I constantly had very much in mind the advice of our highest military authorities who kept emphasizing to us the imperative need of having time to build up preparations for defense vital not only to the United States but to many other countries resisting aggression. Our decision to enter into the conversations with the Japanese was, therefore, in line with our need to rearm for self-defense.

The President and I fully realized that the Japanese government could not, even if it wished, bring about an abrupt transformation in Japan's course of aggression. We realized that so much was involved in a reconstruction of Japan's position that implementation to any substantial extent by Japan of promises to adopt peaceful courses would require a long time. We were, therefore, prepared to be patient in an endeavor to persuade Japan to turn from her course of aggression. We carried no chip on our shoulder, but we were determined to stand by a basic position, built on fundamental principles which we applied not only to Japan but to all countries (tr. 1101–1102).[1]

In his early conversations with Ambassador Nomura, who reached Washington in February 1941, Secretary Hull had expressed the hope that the Japanese Government might have something definite in mind that would offer a practical approach to a general settlement of the problems in the Pacific, and had indicated the willingness of the United States Government to consider any proposal which the Japanese Government might offer that was consistent with the principles to which, the Secretary had made it clear, the United States was committed (ex. 29, vol. II, pp. 331–332). Secretary Hull testified as follows regarding his meeting on April 16, 1941, with Ambassador Nomura:

On April 16, I had a further conversation with the Japanese Ambassador. I pointed out that *the one paramount preliminary question about which our Government was concerned was a definite assurance in advance that the Japanese Government had the willingness and power to abandon its present doctrine of conquest by force and to adopt four principles which our Government regarded as the foundation upon which relations between nations should rest*, as follows:

(1) Respect for the territorial integrity and the sovereignty of each and all nations;
(2) Support of the principle of noninterference in the internal affairs of other countries;
(3) Support of the principle of equality, including equality of commercial opportunity;
(4) Nondisturbance of the *status quo* in the Pacific except as the *status quo* may be altered by peaceful means.

I told the Japanese Ambassador that our Government was willing to consider any proposal which the Japanese Government might offer such as would be consistent with those principles (tr. 1103–1104).

As the result of these early conversations, on May 12 (Washington time), the Japanese Ambassador had presented to Secretary Hull, upon instructions from his Government, a document (Annex A attached hereto) containing a proposal for a general settlement between the United States and Japan (ex. 29, vol. II, pp. 418–425). This document had revealed authoritatively for the first time what the Japanese Government had in mind as the basis for an agreement

---

[1] All references in this appendix indicated in this manner are to pages of the transcript of the hearings before the Committee.

between the United States and Japan (ex. 29, vol. II, p. 332). Between May 12 and June 21, there had taken place a number of conferences between Secretary Hull and the Japanese Ambassador at which the Japanese proposal and related matters were discussed. In the meantime a counterproposal by the United States had been prepared, and on June 21 (Washington time) this counterproposal (Annex B attached hereto) had been handed to the Japanese Ambassador (ex. 29, vol. II, pp. 483–492).

On June 22, 1941, Germany had invaded Russia. The German attack upon Russia had precipitated a series of events in Japan which were to have far-reaching effects upon Japanese-American relations. It had quickened the appetites of those in the Japanese Government who believed that then, or never, Japan's destiny was in her own hands. Intensive consideration had immediately been given in Tokyo to the question whether Japan should not attack Russia at once (ex. 173, Konoye Memoirs, p. 16). Foreign Minister Matsuoka in particular had urged this course. According to the memoirs of Prince Fumimaro Konoye, the Japanese Premier at the time, the attention of the Government became so centered upon this question that the American counterproposal of June 21, which by that time had been received in Tokyo from the Japanese Ambassador in Washington, became completely side-tracked until after an Imperial Conference with Emperor Hirohito on July 2 (Japan time) (ex. 173, Konoye Memoirs, pp. 16, 18). At that conference the question of war with Russia had been temporarily shelved in favor of "an advance into the southern regions," and it had been decided that, first of all, the plans "which have been laid with reference to French Indo-China and Thai will be prosecuted, with a view to consolidating our position in the southern territories" (ex. 173, Konoye Memoirs, p. 70; cf. ex. 1, pp. 1–2.) It is now known that at the Imperial Conference on July 2 (Japan time) it was also decided that, in case the diplomatic negotiations with the United States should break down, "preparations for a war with England and America will also be carried forward"; that all plans, including the plan to use Japan's military strength to settle the Soviet question if the German-Russian war should develop to Japan's advantage, were to be carried out—

in such a way as to place no serious obstacles in the path of our basic military preparations for a war with England and America;

and that—

In case all diplomatic means fail to prevent the entrance of America into the European War, we will proceed in harmony with our obligations under the Tri-Partite Pact. However, with reference to the time and method of employing our armed forces we will take independent action (ex. 173, Konoye Memoirs, p. 71).

The following report of the Imperial Conference on July 2 (Japan time) had been cabled by the Japanese Foreign Minister to the Japanese Ambassadors in the United States, Germany, Italy, and Russia, the same day:

(National Secret)

At the conference held in the presence of the Emperor on July 2nd "The Principal Points in the Imperial Policy for Coping with the Changing Situation" were decided. This Policy consists of the following two parts. The first part "The Policy" and the second part "The Principal Points." (I am wiring merely the gist of the matter.) Inasmuch as this has to do with national defense secrets, keep the information only to yourself.   Please also transmit the content to both the Naval and Military Attachés, together with this precaution.

The Policy.

1. Imperial Japan shall adhere to the policy of contributing to world peace by establishing the Great East Asia Sphere of Co-prosperity, regardless of how the world situation may change.

2. The Imperial Government shall continue its endeavor to dispose of the China incident, *and shall take measures with a view to advancing southward* in order to establish firmly a basis for her self-existence and self-protection.

The Principal Points.

For the purpose of bringing the CHIANG Regime to submission, *increasing pressure shall be added from various points in the south*, and by means of both propaganda and fighting plans for the taking over of concessions shall be carried out.   Diplomatic negotiations shall be continued, and various other plans shall be speeded with regard to the vital points in the south.   *Concomitantly, preparations for southward advance shall be reenforced and the policy already decided upon with reference to French Indo-China and Thailand shall be executed.*   As regards the Russo-German war, although the spirit of the Three-Power Axis shall be maintained, every preparation shall be made at the present and the situation shall be dealt with in our own way.   In the meantime, diplomatic negotiations shall be carried on with extreme care.   Although every means available shall be resorted to in order to prevent the United States from joining the war, if need be, *Japan shall act in accordance with the Three-Power Pact and shall decide when and how force will be employed* (ex. 1, pp. 1–2).[1]

It is worthy of note that this intercepted Japanese message, which was translated and available in Washington[2] on July 8 (Washington time), did not mention the decisions at the Imperial Conference respecting the United States.

Commencing immediately after the Imperial Conference, Japan had proceeded with military preparations on a vast scale, calling up from 1 to 2 million reservists and conscripts, recalling Japanese merchant vessels operating in the Atlantic Ocean, imposing restrictions upon travel in Japan, and carrying out strict censorship of mail and communications.   The Japanese press had dwelt constantly on the theme that Japan was being faced with pressure directed against it never equalled in all Japanese history.   The United States had been charged with using the Philippine Islands as a "pistol aimed at Japan's heart."   The Japanese press had warned that if the United States took further action in the direction of encircling Japan, Japanese-American relations would face a final crisis (ex. 29, vol. II, pp. 339–340).

Largely as a result of disagreements within the Japanese Government regarding the reply to be made to the American proposals of June 21, Premier Konoye and his entire Cabinet had resigned *en bloc* on July 16 (Japan time) (ex. 173, Konoye Memoirs, pp. 20–24). Prince Konoye had then been ordered by Emperor Hirohito to organize the new Cabinet, which he had done, the only important change being the appointment of Admiral Toyoda as Foreign Minister, in place of Yosuke Matsuoka (ex. 173, Konoye Memoirs, p. 25). The views of the latter had been one of the principal causes of the disagreements within the Government regarding its reply to the

---

[1] Unless otherwise noted, all italics in this appendix have been supplied.

[2] The expression "translated and available in Washington," as used in this appendix, means that English translations of the particular intercepted Japanese diplomatic messages were available at the time stated to those officials of the United States Government in Washington to whom the Army and Navy were distributing "Magic" at the time.   It should be borne in mind that all such messages to which reference is made in this appendix were so available; specific reference has been made to the date when a message became available only in those instances where knowledge of the exact date is important.

While the information contained in the intercepted Japanese diplomatic messages was available at the time, the information contained herein which is derived solely from captured Japanese documents (exhibits 8 and 132) and from the memoirs of Prince Konoye (exhibit 173) was not, of course, available at the time.

American proposals of June 21. Following this Cabinet change, while Premier Konoye and the new Foreign Minister in Tokyo and Ambassador Nomura in Washington had made emphatic and repeated protestations of Japan's desire for peace and an equitable settlement of Pacific problems, the messages from Tokyo to Washington had contained such statements as "there is more reason than ever before to arm ourselves to the teeth for all-out war" (ex. 1, p. 8). The bombing of American property in China had continued, including bursts which damaged the American Embassy and the U. S. S. *Tutuila* at Chungking (ex. 29, vol. II, p. 343). An intercepted message of July 19 (Japan time) from Tokyo to Berlin had contained the following estimate of the change in the Japanese Cabinet:

The Cabinet shake-up was necessary to expedite matters in connection with National Affairs and has no further significance. Japan's foreign policy will not be changed and she will remain faithful to the principles of the Tripartite Pact (ex. 1, p. 3).

In the meantime, the movement of Japanese troops and ships in accordance with the Japanese plans for the "southward advance" had begun in earnest, (ex. 29, vol. II, p. 340; ex. 173, Konoye Memoirs, p. 26). Those military and naval movements, plus the failure as yet of the Japanese Government to make any reply to the American proposals of June 21, had led Under Secretary Welles, upon instructions from the Secretary of State, to inform Ambassador Nomura on July 23 (Washington time) that Secretary Hull "could not see that there was any basis now offered for the pursuit of the conversations in which he and the Ambassador had been engaged" (ex. 29, vol. II, p. 525). About this time, Colonel Hideo Iwakuro and Mr. Tadao Wikawa, who had been advising Ambassador Nomura in the conversations, left Washington and returned to Japan. On July 24 (Washington time), in a conference with the Japanese Ambassador attended by Under Secretary Welles and Admiral Harold R. Stark Chief of Naval Operations, President Roosevelt had proposed that, if the Japanese Government would withdraw its forces from French Indochina, he would endeavor to obtain from the British, the Chinese, and the Netherlands Governments, and the United States Government itself would give, a solemn and binding declaration to regard French Indochina as a neutralized country, provided the Japanese Government would give a similar commitment (ex. 29, vol. II, pp. 527–530). Nevertheless, the Japanese troop movements into French Indochina had continued, and on July 26 (Washington time) President Roosevelt had issued an Executive order freezing all Japanese assets in the United States (ex. 29, vol. II, p. 267). The effect of this order had been to bring about very soon the virtual cessation of trade between the United States and Japan (ex. 29, vol. II, p. 343).

In a message dated July 31 (Japan time), which was translated and available in Washington on August 4 (Washington time), the new Foreign Minister had advised Ambassador Nomura that since the Imperial Conference on July 2 (Japan time) the Japanese Government had been devoting every effort to bring about the materialization of the policies there decided upon. He told the Ambassador:

Commercial and economic relations between Japan and third countries, led by England and the United States, are gradually becoming so horribly strained that we cannot endure it much longer. Consequently, our Empire, to save its very life, must take measures to secure the raw materials of the South Seas. Our Empire must immediately take steps to break asunder this ever-strengthening chain of encirclement which is being woven under the guidance and with the participation of England and the United States, acting like a cunning dragon seemingly asleep. That is why we decided to obtain military bases in French Indo-China and to have our troops occupy that territory.

That step in itself, I dare say, gave England and the United States, not to mention Russia, quite a set-back in the Pacific that ought to help Germany, and now Japanese-American relations are more rapidly than ever treading the evil road. This shows what a blow it has been to the United States.

* * * * * * *

We are expending our best efforts to cooperate with Germany. She knows it and ought to understand our actions.

6. Well, the formula for cooperation between Tokyo and Berlin, in order to realize the fundamental spirit of the Tripartite Pact, should be for each country to have a certain flexibility in its conduct. What I mean to say is that each should understand that real cooperation does not necessarily mean complete symmetry of action. In other words, we should trust each other and while striving toward one general objective, each use our own discretion within the bounds of good judgment.

Thus, all measures which our Empire shall take will be based upon a determination to bring about the success of the objectives of the Tripartite Pact. That this is a fact is proven by the promulgation of an Imperial rescript. We are ever working toward the realization of those objectives, and now during this dire emergency is certainly no time to engage in any light unpremeditated or over-speedy action. (Ex. 1, pp. 9–10.)

In the meantime, a reply to the American proposals of June 21 had been transmitted on July 25 (Japan time) to Ambassador Nomura in Washington (ex. 173, Konoye Memoirs, p. 26). He had not presented it to Secretary Hull, however, because of the change in Japanese Cabinets, because he thought it would not be acceptable to the United States Government, and because he had received no instructions from the new Cabinet as to how to proceed under the circumstances (ex. 173, Konoye Memoirs, p. 26). Still another proposal had then been drawn up in Tokyo and this new proposal had been presented to Secretary Hull on August 6 by Ambassador Nomura with the statement that it was intended to be responsive to President Roosevelt's suggestion for the neutralization of French Indochina (ex. 29, vol. II, pp. 546–550). The new Japanese proposal had asked, either expressly or by implication, that the United States—

(1) remove the restrictions it had imposed upon trade with Japan; (2) suspend its defensive preparations in the Philippines; (3) discontinue furnishing military equipment to Great Britain and the Netherlands for the arming of their Far Eastern possessions; (4) discontinue aid to the Chinese Government; and (5) assent to Japan's assertion and exercise of a special military position and a permanent preferential political and economic status in Indochina, involving, as this would, assent to procedures and disposals which menaced the security of the United States and which were contrary to the principles to which this Government was committed. In return the Japanese, Government offered not to station Japanese troops in regions of the southwestern Pacific other than Indochina. It proposed to retain its military establishment in Indochina for an indeterminate period. There thus would still have remained the menace to the security of the United States, already mentioned, as well as the menace to the security of British and Dutch territories in the southwestern Pacific area (ex. 29, vol. II, p. 344).

About this time, in Tokyo, Premier Konoye had determined to propose a personal meeting between himself and President Roosevelt (ex. 173, Konoye Memoirs, p. 29). It is now known that he had presented this idea to the Ministers of War and Navy on August 4 (Japan time). Before that day ended, the Navy Minister had expressed complete accord and had even anticipated the success of the proposed conference (ex. 173, Konoye Memoirs, p. 30). The Minister of War, General Tojo, however, had replied in writing as follows:

If the Prime Minister were to personally meet with the President of the United States, the existing diplomatic relations of the Empire, which are based on the Tripartite Pact, would unavoidably be weakened. At the same time, a considerable domestic stir would undoubtedly be created. For these reasons, the meeting is not considered a suitable move. The attempt to surmount the present critical situation by the Prime Minister's offering his personal services, is viewed with sincere respect and admiration. If, therefore, it is the Prime Minister's intention to attend such a meeting *with determination to firmly support the basic principles embodied in the Empire's Revised Plan to the "N" Plan and to carry out a war against America if the President of the United States still fails to comprehend the true intentions of the Empire even after this final effort is made*, the Army is not necessarily in disagreement.

However, (1) it is not in favor of the meeting if after making preliminary investigations it is learned that the meeting will be with someone other than the President, such as Secretary Hull or one in a lesser capacity. (2) *You shall not resign your post as a result of the meeting on the grounds that it was a failure; rather,— you shall be prepared to assume leadership in the war against America* (ex. 173, Konoye Memoirs, pp. 30–31).

On August 7 (Japan time) Premier Konoye had been instructed by Emperor Hirohito to proceed immediately with arrangements for the meeting (ex. 173, Konoye Memoirs, p. 31). That day the Premier had sent a telegram to Ambassador Nomura, which was translated and available in Washington on August 8 (Washington time), directing him to propose such a meeting (ex. 1, pp. 12–13).

Ambassador Nomura and Secretary Hull had met on August 8 (Washington time), and at that meeting the Ambassador had presented the proposal for a meeting between President Roosevelt and Premier Konoye. Secretary Hull had informed the Ambassador that the new Japanese proposal of August 6 was not responsive to President Roosevelt's suggestion of July 24 (Washington time) mentioned above, and, regarding the proposal for a meeting between the President and Premier Konoye, had said that it remained for the Japanese Government to decide whether it could find means of shaping its policies along lines that would make possible an adjustment of views between the two Governments (ex. 29, vol. II, pp. 550–551).

The next day, August 9 (Washington time), Secretary Hull had conferred with Lord Halifax, the British Ambassador, who had inquired about the amount of aid the United States Government would be able to give in case the Japanese should attack Singapore or the Dutch East Indies. Secretary Hull recorded:

I replied that I myself have visualized the problem and issue in a broader way and that issue is presented by the plan of the Japanese to invade by force the whole of the Indian Ocean and the islands and continents adjacent thereto, isolating China, sailing across probably to the mouth of the Suez Canal, to the Persian Gulf oil area, to the Cape of Good Hope area, thereby blocking by a military despotism the trade routes and the supply sources to the British. I added that this broad military occupation would perhaps be more damaging to British defense in Europe than any other step short of the German crossing of the Channel. I said that this Government visualizes these broad conditions and the problem of resistance which they present; that the activities of this Government in the way of discouraging this Japanese movement and of resistance will be more or less affected by the British defensive situation in Europe and hence by the question of the number of American naval vessels and other American aid that may be needed by Great Britain at the same time. I said that in the event of further Japanese movements south this Government and the British Government should naturally have a conference at once and this Government would then be able to determine more definitely and in detail its situation pertaining to resistance, in the light of the statement I had just made (ex. 28, pp. 710–711).

Except that President Roosevelt had left Washington for the Atlantic Conference meeting with Prime Minister Churchill before either of the two last-mentioned conferences,[1] the foregoing summarizes briefly the immediate background for that Conference so far as relations between the United States and Japan were concerned. The Japanese move into southern French Indochina while at the same time in Washington Ambassador Nomura was engaging in conversations with Secretary Hull looking toward a peaceful settlement of problems in the Pacific, and the consequent breaking off of those conversations, together with the freezing of Japanese assets in the United States, had brought relations between the two countries to a critical stage. Moreover, French Indochina, where the Japanese forces were establishing themselves, was an area of great strategic importance. From it, those forces could strike in many directions, toward major objectives. To the east, across the South China Sea, lay the Philippines. To the west and northwest, across Thailand and the Chinese province of Yunnan, lay Rangoon, Kunming, and the Burma Road, over which American supplies for China were moving. To the south, at the tip of the Malay Peninsula, lay the British naval base at Singapore. Beyond Singapore and the Philippines lay the Netherlands East Indies, with rubber, oil, and other materials needed by Japan for the purposes to which the Japanese Government was committed.

When Under Secretary Welles informed Ambassador Nomura on July 23 (Washington time) that the conversations were at an end, he said that the United States could only assume, first—

that the occupation of Indochina by Japan constituted notice to the United States that the Japanese Government intended to pursue a policy of force and of conquest, and, second, that in the light of these acts on the part of Japan, the United States, with regard to its own safety in the light of its own preparations for self-defense, must assume *that the Japanese Government was taking the last step before proceeding upon a policy of totalitarian expansion in the South Seas and of conquest in the South Seas through the seizure of additional territories in that region* (ex. 29, vol. II, p. 525).

THE ATLANTIC CONFERENCE

(*August 9–14, 1941*)

The meeting between President Roosevelt and Prime Minister Churchill, each accompanied by high officials of their respective Governments, took place at sea near Argentia, Newfoundland, during the second week in August 1941. At it the President and the Prime Minister agreed upon the joint declaration of principles which has since become known as the Atlantic Charter (tr. 1359–1364). Their conversations also dealt with steps which Great Britain and the United States were taking for their safety in the face of the policies of aggression of the German Government and other governments associated with the German Government. They discussed such matters as the proposed occupation of the Canary Islands by the British Government to guard the southern Atlantic convoy route into the

[1] Former Under Secretary of State Sumner Welles testified, however, that he believed he (Welles) left Washington for the Atlantic Conference the evening of August 8 (Washington time) (tr. 1254).

British Isles, a proposal that the Portuguese Government request the Government of the United States for assistance in the defense of the Azores as a means of assurance that those islands would not be occupied by Germany, and the protection of the Cape Verde Islands against Axis aggressors (ex. 22–C).

The President and the Prime Minister also discussed the situation in the Far East. During those discussions Mr. Churchill submitted a proposal for parallel declarations by the United States, British, and Dutch Governments warning Japan against new moves of military aggression.[1] This proposal also contemplated that the Russian Government would be kept fully informed of such steps (ex. 22). The final discussion of Mr. Churchill's proposal occurred on August 11 (ex. 22–C). According to Under Secretary Welles' record of that discussion—

The President gave Mr. Churchill to read copies of the two statements handed to Secretary Hull by the Japanese Ambassador on August 6.

The Prime Minister read them carefully and then remarked that the implication was that Japan, having already occupied Indochina, said that she would move no further provided the United States would abandon their economic and financial sanctions and take no further military or naval defensive measures and further agree to concessions to Japan, including the opportunity for Japan to strangle the Chinese Government, all of which were particularly unacceptable (ex. 22–C).

The President replied that that was about the picture as he saw it, and after expressing his strong feeling that "every effort should be made to prevent the outbreak of war with Japan," he stated the procedure with respect to Japan that he intended to follow upon his return to Washington. He told the Prime Minister that he would inform Ambassador Nomura that if the Japanese Government would give satisfactory assurances that it would not further station its troops in the Southwestern Pacific areas, except French Indochina, and that the Japanese troops now stationed in French Indochina would be withdrawn, the United States Government would resume the informal conversations with the Japanese Government. He said that he would further state that if Japan should refuse to consider this procedure and should undertake further steps in the nature of military expansions, in his belief various steps would have to be taken by the United States notwithstanding his realization that the taking of such measures might result in war between the United States and Japan (ex. 22–C). Mr. Churchill immediately concurred in this procedure (ex. 22–C). There was then discussed—

the desirability of informing Russia of the steps which would be taken as above set forth and of possibly including in the warning to Japan a statement which would cover any aggressive steps by Japan against the Soviet Union (ex. 22–C).

Under Secretary Welles expressed the view that the real issue involved was whether or not Japan would continue its policy of conquest by force in the entire Pacific and suggested that the statement which the President intended to make—

might more advantageously be based on the question of broad policy rather than be premised solely upon Japanese moves in the southwestern Pacific area (ex. 22–C).

---

[1] The record before the Committee also shows that in February 1941, just before the Lend-Lease Act—described by Prime Minister Churchill as "the Bill on which our hopes depend"—was enacted by Congress, the Prime Minister and Lord Halifax, the British Ambassador, had urged upon President Roosevelt and Secretary Hull their desire for some action by the United States "to deter the Japanese" (ex. 158).

The President and Mr. Churchill both agreed to this, and *"it was decided that the step to be taken by the President* [1] would be taken in that sense" (ex. 22–C).

Consideration was then given the question whether or not President Roosevelt should include in his statement to Ambassador Nomura a statement with respect to British policy concerning French Indochina and Thailand (ex. 22–C). However, since the statement ultimately made by the President to Ambassador Nomura did not mention British policy concerning those countries this latter proposal appears to have been dropped (ex. 29, vol. II, pp. 554–559).

Under Secretary Welles returned to Washington from Argentia several days before President Roosevelt, at the latter's request. Upon his arrival, he advised Secretary Hull of what had transpired there, and, at the President's further request, he prepared the initial draft (ex. 22) of the proposed warning to Japan from notes he had made of his final conversation with the President before leaving Argentia (tr. 1259). A revised draft was given to Secretary Hull by Mr. Welles on August 16, 1941 (ex. 22–A), and was further revised by the Secretary and his advisors on Far Eastern affairs before being communicated to Ambassador Nomura by the President (tr. 1272).

President Roosevelt Warns Japan Against Further Aggression and at the Same Time Offers to Resume the Japanese-American Conversations

(August 17, 1941)

President Roosevelt returned to Washington Sunday morning, August 17 (Washington time). Late that afternoon, Ambassador Nomura met with the President and Secretary Hull at the White House, at the President's request (ex. 29, vol. II, p. 554 et seq.; ex. 124).[2] Mr. Roosevelt read and then handed to Admiral Nomura the document

---

[1] The evidence before the Committee is conflicting as to whether or not Prime Minister Churchill promised President Roosevelt that the British Government would take action parallel to that to be taken by the United States Government.

The only contemporaneous records of the Atlantic Conference before the Committee are three memoranda prepared by Under Secretary Welles (ex. 22-B, 22-C, 22-D). Those memoranda show that the procedure outlined by President Roosevelt differed substantially from that envisaged in Prime Minister Churchill's proposal. As there described by Mr. Welles, the President's procedure did not call for parallel action by either the British or Dutch Governments, or for keeping Russia informed, as Mr. Churchill had proposed. Nor, as in the case of Mr. Churchill's proposal, was the precise phraseology of the warning to Japan prescribed, it being left entirely up to the President. Mr. Welles testified that the promise given by the President to Mr. Churchill "was limited to the fact that a warning would be given" (tr. 1422), and that the only agreement reached between the President and the Prime Minister was "that the President made the promise to Mr. Churchill that the Government of the United States, in its own words and in its own way, would issue a warning to the Japanese Government of the character which actually was made by the President on August 17" (tr. 1428).

While it is true that Mr. Welles testified that the promise made by President Roosevelt was to "take parallel action with the British Government in warning the Japanese Government" (tr. 1235-6) and that he "took it for granted Mr. Churchill must have made that statement" (i. e., promised to make a parallel warning) to the President (tr. 1446), it is also true that when asked directly whether the President had told him that Mr. Churchill had promised to make a parallel warning, Mr. Welles said, "the President in his conversation with me, so far as I remember, did not make that specific statement" (tr. 1446). Moreover, as previously noted, the Welles' memoranda neither state nor indicate that any such promise was made by Mr. Churchill (ex. 22-B, 22-C, 22-D), and there is no evidence before the Committee showing that action parallel to the President's warning to Japan was ever taken by the British Government. On the other hand, both "Peace and War" (ex. 28, p. 129) and "Foreign Relations of the United States, Japan 1931–1941" (ex. 29, vol. II, p. 345) refer to an "agreement" to take parallel action made by President Roosevelt and Prime Minister Churchill, though, of course, neither of these purports to be a contemporaneous account of the Atlantic Conference. Likewise, in his testimony before the Committee, Secretary Hull referred to such an "agreement," though again Secretary Hull did not attend the Atlantic Conference (tr. 1116).

[2] This discussion of the meeting referred to in the text, and the discussions in this appendix of other meetings in Washington or Tokyo between representatives of the United States Government and the Japanese Government, are based primarily upon the official State Department records of such meetings appearing in Volumes I and II of "Foreign Relations of the United States, Japan, 1931–1941" (ex. 29) and upon intercepted Japanese messages between Washington and Tokyo reporting such meetings, the Committee exhibits in which such messages appear being indicated in all cases. Reference is made to such records and reports, only the material portions of which have been quoted or summarized here.

drafted by Mr. Welles and the Secretary. It noted that notwithstanding the protracted conversations engaged in by the United States and Japanese Governments looking toward a peaceful settlement in the Pacific and the President's suggestion on July 24, 1941, for the "neutralization" of French Indochina, the Japanese Government had continued to dispose its armed forces at various points in the Far East and had occupied French Indochina. Reading from the document, President Roosevelt said that the United States Government felt that at the present stage "nothing short of the most complete candor on its part in the light of the evidence and indications" in its possession would tend to further the objectives sought. He then warned Japan against further aggression, saying:

Such being the case, this Government now finds it necessary to say to the Government of Japan that if the Japanese Government takes any further steps in pursuance of a policy or program of military domination by force or threat of force of neighboring countries, the Government of the United States will be compelled to take immediately any and all steps which it may deem necessary toward safeguarding the legitimate rights and interests of the United States and American nationals and toward insuring the safety and security of the United States (ex. 29, vol. II, pp. 556–557).

On behalf of his Government, Ambassador Nomura reasserted the sincerity of its desire to bring about an adjustment of Japanese-American diplomatic relations. He expressed his Government's desire to be advised as to the possibility of arranging a meeting between President Roosevelt and Premier Konoye and of resuming the informal conversations which had been terminated by the United States in July because of the Japanese occupation of southern French Indochina. He stated, however, that he felt no further explanations regarding his Government's actions in French Indochina, in addition to the views already expressed to Secretary Hull, were necessary.

The President then read and handed to Ambassador Nomura a second document. It opened with a reference to the Japanese proposal of August 8 (Washington time) for a meeting between himself and Premier Konoye and to the Japanese desire for resumption of the informal conversations. The President said that the United States Government would be prepared to resume the conversations provided the Japanese Government felt that Japan desired and was in a position to suspend its expansionist activities, and to embark upon a peaceful program for the Pacific along the lines of the program to which the United States was committed. His statement concluded:

the Government of the United States, however, feels that, in view of the circumstances attending the interruption of the informal conversations between the two Governments, it would be helpful to both Governments, before undertaking a resumption of such conversations or proceeding with plans for a meeting, if the Japanese Government would be so good as to furnish a clearer statement than has yet been furnished as to its present attitude and plans, just as this Government has repeatedly outlined to the Japanese Government its attitude and plans (ex. 29, vol. II, p. 559).

In Ambassador Nomura's report to Tokyo on this meeting, he emphasized the "graveness with which he (President Roosevelt) views Japanese-U. S. relations." The Ambassador expressed the view that the Japanese proposal for a "leaders' conference" between President Roosevelt and Premier Konoye had "considerably eased" the attitude of the United States Government and that there was no room for doubt "that the President hopes that matters will take a turn for the better" (ex. 124).

The next day, August 18 (Washington time), President Roosevelt sent a message to Prime Minister Churchill describing his meeting with Ambassador Nomura. This message indicates that the President did not learn until after his return to Washington of the Ambassador's request on August 16 (Washington time) for a resumption of the informal conversations. In his message, the President told Mr. Churchill that—

I made to him (Admiral Nomura) a statement covering the position of this Government with respect to the taking by Japan of further steps in the direction of military domination by force along the lines of the proposed statement such as you and I had discussed. The statement I made to him was no less vigorous than and was substantially similar to the statement we had discussed (ex. 70).

The evidence before the Committee does not show whether or not the British Government took "parallel action" to the warning given Japan by President Roosevelt. Under Secretary Welles testified before the Committee that he took it for granted that the British Government took such parallel action and that the records of the State Department would probably show that (tr. 1279), but Secretary Hull testified, and the State Department has advised the Committee, that its files contain no record of any such action (tr. 14, 306; 4480). Furthermore, as late as November 30 (Washington time), Prime Minister Churchill sent a message to the President saying that "one important method *remains unused* in averting war between Japan and our two countries, namely a plain declaration, secret or public as may be thought best, that any further act of aggression by Japan will lead immediately to the gravest consequences. * * * We would, of course, make a similar declaration or share in a joint declaration" (ex. 24); and the evidence further shows that on December 7 the Prime Minister submitted to President Roosevelt a draft of a proposed warning to Japan (tr. 13738–13740). On the other hand, on August 25, 1941, in an address reporting to Parliament on the Atlantic Conference, the Prime Minister said:

But Europe is not the only continent to be tormented and devastated by aggression. For five long years the Japanese military factions, seeking to emulate the style of Hitler and Mussolini, taking all their posturing as if it were a new European revelation, have been invading and harrying the 500,000,000 inhabitants of China. Japanese armies have been wandering about that vast land in futile excursions, carrying with them carnage, ruin and corruption, and calling it "the Chinese incident." Now they stretch a grasping hand into the southern seas of China. They snatch Indo-China from the wretched Vichy French. They menace by their movements Siam, menace Singapore, the British link with Australasia, and menace the Philippine Islands under the protection of the United States.

It is certain that this has got to stop. Every effort will be made to secure a peaceful settlement. The United States are laboring with infinite patience to arrive at a fair and amicable settlement which will give Japan the utmost reassurance for her legitimate interests. We earnestly hope these negotiations will succeed. But this I must say: That if these hopes should fail we shall, of course, range ourselves unhesitatingly at the side of the United States (tr. 1355–1356; 4480–4481).

While Secretary Hull testified that he knew of no parallel action taken by the British other than this address (tr. 14306), which was broadcast by radio, Under Secretary Welles testified that in his opinion this address did not constitute "parallel action" of the kind proposed by Mr. Churchill to the President, and that in Mr. Welles' judgment such action would necessarily have had to have been in the form of an exchange of diplomatic notes (tr. 1356).[1]

On August 21 (Washington time) President Roosevelt sent a message to Congress describing the meeting at Argentia (tr. 1359–1364). This message embodied the text of the "Atlantic Charter" and referred in general terms to other matters discussed at the meeting, but made no specific mention of the proposal to issue a warning to Japan. Under Secretary Welles testified that publication of the proposal to issue a warning to Japan or of the President's warning, itself, would not have been conducive to a successful result in attempting to find a peaceful solution, as it would have inflamed public opinion in Japan (tr. 1277).

JAPAN PROTESTS UNITED STATES SHIPMENTS OF OIL TO RUSSIA

(August 27, 1941)

The Japanese reply to President Roosevelt's request on August 17 (Washington time) for a "clearer statement than has yet been furnished as to its present attitude and plans" was not received until August 28 (Washington time). During the interval between those dates, Ambassador Nomura reported to the Japanese Foreign Office an increasing interest on the part of President Roosevelt in participating in the resumption of the Japanese-American negotiations and stated that, in his opinion, "the President is the one who shows the most interest in the 'leaders conference'" (ex. 124). About the same time the Ambassador received a report from Tokyo concerning the Foreign Minister's talk with Ambassador Grew on August 18 (Japan time) at which Ambassador Grew indicated that he would give the proposed meeting his personal support (ex. 124). On August 23 (Japan time) the Foreign Minister cabled Ambassador Nomura that "everything in our power" was being done "to rush our reply to the United States and at the same time to bring about the 'leaders conference' at an earlier date" (ex. 124). The next day Ambassador Nomura called on Secretary Hull and reported that his Government wanted the "leaders conference" to take place before October 15. The reason he gave for this was the fear in Tokyo that the impression would be created that Japan "had given in in the face of the threat of 'encirclement'" if the proposed Roosevelt-Konoye meeting should follow a reported British-U. S.-Soviet conference to be held at an earlier date (ex. 124; ex. 29, vol. II, p. 568).

At about this time the German Ambassador in Japan, General Ott, received intelligence reports that the United States was preparing to ship oil to Russia via Vladivostok, that the first of the transporting vessels had already sailed, that they would soon sail in rapid succession, and that the oil would undoubtedly be used by Russia for an attack upon Japan. General Ott repeated this information to the Vice Minister for Foreign Affairs during an interview on August 19 (Japan time), and in reply the Vice Minister said that the problem of American oil was receiving very careful attention (ex. 132–A, item C). The next day, and again on August 22 (Japan time), the Foreign

___

[1] There is also before the Committee a memorandum of Dr. Stanley K. Hornbeck, Political Advisor to Secretary Hull, dated, however, February 28, 1944, in which it is stated that toward the end of August 1941, the British and American Governments "served on Japan a strong warning" against further extending her courses of aggression (ex. 108).

Minister cabled Ambassador Nomura requesting him to call the attention of the United States authorities to the fact that if it should become known in Japan that the United States was shipping iron, airplanes, and other materials to Russia by way of Japanese coastal waters, this might have an adverse effect upon Japanese-American relations (ex. 1, p. 19; ex. 124). Ambassador Nomura told Secretary Hull during their conversation on August 23 (Washington time) that the shipment of oil by the United States to Russia through Japanese waters "would naturally give the Japanese real concern at an early date" (ex. 29, vol. II, p. 566). A more urgent message concerning this matter was sent from Tokyo to Ambassador Nomura on August 26 (Japan time) requesting him to "make representations again to the Secretary of State in order that he may reconsider an immediate cessation of these measures from the general viewpoint of the current Japan-American diplomatic relations" (ex. 1, p. 21). Representations of this nature were made to Ambassador Grew in Tokyo the next day (ex. 29, vol. II, p. 569), and on August 27 (Washington time) Ambassador Nomura orally protested to Secretary Hull against American shipments of oil to Russia through Japanese waters. Secretary Hull stated that only two tankers were involved and that the shipments were entirely valid under all the laws of commerce (ex. 29, vol. II, p. 570).

Premier Konoye Sends a Personal Message to President Roosevelt Urging the Proposed "Leaders Conference"

(August 28, 1941)

Premier Konoye replied to President Roosevelt's statement of August 17 (Washington time) in a personal message which Ambassador Nomura handed to the President at a conference at the White House on the morning of August 28 (Washington time). The Premier's message was accompanied by a statement which the Japanese Government intended to be responsive to the President's suggestion that it would be helpful if that Government would furnish a clearer statement of its present attitude and plans than had as yet been given (ex. 29, vol. II, pp. 571-572).

In his message to President Roosevelt, Premier Konoye urged that the meeting between himself and the President be arranged "as soon as possible." He said that while the preliminary informal negotiations that were terminated in July had been "quite appropriate both in spirit and content," nevertheless—

the idea of continuing those conversations and to have their conclusion confirmed by the responsible heads of the two Governments does not meet the need of the present situation which is developing swiftly and may produce unforeseen contingencies.

I consider it, therefore, of urgent necessity that the two heads of the Governments should meet first to discuss from a broad standpoint all important problems between Japan and America covering the entire Pacific area, and to explore the possibility of saving the situation. Adjustment of minor items may, if necessary, be left to negotiations between competent officials of the two countries, following the meeting (ex. 29, vol. II, p. 573).

The statement which accompanied Premier Konoye's message referred, among other things, to the—

principles and directives set forth in detail by the United States Government and envisaged in the informal conversations as constituting a program for the Pacific area—

and continued—

The Japanese Government wishes to state that it considers these principles and the practical application thereof, in the friendliest manner possible, are the prime requisites of a true peace and should be applied not only in the Pacific area but throughout the entire world. Such a program has long been desired and sought by Japan itself (ex. 29, vol. II, p. 575).

However, while the statement contained many assurances regarding Japan's peaceful intentions, the more important assurances were qualified or conditional. Thus, the Japanese Government was prepared to withdraw its troops from Indochina, but only "as soon as the China incident is settled or a just peace is established in East Asia"; concerning Soviet-Japanese relations it was said that Japan would take no military action "as long as the Soviet Union remains faithful to the Soviet-Japanese neutrality treaty and does not menace Japanese Manchukuo or take any action contrary to the spirit of the said treaty"; the Japanese Government had no intention, it was said, of using, "without provocation" military force against any neighboring nation (ex. 29, vol. II, pp. 573–575).

Ambassador Nomura reported to his Government that President Roosevelt "was well pleased" with the Premier's message (ex. 124). The President had said, he cabled, "I am looking forward to having approximately three days talk with Prince Konoye", but that Hawaii was out of the question as a meeting place and that he would prefer Juneau, Alaska. The Ambassador quoted the President as having "smilingly and cynically" said during his reading of the message:

Though I am looking forward to conversations with Prince Konoye, I wonder whether invasion of Thailand can be expected during those conversations just as an invasion of French Indo-China occurred during Secretary Hull's conversations with your Excellency (ex. 124).

The evening of the same day, August 28 (Washington time), Ambassador Nomura called on Secretary Hull and outlined to the Secretary his ideas concerning the arrangements for the proposed Roosevelt-Konoye meeting. During this conversation, the Secretary pointed out to Ambassador Nomura the desirability of there being reached in advance of the proposed meeting "an agreement in principle on the principal questions which were involved in a settlement of Pacific questions between the two nations." The Secretary said that if the proposed meeting should fail to result in an agreement, serious consequences from the point of view of both Governments would ensue. He expressed the view that therefore the purpose of the proposed meeting should be "the ratification of essential points agreed upon in principle" (ex. 29, vol. II, pp. 576–577). Ambassador Nomura concluded his report of this meeting to Tokyo with the comment:

In general, it may be said that the Secretary of State is an exceedingly cautious person. There are indications that he is considering this matter from many angles. I feel that unless we are in fairly close agreement the "leaders conference" will not materialize (ex. 124).

GERMANY SUSPECTS TREACHERY

(August 29–30, 1941)

It became known to the American press, soon after Ambassador Nomura left the White House following his conference with President Roosevelt and Secretary Hull on August 28 (Washington time), that the Ambassador had delivered a personal message to the President from Premier Konoye. Whether this information was given out by Secretary Hull or by Ambassador Nomura is not clear from the record before the Committee (ex. 29, vol. II, pp. 582–583; ex. 124); however, as a result of the disclosure, Foreign Minister Toyoda became greatly concerned that the proposed "leaders conference" should be kept absolutely secret, fearing the project would fail if news of it should leak out before a settlement was reached. The Foreign Minister cabled Ambassador Nomura twice on August 29 (Japan time) urging him "to take every precaution" to guard against leaks (ex. 124).

This concern in Tokyo over the effect of publicity on the conversations and the proposed "leaders conference" was a major reason for calls by the Director of the American Bureau of the Japanese Foreign Office on Ambassador Grew on August 29 and September 3 (Japan time) and for a call by Ambassador Nomura on Secretary Hull on September 1 (Washington time) (ex. 29, vol. II, pp. 579–582, 586–587, 583–585). During his first conversation with Ambassador Grew, the Director, Mr. Terasaki, dwelt at some length on the unfortunate effects of the publicity in Washington about Premier Konoye's message to President Roosevelt, and then communicated to the Ambassador an appeal from Foreign Minister Toyoda that (1) the proposed Roosevelt-Konoye meeting be arranged without delay and (2) pending the outcome of the proposed meeting, the United States postpone the sending oil tankers to the Soviet Union and suspend the order freezing Japanese assets in the United States. Ambassador Grew's memorandum of this meeting noted that he left Mr. Terasaki "under no illusion" that the United States Government would find it possible to agree to either of the "preposterous requests" contained in (2) above (ex. 29, vol. II, p. 582). Ambassador Nomura's conference with Secretary Hull on September 1 (Washington time) was concerned largely with discussion of the effect upon the conversations of the positions taken by the press in Japan and the United States. The Secretary took advantage of the occasion to ask the Ambassador what would happen if an agreement should not be reached at the proposed "leaders conference," and to repeat his suggestion that an effort be made to reach an agreement in principle on fundamental questions before the meeting (ex. 29, vol. II, pp. 583–585).

As a result of the fear in Tokyo of publicity, Ambassador Nomura wrote a brief note to Secretary Hull on August 29 (Washington time) requesting his cooperation in keeping the conversations secret. The Secretary replied on September 2 (Washington time) saying that he would "be glad to conform to the desires of yourself and your Government in the foregoing respect, to every extent practical" (ex. 29, vol. II, pp. 579, 586). However, apparently believing that some official comment was needed in view of the rumors and speculation in Tokyo about Ambassador Nomura's meeting with President Roosevelt, at 2:30 p. m. on August 29 (Japan time), the Japanese Foreign Office released an official statement that Ambassador Nomura had called on President Roosevelt on August 28 and had delivered to the President a message from Premier Konoye stating "Japan's view regarding Pacific problems which are pending between Japan and the United States" (ex. 29, vol. II, p. 579). Ambassador Grew advised Secretary Hull of this announcement later the same afternoon (ex. 29, vol. II, p. 579).

Foreign Minister Toyoda feared publicity because of "the exceedingly complex domestic situation" and the consideration which had to be given to "our relations with Germany and Italy" (ex. 124). What the Foreign Minister had in mind in the first connection is indicated by his cable to Ambassador Nomura on September 3 (Japan time), in which he said:

Since the existence of the Premier's message was inadvertently made known to the public, that gang that has been suspecting that unofficial talks were taking place, has really begun to yell and wave the Tripartite Pact banner (ex. 1, p. 25).

In the second connection, it is now known from captured Japanese documents that less than 4 hours after the Tokyo announcement of Premier Konoye's message to President Roosevelt, General Ott, the German Ambassador, called on the Vice Minister for Foreign Affairs, Mr. Amau, and demanded to know whether the Premier's message departed from the policy determined at the Imperial Conference on July 2, which had been secretly communicated to the German Government, and whether the Cabinet was contemplating any change in that regard (ex. 132–A, item C). The Vice Minister replied that the message did not mean that there had been "a change in Japan's policy, nor that we are contemplating any change in our relations with the Axis." The reason for sending the message, he told the Ambassador, "was to clarify the atmosphere in the Pacific" and to attempt "to start conversations between the two parties." Ambassador Ott suggested that "precautions must be taken against America's scheme to prolong these negotiations, so that this might work to her advantage," to which the Vice Minister replied that "we have given the matter careful thought so that the carrying on of negotiations by Japan with America might not have any disadvantageous consequences upon Germany and Italy." "Our aim," he said, "is to keep her (America) from joining in the war." The German Ambassador then requested an interview with Foreign Minister Toyoda, which took place on the afternoon of August 30 (Japan time). At that interview General Ott again demanded to know whether the intentions of Japan were still as secretly communicated to Germany on July 2. The Foreign Minister denied that there had been any change in Japan's intentions, and stated that Japan's preparations to avail herself of any new developments "are now making headway." The German Ambassador said:

In Foreign Minister Matsuoka's time the Japanese government authorities thought that what America was planning to do was to get Japan to take an attitude in conflict with the Tripartite Pact, that is, to give up taking any positive action in the Pacific area no matter what occasion might arise, and Germany is very grateful that at the time the Japanese government resolutely resisted these American designs, and we hope that it will continue to take that "line." I would like to ask what Your Excellency's views are concerning this point (ex. 132–A, item C).

Admiral Toyoda replied:

In a word I may say that the purpose of the Tripartite Pact is to prevent American participation in the war, and that this view is the same as in the past; nor will it change in the future (ex. 132–A, item C).

The Japanese Ambassador in Berlin reported to Tokyo on October 1, 1941, that because of the Japanese-American negotiations everyone in the German Foreign Office was "thoroughly disgusted with Japan." He said that the fact that the feeling of German leaders and people in general toward Japan was getting bad could not be covered up, and that if Japan were to go ahead with the negotiations without consulting Germany, "there is no telling what steps Germany may take without consulting Japan" (ex. 1, pp. 48–49).

In Italy, the impression created by the Japanese-American talks was not enthusiastic, as the Japanese Ambassador in Rome reported to the Foreign Office on September 30:

Our recent negotiations with the United States have put a bad taste in the mouths of the people of this country. Our attitude toward the Tripartite Alliance appears to them to be faithless. Recently the newspapers have been growing more critical in tone where we Japanese are concerned. Official comment, too, has been none too complimentary. As for Italy's attitude toward the recent celebration of the first anniversary of the conclusion of the Japanese-German-Italian Tripartite Alliance, its coolness reflects the attitude of the whole Italian people (ex. 1, p. 44).

President Roosevelt Replies to Premier Konoye's Message

(September 3, 1941)

President Roosevelt handed to Ambassador Nomura his reply to Premier Konoye at a conference at the White House on the afternoon of September 3 (Washington time) (ex. 29, vol. II, pp. 588–592). The President's reply mentioned the reference in the statement which had accompanied the Premier's message to the basic principles to which the United States Government had long been committed and the President's desire to collaborate in making these principles effective in practice. The President stated that his deep interest in this matter made it necessary for him to observe and take account of developments both in the United States and Japan which had a bearing on Japanese-American relations, and that he could not avoid taking cognizance of indications—

of the existence in some quarters in Japan of concepts which, if widely entertained, would seem capable of raising obstacles to successful collaboration between you and me along the line which I am sure both of us earnestly desire to follow (ex 29, vol. II, p. 592).

The President then suggested:

that it would seem highly desirable that we take precaution, toward ensuring that our proposed meeting shall prove a success, by endeavoring to enter immediately upon preliminary discussion of the fundamental and essential questions on which we seek agreement. The questions which I have in mind for such preliminary discussions involve practical application of the principles fundamental to achievement and maintenance of peace which are mentioned with more specification in the statement accompanying your letter. I hope that you will look favorably upon this suggestion (ex. 29, vol. II, p. 592).

The President also read and handed to Ambassador Nomura a statement which referred to the American proposals of June 21 (Washington time) and to the fact that subsequent conversations had disclosed that there were divergences of view between the two Governments with respect to certain fundamental questions dealt with in those proposals. Reading from the statement, the President expressed the desire of the United States Government "to facilitate progress toward a conclusive discussion" and its belief—

that a community of view and a clear agreement upon the points above mentioned are essential to any satisfactory settlement of Pacific questions. It therefore seeks an indication of the present attitude of the Japanese Government with regard to the fundamental questions under reference (ex. 29, vol. II, p. 591).

In connection with this statement, it will be remembered that the second Konoye Cabinet had resigned on July 16 (Japan time) and had been replaced by the third Konoye Cabinet the next day (ex. 173, Konoye Memoirs, p. 24).

In his memorandum of the conversation with Ambassador Nomura, Secretary Hull wrote:

Both the President and I repeatedly emphasized the necessity for his (i. e., Ambassador Nomura's) Government to clarify its position on the question of abandoning a policy of force and conquest and on three fundamental questions concerning which difficulties had been encountered in our discussion of the Japanese proposal of May twelfth and the discussion of which we had not pursued after the Japanese went into Indochina (ex. 29, vol. II, p. 588).

JAPAN PRESENTS NEW PROPOSALS IN A NEW FORM

(September 6, 1941)

It is now known that about the time President Roosevelt was meeting with Ambassador Nomura, new Japanese proposals were being discussed at a Joint Conference of Japanese Foreign Office and War and Navy officials in Tokyo. According to Premier Konoye, these new proposals were intended by the Foreign Office to bring up only "immediate and concrete problems" and to focus the proposed meeting between President Roosevelt and the Premier on those problems. The Foreign Office took the position that it was difficult to predict how long it would take to consider all of the important fundamental principles dealt with in the proposals which had been under consideration by the two Governments before the freezing orders, and that consequently "the present crisis might not be averted" if it should be necessary to consider all of those principles (ex. 173, Konoye Memoirs, p. 37). The new proposals were approved at the Joint Conference mentioned above and were given to Ambassador Grew by Foreign Minister Toyoda the next day, September 4 (Japan time), with the request that they be transmitted to Secretary Hull by the Ambassador to overcome any possibility of inaccuracy in handling by Ambassador Nomura (ex. 29, vol. II, p. 593).

Ambassador Nomura presented the new proposals to Secretary Hull at a meeting on September 6 (Washington time). He explained that although the new proposals had been prepared by the Japanese Government before it received President Roosevelt's reply of September 3 (Washington time), nevertheless his Government believed that the contents of the new proposals constituted a reply to the President. He said that the proposals were also in response to the view expressed by Secretary Hull at the conference with him on the evening of August 28, namely, that it would be desirable for the two Governments to reach an agreement in principle on the fundamental questions involved before making arrangements for the proposed Roosevelt-Konoye meeting (ex. 29, vol. II, pp. 606–607). As presented to Secretary Hull, the new Japanese proposals were as follows:

DRAFT PROPOSAL HANDED BY THE JAPANESE AMBASSADOR (NOMURA) TO THE SECRETARY OF STATE ON SEPTEMBER 6, 1941

The Government of Japan undertakes:
    (a) that Japan is ready to express its concurrence in those matters which were already tentatively agreed upon between Japan and the United States in the course of their preliminary informal conversations;

(b) that Japan will not make any military advancement from French Indo-China against any of its adjoining areas, and likewise will not, without any justifiable reason, resort to military action against any regions lying south of Japan;

(c) that the attitudes of Japan and the United States towards the European War will be decided by the concepts of protection and self-defense, and, in case the United States should participate in the European War, the interpretation and execution of the Tripartite Pact by Japan shall be independently decided;

(d) that Japan will endeavour to bring about the rehabilitation of general and normal relationship between Japan and China, upon the realization of which Japan is ready to withdraw its armed forces from China as soon as possible in accordance with the agreements between Japan and China;

(e) that the economic activities of the United States in China will not be restricted so long as pursued on an equitable basis;

(f) that Japan's activities in the Southwestern Pacific Area will be carried on by peaceful means and in accordance with the principle of nondiscrimination in international commerce, and that Japan will cooperate in the production and procurement by the United States of natural resources in the said area which it needs;

(g) that Japan will take measures necessary for the resumption of normal trade relations between Japan and the United States, and in connection with the above-mentioned, Japan is ready to discontinue immediately the application of the foreigners' transactions control regulations with regard to the United States on the basis of reciprocity.

The Government of the United States undertakes:

(a) that, in response to the Japanese Government's commitment expressed in point (d) referred to above, the United States will abstain from any measures and actions which will be prejudicial to the endeavour by Japan concerning the settlement of the China Affair;

(b) that the United States will reciprocate Japan's commitment expressed in point (f) referred to above;

(c) that the United States will suspend any military measures in the Far East and in the Southwestern Pacific Area;

(d) that the United States will immediately (upon settlement) reciprocate Japan's commitment expressed in point (g) referred to above by discontinuing the application of the so-called freezing act with regard to Japan and further by removing the prohibition against the passage of Japanese vessels through the Panama Canal (ex. 29, vol. II, pp. 608–609).

Secretary Hull testified that these new Japanese proposals—

were much narrower than the assurances given in the statement communicated to the President on August 28. In the September 6 Japanese draft the Japanese gave only an evasive formula with regard to their obligations under the Tripartite Pact. There was a qualified undertaking that Japan would not "without any justifiable reason" resort to military action against any region south of Japan. No commitment was offered in regard to the nature of the terms which Japan would offer to China; nor any assurance of an intention by Japan to respect China's territorial integrity and sovereignty, to refrain from interference in China's internal affairs, not to station Japanese troops indefinitely in wide areas of China, and to conform to the principle of nondiscrimination in international commercial relations. The formula contained in that draft that "the economic activities of the United States in China will not be restricted so long as pursued on an equitable basis" clearly implied a concept that the conditions under which American trade and commerce in China were henceforth to be conducted were to be a matter for decision by Japan (tr. 1118–1119).

On September 9 (Washington time) Secretary Hull cabled to Ambassador Grew a series of questions to be submitted to Foreign Minister Toyoda regarding the intentions of the Japanese Government in offering certain of the new proposals, especially those relating to China (ex. 29, vol. II, pp. 610–613). The Foreign Minister's replies to these questions were received by Ambassador Grew on September 13 (Japan time) and promptly cabled to Washington (ex. 29, vol. II, pp. 620–624).

On September 15 (Washington time) Ambassador Nomura cabled Foreign Minister Toyoda that it seemed that the matter of the preliminary conversations had been entrusted to Secretary Hull. He said that in such conversations the United States would want to be advised of the peace terms Japan would propose between Japan and China and would refuse to act as intermediary unless the terms were fair and just; therefore, he said, it would be necessary to outline the terms in advance of the proposed "leaders conference." He also reported that the United States wanted to arrange matters with Britain, China, and the Netherlands in advance of the proposed conference, so that those countries would not get the impression the United States was trading them off (ex. 1, p. 27). Two days later, Ambassador Nomura cabled that there were "considerable signs of anticipation of a Japanese-U. S. conference" at a recent United States Cabinet meeting, and that "there is no mistaking the fact that the President is prepared to attend the meeting if the preliminary arrangements can be made" (ex. 1, p. 28). On September 22 (Washington time), he cabled a long report to the Foreign Minister concerning conditions and attitudes in the United States generally. His report concluded with the following estimate:

Finally, though the United States Government does not wish to compromise with Japan at the expense of China, should Japan give up forceful aggressions, Japanese-American trade relations could be restored, and the United States would even go so far as to render economic assistance to Japan (ex. 1, p. 31).

In the meantime, in Tokyo at Joint Conferences on September 6 and 13 (Japan time), the Japanese Government had determined the basic peace terms which it was prepared to offer to China (ex. 132–A, item D). A document containing those terms (Annex C attached hereto) was handed to Secretary Hull by Ambassador Nomura on September 23 (Washington time), having been communicated by the Foreign Minister to Ambassador Grew in Tokyo on September 22 (Japan time) (ex. 29, vol. II, pp. 631–633). During this conference with Secretary Hull, Ambassador Nomura reiterated the desire of his Government to have the Roosevelt-Konoye meeting take place at the earliest possible opportunity. He told the Secretary that the several documents which he had now presented were a full expression of everything the Japanese Government desired to say, and that anything further pertaining to the Tripartite Pact might best be left to the proposed meeting of the heads of the two Governments (ex. 29, vol. II, pp. 634–635). However, on September 27 (Washington time), he delivered to Secretary Hull a further document (Annex D attached hereto), which had been prepared in the form, and along the lines, of the American proposals of June 21 (Washington time) and had been approved at a Joint Conference on September 20 (Japan time). The new document, it was said, incorporated all that the Japanese Government had communicated to the American Government since June 21. A similar document had been delivered to Ambassador Grew on September 25, 1941 (ex. 29, vol. II, pp. 636–641).

On September 27 (Japan time) ceremonies were held in Tokyo celebrating the first anniversary of the Tripartite Pact. That day Foreign Minister Toyoda requested Ambassador Grew to call on him, and asked the Ambassador to convey to President Roosevelt, through Secretary Hull, the anxiety of Premier Konoye and the entire Cabinet lest the proposed Roosevelt-Konoye meeting might be indefinitely delayed, stating that all preparations had been made by the Japanese Government. During this conference he described to Ambassador Grew in considerable detail his Government's position regarding the conversations (ex. 29, vol. II, pp. 641–645). The Foreign Minister cabled his remarks to Ambassador Nomura, saying that "in view of internal and external circumstances in our country, we cannot keep postponing matters forever" (ex. 1, p. 33). Ambassador Nomura communicated the gist of the Foreign Minister's remarks to Secretary Hull on September 29 (Washington time). He said that while he was well aware of the United States Government's position and had communicated it to Tokyo, nevertheless, his Government had instructed him to press for an answer to the Japanese proposal. As his personal opinion, he judged that if nothing came of the proposal for a meeting between the heads of the two Governments, it might be difficult for Premier Konoye to retain his position and that he then would be likely to be succeeded by a less moderate leader (ex. 29, vol. II, p. 652).

AMBASSADOR GREW SUPPORTS THE PROPOSED "LEADERS CONFERENCE"

(August–September 1941)

In Tokyo Ambassador Grew had reached the conclusion that if the Roosevelt-Konoye meeting should not be held, or if it should be long delayed, the Konoye Cabinet might fall. He had first learned of the proposed "leaders conference" at a meeting with Foreign Minister Toyoda on August 18 (Japan time.) During the Foreign Minister's lengthy remarks concerning the proposed meeting, Ambassador Grew had commented on Japan's progressive southward advance and the fact that, in spite of all peaceful assurances, the United States Government in the light of the steps Japan had taken "could only be guided by facts and actions and not words." Notwithstanding the doubts reflected in these statements, at the conclusion of the Foreign Minister's remarks Ambassador Grew had said "that in the interests of peace, (he) would give the proposal (for a meeting) his own personal support" (ex. 29, vol. II, pp. 559–564). Ambassador Grew reported the Foreign Minister's remarks to Secretary Hull the following day in a message which included the following, as paraphrased in the State Department:

that naturally he is not aware of the reaction President Roosevelt will have to the proposal made today orally by the Japanese Minister for Foreign Affairs. The Ambassador urges, however, with all the force at his command, for the sake of avoiding the obviously growing possibility of an utterly futile war between Japan and the United States, that this Japanese proposal not be turned aside without very prayerful consideration. Not only is the proposal unprecedented in Japanese history, but it is an indication that Japanese intransigence is not crystallized completely owing to the fact that the proposal has the approval of the Emperor and the highest authorities in the land. The good which may flow from a meeting between Prince Konoye and President Roosevelt is incalculable. The opportunity is here presented, the Ambassador ventures to believe, for an act of the highest statesmanship, such as the recent meeting of President Roosevelt with Prime Minister Churchill at sea, with the possible overcoming thereby of apparently insurmountable obstacles to peace hereafter in the Pacific (ex. 29, vol. II, p. 565).

A month later, in a personal letter dated September 22 (Japan time) to President Roosevelt, which apparently did not, however, reach

Washington until after the fall of the Konoye Cabinet, he referred to his conversations with Premier Konoye "who," he said—

in the face of bitter antagonism from extremist and pro-Axis elements in the country is courageously working for an improvement in Japan's relations with the United States. He bears the heavy responsibility for having allowed our relations to come to such a pass and he no doubt now sees the handwriting on the wall and realizes that Japan has nothing to hope for from the Tripartite Pact and must shift her orientation of policy if she is to avoid disaster; but whatever the incentive that has led to his present efforts, I am convinced that he now means business and will go as far as is possible, without incurring open rebellion in Japan, to reach a reasonable understanding with us. In spite of all the evidence of Japan's bad faith in times past in failing to live up to her commitments, I believe that there is a better chance of the present Government implementing whatever commitments it may now undertake than has been the case in recent years. It seems to me highly unlikely that this chance will come again or that any Japanese statesman other than Prince Konoye could succeed in controlling the military extremists in carrying through a policy which they, in their ignorance of international affairs and economic laws, resent and oppose. The alternative to reaching a settlement now would be the greatly increased probability of war * * *. I therefore most earnestly hope that we can come to terms, even if we must take on trust, at least to some degree, the continued good faith and ability of the present Government fully to implement those terms." (Ex. 178.)

A week later, on September 29 (Japan time), following his meeting with Foreign Minister Toyoda on September 27 referred to above, Ambassador Grew cabled a long report to Secretary Hull, in which "in all deference to the much broader field of view of President Roosevelt and Secretary Hull and in full awareness that the Ambassador's approach to the matter is limited to the viewpoint of the American Embassy in Japan," he stated at length his appraisal of the existing situation (ex. 29, vol. II, pp. 645–650). The most significant part of this report was the following, as paraphrased in the State Department:

8. Should the United States expect or await agreement by the Japanese Government, in the present preliminary conversations, to clear-cut commitments which will satisfy the United States Government both as to principle and as to concrete detail, almost certainly the conversations will drag along indefinitely and unproductively until the Konoye Cabinet and its supporting elements desiring *rapprochement* with the United States will come to the conclusion that the outlook for an agreement is hopeless and that the United States Government is only playing for time. If the abnormal sensitiveness of Japan and the abnormal effects of loss of face are considered, in such a situation Japanese reaction may and probably will be serious. This will result in the Konoye Government's being discredited and in a revulsion of anti-American feeling, and this may and probably will lead to unbridled acts. The eventual cost of these will not be reckoned, and their nature is likely to inflame Americans, while reprisal and counter-reprisal measures will bring about a situation in which it will be difficult to avoid war. *The logical outcome of this will be the downfall of the Konoye Cabinet and the formation of a military dictatorship which will lack either the disposition or the temperament to avoid colliding head-on with the United States.* There is a question that such a situation may prove to be more serious even than the failure to produce an entirely satisfactory agreement through the proposed meeting between President Roosevelt and Prince Konoye, should it take place as planned (ex. 29, vol. II, pp. 648–649).

In connection with Ambassador Grew's reference to the "viewpoint of the American Embassy in Japan," in his testimony before the Committee he said:

I may say here that we in our Embassy in Tokyo did not have access to any of the secret documents or intercepted telegrams. We didn't even know that they existed (tr. 1481).

And again:

I just want to say once more everything I have said today represents the point of view of one spot, our Embassy in Tokyo, and we were deprived of a great deal of the information which was available to the President and Mr. Hull. We had none of the secret intercepts or telegrams, we had none of the documents that have come into the State Department from time to time, documents of a secret nature, so of course the President and Mr. Hull saw the picture with a great deal more information than we had available to us (tr. 1903–1904).

JAPAN DETERMINES ITS MINIMUM DEMANDS AND ITS MAXIMUM CONCESSIONS IN THE NEGOTIATIONS WITH THE UNITED STATES

(September 6, 1941)

It is now known that in the meantime, in Tokyo, far-reaching decisions had been made. The "Policy of the Imperial Government" which was decided upon at the Imperial Conference on July 2 (Japan time) had provided that in carrying out a southward advance the Government would not be deterred "by the possibility of being involved in a war with England and America." It had also been decided at that conference that in carrying out Japan's preparations for war with Russia and in the use of Japan's military strength against Russia in case the German-Soviet war "should develop to our advantage,"

all plans, especially the use of armed forces, will be carried out in such a way as to place no serious obstacles *in the path of our basic military preparations for a war with England and America* (ex. 173, Konoye Memoirs, pp. 70–71).

When the Japanese advance into southern French Indochina during the latter part of July had brought about the termination of the conversations between Secretary Hull and Ambassador Nomura and the American freezing order, Premier Konoye had come forward early in August with his proposal for a "leaders conference" between President Roosevelt and himself. While this proposal had received the support of the Japanese Navy, it had been supported by the Japanese Army only provided the Premier intended

to carry out a war against America if the President of the United States still fails to comprehend the true intentions of the Empire (ex. 173, Konoye Memoirs, p. 31).

As tension increased in Tokyo, the Japanese Army General Staff began advocating the immediate breaking off of negotiations with the United States and the opening of Japanese-American hostilities, and Premier Konoye discussed this question at innumerable conferences with the Army and Navy Ministers during the latter part of August (ex. 173, Konoye Memoirs, p. 39–40).

It is now known that during those conferences there were developed "Plans for the Prosecution of the Policy of the Imperial Government" which set forth the manner in which the Government would proceed in carrying out the plans "for the southern territories" decided upon at the Imperial Conference on July 2 (Japan time). Premier Konoye submitted these new "Plans" to the Emperor informally on September 5 (Japan time) in the form of an agenda for an Imperial Conference the next day, as follows:

1. Determined not to be deterred by the possibility of being involved in a war with America (and England and Holland), in order to secure our national existence, *we will proceed with war preparations so that they be completed approximately toward the end of October.*

2. At the same time, *we will endeavor by every possible diplomatic means to have our demands agreed to by America and England.* Japan's minimum demands in these negotiations with America (and England), together with the Empire's maximum concessions are embodied in the attached document.

3. *If by the early part of October there is no reasonable hope of having our demands agreed to in the diplomatic negotiations mentioned above, we will immediately make up our minds to get ready for war against America (and England and Holland).*

Policies with reference to countries other than those in the southern territories will be carried out in harmony with the plans already laid. Special effort will be made to prevent America and Soviet Russia from forming a united front against Japan (ex. 173, Konoye Memoirs, p. 77).

According to Premier Konoye, on examining the "Plans", Emperor Hirohito was impressed by the fact that the document seemed "to give precedence to war over diplomatic activities." The Premier explained that the order of business in the agenda did not indicate any differences in degree of importance. The Emperor then summoned the Chiefs of the Army and Navy General Staffs. When they came, he questioned them sharply concerning the probable length of hostilities in the event of a Japanese-American conflict, and then asked whether it was not true that both of them "were for giving precedence to diplomacy." Both answered in the affirmative (ex. 173, Konoye Memoirs, pp. 40–41).

At the Imperial Conference the next day, September 6 (Japan time) the "Plans" were decided upon and approved (ex. 173, Konoye Memoirs, p. 40). However, at the Conference first the President of the Privy Council and then Emperor Hirohito asked for a clarification of the views of the Government as to whether the emphasis was not being placed by the Government upon war rather than diplomacy. When none of the Supreme Command replied, and only the Navy Minister representing the Government, the Emperor is reported to have rebuked the Supreme Command by indicating that he was striving for international peace. After this the Chief of the Navy General Staff assured the Emperor that the Chiefs of the Supreme Command were conscious of the importance of diplomacy, and "advocated a resort to armed force only when there seemed no other way out." According to Premier Konoye, the Conference adjourned "in an atmosphere of unprecedented tenseness" (ex. 173, Konoye Memoirs, p. 41).

Japan's "minimum demands" in the negotiations with America and England, as approved at the Imperial Conference on September 6 (Japan time), were as follows, according to Premier Konoye's memoirs:

1. America and England would be required to agree not to intervene in, or obstruct, the settlement by Japan of the "China Incident", to close the Burma Road, and to cease all aid of any kind to China.

2. America and England would be required to agree to take no action in the Far East which offered a threat to the Japanese Empire, and not to establish military bases in Thailand, the Netherlands East Indies, China, or Far Eastern Soviet Russia or increase their existing Far Eastern military forces over their present strength. In this connection Japan would not consider any demands "for the liquidation of Japan's special relations with French Indo-China."

3. America and England would be required to agree to cooperate with Japan in her attempt to obtain needed raw materials; to restore trade relations with Japan and "furnish her with the

raw materials she needs" from British and American territories in the Southwest Pacific; and to assist Japan in establishing close economic relations with Thai and the Netherlands East Indies (ex. 173, Konoye Memoirs, appendix V, pp. 77–78).

The "maximum concessions" Japan was prepared to make in return for agreement to her "minimum demands" were as follows:

1. Japan would not use French Indochina as a base for operations against any neighboring countries "with the exception of China."

2. Japan would be prepared to withdraw her troops from French Indochina "as soon as a just peace is established in the Far East."

3. Japan would be prepared to guarantee the neutrality of the Philippine Islands (ex. 173, Konoye Memoirs, appendix V, p. 78).

In other words, in an effort to take all possible advantage of the world situation, the Japanese Government determined at the Imperial Conference on September 6 (Japan time) that the least Japan would accept from America and England in return for the withdrawal of her troops from French Indochina would be the agreement of America and England to cease all aid to China, to accept a military and naval status in the Far East inferior to Japan, and to furnish all possible material aid to Japan. Furthermore, Japan did not intend to perform her part of the "bargain" until after "a just peace" had been established in the Far East. From the Japanese standpoint, this latter qualification meant after the settlement of the "China Incident" by Japan on her own terms. The substance of these "minimum demands" was contained in the ultimatum which the Japanese Government later delivered to the United States on November 20 (Washington time).

The evening of the same day, September 6 (Japan time), Premier Konoye, with the knowledge and approval of the Japanese Ministers of War, Navy, and Foreign Affairs met with Ambassador Grew at a private house under conditions of extraordinary secrecy. In his notes of the meeting, Ambassador Grew wrote that the Premier had requested that his statements be transmitted personally to President Roosevelt in the belief that they might amplify and clarify the approach which he had made through Ambassador Nomura. Ambassador Grew noted that the Premier and, consequently, the Government of Japan, conclusively and wholeheartedly agreed with the four principles put forward by Secretary Hull as a basis for the rehabilitation of Japanese-American relations.[1] In his memoirs, however, Prince Konoye stated that when at this meeting Ambassador Grew asked for his views regarding Secretary Hull's four principles he said "that they were splendid as principles but when it came down to actual application a variety of problems arose" and that it was in order to solve those very problems that he deemed it necessary to hold the meeting with President Roosevelt (ex. 173, Konoye Memoirs, p. 42). Ambassador Grew noted that Premier Konoye had strongly urged that no better opportunity for the improvement of Japanese-American relations would be presented, and that the Premier had

[1] In a memorandum dated October 7 (Japan time) recording a conference which he had on that date with the Japanese Foreign Minister, Ambassador Grew noted that the Foreign Minister told him that Ambassador Nomura had been instructed to inform Secretary Hull that the statement in the United States memorandum of October 2 (Washington time) (*see infra*) that Premier Konoye "fully subscribed" to the four principles should be modified to indicate that the Premier subscribed "in principle" (ex. 29, vol. II, p. 664).

said that he had the full support of the responsible chiefs of the Army and Navy, who were already choosing their delegates to the proposed conference. Premier Konoye had said, he noted, that he could control any opposition from within the Government, and that he was determined to spare no effort, despite all elements and factors opposing him to crown his present endeavors with success. The Ambassador wrote that during the conversation he had outlined in general terms—

the bitter lessons of the past to our Government as the result of the failure of the Japanese Government to honor the promises given to me by former Japanese Ministers for Foreign Affairs apparently in all sincerety—

and had stated that, as the result—

the Government of the United States had at long last concluded that it must place its reliance on actions and facts and not on Japanese promises or assurances.

He noted that Premier Konoye had expressed the earnest hope that in view of the present internal situation in Japan the projected meeting with the President could be arranged "with the least possible delay" (ex. 29, vol. II, pp. 604–606).

THE UNITED STATES ASKS JAPAN TO CLARIFY ITS NEW PROPOSALS

(October 2, 1941)

Thus, as September ended the Japanese Government, on the one hand, was vigorously asserting the urgent and pressing need to go forward with the proposed Roosevelt-Konoye meeting at the earliest possible moment. It is now known that this desire for haste reflected the decision of the Imperial Conference on September 6 (Japan time) that—

If *by the early part of October* there is no reasonable hope of having our demands agreed to in the diplomatic negotiations * * *, we will immediately make up our minds to get ready for war against America (and England and Holland) (ex. 173, Konoye Memoirs, p. 77).

On the other hand, the United States Government, knowing nothing of these plans but nonetheless skeptical of Japan's peaceful intentions, was insisting that before the proposed Roosevelt-Konoye meeting should take place the two Governments should preliminarily agree upon the fundamental matters under consideration when the conversations were broken off in July after the Japanese military occupation of southern French Indochina. This latter position had been taken in the reply to Premier Konoye which President Roosevelt handed to Ambassador Nomura on September 3, and had been repeated many times by Secretary Hull in his subsequent conversations with the Ambassador.

The Committee has obtained from the files of President Roosevelt a memorandum in Secretary Hull's handwriting, on White House stationery, apparently written by the Secretary for the President before the latter left Washington for Hyde Park about September 25 (Washington time) (ex. 179; ex. 1, p. 40). This memorandum summarized Secretary Hull's views at the time:

My suggestion on Jap situation—for you to read *later*.

C. H.

When the Jap Prime Minister requested a meeting with you, he indicated a fairly basic program in generalities, but left open such questions as getting troops out of China, Tripartite Pact, nondiscrimination in trade in Pacific.

We indicated desire for meeting, but suggested first an agreement in principle on the vital questions left open, so as to insure the success of the conference.

Soon thereafter, the Japs *narrowed* their position on these basic questions, and now continue to urge the meeting at Juneau.

My suggestion is to recite their more liberal attitude when they first sought the meeting with you, with their much narrowed position *now*, and earnestly ask if they cannot go back to their original liberal attitude so we can start discussions *again* on agreement in principle *before* the meeting, and reemphasizing your desire for a meeting (ex. 179). [Italics in original.]

President Roosevelt sent his comments to Secretary Hull from Hyde Park in the following memorandum dated September 28 (Washington time):

MEMORANDUM FOR THE SECRETARY OF STATE

I wholly agree with your penciled note—to recite the more liberal original attitude of the Japanese when they first sought the meeting, point out their much narrowed position now, earnestly ask if they cannot go back to their original attitude, start discussions again on agreement in principle, and reemphasize my hope for a meeting.

F. D. R.
(ex. 179.)

On October 2 (Washington time), Secretary Hull handed to Ambassador Nomura the United States' reply to the Japanese Government's proposals of September 6 and its subsequent statements of September 23 (Annex C) and September 27 (Annex D). This reply briefly reviewed the course of the conversations thus far, pointing out that developments from early August up to September 6 had seemed to justify the United States Government in concluding that the Japanese Government might be expected to adhere to and to give practical application to a broad progressive program covering the entire Pacific area. The reply continued:

It was therefore a source of disappointment to the Government of the United States that the proposals of the Japanese Government presented by the Japanese Ambassador on September 6, 1941, which the Japanese Government apparently intended should constitute a concrete basis for discussions, appeared to disclose divergence in the concepts of the two Governments. That is to say, those proposals and the subsequent explanatory statements made in regard thereto serve, in the opinion of this Government, to narrow and restrict not only the application of the principles upon which our informal conversations already referred to had been based but also the various assurances given by the Japanese Government of its desire to move along with the United States in putting into operation a broad program looking to the establishment and maintenance of peace and stability in the entire Pacific area (ex. 29, vol. II, pp. 658–659).

It was then noted that the Japanese assurances of peaceful intent continued to be qualified by phrases the need for which was not readily apparent; that in the economic sphere the new proposals were restricted to the countries of the Southwest Pacific area, rather than the entire Pacific area, as before; and that a clear-cut manifestation of Japan's intention in regard to the withdrawal of Japanese troops from China and French Indochina would be most helpful in making known Japan's peaceful intentions, as would additional clarification of the Japanese Government's position with respect to the European war. The reply continued by stating that from what the Japanese Government had so far indicated in regard to its purposes, the United States Government had derived the impression that Japan had in mind a program by which the liberal and progressive principles adhered to by the United States would be circumscribed in their application by qualifications and exceptions. The Japanese Government was then asked whether, under such circumstances, it believed the proposed Roosevelt-Konoye meeting would be likely to contribute to the high purposes "which we have mutually had in mind." The reply concluded by stating that it was the belief of the United States Government that renewed consideration of the fundamental principles which it had long advocated would aid in reaching a meeting of minds in regard to the essential questions on which agreement was sought and would thus lay a firm foundation for the proposed meeting, and that it was the President's earnest hope that a discussion of the fundamental questions might be so developed that the meeting could be held (ex. 29, vol. II, pp. 656–661). After reading the reply, Ambassador Nomura commented that he thought his Government would be disappointed because of its very earnest desire to hold the meeting, but that in any case he would transmit it to his Government, which he did the same day (ex. 29, vol. II, p. 655; ex. 1, p. 50). He added that he was convinced that the Japanese Government was entirely sincere in this matter and had no ulterior purpose. He said, however, that in view of the difficulties of the internal situation in Japan, he did not think his Government could go any further at this time (ex. 29, vol. II, p. 655).

In a memorandum bearing the same date, October 2 (Washington time), which was distributed to President Roosevelt and Secretary Hull in addition to Secretary Stimson, General Marshall and other high officers in the War Department, Colonel Hayes A. Kroncr, Acting Assistant Chief of Staff, G–2, reached the following conclusions:

10. This Division is of the opinion that neither a conference of leaders nor economic concessions at this point would be of any material advantage to the United States unless a definite commitment to withdraw from the Axis were obtained prior to the conference. * * *

11. Since it is highly improbable that this condition can be met by the Japanese Government at the present time our course lies straight before us. This Division still believes that forceful diplomacy vis-a-vis Japan, including the application of ever increasing military and economic pressure on our part, offers the best chance of gaining time, the best possibility of preventing the spread of hostilities in the Pacific Area, and the best hope of the eventual disruption of the Tripartite Pact. The exercise of increasingly strong "power diplomacy" by the United States is still clearly indicated (ex. 33).

The following undated note, in Secretary Stimson's handwriting, appears at the end of his copy of the above memorandum:

Quite independently I have reached similar conclusions and hold them strongly. I believe however that during the next three months while we are rearming the Philippines great care must be exercised to avoid an explosion by the Japanese Army. Put concretely this means, that while I approve of stringing out negotiations during that period, they should not be allowed to ripen into a personal conference between the President and P. M.[1] I greatly fear that such a conference if actually held would produce concessions which would be highly dangerous to our vitally important relations with China (ex. 33–A).

Admiral Stark testified before the Committee that he neither opposed or approved the proposal for a meeting between President Roosevelt and Premier Konoye. He continued:

I do recall when it was discussed my own personal opinion was that the President and Mr. Hull were right in not just going out to discuss something with the Prime Minister without some preliminary agreement regarding the agenda and something which might be accomplished (tr. 6308).

[1] Prime Minister Konoye.

In his testimony before the Committee, Secretary Hull set forth at length the considerations which were taken into account in determining the position to be taken by the United States Government regarding the proposed "leaders conference" (tr. 1120–1124).

The next day, October 3 (Washington time), after he had forwarded the United States reply to Tokyo, Ambassador Nomura cabled Foreign Minister Toyoda a long report on the situation in the United States as he saw it. His report began by stating—

although there is a feeling that the Japanese-U. S. talks have finally reached a deadlock, we do not believe that it should be considered as an absolutely hopeless situation. We are of the impression that the United States worded their memorandum in such a way as to permit a ray of hope to penetrate through (ex. 1, p. 51–52).

He expressed the view that an "understanding" between Japan and the United States hinged on one point, the problem of the evacuation of the Japanese troops from China (ex. 1, p. 53).

During the next 2 weeks the Japanese Foreign Office made repeated efforts both in Washington and in Tokyo to have the United States Government state what further assurances it desired from the Japanese Government, emphasizing that the position of Premier Konoye was daily growing more difficult. Also during this period, Ambassador Nomura appears to have incurred the displeasure of Foreign Minister Toyoda. In a message to the Foreign Minister on October 8 (Washington time), the Ambassador indicated that he agreed with many of Secretary Hull's criticisms of the Japanese proposals of September 6, which the Foreign Office had prepared. He expressed the opinion that—

In our proposal of the 6th and in the explanation thereof, not only did we limit them and narrow what we had discussed in our informal conversations thus far, but we also curtailed extremely the guarantees we offered concerning the aforementioned principles. We equivocated concerning guarantees that we would not engage in armed aggression. We limited the area to which the principle of nondiscriminatory treatment would apply in the Pacific, and on the excuse that China was geographically near to us, we limited the very principle itself. On the question of stationing and evacuating troops in and from China (including French Indo-China), the Americans are making some demands which we in principle have objections to. Moreover, they figure that they must be much surer of our attitude toward the three-power pact. These points you probably already know (ex. 1, p. 59).

As the result of repeated instructions from the Foreign Minister to obtain from Secretary Hull an expression of his views regarding the three major points of difference between the two Governments, i. e., which had developed in the earlier conversations, namely, (1) the withdrawal of troops from China, (2) Japan's obligations under the Tripartite Pact, and (3) nondiscrimination in international trade, Ambassador Nomura called on Secretary Hull on October 9 (Washington time) (vol. II, pp. 670–672). The Ambassador's report of this meeting (ex. 1, p. 61) was plainly unsatisfactory to Foreign Minister Toyoda, for on October 10 (Japan time) the Foreign Minister cabled Ambassador Nomura that he was well aware of the Ambassador's opinions and that what he wanted was "the opinions of the American officials and none other." Saying that "slowly but surely the question of these negotiations has reached the decisive stage," and that he was doing his utmost "to bring about a decision on them and the situation does not permit of this senseless procrastination," he told Ambassador Nomura:

You do not tell me whether or not we have a chance to proceed with these parleys. You do not tell me how Hull answers. You do not tell me anything else I need to know for my future consideration. You must wire me in detail and immediately the minutes of these conversations, what they say and the prospect for negotiations. Hereafter, when you interview Hull or the President of the United States, please take Wakasugi or Iguchi with you and please send me without delay the complete minutes of what transpires (ex. 1, p. 63).

On the same afternoon, October 10 (Japan time), Foreign Minister Toyoda requested Ambassador Grew to call on him, and during their conversation told Ambassador Grew that Ambassador Nomura had been "unable to provide the information" he had asked for and that—

a week of very valuable time had been wasted in an endeavor to elicit through the Japanese Ambassador information which, had it been received, would have measurably accelerated the present conversations (ex. 30, p. 454).

The Foreign Minister told Ambassador Grew that in order to prevent further delay he was requesting the Ambassador to ask his Government to reply to the following question:

The Government of Japan has submitted to the Government of the United States with reference to certain questions proposals which are apparently not satisfactory to the Government of the United States. Will the American Government now set forth to the Japanese Government for its consideration the undertakings to be assumed by the Japanese Government which would be satisfactory to the American Government (ex. 29, vol. II, p. 678)?

He continued by saying that since—

he had the impression that the Japanese Ambassador in Washington was apparently very fatigued, serious consideration was being given to the question of sending to Washington a diplomat of wide experience to assist the Ambassador in carrying on the present conversations. Admiral Toyoda said he had in mind a high-ranking diplomatic official with the personal rank of Ambassador, but he had not yet approached the official in question and was therefore uncertain as to whether he would agree to undertake to accept the mission. It would be of great assistance to the Minister to ascertain whether the Government of the United States, in the event that it was decided to send the official in question to Washington, would be prepared to make available a reservation for him on the airplane from Manila to San Francisco. Admiral Toyoda said that the official in question would not be accredited to the Government of the United-States but would be temporarily and unofficially attached to the Japanese Embassy in Washington. I told the Foreign Minister that I would transmit his inquiry to my Government.

In concluding the conversation, the Minister several times stressed to me, in view of the importance of the time factor, the necessity of expediting the progress of the conversations (ex. 29, vol. II, p. 679).

Ambassador Nomura replied to Foreign Minister Toyoda's message of October 10 (Japan time) on the same date (Washington time):

What they want is the maintenance of peace in the Pacific, and they claim that our policy is semipacific and semiaggressive. They say that our proposal of September 6 diverged greatly from preceding statements and that it will be out of the question to agree on any preparatory talks on the basis of such a proposal. In addition to the three matters mentioned in your message, it seems that there are many other objections. I have repeatedly asked them to clarify what I do not understand, but they won't answer. At any rate, however, I feel safe at least in saying that they are demanding that we compromise in accordance with the lines laid down in their memorandum of October 2. *I am sure that there is not the slightest chance on earth of them featuring a conference of leaders so long as we do not make that compromise.*

In other words, they are not budging an inch from the attitude they have always taken; however, they act as if they were ready to consider at any time any plan of ours which would meet the specifications of their answer of the 2nd (ex. 1, p. 63).

On October 13 (Japan time) Foreign Minister Toyoda cabled instructions to the Counselor of the Japanese Embassy in Washington,

Mr. Wakasugi, who had just returned to Washington after 2 weeks in Japan, to call upon Under Secretary Welles. In his message, the Foreign Minister said that he was particularly anxious to be advised as soon as possible as to whether he could assume that the United States had no particular disagreements other than the three major points and whether the United States would submit a counterproposal to the Japanese proposals of September 27. He said:

> The situation at home is fast approaching a crisis, and it is becoming absolutely essential that the two leaders meet if any adjustment of Japanese-U. S. relations is to be accomplished (ex. 1, p. 64).

Counselor Wakasugi talked with Under Secretary Welles on the afternoon of October 13 (ex. 29, vol. II, pp. 680–686). Admiral Nomura sent two reports of that meeting to Tokyo, on the same day (ex. 1, pp. 66–68). His first report stated that so far as Mr. Welles knew there were no obstacles to the materialization of the leaders' conference other than the three major points, though there might be one or two others, and that the United States had no intention of submitting any counterproposal other than those of June 21 and October 2. His second report was a more detailed description of the Welles-Wakasugi meeting. In reply, the Foreign Minister said that these reports had "clarified many points" and "that there is no need for us to make any further move until the other side decides that it is impossible to clarify the concrete proposal any further" (ex. 1, pp. 69–70).

In Tokyo, the Japanese Government also made frequent overtures to the officials at the American Embassy. Thus, early on October 7 (Japan time), the Premier's private secretary, Mr. Ushiba, called on Counselor Dooman (ex. 29, vol II, pp. 662–663) and complained that the failure of the preliminary conversations to make any progress had made the Premier's position difficult. He concluded his remarks with the comment that—

> the only thing left for the Japanese Government was to ask the American Government to give specifications with regard to the character of the undertakings which Japan was desired to give, and that if a clear-cut reply was not forthcoming to bring the conversations to a close (ex. 29, vol. II, p. 663).

This meeting appears to have been preliminary to a meeting the same morning between Ambassador Grew and the Foreign Minister, at the latter's request. At that meeting, as on the occasion of subsequent calls by Mr. Terasaki on Counselor Dooman and Ambassador Grew on October 8 and 9, the Japanese endeavored to obtain comments on the American reply of October 2. It was again indicated that the Japanese Government wished to know more definitely what undertakings the United States Government wanted it to give. These efforts culminated in Foreign Minister Toyoda's request of Ambassador Grew on October 10 that he submit that question to Secretary Hull. On that occasion Ambassador Grew commented at length on the opinion he had conveyed the day before to the Foreign Minister, that the reports he had received of plans to dispatch additional Japanese troops to Indochina in substantial numbers "could not but seriously and adversely affect these conversations (ex. 29, vol. II, p. 679).

GERMANY DEMANDS THAT JAPAN WARN THE UNITED STATES THAT
WAR BETWEEN GERMANY AND ITALY AND THE UNITED STATES
WOULD LEAD TO WAR BETWEEN JAPAN AND THE UNITED STATES
PURSUANT TO THE TRIPARTITE PACT

(October 1941)

The intercepted Japanese messages show that during the latter part of September and the early part of October both the German and Italian Ambassadors sought to obtain from Foreign Minister Toyoda confidential information regarding the Japanese-American conversations. In contrast with the policy followed by his predecessor, Foreign Minister Matsuoka, from whom the Axis partners had obtained such information, Foreign Minister Toyoda declined to give them any (ex. 1, p. 71).

Failing in this, after the German attacks on American merchant vessels and the movement in the United States for revision of the Neutrality Act, the Germans took a stronger line. This became known to the United States not only from intercepted messages but also through statements made by the Japanese Vice Minister for Foreign Affairs, Mr. Amau, to Ambassador Grew in Tokyo on October 15 (Japan time). Mr. Amau told Ambassador Grew—

that the German Government is insistently pressing for the issuance of a statement by the Japanese Government in confirmation of the interpretation given to the Tripartite Pact by Mr. Matsuoka, to the effect that Japan will declare war on the United States in the event of war occurring between Germany and the United States. As a reply, although it has not yet been decided when or whether such reply will be rendered to the German Government, the Japanese Government is considering a formula of a noncommittal nature to the effect that maintenance of peace in the Pacific is envisaged in the Tripartite Pact and that the attention of the American Government has been sought for its earnest consideration of Japan's obligations under the Pact (ex. 29, vol. II, p. 686).

The following day, however, Foreign Minister Toyoda cabled Ambassador Nomura that early in October—

the German authorities demanded that the Japanese Government submit to the American Government a message to the effect that the Japanese Government observes that if the ROOSEVELT Administration continues to attack the Axis Powers increasingly, a belligerent situation would inevitably arise between Germany and Italy, on the one hand, and the United States, on the other, and this would provide the reasons for the convocation of the duties envisioned in the Three Power agreement and might lead Japan to join immediately the war in opposition to the United States. We have not as yet submitted this message because, in view of the Japanese-American negotiations, we found it necessary to consider carefully the proper timing as well as wording of the message. The German authorities have been repeatedly making the same request, and there are reasons which do not permit this matter to be postponed any longer. While Japan, on the one hand, finds it necessary to do something in the way of carrying out the duties placed upon her by the Three Power Alliance she had concluded with Germany, on the other hand, she is desirous of making a success of the Japanese-American negotiations. Under the circumstances, we can do no other than to warn the United States at an appropriate moment in such words as are given in my separate telegram #672 and as would not affect the Japanese-American negotiations in one way or another. This message is a secret between me and you (ex. 1, p. 71).

The proposed "warning" to the United States sent to Ambassador Nomura in the Foreign Minister's separate telegram #672 was as follows:

The Imperial Japanese Government has repeatedly affirmed to the American Government that the aim of the Tripartite Pact is to contribute toward the prevention of a further extension of the European war. Should, however, the recent tension in the German-American relations suffer aggravation, there would arise a distinct danger of a war between the two powers, a state of affairs over which Japan, as a signatory to the Tripartite Pact, naturally cannot help entertain a deep concern. Accordingly, in its sincere desire that not only the German-American relations will cease further deterioration but the prevailing tension will also be alleviated as quickly as possible, the Japanese Government is now requesting the earnest consideration of the American Government (ex. 1, p. 71).

Foreign Minister Toyoda never had an opportunity to select the "appropriate moment" for the delivery of this warning, because the next day Premier Konoye and his entire Cabinet resigned *en bloc*. The German Ambassador continued to press for action by Foreign Minister Togo, Admiral Toyoda's successor, but by November 11 (Japan time) when the Foreign Minister communicated with Ambassador Nomura concerning it, far more vigorous measures were contemplated by the Japanese. Foreign Minister Togo's reply erred on the side of understatement:

I explained (to the German Ambassador) that there is a good chance that it would be more effective, under the present circumstances, for us to present a determined attitude rather than to merely make representations to the United States. It is exceedingly doubtful, I pointed out, whether a mere representation would bear any fruit (ex. 1, p. 117).

The Konoye Cabinet Falls, and Ambassador Nomura Asks Permission to Return to Japan

(October 16, 1941; October 18–November 5, 1941)

The attitude of the Japanese representatives in the conversations in Washington and in Tokyo during the latter part of September and the early part of October reflected developments within the Japanese Government during that period. In turn, the course of those developments was directly affected by the far-reaching decisions which had been made at the Imperial Conference on September 6 (Japan time). As has been seen, it is now known that at that conference it had been decided that if "by the early part of October" there should be "no reasonable hope" of having the Japanese "demands" agreed to in the diplomatic negotiations—

we will immediately make up our minds to get ready for war against America (and England and Holland) (ex. 173, Konoye Memoirs, p. 77).

This decision, according to Premier Konoye, had established a dead line "beyond which negotiations could not proceed." The Japanese Government "came more and more to feel that we were approaching a show-down" (ex. 173, Konoye Memoirs, p. 43).

As Ambassador Nomura had told Secretary Hull, with the presentation of its new proposals of September 6, its proposals for basic peace terms with China on September 23, and its revision of the American proposals of June 21 which had been delivered to Secretary Hull on September 27, the Japanese Government took the position that there was nothing more that it desired to say and that the next move was up to the United States. In his memoirs, Premier Konoye criticizes the action of the Japanese Foreign Office in submitting three proposals during September without deciding that it would proceed with the September 27 plan "alone, in complete disregard of the plans of the past" (ex. 173, Konoye Memoirs, p. 46).

This action, which left the Japanese intentions confused, was largely responsible for the fact that the United States Government, in its reply of October 2 (Washington time), had asked for a further clarification of the Japanese intentions.

It is now known that before the United States' reply of October 2 was received in Tokyo and as a result of the fact that the dead line set on September 6 was approaching at a faster rate than the conversations were progressing, Premier Konoye began frequent conferences with members of his Cabinet. He conferred on September 24 and 25 (Japan time) with the War Minister, Navy Minister, Foreign Minister, and President of the Navy Planning Board. From September 27 to October 1 (Japan time) he had discussions with the Navy Minister "concerning the atmosphere in his circle." On October 4 (Japan time), after receipt of the United States reply of October 2, Premier Konoye had an audience with Emperor Hirohito, following which there was a Joint Conference attended by the chiefs of the Japanese High Command. On the evening of October 5 (Japan time) he conferred with General Tojo, the War Minister, to whom he expressed the opinion "that he would continue negotiations (with the United States) to the very end" (ex. 173, Konoye Memoirs, p. 49).

On the evening of October 7 (Japan time), General Tojo called on Premier Konoye and declared that the Army would find it difficult to submit to the withdrawal of its troops from China. In view of this attitude, on October 8 (Japan time) Premier Konoye conferred with the Navy Minister and the Foreign Minister concerning "methods of avoiding a crisis." He met twice with Foreign Minister Toyoda on October 10 (Japan time), the day on which the Foreign Minister asked Ambassador Grew to inquire from the United States Government what additional assurances it desired the Japanese Government to give. A Joint Conference was held on October 11 (Japan time) (ex. 173, Konoye Memoirs, p. 49).

On Sunday, October 12 (Japan time), Premier Konoye called a meeting attended by himself and the Ministers of War, Navy, and Foreign Affairs, together with the President of the Planning Board, which he described in his memoirs as "almost the last conference relative to peace or war." Before the meeting he had learned that the Navy, although not desiring a rupture in the negotiations, and wishing as much as possible to avoid war, nevertheless was unwilling to state this publicly, and would therefore leave the question of peace or war up to the Premier. At the meeting, according to Premier Konoye's memoirs, the Navy Minister stated:

We have now indeed come to the crossroads where we must determine either upon peace or war. I should like to leave this decision entirely up to the Premier. And, if we are to seek peace, we shall go all the way for peace. Thus, even if we make a few concessions, we ought to proceed all the way with the policy of bringing the negotiations to fruition. * * * If we are to have war, we must determine upon war here and now. Now is the time. We are now at the final moment of decision. If we decide that we are not to have war, I should like to have us proceed upon the policy that we will bring negotiations to fruition no matter what happens (ex. 173, Konoye Memoirs, p. 50).

In reply to this, Premier Konoye said:

If we were to say that we must determine on war or peace here, today, I myself would decide on continuing the negotiations (ex. 173, Konoye Memoirs, p. 50).

General Tojo, the Minister of War, objected, saying:

This decision of the Premier's is too hasty. Properly speaking, ought we not to determine here whether or not there is any possibility of bringing the negotiations to fruition? *To carry on negotiations for which there is no possibility for fruition, and in the end to let slip the time for fighting, would be a matter of the greatest consequence* (ex. 173, Konoye Memoirs, p. 50).

General Tojo then asked Foreign Minister Toyoda whether he thought there was any possibility of bringing negotiations to fruition. In answer to this question, the Foreign Minister replied that the most difficult problem was the question of the withdrawal of troops from China. He continued:

if in this regard the Army says that it will not retreat one step from its former assertions, then there is no hope in the negotiations. But if on this point the Army states that it will be all right to make concessions, however small they may be, then we cannot say that there is no hope of bringing the negotiations to fruition (ex. 173, Konoye Memoirs, p. 50).

General Tojo, however, would not yield, saying:

The problem of the stationing of troops, in itself means the life of the Army, and we shall not be able to make any concessions at all (ex. 173, Konoye Memoirs, p. 50).

According to Premier Konoye, although the conference lasted 4 hours, no conclusion was arrived at before the meeting adjourned. The following day, October 13 (Japan time), Premier Konoye reported the situation to Emperor Hirohito and Marquis Kido, the Lord Keeper of the Privy Seal and a leader of the "senior statesmen." The next day the Premier met with General Tojo before the Cabinet meeting and again asked his considered opinion concerning the problem of the stationing of troops in China, saying that he had a very great responsibility for the "China Incident," which was still unsettled, and that he found it difficult to agree "to enter upon a greater war the future of which I cannot at all foresee." He then urged, according to his memoirs, that Japan "ought to give in for a time, grant to the United States the formality of withdrawing troops, and save ourselves from the crisis of a Japanese-American war" (ex. 173, Konoye Memoirs, p. 51).

In response to this, General Tojo declared—

if at this time we yield to the United States, she will take steps that are more and more high-handed, and will probably find no place to stop. The problem of withdrawing troops is one, you say, of forgetting the honor and of seizing the fruits, but, to this, I find it difficult to agree from the point of view of maintaining the fighting spirit of the Army (ex. 173, Konoye Memoirs, p. 51).

Premier Konoye records that thus General Tojo did not move from the position he had taken, and the talk ended at odds. According to his memoirs, at the Cabinet meeting which followed, General Tojo at the outset "strongly and excitedly set forth the reasons why the Japanese-American negotiations should no longer be continued." No further reference to the question of continuing the negotiations was made at the Cabinet meeting, as none of the Cabinet ministers would answer General Tojo (ex. 173, Konoye Memoirs, p. 51.)

That evening General Tojo is reported to have sent a message to Premier Konoye in which he said, in effect, that if the Navy's decision to entrust the question of peace or war to the Premier was due to a desire on the part of the Navy not to have a war, then the Imperial Conference on September 6 "will have been fundamentally overturned," as the decisions reached at that conference would not have taken into account such an attitude on the part of the Navy. He then expressed the belief that the entire Cabinet should resign and "declare insolvent everything that has happened up to now and reconsider our plans once more." He said that it was very hard for him to ask the Premier to resign but that, as matters had come to pass, he could not help but do so, and begged the Premier to exert his efforts toward having the Emperor designate Prince Higashikuni, the Chief of the General Staff, as the next Premier, in the belief that only an imperial prince would have power to keep control of the Army and the Navy and to refashion a plan (ex. 173, Konoye Memoirs, p. 52).

The next day, October 15 (Japan time), Premier Konoye was received by Emperor Hirohito, to whom the Premier reported the foregoing developments. The Emperor expressed doubts concerning the desirability of naming Prince Higashikuni the next Premier, saying, according to Premier Konoye:

> In time of peace it would be all right, but in a situation in which we fear that there may be war, and when we also think further of the interests of the Imperial House, I question the advisability of a member of royalty standing forth (ex. 173, Konoye Memoirs, p. 52).

That evening the Premier secretly discussed the situation with Prince Higashikuni, who said he desired several days to think the matter over. However, according to Premier Konoye's memoirs, the situation would not permit further delay, and the following morning all of the Cabinet members submitted their resignations. The next day the "senior statesmen" met in consultation regarding the selection of the next Premier, but Prince Konoye did not attend (ex. 173, Konoye Memoirs, pp. 52–53). Instead, he submitted a long letter explaining in detail the chain of events leading to the resignation of his Cabinet (ex. 173, Konoye Memoirs, appendix IX, pp. 87–91).

Several of the intercepted Japanese messages confirm Prince Konoye's emphasis upon the Army's stand regarding the withdrawal of Japanese troops from China as one of the main causes of the resignation of the Konoye Cabinet. Thus, on October 15 (Washington time), shortly after the Cabinet meetings in Tokyo at which General Tojo refused to make any concessions regarding the evacuation of troops from China, Ambassador Nomura reported to the Foreign Office that the Japanese military attaché at the Japanese Embassy in Washington had been—

> instructed by the Headquarters in Tokyo to advise us not to yield an inch in our stand regarding the question of the evacuation of troops. They are apprehensive that we have not emphasized enough our stand regarding it and urge us to lay special stress on this point (ex. 1, p. 70).

On October 17 (Japan time), Foreign Minister Toyoda cabled Ambassador Nomura that the Cabinet had resigned, saying:

> The resignation was brought about by a split within the Cabinet. It is true that one of the main items on which opinion differed was on the matter of stationing troops or evacuating them from China. However, regardless of the make-up of the new Cabinet, negotiations with the United States shall be continued along the lines already formulated. There shall be no changes in this respect.
> Please, therefore, will you and your staff work in unison and a single purpose, with even more effort, if possible, than before (ex. 1, p. 76).

The Imperial Command to form a new Cabinet was given on October 17 (Japan time) to General Hideki Tojo, who not only became Premier but also took the portfolios of the War and Home Ministries. In addition to having been War Minister in the preceding Cabinet of Premier Konoye, General Tojo was an Army officer on the active list. The same day, Premier Konoye's private secretary, Mr. Ushiba, called on Counselor Dooman at the American Embassy in Tokyo, and through him conveyed to Ambassador Grew from the Premier

a very interesting explanation of the circumstances which had led to the fall of the cabinet and the successful efforts of the Prime Minister to ensure the appointment of a successor who would continue the conversations with the United States. The circumstances were extraordinarily dramatic and constitute what may in future be regarded as one of the really big moments in Japanese history (ex. 30, p. 458).

Mr. Ushiba also delivered to Ambassador Grew a letter from Prince Konoye in which he stated that he felt certain—

that the Cabinet which is to succeed mine will exert its utmost in continuing to a successful conclusion the conversations which we have been carrying on up till today (ex. 30, p. 457).

The following week, a "reliable Japanese informant" gave Ambassador Grew the following account of the events leading up the resignation of the Konoye Cabinet:

The informant called on me at his own request this evening. He told me that just prior to the fall of the Konoye Cabinet a conference of the leading members of the Privy Council and of the Japanese armed forces had been summoned by the Emperor, who inquired if they were prepared to pursue a policy which would guarantee that there would be no war with the United States. The representatives of the Army and Navy who attended this conference did not reply to the Emperor's question, whereupon the latter, with a reference to the progressive policy pursued by the Emperor Meiji, his grandfather, in an unprecedented action ordered the armed forces to obey his wishes. The Emperor's definite stand necessitated the selection of a Prime Minister who would be in a position effectively to control the Army, the ensuing resignation of Prince Konoye, and the appointment of General Tojo who, while remaining in the Army active list, is committed to a policy of attempting to conclude successfully the current Japanese-American conversations (ex. 29, vol. II, p. 697).

On October 16 (Washington time), in a conversation with Lord Halifax, the British Ambassador in the United States, Ambassador Nomura said:

The resignation of the Japanese Cabinet was due to internal differences between on the one hand the Prime Minister and those who wished to reach agreement with the United States by not insisting on the third point mentioned above (the right to station troops in China), and on the other hand those who thought that not to insist on this point would involve too great a loss of face.

But the Ambassador did not anticipate any sudden change of policy. The Emperor was in favour of peace, and even if a general were made Prime Minister, it was unlikely that the Emperor's wishes would be disregarded.

The outburst of a Japanese Navy spokesman as reported in the United States press today was of no importance, and might be disregarded.

Everybody in the Japanese Cabinet wanted understanding with the United States, and the only difference was as to the price that should be paid for it (ex. 158).

Two days later, on October 18 (Washington time), Ambassador Nomura cabled his congratulations to the new Foreign Minister, Shigenori Togo, at the same time expressing his fear that he would not "be able to accomplish much in the future" and asking the new Foreign Minister's approval of his returning to Japan "in the near future so that I may personally report the situation here" (ex. 1, p. 79). He expressed similar views in a message (ex. 1, p. 80) to the Japanese Navy Minister on October 20 (Washington time), and in a message to the new Foreign Minister 2 days later in which he said:

I am sure that I, too, should go out with the former cabinet. * * * Nor do I imagine that you all have any objection. I don't want to be the bones of a dead horse. I don't want to continue this hypocritical existence, deceiving other people. No, don't think I am trying to flee from the field of battle, but as a man of honor this is the only way that is open for me to tread. Please send me your permission to return to Japan. Most humbly do I beseech your forgiveness if I have injured your dignity and I prostrate myself before you in the depth of my rudeness (ex. 1, p. 81).

On October 23 (Japan time), Foreign Minister Togo cabled Ambassador Nomura that the outcome of the negotiations would "have a great bearing upon the decision as to which road the Imperial Government will pursue," and expressed the hope that the Ambassador would see fit "to sacrifice all of (his) personal wishes and remain at (his) post" (ex. 1, p. 82). On November 4 (Japan time), the Foreign Minister cabled Ambassador Nomura to "compose yourself and make up your mind to do your best." Finally, on November 5 (Washington time), Ambassador Nomura cabled the Foreign Minister that after careful consideration "I have decided to continue to put forth my best efforts, however feeble they may be" (ex. 1, p. 100).

THE TOJO CABINET FORMULATES ITS "ABSOLUTELY FINAL PROPOSAL"

(November 5, 1941)

As the result of the Cabinet crisis in Japan, the State Department in Washington considered the dispatch of a personal message from President Roosevelt to Emperor Hirohito urging Japan to join with the United States to preserve peace in the Pacific area, but stating that if Japan should start new military operations the United States "would have to seek, by taking any and all steps which it might deem necessary, to prevent any extension" of the war (ex. 20). Such a message was not sent, however, pending clarification of the situation in Japan and the policies of the new Japanese Government (ex. 20; tr. 4494–4501).

Commencing October 17 (Japan time) the Tojo Cabinet engaged in preparations for a formal determination of the policies it would follow, and such a determination was made at an Imperial Conference on November 5 (Japan time). During the interval between those dates, Ambassador Nomura received only general instructions from the Japanese Foreign Office concerning the course he should follow in further talks with the Americans. He was, however, advised on October 21 (Japan time) that

the new cabinet differs in no way from the former one in its sincere desire to adjust Japanese-United States relations on a fair basis. Our country has said 1 ractically all she can say in the way of expressing of opinions and setting forth our stands. *We feel that we have now reached a point where no further positive action can be taken by us except to urge the United States to reconsider her views.*

We urge, therefore, that, choosing an opportune moment, either you or Wakasugi let it be known to the United States by indirection that our country is not in a position to spend much more time discussing this matter. Please continue the talks, emphasizing our desire for a formal United States counter proposal to our proposal of 27 September (ex. 1, p. 81).

These instructions were concurred in by the Japanese War and Navy Ministers (ex. 1, p. 84).

In accordance with the Foreign Minister's instructions, Minister Wakasugi called on Under Secretary Welles on October 24 (Washington time). The Minister told the Under Secretary that the new Japanese Government desired to follow the policy of the preceding Government and to continue the conversations without delay, adding that in his belief the new Government—

had taken office under such circumstances and was pressed by tense public opinion to such an extent as to make it imminently desirable that the conversations be pressed to a satisfactory conclusion speedily (ex. 29, vol. II, p. 693).

He then asked whether the United States had as yet any counterproposals to make to the suggestions offered by the Japanese Government on September 27. In reply, Mr. Welles made it clear that the United States would be glad to continue the conversations, but suggested that recent belligerent public statements by high Japanese officials and the tone of the Japanese press were not helpful to the atmosphere in which the conversations would take place. When Minister Wakasugi pointed to a recent speech by Secretary of the Navy Knox in which Mr. Knox had said that a Japanese-American war was inevitable and that the United States Navy was on a "24-hour basis," Mr. Welles said that this simply showed the effect on the Navy of the statements being made in Japan. In reply to the Minister's inquiry regarding the possibility of counterproposals being submitted by the United States, Mr. Welles said that the United States position was fully set forth in its draft proposals of June 21 and the statement delivered to Ambassador Nomura on October 2, and that for this reason he did not think any counterproposals by the United States were called for. The conversation concluded with a discussion of the possibility of taking up the three major points of disagreement in the following order: (1) Economic nondiscrimination, (2) Japan's status under the Tri-Partite Pact, and (3) the China question (ex. 29, vol. II, pp. 692–697). A full report on this conversation was immediately sent to Tokyo by Ambassador Nomura (ex. 1, pp. 82–84).

Four days later Minister Wakasugi cabled his own lengthy appraisal of the general attitude of the United States (ex. 1, pp. 86–87). The basic United States policy, he said, was the crushing of the so-called Hitlerism, which he defined as "the establishment of a new order through the force of arms." Because the United States "presumed" that Japan intended to develop the French Indo-China and Thailand area "under the principle of our military's coprosperity sphere, in a monopolistic manner, and through the force of arms," as contrasted with America's principle of economic nondiscrimination, there had arisen "a clash of ideologies." He said that there was every indication that the United States Government was "anxious to adjust the relationship between the two nations," but that he doubted that it would make any concessions from its proposals of June 21 and October 2. He expressed the opinion that the United States had completed its preparations "in the event of the worst," and that "a course of economic pressure plus watchful waiting" had been decided on. He felt, however, that all was not hopeless and that by "good-naturedly" continuing the talks there would be opened up "ways of breaking down differences if we make the best use of world developments." He concluded his report by saying:

However, if we depend on immediate settlement by settling local differences by insisting upon our freedom of action (sic), we must have our minds made up that not only will these negotiations be terminated, but that our national relations will be severed.

The United States has expressed its interest in continuing with the talks after she has been advised of the attitude and policy of the newly formed Cabinet of Japan. I urge, therefore, that the new Cabinet establish its basic policy as speedily as possible, so that we may lay our cards on the table for them to see. I sincerely believe that that would be to our best interest (ex. 1, p. 87).

On October 30 (Japan time) in Tokyo the new Foreign Minister received the diplomatic corps individually, and during the course of his talk with Ambassador Grew he expressed his desire that the Japanese-American conversations be continued and be successfully brought to a conclusion without delay, and he asked Ambassador Grew's cooperation to that end (ex. 29, vol. II, pp. 699–700). Ambassador Grew noted that, compared with Admiral Toyoda who had preceded him, the new Foreign Minister was "grim, unsmiling, and ultra-reserved" (ex. 30, p. 465). The Foreign Minister cabled Ambassador Nomura that he had told Ambassador Grew that if Japanese-American relations got worse, unfortunate results would ensue, a statement substantially similar to the statement he had made to Sir Robert Craigie, the British Ambassador, on October 26 (Japan time) (ex. 1, p. 91).

The great activity in Tokyo during the period immediately after the formation of the Tojo Cabinet, and the attitude with which that Cabinet approached the continuance of the Japanese-American conversations, is illustrated by Foreign Minister Togo's message No. 725 of November 4 (Japan time) to Ambassador Nomura:

1. Well, relations between Japan and the United States have reached the edge, and our people are losing confidence in the possibility of ever adjusting them. In order to lucubrate on a fundamental national policy, *the Cabinet has been meeting with the Imperial Headquarters for some days in succession. Conference has followed conference, and now we are at length able to bring forth a counterproposal for the resumption of Japanese-American negotiations based upon the unanimous opinion of the Government and the military high command* (ensuing Nos. 726 and 727). This and other basic policies of our Empire await the sanction of the conference to be held on the morning of the 5th.

2. Conditions both within and without our Empire are so tense that no longer is procrastination possible, yet in our sincerity to maintain pacific relationships between the Empire of Japan and the United States of America, we have decided, as a result of these deliberations, to gamble once more on the continuance of the parleys, *but this is our last effort. Both in name and spirit this counterproposal of ours is, indeed, the last.* I want you to know that. *If through it we do not reach a quick accord, I am sorry to say the talks will certainly be ruptured. Then, indeed, will relations between our two nations be on the brink of chaos.* I mean that the success or failure of the pending discussions will have an immense effect on the destiny of the Empire of Japan. *In fact, we gambled the fate of our land on the throw of this die.*

When the Japanese-American meetings began, who would have ever dreamt that they would drag out so long? Hoping that we could fast come to some understanding, we have already gone far out of our way and yielded and yielded. The United States does not appreciate this, but through thick and thin sticks to the self-same propositions she made to start with. Those of our people and of our officials who suspect the sincerity of the Americans are far from few. Bearing all kinds of humiliating things, our Government has repeatedly stated its sincerity and gone far, yes, too far, in giving in to them. There is just one reason why we do this—to maintain peace in the Pacific. There seem to be some Americans who think we would make a one-sided deal, but our temperance, I can tell you, has not come from weakness, and naturally there is an end to our long-suffering. Nay, when it come to a question of our existence and our honor, when the time comes we will defend them without recking the cost. If the United States takes an attitude that overlooks or shuns this position of ours, there is not a whit of use in ever broaching the talks. *This time we are showing the limit of our friendship; this time we are making our last possible bargain*, and I hope that we can thus settle all our troubles with the United States peaceably.

3. It is to be hoped earnestly that looking forward *to what may come at the end—at the last day of Japanese-American negotiations*—the Government of the United States will think ever so soberly how much better it would be to make peace with us; how much better this would be for the whole world situation.

4. Your Honor will see from the considerations above how important is your mission. You are at a key post, and we place great hopes in your being able to do something good for our nation's destiny. Will you please think deeply on that and compose yourself and make up your mind to continue to do your best? I hope you will. Now just as soon as the conference is over, I will let you know immediately, and I want you to go and talk to President ROOSEVELT and Secretary HULL. I want you to tell them *how determined we are* and try to get them to foster a speedy understanding.

5. In view of the gravity of these talks, as you make contacts there, so I will make them here. I will talk to the American Ambassador here in Tokyo, and as soon as you have got the consensus of the American officials through talking with them, please wire me. Naturally, as these things develop, in case you take any new steps, I want you to let me know and get in contact with me. In this way we will avoid letting anything go astray. Furthermore, lest anything go awry, *I want you to follow my instructions to the letter. In my instructions, I want you to know there will be no room for personal interpretation* (ex. 1, pp. 92–93).

The day the Foreign Minister sent the long message quoted above, he cabled Ambassador Nomura the substance of two Japanese counterproposals to be used in the conversations, if they should be approved at the Imperial Conference on November 5 (Japan time). The first proposal was designated "Proposal A," and was described as "*our revised ultimatum*"; its provisions were referred to as "*our demands*" (ex. 1, pp. 94–95). The second proposal, designated "Proposal B," was to be used in case of "remarkable" differences between the Japanese and American views, "since the situation does not permit of delays." It was advanced, the Foreign Minister said, with the idea of making "*a last effort to prevent something happening*" (ex. 1, p. 96–97).

At the Imperial Conference in Tokyo on November 5 (Japan time), the counterproposals developed in the conferences and discussions which had gone before were taken up and approved in the form previously sent to Ambassador Nomura. Foreign Minister Togo immediately cabled the Ambassador that he should resume the conversations, and instructed him to submit "Proposal A" first. The Foreign Minister told the Ambassador that if it should become apparent that an agreement based upon "Proposal A" could not be reached, "we intend to submit *our absolutely final proposal*, Proposal B." He continued:

4. As stated in my previous message, *this is the Imperial Government's final step. Time is becoming exceedingly short and the situation very critical. Absolutely no delays can be permitted.* * * *

5. We wish to avoid giving them the impression *that there is a time limit or that this proposal is to be taken as an ultimatum.* In a friendly manner, show them that we are very anxious to have them accept our proposal (ex. 1, p. 99).

The intercepted messages show that the Japanese Government intended to insist not only on a written agreement signed by the United States but also to require the United States to "make Great Britain and the Netherlands sign those terms in which they are concerned" (ex. 1, pp. 98–99). Although the Foreign Minister instructed Ambassador Nomura to avoid giving the Americans the impression that "there is a time limit," he made it clear to the Ambassador (No. 736) that such a dead line had been fixed:

Because of various circumstances, *it is absolutely necessary that arrangements for the signing of this agreement be completed by the 25th of this month.* I realize that this is a difficult order, but under the circumstances it is an unavoidable one. Please understand this thoroughly and tackle the problem of saving the Japanese-U. S. relations *from falling into a chaotic condition.* Do so with great determination and with unstinted effort, I beg of you (ex. 1, p. 100).

The record before the Committee does not show whether or not the decision to submit the foregoing counterproposals was the only decision made at the Imperial Conference on November 5. It is now known, however, that on that date the Navy promulgated its "Combined Fleet Top Secret Operation Order No. 1" to all Japanese Fleet and task force commanders (tr. 482). The record does not show whether the issuance of this order was made known to the Japanese Foreign Office.

Order No. 1, itself, was brief:

COMBINED FLEET ORDER

Combined Fleet Operations in the War Against the UNITED STATES GREAT BRITAIN, and the NETHERLANDS will be conducted in accordance with the Separate Volume (ex. 8).

The separate volume, which was attached to Order No. 1, prescribed the operations to be conducted (*a*) in case war with the United States, Great Britain, and the Netherlands "begins during the China Operations," and (*b*) in case war with Russia "begins during the War with the United States, Great Britain, the Netherlands and China" (ex. 8). It stated: "The Empire is expecting war to break out with the United States, Great Britain and the Netherlands," and provided that, in such event, "In the east the American Fleet will be destroyed" (ex. 8).

Order No. 1 had been in course of preparation since the latter part of August. From September 2–13 (Japan time) a war plans conference had been held continuously at the Naval War College in Tokyo. It was during this same period, on September 6 (Japan time), that an Imperial Conference decided:

If by the early part of October there is no reasonable hope of having our demands agreed to in the diplomatic negotiations * * *, we will immediately make up our minds to get ready for war against America (England and Holland) (ex. 173, Konoye Memoirs, p. 77).

On September 13 (Japan time) an outline containing the essential points of Order No. 1 had been completed at the Naval War College, but the Order itself was not promulgated until immediately after the Imperial Conference on November 5 (Japan time) (ex. 8).

AMBASSADOR GREW WARNS THAT WAR WITH JAPAN MAY COME "WITH DRAMATIC AND DANGEROUS SUDDENNESS"

(*November 3, 1941*)

During the period which immediately preceded the Imperial Conference on November 5 (Japan time), Ambassador Grew was endeavoring to determine what the policies of the Tojo Government would be. Among the sources of his information was "a reliable Japanese informant" who called on the Ambassador on October 25 (Japan time) and again on November 3 (Japan time). On both occasions the information imparted by the informant fell short of disclosing to Ambassador Grew the actual decisions affecting the United States which were being made by the Tojo Cabinet, as described above, but was sufficient to convince the Ambassador that the situation was approaching a crisis. He recorded that on November 3 he was told that the new Japanese Government "had reached a definite decision as to how far it was prepared to go in implementing the desires of the Emperor for an adjustment of relations with the United States," and that "this information had been communicated by the Prime Minister to the Emperor on the afternoon of November 2" (Japan time) (ex. 29, vol. II, p. 701). In his testimony before the Committee, Ambassador Grew said, referring to the period immediately following the fall of the Konoye Cabinet:

I took about two weeks to size up the new situation. I was not quite sure what Tojo's policy was going to be. I had been assured he was going to try to keep on the conversations, going to do his best to come to an agreement with us, and all the rest of it. Frankly, I had my fingers crossed. I was waiting to size it up, and after I had sized it up I sent the telegram of November 3 (tr. 1908).

In the telegram of November 3 (Japan time) to which Mr. Grew referred, he warned Secretary Hull and Under Secretary Welles that—

Japan's resort to measures which might (make) war with the United States inevitable may come *with dramatic and dangerous suddenness* (ex. 15).

The telegram summarized his opinions on the general situation in Japan. In it he noted that the strong policy which he had recommended in his telegram of September 12, 1940 (ex. 26), called the "green light" telegram because it gave the go-ahead signal for economic sanctions against Japan, together with the impact upon Japan of political developments abroad had brought the Japanese Government "to seek conciliation with the United States." If those efforts should fail, he foresaw a probable swing of the pendulum in Japan back once more to its former position "or still further back," leading—

to what I have called an "all out, do or die" attempt to render Japan impervious to foreign economic embargoes, even risking national hara kiri rather than cede to foreign pressure. * * * such a contingency is not only possible but probable (ex. 15).

Ambassador Grew went on to express his opinion that the view that the progressive imposition of drastic economic measures, while attended with some risk of war, would probably avert war, was

a dangerously uncertain hypothesis upon which to base the considered policy and measures of the United States (ex. 15).

Conceding that in discussing the "grave and momentous" subject of whether American needs, policies, and objectives justified war with Japan if diplomacy should fail, he was "out of touch with the Administration's thoughts and intentions thereon," and that his purpose was only to "ensure against my country's getting into war with Japan through any possible misconception of the capacity of Japan to rush headlong into a suicidal conflict with the United States," he warned that—

it would be shortsighted to underestimate Japan's obvious preparations for a program to be implemented if her alternative program for peace should fail. It would be similarly shortsighted to base our policy on the belief that these preparations are merely in the nature of saber rattling (for) the exclusive purpose of giving moral support to Japan's high pressure diplomacy. *Japan's resort to measures which might (make) war with the United States inevitable may come with dramatic and dangerous suddenness* (ex. 15).

The State Department file copy of Ambassador Grew's telegram of November 3 (Japan time) bears the following handwritten note:

Paraphrase of this telegram in full given to Commander Watts, ONI, by telephone on November 8, 1941 (ex. 15).

On November 17 (Japan time) Ambassador Grew cabled Secretary Hull and Under Secretary Welles as follows, referring specifically to the last sentence of his November 3 warning:

In emphasizing need *for guarding against sudden military or naval actions by Japan in areas not at present involved in the China conflict, I am taking into account as a probability that the Japanese would exploit all available tactical advantages, including those of initiative and surprise.* It is important, however, that our Government not (repeat not) place upon us, including the military and naval attachés, major responsibility for giving prior warning.

* * * * * * *

We fully realize that possibly our most important duty at this time is to watch for premonitory indications of military or naval operations which might be forthcoming against such areas and we are taking every precaution to guard against surprise. However, our field of military and naval observation is almost literally restricted to what can be seen with our own eyes, which is negligible. We would, therefore, advise that our Government, from abundance of caution, discount as far as possible the likelihood of our being able to give substantial warning (ex. 15).

Ambassador Grew testified that he had no knowledge or indication whatever of the assembling of the Japanese naval striking force for the attack on Pearl Harbor, or that at the war games conducted by Admiral Yamamoto at the Naval War College in Tokyo between September 2 and 13 (Japan time) the final plans were being formulated for the attack (tr. 1481). He further testified that although he knew that a meeting of the Japanese Cabinet took place on December 1, he "did not (know) and could not have guessed" that the Cabinet had discussed the attack on Pearl Harbor (tr. 1615), and that, with the single exception of the information upon which his message of January 27, 1941 (Japan time) (ex. 15) was based, he had no information of any character prior to the attack on Pearl Harbor which indicated the possibility of such an attack by the Japanese (tr. 1477).

GENERALISSIMO CHIANG KAI-SHEK APPEALS TO GREAT BRITAIN AND THE UNITED STATES FOR AID

(October 28–November 4, 1941)

During the latter part of October, the Japanese began extensive troop concentrations at Haiphong on the coast of northern French Indochina, and steady streams of Japanese military supplies and materials were reported arriving at Hainan (off the northern coast of French Indochina) and at Formosa. As a result of these and other Japanese military movements, which were interpreted in Chungking as foreshadowing an early invasion of Yunnan Province for the purpose of taking the city of Kunming and severing the Burma Road, Generalissimo Chiang Kai-shek made strenuous efforts to obtain British and American air support for his ground forces in that area.

On October 28 at his first meeting in Chungking with General Magruder, the head of the recently arrived United States military mission to China, the Generalissimo asked General Magruder to

---

[1] Ambassador Grew's message of January 27, 1941 (Japan time) follows: "My Peruvian colleague told a member of my staff that he had heard from many sources including a Japanese source that the Japanese military forces planned, in the event of trouble with the United States, to attempt a surprise mass attack on Pearl Harbor using all of their military facilities. He added that although the project seemed fantastic the fact that he had heard it from many sources prompted him to pass on the information" (ex. 15). Paraphrased copies were promptly sent by the State Department to Military Intelligence Division (Army) and Office of Naval Intelligence (Navy) (ex. 15).

inform Washington at once of the threatening situation, and urged that President Roosevelt "intercede with London to make available the Singapore air forces to support his defense." He pled with General Magruder that the President "be urged to bring diplomatic pressure on Japan and to appeal as well to Britain jointly to warn Japan that an attack upon Kunming would be considered inimical to our interests." He insisted that if the Japanese should take Kunming and thus sever the Burma Road, Chinese resistance would end and a Japanese attack on the Malay Peninsula would inevitably follow. He believed his land forces could resist the anticipated attack only with air support, which he did not have and which only the British air forces at Singapore could furnish in time. General Magruder immediately radioed the Generalissimo's plea to Secretary Stimson and General Marshall, after discussing the interview with Ambassador Gauss (ex. 47).

In Washington, on the morning of October 30 (Washington time), Mr. T. V. Soong handed to Secretary of the Treasury Morgenthau, a message from Generalissimo Chiang Kai-shek which repeated the substance of what the Generalissimo had said to General Magruder. Chiang's message urged the United States "to use strong pressure on Britain to send Singapore Air Force to cooperate with Colonel Chennault in order to save democratic position in Far East" and stressed the critical nature of the situation (ex. 16–A). Secretary Morgenthau sent the Generalissimo's message to President Roosevelt on the same day, without written comment, and the President forwarded it to Secretary Hull with this handwritten note:

C. H. Can we do anything along these lines? How about telling Japan a move to close Burma Road would be inimical? F. D. R. (ex. 16–A).

On November 1 (Washington time), Secretary Hull called a conference at the State Department which was attended by, among others, the Secretary, Under Secretary Welles, and Dr. Stanley K. Hornbeck, for that Department, and by General Leonard T. Gerow, Chief of War Plans Division, for the War Department and Admiral R. E. Schuirmann, Director of the Central Division, for the Navy Department. The conference was called for the purpose of discussing what action should be taken in response to Generalissimo Chiang Kai-shek's plea. Secretary Hull expressed the opinion that "there was no use to issue any additional warnings to Japan if we can't back them up," and the Secretary therefore desired to know whether "the military authorities would be prepared to support further warnings by the State Department." A second meeting in the same connection was held at the State Department the following day (ex. 16).

General Gerow submitted a report on these meetings to General Marshall on November 3 (Washington time) in which he pointed out that the Military Intelligence Division's (G–2's) latest estimate did not support Generalissimo Chiang Kai-shek's conclusions as to the imminence of a Japanese move toward Kunming, though agreeing that the fall of Kunming would seriously affect Chinese resistance to Japan. After reviewing the strength of the United States forces in the Philippines and concluding that the dispatch of any considerable portion of the air garrison there would leave the island of Luzon open to serious risk of capture, General Gerow's report summarized certain "strong" opinions of the War Plans Division, which were stated as follows:

a. The policies derived in the American-British Staff conversations remain sound; viz:

(1) The primary objective is the defeat of Germany.

(2) The principal objective in the Far East is to keep Japan out of the war.

(3) Military counter action against Japan should be considered only in case of any of the following actions by Japan (which were then enumerated).

*   *   *   *   *   *   *

d. Political and economic measures should be used wherever effective to deter Japanese action.

e. * * * *Strong diplomatic and economic pressure may be exerted from the military viewpoint, at the earliest, about the middle of December 1941,* when the Philippine Air Force will have become a positive threat to Japanese operations. It would be advantageous, *if practicable,* to delay severe diplomatic and economic pressure until February or March 1942, when the Philippine Air Force will have reached its projected strength, and a safe air route, through Samoa, will be in operation. (ex. 16).

The weekly meeting of the Army-Navy Joint Board scheduled for November 5 (Washington time) was held on the afternoon of November 3 (Washington time). The question of aid to Generalissimo Chiang Kai-shek received more attention than any other item on the agenda (ex. 16). Admiral Royal E. Ingersoll presented the situation as the Navy saw it and General Marshall gave the Army's viewpoint. Admiral Schuirmann reported on the two meetings at the State Department and read a memorandum (tr. 5520–5523) prepared by Dr. Hornbeck in which the latter stated his personal opinion in favor of a firm representation to Japan, even though war might result. Among other things, General Marshall said that it was his information that "the Japanese authorities might be expected to decide upon the national policy by November 5," apparently referring to the intercepted Japanese messages between Washington and Tokyo regarding the Imperial Conference to be held in Tokyo on that date. He expressed the view that—

Until powerful United States Forces had been built up in the Far East, it would take some very clever diplomacy to save the situation. *It appeared that the basis of U. S. policy should be to make certain minor concessions which the Japanese could use in saving face. These concessions might be a relaxation on oil restrictions or on similar trade restrictions* (ex. 16).

Following these discussions the Joint Board decided that—

War Plans Division of the War and Navy Departments would prepare a memorandum for the President, as a reply to the State Department's proposed policy in the Far Eastern situation. The memorandum would take the following lines:

Oppose the issuance of an ultimatum to Japan.

Oppose U. S. military action against Japan should she move into Yunnan.

Oppose the movement and employment of U. S. military forces in support of Chiang Kai-shek.

Advocate State Department action to put off hostilities with Japan as long as possible.

Suggest agreement with Japan to tide the situation over for the next several months.

Point out the effect and cost a U. S.-Japanese war in the Far East would have on defense aid to Great Britain and other nations being aided by the U. S.

Emphasize the existing limitations on shipping and the inability of the U. S. to engage in a Far Eastern offensive without the transfer of the major portion of shipping facilities from the Atlantic to the Pacific (ex. 16).

That evening, November 3 (Washington time), the State Department received a telegram from Ambassador Gauss in Chungking to the effect that while it was not yet certain that Japan would undertake an invasion of Yunnan from Indochina, it was believed certain that in any case large Japanese air forces would operate against the

Burma Road and any volunteer air forces in China, and that accordingly, if Anglo-American air units were sent into Yunnan, they should be in sufficient force to maintain themselves against heavy Japanese air concentrations. "Half or token measures," the Ambassador advised, "would prove dangerous" (ex. 47).

The next morning, November 4 (Washington time), the State Department received from the Chinese Embassy a personal message to President Roosevelt from Generalissimo Chiang Kai-shek (ex. 47). This message quoted a lengthy message which the Generalissimo had sent directly to Prime Minister Churchill, in which the Generalissimo expressed substantially the same views as those he had communicated to General Magruder, and urged that the British air force in Malaya, "with American cooperation," be sent to his assistance to resist the anticipated assault on Yunnan and Kunming. The Generalissmo then urged the United States "to draw on its air arm in the Philippines to provide either an active unit or a reserve force in the combined operation," saying that—

unless Japan is checked sharply and at once, she is on the verge of winning a position from which she can deal with each of us separately and in her own time (ex. 47).

Neither the Generalissimo's message addressed to the Prime Minister nor his message addressed to the President made any further reference to the proposal that a warning to Japan be issued by Britain or the United States. On the 4th Secretary Hull held separate conferences at the State Department with Secretary Knox, and with General Marshall and Admiral Ingersoll (tr. 1171, 1173).

The next day, November 5 (Washington time), President Roosevelt received the following message from Prime Minister Churchill:

I have received Chiang Kai-shek's attached appeal addressed to us both for air assistance. You know how we are placed for air strength at Singapore. Nonetheless, I should be prepared to send pilots and even some planes if they could arrive in time.

What we need now is a deterrent of the most general and formidable character. The Japanese have as yet taken no final decision, and the Emperor appears to be exercising restraint. When we talked about this at Argentia you spoke of gaining time, and this policy has been brilliantly successful so far. But our joint embargo is steadily forcing the Japanese to decisions for peace or war.

It now looks as if they would go into Yunnan cutting the Burma Road with disastrous consequence for Chiang Kai-shek. The collapse of his resistance would not only be a world tragedy in itself, but it would leave the Japanese with large forces to attack north or south.

The Chinese have appealed to us, as I believe they have to you, to warn the Japanese against an attack on Yunnan. I hope you might remind them that such an attack, aimed at China from a region in which we have never recognized that the Japanese have any right to maintain forces, would be in open disregard of the clearly indicated attitude of the United States Government. We should, of course, be ready to make a similar communication.

No independent action by ourselves will deter Japan because we are so much tied up elsewhere. But of course we will stand with you and do our utmost to back you in whatever course you choose. I think, myself, that Japan is more likely to drift into war than to plunge in. Please let me know what you think (ex. 158).

President Roosevelt did not reply to Prime Minister Churchill until 2 days later. In the meantime, General Marshall and Admiral Stark submitted to him, under date of November 5 (Washington time), a joint memorandum (ex. 16) pursuant to the action of the Joint Board referred to above. In their joint memorandum

General Marshall and Admiral Stark referred to the various communications from Generalissimo Chiang Kai-shek which have been mentioned above, and to Secretary Hull's request for advice "as to the attitude which this Government should take" toward a Japanese offensive against Kunming and the Burma Road, and stated that the question they had considered was—

whether or not the United States is justified in undertaking offensive military operations with U. S. forces against Japan, to prevent her from severing the Burma Road. They consider that such operations, however well disguised, would lead to war.

In answering this question, General Marshall and Admiral Stark then advised the President:

At the present time the United States Fleet in the Pacific is inferior to the Japanese Fleet and cannot undertake an unlimited strategic offensive in the Western Pacific. In order to be able to do so, it would have to be strengthened by withdrawing practically all naval vessels from the Atlantic except those assigned to local defense forces. An unlimited offensive by the Pacific Fleet would require tremendous merchant tonnage, which could only be withdrawn from services now considered essential. The result of withdrawals from the Atlantic of naval and merchant strength might well cause the United Kingdom to lose the Battle of the Atlantic in the near future.

The current plans for war against Japan in the Far East are to conduct defensive war, in cooperation with the British and Dutch, for the defense of the Philippines and the British and Dutch East Indies. The Philippines are now being reinforced. The present combined naval, air, and ground forces will make attack on the islands a hazardous undertaking. By about the middle of December 1941, United States air and submarine strength in the Philippines will have become a positive threat to any Japanese operations south of Formosa. The U. S. Army air forces in the Philippines will have reached the projected strength by February or March, 1942. The potency of this threat will have then increased to a point where it might well be a deciding factor in deterring Japan in operations in the areas south and west of the Philippines. By this time, additional British naval and air reinforcements to Singapore will have arrived. The general defensive strength of the entire southern area against possible Japanese operations will then have reached impressive proportions.

Until such a time as the Burma Road is closed, aid can be extended to Chiang Kai-shek by measures which probably will not result in war with Japan. These measures are: continuation of economic pressure against Japan, supplying increasing amounts of munitions under the Lend-Lease, and continuation and acceleration of aid to the American Volunteer Group.

The Chief of Naval Operations and the Chief of Staff are in accord in the following conclusions:

(a) The basic military policies and strategy agreed to in the United States-British Staff conversations remain sound. The primary objective of the two nations is the defeat of Germany. If Japan be defeated and Germany remain undefeated, decision will still have not been reached. In any case, an unlimited offensive war should not be undertaken against Japan, since such a war would greatly weaken the combined effort in the Atlantic against Germany, the most dangerous enemy.

(b) *War between the United States and Japan should be avoided while building up defensive forces in the Far East, until such time as Japan attacks or directly threatens territories whose security to the United States is of very great importance.* Military action against Japan should be undertaken only in one or more of the following contingencies:

(1) A direct act of war by Japanese armed forces against the territory or mandated territory of the United States, the British Commonwealth, or the Netherlands East Indies;

(2) The movement of Japanese forces into Thailand to the west of 100° East or south of 10° North; or into Portuguese Timor, New Caledonia, or the Loyalty Islands.

(c) If war with Japan can not be avoided, it should follow the strategic lines of existing war plans; i. e., military operations should be primarily defensive, with the object of holding territory, and weakening Japan's economic position.

(d) Considering world strategy, a Japanese advance against Kunming, into Thailand, except as previously indicated, or an attack on Russia, would not justify intervention by the United States against Japan.

(e) All possible aid short of actual war against Japan should be extended to the Chinese Central Government.

(f) In case it is decided to undertake war against Japan, complete coordinated action in the diplomatic, economic, and military fields, should be undertaken in common by the United States, the British Commonwealth, and the Netherlands East Indies.

The Chief of Naval Operations and the Chief of Staff recommend that the United States policy in the Far East be based on the above conclusions.

Specifically, they recommend:

That the dispatch of United States armed forces for intervention against Japan in China be disapproved.

That material aid to China be accelerated consonant with the needs of Russia, Great Britain, and our own forces.

That aid to the American Volunteer Group be continued and accelerated to the maximum practicable extent.

That no ultimatum be delivered to Japan (ex. 16).

Secretary Hull testified that he—

was in thorough accord with the views of the Chief of Staff and the Chief of Naval Operations that United States armed forces should not be sent to China for use against Japan. I also believed so far as American foreign policy considerations were involved that material to China should be accelerated as much as feasible, and that aid to the American Volunteer Group should be accelerated. Finally, *I concurred completely in the view that no ultimatum should be delivered to Japan. I had been striving for months to avoid a showdown with Japan, and to explore every possible avenue for averting or delaying war between the United States and Japan. That was the cornerstone of the effort which the President and I were putting forth with our utmost patience.* (tr. 1130).

On November 7 (Washington time), President Roosevelt sent the following reply, prepared in the State Department, to Prime Minister Churchill's message of the 5th:

We have very much in mind the situation to which Chiang Kai-shek's appeal is addressed. While we feel that it would be a serious error to underestimate the gravity of the threat inherent in that situation, we doubt whether preparations for a Japanese land campaign against Kunming have advanced to a point which would warrant an advance by the Japanese against Yunnan in the immediate future. In the meantime we shall do what we can to increase and expedite lend lease aid to China and to facilitate the building up of the American volunteer air force, both in personnel and in equipment. We have noted that you would be prepared to send pilots and some planes to China.

We feel that measures such as the foregoing and those which you have in mind along the lines we are taking, together with continuing efforts to strengthen our defenses in the Philippine Islands, paralleled by similar efforts by you in the Singapore area, will tend to increase Japan's hesitation, whereas in Japan's present mood new formalized verbal warning or remonstrances might have, with at least even chance, an opposite effect.

This whole problem will have our continuing and earnest attention, study, and effort.

I shall probably not, repeat not, make express reply to Chiang Kai-shek before the first of next week. Please keep within the confidence of your close official circle that I have said above (ex. 16–B).

The record shows that on November 8, Secretary Hull conferred at the State Department with General Miles, head of the Military Intelligence Division (G–2), General Staff (tr. 1173), and on November 10 with Secretary Knox (tr. 1171). On the latter date he sent to President Roosevelt a draft of a proposed reply to Generalissimo Chiang Kai-shek. The next day the President dictated the following brief note to his aide, General Watson, which was attached to the Secretary's draft and read:

I want to see Hu Shih for five minutes on Wednesday, and give this to me when he comes (ex. 16).

Written on the same sheet of paper, below the typewritten note to General Watson and apparently after the conference with Dr. Hu Shih, the Chinese Ambassador, appears the following, in the President's handwriting:

C. H. O. K. to send. F. D. R. (ex. 16).

The draft was then returned to the State Department, where the message in final form was handed to Dr. Hu Shih late in the afternoon of November 14 (Washington time) for transmittal to Generalissimo Chiang Kai-shek. In it President Roosevelt described briefly the intensive consideration that had been given to the Generalissimo's appeal, and continued:

Under existing circumstances, taking into consideration the world situation in its political, military, and economic aspects, we feel that the most effective contribution which we can make at this moment is along the line of speeding up the flow to China of our Lend-Lease materials and facilitating the building up of the American Volunteer air force, both in personnel and in equipment. We are subjected at present, as you know, to demands from many quarters and in many connections. We are sending materials not only to China and Great Britain, but to the Dutch, the Soviet Union, and some twenty other countries that are calling urgently for equipment for self-defense. In addition, our program for our own defense, especially the needs of our rapidly expanding Navy and Army, calls for equipment in large amount and with great promptness. Nevertheless, I shall do my utmost toward achieving expedition of incre. sing expedition of increasing amounts of material for your use. Meanwhile we are exchanging views with the British Government in regard to the entire situation and the tremendous problems which are presented, with a view to effective coordinating of efforts in the most practicable ways possible.

I believe that you will share my feeling that measures such as the foregoing, together with such as the British doubtless are considering, adopted and implemented simultaneously with your intensive efforts to strengthen the defenses of Yunnan Province are sound steps toward safeguarding against such threat of an attack upon Yunnan as may be developing. Indirectly influencing that situation: American military and naval defensive forces in the Philippine Islands, which are being steadily increased, and the United States Fleet at Hawaii, lying as they do along the flank of any Japanese military movement into China from Indochina, are ever present and significant factors in the whole situation, as are the increasing British and Dutch defensive preparations in their territories to the south.

This Government has on numerous occasions pointed out to the Government of Japan various consequences inherent in pursuit of courses of aggression and conquest. We shall continue to impress this point of view upon Japan on every appropriate occasion (ex. 16).

In accordance with the joint recommendation that had been made by General Marshall and Admiral Stark, no warning was delivered to Japan as Generalissimo Chiang Kai-shek had urged.

It is clear that the movement of additional Japanese troops into northern French Indochina had a twofold purpose. On the one hand the troops were an immediate threat to China by their proximity to Yunnan Province, the Burma Road, and Kunming on the north and northwest. Generalissimo Chiang Kai-shek's appeal for aid recognized the immediacy of that threat. On the other hand, the additional Japanese forces increased the potential threat to the British Malay States and Singapore, and to the Netherlands East Indies and the Philippines. The price the Japanese Government hoped to exact from the United States and Great Britain for the removal of this latter threat had been determined at the Imperial Conference on September 6 (Japan time). The subsequent fall of the Konoye

Cabinet and accession of General Tojo in October had only increased Japan's determination to use this potential threat to blackmail the United States, if possible, into (1) ceasing all aid to China, (2) accepting a military and naval status in the Far East inferior to that of Japan, and (3) furnishing all possible material aid to Japan. Furthermore, since the Japanese Army at no time evidenced a willingness to withdraw its troops from China, or to agree not to use northern French Indo-China as a base for operations against China, it would seem clear that the Japanese strategy was not only to blackmail the United States into granting those "minimum demands" but also, having accomplished that, to turn on China from northern French Indochina and thus to expedite the liquidation of the "China Incident" and the establishment of a Japanese "just peace" in the Far East.

JAPAN DELIVERS ITS NEXT-TO-LAST PROPOSAL TO THE UNITED STATES

(November 10, 1941)

After the Imperial Conference on November 5 (Japan time) the Japanese-American conversations were "on the last lap" as far as the Japanese Government was concerned (ex. 1, p. 101). Immediately after that conference the final Japanese diplomatic, naval, and military maneuvers began. The instructions Foreign Minister Togo sent to Ambassador Nomura to resume the talks and to present proposal "A" to the United States Government had their counterparts in operational orders issued to the Japanese Navy and, without doubt, to the Japanese Army as well. Those orders contemplated naval, air, and troop dispositions which were commenced immediately. Many of those dispositions were detected and observed by the United States, Great Britain, or the Netherlands, but the major Japanese naval movement was successfully kept secret by the Japanese until the attack on Pearl Harbor on the morning of December 7, 1941.

It is imperative to an accurate appraisal of this closing period of the Japanese-American conversations to keep in mind those Japanese military and naval dispositions. Reports of the military movements toward the south and alarms about Japanese naval movements (except the one toward Pearl Harbor) reached Washington and the State Department during November as the Japanese Ambassadors were presenting their final proposals, and again, as in July, discredited the intentions of the Japanese Government. Commencing in the middle of November the American consuls at Hanoi and Saigon in north and south French Indochina reported extensive new landings of Japanese troops and equipment in Indochina (tr. 1138). About November 21 (Washington time) the State Department received word that the Dutch had information that a Japanese naval force had arrived near Palao, the nearest point in the Japanese mandated islands to the heart of the Netherlands Indies (ex. 21; tr. 1138).

It is now known that at the same time a powerful Japanese naval striking force, its formation and purpose successfully kept secret, was assembling in a northern Japanese harbor for the attack on the United States Pacific Fleet, under orders issued on or about November 14 (Japan time). On November 21 (Japan time) the commander in chief of the combined Japanese fleet was directed to order his forces to advance to the area in which they were to wait in readiness and to station them in such positions that—

in the event of the situation becoming such that commencement of hostilities be inevitable, they will be able to meet the situation promptly (tr. 436–7).

On November 25 (Japan time) the commander in chief issued an order which directed the naval striking force to "advance into Hawaiian waters and upon the very opening of hostilities * * * attack the main force of the United States Fleet in Hawaii and deal it a mortal blow" (tr. 437). The order provided, however, that—

Should it appear certain that Japanese-American negotiations will reach an amicable settlement prior to the commencement of hostile action, all the forces of the Combined Fleet are to be ordered to reassemble and return to their bases (tr. 437).

The striking force sailed from Hitokappu Bay in northern Japan at 9 a. m. November 26 (Japan time), or about 7 p. m. on November 25 (Washington time) (tr. 450).

In the meantime, it had been decided in Tokyo to send Saburu Kurusu, former Japanese Ambassador to Germany, to Washington to assist Ambassador Nomura. On the evening of November 4 (Japan time) Mr. Kurusu told Ambassador Grew that the mission had been broached to him "only yesterday afternoon" (ex. 30, p. 471), although it appears from the comments made by Foreign Minister Toyoda to Ambassador Grew on October 10 (Japan time) that the matter had been under consideration for some time. Arrangements were made by the State Department for the Pan-American clipper to be held in Hong Kong for 2 days to permit Mr. Kurusu to travel on that plane, and he left Tokyo early on November 5 (Japan time). Foreign Minister Togo cabled Ambassador Nomura on November 4 (Japan time) of this development, saying that Ambassador Kurusu was being sent to assist Ambassador Nomura and to be his "right-hand man" in view of "the gravity of the present negotiations and in view of your request on instructions from me" (ex. 1, p. 97). Two days later the Foreign Minister cabled that the reason for Ambassador Kurusu's dispatch "so quickly" was "to show our Empire's sincerity in the negotiations soon to follow." The officials of the Japanese Army and Navy, the Foreign Minister said, were "pleased with the special dispatch of the Ambassador" (ex. 1, p. 101).

In Washington, as soon as he received Foreign Minister Togo's instructions to resume the conversations, Ambassador Nomura arranged a meeting with Secretary Hull. At that meeting, which took place on the morning of November 7 (Washington time), Ambassador Nomura informed the Secretary that he had now received instructions from the new Japanese Government, and that he wished to resume the conversations. He then said that the new Japanese Cabinet had deliberated on the various questions at issue between the two Governments—

with a view to making the utmost concessions that they could make, having due regard for the situation in the Far East and the attitude of public opinion in Japan (vol. II, p. 707).

He said that of the three principal questions on which there were divergent views, he thought that it would not be difficult to reconcile the views of the two Governments on two, namely, nondiscrimination in international trade and Japan's obligations under the Tripartite

Pact. He realized that the difficulties of reaching an agreement on the third, the China question, were greater. So saying, he handed to Secretary Hull a document (ex. 29, vol. II, pp. 709–710) containing formulæ relating to the withdrawal of Japanese troops from China and to nondiscrimination in international trade. This document was, he said, to be taken in conjunction with the United States proposals of June 21 and October 2 and the Japanese proposal delivered to the Secretary on September 27. It embodied the substance of the provisions of proposal "A" regarding those two points, but was silent regarding the question of Japan's obligations under the Tripartite Pact. Secretary Hull expressed the hope that some concrete statement concerning the latter point could be worked out that would be of help, but Ambassador Nomura said it did not seem to him any further statement was necessary than had already been made, considering the attitude of the Japanese Government which "manifestly desired to maintain peace in the Pacific." During the conversation Secretary Hull again mentioned that before entering into any formal negotiations he intended to discuss the matter with the Chinese, the British, and the Dutch (ex. 29, vol. II, p. 708). Ambassador Nomura requested a meeting with President Roosevelt, which was subsequently arranged for November 10 (Washington time).

The afternoon of November 7 (Washington time), Secretary Hull attended a Cabinet meeting at the White House. The situation in the Far East appears to have been uppermost in the minds of those present; especially the President, Secretary Hull, and Secretary Stimson. Secretary Stimson had had a conference with the President the day before, November 6 (Washington time), and had recorded in his daily notes that he and the President had talked—

about the Far Eastern situation and the approaching conference with the messenger who is coming from Japan. The President outlined what he thought he might say. *He was trying to think of something which would give us further time.* He suggested he might propose a truce in which there would be no movement or armament for 6 months and then if the Japanese and Chinese had not settled their arrangement in that meanwhile, we could go on on the same basis. I told him I frankly saw two great objections to that; first, that it tied up our hands just at a time when it was vitally important that we should go on completing out reenforcement of the Philippines; and second, that the Chinese would feel thas any such arrangement was a desertion of them. I reminded him that it has always been our historic policy since the Washington conference not to leave the Chinese and Japanese alone together, because the Japanese were always able to overslaugh the Chinese and the Chinese know it. I told him that I thought the Chinese would refuse to go into such an arrangement (tr. 14414–14415).

The morning of the next day, November 7 (Washington time), Admiral John R. Beardall, President Roosevelt's naval aide, at the President's direction, requested the appropriate officers in the Navy Department to arrange for the delivery to the President of complete translations of the intercepted Japanese messages, rather than memoranda briefly summarizing the messages as had been delivered theretofore under the existing agreement between the Army and the Navy in that connection. Such arrangements were made and, commencing November 12 (Washington time), complete translations were delivered each day to Admiral Beardall for delivery to President Roosevelt. According to reported statements made by Admiral Beardall at the time, the President told him that he (the President) "was in fact either seeing or being told about the material through Hull" (tr. 14525–14526).

According to Secretary Stimson's notes of the Cabinet meeting on November 7 (Washington time), President Roosevelt took—

what he said was the first general poll of his Cabinet and it was on the question of the Far East—whether the people would back us up in case we struck at Japan down there and what the tactics should be. It was a very interesting talk— the best Cabinet meeting I think we have ever had since I have been there. He went around the table—first Hull and then myself, and then around through the whole number and it was unanimous in feeling the country would support us. He said that this time the vote is unanimous, he feeling the same way. Hull made a good presentation of the general situation. I told them I rather narrowed it down into a following-up the steps which had been done to show what needed to be done in the future. The thing would have been much stronger if the Cabinet had known—and they did not know except in the case of Hull and the President—what the Army is doing with the big bombers and how ready we are to pitch in (tr. 14415–14416).

Secretary Hull testified that at this Cabinet meeting, after President Roosevelt turned to him and asked whether he had anything in mind—

I thereupon pointed out for about 15 minutes the dangers in the international situation. I went over fully developments in the conversations with Japan and *emphasized that in my opinion relations were extremely critical and that we should be on the lookout for a military attack anywhere by Japan at any time.* When I finished, the President went around the Cabinet. *All concurred in my estimate of the dangers.* It became the consensus of the Cabinet that the critical situation might well be emphasized in speeches in order that the country would, if possible, be better prepared for such a development.

Accordingly, Secretary of the Navy Knox delivered an address on November 11, 1941, in which he stated that we were not only confronted with the necessity of extreme measures of self-defense in the Atlantic, but we were "likewise faced with grim possibilities on the other side of the world—on the far side of the Pacific"; and the Pacific no less than the Atlantic called for instant readiness for defense.

On the same day Under Secretary of State Welles in an address stated that beyond the Atlantic a sinister and pitiless conqueror had reduced more than half of Europe to abject serfdom and that in the Far East the same forces of conquest were menacing the safety of all nations bordering on the Pacific. The waves of world conquest were "breaking high both in the East and in the West," he said, and were threatening more and more with each passing day "to engulf our own shores." He warned that the United States was in far greater peril than in 1917; that "at any moment war may be forced upon us" (tr. 1131–1132).

Statements which were made by Foreign Minister Togo to Ambassador Grew in Tokyo 3 days later, on November 10 (Japan time), show the attitude with which the Japanese Foreign Office was approaching the conversations during this period immediately following the Imperial Conference on November 5. After informing the Ambassador that new proposals had been sent to Ambassador Nomura for presentation to the United States Government, the Foreign Minister urged the necessity of a speedy settlement, saying that national sentiment would "not tolerate further protracted delay in arriving at some conclusion" and that the position was "daily becoming more pressing." He said that the new proposals represented the "maximum possible concessions by Japan," and handed to the Ambassador the texts of the two documents submitted to Secretary Hull on November 7. During the Foreign Minister's comments on these documents, he expressed the desire that the British Government should conclude an agreement with Japan simultaneously with the United States, in view of Great Britain's interests in the Pacific. The Foreign Minister told Ambassador Grew that he felt that the United States did not adequately appreciate the realities of the situation in the Far East. Referring to the steadily increasing population of Japan, he stated it was necessary to assure the raw materials necessary for the existence of that population and that unless the United States realized this fact as among the realities of the situation, a successful conclusion to the conversations would be difficult. Ambassador Grew told the Minister that his statements penetrated to the heart of the whole problem, since one of the fundamental purposes of the conversations was to open a way for Japan to obtain such necessary supplies, together with a full flow of trade and commerce and market for her industries, but by peaceful means as opposed to the use of force. In reply to this the Minister said, as reported by Ambassador Grew, that—

He did not wish to go into the fundamentals of the question, but he thought that he could advert briefly to the importance of commercial and economic relations between the United States and Japan. The freezing by the United States of Japanese assets had stopped supplies of many important raw materials to Japan. Economic pressure of this character is capable of menacing national existence to a greater degree than the direct use of force. He hoped that the American Government would take into consideration circumstances of this character and realize the possibility that the Japanese people, if exposed to continued economic pressure, might eventually feel obliged resolutely to resort to measures of self-defense (ex. 29, vol. II, p. 714).

The Minister saw no inconsistency between insisting that Japan would not give up the fruits of 4 years of hostilities in China and at the same time accepting the principle of refraining from aggression and the use of force (ex. 29, vol. II, pp. 710–714; ex. 1, pp. 109–111).

Ambassador Nomura's meeting with President Roosevelt took place at the White House on the morning of November 10 (Washington time), with Secretary Hull and Minister Wakasugi present. At this meeting the Ambassador read from a prepared document an explanation of the proposals he had been instructed by his Government to present (i. e., proposal "A"), the substance of which (except as regards the Tripartite Pact) he had already communicated to Secretary Hull on November 7. Regarding the first question, the application of the principle of nondiscrimination in international trade, he said that his Government had now decided to accept its application in all Pacific areas, including China, upon the understanding that the principle would be applied uniformly to the rest of the world as well. As to the second question, the attitude of the two Governments toward the European war, he stated that his Government was not prepared to go further in black and white than the language contained in its proposal of September 27, which was:

Both Governments maintain it their common aim to bring about peace in the world, and, when an opportune time arrives, they will endeavor jointly for the early restoration of world peace.

With regard to developments of the situation prior to the restoration of world peace, both Governments will be guided in their conduct by considerations of protection and self-defense; and, in case the United States should participate in the European War, Japan would decide entirely independently in the matter of interpretation of the Tripartite Pact between Japan, Germany, and Italy, and would likewise determine what actions might be taken by way of fulfilling the obligations in accordance with the said interpretation (ex. 29, vol. II, p. 638).

He added that if the United States was in a position to give assurance that it had no intention of placing too liberal an interpretation on the term "protection and self-defense," his Government would be prepared to reciprocate. Concerning the third question, the stationing and withdrawal of troops from China and French Indochina, Ambassador Nomura submitted the following formula:

With regard to the Japanese forces which have been despatched to China in connection with the China Affair, those forces in specified areas of North China and Mengchiang (Inner Mongolia) as well as in Hainan-tao (Hainan Island) will remain to be stationed for a certain required duration after the restoration of peaceful relations between Japan and China. All the rest of such forces will commence withdrawal as soon as general peace is restored between Japan and China and the withdrawal will proceed according to separate arrangements between Japan and China and will be completed within two years with the firm establishment of peace and order.

The Japanese Government undertake to respect the territorial sovereignty of French Indo-China. The Japanese forces at present stationed there will be withdrawn as soon as the China Affair is settled or an equitable peace is established in East Asia (ex. 29, vol. II, p. 716).

The Ambassador said that this formula clearly indicated that the stationing of Japanese troops in China was not of a permanent nature, and that however desirable the complete and immediate withdrawal of all Japanese troops from China might be, it was "impracticable under the present circumstances." In a written statement, which he then read, Ambassador Nomura said that as viewed from the Japanese side it seemed that the United States had remained adamant in its position and had shown little sign of reciprocation to "concessions" by the Japanese with the result that "in certain quarters in my country some skepticism has arisen as to the true intention of the United States Government." He continued:

People in my country take the freezing of the assets as an economic blockade and they go even so far as to contend that the means of modern warfare are not limited to shooting. No nation can live without the supply of materials vital to its industries. Reports reaching me from home indicate that the situation is serious and pressing and the only way of preserving peace is to reach some kind of amicable and satisfactory understanding with the United States without any unnecessary loss of time. In the face of these mounting difficulties, the Japanese Government bent all its efforts to continue the conversations and bring about a satisfactory understanding solely for the purpose of maintaining peace in the Pacific. *My Government therefore is now submitting certain proposals as its utmost effort* for that purpose, and I shall feel very grateful if I can have the views of your Government on them at the earliest possible opportunity (ex. 29, vol. II, p. 717).

In reply, President Roosevelt read a brief statement which concluded:

We hope that our exploratory conversations will achieve favorable results in the way of providing a basis for negotiations. We shall continue to do our best to expedite the conversations just as we understand that the Japanese Government is anxious to do. We hope that the Japanese Government will make it clear that it intends to pursue peaceful courses instead of opposite courses, as such clarification should afford a way for arriving at the results which we seek (ex. 29, vol. II, p. 718).

The President referred to the improvement of American relations with the South American countries under the "good neighbor policy" as compared to the policy of force that had been employed by the United States in some cases. Then, according to Ambassador Nomura's report to Tokyo the same day—

Speaking on the remark I had made to the effect that economic pressure had aroused the ill feelings of the Japanese people and had made them impatient, the President said, "It is necessary to find a *modus vivendi* if the people are to live," and proceeded to explain that this expression should be translated as "method of living" (ex. 1, p. 116).

Ambassador Nomura reported that it was not clear to him what the phrase "modus vivendi" really meant, and that he intended to ascertain whether the President was referring to, possibly, "a provisional agreement" (ex. 1, p. 116).

Upon receipt of Ambassador Nomura's report, Foreign Minister Togo cabled the Ambassador that there were—

indications that the United States is still not fully aware of the exceedingly criti- calness of the situation here. *The fact remains that the date set forth in my message No. 736 is absolutely immovable under present conditions. It is a definite dead line and therefore it is essential that settlement be realized by about that time.* The session of Parliament opens on the 15th * * *. The government must have a clear picture of things to come, in presenting its case at the session. You can see, therefore, that *the situation is nearing a climax and that time is indeed becoming short.*

I appreciate the fact that you are making strenuous efforts, but in view of the above-mentioned situation, will you redouble them? When talking to the Secre- tary of State and others, drive the points home to them. Do everything in your power to get a clear picture of the U. S. attitude in the minimum of time. At the same time do everything in your power to have them give their speedy approval to our final proposal.

We would appreciate being advised of your opinions on whether or not they will accept our final proposal A (ex. 1, pp. 116–117).

Ambassador Nomura immediately cabled the Foreign Minister that Secretary Hull had agreed to study the Japanese proposals the fol- lowing day, Armistice Day, and that his next meeting with the Sec- retary was scheduled for the afternoon of November 12 (Washington time) (ex. 1, p. 118).

On November 11 (Japan time), as the result of statements made by Foreign Minister Togo to him on October 26 (Japan time) (ex. 1, p. 91), the British Ambassador in Tokyo, Sir Robert Craigie, called on the Foreign Minister upon instructions from the British Foreign Office and urged the desirability of a supreme effort to reach an agree- ment with the United States, saying that when the point of actual negotiations was reached the British Government would be ready to join in seeking an agreement (ex. 1, pp. 117–118; ex. 158). Secretary Hull was informed of the instructions to the British Ambassador in Tokyo during a conversation with Lord Halifax on November 12 (Washington time) (ex. 158). During the conversation between Foreign Minister Togo and Sir Robert Craigie, the Foreign Minister went to great lengths to convince the British Ambassador how critical the situation was, saying that in the view of the Japanese Government the negotiations had reached the final phase, that the Imperial Gov- ernment had made its "maximum concessions," and that if the United States refused to accept those terms and sign the agreement "within a week to ten days," it would be "useless" to continue the negotiations, as the Japanese domestic political situation would permit "no further delays in reaching a decision." He emphasized this latter point in his report of the conversation to Ambassador Nomura, saying that it was "absolutely impossible that there be any further delays," that while there were indications that the United States Government was "still under the impression that the negotiations are in the preliminary stages and that we are still merely exchanging opinions," as far as Tokyo was concerned, "this is the final phase," and expressed the "fervent" hope that Ambassador Nomura would do—

everything in (his) power to make them realize this fact and bring about an agreement at the earliest possible moment (ex. 1, p. 119).

At the meeting between Secretary Hull and Ambassador Nomura on November 12 (Washington time), the Ambassador said that his new Government had asked him to emphasize its desire to expedite a settlement because the internal situation in Japan was difficult, people were becoming impatient and a session of the Diet was impending. He expressed the hope that "within a week or ten days" some agreement could be reached. Secretary Hull commented that the matters submitted on November 10 were being worked on as rapidly as possible, and that as soon as a good basis had been reached in the exploratory conversations the United States could then approach the Chinese Government and sound out their attitude. He had previously handed to the Ambassador a document setting forth his general ideas relating to mutual conciliation between Japan and China. In response to a question from Minister Wakasugi, who was also present, Secretary Hull hinted that Japan and China might be "brought together" by the United States, but did not say in so many words that the United States would mediate between them. The conversation ended with Secretary Hull expressing the hope that he might have something by way of comment on the Japanese proposals on November 14 (ex. 29, vol. II, pp. 722–726). According to Ambassador Nomura's report to Tokyo, Secretary Hull also indicated that the British and the Dutch were being informed generally of the nature of the conversations, and that if a basis for negotiations should be worked out, it was possible that they might sign with the United States, although the Secretary "could not guarantee this" (ex. 1, p. 120). Ambassador Nomura told the Foreign Minister he was not "satisfied with their attitude toward taking up negotiations," and he sent Minister Wakasugi to see one of Mr. Hull's advisors the following day to press for an early decision. During that conversation, Mr. Wakusugi said that the public in Japan was becoming impatient "and almost desperate," and that he hoped for a clear-cut answer the next day as to whether the United States would accept or not the Japanese proposal of September 25 as modified through November 10, or desired changes therein, or whether the United States' proposal of June 21 was its final proposal (ex. 29, vol. II, pp. 729–731; ex. 1, pp. 123–125). Similar representations concerning the need for immediate agreement were made to Ambassador Grew on November 12 (Japan time), including statements that the negotiations had reached their final phase, that Japan had made the greatest possible concessions, and that "a very critical and dangerous state of affairs will result should any appreciable delay be encountered in successfully concluding the negotiations" (ex. 29, vol. II, pp. 719–722).

Secretary Hull testified that:

during those early days in October, it looked more and more like they were prepared to, and were intending to, adhere to their policies * * * the situation floated along until Tojo's government came into power, about the 16th, I think, of October * * * and the Konoye Government fell.

While they started out with a professed disposition to keep up the conversations, we could detect circumstances and facts indicative of duplicity and double dealing, and the real purpose was to go forward more energetically with their plans, as was indicated by numerous demands on us to make haste, and statements that this matter could not go on without something serious happening.

*　　　*　　　*　　　*　　　*　　　*　　　*

The impression we received, at least myself, and some others, was that during those months they tried to prevail on this Government by persuasion and threats and other methods to yield its basic principles, so that Japan could maintain intact her policy and her continued course of aggression and conquest (tr. 1178–1179).

On November 14 (Japan time), although he knew that Ambassador Nomura had scheduled a meeting with Secretary Hull for November 15 (Washington time) at which proposal "A" would be further discussed, Foreign Minister Togo cabled the Ambassador the English text to be used in presenting proposal "B", and told the Ambassador he would be notified when to present that "absolutely final proposal" to the United States Government (ex. 1, pp. 125–126). This message was translated and available in Washington on November 14 (Washington time) (ex. 1, p. 126). The same day Ambassador Nomura cabled the Foreign Minister a long report (No. 1090) in which, although he realized he would be "harshly criticized," he cautioned against precipitate action:

I am telling Your Excellency this for your own information only.

I believe that I will win out in the long run in these negotiations, and I will fight to the end. I will do my very best with infinite patience and then leave the outcome up to God Almighty. However, I must tell you the following:

1. As I told you in a number of messages, the policy of the American Government in the Pacific is to stop any further moves on our part either southward or northward. With every economic weapon at their command, they have attempted to achieve this objective, and now they are contriving by every possible means to prepare for actual warfare.

2. In short, they are making every military and every other kind of preparation to prevent us from a thrust northward or a thrust southward; they are conspiring most actively with the nations concerned and rather than yield on this fundamental political policy of theirs in which they believe so firmly, they would not hesitate, I am sure, to fight us. It is not their intention, I know, to repeat such a thing as the Munich conference which took place several years ago and which turned out to be such a failure. Already I think the apex of German victories has been passed. Soviet resistance persists, and the possibility of a separate peace has receded, and hereafter this trend will be more and more in evidence.

3. The United States is sealing ever-friendlier relations with China, and insofar as possible she is assisting Chiang. For the sake of peace in the Pacific, the United States would not favor us at the sacrifice of China. Therefore, the China problem might become the stumbling block to the pacification of the Pacific and as a result the possibility of the United States and Japan ever making up might vanish.

4. There is also the question of whether the officials of the Japanese Government are tying up very intimately with the Axis or not. We are regarded as having a very flexible policy, ready, nevertheless, in any case, to stab the United States right in the back. Lately the newspapers are writing in a manner to show how gradually we are tying up closer and closer with the Axis.

5. If we carry out a venture southward for the sake of our existence and our lives, it naturally follows that we will have to fight England and the United States, and chances are also great that the Soviet will participate. Furthermore, among the neutral nations, those of Central America are already the puppets of the United States, and as for those of South America, whether they like it or not, they are dependent for their economic existence on the United States, and must maintain a neutrality partial thereto.

6. It is inevitable that this war will be long, and this little victory or that little victory, or this little defeat or that little defeat do not amount to much, and it is not hard to see that whoever can hold out till the end will be the victor.

7. It is true that the United States is gradually getting in deeper and deeper in the Atlantic, but this is merely a sort of convoy warfare, and as things now stand she might at any moment transfer her main strength to the Pacific.

Great Britain, too, in the light of the present condition of the German and Italian Navies, has, without a doubt, moved considerable strength into the area of the Indian Ocean. I had expected in the past that should the United States start warlike activities in the Atlantic, there would be considerable feeling for a compromise in the Pacific, but there has been no evidence of such an inclination as yet. There are even now many arguments against war with Germany as opposed to internal questions, but there is not the slightest opposition to war in the Pacific. It is being thought more than ever that participation will be carried out through the Pacific area.

8. *Though I cannot be a hundred percent sure of the present situation in Japan, having read your successive wires I realize that the condition must be very critical. In spite of the fact that it is my understanding that the people and officials, too, are tightening their belts, I am going to pass on to you my opinion, even though I know that I will be harshly criticized for it. I feel that should the situation in Japan permit, I would like to caution patience for one or two months in order to get a clear view of the world situation. This, I believe, would be the best plan* (ex. 1, pp. 127–129).

The Foreign Minister's reply came back promptly and unequivocally:

For your Honor's own information.
1. I have read your #1090, and you may be sure that you have all my gratitude for the efforts you have put forth, but *the fate of our Empire hangs by the slender thread of a few days,* so please fight harder than you ever did before.
2. What you say in the last paragraph of your message is, of course, so and I have given it already the fullest consideration, but I have only to refer you to the fundamental policy laid down in my #725. Will you please try to realize what that means. In your opinion we ought to wait and see what turn the war takes and remain patient. However, *I am awfully sorry to say that the situation renders this out of the question.* I set the deadline for the solution of these negotiations in my #736, *and there will be no change.* Please try to understand that. *You see how short the time is;* therefore, do not allow the United States to sidetrack us and delay the negotiations any further. Press them for a solution *on the basis of our proposals,* and do your best to bring about an immediate solution (ex. 1 p. 137–8).

The next day, November 15 (Washington time), Ambassador Nomura called on Secretary Hull and the Secretary handed the Ambassador a statement, in writing, regarding the formula proposed by the Japanese Government on November 10 (Washington time) for dealing with the question of nondiscrimination in international trade. After noting that in its proposal, the Japanese Government recognized

the principle of nondiscrimination in international commercial relations to be applied to all the Pacific areas, inclusive of China, *on the understanding that the principle in question is to be applied uniformly to the rest of the entire world as well* (ex. 29, vol. II, p. 734),

the statement suggested that the meaning of the condition attached by the Japanese was not entirely clear. It was assumed that the Japanese Government did not intend to ask the United States Government to accept responsibility for discriminatory practices in areas outside its sovereign jurisdiction, or to propose including in an arrangement with the United States a condition which could be fulfilled only with the consent and cooperation of all other governments. The statement then reviewed the efforts of the United States over recent years to reduce tariff barriers, and suggested that similar action by Japan would be a "long forward step" toward the objective set forth in the Japanese proposal. The need for the proviso noted above was then questioned, and it was suggested that the proviso might well be omitted. The statement was accompanied by a draft of a proposed joint United States-Japanese declaration on economic policy, which Secretary Hull told Minister Wakasugi constituted the United States reply to the Japanese proposal on the question of nondiscrimination in international trade (ex. 29, vol. II, pp. 731–737).

Ambassador Nomura then stated that his Government regarded the conversations as having progressed to the stage of formal negotiations. In reply to this, Secretary Hull said that until the conversations had reached a point where he could call in the British, the Chinese, and the Dutch and say that there was a basis for negotiation, the conversations were exploratory. He pointed out that whereas the United States proposal of June 21 made it clear that the settlement under discussion related to the entire Pacific area, the proposal the previous Japanese Government had submitted on September 27 narrowed the application of the proposals regarding economic nondiscrimination and peaceful intent to the southwestern Pacific, and he then requested that the new Japanese Government give assurances on that point. He said that it would be difficult for him to go to the British and the Dutch and say that Japan was willing to enter upon a peaceful program but at the same time desired to adhere to a fighting alliance with Germany. The Secretary said that if the United States made an agreement with Japan while Japan had an outstanding obligation to Germany which might call upon Japan to go to war with us, this would cause "so much turmoil in the country that he might be lynched." He asked the Ambassador whether the United States Government could assume that if the Japanese Government entered into an agreement with it the Tripartite Pact would become a "dead letter." When Mr. Wakasugi inquired whether this was an answer to the Japanese proposal on the question of Japan's relations under the Tripartite Pact, Secretary Hull said the United States would be better able to reply after receiving an answer to the question he had just raised. Ambassador Nomura said he was afraid the American Government did not trust the Japanese Government, though there was no material difference between the policies of the new Government and the previous Government. Secretary Hull said that the new Japanese Government seemed to be taking the attitude that the United States Government must reply "at once" to their points, and that he did not think that his Government—

should be receiving ultimatums of such a character from the Japanese Government under circumstances where the United States had been pursuing peaceful courses throughout and the Japanese Government had been violating law and order (ex. 29, vol. II, p. 734).

He concluded by saying that when he had heard further from the new Japanese Government regarding its peaceful intentions, and when the question of nondiscrimination could be cleared up as suggested in the proposals he had handed to Ambassador Nomura during the meeting, and also in regard to the Tripartite Pact, he believed that some solution could be reached on the question of stationing troops in China. The Secretary emphasized at the same time that he did not desire any delay and that he was working as hard as he could to bring about a wholly satisfactory and broad settlement. It was agreed that there should be a further meeting after Ambassador Nomura had received instructions from his Government (ex. 29, vol. II, pp. 731–734; ex. 1, p. 132).

In his report of this meeting to Tokyo, Ambassador Nomura said that he had told Mr. Hull he felt his Government would be "very disappointed" over these replies. He continued:

Today's talks can be boiled down to the fact that the United States did clarify their attitude on the trade question. On the other two problems, although we agree in principle, we differ on interpretations. They harbor deep doubts as to the sincerity of our peaceful intentions and apparently they view the China situation through those eyes of suspicion (ex. 1, p. 137).

There is no evidence before the Committee indicating that at that time Ambassador Nomura had any knowledge that the Japanese naval striking force had already started assembling for the attack on Pearl Harbor.

THE TOJO CABINET REFUSES TO CONSIDER ANY SUGGESTION LESS
FAVORABLE TO JAPAN THAN ITS "ABSOLUTELY FINAL PROPOSAL"

(November 18–19, 1941)

Ambassador Kurusu reached Washington on November 15 (Washington time) (tr. 1133). On the morning of November 17 (Washington time), with Ambassador Nomura, he called on Secretary Hull prior to their meeting with President Roosevelt. After he had been introduced, Ambassador Kurusu said, among other things, that he was fully assured of Premier Tojo's desire to reach a peaceful settlement with the United States, and that Premier Tojo was optimistic regarding the possibility of settling the differences in respect to non-discrimination in international trade and Japan's attitude toward the European war, but felt that there were greater difficulties in the question of withdrawing Japanese troops from China. Before the meeting with President Roosevelt, Ambassador Nomura handed Secretary Hull two documents which he said the Japanese Government was submitting in response to the questions that had been raised at the conference on November 12 regarding Japan's peaceful intentions and the scope of the proposed understanding between the two Governments (ex. 29, vol. II, pp. 738–739).

At the meeting at the White House, Ambassador Kurusu was formally received by President Roosevelt. The conversation was largely devoted to a discussion of the relation of Japan and the United States to the war in Europe and to the China problem. Concerning the latter the President said that at a suitable stage the United States would, so to speak, "introduce" Japan and China to each other and tell them to proceed with the remaining adjustments, the Pacific questions having already been determined. Secretary Hull explained at length that America's military preparations were for defense before it was too late, that the United States was on the defense in the present Pacific situation and that Japan was the aggressor. The conference ended with the understanding that both Ambassadors would see Secretary Hull the next morning (ex. 29, vol. II, pp. 740–743).

At that meeting at the White House no effort was made by either side to solve the three major points of difference between the two countries, and there is no evidence before the Committee of any contact between representatives of the two Governments on the afternoon of November 17 (Washington time). However, as Ambassador Nomura reported to Tokyo the next day (No. 1135), that evening the two Japanese Ambassadors "went to call on a certain Cabinet member." "This," they cabled the Foreign Minister, "is what he told us":

The President is very desirous of an understanding between Japan and the United States. In his latest speech he showed that he entertained no ill will towards Japan. I would call that to your attention. Now the great majority of the cabinet members, with two exceptions, in principle approve of a Japanese American understanding. *If Japan would now do something real, such as evacuating French Indo-China, showing her peaceful intentions, the way would be open for us to furnish you with oil and it would probably lead to the reestablishment of normal trade relations.* The Secretary of State cannot bring public opinion in line so long as you do not take some real and definite steps to reassure the Americans (ex. 1, p. 154).

There are indications in the record before the Committee that this meeting between the two Japanese Ambassadors and a member of President Roosevelt's Cabinet on the evening before their meeting with Secretary Hull was more than a coincidence. Under Secretary Welles testified before the Committee in another connection that he had been told by Secretary Hull "and other individuals" that Mr. Frank Walker, then Postmaster General and as such a member of President Roosevelt's Cabinet, was "negotiating" with the Japanese and that he thought Mr. Walker "had conversations both with Admiral Nomura and later, when Kurusu was here, with him, as well" (tr. 1319–1320). Furthermore, the record of outside telephone calls through the White House switchboard shows that at 6:25 p. m. on November 17, before the meeting of the two Japanese Ambassadors with the "certain Cabinet member," Postmaster General Walker talked with Secretary Hull, and that he also talked with Secretary Hull at 9:22 o'clock the next morning, November 18 (Washington time), before Secretary Hull's conference at 10:30 o'clock with the two Ambassadors (ex. 179).

The suggestion made that evening by the Cabinet member—that some action by Japan to show her peaceful intentions, "such as evacuating French Indochina," would open the way for the United States to relax its freezing orders—was substantially the proposal made by the two Ambassadors to Secretary Hull at their meeting with him at 10:30 the next morning. While at that meeting the greatest emphasis was placed on the question of Japan's obligations under the Tripartite Pact, during the discussion of this subject, after Secretary Hull had pointed out that the American public would never understand an agreement between Japan and the United States if Japan continued to adhere to the Tripartite Pact, Ambassador Nomura said that the situation in the southwest Pacific was now critical, with the United States and Great Britain reinforcing their armed forces in Singapore and the Philippine Islands to counter Japan's sending troops to French Indochina. He suggested that if this situation could now be checked, if the tension could be relaxed, an atmosphere could be created in which the talks could continue. Ambassador Kurusu then said that the freezing regulations had caused impatience in Japan and a feeling that Japan had to fight while it could; he said that what was needed now was to do something to enable Japan to change its course. Secretary Hull asked to what extent a relaxation of freezing would enable Japan to adopt peaceful policies. He explained that—

what he had in mind was to enable the peaceful leaders in Japan to get control of the situation in Japan and to assert their influence.

Ambassador Nomura then asked whether there was any hope of a solution—some small beginning toward the realization of "our high ideals"—and continued by suggesting:

the possibility of going back to the status which existed before the date in July when following the Japanese move into southern French Indochina, our freezing measures were put into effect.[1] The Secretary said that if we should make some modifications in our embargo on the strength of a step by Japan such as the Ambassador had mentioned we do not know whether the troops which have been withdrawn from French Indochina will be diverted to some equally objectionable movement elsewhere. The Ambassador said that what he had in mind was simply some move toward arresting the dangerous trend in our relations. *The Secretary said*

---

[1] While the Japanese move that precipitated the United States freezing order was into *southern* French Indochina, Japanese troops had moved into *northern* French Indochina in 1940.

that it would be difficult for him to get this Government to go a long way in removing the embargo unless this Government believed that Japan was definitely started on a peaceful course and had renounced purposes of conquest. The Ambassador said that the Japanese were tired of fighting China and that Japan would go as far as it could along a first step. The Secretary said that he would consult with the British and the Dutch to see what their attitude would be toward the suggestion offered by the Japanese Ambassador (ex. 29, vol. II, p. 750).

Ambassadors Nomura and Kurusu pursued their suggestion further at a conference with Secretary Hull the next day, November 19 (Washington time). Ambassador Nomura told the Secretary that they had reported to their Government the conversation of the preceding day and were momentarily expecting instructions.

The Secretary then asked how the Ambassador (Nomura) felt about the possibilities. *The Ambassador said that yesterday he had made the suggestion in regard to a restoration of the status which prevailed before the Japanese moved into south Indochina in the latter part of July because he felt that, as this action had precipitated our freezing measures which in turn had reacted in Japan to increase the tension, if something could be done on his suggestion, it would serve to relieve that tension and tend to create a better atmosphere in our relations.* The Secretary asked whether the Ambassador contemplated that if a proposal such as the Ambassador had suggested were carried out we would go on with the conversations. The Ambassador replied in the affirmative. The Secretary expressed the view that this might enable the leaders in Japan to hold their ground and organize public opinion in favor of a peaceful course. He said that he recognized that this might take some time.

The Ambassador said that what was in his mind was that both sides now appeared to be preparing for eventualities and that nevertheless the Japanese desired a quick settlement, especially in view of our freezing measures. The Secretary said that he presumed that the Ambassador had in mind, in connection with the continuation of our conversations, further efforts to iron out the important points on which our views had not so far diverged. The Ambassador agreed (ex. 29, vol. II, p. 751).

In reporting to Tokyo on November 18 (Washington time) the substance of their conversation with Secretary Hull on that day, the two Japanese Ambassadors had, in fact, dispatched four separate telegrams (ex. 1, pp. 146, 149, 151, 152), each of which outlined the suggestion they had made, thereby indicating the importance the two Ambassadors attached to it. The sending of four telegrams may also have reflected the fact that they had already received from the Foreign Minister the English text of proposal "B", which was far more drastic than their suggestion and was, they knew, regarded in Tokyo as Japan's "absolutely final proposal." Furthermore, they had been told by the Foreign Minister that they would be notified when to present it to Secretary Hull. The two final telegrams show that both Japanese Ambassadors regarded a return to the status prior to freezing as the only means to success in the negotiations. In his message (No. 1133) Ambassador Kurusu said:

In view of the internal situation in our country, although I think there will be difficulties to be met in trying to reach a settlement in harmony with the wishes of the Americans, I feel that *as a stopgap for the present, we should ask them to consider our strong desires for a "time limit" in connection with the conclusion of such a Japanese-American agreement and for the purpose of breaking the present deadlock, ask them for the removal at once of the freezing act and also for assurances regarding imports of a specified amount of oil.*

In the conference of the 18th both Ambassador Nomura and I suggested the resumption of the status quo prior to 24 July, but in view of the progress of negotiations thus far, the Americans will likely not consent to this merely for our agreeing to not forcefully invade any territory aside from French Indo-China as per Proposal "B" or for our promise in vague terms of evacuation of troops from French Indo-China * * * Please have your mind made up to this. I desire instructions re "time limit" and * * * as we desire to press for a speedy settlement, please give consideration to the above and advise at once (ex. 1, pp. 151–152).

In his message (No. 1134) to the Foreign Minister Ambassador Nomura outlined at greater length what he and Ambassador Kurusu had in mind:

In our conversations of today, *as a practical means of alleviating the ever worsening front with which we are faced and to quiet the fearful situation, as well as, to bring about a return to the situation existing before the application of the freezing legislation, we suggested the evacuation of Japanese troops stationed in the southern part of French Indo-China.*

Hull, showing considerable reluctance replied, "After Japan had clearly demonstrated her intentions to be peaceful I will confer with Britain, the Netherlands and other interested powers."

In the past it would seem that the greatest stumbling block for the American authorities was the question of our troops of occupation in China. Recently, however, the United States, what with her internal situation and, especially insofar as it concerns the revision of the Neutrality Agreement, her increasing involvement in the war in the Atlantic, seems to have undergone a change. She is now, rather, exhibiting a tendency to lay more emphasis on Japan's peace plans insofar as they pertain to the Tri-Partite Alliance. With regard to other questions, too, it seems very clear that they are of a mind to bring about a compromise after making sure of our peaceful intentions. In view of these circumstances, as a result of our deliberations of successive days it would seem that should we present Proposal "B" immediately, an understanding would be more difficult to realize than if we went on with our discussions of Proposal "A". *Therefore, looking at it from a practical point of view, we are of the opinion that prior to presenting of Proposal "B" it would be more advisable to reach a practical settlement, principally on the questions of the acquisition of goods and the cancellation of the freezing legislation mentioned in Proposal "B", and then to try to proceed with the solution of other questions on this basis. Unless we follow this course we are convinced that an immediate solution will be extremely difficult.*

*   *   *   *   *   *   *

The United States, of course, has indicated clearly that she is not interested in mere promises as much as she is in putting said promises in effect. *It is necessary, therefore, for us to be prepared to withdraw our troops as soon as the freezing order is rescinded and materials are made available to us.*

Please advise us as to your intentions after perusing my message #1133 (ex. 1, pp. 152–3).

The temporary arrangement suggested by the two Japanese Ambassadors was summarily rejected by the Japanese Government in Tokyo. On November 19 (Japan time), in a message in which he referred to the Ambassadors' messages No. 1133 and No. 1134 above, Foreign Minister Togo emphasized that in the negotiations consent could be given only "within the scope of the instructions of this office." He told Ambassador Nomura that—

the internal situation in our country is such *that it would be difficult for us to handle it if we withdraw from Southern French Indo-China, merely on assurances that conditions prior to this freezing act will be restored. It would be necessary to have a proposed solution that would come up to the B proposal.* With the situation as urgent as it is now, it is of utmost importance that you play your hand for the amelioration of the situation, to the extent of the proposal in your message, then to push on for an understanding.

The Ambassador (Kurusu) *did not arrange this with us beforehand, but made the proposal contained in your message for the purpose of meeting the tense situation existing within the nation, but this can only result in delay and failure in the negotiations. The Ambassador, therefore, having received our revised instructions,* (after reading our #797, 800 and 801) *will please present our B proposal of the Imperial Government, and no further concessions can be made.*

If the U. S. consent to this cannot be secured, the negotiations will have to be broken off; therefore, with the above well in mind put forth your very best efforts (ex. 1, p. 155).

Ambassador Nomura immediately cabled the Foreign Minister in Tokyo his astonishment at the Japanese Government's unwillingness to consider seriously the suggestion he and Ambassador Kurusu had made. His message (No. 1136), dated November 19 (Washington time) follows in full:

I know that it is beyond our powers to imagine the anxiety felt by the Cabinet leaders who bear the heavy responsibility of saving the nation and succoring the people at this time when relations between Japan and the United States have now at last reached the point of cruciality. There are now three ways which the Empire might take—
    (1) Maintain the status quo.
    (2) Break the present deadlock by an advance under force of arms.
    (3) Devise some means for bringing about a mutual non-agression arrangement.
No. 1 would mean that both sides would continue to increase war preparations and send out larger fleets of war vessels bringing about a state where only a contact would be needed to start a conflagration. In other words this would finally result in an armed clash and it differs from No. 2 only in the matter of the longer or shorter time involved.
No. 3 would mean finding some provisional arrangement by which the present deadlock might be broken, and at the same time attaining our objectives under the peace for which we have been striving. *My #1134 of yesterday was sent with this purpose in mind. The displeasure felt by the government is beyond my power of comprehension*, but as I view it, the present, after exhausting our strength by four years of the China incident following right upon the Manchuria incident, is hardly an opportune time for venturing upon another long drawn out warfare on a large scale. *I think that it would be better to fix up a temporary "truce" now in the spirit of "give and take" and make this the prelude to greater achievements to come later.*
I am thus frankly setting before you my humble opinion as supplementary to my message of yesterday (ex. 1, p. 158).

In a separate message Ambassador Nomura requested the Foreign Minister to "*convey the above* (message) *to the Prime Minister*" (ex. 1, p. 158).

In reply to this Foreign Minister Togo cabled Ambassador Nomura on November 20 (Japan time) that:

under the circumstances here, we regret that *the plan suggested by you, as we have stated in our message, would not suffice for saving the present situation.*
We see no prospects for breaking the deadlock *except for you to push negotiations immediately along the lines of the latter part of our #798.* Please understand this. *The Premier also is absolutely in accord with this opinion* (ex. 1, p. 160).

Message No. 798 referred to in the next preceding paragraph was the message the Foreign Minister had sent on November 19 (Japan time) which rejected Ambassador Nomura's suggestion for a "provisional arrangement" and instructed him to present proposal "B," the Japanese Government's "absolutely final proposal."

Foreign Minister Togo's message of November 20 (Japan time), which thus finally and conclusively rejected the suggestion made by Ambassadors Nomura and Kurusu, was sent not only after the Foreign Minister had received the Ambassadors' four telegrams of November 18 (Washington time), including No. 1133 and No. 1134 quoted in part above, but also after the Foreign Minister had received Ambassador Nomura's message No. 1135 of the same date, reporting on the meeting of the two Ambassadors with the member of President Roosevelt's Cabinet on the evening of November 17 (Washington time). Consequently, the record before the committee shows that the Japanese Government, including Premier Tojo, refused to consider the provisional arrangement suggested by Ambassadors Nomura and

Kurusu with knowledge not only that Secretary Hull had agreed to discuss it with the British and the Dutch—thus indicating, in the light of his prior statements, that he believed a basis for negotiations had been suggested by the two Ambassadors—but with the further knowledge that practically the same suggestion had been made to Ambassadors Nomura and Kurusu by a member of President Roosevelt's Cabinet.

The seriousness with which the Japanese Government regarded the stage that had now been reached in the negotiations is evidenced by the fact that on November 15 (Japan time), the Japanese Foreign Office sent out a circular message to its officials abroad, including those in Washington, prescribing "the order and method of destroying the code machines in the event of an emergency" (ex. 1, p. 137). Four days later the Foreign Office sent out circular messages establishing the so-called "winds code," to be used in case of an emergency and the cutting off of international communications. The receipt of a message implementing this code was to be the signal to "destroy all code papers, etc." (ex. 1, pp. 154–155). Those two messages were sent from Tokyo *before* Japan's "absolutely final proposal" was presented to Secretary Hull, and appear to have been the first Japanese messages intercepted which dealt with the destruction of codes, code machines, et cetera.

JAPAN DELIVERS ITS "ABSOLUTELY FINAL PROPOSAL" TO THE UNITED STATES AND DEMANDS AN AGREEMENT ON THAT BASIS

(November 20, 1941)

On November 20 (Washington time), Thanksgiving Day, Ambassadors Nomura and Kurusu called at the State Department. Ambassador Kurusu told Secretary Hull that they had referred to their Government the suggestion Ambassador Nomura had made at the meeting 2 days before for a return to the status which prevailed prior to the Japanese move into southern French Indochina in July. He said that both he and Ambassador Nomura had anticipated that the Japanese Government might perceive difficulty in moving troops out of Indochina in short order, but that nevertheless the Japanese Government was now prepared to offer a proposal "on that basis." He said that the Japanese proposal represented an amplification of the suggestion Ambassador Nomura had made (ex. 29, vol. II, p. 753).

The proposal which Ambassador Kurusu then read and handed to Secretary Hull was the second formula, proposal "B," approved at the Imperial Conference in Tokyo on November 5 (Japan time) as a "last effort to prevent something happening." In his messages to Ambassador Nomura, Foreign Minister Togo had described it as "an ultimatum" (ex. 1, p. 99), as "our absolutely final proposal" (ex. 1, p. 99), and as "our last possible bargain" (ex. 1, p. 93). As originally drawn up and approved, proposal "B" had consisted of four provisions, each of which was contained in the Japanese proposal of November 20 (ex. 1, pp. 97, 99; ex. 29, vol. II, pp. 755–756). "If necessary," those four provisions were to be supplemented by others dealing with the three points previously at issue in the conversations—i. e., the evacuation of troops from China and French Indochina, the Tripartite Pact, and nondiscrimination in international trade. In the English text of proposal "B" cabled to Ambassador Nomura on November

14 (Japan time), specific provisions covering those three points were added to the original four provisions (ex. 1, p. 126). However, the Foreign Minister's instructions to Ambassador Nomura on November 19 (Japan time) to present proposal "B" had also directed him to delete the provisions dealing with nondiscrimination in international trade and the Tripartite Pact, leaving only the provision relating to evacuation of troops in addition to the four provisions approved on November 5 (Japan time) (ex. 1, p. 156). But whereas the formula concerning the evacuation of troops which Ambassador Nomura had presented to Secretary Hull on November 7 (Washington time) had covered the evacuation of Japanese troops from both China and French Indochina, the provision contained in the Japanese proposal of November 20 covered the evacuation of Japanese troops from French Indochina only. To this, possibly with an eye to the suggestion made by Ambassador Nomura to Secretary Hull on November 18, the Japanese Government had added a provision for the transfer of their troops from southern French Indochina to northern French Indochina "upon the conclusion of the present arrangement." [1]

As read and delivered to Secretary Hull by Ambassador Kurusu, the Japanese proposal follows in full:

1. Both the Governments of Japan and the United States undertake not to make any armed advancement into any of the regions in the Southeastern Asia and the Southern Pacific area excepting the part of French Indo-China where the Japanese troops are stationed at present.

2. The Japanese Government undertakes to withdraw its troops now stationed in French Indo-China upon either the restoration of peace between Japan and China or the establishment of an equitable peace in the Pacific area.

In the meantime the Government of Japan declares that it is prepared to remove its troops now stationed in the southern part of French Indo-China to the northern part of the said territory upon the conclusion of the present arrangement which shall later be embodied in the final agreement.

3. The Government of Japan and the United States shall cooperate with a view to securing the acquisition of those goods and commodities which the two countries need in Netherlands East Indies.

4. The Governments of Japan and the United States mutually undertake to restore their commercial relations to those prevailing prior to the freezing of the assets.

The Government of the United States shall supply Japan a required quantity of oil.

5. The Government of the United States undertakes to refrain from such measures and actions as will be prejudicial to the endeavors for the restoration of general peace between Japan and China (ex. 29, vol. II, pp. 755–756).

When Ambassador Kurusu handed the Japanese proposal to him, Secretary Hull said that he would examine and study it sympathetically. Secretary Hull referred to the fact that the United States was supplying aid to both Great Britain and China, and indicated that until Japan made it perfectly clear that her policy was one of peace it would be impossible to cease aiding China. However, Ambassador Kurusu observed in connection with paragraph 5 of the proposal that it "might be interpreted to mean that American aid to China would be discontinued as from the time that negotiations were started." (Ex. 29, vol. II, pp. 753–755.)

In his testimony before the Committee Secretary Hull summarized the Japanese note of November 20 in these words:

---

[1] Secretary Hull testified that the conditional offer of the Japanese "to withdraw troops from southern Indochina to northern Indochina was meaningless as they could have brought those troops back to southern Indochina within a day or two, and furthermore they placed no limit on the number of troops they might continue to send there." (Tr. 14261.)

The plan thus offered called for the supplying by the United States to Japan of as much oil as Japan might require, for suspension of freezing measures, for discontinuance by the United States of aid to China, and for withdrawal of moral and material support from the recognized Chinese Government. It contained a provision that Japan would shift her armed forces from southern Indochina to northern Indochina, but placed no limit on the number of armed forces which Japan might send into Indochina and made no provision for withdrawal of those forces until after either the restoration of peace between Japan and China or the establishment of an "equitable" peace in the Pacific area. While there were stipulations against further extension of Japan's armed force into southeastern Asia and the southern Pacific (except Indochina), there were no provisions which would have prevented continued or fresh Japanese aggressive activities in any of the regions of Asia lying to the north of Indochina—for example, China and the Soviet Union. The proposal contained no provision pledging Japan to abandon aggression and to revert to peaceful courses (tr. 1137–38).

It is now known that the Japanese note of November 20, was, in fact, a restatement in more peremptory terms of Japan's "minimum demands" determined at the Imperial Conference in Tokyo on September 6 (Japan time). As applied to the United States, the three major Japanese "demands" decided upon at that Imperial Conference were, that the United States would not "intervene in or obstruct a settlement by Japan of the China Incident", i. e., would cease all aid to China; that the United States would "take no action in the Far East which offers a threat to the defense of the Empire"; and that the United States would "cooperate with Japan in her attempt to obtain needed raw materials" (ex. 179, Konoye Memoirs, pp. 77–78). In an intercepted message to Ambassador Nomura which was translated and available in Washington on November 24 (Washington time), Foreign Minister Togo said:

our demand for a cessation of aid to Chiang (the acquisition of Netherlands Indies goods and at the same time the supply of American petroleum to Japan as well) is a most essential condition (ex. 1, p. 172).

Secretary Hull testified that the Japanese must have known that their proposal was—

an utterly impossible proposal for us, in the light of our 4 or 5 years exploration of each others situations and attitudes (tr. 1181).

He continued—

To have accepted the Japanese proposal of November 20 was clearly unthinkable. It would have made the United States an ally of Japan in Japan's program of conquest and aggression and of collaboration with Hitler. It would have meant yielding to the Japanese demand that the United States abandon its principles and policies. It would have meant abject surrender of our position under intimidation (tr. 1140).

Secretary Hull and President Roosevelt, as well as other high officials of the Government, not only knew from the intercepted Japanese messages already mentioned that the note the Japanese delivered on Thanksgiving Day, November 20, was their "absolutely final proposal," they also knew from the same source that the Japanese Government had fixed November 25 (Japan time) as the dead line by which the written agreement of the United States, Great Britain, and the Netherlands to its demands were to be obtained. On November 22 (Washington time), the following intercepted message from Foreign Minister Togo to Ambassador Nomura was translated and available in Washington:

It is awfully hard for us to consider changing the date we set in my #736 (November 25). You should know this, however, I know you are working hard. **Stick** to our fixed policy and do your very best. Spare no efforts and try to bring about the solution we desire. *There are reasons beyond your ability to guess why we wanted to settle Japanese-American relations by the 25th, but if within the next three or four days you can finish your conversations with the Americans; if the signing can be completed by the 29th,* (let me write it out for you—twenty-ninth); *if the pertinent notes can be exchanged; if we can get an understanding with Great Britain and the Netherlands; and in short if everything can be finished, we have decided to wait until that date. This time we mean it, that the dead line absolutely cannot be changed. After that things are automatically going to happen.* Please take this into your careful consideration and work harder than you ever have before (ex. 1, p. 165).

Even with four added days of grace, the situation was, Secretary Hull testified,

critical and virtually hopeless. On the one hand our Government desired to exhaust all possibilities of finding a means to a peaceful solution and to avert or delay an armed clash, especially as the heads of this country's armed forces continued to emphasize the need for time to prepare for resistance. On the other hand, Japan was calling for a show-down.

There the situation stood—the Japanese unyielding and intimidating in their demands and we standing firmly for our principles.

The chances of meeting the crisis by diplomacy had practically vanished. We had reached the point of clutching at straws (tr. 1140).

Neither Secretary Hull nor President Roosevelt, nor any of their advisors, knew, however, that almost simultaneously with the delivery in Washington of the Japanese ultimatum of November 20, the Imperial Japanese General Headquarters in Tokyo had ordered the commander in chief of the Japanese combined fleet to direct the Japanese naval striking force, already assembling in a harbor in northern Japan, to "advance to the area in which they are to wait in readiness" for the attack on Pearl Harbor (tr. 437).

The United States Replies

(November 26, 1941)

The United States reply was handed to Ambassadors Nomura and Kurusu in the late afternoon on November 26 (Washington time), 6 days after the delivery of the Japanese ultimatum (tr. 1147). Those 6 days were a period of intense activity, involving not only the highest officials in the United States Government but also the highest officials of the British, Dutch, Australian, and Chinese Governments.

From time to time Secretary Hull had told the Japanese Ambassadors that when his conversations with them got beyond the exploratory stage he would talk with the representatives of the British, Dutch, and Chinese Governments. On November 18 (Washington time), after the Japanese Ambassadors suggested a return to the status prior to the freezing orders in July, Secretary Hull told them he would consult the British and the Dutch to see what their attitude would be (ex. 29, vol. II, p. 750). Immediately after that conference, Secretary Hull requested the British Minister, Sir Ronald Campbell, to call on him. Secretary Hull's memorandum of his conversation with the Minister is as follows:

I said that I had engaged in a lengthy conference with the two ranking Japanese representatives, including Mr. Kurusu, who is here for the purpose of carrying on conversations with this Government. I added that the conversation related to the question of a proposed peaceful settlement for the Pacific area. I stated that nothing was agreed upon at this meeting and that the discussion included the subject of two opposing policies—of conquest by force on the one hand and a policy of peace, law, and order on the other. I went on to say that the three main points on which we have encountered serious difficulties in former conversations with Ambassador Nomura, namely, the bringing of Japanese troops out of China, the Tripartite Pact and certain phases of commercial policy, were discussed at length; but that the Japanese made no concessions on the troop matter or on the matter of the Tripartite Pact. I told the Minister that the Japanese finally inquired whether a brief temporary partial arrangement could not be worked out that would enable them to improve public sentiment in Japan along the lines of peace rather than of military action. This would also include the idea of Japan's, coming out of China. They said while the United States and maybe Great Britain and the Netherlands East Indies, if they should be so disposed on consultation, would to a partial extent relax embargoes on exports to Japan, Japan on its part would correspondingly take steps in the direction of a peaceful policy and in organizing and educating its public opinion in support of such a policy during the next few months. The Japanese suggested further that the whole question of a general peaceful settlement for the Pacific area would be gradually developed and public opinion in Japan would enable them to meet us more satisfactorily themselves, and presumably satisfactorily to us, on the more difficult questions such as removing their troops from China and the Tripartite Pact. They did not, however, make any definite commitments as to just how far they could comply with our position with respect to these two points.

I said to the British Minister that I had made it clear to the Japanese that if their Government cared to present something on this point, I would give it consideration in the event it appeared to be feasible of consideration, but that I could make no promise, and that if it should be deemed feasible, I would confer with the British, the Dutch, the Chinese and the Australians about any phase of the matter in which they would be interested to which they would give consideration. I also said to the Japanese that, of course, unless Japan decides on a peaceful policy rather than a policy of force and conquest, we could not get far in any kind of discussion but that I could understand why they might need a little time to educate public opinion, as stated (ex. 168).

The next day the Australian and Netherlands Ministers called separately on Secretary Hull, at his request, and to each he gave the substance of his talk with the British Minister (ex. 168).

Before turning to a discussion of the preparation of the United States' reply to the Japanese note of November 20, it is important to recall briefly the evidence before the Committee of the consideration given earlier in November to—

the possibility of reaching some stop-gap arrangement with the Japanese to tide over the immediate critical situation and thus to prevent a breakdown in the conversations, and even perhaps to pave the way for a subsequent general agreement (Hull, tr. 1128).

At the Joint Board meeting on November 3 (Washington time) which followed the conferences called by Secretary Hull to determine whether "the military authorities would be prepared to support further warnings" by the United States to Japan as urged by Generalissimo Chiang Kai-shek, General Marshall had expressed the view that—

the basis of U. S. policy should be to make certain minor concessions which the Japanese could use in saving face. These concessions might be a relaxation on oil restrictions or on similar trade restrictions (ex. 16).

The Joint Board had decided that the War and Navy Departments would prepare a memorandum for President Roosevelt which would, among other things, oppose the issuance of an ultimatum to Japan as urged by the Generalissimo, advocate State Department action to put off hostilities with Japan as long as possible, and suggest that an agreement be made with Japan to tide the situation over for the next several months. However, the joint memorandum which General Marshall and Admiral Stark actually submitted to President Roosevelt on November 5 contained only the first of the Joint Board's recommendations; no reference was made in the memorandum to the second or third points recommended by the Board and mentioned above (ex. 16).

The day after the Marshall-Stark joint memorandum was given to President Roosevelt, Secretary of War Stimson—

had an hour's talk alone with the President with regard to the Far Eastern situation and his approaching conference with Kurusu, who was coming from Japan. The thing uppermost in his mind was how to gain more time (tr. 14386–14387).

In his notes of that talk with the President, Mr. Stimson recorded:

The President outlined what he thought he might say. *He was trying to think of something which would give us further time.* He suggested that he might propose a truce in which there would be no movement of armament for 6 months and then if the Japanese and Chinese had not settled their arrangement in that meanwhile, we could go on on the same basis (tr. 14414).

At the Cabinet meeting the next day, November 7, the President had heard Secretary Hull's estimate of the situation in the Far East and had polled the Cabinet as already described (tr. 14415). On November 10, during his talk with Ambassador Nomura, the President had made reference to a *"modus vivendi,"* and after this meeting, in his report to Tokyo, Ambassador Nomura had said he intended to find out whether the President referred to "possibly, a provisional agreement" (ex. 29, vol. II, p. 718; ex. 1, p. 116). Again, in his report to Tokyo of the meeting with President Roosevelt on November 17, Ambassador Nomura had commented that, in connection with a remark by the President that the United States desired to preserve peace in the Pacific,

I could see that he was outlining some formula in his mind (ex. 1, p. 139).

It was on the evening of the same day that the two Japanese Ambassadors had called on a member of the President's Cabinet and had been told that the President "was very desirous of an understanding between Japan and the United States," and if Japan would do something real to show her peaceful intent, "such as evacuating French Indo-China," the way would be open "for us to furnish you with oil and it would probably lead to the reestablishment of normal trade relations" (ex. 1, p. 154).

Exhibit 18 before the Committee includes the following undated, pencilled memorandum in President Roosevelt's handwriting:

6 months

1. U. S. to resume economic relations—some oil and rice now—more later.
2. Japan to send no more troops to Indo-China or Manchurian border or any place South (Dutch, Brit. or Siam).
3. Japan to agree not to invoke tripartite pact if U. S. gets into European war.
4. U. S. to *introduce* Japs to Chinese to talk things over but U. S. to take no part in their conversations.
Later on Pacific agreements. (ex. 18). [Italics in original.]

Attached to the President's memorandum, which was obtained from the files of the State Department, is a cover sheet on which appears the following typewritten note: "Pencilled memorandum given by the President to the Secretary of State (not dated but probably written shortly after November 20, 1941)" (ex. 18). However, the fact that the memorandum suggests only that Japan should not be permitted to send "more troops to Indochina or Manchurian Border," whereas by November 18 the Japanese Ambassadors were suggesting to Secretary Hull the withdrawal of Japanese troops from at least southern French Indochina, would seem to indicate that the memorandum may have been written by the President before the latter date.

Likewise, since early in November the State Department had been giving intensive study to the possibility of reaching some stopgap arrangement, knowing that—

The presentation to the Japanese of a proposal which would serve to keep alive the conversations would also give our Army and Navy time to prepare and to expose Japan's bad faith if it did not accept. We considered every kind of suggestion we could find which might help or keep alive the conversations and at the same time be consistent with the integrity of American principles (Hull, tr. 1128).

Two of those suggestions were used in preparing the United States' reply to the Japanese note of November 20. On November 11 (Washington time), the Far Eastern Division of the State Department had submitted to Secretary Hull a draft of a proposal intended to serve as a—

transitional arrangement the very discussion of which might serve not only to continue the conversations pending the advent of a more favorable situation, even if the proposal is not eventually agreed to, but also to provide the entering wedge toward a comprehensive settlement of the nature sought providing the proposal is accepted by Japan and provided further that China is able to obtain satisfactory terms from Japan (ex. 18).

This draft proposal consisted of two parts, the first of which contained a statement of principles and mutual pledges with respect to economic relations which followed closely the lines of the counterproposals made to the Japanese on several prior occasions beginning in April. The second part contemplated immediate Japanese-Chinese negotiations during which there would be an armistice between those countries and the United States would hold in abeyance the shipment of supplies of a military character to China and Japan would not increase or supply its military forces in China and French Indochina. Upon the conclusion of a peace settlement between Japan and China the United States was to negotiate with both China and Japan for the resumption of normal trade relations (ex. 18).

On November 18 (Washington time), Secretary of the Treasury Morgenthau sent to President Roosevelt and Secretary Hull a draft of a proposed comprehensive settlement between Japan and the United States (ex. 168). This draft was revised in the Far Eastern Division of the State Department the same day and copies of the revised draft, entitled "Outline of Proposed Basis for Agreement Between the United States and Japan," were sent at once to General Marshall and Admiral Stark for their consideration (ex. 18). As revised, the proposal set forth in summary form various steps "proposed" to be taken by the United States and Japanese Governments, respectively (ex. 18). The evidence before the Committee shows that on the same day, November 19, Secretary Hull had two meetings with Admiral Schuirmann, through whom the State Department maintained liaison with the Navy Department (tr. 1173), and that a conference attended by Admiral Stark for the Navy Department and by General Gerow for the War Department (General Marshall was out of town) was held at the State Department on the morning of November 21 (Washington time) at which the "Outline" was discussed. At that conference Secretary Hull requested both Admiral Stark and General Gerow to submit their comments on the "Outline" from the military and naval standpoint (ex. 18).

This they did the afternoon of the same day, November 21 (Washington·time). In his memorandum General Gerow said that he believed General Marshall would concur in the views which he expressed concerning the "Outline" and advised Secretary Hull that on the basis of a hasty study War Plans Division saw "no objection to its use as a basis for discussion." He said that—

the adoption of its provisions would attain *one of our present major objectives— the avoidance of war with Japan*. Even a temporary peace in the Pacific would permit us to complete defensive preparations in the Philippines and at the same time insure continuance of material assistance to the British—both of which are highly important.

The foregoing should not be construed as suggesting strict adherence to all the conditions outlined in the proposed agreement. *War Plans Division wishes to emphasize it is of grave importance to the success of our war effort in Europe that we reach a modus vivendi with Japan* (ex. 18).

General Gerow suggested the deletion from the "Outline" of a provision which would require Japan to withdraw all Japanese troops from Manchuria except for a few divisions necessary as a police force, provided Russia withdrew all her troops from her far eastern front except for an equivalent remainder, on the ground that such·a provision would probably be unacceptable to Russia. He requested that the War Department be given an opportunity to consider the military aspects of any major changes that might be made in the proposal (ex. 18).

In his memorandum, Admiral Stark objected to provisions in the "Outline" which would place limitations on American naval forces in Pacific waters, commit the United States to use its influence toward causing Great Britain to cede Hong Kong to China, and require Japan to sell to the United States a specified tonnage of merchant vessels. He agreed with General Gerow that the provision concerning the withdrawal of Japanese troops in Manchuria should be deleted. He made several suggestions regarding the phrasing of other provisions, and ended his memorandum with the comment that while the provisions of the "Outline" might be assumed to abrogate the Tripartite Pact on the part of Japan, it would be helpful if that could be specifically stated (ex. 18).

The following day, November 22 (Washington time), there was completed in the State Department the first draft of a counterproposal in reply to the Japanese note of November 20. This draft counterproposal was in two sections. The first section contained a proposed *modus vivendi* as an alternative to the Japanese proposals of November 20, and was prefaced by a brief statement of the circumstances leading to its preparation. Revised drafts of this section were prepared on November 24 and 25. From November 22 to November 26 the *modus vivendi* project was discussed and given intensive consideration within the State Department, by President Roosevelt and by the highest authorities of the Army and Navy, including Secretaries Stimson and Knox and General Marshall and Admiral Stark. The *modus vivendi* was also discussed with the British, Australian, Chinese, and Dutch Governments, principally through their diplomatic representatives in Washington. Such revisions as were made in the original draft of this section are discussed in connection with the final draft of November 25, which is set forth in full below.

The second section of the November 22 draft consisted of two parts. The first part contained the statement of principles and mutual pledges with respect to economic relations which had been prepared by the State Department's Far Eastern Division on November 11. The second part was based primarily upon the "Outline" sent by the State Department to the War and Navy Departments on November 19, modified, however, in accordance with the suggestions made by Admiral Stark and General Gerow in their memoranda of November 21 to Secretary Hull mentioned above. The changes made in this section in the succeeding drafts of November 24 and November 25 were few in number and, as so modified, this section became the reply to the Japanese note of November 20 which was handed by Secretary Hull to the Japanese Ambassadors on November 26 (Washington time). Secretary Hull testified that all who saw the *modus vivendi* section also saw the section which became the United States reply of November 26 (tr. 14363).

The final, November 25 (Washington time), draft of the *modus vivendi* section was as follows:

The representatives of the Government of the United States and of the Government of Japan have been carrying on during the past several months informal and exploratory conversations for the purpose of arriving at a settlement if possible of questions relating to the entire Pacific area based upon the principles of peace, law and order, and fair dealing among nations. These principles include the principle of inviolability of territorial integrity and sovereignty of each and all nations; the principle of non interference in the internal affairs of other countries; the principle of equality, including equality of commercial opportunity and treatment; and the principle of reliance upon international cooperation and conciliation for the prevention and pacific settlement of controversies and for improvement of international conditions by peaceful methods and processes.

It is believed that in our discussions some progress has been made in reference to the general principles which constitute the basis of a peaceful settlement covering the entire Pacific area. Recently the Japanese Ambassador has stated that the Japanese Government is desirous of continuing the conversations directed toward a comprehensive and peaceful settlement in the Pacific area; that it would be helpful toward creating an atmosphere favorable to the successful outcome of the conversations if a temporary *modus vivendi* could be agreed upon to be in effect while the conversations looking to a peaceful settlement in the Pacific were continuing; and that it would be desirable that such *modus vivendi* include as one of its provisions some initial and temporary steps of a reciprocal character in the resumption of trade and normal intercourse between Japan and the United States.

On November 20 the Japanese Ambassador communicated to the Secretary of State proposals in regard to temporary measures to be taken respectively by the Government of Japan and by the Government of the United States, which measures are understood to have been designed to accomplish the purposes above indicated. These proposals contain features which, in the opinion of this Government, conflict with the fundamental principles which form a part of the general settlement under consideration and to which each Government has declared that it is committed.

The Government of the United States is earnestly desirous to contribute to the promotion and maintenance of peace in the Pacific area and to afford every opportunity for the continuance of discussions with the Japanese Government directed toward working out a broad-gauge program of peace throughout the Pacific area. *With these ends in view, the Government of the United States offers for the consideration of the Japanese Government an alternative suggestion for a temporary modus vivendi, as follows:*

MODUS VIVENDI

1. The Government of the United States and the Government of Japan, both being solicitous for the peace of the Pacific, affirm that their national policies are directed toward lasting and extensive peace throughout the Pacific area and that they have no territorial designs therein.

2. They undertake reciprocally not to make from regions in which they have military establishments any advance by force or threat of force into any areas in Southeastern or Northeastern Asia or in the southern or the northern Pacific area.

3. The Japanese Government undertakes forthwith to withdraw its armed forces now stationed in southern French Indochina and not to replace those forces; to reduce the total of its forces in French Indochina to the number there on July 26, 1941; and not to send additional naval, land or air forces to Indochina for replacements or otherwise.

The provisions of the foregoing paragraph are without prejudice to the position of the Government of the United States with regard to the presence of foreign troops in that area.

4. The Government of the United States undertakes forthwith to modify the application of its existing freezing and export restrictions to the extent necessary to permit the following resumption of trade between the United States and Japan in articles for the use and needs of their peoples:

(a) Imports from Japan to be freely permitted and the proceeds of the sale thereof to be paid into a clearing account to be used for the purchase of the exports from the United States listed below, and at Japan's option for the payment of interest and principal of Japanese obligations within the United States, provided that at least two-thirds in value of such imports per month consist of raw silk. It is understood that all American-owned goods now in Japan the movement of which in transit to the United States has been interrupted following the adoption of freezing measures shall be forwarded forthwith to the United States.

(b) Exports from the United States to Japan to be permitted as follows:

(i) Bunkers and supplies for vessels engaged in the trade here provided for and for such other vessels engaged in other trades as the two Governments may agree.

(ii) Food and food products from the United States subject to such limitations as the appropriate authorities may prescribe in respect of commodities in short supply in the United States.

(iii) Raw cotton from the United States to the extent of $600,000 in value per month.

(iv) Medical and pharmaceutical supplies subject to such limitations as the appropriate authorities may prescribe in respect of commodities in short supply in the United States.

(v) Petroleum. The United States will permit the export to Japan of petroleum, within the categories permitted general export, upon a monthly basis for civilian needs. The proportionate amount of petroleum to be exported from the United States for such needs will be determined after consultation with the British and the Dutch Governments. It is understood that by civilian needs in Japan is meant such purposes as the operation of the fishing industry, the transport system, lighting, heating, industrial and agricultural uses, and other civilian uses.

(vi) The above-stated amounts of exports may be increased and additional commodities added by agreement between the two governments as it may appear to them that the operation of this agreement is furthering the peaceful and equitable solution of outstanding problems in the Pacific area.

5. The Government of Japan undertakes forthwith to modify the application of its existing freezing and export restrictions to the extent necessary to permit the resumption of trade between Japan and the United States as provided for in paragraph four above.

6. The Government of the United States undertakes forthwith to approach the Australian, British and Dutch Governments with a view to those Governments' taking measures similar to those provided for in paragraph four above.

7. With reference to the current hostilities between Japan and China, the fundamental interest of the Government of the United States in reference to any discussions which may be entered into between the Japanese and the Chinese Governments is simply that these discussions and any settlement reached as a result thereof be based upon and exemplify the fundamental principles of peace, law, order and justice, which constitute the central spirit of the current conversations between the Government of Japan and the Government of the United States and which are applicable uniformly throughout the Pacific area.

8. This *modus vivendi* shall remain in force for a period of three months with the understanding that the two parties shall confer at the instance of either to ascertain whether the prospects of reaching a peaceful settlement covering the entire Pacific area justify an extension of the *modus vivendi* for a further period (Ex. 18.)

Comparison of this final draft of the *modus vivendi* section and the prior drafts of November 22 and November 24 shows that paragraphs

1, 2, 5, 6, 7, and 8 above were contained in each draft and remained the same in substance throughout, with but few changes in text. In paragraph 3, the final draft added the proviso contained in the second sentence and omitted specific mention of a limitation of 25,000 upon the total number of Japanese troops to remain in French Indochina, retaining from the prior drafts, however, the limitation expressed in terms of "the number there on July 26, 1941." Paragraph 4 was the same in both the final draft and the draft of November 24, but differed from the corresponding provision in the November 22 draft, which had been as follows:

The Government of the United States undertakes forthwith to remove the freezing restrictions which were placed on Japanese assets in the United States on July 26 and the Japanese Government agrees simultaneously to remove the freezing measures which it imposed in regard to American assets in Japan. Exports from each country would thereafter remain subject to the respective export control measures which each country may have in effect for reasons of national defense (ex. 18).

During the 5 days from November 22 to November 26, inclusive, the State Department was the focal point of great activity. After the preparation of the November 22 draft of the *modus vivendi* and in accordance with his conversations with the British Minister on November 18 and the Netherlands and Australian Ministers on November 19, on Saturday, November 22 (Washington time), Secretary Hull arranged a meeting at the State Department with Lord Halifax, the British Ambassador; Dr. Hu Shih, the Chinese Ambassador; Dr. A. Loudon, the Netherlands Minister; and Mr. Richard G. Casey, the Australian Minister. His report of that meeting follows in full:

The British Ambassador, the Australian Minister, and the Netherlands Minister called at my request, the Chinese Ambassador joining us later on. I enumerated the high points in the conversations which I have been carrying on with the Japanese officials here since the spring of this year. They are fully set forth in records of my conversations during that time and need not be repeated here.

I concluded with an account of the Japanese proposal for a *modus vivendi*. I showed it to them to read, with the exception of the Chinese Ambassador who had not yet arrived, and then proceeded to outline my proposed reply in the nature of a substitute for the Japanese proposal. There seemed to be general agreement that a substitute was more desirable than a specific reply to the Japanese proposal, section for section. The substitute reply was substantially what is contained in the present final draft, which I am considering handing to the Japanese. Each of the gentlemen present seemed to be well pleased with this preliminary report to them, except the Chinese Ambassador, who was somewhat disturbed, as he always is when any question concerning China arises not entirely to his way of thinking. This reaction on his part is very natural. He did not show serious concern in view of the provision in our proposed *modus vivendi* which would block a Japanese attack on China in order to destroy the Burma Road. He inquired whether this would commit the Japanese not to further invade China during the coming three months, to which I replied in the negative, adding that this was a question to be decided under the permanent agreement now receiving attention. I made it clear that this proposal was made by the Japanese and that there was probably not one chance in three that they would accept our reply even though it does provide that this proposed temporary arrangement constitutes a part of the general conversations looking toward a general agreement on the basic questions (ex. 18).

Secretary Hull's memoranda of his subsequent conversations with those who attended this meeting show that each of them immediately reported to their respective Governments, for comment, the terms of the Japanese note of November 20 to the United States and of the November 22 draft of the proposed *modus vivendi* (ex. 18).

Later that day, November 22, Ambassadors Nomura and Kurusu called on Secretary Hull. The Secretary told them that he had talked with the representatives of the other Governments mentioned above, and

that there had been a discussion of the question of whether things (meaning Japanese peaceful pledges, et cetera) could be developed in such a way that there could be a relaxation to some extent of freezing. The Secretary said that these representatives were interested in the suggestion and there was a general feeling that the matter could all be settled if the Japanese could give us some satisfactory evidences that their intentions were peaceful.

The Secretary said that in discussing the situation with the representatives of these other countries he found that there had arisen in their minds the same kind of misgivings that had troubled him in the course of the conversations with the Japanese Ambassador. He referred to the position in which the Japanese Government had left the Ambassador and the Secretary as they were talking of peace when it made its move last July into Indochina. He referred also to the mounting oil purchases by Japan last Spring when the conversations were in progress, to the fact that he had endured public criticism for permitting those shipments because he did not wish to prejudice a successful outcome to the conversations and to the fact that that oil was not used for normal civilian consumption.

The Secretary went on to say that the Japanese press which is adopting a threatening tone gives him no encouragement and that no Japanese statesmen are talking about a peaceful course, whereas in the American press advocacy of a peaceful course can always get a hearing. He asked why was there not some Japanese statesmen backing the two Ambassadors by preaching peace. The Secretary pointed out that if the United States and other countries should see Japan coming along a peaceful course there would be no question about Japan's obtaining all the materials she desired; that the Japanese Government knows that.

The Secretary said that while no decisions were reached today in regard to the Japanese proposals he felt that we would consider helping Japan out on oil for civilian requirements only as soon as the Japanese Government could assert control of the situation in Japan as it relates to the policy of force and conquest. He said that if the Ambassador could give him any further assurances in regard to Japan's peaceful intentions it would help the Secretary in talking with senators and other persons in this country (ex. 29, vol. II, pp. 757–758).

Later, Secretary Hull commented that Japan made it very difficult by leaving troops in Indochina. Ambassador Kurusu replied—

that the Japanese desired the troops in northern Indo-China in order to bring about a settlement with China. He said that after the settlement of the China affair Japan promised to bring the troops out of Indo-China altogether.

The Secretary emphasized again that he could not consider this, that also uneasiness would prevail as long as the troops remained in Indo-China, and commented that Japan wanted the United States to do all the pushing toward bringing about a peaceful settlement; that they should get out of Indo-China.

Mr. Kurusu observed that the Japanese Foreign Minister had told Ambassador Grew that we seemed to expect that all the concessions should be made by the Japanese side (ex. 29, vol. II, p. 760).

After further discussion of the troop situation in Indochina, Ambassador Nomura pressed Secretary Hull for an answer to the Japanese proposal of November 20. In reply, the Secretary said—

that if the Japanese could not wait until Monday before having his answer there was nothing he could do about it as he was obliged to confer again with the representatives of the other governments concerned after they had had an opportunity to consult with their governments. He repeated that we were doing our best, but emphasized that unless the Japanese were able to do a little there was no use in talking (ex. 29, vol. II, p. 761).

Ambassador Nomura "disclaimed any desire to press the Secretary too hard for an answer * * * and said that the Japanese would be quite ready to wait until Monday" (ex. 29, vol. II, p. 761). Ambassador Nomura sent two reports of this meeting to Tokyo (ex. 1, pp. 167–169, 170–171), in one of which he observed:

We (Japanese Ambassadors) kept a calm appearance throughout the talk, and at no time became excited, and the opponent's attitude was also the same (ex. 1, p. 171).

The two Ambassadors did not meet with Secretary Hull again until Wednesday afternoon, November 26 (Washington time), when the Secretary gave them the United States reply (ex. 29, vol. II, pp. 764–770).

There is no evidence before the Committee of any meetings or conferences outside the State Department regarding the *modus vivendi* the next day, Sunday, November 23 (Washington time). However, Monday, November 24 (Washington time), like the preceding Saturday, was a day of great activity. A new draft of the entire counterproposal was completed in the Department over the weekend (ex. 18). During the early part of the afternoon Secretary Hull had telephone conversations with Secretary Stimson and Secretary Knox, as well as a conference with Admiral Schuirmann (tr. 1166). At 3:30 p. m., Secretary Hull had a conference at the State Department with General Marshall and Admiral Stark, at which the new draft was discussed in detail (tr. 1166; ex. 18). During this conference General Marshall expressed the opinion that 25,000 Japanese troops in French Indo-China, the maximum permitted under the current draft of the *modus vivendi*, would not be a menace (ex. 18). Following his conference with General Marshall and Admiral Stark at the State Department, Lord Halifax, Dr. Hu Shih, Dr. Loudon, and Mr. Casey called on Secretary Hull at his request, and to each of them he handed copies of the latest draft of the *modus vivendi*. The Secretary's memorandum of that meeting records that they spent an hour reading the draft and taking notes to send back to their Governments. The memorandum continues:

The Chinese Ambassador objected to more than a maximum of 5,000 Japanese troops being left in Indochina. I again stated that General Marshall had a few minutes before expressed to me his opinion that 25,000 troops would be no menace and that, while this Government did not recognize the right of Japan to keep a single soldier in Indochina, we were striving to reach this proposed temporary agreement primarily because the heads of our Army and Navy often emphasize to me that time is the all-important question for them, and that it is necessary to be more fully prepared to deal effectively with the situation in the Pacific area in case of an outbreak by Japan. I also emphasized the point that, even if we agree that the chances of such an outbreak are not great, it must be admitted that there are real possibilities that such an outbreak may soon occur—any day after this week—unless a temporary arrangement is effected that will cause the agitated state of public opinion to become more quiet and thereby make it much more practicable to continue the conversations relative to the general agreement.

The Chinese Ambassador dwelt on the matter of reducing the proposed figure of 25,000 soldiers to remain in Indochina to 5,000. I pointed out and each of the representatives understood the great advantage it would be to our five countries to have Japan committed to a peaceful course for three months and set forth the advantages to each of having additional time in which to make further preparations, et cetera, et cetera. They seemed to be very much gratified. They seemed to be thinking of the advantages to be derived without any particular thought of what we should pay for them, if anything. Finally, when I discovered that none of their governments had given them instructions relative to this phase of the matter, except in the case of the Netherlands Minister, I remarked that each of their Governments was more interested in the defense of that area of the world than this country, and at the same time they expected this country, in case of a Japanese outbreak, to be ready to move in a military way and take the lead in defending the entire area. And yet I said their Governments, through some sort of preoccupation in other directions, do not seem to know anything about these phases of the questions under discussion. I made it clear that I was definitely disappointed at these unexpected developments, at the lack of interest and lack of a disposition to cooperate. They said nothing except the Netherlands Minister who then replied that he had heard from his Government and that it would support the *modus vivendi* proposal. I then indicated that I was not sure that I would present it to the Japanese Ambassador without knowing anything about the views and attitude of their Governments. The meeting broke up in this fashion (ex. 18).

Later that day Secretary Hull sent to President Roosevelt a draft of a proposed message from the President to Prime Minister Churchill. The proposed message summarized the Japanese note of November 20, saying that the Japanese Ambassador had "represented" that the conclusion of such a "modus vivendi" might give the Japanese Government opportunity to develop public sentiment in Japan in support of a liberal and comprehensive program of peace covering the Pacific area and that "the domestic political situation in Japan was so acute as to render urgent some relief such as was envisaged in the proposal." The message pointed out that the Japanese proposal "would apparently not exclude advancement into China from Indo-China." It went on to say that the United States Government proposed to inform the Japanese Government that in its opinion the Japanese proposals contained features "not in harmony with the fundamental principles which underlie the proposed general settlement" to which each Government had declared that it was committed, and then summarized the terms of the *modus vivendi* which was being considered by the United States Government as an alternative proposal. The message advised the Prime Minister that the British Ambassador in Washington had been informed and was informing the British Foreign Minister (ex. 18). President Roosevelt returned the draft message to Secretary Hull with the notation "O. K., see addition. F. D. R." (ex. 18). The "addition" referred to by the President was the following sentence which he had written in longhand for insertion at the end of the message:

This seems to me a fair proposition for the Japanese but its acceptance or rejection is really a matter of internal Japanese politics. I am not very hopeful and we must all be prepared for real trouble, possibly soon (ex. 18).

The message, with the sentence added by the President, was sent to the Prime Minister at 11 p. m. that evening, November 24 (Washington time), through Ambassador Winant in London (ex. 18).

The next day, Tuesday, November 25 (Washington time), the draft counterproposal was once more revised in the State Department. This was the final revision of the section containing the *modus vivendi*. At 9:30 a. m. Secretary Stimson and Secretary Knox met with Secretary Hull at the State Department for their "usual Tuesday morning meeting" (tr. 14,390), which Secretary Stimson described in his notes:

Hull showed us the proposal for a three months' truce, which he was going to lay before the Japanese today or tomorrow. It adequately safeguarded all our interests, I thought as we read it, but I don't think there is any chance of the Japanese accepting it, because it was so drastic. In return for the propositions which they were to do; namely, to at once evacuate and at once to stop all preparations or threats of action, and to take no aggressive action against any of her neighbors, etc., we were to give them open trade in sufficient quantities only for their civilian population. This restriction was particularly applicable to oil. We had a long talk over the general situation (tr. 14,417–14,418).

It is clear that Secretary Stimson's description of the *modus vivendi* as "so drastic" refers to the limited nature of the trade concessions to be made by the United States under it.

At noon that day the so-called "War Council" composed of President Roosevelt, Secretaries Hull, Stimson, and Knox, and General Marshall and Admiral Stark met at the White House. The discussion centered on the Japanese situation. According to Secretary Stimson's notes, the President

brought up the event that we were likely to be attacked perhaps (as soon as) next Monday, for the Japanese are notorious for making an attack without warning, and the question was what we should do. The question was how we should maneuver them into the position of firing the first shot without allowing too much danger to ourselves.[1] It was a difficult proposition. Hull laid out his general broad propositions on which the thing should be rested—the freedom of the seas and the fact that Japan was in alliance with Hitler and was carrying out his policy of world aggression. The others brought out the fact that any such expedition to the South as the Japanese were likely to take would be an encirclement of our interests in the Philippines and cutting into our vital supplies of rubber from Malasia. I pointed out to the President that he had already taken the first steps toward an ultimatum in notifying Japan way back last summer that if she crossed the border into Thailand she was violating our safety and that therefore he had only to point out (to Japan) that to follow any such expedition was a violation of a warning we had already given. So Hull is to go to work on preparing that (tr. 14,418–14,419).

In addition to Secretary Hull's testimony regarding this meeting (tr. 1144), the record before the Committee contains a copy of a letter written by the Secretary to the Roberts Commission a little over a month after the meeting. In that letter, after stating that at the meeting of the War Council on November 25, as well as the meeting on November 28, he had "emphasized the critical nature" of the relations between the United States and Japan, the Secretary continued:

I stated to the conference that there was practically no possibility of an agreement being achieved with Japan; that in my opinion the Japanese were likely to break out at any time with new acts of conquest by force; and that the matter of safeguarding our national security was in the hands of the Army and the Navy. At the conclusion I with due deference expressed my judgment that any plans for our military defense should include an assumption that the Japanese might make the element of surprise a central point in their strategy and also might attack at various points simultaneously with a view to demoralizing efforts of defense and of coordination for purposes thereof (ex. 174).

General Marshall testified that he had "a very distinct recollection of Mr. Hull's saying at one of those meetings, one of the last, 'These fellows mean to fight; you will have to be prepared'" (tr. 3079).

Admiral Stark, who attended the War Council meeting on November 25, added a postscript concerning it to a letter of that date which he sent to Admiral Kimmel at Pearl Harbor. In the postscript, he described the comments of the President and the Secretary of State:

I held this up pending a meeting with the President and Mr. Hull today. I have been in constant touch with Mr. Hull and it was only after a long talk with him that I sent the message to you a day or two ago showing the gravity of the situation. He confirmed it all in today's meeting, as did the President. Neither would be surprised over a Japanese surprise attack (ex. 106).

After the meeting at the White House, Secretary Hull returned to the State Department and Secretary Stimson to the War Department. Secretary Stimson recorded in his notes:

---

[1] With reference to this sentence in Secretary Stimson's notes, General Marshall testified: "* * * they were trying to arrange a diplomatic procedure, rather than firing off a gun, that would not only protect our interests, by arranging matters so that the Japanese couldn't intrude any further in a dangerous way, but also anything they did do, they would be forced to take the offensive action, and what we were to do had to be prepared for the President by Mr. Hull. It was not a military order. It was not a military arrangement" (tr. 13801).

When I got back to the Department I found news from G-2 that an (a Japanese) expedition had started. Five Divisions have come down from Shantung and Shansi to Shanghai and there they had embarked on ships—30, 40, or 50 ships—and have been sighted south of Formosa. I at once called up Hull and told him about it and sent copies to him and to the President of the message from G-2 (tr. 14419).

Secretary Hull's record of telephone calls shows a call on that day from Secretary Stimson at 4:30 p. m. (tr. 1166), and the record of outside telephone calls through the White House switchboard shows such a call at 4:25 p. m. and that the call was completed (tr. 5545). The latter record also shows that Postmaster General Walker telephoned Secretary Hull four times that afternoon (tr. 5545–5546). The first call was at 12:27 p. m., while the meeting at the White House was in progress, and was not completed. The other calls, which were completed, were at 3:30, 4:05, and 5:30 p. m.

In the meantime reports were reaching Washington of the reactions of the Chinese, Dutch, and British Governments to the terms of the proposed *modus vivendi*. As noted above, the Netherlands Minister informed Secretary Hull at the conference on the afternoon of November 24 (Washington time) that his Government would support the *modus vivendi* proposal. The next day the Minister formally transmitted to Secretary Hull his Government's comments on the Japanese note of November 20 and the proposed *modus vivendi* (tr. 4471–4474). The comments of the British Foreign Secretary, Sir Anthony Eden, were contained in a memorandum handed to Secretary Hull on the same day by Lord Halifax, the British Ambassador (ex. 18). That memorandum expressed the willingness of the British Foreign Office to leave to Secretary Hull the decision whether to reject the Japanese proposals or make a counterproposal. It took the position that the Japanese proposals should be regarded "as the opening movement in a process of bargaining," and suggested that if a counterproposal should be made, "our demands should be pitched high and our price low." On this basis it was suggested "for the consideration of the United States Government" that any counterproposal—

should stipulate for the total withdrawal from Indo-China not merely of the Japanese "troops" as in the Japanese proposal but of Japanese naval, military and air forces with their equipment and for the *suspension of further military* advances in China in addition to satisfactory assurances regarding other areas in South East Asia, the Southern Pacific and Russia; the quid pro quo being legitimate relaxation of existing economic measures so as to allow the export of limited quantities of goods to ensure the welfare of the Japanese civilian population, but excluding goods of direct importance to the war potential, in particular oil, of which we know the Japanese have no shortage except for military purposes. These relaxations would of course only become effective as and when withdrawal of Japanese armed forces took place, and we should expect in return to receive goods of a similar nature from Japan if we required them.

Mr. Hull has of course made it perfectly clear to the Japanese that any interim arrangement is only a first step in a wider settlement which must be in conformity with basic principles acceptable to the United States. We feel that to prevent misrepresentation by Japan it will have to be made public that any interim agreement is purely provisional and is only concluded to facilitate negotiation of an ultimate agreement on more fundamental issues satisfactory to all parties concerned (ex. 18). (Italics in original.)

Prime Minister Churchill's reply to President Roosevelt's message of November 24 reached the State Department early on the morning of November 26 (ex. 23). In it the Prime Minister said:

Your message about Japan received tonight. Also full accounts from Lord Halifax of discussions and your counter project to Japan on which Foreign

Secretary has sent some comments. Of course, it is for you to handle this business and we certainly do not want an additional war. There is only one point that disquiets us. What about Chiang Kai Shek? Is he not having a very thin diet? Our anxiety is about China. If they collapse our joint dangers would enormously increase. We are sure that the regard of the United States for the Chinese cause will govern your action. We feel that the Japanese are most unsure of themselves (ex. 23).

The views of the Chinese Government had already been made known to the United States Government. The Chinese Foreign Minister, to whom on November 22 the Chinese Ambassador in Washington had cabled the substance of the Japanese note of November 20 and the proposed *modus vivendi*, sent the following message to the Chinese Ambassador on November 24:

After reading your telegram, the Generalissimo showed strong reaction. He got the impression that the United States Government has put aside the Chinese question in its conversations with Japan instead of seeking a solution, and is still inclined to appease Japan at the expense of China. * * * We are * * * firmly opposed to any measure which may have the effect of increasing China's difficulty in her war of resistance, or of strengthening Japan's power in her aggression against China. Please inform the Secretary of State (ex. 18).

On November 25, Owen Lattimore, Generalissimo Chiang Kai-shek's American advisor, cabled Lauchlin Currie, one of President Roosevelt's administrative assistants:

After discussing with the Generalissimo the Chinese Ambassador's conference with the Secretary of State, I feel you should urgently advise the President of the Generalissimo's very strong reaction. I have never seen him really agitated before. Loosening of economic pressure or unfreezing would dangerously increase Japan's military advantage in China. A relaxation of American pressure while Japan has its forces in China would dismay the Chinese. Any "Modus Vivendi" now arrived at with Japan would be disastrous to Chinese belief in America and analogous to the closing of the Burma Road, which permanently destroyed British prestige. Japan and Chinese defeatists would instantly exploit the resulting disillusionment and urge oriental solidarity against occidental treachery. It is doubtful whether either past assistance or increasing aid could compensate for the feeling of being deserted at this hour. The Generalissimo has deep confidence in the President's fidelity to his consistent policy but I must warn you that even the Generalissimo questions his ability to hold the situation together if the Chinese national trust in America is undermined by reports of Japan's escaping military defeat by diplomatic victory (ex. 18).

The same day, Generalissimo Chiang Kai-shek cabled Mr. T. V. Soong in Washington the following message, which the latter promptly delivered to Secretary Stimson and Secretary Knox:

I presume Ambassador Hu Shih has given you a copy of my telegram yesterday. Please convey contents of the message to Secretaries Knox and Stimson immediately.

Please explain to them the gravity of the situation. If America should relax the economic blockade and freezing of Japanese assets, or even if reports that the United States is considering this should gain currency, the morale of our troops will be sorely shaken. During the past two months the Japanese propaganda have spread the belief that in November an agreement will be successfully reached with the United States. They have even come to a silent but nonetheless definite understanding with the doubtful elements in our country. If, therefore, there is any relaxation of the embargo or freezing regulations, or if a belief of that gains ground, then the Chinese people would consider that China has been completely sacrificed by the United States. The morale of the entire people will collapse and every Asiatic nation will lose faith, and indeed suffer such a shock in their faith in democracy that a most tragic epoch in the world will be opened. The Chinese army will collapse, and the Japanese will be enabled to carry through their plans, so that even if in the future America would come to our rescue the situation would be already hopeless. Such a loss would not be to China alone.

We could therefore only request the United States Government to be uncompromising, and announce that if the withdrawal of Japanese armies from China, is not settled, the question of relaxing of the embargo or freezing could not be considered. If, on the other hand, the American attitude remains nebulous Japanese propaganda will daily perform its fell purpose so that at no cost to them this propaganda will effect the break-down of our resistance. Our more than four years of struggle with the loss of countless lives and sacrifices and devastation unparalleled in history would have been in vain. The certain collapse of our resistance will be an unparalleled catastrophe to the world, and I do not indeed know how history in future will record this episode (ex. 18).

The evening of November 25 (Washington time), Dr. Hu Shih, the Chinese Ambassador, called on Secretary Hull and delivered to him a copy of the Chinese Foreign Minister's telegram quoted above. According to Secretary Hull's memorandum of the conversation, the Ambassador endeavored to explain Generalissimo Chiang Kai-shek's opposition to the *modus vivendi* on the ground that the Generalissimo was not thoroughly acquainted with the over-all international aspects of the Japanese situation, and viewed it only from his own situation in Chungking (ex. 18). The Secretary's memorandum continued:

I replied that in the first place the official heads of our Army and Navy for some weeks have been most earnestly urging that we not get into war with Japan until they have had an opportunity to increase further their plans and methods and means of defense in the Pacific area. In the second place, at the request of the more peaceful elements in Japan for conversations with this Government looking toward a broad peaceful settlement for the entire Pacific area, we have been carrying on conversations and making some progress thus far; and the Japanese are urging the continuance of these general conversations for the purpose of a broad Pacific area settlement. The situation, therefore, is that the proposed *modus vivendi* is really a part and parcel of the efforts to carry forward these general conversations for the reasons that have been fully stated from time to time, and recently to the Chinese Ambassador and to others.

I said that very recently the Generalissimo and Madame Chiang Kai-shek almost flooded Washington with strong and lengthy cables telling us how extremely dangerous the Japanese threat is to attack the Burma Road through Indochina and appealing loudly for aid, whereas practically the first thing this present proposal of mine and the President does is to require the Japanese troops to be taken out of Indochina and thereby to protect the Burma Road from what Chiang Kai-shek said was an imminent danger. Now, I added, Chiang Kai-shek ignores that situation which we have taken care of for him and inveighs loudly about another matter relating to the release of certain commodities to Japan corresponding to the progress made with our conversations concerning a general peace agreement. He also overlooks the fact that our proposal would relieve the menace of Japan in Indochina to the whole South Pacific area, including Singapore, the Netherlands East Indies, Australia, and also the United States, with the Philippines and the rubber and tin trade routes. All of this relief from menace to each of the countries would continue for ninety days. One of our leading admirals stated to me recently that the limited amount of more or less inferior oil products that we might let Japan have during that period would not to any appreciable extent increase Japanese war and naval preparations. I said that, of course, we can cancel this proposal but it must be with the understanding that we are not to be charged with failure to send our fleet into the area near Indochina and into Japanese waters, if by any chance Japan makes a military drive southward.

The Ambassador was very insistent in the view that he would send back to his Government a fuller explanation which he hoped might relieve the situation more or less. Our conversation was, of course, in a friendly spirit (ex. 18).

The same evening, whether before or after his talk with Secretary Hull is not clear from the record before the Committee, Dr. Hu Shih called on Dr. Stanley K. Hornbeck, political advisor to the Secretary. After expressing to Dr. Hornbeck his complete confidence that the United States "would yield nothing in the field of principles and pursue no course of 'appeasement' ", the Chinese Ambassador repeated what he had said at the conference the preceding day regarding the second and third points of the *modus vivendi*, evidencing the concern of his Government that point 2 would leave Japan free to continue operations against China and that point 3 would not sufficiently limit the number of Japanese troops in Indo-China to dispel the Japanese threat to the Burma Road. He expressed the hope that the *modus vivendi* would be made more restrictive (ex. 18).

In the meantime, other intercepted Japanese messages available to Secretary Hull before delivery of the United States reply on November 26 (Washington time), in addition to the messages (ex. 1, pp. 155, 160) in which the Japanese Foreign Minister told Ambassador Nomura that a return to the status prior to the freezing orders was not enough and that it would be necessary to have a solution that would "come up to the B proposal," had indicated that the Japanese Government would accept nothing less than the terms of that proposal. Thus, on November 24 (Japan time), the Japanese Foreign Minister cabled Ambassador Nomura:

Our expectations, as I told you in my #798, go beyond the restoration of Japan-American trade and a return to the situation of the freezing legislation and require the realization of all points of Proposal B with the exception of clauses 6 and 7. (*Note.* Clauses 6 and 7 were not included in the Japanese proposal of November 20.) Therefore, our demand for a cessation of aid to Chiang (the acquisition of Netherlands Indies goods and at the same time the supply of American petroleum to Japan as well) is a most essential condition (ex. 1, p. 172).

Again on November 26 (Japan time) Foreign Minister Togo cabled Ambassador Nomura that "our final proposal envisages an agreement on the basis of the 'B' proposal *in toto*" with the two exceptions already noted (ex. 1, p. 176). The same day the Foreign Minister cabled Ambassador Nomura that as soon as he reached a settlement on the basis of the November 20 note—

it is essential that you secure guarantees for the acquisition of goods in connection with clauses 2 and 3 (*Note:* clauses 3 and 4 of the November 20 note) of that proposal. Of these goods the acquisition of petroleum is one of the most pressing and urgent requirements of the Empire. Therefore, * * * prior to the signing of an understanding, and at as early a date as possible, I would like to have you make our wishes known insofar as petroleum imports are concerned along the following lines:
4,000,000 tons per year from the United States (ex. 1, p. 177).

On November 21 (Washington time) Ambassador Kurusu had called on Secretary Hull and handed him a letter which he proposed to sign as a clarification of Japan's interpretation of the Tripartite Pact. The proposed letter asserted that the Pact did not in any way infringe the sovereign rights of Japan as an independent state; that Japan was free to make its own interpretation; that the Japanese Government would not become involved in war "at the behest of any foreign power"; and that it would "accept warfare only as the ultimate, inescapable necessity for the maintenance of its security and the preservation of its national life against active injustice" (ex. 29, vol. II, p. 757). The record of the conversations shows that the substance of all of these assertions had been made by the Japanese many times before. Secretary Hull asked the Ambassador whether he had anything more to offer on the whole subject of a peaceful settlement, and Mr. Kurusu replied that he did not (ex. 29, vol. II, p. 756). Secretary Hull described this incident in his testimony:

The next morning, Kurusu came to my apartment in the hotel and was talking about the Tripartite Agreement, endeavoring to minimize that, and I suddenly inquired of him if his government had anything more to offer on the general peace situation, and he quickly said, "No."

So there we had nailed down what he said was the last proposal and what their interceptions had informed us was very final in the matter (tr. 1181).

Secretary Hull had also received a report from Ambassador Grew of his talk with Foreign Minister Togo on November 24 (Japan time), during which the Foreign Minister stated that the withdrawal of the Japanese troops from southern to northern Indochina was the maximum concession Japan could make "in any event", and that Japan would be willing to have President Roosevelt act as "introducer" between Japan and China "with the understanding that then the United States would refrain from action prejudicial to restoring peace between China and Japan," i. e., cease all aid to China (ex. 29, vol. II, pp. 762–763).

On Wednesday, November 26 (Washington time), Secretary Stimson talked with Secretary Hull at 9:15 a. m. and again at 9:50 a. m., according to the White House telephone records (tr. 5546). Mr. Stimson summarized the conversations in his notes:

Hull told me over the telephone this morning that he had about made up his mind not to give (make) the proposition that Knox and I passed on the other day to the Japanese but to kick the whole thing over—to tell them that he has no other proposition at all. The Chinese have objected to that proposition—when he showed it to them; that is, to the proposition which he showed to Knox and me, because it involves giving to the Japanese the small modicum of oil for civilian use during the interval of the truce of the three months. Chiang Kai-shek had sent a special message to the effect that that would make a terrifically bad impression in China; that it would destroy all their courage and that they (it) would play into the hands of his, Chiang's, enemies and that the Japanese would use it. T. V. Soong had sent me this letter and has asked to see me and I had called Hull up this morning to tell him so and ask him what he wanted me to do about it. He replied as I have just said above—that he had about made up his mind to give up the whole thing in respect to a truce and to simply tell the Japanese that he had no further action to propose (tr. 14,420).

On his return to the State Department from the War Council meeting the preceding day, Secretary Hull had been told by Secretary Stimson that the Japanese were embarking a large expeditionary force of 30, 40, or 50 ships at Shanghai and that this expedition was proceeding along the China coast south of Formosa. Secretary Stimson had also telephoned President Roosevelt about this, and had sent copies of the intelligence report to him. A few minutes after his telephone conversations with Secretary Hull on the morning of November 26, Secretary Stimson telephoned the President to inquire whether he had received the report on the Japanese expedition. According to Secretary Stimson's notes, the President—

fairly blew up—jumped up into the air, so to speak, and said he hadn't seen it and that that changed the whole situation because it was an evidence of bad faith on the part of the Japanese that while they were negotiating for an entire truce—an entire withdrawal (from China)—they should be sending this expedition down there to Indo-China. I told him that it was a fact that had come to me through G–2 and through the Navy Secret Service and I at once got another copy of the paper I had sent last night and sent it over to him by special messenger (tr. 14,420–14,421).

The record before the Committee contains the following "Memorandum for the President," dated November 26 (Washington time) and signed by Secretary Stimson:

Japanese Convoy Movement Towards Indo-China

About a month and a half ago we learned through Magic that the Japanese Government informed the Vichy Government that they proposed to move approximately 50,000 troops into Indo-China in addition to the 40,000 already there by previous agreement.

Today information has accumulated to the effect that a convoy of from ten to thirty ships, some of 10,000 tons displacement, has been assembled near the mouth of the Yangtse River below Shanghai. This could mean a force as great as 50,000 but more probably a smaller number. Included in this ship concentration was at least one landing-boat carrier. The deck-load of one vessel contained heavy bridge equipment. Later reports indicate that this movement is already under way and ships have been seen south of Formosa.

The officers concerned in the Military Intelligence Division feel that unless we receive other information, this is more or less a normal movement, that is, a logical follow-up of their previous notification to the Vichy Government.

I will keep you informed of any other information in this particular field (ex. 98).

At 6:54 p. m. that day the following priority message was dispatched from the Navy Department:

From the President. For the High Commissioner Philippines

Admiral Hart will deliver to you a copy of a despatch which with my approval the CNO and the COS addressed to the senior Army and Navy commanders in the Philippines. In addition you are advised that the Japanese are strongly reenforcing their garrisons and naval forces in the Mandates in a manner which indicates they are preparing this region as quickly as possible against a possible attack on them by US Forces. However, I am more particularly concerned over increasing opposition of Japanese leaders and by current southward troop movements from Shanghai and Japan to the Formosa area. Preparations are becoming apparent in China, Formosa, and Indo China for an early aggressive movement of some character although as yet there are no clear indications as to its strength or whether it will be directed against the Burma Road, Thailand, Malay Peninsula, Netherlands East Indies, or the Philippines. Advance against Thailand seems the most probable. I consider it possible that this next Japanese aggression might cause an outbreak of hostilities between the U. S. and Japan. I desire that after further informing yourself as to the situation and the general outlines of naval and military plans through consultation with Admiral Hart and General MacArthur you shall in great confidence present my views to the President of the Philippine Commonwealth and inform him that as always I am relying upon the full cooperation of his Government and his people. Please impress upon him the desirability of avoiding public pronouncement or action since that might make the situation more difficult. Roosevelt (tr. 13,861–13,862).

The evidence before the Committee shows that at about 1:20 p. m. that day, November 26, Secretary Hull telephoned Admiral Stark (tr. 1166, 5546), that Admiral Stark called Secretary Hull at 2:35 p. m. after attempting to telephone General Marshall (who was out of town) at 1:28 (tr. 5546), and that late that afternoon Secretary Hull conferred at the White House with President Roosevelt (tr. 1147). The Secretary was preceded at the White House by the Chinese Ambassador, Dr. Hu Shih, and Mr. T. V. Soong (ex. 179). Secretary Hull testified that on November 26 he recommended to President Roosevelt—and that the President approved—the Secretary's calling in the two Japanese Ambassadors and handing them the proposals contained in the second section of the counterproposal that had been under consideration at the State Department, while withholding the *modus vivendi* plan (tr. 1147). President Roosevelt was, Secretary Hull testified, "thoroughly familiar" with both sections of the counterproposal (tr. 14, 312). The record before the Committee contains the following memorandum dated November 26 (Washington time) from Secretary Hull for President Roosevelt:

MEMORANDUM FOR THE PRESIDENT

With reference to our two proposals prepared for submission to the Japanese Government, namely:

(1) A proposal in the way of a draft agreement for a broad, basic, peaceful settlement for the Pacific area, which is henceforth to be made a part of the general conversations now going on and to be carried on, if agreeable to both Governments, with a view to a general agreement on this subject.

(2) The second proposal is really closely connected with the conversations looking toward a general agreement, which is in the nature of a *modus vivendi* intended to make more feasible the continuance of the conversations.

In view of the opposition of the Chinese Government and either the half-hearted support or the actual opposition of the British, the Netherlands, and the Australian Governments, and in view of the wide publicity of the opposition and of the additional opposition that will naturally follow through utter lack of an understanding of the vast importance and value otherwise of the *modus vivendi*, without in any way departing from my views about the wisdom and the benefit of this step to all of the countries opposed to the aggressor nations who are interested in the Pacific area, I desire very earnestly to recommend that at this time I call in the Japanese Ambassadors and hand to them a copy of the comprehensive basic proposal for a general peaceful settlement, and at the same time withhold the *modus vivendi* proposal.

/s/ CORDELL HULL (ex. 18).

In his testimony before the Committee, Secretary Hull gave a more detailed statement of the considerations which led to his recommendation to the President:

I and other high officers of our Government knew that the Japanese military were poised for attack. We knew that the Japanese were demanding—and had set a time limit, first of November 25 and extended later to November 29, for—acceptance by our Government of their extreme last-word proposal of November 20.

It was therefore my judgment, as it was that of the President and other high officers, that the chance of the Japanese accepting our proposal was remote.

So far as the *modus vivendi* aspect would have appeared to the Japanese, it contained only a little chicken feed in the shape of some cotton, oil, and a few other commodities in very limited quantities as compared with the unlimited quantities the Japanese were demanding.

It was manifest that there would be widespread opposition from American opinion to the *modus vivendi* aspect of the proposal especially to the supplying to Japan of even limited quantities of oil. The Chinese Government violently opposed the idea. The other interested governments were sympathetic to the Chinese view and fundamentally were unfavorable or lukewarm. Their cooperation was a part of the plan. It developed that the conclusion with Japan of such an arrangement would have been a major blow to Chinese morale. In view of these considerations it became clear that the slight prospects of Japan's agreeing to the *modus vivendi* did not warrant assuming the risks involved in proceeding with it, especially the serious risk of collapse of Chinese morale and resistance and even of disintegration of China. It therefore became perfectly evident that the modus vivendi aspect would not be feasible.

The Japanese were spreading propaganda to the effect that they were being encircled. On the one hand we were faced by this charge and on the other by one that we were preparing to pursue a policy of appeasing Japan. In view of the resulting confusion, it seemed important to restate the fundamentals. We could offer Japan once more what we offered all countries, a suggested program of collaboration along peaceful and mutually beneficial and progressive lines. It had always been open to Japan to accept that kind of a program and to move in that direction. It still was possible for Japan to do so. That was a matter for Japan's decision. Our hope that Japan would so decide had been virtually extinguished. Yet it was felt desirable to put forth this further basic effort in the form of one sample of a broad but simple settlement to be worked out in our future conversations, on the principle that no effort should be spared to test and exhaust every method of peaceful settlement (tr. 1145–1147).

Upon his return to the State Department from his conference with President Roosevelt, at 5 p. m. Secretary Hull met with Ambassadors

Nomura and Kurusu at the Department and handed them, in reply to the Japanese note of November 20, the second section of the counterproposal which had been under consideration since November 22, together with an explanatory statement. The explanatory statement was the first section of that counterproposal as quoted herein (pp. 70–71) modified by the deletion of the *modus vivendi* and with further changes made necessary thereby. It reviewed briefly the objectives sought in the exploratory conversations, and stated that it was believed that some progress had been made with respect to the general principles involved. Note was taken of the recent statements of the Japanese Ambassadors that it would be helpful toward creating an atmosphere favorable to the successful outcome of the conversations if a temporary *modus vivendi* could be agreed upon, to be in effect while the conversations looking toward a comprehensive and peaceful settlement in the Pacific area were continuing. It was stated that the United States Government most earnestly desired to afford every opportunity for the continuance of the discussions to this end. The statement continued:

The proposals which were presented by the Japanese Ambassador on November 20 contain some features which, in the opinion of this Government, conflict with the fundamental principles which form a part of the general settlement under consideration and to which each Government has declared that it is committed. The Government of the United States believes that the adoption of such proposals would not be likely to contribute to the ultimate objectives of ensuring peace under law, order, and justice in the Pacific area, and it suggests that further effort be made to resolve our divergences of views in regard to the practical application of the fundamental principles already mentioned.

With this object in view *the Government of the United States offers for the consideration of the Japanese Government a plan of a broad but simple settlement covering the entire Pacific area as one practical exemplification of a program which this Government envisages as something to be worked out during our further conversations.*

The plan therein suggested represents an effort to bridge the gap between our draft of June 21, 1941, and the Japanese draft of September 25, by making a new approach to the essential problems underlying a comprehensive Pacific settlement. *This plan contains provisions dealing with the practical application of the fundamental principles which we have agreed in our conversations constitute the only sound basis for worth-while international relations.* We hope that in this way progress toward reaching a meeting of minds between our two Governments may be expedited (ex. 29, vol. II, p. 767).

The outline of a proposed basis for agreement which Secretary Hull handed to the Japanese Ambassadors follows, in full:

Strictly Confidential, Tentative and Without Commitment.

WASHINGTON, *November 26, 1941.*

OUTLINE OF PROPOSED BASIS FOR AGREEMENT BETWEEN THE UNITED STATES AND JAPAN

SECTION I

Draft Mutual Declaration of Policy

The Government of the United States and the Government of Japan both being solicitous for the peace of the Pacific affirm that their national policies are directed toward lasting and extensive peace throughout the Pacific area, that they have no territorial designs in that area, that they have no intention of threatening other countries or of using military force aggressively against any neighboring nation, and that, accordingly, in their national policies they will actively support and give practical application to the following fundamental principles upon which their relations with each other and with all other governments are based:

(1) The principle of inviolability of territorial integrity and sovereignty of each and all nations.

(2) The principle of noninterference in the internal affairs of other countries.

(3) The principle of equality, including equality of commercial opportunity and treatment.

(4) The principle of reliance upon international cooperation and conciliation for the prevention and pacific settlement of controversies and for improvement of international conditions by peaceful methods and processes.

The Government of Japan and the Government of the United States have agreed that toward eliminating chronic political instability, preventing recurrent economic collapse, and providing a basis for peace, they will actively support and practically apply the following principles in their economic relations with each other and with other nations and peoples:

(1) The principle of nondiscrimination in international commercial relations.

(2) The principle of international economic cooperation and abolition of extreme nationalism as expressed in excessive trade restrictions.

(3) The principle of nondiscriminatory access by all nations to raw material supplies.

(4) The principle of full protection of the interests of consuming countries and populations as regards the operation of international commodity agreements.

(5) The principle of establishment of such institutions and arrangements of international finance as may lend aid to the essential enterprises and the continuous development of all countries and may permit payments through processes of trade consonant with the welfare of all countries.

SECTION II

Steps to be Taken by the Government of the United States and by the Government of Japan

The Government of the United States and the Government of Japan propose to take steps as follows:

1. The Government of the United States and the Government of Japan will endeavor to conclude a multilateral nonaggression pact among the British Empire, China, Japan, the Netherlands, the Soviet Union, Thailand, and The United States.

2. Both Governments will endeavor to conclude among the American, British, Chinese, Japanese, the Netherland, and Thai Governments an agreement whereunder each of the Governments would pledge itself to respect the territorial integrity of French Indochina and, in the event that there should develop a threat to the territorial integrity of Indochina, to enter into immediate consultation with a view to taking such measures as may be deemed necessary and advisable to meet the threat in question. Such agreement would provide also that each of the Governments party to the agreement would not seek or accept preferential treatment in its trade or economic relations with Indochina and would use its influence to obtain for each of the signatories equality of treatment in trade and commerce with French Indochina.

3. The Government of Japan will withdraw all military, naval, air, and police forces from China and from Indochina.

4. The Government of the United States and the Government of Japan will not support—militarily, politically, economically—any government or regime in China other than the National Government of the Republic of China with capital temporarily at Chungking.

5. Both Governments will give up all extraterritorial rights in China, including rights and interests in and with regard to international settlements and concessions, and rights under the Boxer Protocol of 1901.

Both Governments will endeavor to obtain the agreement of the British and other governments to give up extraterritorial rights in international settlements and in concessions and under the Boxer Protocol of 1901.

6. The Government of the United States and the Government of Japan will enter into negotiations for the conclusion between the United States and Japan of a trade agreement, based upon reciprocal most-favored-nation treatment and reduction of trade barriers by both countries, including an undertaking by the United States to bind raw silk on the free list.

7. The Government of the United States and the Government of Japan will, respectively, remove the freezing restrictions on Japanese funds in the United States and on American funds in Japan.

8. Both Governments will agree upon a plan for the stabilization of the dollar-yen rate, with the allocation of funds adequate for this purpose, half to be supplied by Japan and half by the United States.

9. Both Governments will agree that no agreement which either has concluded with any third power or powers shall be interpreted by it in such a way as to conflict with the fundamental purpose of this agreement, the establishment and preservation of peace throughout the Pacific area.

10. Both Governments will use their influence to cause other governments to adhere to and to give practical application to the basic political and economic principles set forth in this agreement (ex. 167; ex. 29, vol. II, pp. 768–770).

Ambassador Grew was fully informed the same evening of the substance of the United States' reply.   (Tr. 4513–4522; ex. 75.)

The record before the Committee shows that, commencing with the first draft of an American counterproposal on November 22 (Washington time), all the officials of the United States Government who were consulted by Secretary Hull regarding the proposed *modus vivendi* necessarily saw and considered the successive drafts of the foregoing so-called "Ten Point" note, since from the outset the provisions which, as revised, became the "Ten Point" note had constituted the second section of the counterproposal and had been attached to the first section containing the *modus vivendi*.   The record also shows that the provisions of the "Ten Point" note probably received more attention from the high officers of the Army and Navy than did the terms of the *modus vivendi*, since the part containing the so-called "Ten Points" was based primarily upon the State Department's revision of the Morgenthau suggestions of November 18.   It will be recalled that that revision was sent to the Army and Navy for comment on November 19, and was the subject of the conference at the State Department on November 21 attended by General Gerow and Admiral Stark, who thereafter submitted their comments and suggestions to Secretary Hull in memoranda of the same date.   As has already been pointed out, the first section of the "Ten Point" note was based almost entirely upon the statement of principles contained in the draft proposal submitted by the State Department's Far Eastern Division to Secretary Hull on November 11, which in turn had been frequently discussed with the Japanese during the six months since the conversations began in the spring of 1941.

Returning to Secretary Hull's meeting with Ambassadors Nomura and Kurusu, after the Japanese had read the documents handed them by the Secretary, Ambassador Kurusu asked whether this was the United States reply to their proposal.

The Secretary replied that we had to treat the proposal as we did, as there was so much turmoil and confusion among the public both in the United States and in Japan.   He reminded the Japanese that in the United States we have a political situation to deal with just as does the Japanese Government, and he referred to the fire-eating statements which have been recently coming out of Tokyo, which he said had been causing a natural reaction among the public in this country. *He said that our proposed agreement would render possible practical measures of financial cooperation, which, however, were not referred to in the outline for fear that this might give rise to misunderstanding.*   He also referred to the fact that he had earlier in the conversations acquainted the Ambassador of the ambition that had been his *of settling the immigration question* but that the situation had so far prevented him from realizing that ambition (ex. 29, vol. II, p. 764).

Ambassador Kurusu then commented adversely on various provisions of the American note, saying among other things that he did not see how his Government could consider paragraphs (3) and (4), and that if this represented the idea of the American Government he did not see how any agreement was possible.   He said that when they reported the United States' answer to their Government "it would be likely to throw up its hands". He suggested that it might be better if they did not refer it to their Government before discussing its contents further informally in Washington. Later, he said that he felt the reply could be interpreted "as tantamount to meaning the end." He asked whether the United States was interested in a *modus vivendi*. Secretary Hull replied that he had explored that and that he had done his best in the way of exploration (ex. 29, vol. II, pp. 764–766).

In reply to Ambassador Kurusu's suggestion that the document should be discussed informally before reporting it to Tokyo—

The Secretary suggested that they might wish to study the documents carefully before discussing them further. He repeated that we were trying to do our best to keep the public from becoming uneasy as a result of their being harangued. He explained that in the light of all that has been said in the press, our proposal was as far as we would go at this time in reference to the Japanese proposal; that there was so much confusion among the public that it was necessary to bring about some clarification; that we have reached a stage when the public has lost its perspective and that it was therefore necessary to draw up a document which would present a complete picture of our position by making provision for each essential point involved.

The Secretary then referred to the oil question. He said that public feeling was so acute on that question that he might almost be lynched if he permitted oil to go freely to Japan. He pointed out that if Japan should fill Indochina with troops our people would not know what lies ahead in the way of a menace to the countries to the south and west. He reminded the Japanese that they did not know what tremendous injury they were doing to us by keeping immobilized so many forces in countries neighboring Indochina. He explained that we are primarily out for our permanent futures, and the question of Japanese troops in Indochina affects our direct interests (ex. 29, vol. II, p. 765).

At the conclusion of the meeting, Ambassador Nomura asked whether the two Ambassadors could see President Roosevelt, and Secretary Hull replied that he had no doubt the President would be glad to see them at any time. The Ambassador also said that he would like to have the counselor of the Japanese Embassy call on Mr. Joseph W. Ballantine, one of the Secretary's principal advisors on Far Eastern affairs, the next day "to discuss further details" (ex. 29, vol. II, p. 766).

Secretary Hull testified:

The document handed the Japanese on November 26 was essentially a restatement of principles which have long been basic in this country's foreign policy. The practical application of those principles to the situation in the Far East, as embodied in the ten points contained in the document, was along lines which had been under discussion with the Japanese representatives in the course of the informal exploratory conversations during the months preceding delivery of the document in question. Our Government's proposal embodied mutually profitable policies of the kind we were prepared to offer to any friendly country and was coupled with the suggestion that the proposal be made the basis for further conversations.

* * * * * * *

Our Government's proposal was offered for the consideration of the Japanese Government as one practical example of a program to be worked out. It did not rule out other practical examples which either Government was free to offer.

We well knew that, in view of Japan's refusal throughout the conversations to abandon her policy of conquest and domination, there was scant likelihood of her acceptance of this plan. But it is the task of statesmanship to leave no possibility for peace unexplored, no matter how slight. It was in this spirit that the November 26 document was given to the Japanese Government (tr. 1151–1152).

Before their meeting with Secretary Hull late in the afternoon of November 26 (Washington time), the two Japanese Ambassadors had sent a joint telegram to Foreign Minister Togo in which they recognized, even before Secretary Hull delivered the "Ten Point" note to them, that the negotiations were for all practical purposes at an end. They told the Foreign Minister:

"As we have wired you several times, there is hardly any possibility of having them consider our "B" proposal in toto. On the other hand, if we let the situation remain tense as it is now, sorry as we are to say so, the negotiations will inevitably be ruptured, *if indeed they may not already be called so. Our failure and humiliation are complete* (ex. 1, p. 180).

They then asked the approval of the Foreign Minister of the only remaining suggestion they had to offer, as a device to obtain more time. The Ambassadors suggested, with "grave misgivings," that they be permitted to propose to Secretary Hull that President Roosevelt wire Foreign Minister Togo (not Emperor Hirohito) that "for the sake of posterity he hopes that Japan and the United States will cooperate for the maintenance of peace in the Pacific * * * and that you in return reply with a cordial message." The Ambassadors asked that their request be shown to the Navy Minister (ex. 1, p. 182).

While Ambassador Nomura and Ambassador Kurusu were meeting with Secretary Hull at the State Department, and at their direction, the counselor of the Japanese Embassy, Mr. Wakasugi, using the trans-Pacific telephone, informed the Foreign Office in Tokyo that the meeting was in progress and that "the future of the present talks would be decided during the course of today's conversation" (ex. 1, p. 179). In making this call, Mr. Wakasugi used a telephone code established earlier that day in a message from the Foreign Minister which said "the situation is momentarily becoming more tense and telegrams take too long" (ex. 1, p. 178). There is no evidence before the Committee of the use of a trans-Pacific telephone code in connection with the negotiations prior to the establishment of this code by the Japanese Foreign Office before the American note was delivered on November 26 (Washington time).

Almost immediately upon his return to the Japanese Embassy, Ambassador Kurusu telephoned the Japanese Foreign Office in Tokyo, using the trans-Pacific telephone. He told the Chief of the American Division, Kumaicho Yamamoto:

I have made all efforts, *but they will not yield*. I sent a cable expressing my opinions to the Foreign Minister this morning.[1] The situation is just like that. Otherwise there is no means of accomplishing it (ex. 1, p. 179).

He continued—

I rather imagine you had expected this outcome (ex. 1, p. 180).

To which Bureau Chief Yamamoto replied:

Yes, I had expected it, but I wished to exert every effort up to the final moment in the hope that something might be accomplished (ex. 1, p. 180).

That evening Ambassador Nomura cabled three reports to the Foreign Minister of the Ambassadors' meeting with Secretary Hull. The first was a brief résumé of the "Ten Point" note, accompanied by this comment:

In view of our negotiations all along, we were both dumbfounded and said we could not even cooperate to the extent of reporting this to Tokyo. We argued back furiously, but HULL remained solid as a rock. Why did the United States have to propose such hard terms as these? Well, England, the Netherlands, and China doubtless put her up to it. Then, too, we have been urging them to quit helping CHIANG, and lately a number of important Japanese in speeches have

---

[1] The message referred to above in which the Ambassadors said "Our failure and humiliation are complete".

been urging that we strike at England and the United States. Moreover, there have been rumors that we are demanding of Thai that she give us complete control over her national defense. All that is reflected in these two hard proposals, or we think so (ex. 1, p. 182).

The third telegram was a detailed account of the meeting (ex. 1, pp. 183–185). The second telegram consisted of general comments on the situation (ex. 1, pp. 182–183). In it Ambassador Nomura showed great concern lest some "independent action" taken by Japan *while the negotiations were continuing* should place upon Japan the responsibility "for the rupture of the negotiations." He pointed out that "up to the present we have only been able to press them for an early solution. During this time we have not expressed any final intention!" Recognizing that "such a thing as the clarification of our intention is a strict military secret," the Ambassador recommended:

consequently, *I think that it might be the better plan, dependent of course on the opinions of the Government, that the current negotiations be clearly and irrevocably concluded either through an announcement to the American Embassy in Tokyo or by a declaration for internal and external consumption.* I would like, if such a course is followed, to make representations here at the same time (ex. 1, p. 183).

THE TOJO CABINET MAKES A PRETENSE OF CONTINUING THE JAPANESE-AMERICAN CONVERSATIONS AND AT THE SAME TIME MOVES ADDITIONAL JAPANESE TROOPS INTO SOUTHERN INDOCHINA

(November 27–December 7, 1941)

The record before the Committee thus shows that there was little hope or expectation in Washington on November 27, either among those in the United States Government who were familiar with the Japanese-American conversations or on the part of the two Japanese Ambassadors, that the Tojo Government in Tokyo would continue the conversations. Nevertheless, as requested by Ambassador Kurusu the day before, a meeting with President Roosevelt was arranged for 2:30 p. m. on November 27 (Washington time) at the White House.

That morning, before the White House conference, Secretary Hull held a "special and lengthy" press conference at which he reviewed the Far Eastern situation and particularly the state of the Japanese-American conversations in much greater detail than had been true of the statement made to the press late the preceding afternoon, following his conference with the two Japanese Ambassadors (tr. 1154–1161). That statement had said only that the Japanese Ambassadors had been handed for their consideration a document that was the culmination of conferences back and forth during recent weeks, and that it was unnecessary to repeat what had been said so often in the past that it rested on certain basic principles with which the correspondents should be entirely familiar in the light of many repetitions (ex. 167). At Secretary Hull's press conference on the morning of November 27, he emphasized that from the beginning he had kept in mind that the groups in Japan led by the military leaders had a plan to conquer by force half of the earth with half its population; that this movement had started in earnest in 1937, and carried with it a policy of non-observance of any standards of conduct in international relations or of any law or of any rule of justice or fair play. The Secretary said that from the beginning, as the world was going more and more to a state of international anarchy, the United States had sought to keep alive the basic philosophy and principles governing the opposing viewpoint in international relations, but that it was no easy undertaking. He then briefly reviewed the nature of the conversations he had had with the Japanese, commencing in the spring of 1941, to determine whether a peaceful settlement relating to the entire Pacific area might not be possible. He said that while the conversations during the preceding several months had been purely exploratory, for the past 10 days or so all phases of the basic questions presented and of suggestions or ideas or methods of bringing Japan and the United States as close together as possible had been explored, on the theory there might thus be reached the beginning of some peaceful and cordial relations between Japan and other nations in the Pacific area, including the United States. He said that during the conversations it had been necessary to keep in mind not only the political situation in Japan but also the activities of the Japanese Army and Navy, and he cited the fact:

that we had known for some days　＊　＊　＊　that the Japanese were pouring men and materials and boats and all kinds of equipment into Indo-China.　＊　＊　＊ There was a further report that the Japanese Navy might make attacks somewhere there around Siam, any time within a few days (tr. 1156–1157).

He said that if the Japanese established themselves in Indochina in adequate numbers, which they seemed to be doing, they would have a base not only for operations against China but the whole South Sea area. The Secretary said that the United States Government had exhausted all its efforts to work out phases of this matter with the Japanese; and that those efforts had been put forth to facilitate the making of a general agreement. On November 26, he continued, because he had found there was so much confusion and so many collateral manners brought in, while at the same time high Japanese officials in Tokyo continued to proclaim their old doctrine of force, he had thought it important to bring the situation to a clear perspective by restating the fundamental principles to which the United States was committed and at the same time show how those principles could be applied to a number of specific conditions which would logically be a part of a broad basic settlement in the entire Pacific area. When he was asked whether he expected the Japanese to come back and talk further on the basis of what he had given them on November 26, Secretary Hull replied that he did not know, but that the Japanese might not do that. In reply to a question whether it could be assumed there was not much hope that the Japanese would accept the principles to which he had referred and go far enough to afford a basis for continuing the conversations, the Secretary said there was always a possibility but that he would not say how much probability there might be.

Secretary Hull's press conference took place at about 10 o'clock that morning. Both before and after it, at 9:17 and 11 o'clock, the Secretary talked with Secretary Stimson regarding the state of the negotiations; he also talked with Admiral Stark that morning (tr. 1167, 5547). Secretary Stimson's notes for that day (November 27) describe his two conversations with Secretary Hull:

A very tense, long day. News is coming in of a concentration and movement south by the Japanese of a large Expeditionary Force moving south from Shanghai and evidently headed towards Indo-China, with a possibility of going to the Philippines or to Burma, or to the Burma Road or to the Dutch East Indies, but probably a concentration to move over into Thailand and to hold a position from which they can attack Singapore when the moment arrives.

The first thing in the morning I call up Hull to find out what his finale has been with the Japanese—whether he had handed them the new proposal which we passed on two or three days ago or whether, as he suggested yesterday he would, he broke the whole matter off. He told me now that he had broken the whole matter off. As he put it, "I have washed my hands of it and it is now in the hands of you and Knox—the Army and the Navy." I then called up the President. The President gave me a little different view. He said they had ended up, but they ended up with a magnificent statement prepared by Hull. I found out afterwards that this was not a reopening of the thing but a statement of our constant and regular position.

General Arnold came in to present the orders for the movement of two of our biggest planes out from San Francisco and across the Mandated Islands to Manila. There is a concentration going on by the Japanese in the Mandated Islands and these planes can fly high over them, beyond the reach of their pursuit planes and take photographs.

Knox and Admiral Stark came over and conferred with me and General Gerow. Marshall is down at the maneuvers today and I feel his absence very much. There was a tendency, not unnatural, on the part of Stark and Gerow to seek for more time. I said that I was glad to have time but I didn't want it at any cost of humility on the part of the United States or of reopening the thing which would show a weakness on our part. The main question has been over the message that we shall send to MacArthur. We have already sent him a quasi alert, or the first signal for an alert, and now, on talking with the President this morning over the telephone, I suggested and he approved the idea that we should send the final alert; namely, that he should be on the *qui vive* for any attack and telling him how the situation was. So Gerow and Stark and I went over the proposed message to him from Marshall very carefully; finally got it in shape and with the help of a telephone talk I had with Hull, I got the exact statement from him of what the situation was (tr. 14,421–14,423).

Because of its relationship to events which followed, it is necessary here to refer briefly to the background of Secretary Stimson's observation in his notes that General Gerow and Admiral Stark desired "to seek for more time." It will be recalled that on November 5, in connection with Generalissimo Chiang Kai-shek's appeal for British and American aid, General Marshall and Admiral Stark had concluded that—

war between the United States and Japan should be avoided while building up defensive forces in the Far East, until such time as Japan attacks or directly threatens territories whose security to the United States is of very great imp-or tance (ex. 16).

As has been seen, one of the major considerations in the *modus vivendi* proposal was the desire of the military and naval authorities "for more time." However, at the War Council meeting on November 25 attended by General Marshall and Admiral Stark, Secretary Hull stated that there was "practically no possibility of an agreement being achieved with Japan" (ex. 174, Item 13). The next day, at an Army-Navy Joint Board meeting, General Marshall and Admiral Stark directed the preparation of a memorandum to President Roosevelt regarding what steps should be taken if the negotiations with Japan should end without agreement. The meeting on November 27 described by Secretary Stimson in his notes for that day was also described in a memorandum for General Marshall prepared the same day by General Gerow:

2. Later in the morning, I attended a conference with the Secretary of War Secretary of Navy, and Admiral Stark. The various messages to the Army and Navy Commanders and to Mr. Sayre were discussed. A joint message for General MacArthur and Admiral Hart was approved (copy attached). The Secretaries were informed of the proposed memorandum you and Admiral Stark

directed be prepared for the President.   The Secretary of War wanted to be sure that the memorandum would not be construed as a recommendation to the President that he request Japan to reopen the conversations.   He was reassured on that point.   It was agreed that the memorandum would be shown to both Secretaries before dispatch.

3. Both the message and the memorandum were shown to the Secretary of War. He suggested some minor changes in the memorandum.   These were made (copy attached) (ex. 45).

In his prepared statement submitted to the Committee, Secretary Stimson stated that at the meeting with General Gerow and Admiral Stark,

I told them, which was the fact, that I also would be glad to have time but I did not want it at the cost of humiliation of the United States or of backing down on any of our principles which would show a weakness on our part (tr. 14, 394).

General Marshall summed up his viewpoint and that of Secretary Stimson in his testimony before the committee:

He (Secretary Stimson) was very much afraid—he feared that we would find ourselves involved in the developing situation where our disadvantages would be so great that it would be quite fatal to us when the Japanese actually broke peace.

He also felt very keenly that, and thought about this part a great deal more than I did, because it was his particular phase of the matter, that we must not go so far in delaying actions of a diplomatic nature as to sacrifice the honor of the country.   He was deeply concerned about that.

My approach to the matter, of course, was much more materialistic.   I was hunting for time.   Hunting for time, so that whatever did happen we would be better prepared than we were at that time, that particular time.

So it was a question of resolving his views as to the honor, we will say, of the United States, and his views of a diplomatic procedure which allowed the Japanese to continue movements until we would be in a hopeless situation before the peace was broken, and mine, which as I say, were much more materialistic, as I think they should have been, that we should get as much time as we could in order to make good the terrible deficiencies in our defensive arrangements (tr. 13,820–13,821).

The memorandum for President Roosevelt, although dated November 27 (Washington time), was signed by General Marshall upon his return to Washington on November 28 (Washington time), with the minor changes suggested by Secretary Stimson, and was as follows:

Memorandum for the President

Subject: Far Eastern Situation.

If the current negotiations end without agreement, Japan may attack: the Burma Road; Thailand; Malaya; the Netherlands East Indies; the Philippines; the Russian Maritime Provinces.

There is little probability of an immediate Japanese attack on the Maritime Provinces because of the strength of the Russian forces.   Recent Japanese troop movements all seem to have been southward.

The magnitude of the effort required will militate against direct attack against Malaya and the Netherlands East Indies until the threat exercised by United States forces in Luzon is removed.

Attack on the Burma Road or Thailand offers Japanese objectives involving less risk of major conflict than the others named, and clearly within the means available, if unopposed by major powers.   Attack on the Burma Road would, however, be difficult and might fail.   If successful, the Chinese Nationalist Government might collapse.   Occupation of Thailand gains a limited strategic advantage as a preliminary to operations against Malaya or the Netherlands East Indies; might relieve internal political pressure, and to a lesser extent, external economic pressure.   Whether the offensive will be made against the Burma Road, Thailand, or the Philippines cannot now be forecast.

The most essential thing now, from the United States viewpoint, is to gain time.   Considerable Navy and Army reinforcements have been rushed to the

Philippines but the desirable strength has not yet been reached. The process of reinforcement is being continued. Of great and immediate concern is the safety of the Army convoy now near Guam, and the Marine Corps' convoy just leaving Shanghai. Ground forces to a total of 21,000 are due to sail from the United States by December 8, 1941, and it is important that this troop reinforcement reach the Philippines before hostilities commence.

Precipitance of military action on our part should be avoided so long as consistent with national policy. The longer the delay, the more positive becomes the assurance of retention of these islands as a naval and air base. Japanese action to the south of Formosa will be hindered and perhaps seriously blocked as long as we hold the Philippine Islands. War with Japan certainly will interrupt our transport of supplies to Siberia, and probably will interrupt the process of aiding China.

After consultation with each other, United States, British, and Dutch military authorities in the Far East agreed that joint military counteraction against Japan should be undertaken only in case Japan attacks or directly threatens the territory or mandated territory of the United States, the British Commonwealth, or the Netherlands East Indies, or should the Japanese move forces into Thailand west of 100° east or south of 10° north, Portuguese Timor, New Caledonia, or the Loyalty Islands.

Japanese involvement in Yunnan or Thailand up to a certain extent is advantageous, since it leads to further dispersion, longer lines of communication, and an additional burden on communications. However, a Japanese advance to the west of 100° east or south of 10° north, immediately becomes a threat to Burma and Singapore. Until it is patent that Japan intends to advance beyond these lines, no action which might lead to immediate hostilities should be taken.

It is recommended that:

prior to the completion of the Philippine reinforcement, military counteraction be considered only if Japan attacks or directly threatens United States, British, or Dutch territory as above outlined;

in case of a Japanese advance into Thailand, Japan be warned by the United States, the British, and the Dutch governments that advance beyond the lines indicated may lead to war; prior to such warning no joint military opposition be undertaken;

steps be taken at once to consummate agreements with the British and Dutch for the issuance of such warning.

[s] G. C. MARSHALL   [s] H. R. STARK (ex. 17).

Before the meeting at the White House at 2 p. m. on November 27 (Washington time), Secretary Hull conferred briefly alone with President Roosevelt (ex. 58). When the two Japanese Ambassadors arrived, Ambassador Nomura seized the first opportunity to say that they were disappointed over the failure of any agreement for a *modus vivendi.* President Roosevelt expressed his grateful appreciation and that of the United States Government to the peace element in Japan which had worked hard in support of the movement for a peaceful settlement in the Pacific area, and made it clear that the United States was not overlooking what that element had done and was still ready to do. He added that most people in the United States wanted a peaceful solution of the Pacific problems, and that while he had not given up yet, the situation was serious and that fact should be recognized. He pointed out that the Japanese occupation of French Indo-China had had the effect of a cold bath on the people of the United States as well as on the United States Government, and intimated that a second such bath appeared to be in the offing. He said that throughout the conversations there had been no real indication of a desire for peace by any of Japan's leaders, and that this also had had its effect on the conversations. According to his memorandum of the meeting, Secretary Hull then

made it clear that unless the opposition to the peace element in control of the Government should make up its mind definitely to act and talk and move in a peaceful direction, no conversations could or would get anywhere as has been so clearly demonstrated; that everyone knows that the Japanese slogans of co-prosperity, new order in East Asia and a controlling influence in certain areas, are all terms to express in a camouflaged manner the policy of force and conquest by Japan and the domination by military agencies of the political, economic, social, and moral affairs of each of the populations conquered; and that so long as they move in that direction and continue to increase their cultural relations, military and otherwise with Hitler through such instruments as the Anti-Comintern Pact and the Tripartite Pact, et cetera, et cetera, there could not be any real progress made on a peaceful course (ex. 29, vol. II, p. 772).

During the conversation, Ambassador Kurusu suggested that the trouble was not with fundamentals so much as with their application. However, with reference to a recent remark of President Roosevelt about "introducing" Japan and China, when the Ambassador asked who would take such action and the President said "both sides"—meaning Japan as well as China—the Ambassador pointed out "that from a practical standpoint that would be very difficult to accomplish" (ex. 29, vol. II, pp. 770–772).

According to Ambassador Nomura's report to Tokyo, as the meeting ended, President Roosevelt told the Ambassadors that he was leaving the next day, Friday, for Warm Springs, Ga., for a rest and was planning to return the following Wednesday. He said that he would like to talk with the Ambassadors then and would be very gratified if some means of settlement could be discovered in the meantime (ex. 1, pp. 192–194). In addition to Ambassador Nomura's cabled report of the meeting, Ambassador Kurusu telephoned the Japanese Foreign Office in Tokyo, using the voice code previously arranged, and said that in the conversation with the President "there wasn't much that was different from Hull's talks of yesterday." He asked how things were in Tokyo, and was told that a crisis appeared "imminent." The Ambassador reported that the United States wanted to continue the negotiations, but Bureau Chief Yamamoto said "we can't yield." The Ambassador concluded by saying that there was nothing of particular interest in the day's talk with President Roosevelt, except that the southward advance of Japanese troops was "having considerable effect" (ex. 1, pp. 188–191).

The record shows that President Roosevelt had an appointment with Admiral Ernest J. King at 3:45 p. m. immediately after his conference with the two Japanese Ambassadors (ex. 58), and that at about 4:00 p. m. Secretary Stimson telephoned and talked with Secretary Hull (tr. 1167, 5547). At 5:00 p. m. Secretary Hull telephoned Admiral Stark, but was unable to reach him and talked with Admiral Schuirmann instead (tr. 5547).

In addition to the conversations Secretary Hull had with officials of the United States Government on November 27 (Washington time), the Secretary and Under Secretary Welles also conferred that day with representatives of three of the governments that had been consulted in connection with the proposed *modus vivendi*. The Netherlands Minister called and handed Secretary Hull a memorandum of the same date in which the Netherlands Foreign Minister took the position that inasmuch as the *modus vivendi* proposal was only the beginning of negotiations, the military and economic concessions suggested therein as a start seemed to be "quite far reaching" and that it was "most unlikely" that Japan would at the present moment leave the Axis (ex. 18). The Australian Minister, Mr. Casey, also called on Secretary Hull and asked whether the *modus vivendi* had been abandoned permanently. When Secretary Hull said he so considered it, Mr. Casey

expressed great concern and desired to know more about the movements of Chiang Kai-shek and others intended to discourage the further consideration of the *modus vivendi*. I referred to copies of British communications on the subject, adding that Ambassador Halifax was strong for the proposal all the way and that I sympathized with his situation but I did not feel that the communications from Churchill and Eden, with qualifications such as were in them, would be very helpful in a bitter fight that would be projected by Chiang Kai-shek and carried forward by all of the malcontents in the United States, although I felt unreservedly that Churchill and Eden, like the British Ambassador here, would be for whatever we might do, even though not entirely to their liking in every way. The Minister inquired whether I thought it would be feasible to take up this matter further with the Chinese, and I replied that I did not think so, so far as I am concerned. I thanked the Minister for his cooperation and that of his Government (ex. 18).

Also that morning the British Ambassador "urgently" called on Under Secretary Welles. The Under Secretary's memorandum of their conversation noted that Lord Halifax said that Secretary Hull had telephoned him the previous evening and told him the nature of the United States' reply to Japan, and continued:

The Ambassador said that he was not quite clear in his own mind as to the reasons which prompted this sudden change in presenting the Japanese Government with a document other than the *modus vivendi* document which had so recently been under discussion.

I said that Secretary Hull had requested me to say to the Ambassador in this regard that one of the reasons for the determination reached was the half-hearted support given by the British Government to the earlier proposal which had been under discussion and the raising of repeated questions by the British Government in regard thereto.

Lord Halifax said he could not understand this inasmuch as he had communicated to Secretary Hull the full support of the British Government.

To that I replied that the message sent by Mr. Churchill to the President yesterday could hardly be regarded as "full support," but on the contrary, very grave questioning of the course then proposed.

Lord Halifax said that this message had been intended merely to express the objections on the part of the Chinese Government. He went on to say that he himself had been surprised by the vigor of the Chinese objections and that he had, in fact, stated to the Chinese Ambassador that in view of the fact that only ten days ago General Chiang Kai-shek was imploring the British and the United States Government to prevent the closing of the Burma Road, it would seem to him, Lord Halifax, that the course proposed by Secretary Hull gave positive assurances to the Chinese Government that the Burma Road would in fact be kept open if the *modus vivendi* agreement with Japan could be consummated. He said that he felt that the attitude taken by the Chinese Government was based partly on faulty information and partly on the almost hysterial reaction because of the fear that any kind of an agreement reached between Japan and the United States at this time would result in a complete breakdown of Chinese morale.

I told Lord Halifax that information received this morning tended to show that Japanese troop movements in southern Indochina were already very active and that Japanese forces there were being quickly increased in number. I said these reports likewise indicated that the threat against Thailand was imminent. I said, in conclusion, that it was evident from the information received here that the Japanese were preparing to move immediately on a very large scale. The gravity of the situation, I thought, could not be exaggerated (ex. 18).

While on November 27 (Washington time) both Secretary Hull and Under Secretary Welles thus believed the situation could not be more serious, the record before the Committee indicates that the political adviser to the Secretary, Dr. Stanley K. Hornbeck, was less concerned. In a memorandum of that date entitled "Problem of Far Eastern relations—Estimate of Situation and certain probabilities," Dr.

Hornbeck expressed the opinion that he did not believe the United States was "on the immediate verge of 'war' in the Pacific." He stated that in his opinion there was less reason on November 27 than there was a week before for the United States to be apprehensive lest Japan make war on the United States. "Were it a matter of placing bets," he wrote, "the undersigned would give odds of five to one that the United States and Japan will *not* be at 'war' on or before Decem- 15." (tr. 5523–5537). [Italics in original.]

Apart from the remark of Bureau Chief Yamamoto during his· telephone conversation with Ambassador Kurusu the evening of November 26 (Washington time), when Yamamoto told the Ambassador that he had expected that the United States would not yield to the demands made by the Japanese Government in its note of November 20, and Yamamoto's remark the next day in his telephone conversation with the Ambassador that Japan "can't yield," there is no evidence before the Committee that the Japanese Foreign Office furnished the two Japanese Ambassadors any official comment or instructions as to their next step until November 28 (Japan time). That day Foreign Minister Togo cabled the following instructions:

> Well, you two Ambassadors have exerted superhuman efforts but, in spite of this, the United States has gone ahead and presented this humiliating proposal. This was quite unexpected and extremely regrettable. *The Imperial Government can by no means use it as a basis for negotiations.* Therefore, with a report of the views of the Imperial Government on this American proposal which I will send you in two or three days, the negotiations *will be de facto ruptured. This is inevitable. However, I do not wish you to give the impression that the negotiations are broken off.* Merely say to them that you awaiting instructions and that, although the opinions of your Government are not yet clear to you, to your own way of thinking the Imperial Government has always made just claims and has borne great sacrifices for the sake of peace in the Pacific. Say that we have always demonstrated a long-suffering and conciliatory attitude, but that, on the other hand, the United States has been unbending, making it impossible for Japan to establish negotiations. Since things have come to this pass, I contacted the man you told me to in your #1180 and he said that under the present circumstances what you suggest is entirely unsuitable.[1] From now on do the best you can (ex. 1, p. 195).

This message, in the above form, was available in Washington on November 28 (Washington time) (ex. 1, p. 195), whether before or after the War Council meeting that day is not known definitely, although, as noted below, there is some indication that it was not available until afterward.

The War Council met at noon at the White House, with President Roosevelt, Secretary of State Hull, Secretary of War Stimson, Secretary of the Navy Knox, and General Marshall and Admiral Stark present. Secretary Hull repeated the comments he had made 3 days before, at the War Council meeting on November 25, emphasizing again that there was "practically no possibility of an agreement being achieved with Japan," that the Japanese were likely "to break out at any time with new acts of conquest," employing the element of surprise as "a central point in their strategy," and that the "safeguarding of our national security was in the hands of the Army and the Navy" (Tr. 1203). Earlier that day Secretary Stimson had received from the Military Intelligence Division (G–2) a summary of the available information regarding Japanese military and naval move-

---

[1] This has reference to the suggestion made by the two Ambassadors on November 26 (Washington time) that they be permitted to propose to Secretary Hull that President Roosevelt send a personal message to Foreign Minister Togo (ex. 1, p. 180).

ments in the Far East, and had taken it to President Roosevelt and suggested that he read it before the War Council meeting, which the President had called. In his notes of the meeting, Secretary Stimson said:

When we got back there at 12:00 o'clock he had read the paper that I had left with him. The main point of the paper was a study of what the Expeditionary Force, which we know has left Shanghai and is headed South, is going to do. G–2 pointed out that it might develop into an attack on the Philippines or a landing of further troops in Indo-China, or an attack on Thailand or an attack on the Dutch Netherlands, or on Singapore. After the President had read these aloud, he pointed out that there was one more. It might, by attacking the Kra Isthmus, develop into an attack on Rangoon, which lies only a short distance beyond the Kra Isthmus and the taking of which by the Japanese would effectually stop the Burma Road at its beginning. This, I think, was a very good suggestion on his part and a very likely one. It was the consensus that the present move—that there was an Expeditionary Force on the sea of about 25,000 Japanese troops aimed for a landing somewhere—completely changing the situation when we last discussed whether or not we could address an ultimatum to Japan about moving the troops which she already had on land in Indo-China. It was now the opinion of everyone that if this expedition was allowed to get around the southern point of Indo-China and to go off and land in the Gulf of Siam, either at Bangkok or further west, it would be a terrific blow at all of the three Powers, Britain at Singapore, the Netherlands, and ourselves in the Philippines. It was the consensus of everybody that this must not be allowed. Then we discussed how to prevent it. It was agreed that if the Japanese got into the Isthmus of Kra, the British would fight. It was also agreed that if the British fought, we would have to fight. And it now seems clear that if this expedition was allowed to round the southern point of Indo-China, this whole chain of disastrous events would be set on foot of going.

It further became a consensus of views that rather than strike at the Force as it went by without any warning on the one hand, which we didn't think we could do; or sitting still and allowing it to go on, on the other, which we didn't think we could do; that the only thing for us to do was to address it a warning that if it reached a certain place, or a certain line, or a certain point, we should have to fight. The President's mind evidently was running towards a special telegram from himself to the Emperor of Japan. This he had done with good results at the time of the Panay incident, but for many reasons this did not seem to me to be the right thing now and I pointed them out to the President. In the first place, a letter to the Emperor of Japan could not be couched in terms which contained an explicit warning. One does not warn an Emperor. In the second place it would not indicate to the people of the United States what the real nature of the danger was. Consequently I said there ought to be a message by the President to the people of the United States and I thought that the best form of a message would be an address to Congress reporting the danger, reporting what we would have to do if the danger happened. The President accepted this idea of a message but he first thought of incorporating in it the terms of his letter to the Emperor. But again I pointed out that he could not publicize a letter to an Emperor in such a way; that he had better send his letter to the Emperor separate as one thing and a secret thing, and then make his speech to the Congress as a separate and a more understandable thing to the people of the United States. This was the final decision at that time and the President asked Hull and Knox and myself to try to draft such papers (tr. 14,424–14,426).

Shortly after the meeting ended, President Roosevelt left for Warm Springs, Ga., telling reporters that the Japanese situation might require his return at any time.[1]

Also on November 28, the Netherlands Minister called on Secretary Hull to inquire what reactions the Secretary had had from the Japanese situation. The Secretary recorded that he handed the Minister—

three cables from Saigon and other localities in the French Indochina area indicating that tens of thousands of Japanese troops with equipment, vessels, trans-

---

[1] Earlier that day he had informed the press that American merchant vessels sailing the Pacific would not be armed "under existing circumstances." When asked how long he expected the existing circumstances to prevail, the President had replied that that question "should be asked in Tokyo" (Washington Post, November 29, 1941).

ports, et cetera, were proceeding to that area from the north. He examined the cables carefully and appeared much disturbed about the Japanese troop movements. The Minister stated that this presented a very serious situation.

The Minister wanted to make clear that he had supported me unequivocally in connection with the proposed *modus vivendi* arrangement which I abandoned on Tuesday evening, November twenty-fifth, or practically abandoned when the Chinese had exploded without knowing half the true facts or waiting to ascertain them. I said that I had determined early Wednesday morning, November twenty-sixth, to present to the Japanese later in the day the document containing a proposed draft of an agreement which set forth all of the basic principles for which this Government stands and has stood for, for many years, especially including the maintenance of the territorial integrity of China. I reminded the Minister that the central point in our plan was the continuance of the conversations with Japan looking toward the working out of a general agreement for a complete peaceful settlement in the Pacific area and that the so-called *modus vivendi* was really a part and parcel of these conversations and their objectives, intended to facilitate and keep them alive and that, of course, there was nothing that in any way could be construed as a departure from the basic principles which were intended to go into the general peace agreement. The Minister said he understood the situation (tr. 4475–4476).

The British Minister, Sir Ronald Campbell, called on Dr. Hornbeck that day to inquire whether the Japanese-American negotiations had in fact "broken down" as, he said, was stated in a message the British armed authorities had received from the United States armed authorities.[2] Dr. Hornbeck told the Minister that so far as he was aware neither Government had "declared or indicated" that the negotiations were terminated, but that he was not in a position to confiim or deny the statement referred to by the Minister (ex. 18). At 7 o'clock that evening the State Department sent a telegram to Ambassador Gauss in Chungking which summarized the Japanese demands of November 20 and the terms of the proposed *modus vivendi*. The telegram briefly reviewed the circumstances which led to the decision to withhold the *modus vivendi* from the United States reply of November 26, concerning which Ambassador Gauss had been previously informed, describing in some detail for the Ambassador's information the position regarding the *modus vivendi* taken by the Chinese Government (ex. 18).

According to Secretary Stimson, the rest of the week-end after the war council meeting on Friday "was largely taken up with preparing a suggested draft of a message for the President to deliver to Congress" (Tr. 14403). The record before the Committee shows that Friday afternoon Admiral Stark called Secretary Hull on the White House telephone at 2:49 o'clock and talked with one of the officials of the State Department's Far Eastern Division, and that at 5:25 o'clock Secretary Stimson called Secretary Hull and talked with Dr. Hornbeck (Tr. 5548). The next day, Saturday, November 29 (Washington time), Secretary Stimson and Secretary Knox sent to Secretary Hull suggested drafts, which they had prepared, of the proposed message to Congress decided upon the day before (ex. 161). In an attached note in his handwriting, Secretary Stimson described his suggestions as a "memo which may be helpful as to certain portions of the message to the Congress." Secretary Knox also forwarded a copy of his suggestions to President Roosevelt en route to Warm Springs, with an accompanying letter in which he said that he had had the assistance of both Admiral Stark and Admiral Turner in preparing the summation of the military situation contained in his draft. He told the President:

<hr>

[2] The message referred to appears to have been the Navy "war warning" dispatch of November 27 (Washington time) to Admiral Hart and Admiral Kimmel, which was sent to the United States Naval Observer in London with instructions to "inform British" (ex. 37).

The news this morning indicates the Japs are going to deliberately stall for two or three days, so unless this picture changes, I am extremely hopeful that you will get a two or three day respite down there and will come back feeling very fit (ex. 161).

It seems probable that Secretary Knox's information that the Japs were stalling "for two or three days" was based on Foreign Minister Togo's message quoted above, in which the Foreign Minister told Ambassador Nomura that with a report of his Government's views on the United States' reply of November 26 "which I will send you in two or three days, the negotiations will be de facto ruptured" (ex. 1, p. 195). While this is not conclusive as to whether or not that message was available before the War Council meeting on November 28 (Washington time), it does indicate that, although the message was translated by the Navy on November 28, it was not seen by Secretary Knox until "this morning", i. e., November 29 (Washington time).

The suggestions sent by Secretary Stimson and Secretary Knox to Secretary Hull were combined in a single draft (ex. 161–A), which then underwent extensive revision and modification. The revised draft was ready by noon the same day, Saturday, November 29 (Washington time), according to a handwritten note accompanying a copy of it which Dr. Hornbeck sent to Secretary Stimson the next day (ex. 161–A). It was accompanied by a draft of a proposed message to Emperor Hirohito and by the following memorandum for President Roosevelt dated November 29 (Washington time):

MEMORANDUM FOR THE PRESIDENT

There is attached a draft of a proposed message to Congress, to which draft the Secretary of the Navy and the Secretary of War made material contributions, and the officers of the Department made further contributions, which together comprise the draft of proposed message.

In order to get this to you today it has not been possible carefully to go over this draft a second time. In fact, I myself have not had time to read it at all critically, but expect to do so over the week-end and give you the benefit of any further comment or suggestions.

I also enclose a draft by the Far Eastern officials of a possible message from you to the Emperor of Japan. My personal view continues as on yesterday to be that its sending will be of doubtful efficacy, except for the purpose of making a record. It might even cause such complications as Col. Stimson and I referred to on yesterday.

If you should send this message to the Emperor it would be advisable to defer your message to Congress until we see whether the message to the Emperor effects any improvement in the situation. I think we agree that you will not send message to Congress until the last stage of our relations, relating to actual hostility, has been reached.

I think you will desire to have any message to the Emperor dispatched in code to Ambassador Grew for communication by him to the Emperor through appropriate channels (ex. 19).

The draft of a message to Emperor Hirohito was brief. In it, after referring to the long period of unbroken peace between the United States and Japan, the President was to state that he was addressing the Emperor "because of the deep and far-reaching emergency which appears to be in formation." He was then to continue:

Developments are occurring in the Pacific area which threaten to deprive each of our nations and all humanity of the beneficial influence of the long peace between our two countries. Those developments contain tragic possibilities.

The history of both our countries affords brilliant examples in which your and my predecessors have, at other times of great crisis, by their enlightened decisions and acts, arrested trends and directed national policies along new and better courses—thereby bringing blessings to the peoples of both countries and to the peoples of other lands.

Feeling deeply concerned over the present trend of events, I address myself to Your Majesty at this moment in the fervent hope that Your Majesty may, as I am doing, give thought to ways of dispelling the dark clouds which loom over the relations between our two countries and of restoring and maintaining the traditional state of amity wherein both our people may contribute to lasting peace and security throughout the Pacific area (ex. 19).

The draft of the proposed message to Congress was longer, a document of some twenty typewritten pages (ex. 19). It will be remembered that the War Council had decided on November 28 that the message was to be a message "to the people of the United States" as well as "an address to Congress reporting the danger, reporting what we would have to do if the danger happened" (tr. 14426). If the President should send the message to Emperor Hirohito, that, the War Council had decided, was to be "one thing and a secret thing," as a message to an Emperor could not be publicized as a message to Congress could, and the President was to make his speech to Congress "as a separate and more understandable thing to the people of the United States" (tr. 14426). The proposed message began with these words:

GENTLEMEN OF THE CONGRESS: I come before you to report to you on serious danger which is threatening this country and its interests in the Far East. Relations between the United States and the Japanese Empire have reached a stage where I consider it incumbent upon me to lay before you the essential facts of the situation and their extremely serious implications (ex. 19).

It then briefly reviewed the development of American foreign policy in the Far East since 1833, discussing American relations with China, the acquisition by the United States of sovereignty over the Philippines with its attendant responsibilities, and the relations between the United States and Japan since 1908, including a brief discussion of the Nine Power Treaty of 1921. It considered the policy of aggression followed by the Japanese first in Manchuria commencing in 1931 and then in China, during the course of which American lives and property had been imperiled and damaged in disregard for American rights under existing treaties.

The proposed message then took up the relationship of Japan to Germany and Italy in their scheme of world-wide conquest. It pointed out that in flat defiance of its covenants Japan had invaded and sought to overthrow the Government of China and that step by step the Japanese armed forces, passing through the China Sea in the immediate proximity of the Philippine Islands, had invaded and taken possession of French Indo-China. It continued:

Today they are openly threatening an extension of this conquest into the territory of Thailand. That step, if taken, would place them where they would directly menace, to the North, the Burma Road, China's lifeline, and, to the South, the port and Straits of Singapore through which gateway runs the commerce of the world, including our own, between the Pacific and the Indian Ocean.

To the eastward of the Philippines, Japan has extended her threatening activities through the Caroline and Marshall Islands where, in violation of the mandate under which she received the custody of those islands, she has been secretly establishing naval and air bases and fortifications directly on the line between the United States and the Philippines.

By these steps Japan has enveloped with threatening forces the western, northern, and eastern approaches to the Philippines. Should this process go further, it will completely encircle and dangerously menace vital interests of the United States.

*   *   *   *   *   *   *

This situation, precipitated solely by Japanese aggression, holds unmistakable threats to our interests, especially our interest in peace and in peaceful trade, and to our responsibility for the security of the Philippine Archipelago. The successful defense of the United States, in a military sense, is dependent upon supplies of vital materials which we import in large quantities from this region of the world. To permit Japanese domination and control of the major sources of world supplies of tin and rubber and tungsten would jeopardize our safety in a manner and to an extent that cannot be tolerated. Along with this would go practical Japanese control of the Pacific.

Unless the present course of events in the Far East is halted and considerations of justice, humanity, and fair dealing are restored, we will witness in that region of the world precisely what has already transpired throughout the continental limits of Europe where Hitler seeks dominion by ruthless force (ex. 19).

It was then pointed out that throughout the period in which Japan had been making it clear that this was her program, the Government of the United States had endeavored to persuade the Government of Japan that Japan's best interests lay in maintaining and cultivating friendly relations with the United States and other countries that believe in orderly and peaceful processes. Reference was made to the 8 months of conversations with the Japanese which had been carried on by the Secretary of State and the President for the purpose of arriving, if possible, at some understanding agreeable to both Governments, and the principles for which the United States had stood, as set forth in the United States note of November 26 to Japan, were summarized. It was stated that in this effort the United States Government had had the agreement and support of the Governments of Great Britain, Australia, the Netherlands, and China. Every effort had been made, it was said, toward reaching a fair and workable agreement, and to commit Japan to practices in line with the principles advocated by the United States.

These efforts, the proposed message continued, had failed, and Japan had refused to change her position or her practices, and relations between the two nations were threatened with rupture. The supreme question presented to the United States, it was said, was the question of self-defense; the immediate question was whether the United States would, or would not, stand by while Japan went forward with a program of conquest. The effects of that program of conquest, if successful, on China and the Philippines were then described, and it was said that—

If the Japanese should carry out their now threatened attacks upon, and were to succeed in conquering, the regions which they are menacing in the southwestern Pacific, our commerce with the Netherlands East Indies and Malaya would be at their mercy and probably be cut off. Our imports from those regions are of vital importance to us. We need those imports in time of peace. With the spirit of exploitation and destruction of commerce which prevails among the partners in the Axis Alliance, and with our needs what they are now in this period of emergency, an interruption of our trade with that area would be catastrophic (ex. 19).

The proposed message then concluded by stating that the United States did not want war with Japan, but that if war should come, the fault and responsibility would be those of Japan, and that the primary cause would have been the pursuit by Japan of a policy of aggression. The policy of the United States and its relation with Japan should not be influenced by fear of what attacks, acting unlawfully and with resort to force, Japan might make upon the United States—

but by determination on our part to give the utmost support of which we are reasonably capable to the fundamental principles of order and security and justice to which we have been and are committed, with confidence that it is within our capacity to withstand any attack which anyone may make upon us because of our pursuit of that course (ex. 19).

Also on November 29 (Washington time), the British Ambassador called on Secretary Hull to learn of any further developments in the Japanese situation, especially with reference to the question of the proposed *modus vivendi.* As Secretary Hull described the conversation:

This caused me to remark in a preliminary way that the mechanics for the carrying on of diplomatic relations between the governments resisting aggressor nations are so complicated that it is nearly impossible to carry on such relations in a manner at all systematic and safe and sound. I referred to the fact that Chiang Kai-shek, for example, has sent numerous hysterical cable messages to different Cabinet officers and high officials in the Government other than the State Department, and sometimes even ignoring the President, intruding into a delicate and serious situation with no real idea of what the facts are. I added that Chiang Kai-shek has his brother-in-law, located here in Washington, disseminate damaging reports at times to the press and others, apparently with no particular purpose in mind; that we have correspondents from London who interview different officials here, which is entirely their privilege to do, except that at times we all move too fast without fully understanding each other's views, et cetera, et cetera. I stated that this was well illustrated in the case of the recent outburst by Chiang Kai-shek. In referring to this I remarked that it would have been better if, when Churchull received Chiang Kai-shek's loud protest about our negotiations here with Japan, instead of passing the protest on to us without objection on his part, thereby qualifying and virtually killing what we knew were the individual views of the British Government toward these negotiations, he had sent a strong cable back to Chiang Kai-shek telling him to brace up and fight with the same zeal as the Japanese and the Germans are displaying instead of weakening and telling the Chinese people that all of the friendly countries were now striving primarily to protect themselves and to force an agreement between China and Japan, every Chinese should understand from such a procedure that the best possible course was being pursued and that this calls for resolute fighting until the undertaking is consummated by peace negotiatons which Japan in due course would be obliged to enter into with China.

I expressed the view that the diplomatic part of our relations with Japan was virtually over and that the matter will now go to the officials of the Army and the Navy with whom I have talked and to whom I have given my views for whatever they are worth. Speaking in great confidence, I said that it would be a serious mistake for our country and other countries interested in the Pacific situation to make plans of resistance without including the possibility that Japan may move suddenly and with every possible element of surprise and spread out over considerable areas and capture certain positions and posts before the peaceful countries interested in the Pacific would have time to confer and formulate plans to meet these new conditions; that this would be on the theory that the Japanese recognize that their course of unlimited conquest now renewed all along the line probably is a desperate gamble and requires the utmost boldness and risk.

I also said to the Ambassador that a calm deliberate Japanese Government would more than ever desire to wait another thirty days to see whether the German Army is driven out of Russia by winter. I added that the extremist fire-eating elements in Japan, who have preached a general forward movement supported by the Army and Navy have influenced a vast portion of the Japanese public to clamor for such a movement, would probably take no serious notice of the Russian-German situation, but would go forward in this desperate undertaking which they have advocated for some time; that at least it would be a mistake not to consider this possibility as entirely real, rather than to assume that they would virtually halt and engage in some movements into Thailand and into the Burma Road while waiting the results on the Russian front. The Ambassador, I think, had his reservations on this latter point. He did not disagree with what I said about the badly confused mechanics for the conduct of diplomatic relations between several of our countries in these critical times (ex. 18).

Also that day the Australian Minister, Mr. Casey, called on Secretary Hull and intimated that he was prepared to suggest to the Japanese Ambassador that Australia would be glad to act as mediator between Japan and the United States. In his memorandum of the conversation, Secretary Hull noted that he gave the matter no serious attention, except to tell the Minister—

that the diplomatic stage was over and that nothing would come of a move of that kind. I interrupted him to make this conclusive comment before the Minister could make a detailed statement of the matter on the assumption that he would develop a set of facts along lines that he began to intimate (ex. 174).

That afternoon the State Department received from Ambassador Grew the text of a Japanese note protesting the alleged flight of an American airplane over the island of Formosa on November 20, claiming this was a violation of Japanese territory and requesting that the matter "be brought to the attention of the United States authorities concerned." Ambassador Grew was informed on December 6 (Washington time) that the requested action had been taken, and that on November 24 an unidentified airplane had carried out a reconnaissance of Guam (ex. 130). The same afternoon (November 29) Secretary Hull received a request from the British Ambassador for a copy of the text of the United States' note of November 26 to send to the British Foreign Minister, to whom the general character of the note had previously been communicated (ex. 158). A copy of the note was sent to the Ambassador by Under Secretary Welles the following Tuesday (tr. 1338). Also that afternoon the State Department instructed American diplomatic and consular offices at Saigon, Bangkok and Singapore to report "all movements of military or naval units" promptly to the American Consul at Manila, who was told to transmit such information to Admiral Hart, the Commander in Chief of the Asiatic Fleet (ex. 21).

Overshadowing the other events of the day, however, was an Associated Press report of a speech made by Premier Tojo in Tokyo before a rally sponsored by the "Imperial Rule Assistance Association" and the "Dai Nippon East Asia League," in commemoration of the first anniversary of the Joint Declaration by the Governments of Japan and Manchukuo and the Wang Ching-wei Regime in Japanese-occupied China (ex. 29, vol. II, p. 122).[1] In his speech, Premier Tojo said:

It is certainly the most fortunate lot of the three powers to have the privilege of collaborating together under this banner for cutting open the thorny way, and 1 year has already gone by since we started this honorable work together, and if it is not the greatest task of the present century what else can it be.

However if we look around we find that there are still many countries who are indulging in actions hostile to us. In fact they are trying to throw obstacles in the way of the construction of the East Asia co-prosperity sphere and are trying to enjoy the dream of exploitation of East Asia at the cost of the 1,000 million populace of the East Asiatic peoples to satisfy their greed of possession.

The fact that Chiang Kai-shek is dancing to the tune of Britain, America, and communism at the expense of able-bodied and promising young men in his futile resistance against Japan is only due to the desire of Britain and the United States to fish in the troubled waters of East Asia by pitting the East Asiatic peoples against each other and to grasp the hegemony of East Asia. This is a stock in trade of Britain and the United States.

For the honor and pride of mankind we must purge this sort of practice from East Asia with a vengeance (ex. 29, vol. II, p. 148).

The reports of this speech by Premier Tojo commenced coming in on November 29, the date fixed by Foreign Minister Togo as the final deadline before which Ambassador Nomura was to obtain the written

---

[1] Extracts from Premier Tojo's speech were carried in American newspapers on November 30 under such headlines as "Japan Threatens to Purge Asia of U. S. and Britain" (Washington Post, November 30, 1941).

agreement of the United States to the Japanese demands of November 20 or else things would "automatically" begin to happen (ex. 1, p. 165). It must be assumed Secretary Hull was aware of this and of the Foreign Minister's message to Ambassador Nomura stating that the negotiations would be de facto ruptured within 2 or 3 days (ex. 1, p. 195).

Late Saturday evening, November 29 (Washington time), Secretary Hull telephoned President Roosevelt at Warm Springs and had a lengthy conversation with him, after which the President's press secretary told reporters:

> In view of the reported statement—an Associated Press dispatch by the Premier of Japan, the President tonight is of the opinion that he may have to leave Warm Springs tomorrow afternoon, arranging the railroad schedule so as to arrive in Washington Monday before noon (tr. 14337).

Secretary Hull testified that "the gravity of the situation was evident from many sources", and that as Premier Tojo's statement reflected the extreme acuteness of the situation, "in that sense it may be said that the statement prompted my telephone call and the President's return" (Tr. 14,340).

In the meantime, after cabling Ambassador Nomura on November 28 (Japan time) that he did not wish the Ambassador "to give the impression that the negotiations are broken off" (ex. 1, p. 195), Foreign Minister Togo had followed up that message with another the next day in which he instructed the Ambassador:

> *We wish you would make one more attempt verbally along the following lines:*
>
> The United States government has (always?) taken a fair and judicial position and has formulated its policies after full consideration of the claims of both sides.
>
> However, the Imperial Government is at a loss to understand why it has now taken the attitude that the new proposals we have made cannot be made the basis of discussion, but instead has made new proposals which ignore actual conditions in East Asia and would greatly injure the prestige of the Imperial Government.
>
> With such a change of front in their attitude toward the China problem, what has become of the basic objectives that the U. S. government has made the basis of our negotiations during these seven months? On these points we would request careful self-reflection on the part of the United States government.
>
> (*In carrying out this instruction, please be careful that this does not lead to anything like a breaking off of negotiations*) (ex. 1, p. 199).

This message was translated and available in Washington on Sunday, November 30 (Washington time). Late that evening Ambassador Kurusu telephoned Bureau Chief Yamamoto in Tokyo that arrangements had been made for the two Ambassadors to meet with Secretary Hull the next morning, Monday. The Ambassador reported that President Roosevelt was returning to Washington the next day because of Premier Tojo's speech, and cautioned against such "ill-advised statements," saying that it put the two Ambassadors "in a very difficult position." When Yamamoto urged the Ambassador to continue the negotiations, Ambassador Kurusu said they would need Tokyo's help, and both the Premier and the Foreign Minister would need "to change the tone of their speeches." The Ambassador continued:

> Actually the real problem we are up against is the effects of happenings in the South. You understand don't you? (ex. 1, p. 207).

Yamamoto replied:

> Yes, yes (ex. 1, p. 207).

Secretary Hull testified that he telephoned the President that Sunday [1] "after conferring with our military regarding the Japanese Prime Minister's bellicose statement and the increasing gravity of the Far Eastern situation" (tr. 1163). The record shows that the Secretary had two telephone conversations that morning with Admiral Stark at 10:30 and 12:08 o'clock (tr. 1167). Admiral Stark attended the Secretary's conference with President Roosevelt at 11:45 a. m. the next day immediately following the President's return to Washington, and it would seem probable that the arrangement for Admiral Stark to attend that conference was made during the Secretary's telephone conversations with him.

At 1:28 o'clock Sunday afternoon there was received in the State Department, through Ambassador Winant in London, the following message from Prime Minister Churchill for President Roosevelt:

It seems to me that one important method remains unused in averting war between Japan and our two countries, namely a plain declaration, secret or public as may be thought best, that any further act of aggression by Japan will lead immediately to the gravest consequence. I realize your constitutional difficulties but it would be tragic if Japan drifted into war by encroachment without having before her fairly and squarely the dire character of a further aggressive step. I beg you to consider whether, *at the moment which you judge right which may be very near,* you should not say that "any further Japanese aggression would compel you to place the gravest issues before Congress", or words to that effect. We would, of course, make a similar declaration or share in a joint declaration, and in any case arrangements are being made to synchronize our action with yours. Forgive me, my dear friend, for presuming to press such a course upon you, but I am convinced that it might make all the difference and prevent a melancholy extension of the war (ex. 24).

Also that Sunday both the Australian Minister, Mr. Casey, and the British Ambassador, Lord Halifax, called on Secretary Hull. The Australian Minister gave the Secretary the substance of a talk he had had with Ambassador Kurusu. Secretary Hull recorded:

This amounted to very little and there was really nothing new in what he said except that Kurusu made it repeatedly clear that the Japanese were very desirous of continuing conversations with this Government. The Minister then referred to his notes and said that the British Ambassador desired to urge, along with him, the Australian Minister, that I do the best possible to continue our relations with Japan so as to avoid a military conflict at this time, the idea being that they needed more time for preparation to resist in the Pacific area. This view has been asserted constantly during recent weeks by the British Ambassador, the Australian Minister, and twice by the Netherlands Minister (ex. 168).

One of the purposes of the British Ambassador's call was to hand Secretary Hull the following memorandum:

MOST SECRET

There are important indications that Japan is about to attack Thailand and that this attack will include a sea-borne expedition to seize strategic points in the Kra isthmus.

We have plans for the rapid movement of a force from Malaya to hold a line across the Kra isthmus in the neighborhood of Singora. Time is the essence of this plan, particularly at this season of the year when the Kra isthmus is water logged. Consequently great tactical advantage lies with the side which gets there first.

R. A. F. are reconnoitering on arc of 180 miles from Tedta Bharu for three days commencing November 29th and our Commander in Chief, Far East has requested Commander in Chief, Asiatic Fleet at Manila to undertake air recon-

---

[1] Newspaper accounts of Secretary Hull's activities that Sunday state that the Secretary *again* telephoned President Roosevelt at Warm Springs before his departure for Washington (Washington Post, December 1, 1941).

naissance on line Manila-Camranh Bay on the same days.　Commander in Chief Far East, has asked for permission to move into Kra isthmus, if air reconnaissance establishes the fact that escorted Japanese ships are approaching the coast of Thailand, and he asks for an immediate decision on this point.

To allow the Japanese to establish themselves so near the Malay frontier would be an obvious threat to Singapore even though at the present season it might not develop at once.　We have also to bear in mind the encouragement which the Japanese success would give to their extremists.　Demands of appetite would grow and other Far East peoples would be correspondingly depressed.　It looks therefore as though, to ensure the defense of Singapore and for wider reasons, we might have to take the proposed action to forestall the Japanese (ex. 21).

In his memorandum of his conversation with the British Ambassador Secretary Hull stated that the Ambassador—

was very desirous of ascertaining what the United States would do if the British should resist any Japanese undertaking to establish a base on the Kra Isthmus. *I said that the President was returning tomorrow morning and that I would lay all phases of the situation before him on Monday noon.　This I proceeded later to do and the President agreed to notify and see the Ambassador later with respect to his inquiry.* *　*　* The Ambassador continued his attitude of desiring more time for his Government to make preparations to resist in the Pacific area.　He assured me that his Government would be in harmony with any steps that we might pursue to this end (ex. 21).

The next day Lord Halifax sent Secretary Hull a copy of a telegram he had received from the British Foreign Office, "as the point may possibly arise in the course of your discussions this morning." "You will remember," he wrote the Secretary, "you mentioned the point to me as I was leaving your office yesterday" (ex. 158).　The Foreign Office telegram was as follows:

It is conceivable that United States Government may raise with you the question of the compatibility of the operation referred to with our treaty of non-aggression with Thailand.　It may be useful for you to know therefore that we have given careful consideration to this point.

In July last we informed the Thai Government that we should regard the grant of bases to Japan as an infraction of that treaty.　Similarly (although we have as yet made no communication to the Thai Government) we should not feel we could allow the treaty to be a bar to our entering Thailand if a Japanese invasion occurred or was clearly impending.　But it would be greatly preferable if in these eventualities we could act in co-operation with the Thai Government.　If therefore it were decided to undertake the operation, we should naturally do our best to secure Thai's consent.　It would be important however not to reveal to the Thai Government prematurely the existence of our plan owing to the danger of leakage to the Japanese (ex. 158).

Thus, the record before the Committee shows that as President Roosevelt returned to Washington from Warm Springs, the information available to his advisors in Washington indicated that a crisis was fast approaching, if not already at hand.

A series of intercepted Japanese messages that were translated and available in Washington the next day, December 1 (Japan time), fully confirmed this view.　In a telegram dated December 1 (Japan time) to Ambassador Nomura, the Japanese Foreign Minister told the Ambassador that—

The date set in my message No. 812 has come and gone and the situation continues to be increasingly critical.　However, to prevent the United States from becoming unduly suspicious, we have been instructing the Press and others that though there are some wide differences between Japan and the United States, the negotiations are continuing.

(The above is for only your information) (ex. 1, p. 208).

That same day the Japanese Foreign Office informed the Ambassador that its four offices "in London, Hongkong, Singapore, and Manila have been instructed to abandon the use of the code machines and to dispose of them," and that the machine in Batavia had been returned to Japan (ex. 1, p. 209). From a message dated November 29 from the Japanese Ambassador in Thailand to Foreign Minister Togo in Tokyo, it was learned that the Ambassador was conspiring with the pro-Japanese faction in Thailand to place that country in a position where it would be compelled to declare war on Great Britain. The Japanese Ambassador in Thailand reported to Tokyo that the question of joint military action between Thailand and Japan had been brought up in the Thai Government, but that the Government had expressed a desire to pursue a course of strict neutrality. He told Foreign Minister Togo that the Thai Government—

had taken a fairly firm stand that the first one, regardless of whether they be Britain or Japan, who makes the first move shall be considered Thai's enemy. Therefore, for Japan to be looked upon as Thai's helper, she should put Britain in a position to be the first aggressor. *For the purpose of accomplishing this, Japan should carefully avoid Thai territory, and instead, land troops in the neighborhood of Kotaparu in British territory, which would almost certainly force Britain to invade Thailand from Patanbessa.*

The consequence would be Thai's declaration of war on Britain. This strategy is being given careful consideration. Apparently this plan has the approval of Chief of Staff Bijitto. Our naval Attaché has advised the Naval General Staff, also, I think (ex. 1, p. 203).

While the record before the committee shows that all of these Japanese messages were translated and available in Washington on December 1, it does not show the exact hour when translation was completed. It therefore cannot be said with certainty which, if any, of the messages were seen by Secretary Hull before his conference with the Japanese Ambassadors that morning, or which of the messages were seen by President Roosevelt, Secretary Hull, and Admiral Stark before their conference immediately after the President's return to Washington from Warm Springs.

THE INVASION OF THAILAND BY JAPANESE FORCES FROM FRENCH INDOCHINA APPEARS IMMINENT

(December 1–7, 1941)

Thus on December 1 (Washington time) there was much information in Washington that pointed toward Thailand as the next objective of Japanese aggression. Geographically, Thailand lies between French Indochina on the east and Burma on the west, and, with the Gulf of Siam, between French Indochina on the northeast and the British Malay States on the south. After the Japanese occupation of southern French Indochina in late July, Thailand thus became a barrier between those forces and two possible objectives, the Burma Road on the one hand and Singapore on the other. This strategic location of Thailand had been emphasized by General Marshall and Admiral Stark in their joint memorandum of November 5 (Washington time) when they concluded that no military action against Japan should be undertaken by the United States unless, among other contingencies, the Japanese should move their forces "into Thailand to the west of 100° east (i. e., toward the Burma Road) or south of 10° north" (i. e., toward Singapore) (ex. 16).

It is desirable here to review briefly the situation with respect to Thailand as it had developed since July. The record before the Committee shows that after the Japanese invasion and occupation of French Indochina late in July, the Thai Government, fully aware of Thailand's strategic position and importance to the Japanese, on August 12 (Washington time) had formally asked the State Department whether, in the event Thailand should be attacked and should resist attack, the United States Government would extend material assistance to it, the Thai Government having determined and formally announced that it would defend itself against attack by any other country.   Mr. Maxwell M. Hamilton, then Chief of the State Department's Far Eastern Division, to whom the question was presented, had advised the Thai Minister that the matter would be taken up with higher officers of the Department and that he would then communicate further with the Minister (ex. 169, item 6).   The Thai Minister had previously made informal inquiry of the State Department to the same effect, after Secretary Hull had stated at a press conference on August 6 (Washington time) that the United States was becoming increasingly concerned over events in the southwestern Pacific area (ex. 169, item 1–6).   Again on August 14, the Thai Minister had called at the State Department and stated that he had received another telegram from his Government which, "in the gravity of its tone, indicated that a critical state had been reached in respect of the threat of invasion."   He had further stated that he had been instructed "to spare no effort to obtain an expression of the views of the American Government in this situation," and that the Thai Government was ready and able to purchase in America the arms it needed (ex. 169, item 7).

On August 15 (Washington time) the State Department had received from the United States Minister at Batavia in the Netherlands East Indies a telegram containing the substance of a message from the Netherlands Minister of Colonies in London to the Governor-General of the Netherlands East Indies.   In it the Minister of Colonies advised the latter that he had been assured by the British Foreign Minister that in the event of an attack by Japan upon the Netherlands East Indies, the British Empire would back up the Netherlands completely. The Governor-General was also advised that a further conference would soon be held in London with the British Foreign Minister in this connection—

since it has become clear now that the United States and England will not resist Japanese occupation of Thailand with force of arms.   It is also brought to your attention that any guarantee or certainty of United States participation by force of arms is absolutely excluded (ex. 169, item 8).

Secretary Hull had conferred with the Thai Minister in Washington on August 18 (Washington time).   In reply to the Minister's previous inquiries as to the attitude of the United States Government toward Thailand if Thailand should be attacked and should endeavor in good faith to defend itself, Secretary Hull had stated that the United States had been aiding China in many ways against the aggression of Japan and that, in the contingencies mentioned, the United States Government would place Thailand in the same category (ex. 169, item 9).

The next action of importance in connection with Thailand appears to have occurred on October 27 (Washington time), when the British Minister in Washington, Sir Ronald Campbell, discussed the Thailand situation with Under Secretary Welles and left with him two memoranda dated October 25 dealing with possible material aid to

Thailand, including guns, ammunition, planes and aviation gasoline and lubricating oil, by Great Britain and the United States (ex. 169, item 13). It will be recalled that it was about this time that Generalissimo Chiang Kai-shek had appealed to Great Britain and the United States for planes and pilots to defend the Burma Road against an anticipated attack by the Japanese from northern French Indochina. The American reply to the British memoranda of October 25 had been delayed in order that both of these matters could be considered at the same time (ex. 169, item 11). On November 6 (Washington time), that reply, in the form of an aide memoire, had been handed to the British Minister (ex. 169, item 13). The aide memoire pointed out that for some weeks it had been the policy of the United States Government to give sympathetic consideration to priority and export applications filed on behalf of the Thai Government and, whenever practicable in the face of demand from other areas upon American production, to take favorable action upon such applications. Regarding the proposals contained in the British memoranda, the United States reply commented that the British proposal to require the acceptance of British instructors along with the howitzers and field guns which were to be offered to the Thai Government might serve as a pretext upon which the Japanese Government might exert additional pressure upon Thailand. As to planes, the memoranda suggested that the British might wish to consider the release to Thailand of a number of airplanes at Singapore which it was understood were in excess of the number for which pilots were available there. If this should not be practicable, it was suggested that if the British should decide to make available to Thailand planes from those being supplied to it from the United States, the United States Government would be agreeable to such an arrangement. Concerning aviation gasoline and lubricating oil, it was stated that a reply would be made in the near future, after further investigation (ex. 169, item 13).

On November 18 (Washington time) the State Department had advised the American Minister at Bangkok that it had explored the possibility of making available to the Thai Government antitank and antiaircraft guns and ammunition, but that it had been found impossible to spare any of such items at the moment (ex. 169, item 15). Four days later, on November 22 (Washington time), the State Department had advised the American Minister at Bangkok that the question of supplying planes to Thailand had been under active consideration by the British and the United States Governments but that neither Government was in a position to supply any planes to Thailand at the present time. The Minister had been advised that the supplying of aviation gasoline and aviation lubricating oil had also been under consideration, and that the British Government was prepared to furnish limited amounts of aviation gasoline and the United States Government was endeavoring to arrange to supply aviation lubricating oil (ex. 169, item 16). The same day reports had reached the State Department from the British Embassy of Japanese requests for the use of Thai airfields for "survey flights" and for aviation gasoline, presumably for such flights (ex. 169, item 17).

The British Ambassador, Lord Halifax, had called on Under Secretary Welles on November 25 (Washington time) regarding a report from the British Minister at Bangkok that the Thai Government was again becoming very shaky and that unless some practical action were taken by Great Britain and the United States the Japanese influence would again become predominant. The British Ambassador had reported that the aviation gasoline and artillery the British had given the Thai Government had been regarded by the latter as completely insufficient "and had had no appreciably beneficial effects." When Lord Halifax had said that the Thai Government was urgently desirous of obtaining airplanes, the Under Secretary had said that the United States was building up its air strength as rapidly as possible in the Philippines and that he had been informed by both General Marshall and Admiral Stark that the planes the United States had in the Philippines were infinitely more valuable to the United States there than they would be in Thailand. The British Ambassador had then suggested on behalf of his Government that the situation "might be ameliorated by a credit of $10,000,000 to Thailand by the United States." Under Secretary Welles had said that this matter would be given immediate consideration (ex. 169, item 18).

On November 27 (Washington time) the State Department had advised the American Minister at Bangkok concerning renewed instructions which were given on November 22 to American diplomatic and consular officers in Japanese-occupied areas of China, Hongkong and French Indochina regarding the withdrawal of American citizens from those areas, and had authorized him to inform American citizens in Thailand of those instructions (ex. 169, item 20). The next day the Thai Minister had called at the State Department and stated that he feared a Japanese attack on Thailand was imminent. He had said that Thailand would resist any such attack with all its forces. Referring to the statement previously made to him that the United States would place Thailand in the same category as China and would offer assistance in the case of an attack by an aggressor, he had suggested that immediate consideration be given to making planes and other supplies available to Thailand. He had been advised that the matter would be promptly brought to the attention of the appropriate authorities (ex. 169, item 23).

On November 29 (Washington time) the State Department had received a telegram from the American Minister at Bangkok stating that on the previous day the Thai Prime Minister had urged his people to be neutral but to prepare to fight if war became inevitable. The Thai Prime Minister had been reported as saying—

that Great Britain and the United States had promised not to attack Thailand and that the Japanese Ambassador had guaranteed that Japanese troops in Indo-China are not intended for attack on this country in any circumstances (ex. 169, item 28).

On December 1 (Washington time), the day President Roosevelt returned to Washington, from Warm Springs, the Thai Minister, accompanied by his military attaché, called at the State Department and described in detail the general military situation in Thailand, stating that the military equipment now most urgently needed by Thailand was heavy artillery, bombing planes, and pursuit planes. The Minister expressed the hope that means could be found to make this equipment available immediately in order that Thailand might be better able to resist aggression by Japan (ex. 169, item 26).

The following day the State Department sent a telegram to the American Consul at Singapore requesting him to render all possible assistance in connection with the immediate delivery of small quantities of appropriate aviation lubricating oils to Thailand, arrangements for which, the Department said, had been tentatively agreed upon between representatives of this Government and representatives in Washington of the British and the Netherland Governments (ex. 169, item 28).

GERMANY TELLS JAPAN THE TIME IS RIPE TO STRIKE AT THE UNITED STATES, AND PROMISES TO JOIN WITH JAPAN IN WAR AGAINST THE UNITED STATES

(November 29, 1941)

Several additional intercepted Japanese messages between Tokyo and Berlin that were translated and available in Washington on December 1 (Washington time) disclosed that Germany once again was exercising pressure upon Japan under the Tripartite Pact. In a message dated November 29, 1941, from the Japanese Ambassador, Oshima, in Berlin to Foreign Minister Togo, the Ambassador reported a conversation he had had with Foreign Minister von Ribbentrop the day before, following a conference of high German Government and military officials at the official residence of Chancellor Hitler. The Ambassador reported that it was an absolute certainty that at that conference Japan's moves were discussed in connection with discussion of the German war against Russia. He quoted von Ribbentrop as saying:

It is essential that Japan effect the New Order in East Asia without losing this opportunity. There never has been and probably never will be a time when closer cooperation under the Tripartite Pact is so important. If Japan hesitates at this time, and Germany goes ahead and establishes her European New Order, all the military might of Britain and the United States will be concentrated against Japan.

As Fuehrer Hitler said today, there are fundamental differences in the very right to exist between Germany and Japan, and the United States. We have received advice to the effect that there is practically no hope of the Japanese–U. S. negotiations being concluded successfully, because of the fact that the United States is putting up a stiff front.

If this is indeed the fact of the case, and if Japan reaches a decision to fight Britain and the United States, I am confident that that will not only be to the interest of Germany and Japan jointly, but would bring about favorable results for Japan herself (ex. 1, p. 200).

The Japanese Ambassador informed the Foreign Minister in Tokyo that von Ribbentrop had said that the Germans would like to end their war with Russia during the next year, and that he had then continued

should Japan become engaged in a war against the United States, Germany, of course, would join the war immediately. There is absolutely no possibility of Germany's entering into a separate peace with the United States under such circumstances. The Fuehrer is determined on that point (ex. 1, p. 202).

Foreign Minister Togo replied to this message on November 30 (Japan time). His message was in three parts, only the first and third of which were ever intercepted.[1] Both of those parts were translated and available in Washington, however, on December 1 (Washington time):

1. The conversations begun between Tokyo and Washington last April during the administration of the former cabinet, in spite of the sincere efforts of the

---

[1] In this connection, the War Department advised the Committee that the microfilms of Japanese files received from General MacArthur's headquarters did not contain the second part of this message (tr. 13665).

Imperial Government, now stand ruptured—broken. (I am sending you an outline of developments in separate message #986.) In the face of this, our Empire faces a grave situation and must act with determination. Will Your Honor, therefore, immediately interview Chancellor Hitler and Foreign Minister Ribbentrop and confidentially communicate to them a summary of the developments. Say to them that lately England and the United States have taken a provocative attitude, both of them. Say that they are planning to move military forces into various places in East Asia and that we will inevitably have to counter by also moving troops. *Say very secretly to them that there is extreme danger that war may suddenly break out between the Anglo-Saxon nations and Japan through some clash of arms and add that the time of the breaking out of this war may come quicker than anyone dreams.*

*   *   *   *   *   *   *

4. If, when you tell them this, the Germans and Italians question you about our attitude toward the Soviet, say that we have already clarified our attitude toward the Russians in our statement of last July. Say that by our present moves southward we do not mean to relax our pressure against the Soviet and that if Russia joins hands tighter with England and the United States and resists us with hostilities, we are ready to turn upon her with all our might; however, right now, it is to our advantage to stress the south and for the time being we would prefer to refrain from any direct moves in the north.

5. This message is important from a strategic point of view and must under all circumstances be held in the most absolute secrecy. This goes without saying. Therefore, will you please impress upon the Germans and Italians how important secrecy is.

6. As for Italy, after our Ambassador in Berlin has communicated this to the Germans, he will transmit a suitable translation to Premier Mussolini and Foreign Minister Ciano. As soon as a date is set for a conference with the Germans and Italians, please let me know.

Will you please send this message also to Rome, together with the separate message (ex. 1, pp. 204–205).

In the separate message (#986) referred to above, Foreign Minister Togo reviewed the course of the Japanese-American negotiations for Ambassador Oshima's benefit. He stated that during the 6 months of negotiations

the Imperial Government adamantly stuck to the Tripartite Alliance as the cornerstone of the international policy regardless of the vicissitudes of the international situation, and that Japan had based her hopes for a solution between Japan and the United States definitely within the scope of that Alliance (ex. 1, p. 205).

The Foreign Minister said that the American and Japanese views on the question of the evacuation of Japanese troops from China and French Indochina "were completely in opposition to each other." He said that the United States had taken the position that as long as the Imperial Government of Japan was in alliance with Germany and Italy there could be no maintenance of friendly relations between Japan and the United States, and that the United States had begun to demonstrate a tendency to demand the divorce of the Japanese Government from the Tripartite Alliance. "That is to say," the Foreign Minister continued,

it has become gradually more and more clear that the Imperial Government could no longer continue negotiations with the United States. It became clear, too, that a continuance of negotiations would inevitably be detrimental to our cause.

3. The proposal presented by the United States on the 26th made this attitude of theirs clearer than ever. In it there is one insulting clause which says that no matter what treaty either party enters into with the third power it will not be interpreted as having any bearing upon the basic object of this treaty, namely the maintenance of peace in the Pacific. This means specifically the Three-Power Pact. It means that in case the United States enters the European war at any time the Japanese Empire will not be allowed to give assistance to Germany and Italy. It is clearly a trick. This clause alone, let alone others, makes it impossible to find any basis in the American proposal for negotiations. What is

more, before the United States brought forth this plan, they conferred with England, Australia, the Netherlands, and China—they did so repeatedly. Therefore, it is clear that the United States is now in collusion with those nations and has decided to regai d Japan along with Germany and Italy, as an enemy (ex. 1, p. 206).

PRESIDENT ROOSEVELT RETURNS TO WASHINGTON AS THE FAR EASTERN SITUATION MOVES RAPIDLY TOWARD A CLIMAX

(December 1, 1941)

When the two Japanese Ambassadors called on Secretary Hull on Monday morning, December 1 (Washington time), it was their first conference with the Secretary since their meeting with him and President Roosevelt 5 days before. Ambassador Nomura's description of their arrival at the State Department shows that many assumed the Ambassadors had requested the meeting with the Secretary to present the Japanese Government's reply to the American note of November 26. Ambassador Nomura reported to Tokyo:

Upon our arrival at the State Department we found not only newspapermen, but even some members of the Departmental staff crowding the corridors. Some of these spectators were of the opinion that the issue of war or peace was to be immediately decided upon. In general, the scene was highly dramatic (ex. 1, p. 210).

At the start of the conference Ambassador Kurusu asked the reason for President Roosevelt's sudden return to Washington, and Secretary Hull indicated that one of the reasons was the recent "loud talk" of the Japanese Premier. The Ambassador endeavored to minimize the Premier's recent speech and stated, in accordance with the instructions he had received from Tokyo, that the American note of November 26 had been communicated to his Government and that within a few days the Japanese Government's observations concerning it would be presented to the Secretary. He said that his Government believed its proposals of November 20 to be equitable, and had found it difficult to understand the position taken by the United States Government. He had been directed, he said, to inquire what was the ultimate aim of the United States in the conversations and to request the United States Government to make "deep reflection of this matter." He said that the Japanese offer to withdraw its troops from southern French Indo-China still stood (ex. 29, vol. II, pp. 772–774).

Secretary Hull replied that the United States Government had to take into account the "bellicose utterances emanating from Tokyo" and that there never would be possible any peaceful arrangements if such arrangements had to be based upon principles of force. Later, the Secretary called attention to reports received from the press and other sources—

of heavy Japanese troop movements into Indochina and endeavored to make it clear that, when a large Japanese army is anywhere in Indochina, we have to give that situation all the more attention when Japanese statesmen say that they will drive us out of east Asia. He pointed out that we cannot be sure what the Japanese military leaders are likely to do, that we do not know where the Japanese Army intends to land its forces, and that for this reason we cannot sit still but will have to puzzle these things out in some way. The Secretary explained that this situation had been very painful to him and he did not know whether the Ambassador could do anything in the matter of influencing the Japanese Government. Mr. Kurusu said that he felt it was a shame that nothing should come out of the efforts which the conversations of several months had represented. He said he felt that the two sides had once been near an agreement except for two or three points, but that our latest proposals seem to carry the two sides further away than before.

The Secretary pointed out that every time we get started in the direction of progress the Japanese military does something to overturn us. The Secretary expressed grave doubts whether we could now get ahead in view of all the threats that had been made. He pointed out that the acts of the Japanese militarists had effectively tied the hands of the Ambassadors and he did not know whether the Ambassadors could succeed in having anything accomplished toward untying their hands. Mr. Kurusu brought up again his contention made on previous occasions that China had taken advantage of the Washington Conference treaties to flaunt Japan, and commented that if we don't look out China will sell both the United States and Japan down the river. The Secretary observed that he has been plowing through various contradictions in Japanese acts and utterances. He pointed out that the Japanese had been telling us that if something quick is not done something awful was about to happen; that they kept urging upon the Secretary the danger of delay, and kept pressing the Secretary to do something. He said that in view of all the confusion, threats and pressure, he had been brought to the stage where he felt that something must be done to clear the foggy atomsphere; that his conclusion was that he must bring us back to fundamentals; and that these fundamentals were embodied in the propsal which we had offered the Japanese on November 26. He said that we have stood from the first on the points involved in this proposal. He pointed out that everything that Japan was doing and saying was in precisely the opposite direction from the course we have been talking about in our conversations, and that these should be reversed by his government before we can further seriously talk peace (vol. II, pp. 775–776).

The Secretary asked what possibility there was of peace-minded people coming out in Japan and expressing themselves, whether anybody in Japan would be free to speak unless he preached conquest. When the Ambassador commented that the Japanese people were not talking about conquest, Secretary Hull pointed out that everyone in America understood the implications of such terms as "New Order in East Asia" and "Co-prosperity sphere". The Secretary went on to say:

that there was no reason for conflict between the United States and Japan, that there was no real clash of interests. He added that Japan does not have to use a sword to gain for herself a seat at the head of the table. He pointed out that equality of opportunity is in our opinion the key to the future peace and prosperity of all nations (ex. 29, vol II, pp. 776–777).

When Ambassador Kurusu, after remarking that war in the Pacific would be a tragedy, added that the Japanese people believed that the United States wanted to keep Japan fighting China, and to keep Japan strangled, and that they believed they were faced with the alternative of surrendering to the United States or fighting, Secretary Hull said that he had practically exhausted himself here, that the American people were going to assume that there was real danger to this country in the situation, and that there was nothing he could do to prevent it (ex. 29, vol. 2, p. 777).

Ambassador Nomura reported to Foreign Minister Togo that during the conference Secretary Hull had emphasized:

The tone and trend of the Japanese Government's expressions and movements and that of the general public opinion organs, and the increase in strength of the garrisons in French Indo-China (ex. 1, p. 210).

He reported that from the beginning of the conference the Secretary had worn "a deeply pained expression," but that during the course of their explanations the Secretary "showed visible signs of relief (ex. 1, p. 210).

President Roosevelt reached Washington from Warm Springs shortly before noon on Monday, December 1, and went directly to the White House for his conference with Secretary Hull and Admiral Stark.[1] It will be recalled that in Secretary Hull's memorandum of his conversation with the British Ambassador the day before, the Secretary stated that he laid before President Roosevelt on Monday "all phases" of the matters he discussed with the British Ambassador, which had included the Ambassador's inquiry as to "what the United States would do if the British should resist any Japanese undertaking to establish a base on the Kra Isthmus", and that "the President agreed to notify and see the Ambassador later with respect to his inquiry" (ex. 21). Clearly, a further subject discussed at the White House conference was Secretary Hull's conversation that morning with the Japanese Ambassadors. It would also seem probable that at the conference the other events mentioned above that had occurred after the President's departure the preceding Friday were discussed. These included Secretary Hull's revised draft of the proposed message to Congress and the accompanying draft of a message to Hirohito; the significance of Premier Tojo's speech; the information received from the British Ambassador concerning a possible Japanese move into Thailand, which appeared to be confirmed that day by the intercepted Japanese message revealing the intrigues of the Japanese Ambassador in Thailand; Prime Minister Churchill's plea for similar or joint declarations by the United States and Great Britain that "any further act of aggression" would "lead immediately to the gravest consequence," at whatever moment the President should judge right "which may be very near"; and the intercepted Japanese messages showing that the Japanese Government was only making a pretense of continuing the conversations. In addition, the President, Secretary Hull, and Admiral Stark must be assumed to have seen either before or after the White House conference the exchange of messages between the Japanese Foreign Minister in Tokyo and the Japanese Ambassador in Berlin showing the strong German pressure on Japan to make war on Great Britain and the United States and the Japanese reply that *"war may suddenly break out between the Anglo Saxon nations and Japan * * * quicker than anyone dreams."*

There is no evidence before the Committee of any meeting between President Roosevelt and the British Ambassador, Lord Halifax, during the period December 1–7 (Washington time), and no reference to such a meeting has been found in newspaper accounts of President Roosevelt's activities that week. However, the Washington Post reported on December 2 that after the President's conference on December 1 with Secretary Hull and Admiral Stark, the President had a luncheon conference with Mr. Harry Hopkins, who had been driven to the White House from the Naval Hospital for that purpose, returning to the Naval Hospital after the conference; that thereafter

---

[1] The next day, referring to this meeting, the Washington Post reported:

"President Roosevelt yesterday assumed direct command of diplomatic and military moves relating to Japan as the lights of peace flickered low in the Orient and Kichisaburo Nomura, Japanese Ambassador told reporters that 'there must be wise statesmanship to save the situation.'

"It was in a tense atmosphere that the President reached the White House from Warm Springs shortly before noon to receive a report from Secretary of State Hull on his conversation yesterday morning with official Japanese representatives and to confer with diplomatic, naval and personal advisers.

"Washington reports indicate that Japan is massing troops in southern Indochina for a possible military move into Thailand, which an authoritative statement made here last week indicated the United States could not tolerate. In Manila the leaves of United States naval and military forces have been cancelled and London reports said military and air forces are being mobilized in the Netherlands East Indies" (Washington Post, December 2, 1941).

the President called Under Secretary Welles to the White House for a brief conference, after which the Under Secretary "on orders" conferred briefly with Lord Halifax; and that after the latter conference Mr. Welles returned to the White House for a further conference with the President that lasted an hour and a half. The record before the Committee does not show what matters were discussed at the conference between Under Secretary Welles and the British Ambassador.[1]

In the absence of other evidence concerning the subjects discussed at the White House conference that noon, the evidence before the Committee of action taken that evening and the next morning at the direction of President Roosevelt is important. Just before midnight that day, December 1 (Washington time), the Navy Department sent the following dispatch, marked priority, to Admiral Hart, Commander in Chief of the United States Asiatic Fleet:

President directs that the following be done as soon as possible and within two days if possible after receipt this despatch. Charter 3 small vessels to form a "defensive information patrol." Minimum requirements to establish identity as U. S. men-of-war are command by a naval officer and to mount a small gun and 1 machine gun would suffice. Filipino crews may be employed with minimum number naval ratings to accomplish purpose which is to observe and report by radio Japanese movements in west China Sea and Gulf of Siam. One vessel to be stationed between Hainan and Hue, one vessel off the Indo-China coast between, Camranh Bay and Cape St. Jaques and one vessel off Pointe De Camau. Use of *Isabel* authorized by President as one of the three but not other naval vessels. Report measures taken to carry out President's views. At the same time inform me as to what reconnaissance measures are being regularly performed at sea by both Army and Navy whether by air surface vessels or submarines and your opinion as to the effectiveness of these latter measures (ex. 37).

In Tokyo on December 1 (Japan time) the Japanese Cabinet met at the official residence of Premier Tojo. Domei, the authoritative Japanese news agency, issued a report stating that at the meeting the Japanese Cabinet had decided to continue negotiations with the United States, despite the divergence of views of the two Governments. In a telegram to Secretary Hull received the evening of December 1 (Washington time), Ambassador Grew reported that—

Tonight's newspapers reported that the Cabinet at its meeting today, while realizing the difficulty of adjusting the respective positions of the two countries, nevertheless determined to continue the Washington conversations (ex. 25).

As already noted, Ambassador Grew testified before the Committee that although he knew that the Cabinet meeting took place, he "did not (know) and could not have guessed" that the Cabinet had discussed the attack on Pearl Harbor (tr. 1615).

[1] The record before the Committee does, however, contain the following: On December 6, 1941, Captain John Creighton, the United States Naval Attaché at Singapore, sent a message to Admiral Hart, commander in chief of the Asiatic Fleet, at Manila which stated, among other things, that "Brooke Popham (the British commander in chief at Singapore) received Saturday from War Department London quote: 'W have now received assurance of American armed support in cases as follows: 1. We are obliged execute our plans to forestall Japs landing Isthmus of Kra or take action in reply to Nips invasion any other part of Siam * * *.' " (tr. 13520–13521) Captain Creighton testified before the Committee that he did not know or recall who it was that gave him the information upon which this message was based, or where that person had obtained the information, and that it was "really nothing more than rumor" (tr. 13530). Upon receipt of this message, Admiral Hart, on December 6, 1941, sent the following message to Admiral Stark in Washington: "Learn from Singapore we have assured Britain armed support under three or four eventualities. Have received no corresponding instructions from you." (ex. 40) Admiral (now Senator) Hart testified that he never received a reply to his message (tr. 12850–12851). In this connection see also the discussion *infra* of the second message received by the State Department on December 6 (Washington time) from Ambassador Winant in London regarding the two Japanese naval convoys moving toward the Kra Isthmus, in which Ambassador Winant said, among other things: "British feel pressed for time in relation to guaranteeing support Thailand, fearing Japan might force them to invite invasion on pretext protection before British have opportunity to guarantee support but wanting to carry out President's wishes in message transmitted by Welles to Halifax" (ex. 21) and Under Secretary Welles' testimony before the Committee in connection therewith.

However, it is now known that at this meeting the Japanese Cabinet gave its formal approval to the commencement of hostilities against the United States, and that immediately thereafter an Imperial Naval Order was issued on instructions from the Imperial General Headquarters:

Japan, under the necessity of her self-preservation and self-defense, has reached a position to declare war on the United States of America (tr. 438).

By that time, the Japanese naval striking force which had left its rendezvous in northern Japan on November 25 (Washington time) had steamed nearly half the distance to Pearl Harbor.

In Washington, however, Ambassador Nomura that day cabled the Foreign Minister there were indications that the United States desired to continue the negotiations "even if it is necessary to go beyond their stands on the so-called basic principles" (ex. 1, p. 213).

He continued:

If it is impossible from the broad political viewpoint, to conduct a leaders' meeting at this time, would it not be possible to arrange a conference between persons in whom the leaders have complete confidence (for example, Vice President Wallace or Hopkins from the United States and the former Premier Konoye, who is on friendly terms with the President, or Adviser to the Imperial Privy Council Ishii). The meeting could be arranged for some midway point, such as Honolulu. High army and navy officers should accompany these representatives. Have them make one final effort to reach some agreement, using as the basis of their discussions the latest proposals submitted by each.

We feel that this last effort may facilitate the final decision as to war or peace (ex. 1, p. 213)

It seems doubtful that Ambassador Nomura would have sent this message, if in fact he knew that that day the Tojo Cabinet had formally approved the commencement of hostilities against the United States. The Foreign Minister's message in reply to the Ambassador's suggestion, which was translated and available in Washington on December 3 (Washington time), avoided any reference to the Cabinet's action:

As you are well aware, during the tenure of the previous cabinet, a meeting between the leaders of the two countries was suggested by us but the proposals failed to materialize. It is felt that it would be inappropriate for us to propose such a meeting again at this time. Please be advised of this decision (ex. 1, p. 224).

PRESIDENT ROOSEVELT ASKS THE JAPANESE GOVERNMENT TO EXPLAIN ITS PURPOSE IN MOVING ADDITIONAL TROOPS INTO SOUTHERN INDO-CHINA

(December 2, 1941)

The next day, Tuesday, December 2 (Washington time), the two Japanese Ambassadors called on Under Secretary Welles at the latter's request, Secretary Hull being ill and absent from the State Department. Under Secretary Welles told the Ambassadors that he had been asked by President Roosevelt to communicate to them the following, which he then read and handed to Ambassador Nomura:

I have received reports during the past days of continuing Japanese troop movements to southern Indochina. These reports indicate a very rapid and material increase in the forces of all kinds stationed by Japan in Indochina.

It was my clear understanding that by the terms of the agreement—and there is no present need to discuss the nature of that agreement—between Japan and the French Government at Vichy that the total number of Japanese forces permitted by the terms of that agreement to be stationed in Indochina was very considerably less than the total amount of the forces already there.

The stationing of these increased Japanese forces in Indochina would seem to imply the utilization of these forces by Japan for purposes of further aggression, since no such number of forces could possibly be required for the policing of that region. Such aggression could conceivably be against the Philippine Islands; against the many islands of the East Indies; against Burma; against Malaya or either through coercion or through the actual use of force for the purpose of undertaking the occupation of Thailand. Such new aggression would, of course, be additional to the acts of aggression already undertaken against China, our attitude towards which is well known, and has been repeatedly stated to the Japanese Government.

Please be good enough to request the Japanese Ambassador and Ambassador Kurusu to inquire at once of the Japanese Government what the actual reasons may be for the steps already taken, and what I am to consider is the policy of the Japanese Government as demonstrated by this recent and rapid concentration of troops in Indochina. This Government has seen in the last few years in Europe a policy on the part of the German Government which has involved a constant and steady encroachment upon the territory and rights of free and independent peoples through the utilization of military steps of the same character. It is for that reason and because of the broad problem of American defense that I should like to know the intention of the Japanese Government (vol. II, p. 779).

Ambassador Kurusu said that he was not informed by the Japanese Government of its intentions but that he would communicate the foregoing statement immediately to his Government. Then followed an inconclusive discussion of the general situation, during which Under Secretary Welles pointed out that the settlement which the United States was offering Japan in the United States note of November 26 (Washington time) was one which would assure Japan of peace and the satisfaction of Japanese economic needs much more certainly than any other alternative which Japan might feel was open to her. Ambassador Kurusu said that in view of the actual situation in the Far East there were points in the United States proposal of November 26 which the Japanese Government would find it difficult to accept. When asked by Under Secretary Welles whether a reply to the American proposal would be received from the Japanese Government, Ambassador Nomura answered in the affirmative, but said that it might take a few days in view of the important questions which it raised for the Japanese Government (ex. 29, vol. II, pp. 778–781).

In his report of this conversation to Foreign Minister Togo, Ambassador Nomura said:

Judging by my interview with Secretary of State HULL on the 1st and my conversations of today, it is clear that the United States, too, is anxious to peacefully conclude the current difficult situation. I am convinced that they would like to bring about a speedy settlement. Therefore, please bear well in mind this fact in your considerations of our reply to the new American proposals and to my separate wire #1233 (ex. 1, pp. 222–223).

Soon after his meeting with the two Japanese Ambassadors, Under Secretary Welles attended a meeting at noon at the White House at which, in addition to President Roosevelt and Mr. Welles, only Secretary Stimson and Secretary Knox were present. Secretary Stimson described the meeting in his notes as follows:

I left for the White House conference at 12:00 o'clock and there were present there just Knox, Sumner Welles and myself, as Hull is laid up with a cold. The President went step by step over the situation and I think has made up his mind to go ahead. He has asked the Japanese through Sumner Welles what they intend by this new occupation of southern Indo-China—just what they are going to do—and has demanded a quick reply. The President is still deliberating the possibility of a message to the Emperor, although all the rest of us are rather against it, but in addition to that he is quite settled, I think, and he will make a Message to the Congress and will perhaps back that up with a speech to the country. He said that he was going to take the matters right up when he left us (tr. 14,427).

That afternoon, at his press conference, President Roosevelt was asked—

if the Japanese marched into Thailand what would the United States Government do? The President evaded the question. Another correspondent asked if the President could give any indication of the nature of the information requested from the Japanese representatives this morning. The President said let us put it this way, and this answers again many questions at the same time. Since last April we have been discussing with the Japanese some method to arrive at an objective that is permanent peace in the whole area in the Pacific and at times it seemed that progress was being made. During the whole period up to the end of June we assumed that as both nations were negotiating toward that objective— there would be no act contrary to the desired end of peace. We were therefore somewhat surprised when the Japanese Government sent troops to a specific over-all total into Indo-China after very brief negotiations with the Vichy Government at the conclusion of which the Vichy Government let it be understood clearly that they had agreed to this number of troops principally because they were powerless to do anything else.

Sometime later conversations were resumed with the United States and again we made it perfectly clear that the objective we were seeking meant the taking of no additional territory by anyone in the Paicfic area. We received word the other day that there were large additional bodies of Japanese forces of various kinds, including troops, planes, war vessels, etc., in Indo-China and that other forces were on the way. Before these forces had arrived the number of forces already there had greatly exceeded the original amount agreed to by the French and the number on the way were much greater, and the question asked this morning very politely, at my request, was as to what the purpose and intention of the Japanese Government was as to the future, eliminating the necessity of policing Indo-China which is a very peaceful spot and we hope to receive a reply in the near future.

In reply to a question as to whether any time for a reply had been set, the President said that there had naturally been no time limit set (ex. 167).

The same day Ambassador Nomura sent a special report to the Japanese Foreign Office concerning this press conference, as follows:

On the 2d in a press interview the President stated that he had sent us an inquiry that day concerning our increasing troops in French Indo-China. Expressing his own views for the first time, he briefly stated that the trend of Japanese-American negotiations for the past few days and our rumored increasing of troops in southern French Indo-China had both thrown obstacles in the way of the progress of the negotiations (see special intelligence from Washington). This was the first interview since returning from Warm Springs, and particular attention is to be paid to the fact that he referred directly to negotiations (ex. 1, p. 223).

Also that day the first secretary of the Japanese Embassy, Mr. Terasaki, called on officials of the State Department's Far Eastern Division and delivered a document in which it was denied that Premier Tojo had ever made the speech attributed to him on November 30. Mr. Terasaki claimed that when Ambassador Kurusu referred to the Premier's speech in his telephone conversation with Bureau Chief Yamamoto the preceding Sunday evening, Yamamoto had been nonplused and had asked "What speech?" (ex. 29, vol. II, pp. 777–778). The record of that telephone conversation before the Committee shows no such statement by Yamamoto; on the contrary Yamamoto is shown to have taken no exception to Ambassador Kurusu's references to the Premier's speech (ex. 1, pp. 206–207). That day the Chinese Ambassador, Dr. Hu Shih, delivered to the State Department a memorandum in further explanation of the position of the Chinese

Government on the *modus vivendi*, which ended by stating that the Chinese Foreign Minister had expressed—

great gratification in the latest reply of the Secretary (Hull) to the Japanese envoys, which, he understands, reaffirms the fundamental principles repeatedly enunciated by the United States Government (ex. 18).

Two intercepted Japanese messages bearing on Japanese-American relations generally were translated and available in Washington on Tuesday, December 2 (Washington time). One was a message sent from the Foreign Office in Tokyo to Washington on November 27 (Japan time), for retransmittal by Washington to Japanese diplomatic establishments in various North and South American cities. "With international relations becoming more strained," the message set up an emergency system of dispatches in hidden word codes to be used in communicating with those establishments. These emergency dispatches consisted of instructions regarding radio communications and the evacuation of Japanese Embassies, messages stating that relations between Japan and countries whose names were to be inserted were not in accordance with expectations or had been severed, and messages stating that Japan's armed forces had clashed with the armed forces of countries whose names were to be inserted or that Japan and countries whose names were to be inserted were entering a "full fledged general war" (ex. 1, pp. 186–188). The second message was from Hsinking to Tokyo, dated November 28, and contained the following:

In view of the situation, after conferring with the competent authorities, the following measures having to do with the treatment of British and American nationals in Manchukuo *in the event that war breaks out with England and the United States* are as outlined below. We are unanimously agreed on these matters. Should there be any questions regarding them, please wire me at once.
I. Policy. *On the outbreak of war with England and the United States,* after you have at the appropriate time gathered all these nationals together, they are to be returned each to his own homeland at as early a date as possible. However, until this return can be arranged, they are to be interned in places of concentration in Manchukuo.
"The control of such property as they might leave behind will be administered by the Manchukuo Government (ex. 1, p. 198).

On December 3 (Washington time) Secretary Hull held a press conference at which he repeated in large measure the statements he had made at his press conference on November 27 (Washington time), making it plain that at no time had the Japanese Government shown any disposition to modify its basic policies, which he described as at complete variance with those of the United States (tr. 1163).[1] That afternoon the Secretary had a telephone conversation with Admiral Stark at 4:45 o'clock (tr. 1167).

That day, and again the next day, the State Department received telegrams from the American Minister at Bangkok expressing the hope of the Thai Government—

that the American and British Governments will issue public statements to the effect that Japan by invading Thailand would incur the enmity and armed resistance of those two countries in addition to Thailand (ex. 169, item 30).

Other than Ambassador Nomura's report on his and Ambassador Kurusu's conference with Under Secretary Welles on December 3, and Foreign Minister Togo's reply to Ambassador Nomura's suggestion regarding a "leaders conference", both of which have been mentioned above, there is no evidence before the Committee of other

---

[1] Cf. Washington Post, December 4, 1941.

intercepted Japanese messages bearing on Japanese-American relations generally that were translated and available in Washington on December 3 (Washington time).

The next morning, Thursday, December 4 (Washington time), six majority and minority leaders of the Senate and House met with President Roosevelt for 2 hours and thoroughly canvassed the Far Eastern situation "in connection with the defense of our own territories and vital interests in the Far East", and were reported to have left the White House "with the impression that the situation is critical, but will not necessarily come to a show-down with the presentation of Japan's reply" to the President's request for an accounting for the continued Japanese troop movements into southern French Indochina (Washington Post, December 5, 1941). That afternoon at 2:15 o'clock the President conferred for an hour with Secretary Knox (ex. 58). As he left the meeting Secretary Knox told reporters that, among other things, he knew definitely that there would be an investigation of the publication that day by the Chicago Tribune, practically in full, of a copy of United States plans for fighting a global war if it should eventuate, "the most highly secret paper in the possession of the Government" (tr. 14, 411; Washington Post, December 5, 1941). At 3:30 o'clock, President Roosevelt conferred at the White House with Secretary Hull (ex. 58). That evening, according to a message dated December 6 (Washington time) from Ambassador Nomura to Foreign Minister Togo—

those engaged in Plan "A" dined with the President and advised him against a Japanese-American war and urged him to do the 'introducing' at once between Japan and China. However, the President did not make known what he had in mind. According to these men, this attitude of the President is his usual attitude (ex. 1, p. 247).

In explanation of this information, Ambassador Nomura told the Foreign Minister that—

In addition to carrying on frontal negotiations with the President and Hull we also worked directly and indirectly through Cabinet members having close relations with the President and through individuals equally influential (because of its delicate bearing upon the State Department, please keep this point strictly secret) (ex. 1, p. 247).

That day, Thursday, December 4, there were translated and available in Washington the first intercepted Japanese messages from Tokyo directing the destruction of code machines and machine codes by the Japanese Embassy in Washington. As already noted, there had been translated and available in Washington on December 1 (Washington time) a message sent from Tokyo on December 1 (Japan time) which informed the Japanese Embassy in Washington that the Japanese diplomatic offices in London, Hongkong, Singapore, and Manila had been instructed to abandon the use of code machines and to "dispose of them." This message had specifically stated, however, that regardless of other instructions, "the U. S. (office) retains the machines and the machine codes" (ex. 1, p. 209). However, on December 2 (Japan time), in one of the intercepted messages translated and available in Washington on December 4 (Washington time), the Japanese Foreign Office had instructed the Japanese Embassy in Washington to destroy one code machine unit completely, as well as to burn all telegraphic codes except "those now used with the machine," and the various other codes. The Embassy was also instructed to dispose of "all files of messages coming and going and all other secret documents" at the time and in the manner "you deem most proper" (ex. 1, p. 215). This message was followed by a second message on December 4 (Japan time) which gave more detailed instructions concerning the burning of certain codes recently brought to Washington by a Japanese official from the Japanese Embassy in Mexico City, and directed that a certain code keying be kept in Ambassador Nomura's custody "until the last moment" (ex. 1, p. 231).

Admiral Beardall, the Naval Aide to the President, testified that about the 4th or 5th of December, in connection with the delivery of "Magic" to the President, he called the President's particular attention to a message about the burning of codes. He testified that to the best of his recollection the gist of his conversation with the President was as follows:

I said, "Mr. President, this is a very significant dispatch," which he read very carefully, and he said "Well, when do you think it will happen?" I said, "Most any time" (tr. 14035–14036).

He testified that when the President said, "When do you think it will happen," he understood the President to mean, "When is war going to break out, when are we going to be attacked, or something" (tr. 14037).

A third intercepted message translated and available in Washington on December 4 (Washington time) was from Ambassador Nomura to the Japanese Foreign Office, in which the Ambassador said:

If we continue to increase our forces in French Indo-China, it is expected that the United States will close up our Consulates, therefore consideration should be given to steps to be taken in connection with the evacuation of the Consuls (ex. 1, p. 227).

Also that day there was translated and available in Washington Foreign Minister Togo's reply, dated December 3 (Japan time), to Ambassador Nomura's report of his and Ambassador Kurusu's conference with Secretary Hull on December 1 (Washington time). In it, the Foreign Minister put forward arguments for the Ambassadors' use in their forthcoming meeting with Secretary Hull. The Foreign Minister claimed that the United States was using the recent statements of Japanese officials and the Japanese troop movements in the South "as an excuse to doubt our sincerity in wanting to bring about a successful settlement in the Japanese-U. S. negotiations," and complained that Britain, the United States and others had been making military preparations against Japan "at an increasing tempo" and had been acting in a "more and more antagonistic manner of late. "We are insisting", the Foreign Minister said, "that all aid to Chiang cease as soon as Japanese-Chinese negotiations, at the instigation of the United States are launched" (ex. 1, pp. 225–226).

On December 5 (Japan time) Ambassador Grew sent a rush telegram to Secretary Hull in which he stated:

You will no doubt be aware that the American proposal is being represented here to the press and to the public as a mere restatement of "fanciful principles which ignore the realities of the situation", and that no intimation whatever has been given out that the proposal, if implemented, would provide Japan by peaceful and orderly processes with that security—political as well as economic—which she affects to seek by exercise of force. The response of most Japanese to whom we have said that the American proposal, far from being a formulation of fanciful principles designed to preserve the old order of things, is a well-balanced, constructive, practical and forward-looking plan for creating order out of the disorders of the past, has been to express strong disappointment that the private individual is not in a position to form any intelligent opinion with regard to a matter of such supreme importance, while some have said that if the American proposal is actually such as we have described it to be, an attitude of intransigence on the part of the Japanese would be viewed with regret by the masses.

It is impossible to forecast precisely what effect publication of our proposal would have. Undoubtedly reaction to certain phases of the proposal, notably complete evacuation of China, would be strong and indeed might be so violent as to eliminate the last possibility of an agreement. However, there would seem to be even greater risks of the elimination of that possibility if the points at issue continue in Japan to be befogged by ignorance and misrepresentation. I feel sure that you will have considered the wisdom of publishing the proposal as soon as possible after consultation with the Japanese Government, but even without the latter's assent if that should not be forthcoming (tr. 1821–1823).

The Japanese Government Claims its Troop Movements in French Indochina are for the Purpose of Defense Against an Attack by the Chinese

(December 5, 1941)

In the meantime, on December 3 (Japan time), Foreign Minister Togo had sent Ambassador Nomura his message No. 875 containing the Japanese Government's formal reply to President Roosevelt's inquiry regarding the movement of additional Japanese troops into southern French Indochina (ex. 1, p. 224). This reply took the position that the Japanese reinforcements were a precautionary measure against Chinese troops in bordering Chinese territory. Ambassador Nomura had regarded the reply as unsatisfactory, and had at once cabled the Foreign Minister:

I received your reply immediately. I presume, of course, that this reply was a result of consultations and profound consideration. The United States Government is attaching a great deal of importance on this reply. Especially since the President issued his statement yesterday, it is being rumored among the journalists that this reply is to be the key deciding whether there will be war or peace between Japan and the United States. There is no saying but what the United States Government will take a bold step depending upon how our reply is made. If it is really the intention of our government to arrive at a settlement, the explanation you give, I am afraid, would neither satisfy them nor prevent them taking the bold step referred to—even if your reply is made for the mere purpose of keeping the negotiations going. Therefore, in view of what has been elucidated in our proposal which I submitted to the President on November 10th, I would like to get a reply which gives a clearer impression of our peaceful intentions. Will you, therefore, reconsider this question with this in mind and wire me at once (ex. 1, pp. 227–228).

The Foreign Minister's reply to Ambassador Nomura had come back the next day:

What you say in your telegram is, of course, true, but at present it would be a very delicate matter to give any more explanations than set forth in my #875. I would advise against it because unfortunate results might follow, so please reply in accordance with my aforementioned message (ex. 1, p. 232).

Accordingly, on December 5 (Washington time), the Japanese Ambassadors called on Secretary Hull and presented their Government's reply to President Roosevelt's inquiry[1] (ex. 29, vol. II, pp.

---

[1] It is significant that press reports which reached Washington early in the morning of December 5 (Washington time), stated that in Tokyo that day the authoritative Japanese news agency had announced that "Japan cannot accept" the provisions of the United States' note of November 26. Domei was reported to have said: "Such a document cannot serve as a basic datum in Japanese-American negotiations henceforth". These statements, together with Japanese comment critical of Secretary Hull's remarks at his press conference on December 3 (Washington time), were carried in morning newspapers in Washington on December 5 under such headlines as "JAPAN 'CAN'T ACCEPT' TERMS" and "JAPAN EXPECTED TO REJECT TERMS" (Washington Post, December 5, 1941). Secretary Hull conferred for a short time with President Roosevelt before his meeting with the Japanese Ambassadors (Washington Post, December 6, 1941).

781–783). The Japanese reply as handed to the Secretary follows in full:

Reference is made to your inquiry about the intention of the Japanese Government with regard to the reported movements of Japanese troops in French Indochina. Under instructions from Tokyo I wish to inform you as follows:

As Chinese troops have recently shown frequent signs of movements along the northern frontier of French Indo-china bordering on China, Japanese troops, with the object of mainly taking precautionary measures, have been reinforced to a certain extent in the northern part of French Indochina. As a natural sequence of this step, certain movements have been taken on the part of the Japanese Government that may transgress the stipulations of the Protocol of Joint Defense between Japan and France (vol. II, p. 784).

After reading the reply, Secretary Hull said:

that he understood that Japan had been putting forces into northern Indochina for the purpose of attacking China from there. He said that he had never heard before that Japan's troop movements into northern Indochina were for the purpose of defense against Chinese attack. The Secretary added that it was the first time that he knew that Japan was on the defensive in Indochina (vol. II, p. 781).

Ambassador Nomura then repeated to the Secretary the gist of the Foreign Minister's message of December 3 (Japan time) mentioned above, claiming that the Japanese were alarmed over increasing naval and military preparation of the "ABCD" powers in the southwest Pacific, and asserting that the Japanese Government was "very anxious" to reach an agreement with this Government and that the United States ought to be willing to agree to discontinue aid to China as soon as conversations between China and Japan were initiated. The remainder of the conversation consisted largely of a repetition of matters expressed many times before by both the Japanese and the Secretary (ex. 29, vol. II, pp. 781–783).

That morning, December 5 (Washington time), President Roosevelt had received a memorandum from Under Secretary Welles passing on to him a suggestion from the Australian Prime Minister that if Mr. Wendell Willkie should visit Australia with the "imprimateur" of the President, his visit would be most welcome to the Australian Government. The President had immediately dictated a letter to Mr. Willkie regarding this, in which he said:

There is always the Japanese matter to consider. The situation is definitely serious and there might be an armed clash at any moment if the Japanese continued their forward progress against the Philippines, Dutch Indies or Malaya or Burma. Perhaps the next four or five days will decide the matter (ex. 111).

Following his conference with the Japanese Ambassadors, Secretary Hull had lunch at 1 o'clock at the White House with President Roosevelt, after which both the President and the Secretary attended a full Cabinet meeting at 2 o'clock (ex. 58).

That day the American Minister at Bangkok reported to the State Department that he had been informed by the Thai Minister for Foreign Affairs that the Japanese Ambassador in Thailand had told the Minister that the Japanese forces in Indochina "definitely would not be used to invade Thailand and that they were concentrated for use against the Burma Road" (ex. 169, item 31). Also that day, Lord Halifax, the British Ambassador, called on Secretary Hull, who recorded that the Ambassador—

said he had a message from Eden, head of the British Foreign Office, setting forth the British view that the time has now come for immediate cooperation with the Dutch East Indies by mutual understanding. This of course relates to the matter of defense against Japan. I expressed my appreciation (tr. 14,515).

The evening of December 5 (Washington time) the State Department sent a telegram to the American Embassy in Tokyo via Peiping by naval radio for the information of the American Embassy in Chungking and the American consul at Hong Kong containing instructions applicable to all offices in Japan, Japanese-occupied areas in China, Hong Kong, Indochina, and Thailand. Those instructions were—

intended to enable officers, in the event of sudden emergency and in case communications with the Department are delayed or severed, to take appropriate action concerning Government property, alien employees, archives, leases, the evacuation of the American members of the staff, et cetera (tr. 1967–A).

The telegram included the following paragraph concerning the destruction of codes:

It is of the utmost importance that all confidential files, seals, codes, ciphers, true readings, protectograph dies, et cetera, should be destroyed. Fee stamps should be destroyed by burning in the presence of at least two competent witnesses whose affidavits should be obtained (tr. 1967–D).

It ended as follows:

The sending of this instruction is in the nature of a precautionary measure and the authority granted in the foregoing paragraphs is intended to enable the officers concerned to deal with a sudden emergency. The concerned officers should quietly formulate plans to deal with an emergency if and when it arises. It is highly desirable that discussion be kept to a minimum and that publicity be avoided (tr. 1967–E).

Previously, on November 27 (Washington time), the day after the delivery of the United States reply, the State Department had sent a telegram to Ambassador Grew which strongly suggested the probability that the Japanese-American conversations might "lapse" and result "in withdrawal of our diplomatic and consular representation from Japan," and that he should quietly prepare for that eventuality (ex. 18). Also, on November 19 (Washington time), the State Department had sent a telegram to the American Embassy in Tokyo via Shanghai by naval radio, for the information of the American Embassies at Chungking, Peiping, and the American consul at Hong Kong, in which it was stated that the Department desired that—

the American diplomatic and consular officers concerned call to the attention of American citizens in the Japanese Empire, Japanese-occupied areas of China, Hong Kong, Macao, and French Indochina the advice previously given in regard to withdrawal and in so doing emphasize that the shipping problem in the Pacific is very difficult and that because of urgent demands elsewhere there is no assurance that it will be possible to retain in the Pacific even the the present facilities (tr. 4508–4509).

The telegram of November 19 (Washington time) was the last of three major warnings sent by the State Department during 1940 and 1941 advising American nationals to leave the Orient, the other major warnings have been sent on October 6, 1940, and February 11, 1941 (tr. 4502–4508).

On December 5 (Washington time), there was translated and available in Washington a message sent 2 days earlier by Ambassador Nomura to Foreign Minister Togo in which the Ambassador said:

Judging from all indications, we feel that some joint military action between Great Britain and the United States, with or without a declaration of war, is a definite certainty in the event of an occupation of Thailand (ex. 1, p. 227).

At the Japanese Embassy in Washington that day, Councilor Iguchi cabled the Japanese Foreign Office, in response to its instructions to destroy one code machine unit and to burn all telegraphic codes except those used with the machine:

We have completed destruction of codes, but since the U. S.-Japanese negotiations are still continuing I request your approval of our desire to delay for a while yet the destruction of the one code machine (ex. 1, p. 236).

The Foreign Office promptly replied that its instructions regarding code machines were:

of the two sets of "B" code machines with which your office is equipped, you are to burn one set and *for the time being* to continue the use of the other (ex. 1, p. 237).

Both of these intercepted Japanese messages were translated and available in Washington the next day.

The Last Hours

(December 6–8, 1941)

The next day was Saturday, December 6 (Washington time). In the southwest Pacific, the Japanese naval and military forces whose movements in and toward French Indochina had commenced in earnest soon after the Imperial Conference in Tokyo on November 5 (Japan time) and had been observed both by British and American forces based in Malaya and in the Philippines, had begun their final dispositions. It is now known that at the same time, in the mid-Pacific some 6,000 miles away, the Japanese naval force that had left its rendezvous in northern Japan on November 25 (Washington time)—still undiscovered and now almost within striking distance of the Hawaiian Islands—was steaming at high speed toward its target, the United States Pacific Fleet in Pearl Harbor.

While reports of the final Japanese movements in the southwest Pacific began to reach Washington before noon on December 6 (Washington time), the record before the Committee conclusively shows that no one in the United States Government or in its military and naval forces, either in Washington or in the field, knew of the approach of the Japanese naval striking force to the Hawaiian Islands.

That morning, at 10:40 o'clock, the State Department received the following telegram from Ambassador Winant in London, marked "Triple priority and most urgent" and "Personal and secret to the Secretary and the President":

British Admiralty reports that at 3 a. m. London time this morning two parties seen off Cambodia Point, sailing slowly westward toward Kra 14 hours distant in time. First party 25 transports, 6 cruisers, 10 destroyers. Second party 10 transports, 2 cruisers, 10 destroyers (ex. 21).

The State Department file copy of this message bears the stamp "Sent to the President," but does not indicate the hour when that action was taken. The same information had been received in Washington by the Navy Department earlier that morning in a message sent by Admiral Hart from Manila at 7:55 a. m. (Washington time) to Admiral Stark (tr. 4344, ex. 66). The information so received by the Navy Department was communicated to the State Department in a memorandum of December 6 signed by Admiral Schuirmann (ex. 66). Secretary Hull's engagement books for that day show that he had an appointment with Admiral Schuirmann at 1:50 p. m. (tr. 1168), at which time the memorandum was presumably handed to the Secretary by Admiral Schuirmann. Similar information was received in the State Department from the War Department early the next morning (tr. 14,290). The record of outside telephone calls through the White House switchboard on December 6 shows that Secretary Hull was again called by Secretary Stimson at 12:58 p. m. and by Admiral Stark at 1:09 p. m. (ex. 58; tr. 1168). At 3:05 p. m. that afternoon the State Department received a second message from Ambassador Winant, marked "Triple priority and most urgent" and "Personal and secret for the Secretary," containing additional information concerning the Ambassador's earlier message regarding the Japanese naval movement. The second message follows in full:

Again from Cadogan. Admiralty conference on information just forwarded, Cadogan attending. They were uncertain as to whether destination of parties is Kra or Bangkok. Latter would not be reached before Monday.

Note a discrepancy in time reported by me and time reported in our naval despatch, latter stating 3 a. m. Greenwich time, by despatch as given me 3 a. m. London time. Believe former correct.

British feel pressed for time in relation to guaranteeing support Thailand fearing Japan might force them to invite invasion on pretext protection before British have opportunity to guarantee support but wanting to carry out President's wishes in message transmitted by Welles to Halifax.

Leaving to spend evening with Eden in order to go over with him your number 5682, December 5 although I had previously pressed on him each of the points you outlined prior to reception your message with the exception of paragraph seven which I agree is not clear and which I will clear up with him this evening. I want you to know that I had nothing to do with the insertion of the reference to the I. L. O.

I am having lunch with the Prime Minister tomorrow at his usual place in the country and will be constantly in contact with the Embassy over private wires in case you wish to communicate with me [1] (ex. 21).

At 5:15 o'clock that afternoon Secretary Hull again telephoned Admiral Stark (tr. 1168).

That morning at 11 o'clock the State Department received the following telegram from Ambassador Gauss in Chungking:

The Chief of the Information Department of the Foreign Office informed a member of my staff yesterday that "the British wanted to move into Thailand but hesitated to do so in the absence of a clear indication of the American attitude." He said that this report came from a very reliable source in the United States. I attach no significance to the report except as indicative of an interesting and somewhat prevalent tendency to play up the situation (ex. 169, item 32).

At 6 p. m. that day the Department sent a telegram to the American Minister at Bangkok informing him that he might assure the Thai authorities that the extension of credit to Thailand for its current needs was fully agreed to in principle and that the Department expected no delay in working out the details with the appropriate lending agencies of the United States Government (ex. 169, item 33).

In the meantime, both President Roosevelt and Secretary Hull had given renewed attention to the proposal to send a message to Emperor Hirohito. It will be recalled that a draft of such a message had been prepared the preceding Saturday and probably discussed the next

[1] Under Secretary Welles was questioned at length by Senator Ferguson regarding the "message transmitted by Welles to Halifax" referred to in Ambassador Winant's telegram quoted above (tr. 1300–1316; 1337–1340). At Senator Ferguson's request, Mr. Welles undertook to make a special search for the message (tr. 1316), after which he reported to the Committee that it was his understanding that the message in question was the message from President Roosevelt which he communicated to the Japanese Ambassadors on December 2 (Washington time) and a copy of which he sent to the British Ambassador the same day (tr. 1338). The State Department advised Committee counsel that no written record of the message referred to in Ambassador Winant's telegram could be found in its files, and that accordingly it must be assumed the message was oral (tr. 1300). See in this connection the discussion *supra* of Under Secretary Welles reported conference with Lord Halifax on December 1 (Washington time).

Telegram number 5682 referred to in Ambassador Winant's telegram appears in the record before the Committee as exhibit No. 166. It does not deal with the situation in the Far East in any way.

Monday by the Secretary with the President upon his return from Warm Springs. The next day, Tuesday (December 2), Secretary Stimson had recorded in his notes:

The President is still deliberating the possibility of a message to the Emperor, although all the rest of us are rather against it, but in addition to that he is quite settled, I think, that he will make a message to the Congress and will perhaps back that up with a speech to the country (tr. 14,427).

Secretary Hull testified that he was in consultation with President Roosevelt at all stages of the drafting of the President's message to the Emperor (tr. 14,297). The record contains a note in President Roosevelt's handwriting, undated but bearing a stamp showing that it was received in Secretary Hull's office on December 6, which reads:

DEAR CORDELL: Shoot this to Grew—I think can go in grey code—saves time— I don't mind if it gets picked up.

F. D. R. (ex. 20).

The message to Emperor Hirohito attached to the President's memorandum was returned to the President attached to a "Memorandum for the President," also dated December 6 and initialled by Secretary Hull, as follows:

There is attached your message to the Emperor of Japan with page three of the message amended to take care of the point with regard to which I spoke to you on the telephone.
If you approve the draft as it now stands, we shall see that it gets off to Grew at once (ex. 20).

Beneath Secretary Hull's initials appears the following in President Roosevelt's handwriting:

C. H.   O K—send the amended p. 3 to the British Ambassador & send a copy to me.   F. D. R. (ex. 20).

The amended page 3 bears the President's handwritten "O. K.," followed by his initials (ex. 20). There is no explanation in the record before the Committee of the reason for the President's instruction to send a copy of the amended page three to the British Ambassador.

The first three and last paragraphs of the message as thus finally revised were substantially the same as those of the draft message attached to Secretary Hull's memorandum of November 29 to the President. The remainder of the message sent—comprising the main part—consisted of material that is not found in any of the drafts in evidence before the Committee. Secretary Hull testified that the message actually sent to the Emperor—

was prepared in final form on December 6, and included contributions made in the White House as well as material contained in the drafts prepared in the State Department during the preceding weeks (tr. 14,264).

At 8 o'clock that evening (December 6), the State Department dispatched to Ambassador Grew a brief telegram stating that an important telegram to him was being encoded and that it contained the text of a message from President Roosevelt to Emperor Hirohito, to be communicated by Ambassador Grew to the Emperor at the "earliest possible moment" (ex. 20). Both messages were initialled for Secretary Hull by Dr. Hornbeck (ex. 20), which may indicate that after approving the message in final form the Secretary had left the Department for the day. The telegram containing President Roosevelt's message to Emperor Hirohito was dispatched from the State Department at 9 o'clock that evening (ex. 20). The message follows in full:

Almost a century ago the President of the United States addressed to the Emperor of Japan a message extending an offer of friendship of the people of the United States to the people of Japan. That offer was accepted, and in the long period of unbroken peace and friendship which has followed, our respective nations, through the virtues of their peoples and the wisdom of their rulers have prospered and have substantially helped humanity.

Only in situations of extraordinary importance to our two countries need I address to Your Majesty messages on matters of state. I feel I should now so address you because of the deep and far-reaching emergency which appears to be in formation.

Developments are occurring in the Pacific area which threaten to deprive each of our nations and all humanity of the beneficial influence of the long peace between our two countries. Those developments contain tragic possibilities.

The people of the United States, believing in peace and in the right of nations to live and let live, have eagerly watched the conversations between our two Governments during these past months. We have hoped for a termination of the present conflict between Japan and China. We have hoped that a peace of the Pacific could be consummated in such a way that nationalities of many diverse peoples could exist side by side without fear of invasion that unbearable burdens of armaments could be lifted for them all; and that all peoples would resume commerce without discrimination against or in favor of any nation.

I am certain that it will be clear to Your Majesty, as it is to me, that in seeking these great objectives both Japan and the United States should agree to eliminate any form of military threat. This seemed essential to the attainment of the high objectives.

More than a year ago Your Majesty's Government concluded an agreement with the Vichy Government by which five or six thousand Japanese tropos were permitted to enter into Northern French Indo-China for the protection of Japanese troops which were operating against China further north. And this Spring and Summer the Vichy Government permitted further Japanese military forces to enter into Southern French Indo-China for the common defense of French Indo-China. I think I am correct in saying that no attack has been made upon Indo-China, nor that any has been contemplated.

During the past few weeks it has become clear to the world that Japanese military, naval, and air forces have been sent to Southern Indo-China in such large numbers as to create a reasonable doubt on the part of other nations that this continuing concentration in Indo-China is not defensive in its character.

Because these continuing concentrations in Indo-China have reached such large proportions and because they extend now to the southeast and the southwest corners of that Peninsula, it is only reasonable that the people of the Philippines, of the hundreds of Islands of the East Indies, of Malaya and of Thailand itself are asking themselves whether these forces of Japan are preparing or intending to make attack in one or more of these many directions.

I am sure that Your Majesty will understand that the fear of all these peoples is a legitimate fear inasmuch as it involves their peace and their national existence. I am sure that Your Majesty will understand why the people of the United States in such large numbers look askance at the establishment of military, naval, and air bases manned and equipped so greatly as to constitute armed forces capable of measures of offense.

It is clear that a continuance of such a situation is unthinkable.

None of the peoples whom I have spoken of above can sit either indefinitely or permanently on a keg of dynamite.

There is absolutely no thought on the part of the United States of invading Indo-China if every Japanese soldier or sailor were to be withdrawn therefrom.

I think that we can obtain the same assurance from the Governments of the East Indies, the Governments of Malaya and the Government of Thailand. I would even undertake to ask for the same assurance on the part of the Government of China. Thus a withdrawal of the Japanese forces from Indo-China would result in the assurance of peace throughout the whole of the South Pacific area.

I address myself to Your Majesty at this moment in the fervent hope that Your Majesty may, as I am doing, give thought in this definite emergency to ways of dispelling the dark clouds. I am confident that both of us, for the sake of the peoples not only of our own great countries but for the sake of humanity in neighboring territories, have a sacred duty to restore traditional amity and prevent further death and destruction in the world (vol. II, pp. 784–786).

Also at 9 o'clock that evening a telegram from Secretary Hull to Ambassador Gauss at Chungking was dispatched by the State Department, instructing the Ambassador to communicate to Generalissimo Chiang Kai-shek a copy of President Roosevelt's message to Emperor Hirohito, for the Generalissimo's confidential information. This telegram was also initialled for the Secretary by Dr. Hornbeck. After quoting the President's message in full, the telegram concluded:

In communicating copy of this message to Chiang Kai-shek, please state orally as from the President that the quoted message has already been sent by the President to the Emperor; that this message, as the situation now stands, would seem to represent very nearly the last diplomatic move that this Government can make toward causing Japan to desist from its present course; that if the slender chance of acceptance by Japan should materialize, a very effective measure would have been taken toward safeguarding the Burma Road; and that it is very much hoped that Chiang Kai-shek will not make or allow to be spread in Chinese Government circles adverse comment (tr. 14,517).

The final comment may well have been intended to forestall comment such as the Generalissimo had made at the time the *modus vivendi* was under consideration.

Ambassador Grew testified that he first learned of the President's message the evening of December 7 (Japan time) while listening to a radio broadcast from San Francisco (tr. 1501–1503; ex. 30, pp. 486–487). He immediately instructed Mr. Dooman, the Embassy Counselor, to stand by, and not long thereafter the first, short telegram from Secretary Hull was received. Although it showed on its face it had been received in Tokyo at 12 noon (Japan time), an hour after its dispatch from Washington at 11 a. m. (Japan time), the Secretary's second telegram containing President Roosevelt's message to the Emperor was not delivered at the Embassy until 10:30 p. m. "In other words," Ambassador Grew testified, "the telegram appears to have been delivered to the Japanese post office, which handled telegrams, 1 hour after its receipt, and they held it up throughout that day, from 12 noon until 10:30 p. m." (Japan time) (tr. 1501), or 8:30 a. m. December 7 (Washington time). Ambassador Grew saw Foreign Minister Togo at about a quarter past 12 that night. He read President Roosevelt's message aloud to the Foreign Minister, handed him a copy, and then requested an audience with the Emperor to present the President's message personally. Not until after Ambassador Grew had found it necessary to repeat his request did the Foreign Minister agree to present the matter to the Throne, (tr. 14,516).

To return to events in Washington, President Roosevelt's appointments for Saturday, December 6, as shown by his engagement book were two, both at the White House and both in the morning. The first was at 10 o'clock with Justice William O. Douglas, and the second was at 11:15 o'clock with Budget Director Harold O. Smith (ex. 58). The President had no scheduled appointments that afternoon. That evening the President and Mrs. Roosevelt entertained at dinner at 8 o'clock at the White House (ex. 58). Apart from the evidence already mentioned of the President's activities that day in connection with his message to Emperor Hirohito, the only other evidence before the Committee affirmatively showing the President's activities before the White House dinner that evening is a statement contained in a letter dated May 22, 1946, from an official of the Australian Legation in Washington in answer to certain inquiries made by the Committee through the State Department (tr. 14,631–14,632). Referring to a telegram from the Australian Minister for

External Affairs in Canberra to the British Secretary of State for Dominion Affairs of the United Kingdom in London, a paraphrase of which is quoted below, that letter states:

"The telegram contains the substance of a message which the Australian Minister for External Affairs had received from the Australian Minister at Washington. This message was despatched from Washington at 9:30 p. m. on December 6th, 1941. *The information contained therein regarding the procedure to be followed by the President had come orally from the President late in the afternoon of December 6th.*" (Tr. 14,631).

The paraphrase of the Australian Minister for External Affairs' telegram is as follows:

Subject to conditions that President gives prior approval to text of warning as drafted and also gives signal for actual delivery of warning, we concur in draft as a joint communication from all His Majesty's Governments. I point out that message from Australian Minister at Washington just received notes that,
1. President has decided to send message to Emperor.
2. President's subsequent procedure is that if no answer is received by him from the Emperor by Monday evening,
(a) he will issue his warning on Tuesday afternoon or evening,
(b) warning or equivalent by British or others will not follow until Wednesday morning, i. e., after his own warning has been delivered repeatedly to Tokyo and Washington (tr. 13, 741–13, 742).

It would seem clear that the "draft" referred to in the telegram quoted above was the document, a copy of which was obtained by the Committee from the files of President Roosevelt, attached to an unsigned memorandum dated December 7, 1941, on stationery bearing the official seal of the British Government (tr. 13,738). The memorandum was as follows:

The Prime Minister would be very glad of any comments which the President may have on the attached draft of a declaration to the Japanese Government.
The Dominion Governments have yet to give their views on this text. They are being consulted urgently.
The Netherlands government have been given a copy of the draft (tr. 13,738)

The draft declaration to the Japanese Government which was attached to this memorandum was as folllows:

Your Excellency:
I have the honour to inform Your Excellency that I have been instructed to make the following communication to the Imperial Japanese Government on behalf of His Majesty's Governments in the United Kingdom, Canada, the Commonwealth of Australia, New Zealand, and the Union of South Africa.
His Majesty's Governments in the United Kingdom, Canada, Commonwealth of Australia, New Zealand, Union of South Africa have followed closely in consultation with the United States Government the negotiations in which the latter have been engaged with the Japanese Government with a view to relieving the present tension in the Far East. His Majesty's Governments viewed with the same concern as the United States Government the rapidly growing concentration of Japanese forces in Indo-China which prompted the enquiry by the United States Government to the Japanese Government on December 2nd. They have found Japanese reply to that enquiry extremely disquieting. However valid the explanations in regard to North Indo-China as to which they expressly reserve their views the reply entirely fails to explain the fact that the bulk of Japanese forces are stationed in South Indo-China and are being constantly and heavily augmented.
There is no threat from any quarter against Indo-China and this concentration in South Indo-China is only explicable on the assumption that the Japanese Government are preparing for some further aggressive move directed against the Netherlands East Indies, Malaya, or Thailand.
Relations between the Governments of the British Commonwealth and the Netherlands Government are too well known for the Japanese Government to

be under any illusion as to their reaction to any attack on territories of the Netherlands. In the interest of peace His Majesty's Governments feel it incumbent upon them, however, to remove any uncertainty which may exist as regards their attitude in the event of attack on Thailand.

His Majesty's Governments have no designs against Thailand. On the contrary, preservation of full independence and sovereignty of Thailand is an important British interest. Any attempt by Japan to impair that independence or sovereignty would affect the security of Burma and Malay and His Majesty's Governments could not be indifferent to it. They feel bound therefore to warn the Japanese Government in the most solemn manner that if Japan attempts to establish her influence in Thailand by force or threat of force she will do so at her own peril and His Majesty's Governments will at once take all appropriate measures. Should hostilities unfortunately result the responsibility will rest with Japan (tr. 13738–13740).

It would seem clear that the foregoing draft is the draft warning to Japan "concurred in" by the Australian Minister for External Affairs in his telegram to the British Secretary of State for Dominion Affairs, which was dispatched from Canberra the evening of December 7 (tr. 14, 631–14, 632).

In connection with these documents, it will be recalled that the Marshall-Stark joint memorandum of November 27 to President Roosevelt had recommended that—

prior to the completion of the Philippine reinforcement, military counteraction be considered only if Japan attacks or directly threatens United States, British, or Dutch territory as above outlined;

in case of a Japanese advance into Thailand, Japan be warned by the United States, the British, and the Dutch governments that advance beyond the lines indicated may lead to war; prior to such warning no joint military opposition be undertaken;

steps be taken at once to consummate agreements with the British and Dutch for the issuance of such warning (ex. 17).

It will be also recalled that on Sunday, November 30 (Washington time), the State Department had received through Ambassador Winant a message from Prime Minister Churchill to President Roosevelt in which the Prime Minister, while stating that he realized the President's "constitutional difficulties," begged the President to consider at such moment as the President should judge right "which may be very near," the President should not tell Japan "that any further Japanese aggression would compel you to place the gravest issues before Congress or words to that effect." The Prime Minister had said that this was the one important method that remained "unused in averting war between Japan and our two countries," and that Great Britain would "make a similar declaration or share in a joint declaration" (ex. 24).

There is thus evidence before the Committee that by the late afternoon of December 6 the President had determined upon a procedure which contemplated that his message to Emperor Hirohito, as the first step (which he took despite the views of those of his advisors who felt that it would have little effect), would be followed, as recommended by General Marshall and Admiral Stark and previously discussed at length with his principal Cabinet advisors, and as urged by Prime Minister Churchill, by a warning to Japan by the United States Government, with similar warnings by the Governments of Great Britain and the Netherlands. The warning recommended by General Marshall and Admiral Stark was to be given "in case of a Japanese advance into Thailand," and by late Saturday afternoon the progress of the Japanese naval force around Cambodia Point had made such an advance an imminent probability. While both General Marshall (tr. 13809) and Admiral Stark (tr. 13760) testified that to the best of their recollection they were not consulted regarding the President's procedure outlined in the Australian message quoted above, that procedure followed the recommendation made in their joint memorandum of November 27 to the President so far as a warning to Japan was concerned.

In this connection it should be noted that according to Secretary Stimson, President Roosevelt planned to give his warning to Japan in his proposed message to Congress. He said:

The final view was that an additional warning to Japan should be given (tr. 14482).

*   *   *   *   *   *   *

The President was in fact during the early part of December engaged in preparing an address to Congress which would incorporate such a warning, and was also considering a special telegram to the Emperor. Before the address to the Congress was delivered, however, the Japanese struck on December 7th (tr. 14478).

*   *   *   *   *   *   *

The proposal was to go to Congress in advance, and through the address to Congress to give the Japanese a final warning (tr. 14487).

Both the State Department, with respect to its files, and Miss Tully, as custodian of the President's files, were requested by the Committee to furnish it with all information and documents relating to the proposed British warning and the telegram from the Australian Minister for External Affairs mentioned above (tr. 14628–14629; 14632–14633). The State Department searched its files twice and after the second search advised the Committee that no material relevant to those documents had been found (tr. 14629). Miss Tully advised the Committee that a further search of President Roosevelt's files had not disclosed any additional documents or memoranda regarding the documents in question. Regarding the message from the Australian Minister at Washington to Canberra, Miss Tully reported that she believed that "he and the late President discussed the subject but, of course, no record was ever made of such conversations" (tr. 14634).

The preceding day, perhaps at the meeting of his Cabinet, President Roosevelt had requested Secretaries Hull, Stimson, and Knox to compile for him the information available in their respective Departments concerning Japanese air, ground, and naval forces in French Indochina and adjacent areas. A memorandum dated December 5, 1941, based on Office of Naval Intelligence estimates, was transmitted by Secretary Knox to Secretary Hull with a covering, undated memorandum signed by the Secretary stating that the figures attached were those concerning which he had just talked with Secretary Hull on the telephone (ex. 175). A similar memorandum, dated December 6, and prepared by the Military Intelligence Division, was transmitted by Secretary Stimson to Secretary Hull on the same day with a covering letter in which Secretary Stimson specifically referred to the President's request of "yesterday" (ex. 175). The information contained in the memoranda, together with information received in the State Department from American diplomatic and consular sources, was combined in the State Department in a "Memorandum for the President," dated December 6, as follows:

Japanese Forces and Recent Increase in Japanese Military Material and Equipment in Indochina

According to information reported by our Consuls at Hanoi and Saigon, received by them from French military sources in Indochina and not confirmed, it is estimated that there are at present in northern Indochina (Tongking) 25,000 Japanese troops and 80,000 in southern Indochina, making a total of 105,000, and that there are at the outside some 450 Japanese planes in Indochina. According to a statement made December 4 by the Governor General of Indochina to our Consul at Hanoi, there are approximately 70,000 Japanese troops in Indochina, a little less than 30,000 being in Tongking and the balance in the south. The estimate of 105,000 is considered to be approximately correct by the Military Intelligence Division of the War Department.

According to the Office of Naval Intelligence of the Navy Department, 21 transports were sighted in Camranh Bay on December 2 by an air patrol from Manila, 12 submarines were sighted at sea northeast of Saigon proceeding south and nine of these submarines are now in Camranh Bay with other naval units including several destroyers. Our Consul at Hanoi reported on December 5 information from a reportedly reliable source that there were in Camranh Bay 30 transports carrying an estimated division of troops. Our Consul at Tsingtao reported on December 1 that for the preceding ten days an average of about three transports had left Tsingtao daily loaded with troops in summer uniforms.

An official of the French Foreign Office at Vichy stated to an officer of our Embassy on December 3 that the Japanese recently had been sending large amounts of military equipment and material into Indochina. According to our Consul at Hanoi Japanese military equipment recently landed in Indochina includes, as estimated by French military sources, 3,400 trucks and tractors, 600 automobiles, 500 motorcycles, 260 tanks (categories unspecified), 300 cannon, 2,000 machine guns, 1,300 submachine guns, 2,100 pack horses and a large number of bicycles.

The marked increase in Japanese troops in Indochina reportedly began November 21 with the arrival of 21 troop and supply ships at Saigon, the landing of 20,000 troops there, the transfer of 10,000 troops from northern Indochina southward and the subsequent landing of additional troops at both Saigon and Haiphong, those landed at the latter place proceeding southward by train.

At nearby Hainan Island there are estimated by the Military Intelligence Division of the War Department to be some 30,000 Japanese troops and an unknown number of planes. Pursuit planes as well as bombers can fly from Hainan Island to northern Indochina, either direct or via Waichow Island off Pakhoi, Kwantung Province of China (ex. 175).

Secretary Hull testified that he was most invariably at home in the evening "working on Departmental matters," and that while it was possible he might be mistaken, it was his best recollection that he was "at home on the night of December 6, 1941" (tr. 14, 315–14, 317). The record before the Committee shows that at 8:45 o'clock that evening Secretary Hull had a telephone conversation with Secretary Knox, lasting not over 2 minutes (ex. 58; tr. 1168). While Secretary Hull's records indicate that he called Secretary Knox (tr. 1168), the records of the While House switchboard operators indicate that Secretary Knox called Secretary Hull that evening at 8:45 p. m., between two calls to Secretary Stimson made by Secretary Knox at 8:30 and 8:47 p. m. (ex. 58). It is not clear from the record [1] before the Com-

---

[1] Captain Kramer testified that before delivering copies of the first 13 parts to the White House, to Secretary Knox, and to Admiral Theodore S. Wilkinson (then Director of Naval Intelligence), he telephoned the several persons to whom he customarily made deliveries of intercepted Japanese messages, and that he commenced these phone calls "at about a quarter of 9" (tr. 10446–10450). He testified that he did not begin deliveries that evening until after 9 a. m., and that he did not reach Secretary Knox's apartment until after 9:15 p. m. (tr. 10451). He further testified that Secretary Knox read the lengthy 13 parts before making any telephone calls (tr. 14454). On the basis of this testimony, Secretary Knox's phone calls could not have been made before 9:30 p. m., whereas the actual records made at the time show that the first of Secretary Knox's three calls to Secretary Stimson and Secretary Hull was made an hour earlier, at 8:30 p. m., and that his telephone conversation with Secretary Hull occurred at 8:45 p. m. (ex. 58; tr. 1168). This evidence leaves two major alternatives: (1) Captain Kramer's memory with respect to times that evening was faulty and the times he gave should all be moved back at least an hour, making his arrival at Secretary Knox's apartment prior to 8:30 p. m. Under such circumstances it would have been possible for Secretary Knox's reading of the 13-part message to have been the immediate reason for arranging the meeting of the three Secretaries the next morning, provided it is also assumed that the meeting was not arranged during the several conversations among the three Secretaries earlier that Saturday; and (2) Captain Kramer's memory

mittee whether or not Secretary Knox's three telephone calls through the White House switchboard were the calls, "apparently to Mr. Hull and Mr. Stimson" according to Captain Kramer (tr. 10676), made by Secretary Knox after he received and read that evening the first 13 parts (Annex E attached hereto) of the intercepted message from Foreign Minister Togo to Ambassador Nomura containing the Japanese Government's reply to the United States note of November 26. Secretary Knox gave instructions that the first 13 parts of that message, together with any additional intercepted messages that might become available during the night, should be brought to him at the meeting at 10 o'clock the next morning at the State Department which had been arranged with Secretaries Hull and Stimson (tr. 10676–10677). Captain Kramer, who delivered the 13 parts to Secretary Knox that evening, testified that the Secretary agreed with the conclusion he had placed on it, "that it aimed toward a conclusion of negotiations" (tr. 10676), and that nothing was said by the Secretary with respect to taking any action on the message (tr. 10454–10455).

There is no evidence before the Committee that Secretary Hull saw the intercepted Japanese message containing the first 13 parts of the Japanese reply before Sunday. Secretary Hull testified that he could not "recall definitely the exact time" when he first saw that message (tr. 14299). Regarding the so-called "pilot message" which preceded it, Colonel Bratton, Chief of the Far Eastern Section, Military Intelligence Division, who was in charge of the delivery of "magic" to the Secretary of State, testified before the Committee that the "pilot" message, which was sent by the Japanese Foreign Minister to Ambassador Nomura on December 6 (Japan time) and was translated and available in Washington the afternoon of December 6 (Washington time), was distributed to the Secretary of State around 3 p. m. that afternoon (tr. 12049–12050). That message (#901) was as follows:

1. The Government has deliberated deeply on the American proposal of the 26th of November and as a result we have drawn up a memorandum for the United States contained in my separate message #902 (in English).

2. This separate message is a very long one. I will send it in fourteen parts and I imagine you will receive it tomorrow. However, I am not sure. The situation is extremely delicate, and when you receive it I want you to please keep it secret for the time being.

3. Concerning the time of presenting this memorandum to the United States, I will wire you in a separate message. However, I want you in the meantime to put it in nicely drafted form and make every preparation to present it to the Americans just as soon as you receive instructions (ex. 1, pp. 238–239).

Colonel Bratton's testimony in this regard is uncontradicted, and it is therefore reasonable to conclude, since deliveries of "magic" were made directly to the Secretary of State's office, that Secretary Hull

---

with respect to times that evening was correct. Under such circumstances it must follow that the meeting of the three Secretaries the next morning had been arranged before Secretary Knox knew of or saw the 13-part message, unless the assumption is also made that Secretary Knox made a second series of calls after 9:30 p. m. to Secretary Hull and Secretary Stimson that were not made through the White House switchboard and, in the case of Secretary Hull, went unrecorded.

In this general connection, Secretary Hull testified:

"As I recall it, the meeting in my office on December 7 was the result of a mutual agreement on the part of Mr. Stimson, Mr. Knox, and myself. It might have been suggested in the first instance by any one or two of us three. According to my best recollection, the proposal for a meeting grew out of a desire to continue our discussion of the situation created by the movement of the huge Japanese armada southward and westward of the southernmost point of Indo-China" (tr. 14318).

The log of the duty officer at the Navy Department that Saturday evening contains an entry showing that *at 8 p. m.* Secretary Stimson's aide telephoned that Secretary Stimson desired certain specified information regarding American, British, Dutch, Japanese, and Russian naval vessels in the Pacific before 9 a. m. the next morning; that Secretary Knox, among others, was consulted in regard to this, and that Secretary Knox directed that the information be compiled and delivered to him prior to 10 a. m. the next morning (tr. 13946–13947; ex. 162). This would seem to indicate that the meeting of the three Secretaries had been arranged prior to 8 p. m. on Saturday, December 6.

saw the "pilot" message that afternoon before leaving the State Department. In the case of the first 13 parts of the 14-part message, however, the evidence before the Committee as to whether or not the first 13 parts were delivered to the State Department before the morning of December 7 (Washington time) is contradictory [1] and as stated above there is no evidence before the Committee that the first 13 parts were seen by Secretary Hull Saturday evening, December 6 (Washington time).

The evidence before the Committee is uncontradicted, however, that the first 13 parts were delivered to President Roosevelt a little after 9:30 o'clock the evening of December 6 (Washington time). At that time, the President and Mr. Harry Hopkins, who was one of the guests at the White House dinner party, were in the President's study on the second floor of the White House. Commander Schultz, an assistant to Admiral Beardall, naval aide to the President, who personally handed the intercepted messages to the President, testified that he gained the impression the President was expecting them, and that the President read the messages and then handed them to Mr. Hopkins, who was pacing back and forth slowly. His testimony continued:

Commander SCHULZ. Mr. Hopkins then read the papers and handed them back to the President. The President then turned toward Mr. Hopkins and said in substance—I am not sure of the exact words, but in substance—"This means war." Mr. Hopkins agreed, and they discussed then, for perhaps 5 minutes, the situation of the Japanese forces; that is, their deployment and——

Mr. RICHARDSON. Can you recall what either of them said?

Commander SCHULZ. In substance I can. There are only a few words that I can definitely say I am sure of, but the substance of it was that—I believe Mr. Hopkins mentioned it first—that since war was imminent, that the Japanese intended to strike when they were ready, at a moment when all was most opportune for them——

The CHAIRMAN. When all was what?

Commander SCHULZ. When all was most opportune for them. That is, when their forces were most properly deployed for their advantage. Indochina in particular was mentioned, because the Japanese forces had already landed there and there were implications of where they should move next.

The President mentioned a message that he had sent to the Japanese Emperor concerning the presence of Japanese troops in Indochina, in effect requesting their withdrawal.

Mr. Hopkins then expressed a view that since war was undoubtedly going to come at the convenience of the Japanese, it was too bad that we could not strike the first blow and prevent any sort of surprise. The President nodded and then said, in effect, "No, we can't do that. We are a democracy and a peaceful people."

---

[1] Colonel Bratton testified that the last of the 13 parts came into his office some time between 9 and 10 o'clock that night, and that he was in his office when the last of the 13 parts came in (tr. 12049). He further testified that he personally delivered the 13 parts to the night duty officer at the State Department some time after 10 o'clock that night, telling the duty officer that it was a "highly important message as far as the Secretary of State was concerned" and that it should be sent out to Secretary Hull's quarters, which he was assured would be done (tr. 12052–12053). This testimony is directly contrary to the affidavit of Col. Clyde Dusenberry, then Colonel Bratton's chief assistant, in the Clausen investigation. In his affidavit, Colonel Dusenberry stated that he specifically recalled the intercepted message in question and that "it started coming in the night of 6 December 1941 when I was on duty. Colonel Bratton was also on duty then and saw the message coming in and he remained until about half of it had been received. Thereupon he left and went home at about 9 p. m. I stayed so he could go home and sleep. I waited for the remainder. The fourteenth part, being the final part of the message, was received about 12 that night. Thereupon I left and went home. I returned the next morning *to begin the distribution of this intercept consisting of the fourteen parts* and *I began the distribution of the fourteen parts comprising this intercept* about 9 a. m. on 7 December 1941 and finished with the delivery to the State Department *as Kurusu and Nomura were meeting with the Secretary of State.* When I delivered the copy for OPD that morning I handed it to then Colonel Thomas D. Handy who, upon reading it, said to me: "This means war," or words to that effect. *None of these parts comprising this intercept was delivered before the morning of 7 December 1941* because the first half had been received while Colonel Bratton was on duty and he had seen this and had not had it delivered that night" (Clausen, p. 50).

Colonel Dusenberry's statements in his affidavit are in accord with the testimony of Gen. Sherman Miles, then Chief of the Military Intelligence Division and the superior officer of Colonel Bratton and Colonel Dusenberry, who stated that Secretary Hull, Secretary Stimson, and the others on the War Department's "magic" distribution list received on December 6 all intercepted Japanese messages that were translated that day up to midnight "*except the first 13 parts of the 14-part message*" (tr. 4123–4124).

Then he raised his voice, and this much I remember definitely. He said, "But we have a good record."

The impression that I got was that we would have to stand on that record, we could not make the first overt move. We would have to wait until it came.

During this discussion there was no mention of Pearl Harbor. The only geographic name I recall was Indochina. The time at which war might begin was not discussed, but from the manner of the discussion there was no indication that tomorrow was necessarily the day. I carried that impression away because it contributed to my personal surprise when the news did come.

Mr. RICHARDSON. Was there anything said, Commander, with reference to the subject of notice or notification as a result of the papers that were being read?

Commander SCHULZ. There was no mention made of sending any further warning or alert. However, having concluded this discussion about the war going to begin at the Japanese convenience, then the President said that he believed he would talk to Admiral Stark. He started to get Admiral Stark on the telephone. It was then determined—I do not recall exactly, but I believe the White House operator told the President that Admiral Stark could be reached at the National Theater.

Mr. RICHARDSON. Now, was it from what was said there that you draw the conclusion that that was what the White House operator reported?

Commander SCHULZ. Yes, sir. I did not hear what the operator said, but the National Theater was mentioned in my presence, and the President went on to state, in substance, that he would reach the Admiral later, that he did not want to cause public alarm by having the Admiral paged or otherwise when in the theater, where, I believe, the fact that he had a box reserved was mentioned and that if he had left suddenly he would surely have been seen because of the position which he held and undue alarm might be caused, and the President did not wish that to happen because he could get him within perhaps another half an hour in any case.

Mr. RICHARDSON. Was there anything said about telephoning anybody else except Stark?

Commander SCHULZ. No, sir; there was not (tr. 12436–12444).

Captain Krick, who testified that he was at the National Theater that evening with Admiral Stark, recalled that when he and Admiral Stark returned to the latter's home, one of Admiral Stark's servants advised the admiral that there had been a White House call during the evening (tr. 14757). According to Captain Krick's testimony, Admiral Stark retired immediately to his study on the second floor where he had a White House phone (tr. 14755). He returned between 5 and 10 minutes later, and told Captain Krick that—

conditions in the Pacific were serious; that was the substance of it, that conditions with Japan were in a critical state, something of that sort (tr. 14757).

Captain Krick testified that while he could not recall that Admiral Stark had said upon his return, "I have talked with the President of the United States", he had—

heard, of course, the statement of the servant that there had been a White House call, and the Admiral retired immediately, and he may have stated that he was going to call the White House; but I have the distinct impression that the conversation was with the White House (tr. 14758).

There is no evidence before the Committee of any other action taken by President Roosevelt the night of December 6 (Washington time).

A report that the Japanese Embassy in Washington had burned its codes and ciphers the preceding evening was received in the State Department from the Navy Department on December 6 (Washington time) (ex. 174). Intercepted Japanese messages which were translated in Washington that day, in addition to the first 13 parts of the 14-part message, included a message dated December 3 (Japan time) instructing the Japanese Embassy in Washington to keep its "hidden word" code lists "until the last moment" (ex. 1, p. 226); a message requesting Ambassador Nomura to have certain Embassy officials "leave (Washington) by plane within the next couple of days" (ex. 1, p. 234); Ambassador Nomura's report on his and Ambassador Kurusu's meeting with Secretary Hull the day before; and a message dated December 3 from the Japanese Ambassador in Rome to Foreign Minister Togo reporting on his conference that day with Premier Mussolini and Foreign Minister Ciano (ex. 1, pp. 228–229). In the latter report the Ambassador stated that at the conference he had described the developments in the Japanese-American negotiations as set out in message No. 986 from Foreign Minister Togo to the Japanese Ambassador in Berlin (which was translated and available in Washington on December 1 (Washington time) as has already been described). During the course of the conference in Rome, the Japanese Ambassador asked Mussolini and Ciano, if Japan should declare war on the United States and Great Britain,

would Italy do likewise immediately? Mussolini replied: "Of course. She is obligated to do so under the terms of the Tripartite Pact. Since Germany would also be obliged to follow suit, we would like to confer with Germany on this point" (ex. 1, p. 229).

The fourteenth and final part of the intercepted Japanese message containing the text of the Japanese Government's reply to the United States' note of November 26 was translated and available in Washington the next morning, Sunday, December 7 (Washington time). The record before the Committee shows that it was delivered to President Roosevelt in his bedroom at the White House about 10 o'clock that morning by Admiral Beardall, the President's naval aide (tr. 14010; 14033). Admiral Beardall testified that when the President had read it and such other messages as accompanied it in the delivery pouch, he turned to the admiral and remarked that it looked as if the Japanese were going to break off negotiations (tr. 14011; 14034). While Captain Kramer testified that he made a second delivery of "magic" to the White House that morning, at about 11 o'clock, Admiral Beardall testified that he had no recollection of delivering any other "magic" messages to the President (tr. 14034), or of seeing the President again, until after he received word at home about 2 o'clock that afternoon of the Japanese attack on Pearl Harbor (tr. 14015).

Secretary Hull testified that he had no record of nor did he recall—

having seen or having talked with the President between 9:30 p. m. on December 6, 1941 and the moment of the Japanese attack on Pearl Harbor. According to my best recollection, I was available during all that period (tr. 14319).

He testified that on Saturday and Sunday up to the time of the Japanese attack he—

was in constant contact * * * with officers of the State Department and of the Army and Navy * * *. It would be impossible to recall the details of all the conversations which took place, but I might say that the Japanese large-scale military movement from the jumping-off place in Southern Indo-China was very much in the minds of all of us who were called upon to consider that situation. We were striving to ascertain the full significance of those military movements, their probable destination, etc. (tr. 14319–14321).

That Sunday morning Secretaries Knox and Stimson met with Secretary Hull at the State Department. Secretary Hull testified that, according to his best recollection, the subject of that conference—

was in line with our increasingly frequent conferences over the telephone or in person as the dangers and the threatened outbreak in Japan increased.

For instance, on the day just before we had received all of this information from our consuls and from a British dispatch that this Japanese armada had left its jumping-off point and was sailing toward the Kra Isthmus and * * * Prime Minister Tojo had made a speech * * * a little before this. But that, along with these actual movements, especially these movements, was the occasion, the chief occasion, I think of our conference.

   *   *   *   *   *   *   *

Senator LUCAS. In the conversations that you had with Secretary Knox and Secretary Stimson on Sunday morning of the 7th was there anything said in that conversation about the likelihood of Japan attacking Pearl Harbor?

Mr. HULL. Nothing. As you understand, the attack was then on apparently. The fleet was moving toward the Kra Peninsula, which would greatly endanger the situation.

Mr. KEEFE. Pardon me, Mr. Chairman; I could not get your last answer. Will you read it, please?

Mr. HULL. I said the attack was under way, according to the dispatches, on the sixth. This fleet was moving, not up north in the Bay of Siam or Thailand, but it was, so far as my impression extended, moving toward the Kra Isthmus, which was probably a threat all the way down toward Singapore, down the peninsula, and not far from Malaya (tr. 1605–1606).

The record before the Committee shows that all 14 parts (Annex E) of the intercepted Japanese message containing the Japanese reply to the. United States note of November 26 were delivered to Secretary Knox at the State Department a few minutes before the meeting of the three Secretaries (tr. 10468), and that the intercepted message in which Foreign Minister Togo directed Ambassador Nomura to deliver the Japanese reply to Secretary Hull at 1 p. m. that day (ex. 1, p. 248) was handed to one of Secretary Hull's private secretaries at about 10:45 o'clock (tr. 10473). These deliveries were made by Captain Kramer, who testified that at the time of the second delivery he mentioned to Mr. Hull's private secretary the tie-up between 1 p. m. Washington time and "the scheme that had been developing for the past week or so in the Southwest Pacific with reference to Malaya and the Kra Peninsula" (tr. 10472).

A further indication of the matters discussed at the conference of the three Secretaries at the State Department that Sunday morning is a memorandum entitled "Location of U. S. Naval Forces in the Pacific and Far East, as of 7 December 1941" in evidence before the Committee (ex. 176). In the upper right hand corner of this memorandum appears the following handwritten note: "SECNAV (2), 1000", meaning, apparently, two copies for the Secretary of the Navy at 10 o'clock. This note, considered in conjunction with the log of the duty officer at the Navy Department the preceding evening (ex. 162), leaves little doubt that the memorandum was prepared expressly for the conference at the State Department that morning. The memorandum listed the major ships of the United States, Japanese, British, Dutch, and Russian fleets in the Pacific Ocean by name, and the destroyers and submarines in those fleets by number, giving their location "as of 7 Dec. 1941". The Japanese cruisers and destroyers referred to in the Hart message to the Navy Department and the Winant telegrams to the State Department the day before were listed as "off southern Indochina." The bulk of the Japanese Navy was listed as in the two major Japanese naval stations at Kure and Sasebo on the main Japanese islands of Honshu and Kyushu. Included among the Japanese ships listed by name as in those two Japanese naval stations that morning were all of the ships which, it is now known, were at that very moment less than 300 miles north of the Hawaiian Islands in the act of launching their bombers and torpedo planes for the Japanese attack on the United States Pacific Fleet in Pearl Harbor.

Secretary Stimson's notes for that day, which appear to have been written the following day, describe in greater detail the meeting of the three Secretaries.

Today is the day that the Japanese are going to bring their answer to Hull, and everything in MAGIC indicated they had been keeping the time back until now in order to accomplish something hanging in the air. Knox and I arranged a conference with Hull at 10:30 and we talked the whole matter over. Hull is very certain that the Japs are planning some deviltry and we are all wondering where the blow will strike. We three stayed together in conference until lunch time, going over the plans for what should be said or done. The main thing is to hold the main people who are interested in the Far East together—the British, ourselves, the Dutch, the Australians, the Chinese. Hull expressed his views, giving the broad picture of it, and I made him dictate it to a stenographer and I attach it to the end of this. Knox also had his views as to the importance of showing immediately how these different nations must stand together and I got him to dictate that and that is attached hereto. Hull was to see the Japanese envoys at one o'clock but they were delayed in keeping the appointment and did not come until later—as it turned out, till 2:00 o'clock or after. * * * The messages which we have been getting through Saturday and yesterday and this morning are messages which are brought by the British patrol south of Indo-China, showing that large Japanese forces were moving up into the Gulf of Siam. This itself was enough excitement and that was what we were at work on our papers about. The observer thought these forces were going to land probably either on the eastern side of the Gulf of Siam, where it would be still in Indo-China, or on the western side, where it would be the Kra Peninsula, or probably Malaya. The British were very much excited about it and our efforts this morning in drawing our papers was to see whether or not we should all act together. The British will have to fight if they attack the Kra Peninsula. We three all thought that we must fight if the British fought (tr. 14428–14429).

The statement dictated by Secretary Hull as referred to in Secretary Stimson's notes, follows:

Proposed Statement for President by Hull

(See Record, December 7)

The Japanese Government, dominated by the military fire-eaters, is deliberately proceeding on an increasingly broad front to carry out its long proclaimed purpose to acquire military control over one-half of the world with nearly one-half its population. This inevitably means Japanese control of islands, continents, and seas from the Indies back near Hawaii, and that all of the conquered peoples would be governed militarily, politically, economically, socially, and morally by the worst possible military despotism with barbaric, inhuman, and semislavery methods such as Japan has notoriously been inflicting on the people in China and Hitler on the peoples of some fifteen conquered nations of Europe. This would virtually drive and force all free and peaceful peoples off the high seas.

At this moment of serious, threatened, and imminent danger, it is manifest that control of the South Sea area by Japan is the key to the control of the entire Pacific area, and therefore defense of life and commerce and other invaluable rights and interests in the Pacific area must be commenced within the South Sea area at such times and places as in the judgment of naval and military experts would be within sufficient time and at such strategic points as would make it most effective. In no other way can it be satisfactorily determined that the Pacific area can be successfully defended.

More than ever is the cohesive, closely related world movement to conquer and destroy, with Hitler moving across one-half of the world and the Government of Japan under the military group moving across the other half of the world by closely synchronizing their efforts and collaborating and cooperating whenever to their individual or their mutual advantage.

This at once places at stake everything that is precious and worth while. Self-defense, therefore, is the key point for the preservation of each and all of our civilized institutions (tr. 14433–14434).

Secretary Knox's statement was as follows:

(See Record, December 7)

1. We are tied up inextricably with the British in the present world situation.
2. The fall of Singapore and the loss to England of Malaya will automatically not only wreck her far eastern position but jeopardize her entire effort.
3. If the British lose their position the Dutch are almost certain to lose theirs.
4. If both the British and the Dutch lose their positions we are almost certain to be next, being then practically Japanese-surrounded.
5. If the above be accepted, then any serious threat to the British or the Dutch is a serious threat to the United States; or it might be stated any threat to any one of the three of us is a threat to all of us. We should therefore be ready jointly to act together and if such understanding has not already been reached, it should be reached immediately. Otherwise we may fall individually one at a time (or somebody may be left out on a limb).
6. I think the Japanese should be told that any movement in a direction that threatens the United States will be met by force. The President will want to reserve to himself just how to define this. The following are suggestions to shoot at: Any movement into Thailand; or any movement into Thailand west of 100° east and South of 10° North—this in accordance with the recommendations of the British and Dutch and United States military authorities in the Far East; or any movement against British, Dutch, United States, Free French, or Portuguese territory in the Pacific area (tr. 14435–14436).

After the meeting at the State Department, Secretary Stimson went to his home for lunch (tr. 14428). Secretary Knox returned to the Navy Department. Both his aide, Admiral Beatty, and his confidential assistant, Major Dillon, testified that he arrived there from the State Department probably about 11:30 o'clock, possibly a little later (tr. 10239, 10253, 10260). Secretary Hull remained at the State Department. At about noon, the Japanese Embassy telephoned the State Department and asked for an appointment for Ambassador Nomura with Secretary Hull at 1 p. m. that afternoon. Somewhat later the Embassy telephoned again and requested that the appointment be postponed to 1:45 p. m., as Ambassador Nomura was not quite ready (ex. 29, vol. II, p. 786).

That morning the First Secretary of the British Embassy in Washington, Mr. W. G. Hayter, called at the State Department on an official of the Far Eastern Division. In response to an inquiry whether there was any news, Mr. Hayter is reported to have said—

after some hesitation, that the British Minister in Thailand had sent a message to the (British) Foreign Office, which began "For God's sake" and which was endorsed by the Thai Foreign Minister requesting that British armed forces *not* move into Thailand" (ex. 169, item 34). [Italics in original.]

At 1:50 o'clock that afternoon the Navy Department received the following dispatch from Admiral Husband E. Kimmel, commander in chief of the United States Pacific Fleet at Pearl Harbor, T. H.:

Air raid on Pearl Harbor. This is not drill (tr. 14204).

When this message was brought to Secretary Knox, he was talking with Admiral Stark and Admiral Turner, in Major Dillon's office, who testified that after reading the message, the Secretary exclaimed: "My God, this can't be true, this must mean the Philippines" (tr. 10262).

Secretary Stimson recorded in his notes for that day that—

just about 2 o'clock, while I was sitting at lunch, the President called me up on the telephone and in a rather excited voice asked me, "Have you heard the news?" I said, "Well, I have heard the telegrams which have come in about the Japanese advances in the Gulf of Siam." He said, "Oh no, I don't mean that. They have attacked Hawaii. They are now bombing Hawaii." Well, that was an excitement indeed (tr. 14428–14429).

Secretary Hull testified that President Roosevelt telephoned him before the Japanese Ambassadors reached the State Department and told him "There was a report that Pearl Harbor had been attacked" [1] (tr. 1594). He continued:

I discussed before they came whether I would accredit that report as the unquestioned truth of the situation and refuse to admit them or whether in view of the extremely delicate relations I would leave open the one chance in ten or more that the report was not correct. I proceeded to receive and confer with them although I felt that the chances were altogether virtually certain that the report was true (tr. 1594).

The Japanese Ambassadors arrived at the State Department at 2:05 p. m., but were not admitted to Secretary Hull's office until 2:20 p. m. (ex. 29, vol. II, p. 786). According to the official State Department record of the meeting Ambassador Nomura stated—

that he had been instructed to deliver at 1:00 p. m. the document which he handed the Secretary, but that he was sorry that he had been delayed owing to the need of more time to decode the message. The Secretary asked why he had specified one o'clock. The Ambassador replied that he did not know but that that was his instruction.
The Secretary said that anyway he was receiving the message at two o'clock (ex. 29, vol. II, pp. 786–787).

The document Ambassador Nomura handed Secretary Hull was the full text of the memorandum contained in the 14-part message that had been before the three Secretaries at their conference that morning, the first 13 parts of which had been seen by Secretary Knox and President Roosevelt the evening before. The full message as intercepted before its delivery to Secretary Hull is printed as Annex E attached hereto. Secretary Hull testified that the first few pages defined "the Japanese attitude just the reverse of what it was," as "Peace, peace, peace," and the next few pages defined the American attitude "as just the reverse of what it was" (tr. 1594). The final paragraph, which had been contained in the fourteenth part of the intercepted message and had not been seen by either the President or any of the three Secretaries before 10 o'clock that morning, was as follows:

7. Obviously it is the intention of the American Government to conspire with Great Britain and other countries to obstruct Japan's efforts toward the establishment of peace through the creation of a New Order in East Asia, and especially to preserve Anglo-American rights and interests by keeping Japan and China at war. This intention has been revealed clearly during the course of the present negotiations. Thus, the earnest hope of the Japanese Government to adjust Japanese-American relations and to preserve and promote the peace of the Pacific through cooperation with the American Government has finally been lost.
The Japanese Government regrets to have to notify hereby the American Government that in view of the attitude of the American Government it cannot but consider that it is impossible to reach an agreement through further negotiations (ex. 1, p. 245; ex. 29, vol. II, p. 792).

Secretary Hull testified that at the time he—

felt and knew of the extreme probability that the Pearl Harbor report was true. I felt like taking liberties in talking to them about their government in what would not be diplomatic language in ordinary times (tr. 1595).

Secretary Hull interrupted his reading of the memorandum to ask Ambassador Nomura whether the memorandum was presented under

---

[1] Under Secretary Welles also testified that he first learned of the attack through a telephone call from President Roosevelt (tr. 1322; 1362–1373).

instructions from the Japanese Government. The Ambassador replied that it was. When he finished reading, Secretary Hull turned to the Japanese Ambassador and said:

I must say that in all my conversations with you during the last nine months I have never uttered one word of untruth. This is borne out absolutely by the record. In all my fifty years of public service I have never seen a document that was more crowded with infamous falsehoods and distortions—infamous falsehoods and distortions on a scale so huge that I never imagined until today that any Government on this planet was capable of uttering them (ex. 29, vol. II, p. 787).

According to the official State Department records of the meeting the two Japanese Ambassadors "then took their leave without making any comment" (ex. 29, vol. II, p. 787).

Later that afternoon, Secretary Hull issued the following statement:

Japan has made a treacherous and utterly unprovoked attack upon the United States.

At the very moment when representatives of the Japanese Government were discussing with representatives of this Government, at the request of the former, principles and courses of peace, the armed forces of Japan were preparing and assembling at various strategic points to launch new attacks and new aggressions upon nations and peoples with which Japan was professedly at peace including the United States.

I am now releasing for the information of the American people the statement of principles governing the policies of the Government of the United States and setting out suggestions for a comprehensive peaceful settlement covering the entire Pacific area, which I handed to the Japanese Ambassador on November 26, 1941.

I am likewise releasing the text of a Japanese reply thereto which was handed to me by the Japanese Ambassador today. Before the Japanese Ambassador delivered this final statement from his Government the treacherous attack upon the United States had taken place.

This Government has stood for all the principles that underlie fair dealing, peace, law and order, and justice between nations and has steadfastly striven to promote and maintain that state of relations between itself and all other nations.

It is now apparent to the whole world that Japan in its recent professions of a desire for peace has been infamously false and fraudulent (ex. 29, vol. II, p. 793).

The surprise Japanese attack on Pearl Harbor had begun at 1:25 o'clock that Sunday afternoon (Washington time). It was followed almost immediately by a Japanese attack upon Thailand at various places on its land and sea frontiers. Five and half hours after the attack on Thailand commenced the Thai Government gave the order to cease fire (ex. 169). At 3 p. m. on December 7 (Washington time) the first Japanese attacks on Singapore were made; at 3:40 p. m. (Washington time) the Japanese attacked Khota Baru in British Malaya; at 6:10 p. m. (Washington time) they attacked the Gulf of Davao in the Philippine Islands and the Island of Guam (tr. 14127).

In Tokyo, in the meantime, after receiving from Ambassador Grew a copy of President Roosevelt's message to Emperor Hirohito, Foreign Minister Togo had gone to Premier Tojo's official residence with a summary translation of the President's message, and there, at an emergency conference with the Premier and the other members of the Cabinet, had determined the line of action to be taken (ex. 132, item 1, p. 2). At 7 a. m., December 8 (Japan time) Ambassador Grew was awakened by a telephone call from an official of the Japanese Foreign Office who requested him to call on Foreign Minister Togo as soon as possible (ex. 30, p. 493). When Ambassador Grew arrived, Foreign Minister Togo, "grim and formal," handed him the Japanese Government's memorandum breaking off the negotiations. The Foreign Minister said that he had been in touch with Emperor Hirohito, who desired that the memorandum be regarded as his reply to President Roosevelt's message. Ambassador Grew reported to the State Department that the Foreign Minister thereupon made to him the following oral statement:

His Majesty has expressed his gratefulness and appreciation for the cordial message of the President. He has graciously let known his wishes to the Foreign Minister to convey the following to the President as a reply to the latter's message:

"Some days ago, the President made inquiries regarding the circumstances of the augmentation of Japanese forces in French Indochina to which His Majesty has directed the Government to reply. Withdrawal of Japanese forces from French Indochina constitutes one of the subject matters of the Japanese-American negotiations. His Majesty has commanded the Government to state its views to the American Government also on this question. It is, therefore, desired that the President will kindly refer to this reply.

"Establishment of peace in the Pacific, and consequently of the world, has been the cherished desire of His Majesty for the realization of which he has hitherto made his Government to continue its earnest endeavors. His Majesty trusts that the President is fully aware of this fact" (ex. 178).

Following his conference with Ambassador Grew, Foreign Minister Togo arranged a conference with the British Ambassador, Sir Robert Craigie. Upon his arrival, the Foreign Minister informed the British Ambassador that it had become necessary to break off the Japanese-American negotiations, and handed him a copy of the memorandum he had previously given to Ambassador Grew (ex. 132, item 2).

While Foreign Minister Togo was holding his conferences with the American and British Ambassadors, a meeting of the Committee of Advisement of the Privy Council, attended by all of the other members of the Japanese Cabinet and certain other Japanese governmental officials, was in progress in the Imperial Palace. At this meeting the committee considered and approved an Address of Advisement to the Throne and a draft of an Imperial Rescript declaring war against the United States and Great Britain. One of the officials present at the meeting asked Premier Tojo what Germany's attitude would be. Premier Tojo replied that "Germany's entrance in the war in our support is almost certain, and negotiations to that effect are now in progress" (ex. 132, item 3). Following the meeting of the Committee of Advisement, a full session of the Privy Council in the presence of Emperor Hirohito, was held in the Imperial Palace. At this meeting the address to the Throne was presented and unanimously approved. Later that morning, Ambassador Grew received the following communication:

EXCELLENCY:

I have the honor to inform Your Excellency that there has arisen a state of war between Your Excellency's country and Japan beginning today.

I avail myself of this opportunity to renew to Your Excellency the assurances of my highest consideration.

SHIGENORI TOGO,
Minister of Foreign Affairs.
(Ex. 30, p. 499.)

In Washington, Sunday evening, December 7 (Washington time), a meeting of the Cabinet called by President Roosevelt took place in the White House at 8:30 o'clock (tr. 14430). The President opened the meeting by stating that it was the most serious Cabinet meeting that had taken place since 1861, and he then described the Japanese attack at Pearl Harbor so far as it was known at the time. After this the President read a draft of a brief message to Congress which he had prepared. According to Secretary Stimson's notes, the draft presented much the same thoughts as were actually presented the following day to Congress (tr. 14431). The Cabinet meeting lasted over three-quarters of an hour, after which the majority and minority leaders of Congress joined the President and the Cabinet for a meeting which lasted for over 2 hours. At this meeting the President reviewed the events of the preceding weeks and described the events of that Sunday in Washington and at Pearl Harbor. The President asked whether the members of Congress would invite him to appear before a joint session the following day and was told that they would. He said that he could not tell them exactly what he was going to say, because events were changing so rapidly (tr. 14431–14432; ex. 160).

The next day, December 8 (Washington time), shortly after noon, President Roosevelt delivered the following address before a joint session of Congress:

To the Congress of the United States:

Yesterday, December 7, 1941—a date which will live in infamy—the United States of America was suddenly and deliberately attacked by naval and air forces of the Empire of Japan.

The United States was at peace with that Nation and, at the solicitation of Japan, was still in conversation with its Government and its Emperor looking toward the maintenance of peace in the Pacific. Indeed, one hour after Japanese air squadrons had commenced bombing in Oahu, the Japanese Ambassador to the United States and his colleague delivered to the Secretary of State a formal reply to a recent American message. While this reply stated that it seemed useless to continue the existing diplomatic negotiations, it contained no threat or hint of war or armed attack.

It will be recorded that the distance of Hawaii from Japan makes it obvious that the attack was deliberately planned many days or even weeks ago. During the intervening time the Japanese Government has deliberately sought to deceive the United States by false statements and expressions of hope for continued peace.

The attack yesterday on the Hawaiian Islands has caused severe damage to American naval and military forces. Very many American lives have been lost. In addition, American ships have been reported torpedoed on the high seas between San Francisco and Honolulu.

Yesterday the Japanese Government also launched an attack against Malaya.

Last night Japanese forces attacked Hong Kong.

Last night Japanese forces attacked Guam.

Last night Japanese forces attacked the Philippine Islands.

Last night the Japanese attacked Wake Island.

This morning the Japanese attacked Midway Island.

Japan has, therefore, undertaken a surprise offensive extending throughout the Pacific area. The facts of yesterday speak for themselves. The people of the United States have already formed their opinions and well understand the implications to the very life and safety of our Nation.

As Commander-in-Chief of the Army and Navy I have directed that all measures be taken for our defense.

Always will we remember the character of the onslaught against us.

No matter how long it may take us to overcome this premeditated invasion, the American people in their righteous might will win through to absolute victory.

I believe I interpret the will of the Congress and of the people when I assert that we will not only defend ourselves to the uttermost but will make very certain that this form of treachery shall never endanger us again.

Hostilities exist. There is no blinking at the fact that our people, our territory, and our interests are in grave danger.

With confidence in our armed forces—with the unbounded determination of our people—we will gain the inevitable triumph—so help us God.

I ask that the Congress declare that since the unprovoked and dastardly attack by Japan on Sunday, December seventh ,a state of war has existed between the United States and the Japanese Empire (ex. 29, vol. II, pp. 793–794).

Within an hour after President Roosevelt finished his address, the Senate and House of Representatives, acting independently, passed the following resolution, the Senate by a vote of 82 to 0 and the House of Representatives by a vote of 388 to 1:

JOINT RESOLUTION Declaring that a state of war exists between the Imperial Government of Japan and the Government and the people of the United States and making provisions to prosecute the same

Whereas the Imperial Government of Japan has committed unprovoked acts of war against the Government and the people of the United States of America: Therefore be it

Resolved by the Senate and House of Representatives of the United States of America in Congress assembled, That the state of war between the United States and the Imperial Government of Japan which has thus been thrust upon the United States is hereby formally declared; and the President is hereby authorized and directed to employ the entire naval and military forces of the United States and the resources of the Government to carry on war against the Imperial Government of Japan; and, to bring the conflict to a successful termination, all of the resources of the country are hereby pledged by the Congress of the United States (ex. 29, vol. II, p. 795).

The declaration of war against Japan was signed by President Roosevelt at 4:10 p. m. that afternoon, December 8 (Washington time).

*Draft Proposal Handed by Ambassador Nomura to Secretary Hull on
May 12 (Washington time)*

CONFIDENTIAL MEMORANDUM AGREED UPON BETWEEN THE GOVERN-
MENT OF THE UNITED STATES OF AMERICA AND THE GOVERNMENT
OF JAPAN

The Governments of the United States and of Japan accept joint
responsibility for the initiation and conclusion of a general agreement disposing the resumption of our traditional friendly relations.

Without reference to specific causes of recent estrangement, it is
the sincere desire of both Governments that the incidents which led
to the deterioration of amicable sentiment among our peoples should
be prevented from recurrence and corrected in their unforeseen and
unfortunate consequences.

It is our present hope that, by a joint effort, our nations may
establish a just peace in the Pacific; and by the rapid consummation
of an *entente cordiale* [*amicable understanding*], arrest, if not dispel,
the tragic confusion, that now threatens to engulf civilization.

For such decisive action, protracted negotiations would seem ill-
suited and weakening. Both Governments, therefore, desire that
adequate instrumentalities should be developed for the realization
of a general agreement which would bind, meanwhile, both Governments in honor and in act.

It is our belief that such an understanding should comprise only
the pivotal issues of urgency and not the accessory concerns which
could be deliberated at a conference and appropriately confirmed by
our respective Governments.

Both Governments presume to anticipate that they could achieve
harmonious relations if certain situations and attitudes were clarified or improved; to wit:

1. The concepts of the United States and of Japan respecting
   international relations and the character of nations.
2. The attitude of both Governments toward the European War.
3. The relations of both nations toward the China Affair.
4. Commerce between both nations.
5. Economic activity of both nations in the Southwestern
   Pacific area.
6. The policies of both nations affecting political stabilization
   in the Pacific area.

Accordingly, we have come to the following mutual understanding:—

*I. The concepts of the United States and of Japan respecting inter-
national relations and the character of nations.*

The Governments of the United States and of Japan jointly
acknowledge each other as equally sovereign states and contiguous
Pacific powers.

445

Both Governments assert the unanimity of their national policies as directed toward the foundation of a lasting peace and the inauguration of a new era of respectful confidence and cooperation among our peoples.

Both Governments declare that it is their traditional, and present, concept and conviction that nations and races compose, as members of a family, one household; each equally enjoying rights and admitting responsibilities with a mutuality of interests regulated by peaceful processes and directed to the pursuit of their moral and physical welfare, which they are bound to defend for themselves as they are bound not to destroy for others; they further admit their responsibilities to oppose the oppression or exploitation of backward nations.

Both Governments are firmly determined that their respective traditional concepts on the character of nations and the underlying moral principles of social order and national life will continue to be preserved and never transformed by foreign ideas or ideologies contrary to these moral principles and concepts.

II. The attitude of both Governments toward the European War.

The Governments of the United States and Japan make it their common aim to bring about the world peace; they shall therefore jointly endeavour not only to prevent further extension of the European War but also speedily to restore peace in Europe.

The Government of Japan maintains that its alliance with the Axis Powers was, and is, defensive and designed to prevent the nations which are not at present directly affected by the European War from engaging in it.

The Government of Japan maintains that its obligations of military assistance under the Tripartite Pact between Japan, Germany and Italy will be applied in accordance with the stipulation of Article 3 of the said Pact.

The Government of the United States maintains that its attitude toward the European War is, and will continue to be, directed by no such aggressive measures as to assist any one nation against another. The United States maintains that it is pledged to the hate of war, and accordingly, its attitude toward the European War is, and will continue to be, determined solely and exclusively by considerations of the protective defense of its own national welfare and security.

III. The relations of both nations toward the China Affair.

The Government of the United States, acknowledging the three principles as enunciated in the Konoe Statement and the principles set forth on the basis of the said three principles in the treaty with the Nanking Government as well as in the Joint Declaration of Japan, Manchoukuo and China and relying upon the policy of the Japanese Government to establish a relationship of neighborly friendship with China, shall forthwith request the Chiang Kai-shek regime to negotiate peace with Japan.

IV. Commerce between both nations.

When official approbation to the present Understanding has been given by both Governments, the United States and Japan shall assure each other to mutually supply such commodities as are, respectively, available or required by either of them. Both Governments further consent to take necessary steps to the resumption of normal trade relations as formerly established under the Treaty of Commerce and Navigation between the United States and Japan.

V. Economic activity of both nations in the Southwestern Pacific area.

Having in view that the Japanese expansion in the direction of the Southwestern Pacific area is declared to be of peaceful nature, American cooperation shall be given in the production and procurement of natural resources (such as oil, rubber, tin, nickel) which Japan needs.

VI. The policies of both nations affecting political stabilization in the Pacific area.

a. The Governments of the United States and Japan jointly guarantee the independence of the Philippine Islands on the condition that the Philippine Islands shall maintain a status of permanent neutrality. The Japanese subjects shall not be subject to any discriminatory treatment.

b. Japanese immigration to the United States shall receive amicable consideration—on a basis of equality with other nationals and freedom from discrimination.

Addendum.

The present Understanding shall be kept a confidential memorandum between the Governments of the United States and of Japan.

The scope, character and timing of the announcement of this Understanding will be agreed upon by both Governments.

ORAL EXPLANATION FOR PROPOSED AMENDMENTS TO THE ORIGINAL DRAFT

II. Par. 2.

Attitude of Both Governments toward the European War.

Actually the meaning of this paragraph is virtually unchanged but we desire to make it clearer by specifying a reference to the Pact. As long as Japan is a member of the Tripartite Pact, such stipulation as is mentioned in the Understanding seems unnecessary.

If we must have any stipulation at all, in addition, it would be important to have one which would clarify the relationship of this Understanding to the aforementioned Pact.

III.

China Affair.

The terms for China-Japan peace as proposed in the original Understanding differ in no substantial way from those herein affirmed as the "principles of Konoe." Practically, the one can be used to explain the other.

We should obtain an understanding, in a separate and secret document, that the United States would discontinue her assistance to the Chiang Kai-shek regime if Chiang Kai-shek does not accept the advice of the United States that he enter into negotiations for peace.

If, for any reason, the United States finds it impossible to sign such a document, a definite pledge by some highest authorities will suffice.

The three principles of Prince Konoe as referred to in this paragraph are:

1. Neighborly friendship;
2. Joint defense against communism;

3. Economic cooperation—by which Japan does not intend to exercise economic monopoly in China nor to demand of China a limitation in the interests of Third Powers.

The following are implied in the aforesaid principles:

1. Mutual respect of sovereignty and territories;
2. Mutual respect for the inherent characteristics of each nation cooperating as good neighbors and forming a Far Eastern nucleus contributing to world peace;
3. Withdrawal of Japanese troops from Chinese territory in accordance with an agreement to be concluded between Japan and China;
4. No annexation, no indemnities;
5. Independence of Manchoukuo.

III.

Immigration to China.

The stipulation regarding large-scale immigration to China has been deleted because it might give an impression, maybe a mistaken impression, to the Japanese people who have been offended by the past immigration legislation of the United States, that America is now taking a dictating attitude even toward the question of Japanese immigration in China.

Actually, the true meaning and purpose of this stipulation is fully understood and accepted by the Japanese Government.

IV.

Naval, Aerial and Mercantile Marine Relations.

(a) and (c) of this section have been deleted not because of disagreement but because it would be more practical, and possible, to determine the disposition of naval forces and mercantile marine after an understanding has been reached and relations between our two countries improved; and after our present China commitments are eliminated. Then we will know the actual situation and can act accordingly.

Courtesy visit of naval squadrons.

This proposal, (b) of IV might better be made a subject of a separate memorandum. Particular care must be taken as to the timing, manner and scope of carrying out such a gesture.

V.

Gold Credit.

The proposal in the second paragraph of V has been omitted for the same reasons as suggested the omission of paragraphs (a) and (c).

VI.

Activity in Southwestern Pacific Area.

The words, in the first paragraph, "without resorting to arms" have been deleted as inappropriate and unnecessarily critical. Actually, the peaceful policy of the Japanese Government has been made clear on many occasions in various statements made both by the Premier and the Foreign Minister.

VIII. [*VII.*]
Political Stabilization in the Pacific Area.

As the paragraph (*a*) implying military and treaty obligation would require, for its enactment, such a complicated legislative procedure in both countries, we consider it inappropriate to include this in the present Understanding.

Paragraph (*b*) regarding the independence of the Philippine Islands has been altered for the same reason.

In paragraph (*c*) [(*d*)] the words "and to the Southwestern Pacific Area" have been omitted because such questions should be settled, as necessity arises, through direct negotiation with the authorities in the Southwestern areas by the Government of the United States and of Japan respectively.

Conference.

The stipulation for holding a Conference has been deleted. We consider that it would be better to arrange, by an exchange of letters, that a conference between the President and the Premier or between suitable representatives of theirs will be considered when both the United States and Japan deem it useful to hold such a conference after taking into due consideration the effect resulting from the present Understanding.

Announcement.

In regard to the statement to be issued on the successful conclusion of the present Understanding a draft will be prepared in Tokio and cabled to Washington for the consideration of the United States Government.

(Ex. 29, Vol. II, pp. 420–425.)

Draft Proposal Handed by Secretary Hull to Ambassador Nomura on
June 21 (Washington time)

Unofficial, Exploratory   [WASHINGTON,] June 21, 1941.
and Without Commitment

The Governments of the United States and of Japan accept joint responsibility for the initiation and conclusion of a general agreement of understanding as expressed in a joint declaration for the resumption of traditional friendly relations.

Without reference to specific causes of recent estrangement, it is the sincere desire of both Governments that the incidents which led to the deterioration of amicable sentiment between their countries should be prevented from recurrence and corrected in their unforeseen and unfortunate consequences.

It is our earnest hope that, by a cooperative effort, the United States and Japan may contribute effectively toward the establishment and preservation of peace in the Pacific area and, by the rapid consumation of an amicable understanding, encourage world peace and arrest, if not dispel, the tragic confusion that now threatens to engulf civilization.

For such decisive action, protracted negotiations would seem ill-suited and weakening. Both Governments, therefore, desire that adequate instrumentalities should be developed for the realization of a general understanding which would bind, meanwhile, both Governments in honor and in act.

It is the belief of the two Governments that such an understanding should comprise only the pivotal issues of urgency and not the accessory concerns which could be deliberated later at a conference.

Both Governments presume to anticipate that they could achieve harmonious relations if certain situations and attitudes were clarified or improved; to wit:

1. The concepts of the United States and of Japan respecting international relations and the character of nations.

2. The attitudes of both Governments toward the European war.

3. Action toward a peaceful settlement between China and Japan.

4. Commerce between both nations.

5. Economic activity of both nations in the Pacific area.

6. The policies of both nations affecting political stabilization in the Pacific area.

7. Neutralization of the Philippine Islands.

Accordingly, the Government of the United States and the Government of Japan have come to the following mutual understanding and declaration of policy:

I. The concepts of the United States and of Japan respecting international relations and the character of nations.

Both governments affirm that their national policies are directed toward the foundation of a lasting peace and the inauguration of a new era of reciprocal confidence and cooperation between our peoples.

Both Governments declare that it is their traditional, and present concept and conviction that nations and races compose, as members of a family, one household living under the ideal of universal concord through justice and equity; each equally enjoying rights and admitting responsibilities with a mutuality of interests regulated by peaceful processes and directed to the pursuit of their moral and physical welfare, which they are bound to defend for themselves as they are bound not to destroy for others; they further admit their responsibilities to oppose the oppression or exploitation of other peoples.

Both Governments are firmly determined that their respective traditional concepts on the character of nations and the underlying-moral principles of social order and national life will continue to be preserved and never transformed by foreign ideas or ideologies contrary to those moral principles and concepts.

II. The attitudes of both Governments toward the European war.

The Government of Japan maintains that the purpose of the Tripartite Pact was, and is, defensive and is designed to contribute to the prevention of an unprovoked extension of the European war.

The Government of the United States maintains that its attitude toward the European hostilities is and will continue to be determined solely and exclusively by considerations of protection and self-defense: its national security and the defense thereof.

> NOTE (There is appended a suggested draft of an exchange of letters as a substitute for the Annex and Supplement on the Part of the Government of the United States on this subject which constituted a part of the United States draft of May 31, 1941.

III. Action toward a peaceful settlement between China and Japan.

The Japanese Government having communicated to the Government of the United States the general terms within the framework of which the Japanese Government will propose the negotiation of a peaceful settlement with the Chinese Government, which terms are declared by the Japanese Government to be in harmony with the Konoe principles regarding neighborly friendship and mutual respect of sovereignty and territories and with the practical application of those principles, the President of the United States will suggest to the Government of China that the Government of China and the Government of Japan enter into a negotiation on a basis mutually advantageous and acceptable for a termination of hostilities and resumption of peaceful relations.

> NOTE (The foregoing draft of Section III is subject to further discussion of the question of cooperative defense against communistic activities, including the stationing of Japanese troops in Chinese territory, and the question of economic cooperation between China and Japan. With regard to suggestions that the language of Section III be changed, it is believed that consideration of any suggested change can most advantageously be given

after all the points in the annex relating to this section have been satisfactorily worked out, when the section and its annex can be viewed as a whole.)

IV. *Commerce between both nations.*

When official approbation to the present understanding has been given by both Governments, the United States and Japan shall assure each other mutually to supply such commodities as are, respectively, available and required by either of them. Both Governments further consent to take necessary steps to resume normal trade relations as formerly established under the Treaty of Commerce and Navigation between the United States and Japan. If a new commercial treaty is desired by both Governments, it would be negotiated as soon as possible and be concluded in accordance with usual procedures.

V. *Economic activity of both nations in the Pacific area.*

On the basis of mutual pledges hereby given that Japanese activity and American activity in the Pacific area shall be carried on by peaceful means and in conformity with the principle of non-discrimination in international commercial relations, the Japanese Government and the Government of the United States agree to cooperate each with the other toward obtaining non-discriminatory access by Japan and by the United States to commercial supplies of natural resources (such as oil, rubber, tin, nickel) which each country needs for the safeguarding and development of its own economy.

VI. *The policies of both nations affecting political stabilization in the Pacific area.*

Both Governments declare that the controlling policy underlying this understanding is peace in the Pacific area; that it is their fundamental purpose, through cooperative effort, to contribute to the maintenance and the preservation of peace in the Pacific area; and that neither has territorial designs in the area mentioned.

VII. *Neutralization of the Philippine Islands.*

The Government of Japan declares its willingness to enter at such time as the Government of the United States may desire into negotiation with the Government of the United States with a view to the conclusion of a treaty for the neutralization of the Philippine Islands, when Philippine independence shall have been achieved.

[Annex 1 to Annex B]

ANNEX AND SUPPLEMENT ON THE PART OF THE JAPANESE GOVERNMENT

III. *Action toward a peaceful settlement between China and Japan.*

The basic terms as referred to in the above section are as follows:
1. Neighborly friendship.
2. (Cooperative defense against injurious communistic activities— including the stationing of Japanese troops in Chinese territory.) Subject to further discussion.
3. (Economic cooperation.) Subject to agreement on an exchange of letters in regard to the application to this point of the principle of non-discrimination in international commercial relations.
4. Mutual respect of sovereignty and territories.

5. Mutual respect for the inherent characteristics of each nation cooperating as good neighbors and forming an East Asian nucleus contributing to world peace.

6. Withdrawal of Japanese armed forces from Chinese territory as promptly as possible and in accordance with an agreement to be concluded between Japan and China.

7. No annexation.

8. No indemnities.

9. Amicable negotiation in regard to Manchoukuo.

[Annex 2 to Annex B]

ANNEX AND SUPPLEMENT ON THE PART OF THE GOVERNMENT OF THE UNITED STATES

IV. Commerce between both nations.

It is understood that during the present international emergency Japan and the United States each shall permit export to the other of commodities in amounts up to the figures of usual or pre-war trade, except, in the case of each, commodities which it needs for its own purposes of security and self-defense. These limitations are mentioned to clarify the obligations of each Government. They are not intended as restrictions against either Government; and, it is understood, both Governments will apply such regulations in the spirit dominating relations with friendly nations.

[Annex 3 to Annex B]

SUGGESTED EXCHANGE OF LETTERS BETWEEN THE SECRETARY OF STATE AND THE JAPANESE AMBASSADOR

The Secretary of State to the Japanese Ambassador:

EXCELLENCY: In Section II of the Joint Declaration which was entered into today on behalf of our two Governments, statements are made with regard to the attitudes of the two Governments toward the European war. During the informal conversations which resulted in the conclusion of this Joint Declaration I explained to you on a number of occasions the attitude and policy of the Government of the United States toward the hostilities in Europe and I pointed out that this attitude and policy were based on the inalienable right of self-defense. I called special attention to an address which I delivered on April 24 setting forth fully the position of this Government upon this subject.

I am sure that you are fully cognizant of this Government's attitude toward the European war but in order that there may be no misunderstanding I am again referring to the subject. I shall be glad to receive from you confirmation by the Government of Japan that, with regard to the measures which this nation may be forced to adopt in defense of its own security, which have been set forth as indicated, the Government of Japan is not under any commitment which would require Japan to take any action contrary to or destructive of the fundamental objective of the present agreement, to establish and to preserve peace in the Pacific area.

Accept, Excellency, the renewed assurances of my highest consideration.

The Japanese Ambassador to the Secretary of State:

EXCELLENCY: I have received your letter of June—.

I wish to state that my Government is fully aware of the attitude of the Government of the United States toward the hostilities in Europe as explained to me by you during our recent conversations and as set forth in your address of April 24. I did not fail to report to my Government the policy of the Government of the United States as it had been explained to me, and I may assure you that my Government understands and appreciates the attitude and position of the Government of the United States with regard to the European war.

I wish also to assure you that the Government of Japan, with regard to the measures which the Government of the United States may be forced to adopt in defense of its own security, is not under any commitment requiring Japan to take any action contrary to or destructive of the fundamental objective of the present agreement.

The Government of Japan, fully cognizant of its responsibilities freely assumed by the conclusion of this agreement, is determined to take no action inimical to the establishment and preservation of peace in the Pacific area.

Accept, Excellency, the assurances of my most distinguished consideration.

[Annex 4 to Annex B]

SUGGESTED LETTER TO BE ADDRESSED BY THE SECRETARY OF STATE TO THE JAPANESE AMBASSADOR IN CONNECTION WITH THE JOINT DECLARATION

EXCELLENCY: In the informal conversations which resulted in the conclusion of a general agreement of understanding between our two Governments, you and your associates expressed fully and frankly views on the intentions of the Japanese Government in regard to applying to Japan's proposed economic cooperation with China the principle of non-discrimination in international commercial relations. It is believed that it would be helpful if you could be so good as to confirm the statements already expressed orally in the form of replies on the following points:

1. Does the term "economic cooperation" between Japan and China contemplate the granting by the Government of China to the Japanese Government or its nationals of any preferential or monopolistic rights which would discriminate in favor of the Japanese Government and Japanese nationals as compared with the Government and nationals of the United States and of other third countries? Is it contemplated that upon the inauguration of negotiations for a peaceful settlement between Japan and China the special Japanese companies, such as the North China Development Company and the Central China Promotion Company and their subsidiaries, will be divested, in so far as Japanese official support may be involved, of any monopolistic or other preferential rights that they may exercise in fact or that may inure to them by virtue of present circumstances in areas of China under Japanese military occupation?

2. With regard to existing restrictions upon freedom of trade and travel by nationals of third countries in Chinese territory

under Japanese military occupation, could the Japanese Government indicate approximately what restrictions will be removed immediately upon the entering into by the Government of Chungking of negotiations with the Government of Japan and what restrictions will be removed at later dates, with an indication in each case in so far as possible of the approximate time within which removal of restrictions would be effected?

3. Is it the intention of the Japanese Government that the Chinese Government shall exercise full and complete control of matters relating to trade, currency and exchange? Is it the intention of the Japanese Government to withdraw and to redeem the Japanese military notes which are being circulated in China and the notes of Japanese-sponsored regimes in China? Can the Japanese Government indicate how soon after the inauguration of the contemplated negotiations arrangements to the above ends can in its opinion be carried out?

It would be appreciated if as specific replies as possible could be made to the questions above listed.

Accept, Excellency, the renewed assurances of my highest consideration.

(Ex. 29, Vol. II, pp. 486–492.)

ANNEX C

Text of Basic Japanese Terms of Peace With China

1. Neighborly friendship.
2. Respect for sovereignty and territorial integrity.
3. Cooperative defense between Japan and China.

Cooperation between Japan and China for the purposes of preventing communistic and other subversive activities which may constitute a menace to the security of both countries and of maintaining the public order in China.

Stationing of Japanese troops and naval forces in certain areas in the Chinese territory for a necessary period for the purposes referred to above and in accordance with the existing agreements and usages.

4. Withdrawal of Japanese armed forces.

The Japanese armed forces which have been dispatched to China for carrying out the China Affairs will be withdrawn from China upon the settlement of the said Affairs, excepting those troops which come under point 3.

5. Economic cooperation.

(a) There shall be economic cooperation between Japan and China, having the development and utilization of essential materials for national defense in China as its principal objective.

(b) The preceding paragraph does not mean to restrict any economic activities by third Powers in China so long as they are pursued on an equitable basis.

6. Fusion of the Chiang Kai-shek regime and the Wang Ching-wei Government.
7. No annexation.
8. No indemnities.
9. Recognition of Manchoukuo.

(Ex. 29, Vol. II, p. 633)

456

Japanese Proposals Submitted to Secretary Hull on September 27
(Washington time)

The Governments of Japan and of the United States accept joint responsibility for the initiation and conclusion of a general agreement of understanding as expressed in a joint declaration for the resumption of traditional friendly relations.

Without reference to specific causes of recent estrangement, it is the sincere desire of both Governments that the incidents which led to the deterioration of the amicable sentiment between their countries should be prevented from recurrence and corrected in their unforeseen and unfortunate consequences.

It is the earnest hope of both Governments that, by a cooperative effort, Japan and the United States may contribute effectively toward the establishment and preservation of peace in the Pacific area and, by the rapid consummation of an amicable understanding, encourage world peace and arrest, if not dispel, the tragic confusion that now threatens to engulf civilization.

For such decisive action, protracted negotiations would seem ill-suited and weakening. Both Governments, therefore, desire that adequate instrumentalities should be developed for the realization of a general understanding which would bind, meanwhile, both Governments in honor and in act.

It is the belief of both Governments that such an understanding should comprise only the pivotal issues of urgency and not the accessory concerns which could be deliberated later at a conference.

Both Governments presume to anticipate that they could achieve harmonious relations if certain situations and attitudes were clarified or improved; to wit:

1. The concepts of Japan and of the United States respecting international relations and the character of nations.

2. The attitudes of both Governments toward the European War.

3. Action toward a peaceful settlement between Japan and China.

4. Commerce between both nations.

5. Economic problems in the Southwestern Pacific area.

6. The policies of both nations affecting political stabilization in the Pacific area.

Accordingly, the Government of Japan and the Government of the United States have come to the following mutual understanding and declaration of policy:

I. The concepts of Japan and of the United States respecting international relations and the character of nations.

Both Governments affirm that their national policies are directed toward the foundation of a lasting peace and the inauguration of a

457

new era of reciprocal confidence and cooperation between the peoples of both countries.

Both Governments declare that it is their traditional, and present, concept and conviction that nations and races compose, as members of a family, one household living under the ideal of universal concord through justice and equity; each equally enjoying rights and admitting responsibilities with a mutuality of interests regulated by peaceful processes and directed to the pursuit of their moral and physical welfare, which they are bound to defend for themselves as they are bound not to destroy for others; they further admit their responsibilities to oppose the oppression or exploitation of other peoples.

Both Governments are firmly determined that their respective traditional concepts on the character of nations and the underlying moral principles of social order and national life will continue to be preserved and never transformed by foreign ideas or ideologies contrary to those moral principles and concepts.

II. The attitudes of both Governments toward the European War.

Both Governments maintain it their common aim to bring about peace in the world, and, when an opportune time arrives, they will endeavor jointly for the early restoration of world peace.

With regard to developments of the situation prior to the restoration of world peace, both Governments will be guided in their conduct by considerations of protection and self-defense; and, in case the United States should participate in the European War, Japan would decide entirely independently in the matter of interpretation of the Tripartite Pact between Japan, Germany and Italy, and would likewise determine what actions might be taken by way of fulfilling the obligations in accordance with the said interpretation.

III. Action toward a peaceful settlement between Japan and China.

Both Governments, taking cognizance of the fact that the settlement of the China Affair has a vital bearing upon the peace of the entire Pacific area and consequently upon that of the world, will endeavor to expedite a rapid realization of the settlement of the said Affair.

The Government of the United States, recognizing the effort and the sincere desire on the part of the Japanese Government concerning the peaceful settlement of the China Affair, will, with the intention of facilitating the realization of the settlement, render its good offices in order that the Chungking Government may promptly enter into negotiations with the Government of Japan for a termination of hostilities and a resumption of peaceful relations, and will refrain from resorting to any measures and actions which might hamper the measures and efforts of the Government of Japan directed toward the settlement of the China Affair.

The Government of Japan maintains that the basic general terms of peace for the settlement of the China Affair will be in harmony with the principles embodied in the Konoye statement, and those agreements between Japan and China and those matters which have been put into effect in accordance with the said statement; that the economic cooperation between Japan and China will be carried on by peaceful means and in conformity with the principle of non-discrimination in the international commercial relations and also with the principle of especially close relationship which is natural between neighboring countries; and that the economic activities of third Powers in China will not be excluded so long as they are pursued on an equitable basis.

NOTE: There is appended a draft of the basic terms of peace between Japan and China.

IV. Commerce between Japan and the United States.

Both Governments agree to take without delay measures necessary for resuming normal trade relations between the two countries.

Both Governments guarantee each other that they will, as the first of the measures envisaged in the preceding paragraph, discontinue immediately the measures of freezing assets now being enforced, and that they will supply mutually such commodities as are, respectively, available and required by either of them.

V. Economic problems in the Southwestern Pacific area.

Both Governments mutually pledge themselves that the economic activities of Japan and the United States in the Southwestern Pacific area shall be carried on by peaceful means and in conformity with the principle of non-discrimination in the international commercial relations in pursuance of the policy stated in the preceding paragraph, both Governments agree to cooperate each with the other towards the creation of conditions of international trade and international investment under which both countries will have a reasonable opportunity to secure through the trade process the means of acquiring those goods and commodities which each country needs for the safeguarding and development of its own economy.

Both Governments will amicably cooperate for the conclusion and execution of agreements with the Powers concerned in regard to the production and supply, on the basis of non-discrimination, of such specific commodities as oil, rubber, nickel, and tin.

VI. The policies of both nations affecting political stabilization in the Pacific area.

Both Governments, taking cognizance of the fact that it is a matter of vital importance to stabilize promptly the situation in the Southwestern Pacific area, undertake not to resort to any measures and actions which may jeopardize such stabilization. The Government of Japan will not make any armed advancement, using French Indo-China as a base, to any adjacent area thereof (excluding China), and, upon the establishment of an equitable peace in the Pacific area, will withdraw its troops which are now stationed in French Indo-China.

The Government of the United States will alleviate its military measures in the Southwestern Pacific area.

Both Governments declare that they respect the sovereignty and territorial integrity of Thailand and Netherland East Indies, and that they are prepared to conclude an agreement concerning the neutralization of the Philippine Islands when its independence will have been achieved.

The Government of the United States guarantees non-discriminatory treatment of the Japanese nationals in the Philippine Islands.

[Here follows text of basic terms of peace between Japan and China set forth in Annex C above.]

(Ex. 29, Vol. II, pp. 637–640.)

(TEXT OF JAPANESE GOVERNMENT'S REPLY TO UNITED STATES NOTE OF NOVEMBER 26, 1941, AS INTERCEPTED AND DECODED IN WASHINGTON PRIOR TO DELIVERY TO SECRETARY HULL BY THE JAPANESE AMBASSADORS)

(Part 1 of 14)

MEMORANDUM

1. The Government of Japan, prompted by a genuine desire to come to an amicable understanding with the Government of the United States in order that the two countries by their joint efforts may secure the peace of the Pacific area and thereby contribute toward the realization of world peace, has continued negotiations with the utmost sincerity since April last with the Government of the United States regarding the adjustment and advancement of Japanese-American relations and the stabilization of the Pacific area.

The Japanese Government has the honor to state frankly its views, concerning the claims the American Government has persistently maintained as well as the measures the United States and Great Britain have taken toward Japan during these eight months.

2. It is the immutable policy of the Japanese Government to insure the stability of East Asia and to promote world peace, and thereby to enable all nations to find each its proper place in the world.

Ever since the China Affair broke out owing to the failure on the part of China to comprehend Japan's true intentions, the Japanese Government has striven for the restoration of peace and it has consistently exerted its best efforts to prevent the extension of war-like disturbances. It was also to that end that in September last year Japan concluded the Tri Partite Pact with Germany and Italy.

(Part 2 of 14)

However, both the United States and Great Britain have resorted to every possible measure to assist the Chungking regime so as to obstruct the establishment of a general peace between Japan and China, interfering with Japan's constructive endeavours toward the stabilization of East Asia, exerting pressure on The Netherlands East Indies, or menacing French Indo-China, they have attempted to frustrate Japan's aspiration to realize the ideal of common prosperity in cooperation with these regions. Furthermore, when Japan in accordance with its protocol with France took measures of joint defense of French Indo-China, both American and British governments, willfully misinterpreted it as a threat to their own possession and inducing the Netherlands government to follow suit, they enforced the assets freezing order, thus severing economic relations with Japan. While manifesting thus an obviously hostile attitude, these countries have strengthened their military preparations perfecting an encirclement of Japan, and have brought about a situation which endangers the very existence of the empire.

(Part 3 of 14)

Nevertheless, facilitate a speedy settlement, the Premier of Japan proposed, in August last, to meet the President of the United States for a discussion of important problems between the two countries covering the entire Pacific area. However, while accepting in principle the Japanese proposal, insisted that the meeting should take place after an agreement of view had been reached on fundamental —(75 letters garbled)—The Japanese government submitted a proposal based on the formula proposed by the American government, taking fully into consideration past American claims and also incorporating Japanese views. Repeated discussions proved of no avail in producing readily an agreement of view. The present cabinet, therefore, submitted a revised proposal, moderating still further the Japanese claims regarding the principal points of difficulty in the negotiation and endeavoured strenuously to reach a settlement. But the American government, adhering steadfastly to its original proposal, failed to display in the slightest degree a spirit of conciliation. The negotiation made no progress.

(Part 4 of 14)

Thereupon, the Japanese Government, with a view to doing its utmost for averting a crisis in Japanese-American relations, submitted on November 20th still another proposal in order to arrive at an equitable solution of the more essential and urgent questions which, simplifying its previous proposal, stipulated the following points:

(1) The Governments of Japan and the United States undertake not to dispatch armed forces into any of the regions, excepting French Indo-China, in the Southeastern Asia and the Southern Pacific area.

(2) Both Governments shall cooperate with a view to securing the acquisition in the Netherlands East Indies of those goods and commodities of which the two countries are in need.

(3) Both Governments mutually undertake to restore commercial relations to those prevailing prior to the freezing of assets.

The Government of the United States shall supply Japan the required quantity of oil.

(4) The Government of the United States undertakes not to resort to measures and actions prejudicial to the endeavours for the restoration of general peace between Japan and China.

(5) The Japanese Government undertakes to withdraw troops now stationed in French Indo-China upon either the restoration of peace between Japan and China or the establishment of an equitable peace in the Pacific area; and it is prepared to remove the Japanese troops in the southern part of French Indo-China to the northern part upon the conclusion of the present agreement.

(Part 5 of 14)

As regards China, the Japanese Government, while expressing its readiness to accept the offer of the President of the United States to act as "Introducer" of peace between Japan and China as was previously suggested, asked for an undertaking on the part of the United States to do nothing prejudicial to the restoration of Sino-Japanese peace when the two parties have commenced direct negotiations.

The American government not only rejected the above-mentioned new proposal, but made known its intention to continue its aid to Chiang Kai-Shek; and in spite of its suggestion mentioned above, withdrew the offer of the President to act as the so called "Introducer" of peace between Japan and China, pleading that time was not yet ripe for it. Finally, on November 26th, in an attitude to impose upon the Japanese government those principles it has persistently maintained, the American government made a proposal totally ignoring Japanese claims, which is a source of profound regret to the Japanese Government.

(Part 6 of 14)

4. From the beginning of the present negotiation the Japanese Government has always maintained an attitude of fairness and moderation, and did its best to reach a settlement, for which it made all possible concessions often in spite of great difficulties.

As for the China question which constituted an important subject of the negotiation, the Japanese Government showed a most conciliatory attitude.

As for the principle of Non-Discrimination in International Commerce, advocated by the American Government, the Japanese Government expressed its desire to see the said principle applied throughout the world, and declared that along with the actual practice of this principle in the world, the Japanese Government would endeavor to apply the same in the Pacific area, including China, and made it clear that Japan had no intention of excluding from China economic activities of third powers pursued on an equitable basis.

Furthermore, as regards the question of withdrawing troops from French Indo-China, the Japanese government even volunteered, as mentioned above, to carry out an immediate evacuation of troops from Southern French Indo-China as a measure of easing the situation.

(Part 7 of 14)

It is presumed that the spirit of conciliation exhibited to the utmost degree by the Japanese Government in all these matters is fully appreciated by the American government.

On the other hand, the American government, always holding fast to theories in disregard of realities, and refusing to yield an inch on its impractical principles, caused undue delays in the negotiation. It is difficult to understand this attitude of the American government and the Japanese government desires to call the attention of the American government especially to the following points:

1. The American government advocates in the name of world peace those principles favorable to it and urges upon the Japanese government the acceptance thereof. The peace of the world may be brought

about only by discovering a mutually acceptable formula through recognition of the reality of the situation and mutual appreciation of one another's position. An attitude such as ignores realities and imposes one's selfish views upon others will scarcely serve the purpose of facilitating the consummation of negotiations.

(Part 8 of 14)

Of the various principles put forward by the American government as a basis of the Japanese-American agreement, there are some which the Japanese government is ready to accept in principle, but in view of the world's actual conditions, it seems only a Utopian ideal, on the part of the American government, to attempt to force their immediate adoption.

Again, the proposal to conclude a multilateral non-aggression pact between Japan, the United States, Great Britain, China, the Soviet Union, The Netherlands, and Thailand, which is patterned after the old concept of collective security, is far removed from the realities of East Asia.

The American proposal contains a stipulation which states: "Both governments will agree that no agreement, which either has concluded with any third powers, shall be interpreted by it in such a way as to conflict with the fundamental purpose of this agreement, the establishment and preservation of peace throughout the Pacific area." It is presumed that the above provision has been proposed with a view to restrain Japan from fulfilling its obligations under the Tripartite Pact when the United States participates in the war in Europe, and, as such, it cannot be accepted by the Japanese Government.

(Part 9 of 14)

The American Government, obsessed with its own views and opinions, may be said to be scheming for the extension of the war. While it seeks, on the one hand, to secure its rear by stabilizing the Pacific area, it is engaged, on the other hand, in aiding Great Britain and preparing to attack, in the name of self-defense, Germany and Italy, two powers that are striving to establish a new order in Europe. Such a policy is totally at variance with the many principles upon which the American Government proposes to found the stability of the Pacific area through peaceful means.

3. Where as the American Government, under the principles it rigidly upholds, objects to settling international issues through military pressure, it is exercising in conjunction with Great Britain and other nations pressure by economic power. Recourse to such pressure as a means of dealing with international relations should be condemned as it is at times more inhuman than military pressure.

(Part 10 of 14)

4. It is impossible not to reach the conclusion that the American Government desires to maintain and strengthen, in collusion with Great Britain and other powers, its dominant position it has hitherto occupied not only in China but in other areas of East Asia. It is a

fact of history that one countr—(45 letters garbled or missing)—been compelled to observe the status quo under the Anglo-American policy of imperialistic exploitation and to sacrifice the —es to the prosperity of the two nations.   The Japanese Government cannot tolerate the perpetuation of such a situation since it directly runs counter to Japan's fundamental policy to enable all nations to enjoy each its proper place in the world.

(Part 11 of 14)

The stipulation proposed by the American Government relative to French Indo-China is a good exemplification of the above-mentioned American policy.   That the six countries,—Japan, the United States, Great Britain, The Netherlands, China and Thailand,—excepting France, should undertake among themselves to respect the territorial integrity and sovereignty of French Indo-China and equality of treatment in trade and commerce would be tantamount to placing that territory under the joint guarantee of the governments of those six countries.   Apart from the fact that such a proposal totally ignores the position of France, it is unacceptable to the Japanese government in that such an arrangement cannot but be considered as an extension to French Indo-China of a system similar to the n—(50 letters missed)—sible for the present predicament of East Asia.

(Part 12 of 14)

5. All the items demanded of Japan by the American government regarding China such as wholesale evacuation of troops or unconditional application of the principle of Non-Discrimination in International Commerce ignore the actual conditions of China, and are calculated to destroy Japan's position as the stabilizing factor of East Asia.   The attitude of the American government in demanding Japan not to support militarily, politically or economically any regime other than the regime at Chunking, disregarding thereby the existence of the Nanking government, shatters the very basis of the present negotiation.   This demand of the American government falling, as it does, in line with its above-mentioned refusal to cease from aiding the Chunking regime, demonstrates clearly the intention of the American government to obstruct the restoration of normal relations between Japan and China and the return of peace to East Asia.

(Part 13 of 14)

5. In brief, the American proposal contains certain acceptable items such as those concerning commerce, including the conclusion of a trade agreement, mutual removal of the freezing restrictions, and stabilization of the Yen and Dollar exchange, or the abolition of extraterritorial rights in China.   On the other hand, however, the proposal in question ignores Japan's sacrifices in the four years of the China Affair, menaces the empire's existence itself and disparages its honour and prestige.   Therefore, viewed in its entirety, the Japanese government regrets that it cannot accept the proposal as a basis of negotiation.

6. The Japanese government, in its desire for an early conclusion of the negotiation, proposed that simultaneously with the conclusion of the Japanese-American negotiation, agreements be signed, with Great Britain and other interested countries. The proposal was accepted by the American government. However, since the American government has made the proposal of November 26th as a result of frequent consultations with Great Britain, Australia, The Netherlands and Chungking, *ANDND** presumably by catering to the wishes of the Chungking regime on the questions of *CHTUAL YLOKMMTT*** be concluded that all these countries are at one with the United States in ignoring Japan's position.

(Part 14 of 14)

7. Obviously it is the intention of the American Government to conspire with Great Britain and other countries to obstruct Japan's efforts toward the establishment of peace through the creation of a New Order in East Asia, and especially to preserve Anglo-American rights and interests by keeping Japan and China at war. This intention has been revealed clearly during the course of the present negotiations. Thus, the earnest hope of the Japanese Government to adjust Japanese-American relations and to preserve and promote the peace of the Pacific through cooperation with the American Government has finally been lost.

The Japanese Government regrets to have to notify hereby the American Government that in view of the attitude of the American Government it cannot but consider that it is impossible to reach an agreement through further negotiations.

(Ex. 1, pp. 239–245)

Appendix E

THE "WINDS CODE"

468

THE "WINDS CODE"

Establishment and Nature of "Winds Code"

The "Winds code" was established and confirmed by five communications, two of which were processed by the Navy; i. e., Circulars 2353 and 2354, as follows: [1]

From: Tokyo
To: Washington
19 November 1941
Circular #2353
Regarding the broadcast of a special message in an emergency.
In case of emergency (danger of cutting off our diplomatic relations), and the cutting off of international communications, the following warnings will be added in the middle of the daily Japanese-language short-wave news broadcast.
(1) In case of a Japan-U. S. relations in danger: HIGASHI NO KAZEAME.*
(2) Japan-U. S. S. R. relations: KITANOKAZE KUMORI.**
(3) Japan-British relations: NISHI NO KAZE HARE.***
This signal will be given in the middle and at the end as a weather forecast, and each sentence will be repeated twice. When this is heard please destroy all code papers, etc. This is as yet to be a completely secret arrangement.
Forward as urgent intelligence.
25432
JD-1: 6875   (Y) Navy Trans. 11–28–41 (S–TT)

*East wind, rain
**North wind, cloudy
***West wind, clear

From: Tokyo
To: Washington
19 November 1941
Circular #2354
When our diplomatic relations are becoming dangerous, we will add the following at the beginning and end of our general intelligence broadcasts:
(1) If it is Japan-U. S. relations, "HIGASHI".
(2) Japan-Russia relations, "KITA".
(3) Japan-British relations (including Thai, Malaya, and N. E. I.); "NISHI".
The above will be repeated five times and included at beginning and end.
Relay to Rio de Janeiro, Buenos Aires, Mexico City, San Francisco.
25392
JD-1: 6850   (Y) Navy Trans. 11–26–41 (S)

By way of confirming the winds code and reflecting its nature the following dispatch, No. 281430, was received from the Commander in chief of the Asiatic Fleet:[2]

[1] Committee exhibit No. 1, pp. 154, 155.
[2] Id., No. 142.

TOP SECRET

28 NOVEMBER 1941
FROM: CINCAF [3]
ACTION: OPNAV [4]
INFO: COMSIXTEEN CINCPAC COMFOURTEEN [5]
281430
FOLLOWING TOKYO TO NET INTERCEPT TRANSLATION RECEIVED
FROM SINGAPORE X IF DIPLOMATIC RELATIONS ARE ON VERGE
OF BEING SEVERED FOLLOWING WORDS REPEATED FIVE TIMES
AT BEGINNING AND END OF ORDINARY TOKYO NEWS BROAD-
CASTS WILL HAVE SIGNIFICANCE AS FOLLOWS X HIGASHI HIGASHI
JAPANESE AMERICAN X KITA KITA RUSSIA X NISHA NISHI ENG-
LAND INCLUDING OCCUPATION OF THAI OR INVASION OF MALAYA
AND NEI XX ON JAPANESE LANGAUGE FOREIGN NEWS BROAD-
CASTS THE FOLLOWING SENTENCES REPEATED TWICE IN THE
MIDDLE AND TWICE AT THE END OF BROADCASTS WILL BE USED
XX AMERICA HIGASHI NO KAZE KUMORI [6] XX ENGLAND X NISHI
NO KAZE HARE X UNQUOTE X BRITISH AND COMSIXTEEN MON-
ITORING ABOVE BROADCASTS

Two further dispatches relate significantly to the winds code, the
first from Consul General Foote, our senior diplomatic representative
in the Netherlands East Indies, the second from Colonel Thorpe, our
senior Army intelligence officer in Java.[7]

TELEGRAM RECEIVED

BF
This telegram must be
closely paraphrased be-
fore being communicated
to anyone. (SC)

FROM

---------- Batavia
Dated December 4, 1941
Rec'd. 9:19 a. m.

Secretary of State,
　　Washington.
　　　220, December 4, 10 a. m.
War Department at Bandoeng claims intercepted and decoded following from
Ministry Foreign Affairs Tokyo:
"When crisis leading to worst arises following will be broadcast at end weather
reports; one east wind rain war with United States, two north wind cloudy war
with Russia, three west wind clear war with Britain including attack on Thailand
or Malaya and Dutch Indies. If spoken twice burn codes and secret papers."
Same re following Japanese Ambassador Bangkok to Consul General Batavia:
"When threat of crises exists following will be used five times in texts of general
reports and radio broadcasts: one Higashi east America, two Kita north Russia,
three Nishi west Britain with advance into Thailand and attack on Malaya and
Dutch Indies."
Thorpe and Slawson cabled the above to War Department. I attach little or no
importance to it and view it with some suspicion. Such have been common since
1936.
HSM　　　　　　　　　　　　　　　　　　　　　　　　　　　　FOOTE

---

[3] Commander in chief, Asiatic Fleet.
[4] Office of Naval Operations.
[5] Commandant Sixteenth Naval District; commander in chief, Pacific Fleet; commandant, Fourteenth
Naval District.
[6] It is to be noted that, apparently through inadvertence in transmitting the message, the code phrase
referring to Russian has been improperly comingled with that referring to the United States.
[7] See committee exhibit No. 142.

FROM ALUSNA BATAVIA   OPNAV   RRRRR
DATE 5 DEC 1941 [8]
DECODED BY KALAIDJIAN
PARAPHRASED BY PURDY

Ø31Ø3Ø   CRØ222

FROM THORPE FOR MILES WAR DEPT. CODE INTERCEPT: JAPAN WILL NOTIFY HER CONSULS OF WAR DECISION IN HER FOREIGN BROADCASTS AS WEATHER REPORT AT END. EAST WIND RAIN XXXXXX UNITED STATES: NORTH WIND CLOUDY RUSSIA: WEST WIND CLEAR ENGLAND WITH ATTACK ON THAILAND MALAY AND DUTCH EAST INDIES. WILL BE REPEATED TWICE OR MAY USE COMPASS DIRECTIONS ONLY. IN THIS CASE WORDS WILL BE INTRODUCED FIVE TIMES IN GENERAL TEXT.

(Signature illegible)

DISTRIBUTION:
WAR DEPT_____ACTION   FILES: CNO_____ 2ØOP_____ 2ØA_____
RECORD COPY: __2ØC_____X   SHOW OPDO_____

TOP SECRET   SECRET

EFFORTS TO MONITOR

The evidence is undisputed that both services extended themselves in an effort to intercept a message, in execution of the winds code, not only through their own monitoring stations but through facilities of the Federal Communications Commission as well. While only fragmentary evidence of a documentary nature is available to indicate the nature of instructions to monitor for an implementing or execute message, the Federal Communications Commission file is complete and, as indicated, there is no contention that every effort was not made to intercept an execute message.[9]

CONSIDERATIONS BEARING ON THE POSSIBILITY OF A MESSAGE IN EXECUTION OF THE "WINDS CODE" HAVING BEEN RECEIVED PRIOR TO DECEMBER 7, 1941

1. Capt. L. F. Safford in a prepared statement (read before the joint committee) [10] has set forth a positive assertion that a winds execute message was received in the Navy Department *on the morning of December 4, 1941*, and has elaborated on the circumstances which serve, in his opinion, to indicate that a winds execute was dispatched and why such a message would have been dispatched from Tokyo.

Safford asserted that when he first saw the message it had already been translated by Kramer; that Kramer had underscored all three "code phrases" on the original incoming teletype sheet; and that he had written in pencil or colored crayon the free translation: "War with England (including NEI,[11] etc.); war with the U. S.; peace with Russia." Safford has persistently testified that an authentic implementing message was received.

---

[8] It is to be noted that this message bears the date December 5, 1941, whereas the "number group" is 031030, indicating December 3, 1941. From evidence available (see discussion, *infra*) it appears this message was dispatched from Batavia on December 3, 1941, but was not processed in the Navy Department until December 5, 1941, inasmuch as the message was sent "deferred."

[9] See committee record, pp. 9809, 9810.

[10] I d., at pp. 9622–9654.

[11] Netherlands East Indies.

2. Capt. A. D. Kramer testified before the committee that *on the morning of December 5* the GY Watch Officer, thought by him possibly to be Lieutenant Murray, came to the door of his office and showed him a message which he, Kramer, regarded as an implementation of the winds code; that he saw this message only briefly, relying on the evaluation of the GY watch officer as to the authenticity of the message; that he had no recollection of writing on the message but that had he written anything he positively would not have used the word "war"; that he proceeded to Captain Safford's office with the GY watch officer when the message was delivered to Safford; that he never saw the message again.[12]

It should be noted that Kramer testified the message he saw was on a piece of teletype paper torn off from the machine and was not more than a line or two, possibly three lines; that in no case did the message contain some 200 words as alleged by Captain Safford in his statement.[13] Further, that the message he saw referred to only one country, which to the best of his belief was England.[14] This testimony must, of course, be considered along with Kramer's testimony before the Navy Court of Inquiry. When asked what Japanese language words were used in the execute message he saw, he replied:[15] "*Higashi No Kazeame,* I am quite certain. The literal meaning of *Higashi No Kazeame* is East Wind, Rain. That is plain Japanese language. The sense of that, however, meant strained relations or a break in relations, possibly even implying war with a nation to the eastward, the United States."

3. Admiral R. E. Ingersoll testified that during December of 1941 he was Assistant Chief of Naval Operations; that he saw "messages" which were supposed to implement the winds code, they being brought to his office; that he did not recall definitely whether he saw them prior to December 7 or thereafter; that an implementation of the code received prior to December 7, if genuine, would simply have confirmed what had already been dispatched to the Fleet regarding destruction of codes by the Japanese and would have required no action; that he thought the message he saw referred to all three countries; i. e. England, United States, and Russia.[16]

4. Col. Otis K. Sadtler, in charge of the military branch of the Army Signal Corps in December of 1941, testified that about 9 a. m. or shortly thereafter on Friday, December 5, Admiral Noyes telephoned him to the effect that the "message was in" (referring to an implementing winds message); that Noyes told him "it was the word that implied a break in relations between Japan and Great Britain"; that he went to General Miles' office, informing Miles that the "word was in"; that Miles sent for Colonel Bratton and when Bratton came in, he, Sadtler, told Bratton word had been received from Admiral Noyes to the effect that diplomatic relations between Japan and Great Britain were in danger; that Bratton asked him to verify receipt of the message; that he called Admiral Noyes again, asking him to verify the "Japanese word" and Noyes replied that he did not know any Japanese but it was the one that "meant Japan and Great Britain"; that upon reporting this information to General Miles'

12 Committee record, pp. 10481 *et seq.*
13 Id., at p. 10491.
14 Id., at p. 10501.
15 Navy court of inquiry (top secret) record, p. 957.
16 Committee record, pp. 11278 *et seq.*

office he did not thereafter get in touch with Admiral Noyes concerning the message; that he never saw the message Noyes reported to him; and that insofar as he could ascertain it did "not come over", i. e. to his office or the Army.[17]

5. Col. Rufus S. Bratton, Chief of the Far Eastern Section of the Intelligence Branch of the Military Intelligence Division in December of 1941, testified that sometime around 9 or 10 a. m. on the morning of December 5 he was called to General Miles' office where Sadtler stated Noyes had just called to say "it is in" (the winds execute message); that Miles, at his suggestion, requested Sadtler to get from Noyes a copy either of the Japanese text or of the English translation so a determination could be made as to whether the message was a genuine execute or another false alarm; that he did not again see Sadtler concerning the matter; that he, Bratton, called up the Navy, talking to either Captain McCollum or Kramer to inquire if they had received a winds execute message and was advised that no such message had been received; that he contacted Army SIS [18] and was likewise advised that no execute had been received; that the Army continued to monitor for an implementing message up to and after the December 7 attack.[19]

6. Admiral Richmond K. Turner, Chief of War Plans in December of 1941, testified before the committee as follows:

> On Friday afternoon, I think it was, of December 5, Admiral Noyes called on the telephone or the interphone, I do not know which, and said "The weather message", or words to this effect, "the first weather message has come in" and I said, "What did it say?" And he said, "North wind clear." And I said, "Well, there is something wrong about that," and he said, "I think so, too", and he hung up.
> I never saw a draft of that, I do not know from my own knowledge where he got it from. I assumed until recently that it it was an authentic message. From what I can determine since coming back here it was something entirely different, but it was never told to me. If it had come in and had been authentic I am certain that I would have received a copy of it.

Turner testified that he did not see an implementation of the winds code applying to the United States.[20]

7. To complete the picture it would seem apropos to set forth the testimony of Rear Adm. Leigh Noyes at this point.

Noyes, in December of 1941, Director of Naval Communications, testified before the committee that prior to December 7, 1941, no genuine winds execute message was brought to him or to his attention by anyone in the Navy Department; that prior to the Pearl Harbor attack there were several instances when messages were brought to him which were first thought to be winds execute messages but were determined not to be genuine; that the message described by Captain Safford in his statement, if received, would not have been regarded as an authentic execute message since (1) it is alleged to have been in Morse code and not by voice (2) no provision was made for a negative expression in the winds code (3) an execute would not have been

---

[17] Id., at pp. 12357–12363.
[18] Signal Intelligence Service.
[19] Committee record, pp. 12068–12077:
Colonel Bratton testified: "I can state most positively that no execute of the winds codes was ever received by me prior to the attack on Pearl Harbor. I find it hard to believe that any such execute message could get into the War Department without passing over my desk.
"It is inconceivable to me. I might have missed it but I had some assistants who were on the watch for it, and there were some people in the Army SIS who were also on the watch for it. They couldn't all have missed it. It is simply inconceivable to me that such a message could have been in the War Department without some one of us knowing about it or seeing it." Committee record, p. 12089.
[20] Committee record, p. 5214.

interpreted to mean war, and (4) Circular 2353 made no provision for N. E. I. as stated by Safford.

With respect to Colonel Sadtler's testimony that Noyes called him saying "The message is in," or words to that effect, Noyes stated he had no present recollection of having made such a statement although he would not say it did not occur inasmuch as he talked with the chief signal officer a number of times each day.[21]

Further, Noyes testified that he was directed to prepare a folder for the Roberts Commission but that it did not include a winds execute message and the folder in fact was supposed to contain no magic nor any reference to it; that the McCollum message,[22] to his knowledge, contained no reference to a winds execute message.[23]

8. The "Rochefort Message."

On December 5, 1941, a dispatch signed "Miles" was sent by the War Department to the assistant chief of staff headquarters G–2, Hawaiian Department, as follows: [24]

> Contact Commander Rochefort immediately thru Commandant Fourteenth Naval District regarding broadcasts from Tokyo reference weather.

At first blush, the foregoing dispatch would suggest, inferentially at least, the possibility of an execute message having been received. Colonel Bratton, upon whose recommendation the dispatch was sent, testified, however: [25]

> I had a discussion with Commander McCollum, now Captain McCollum, as to the amount of knowledge that the Navy had in Hawaii. He assured me his man Rochefort there at that time knew practically everything that there was to be known about the U. S.-Japanese relations through one means or another. I knew that suitable warning messages had been sent out to Hawaii and elsewhere. I had not read the messages and did not know their exact contents. I wanted to make sure that our G–2 in Hawaii got in touch with the ONI man in Hawaii, to get from him all the intelligence that he had in his possession, and I knew that if they got together on the subject of this winds message—I did not know, but I felt that they were going from there, and that there would be a complete exchange of intelligence and that the Army G–2 would then be in possession of just as much intelligence as Rochefort, the ONI man, had.

Colonel Bratton's testimony is to the effect that the dispatch of the message to G–2 to contact Rochefort had nothing whatever to do with receipt of a message in execution of the winds code. In this regard Captain McCollum stated:[26]

> I understood that G–2 was very anxious for their G–2 in Hawaii to have direct access with Commander Rochefort, who had the only agency capable of intercepting the winds message in Hawaii, sir. The Army, as I understand it, had no parallel set-up in Hawaii at that time.

[21] In a statement submitted to the committee under date of February 25, 1946, in amplification of his testimony, Admiral Noyes said: "In reading over my testimony I noted that I failed to bring out the following point, which, however, is supported by my previous testimony and by documentary evidence.

"In connection with the alleged telephone conversation with me on 5 December to which Colonel Sadtler testified and which I did not recall in that form:

"On 5 December there was received from Colonel Thorpe in Batavia addressed to General Miles in the War Department. This message was transmitted by the *Naval Attaché* to *Navy Department* for delivery to General Miles. As I have already testified, the subject matter was under discussion between me and the War Department during that day. It is very probable that I would have called Colonel Sadtler and notified him of the fact that this message had been received and was being delivered to the War Department for General Miles on account of its importance. Since discussion took place between me and the War Department during that day on the subject matter of this message and the War Department recommended that we should make no change in our original translation of the set-up of the Winds Code (see previous testimony), it would appear that any possible authentic or false execute of the winds message would have also been discussed and settled during that day." Committee record, pp. 14101, 14102.
[22] See discussion, *infra.*
[23] Committee record, pp. 12605–12620.
[24] Committee exhibit No. 32, p. 20.
[25] Committee record, p. 12120, 12121.
[26] Id., at pp. 9271, 9272.

CONSIDERATIONS MILITATING AGAINST LIKELIHOOD OF "WINDS CODE" EXECUTE MESSAGE HAVING BEEN RECEIVED PRIOR TO DECEMBER 7, 1941

1. Examination of Circular 2353 (to which Captain Safford admits the alleged winds execute was responsive) reflects that an execute warning would be added in the middle and at the end of the daily Japanese language short wave news broadcast "in case of emergency (danger of cutting off our diplomatic relations), and *the cutting off of international communications.*" When the execute was heard "all code papers, etc." were to be destroyed.

A reasonable construction of this circular would indicate that the winds code was an emergency arrangement designed to be employed in the event ordinary commercial means of international communications were no longer available to the Japanese Government. Contemplating that such commercial means conceivably might not be available to her, it would appear natural that Japan should devise a means such as the winds code to direct her diplomatic establishments to destroy their codes and secret papers. Manifestly and quite naturally the winds code should provide for destruction of *all* code papers inasmuch as the necessity for having any codes whatever of the type outstanding would be precluded by the cutting-off of international communications.

Ordinary commercial means of communications were available to Japan up to the December 7 attack on Pearl Harbor and in fact committee exhibit 1 is replete with instructions to Japanese diplomatic establishments with respect to destruction of codes.[27] Accordingly, it can fairly be concluded that recourse to the emergency system provided by the winds code was not necessitated and in consequence was not resorted to prior to December 7 inasmuch as the contingency contemplating its use (cutting off of international communications) did not materialize prior to the Pearl Harbor attack.

2. It is admitted and of course definitely known that a winds execute message (*Nishi No Kaze Hare*—west wind, clear) applying to England was transmitted from Tokyo stations JLG4 and JZJ between 0002 and 0035 GMT, December 8, 1941.[28] Such a message was of course reasonable inasmuch as Japan could very well contemplate that ordinary commercial means of communications would no longer be available after the Pearl Harbor attack.

Inasmuch as a genuine winds execute message applying to England was transmitted after the Pearl Harbor attack, it would appear anomalous that such a message should also have been sent prior to December 7.[29]

3. The investigation conducted in Japan by headquarters of the supreme allied commander reflected that a signal implementing Circulars 2353 and 2354 was probably not transmitted prior to December 8, Tokyo time, but was transmitted by radio voice broadcast at some hour after 0230, December 8, Tokyo time.[30] No evidence could be obtained that an implementing signal was transmitted by radio telegraph. Significantly, those who conducted the interrogation

[27] See sections relating to destruction of codes, pts. III and IV, this report.
[28] See committee exhibit No. 142.
[29] Admiral Noyes suggested that Japan's sending an execute on December 7 was probably occasioned by reason of the fact that some Japanese diplomatic establishment had failed to respond to instructions to destroy their codes which had been dispatched through ordinary channels of communication.
[30] December 7, Washington time.

in Japan had no knowledge prior to the interrogation that the United States had information that the winds code was used on December 8, Tokyo time.[31]

Mr. Shinroku Tanomogi was head of the overseas department of the Japan Radio Broadcasting Corporation in December 1941, and as such was in charge of programs, including news programs, beamed to foreign countries. Upon interview he stated he had no recollection at all of any "east wind rain" report or any similar phrase being broadcast prior to December 8.[32]

4. Inquiry made through the State Department reflects that no winds execute message was intercepted prior to the Pearl Harbor attack by the British, Dutch, or Australians.[33]

5. In his statement submitted for the committee's consideration, Captain Safford definitely states that the alleged implementing winds message was part of a Japanese overseas "news" broadcast from station JAP (Tokyo) on 11980 kilcoycles beginning at 1330 Greenwich civil time on Thursday, December 4, 1941, this time corresponding to 10:30 p. m., Tokyo time, and 8:30 a. m., Washington time, December 4, 1941; that the winds message broadcast was forwarded by teletype from Cheltenham to the Navy Department shortly before 9 a. m. on December 4, 1941. Further, that when he first saw the message it had already been translated by Kramer; that Kramer had underscored all three "code phrases" on the original incoming teletype sheet; and that he had written in pencil or colored crayon the following free translations:

> War with England (including NEI, etc.)
> War with the U. S.
> Peace with Russia.

Kramer has testified that had he seen such a message, as alleged by Safford, he would in no case have interpreted a winds execute to mean war.[34]

In this regard, the Thorpe and Foote messages, which interpreted the winds code as meaning war, were not available to the Navy Department until after the time Safford alleges the winds execute came in and was interpreted by Kramer to mean war. The Thorpe dispatch, while intended for General Miles of the War Department, was sent by Naval Communications and was received at the Navy Department at 1:21 a. m., December 4, 1941.[35] It was not decoded until 1:45 a. m., December 5, 1941, the delay being occasioned by the fact that the dispatch was sent "deferred," the lowest priority in handling.[36] The Foote dispatch, it is to be noted, was not received in the State Department until 9:19 a. m., December 4. Consequently, as indicated, no information was available in the Navy Department on the morning of December 4 as alleged by Safford serving as basis for interpreting a winds execute message to mean war. Even conceding the availability of the Thorpe and Foote dispatches, it would scarcely appear likely that the Navy Department would disregard its own translation of the winds code and be guided solely by the dispatches from outside sources.

[31] See committee exhibit No. 142.
[32] Id., sec. 4B.
[33] Committee exhibit No. 142, secs. 4c, 4d, 4e. See also committee record, p. 11564.
[34] See Navy Court of Inquiry (top secret) record, pp. 968, 969, 975, 987; committee record, p. 10492.
[35] Committee record, p. 10135.
[36] Id., at pp. 11255, 11256.

6. The winds execute message Safford alleges he saw on the morning of December 4, bore the "negative form for war with Russia" and mixed up the plain language broadcast with the Morse broadcast.[37] It is thus clear that the alleged winds execute of December 4 was not responsive to the establishing winds code.

Captain Kramer, it should be noted, testified before the joint committee that had the "negative form" been employed with respect to Russia, he would have regarded such fact as nullifying any credence to be placed in a broadcast purporting to be a winds execute message. It would appear agreed that the implementation of an establishing code must conform in meticulous detail to the code as originally established.

7. Referring to Captain Safford's statement, the following matters appear to be subject to serious question:

A. Safford relies on Cincaf 281430 [38] as basis for evaluation of a winds execute message to mean war, pointing out that this dispatch contained the statement "Nishi nishi England *including occupation of Thai or Invasion of Malay and N. E. I.*"

It should be noted, however, that Cincaf 281430 indicates the winds code would be employed "if diplomatic relations are on verge of being severed." In any event the interpretation of Cincaf 281430 as relied upon by Safford while possibly indicating war with England does not by any reasonable construction indicate war with the United States.[38a]

B. Safford's reliance in his statement on Cincaf 281430 as providing basis for evaluating a winds execute as meaning war is in contradiction of his testimony before the Navy Court of Inquiry where reliance was placed on the Thorpe and Foote dispatches.[39]

While denied by Safford, the suggestion was made by counsel before the committee that Safford may have shifted reliance on the Thorpe and Foote dispatches to Cincaf 281430 by reason of the fact that he had learned that both the Thorpe and Foote dispatches were not available to the Navy Department until after the morning of December 4.[40]

C. Safford seeks to bring out that the alleged winds execute was intended for the Japanese London Embassy inasmuch as the latter had destroyed its codes 3 days previously and a winds message was the only way that Tokyo could get news to its London Ambassador secretly.[41]

This statement is not true insofar as it implies that no other means of communication between Tokyo and London was available. By Circular 2409 of November 27, 1941,[42] the Japanese established the "hidden word" code and by Circular 2461 [43] instructed that this code be kept

---

[37] That is. Circular 2353 with Circular 2354.
[38] Set forth, supra.
[38a] See committee record, p. 9670.
[39] Navy Court of Inquiry (top secret) record, p. 748; see also committee record, p. 9667.
[40] Committee record, pp. 9667, 9668.
[41] Id., at p. 9639.
[42] Committee exhibit No. 1, p. 186.
[43] Id., at p. 226.

until the last moment. This code system of communication was clearly available to the Japanese in communicating with their London Ambassador and was in fact
employed on December 7 in Circular 2494.[44] Safford
admitted in his testimony before the joint committee the
availability in the London Embassy of the hidden word
code.

Furthermore, in Circular 2443, dated December 1,[45]
to London instructions were issued to discontinue use of the
code machine and to dispose of it immediately. Ostensibly
other code systems were still available after destruction of
the code machine and it is known that coded traffic in
the system referred to as PA–K2 passed from the Japanese
London Embassy to Tokyo December 6, 1941.[46]

D. By way of lending credence to his assertion that a winds
execute was received, Safford has testified that Mc-
Collum's dispatch of December 4 (not sent) was predicated
on such a winds execute and mentioned the execute in the
last portion.[47]

McCollum definitely contradicted this in testifying
before the committee, asserting that his dispatch was
based on a memorandum he, McCollum, had prepared
under date of December 1 [48] and bore no relationship
to a winds execute message; that he neither saw nor
received knowledge of a true winds execute prior to
December 7.[49]

E. In further substantiation of his allegation that a winds
execute was received on the morning of December 4,
Safford has referred to the fact that the dispatches from
OpNav to our own establishments to destroy their codes
was based on a winds execute.

This assertion is diametrically contrary to testimony of
Noyes [50] and Kramer [51] who declared that OpNav instructions to our establishments to destroy their codes
was based on instructions sent out by the Japanese [52] to
their diplomatic establishments to destroy codes, and
bore no relationship to a winds execute. The testimony
of McCollum and Ingersoll tends to confirm the foregoing.

F. Safford points out that the individual smooth translations
of the alleged winds execute for authorized Navy Department officials and the White House were distributed at
noon on December 4, 1941, in accordance with standard
operating procedure.[53]

Kramer, in testifying before the joint committee,
categorically denied that any copies of a winds execute
message were prepared for distribution by his section, it

[44] Id., at p. 251.
[45] Id., at p. 209.
[46] Committee record, p. 9740.
[47] See pt. IV, this report, for discussion of so-called McCollum dispatch.
[48] Committee exhibit No. 81.
[49] Committee record, pp. 9124–9134.
[50] Id., at p. 12623.
[51] Id., at p. 10504.
[52] Committee exhibit No. 1.
[53] Committee record, pp. 9763 et seq.

being noted that it was the responsibility of Kramer to prepare and distribute the smooth translations.[54]

G. Captain Safford has pointed out that a winds-execute was dispatched in Morse code. Captain Rochefort, who was in charge of the Communications Intelligence Unit at Pearl Harbor in December of 1941, testified that all of the broadcast schedules giving the various frequencies furnished by Washington were all voice frequencies; that to him the very setting up of the winds code implied "voice"; that if an execute message were sent in Morse code it would have meant that every Japanese Embassy (and consulate) in every Japanese location throughout the world for whom the message was intended by the Japanese Government would "have had to maintain Morse code operators, people capable of receiving Morse code. I do not think so." [55]

Rochefort further testified that they were monitoring for a winds execute message at Honolulu and continued to do so until after the attack; that four of his best language officers were on a 24-hour watch for an execute; that no winds implementing message was intercepted.[56]

H. Admiral Noyes testified that he would not have regarded the message which Safford alleges was received as an authentic execute message inasmuch as (1) Morse code was allegedly used and in consequence not responsive to Circular 2353; (2) no provision was made in the winds code for a "negative form" with respect to Russia; (3) an execute message would not have been interpreted to mean war; and (4) no reference is made in Circular 2353 to N. E. I., although the alleged execute was responsive to Circular 2353 and Safford indicates reference was made to. N. E. I.[57]

8. Safford, in testifying before the joint committee, placed emphasis on the fact that the winds code provided for destruction of *all* codes (Circular 2353) and by reason thereof a winds execute message would have more significance than the itercepts contained in committeee exhibit 1 which gave instructions with respect to destruction of particular codes.[58]

If a winds execute message was dispatched for the Japanese London Embassy on December 4, as alleged by Safford, it would necessarily

[54] Committee record, p. 10496.
[55] Id., at p. 12548.
[56] Id., at pp. 12532–12534.
[57] Id., at pp. 12614, 12615.
[58] When asked what there was in the winds execute message alleged by him to have been received which indicated *war*, Captain Safford testified: "For one thing there is instruction to destroy all code papers. If that is regarded as synonymous with the outbreak of war, as I have heard testified in this room, that by itself means something more than the wording of these three paragraphs above * * *. Tokyo had sent out instructions to various people telling them to burn their most important codes but to leave two codes open. One was the so-called PA-K2 code and the other was the LA code. Now, with those two exceptions all codes had been burnt, but this said, '*Please destroy all code papers,*' and so forth. In other words, there was no exceptions in this one." Committee record, p. 9778.

In marked contradiction of the foregoing testimony is the explanation of Captain Safford as to the reason for Japan's London Embassy having the PA-K2 code system after the alleged winds execute message was received. He stated: "There were two systems that were exempt from destruction. One was PA-K2, and the other was LA, neither of which were considered by ourselves as secret, and we presumed the Japanese did not consider them secret." Committee record, p. 9741.

It is to be noted, however, that the Honolulu consulate, as well as Tokyo, used the PA-K2 system for some of the most vital messages shortly before December 7 (see committee exhibit No. 2). While this was virtually the only system left after the messages ordering the destruction of various codes, the PA-K2 system was employed for the sending of messages which would probably have tipped off the attack on Pearl Harbor, had it not been for the fact they were not translated until after the attack.

mean that *all* codes were to be destroyed by Japan's London Ambassador. It is definitely known, as earlier indicated, that London sent a dispatch to Tokyo in the system known as PA–K2 on December 6, 1941. Such fact would indicate strongly that no winds execute was dispatched on December 4 with consequent destruction of *all* codes.[59]

9. It appears clear that both the Navy and Army were still looking for a winds execute message after the morning of December 4, based on records of the Federal Communications Commission.[60]

In this connection at 7:50 p. m. on December 5, 1941, the watch officer of FCC phoned Colonel Bratton of the Army with respect to a false winds message received from the FCC Portland monitoring station. The FCC watch officer submitted the following memorandum for his superior with respect to Bratton's remarks:

> Remarks by Col. Bratton:
> Results still negative but am pleased to receive the negative results as it means we have that much more time. The information desired will occur in the middle of a program and possibly will be repeated at frequent intervals. (Asked Col. Bratton if I should communicate the information to Portland—concerning the fact that the desired data will be in the middle of a program.) No, I will have a conference with Lt. Col. Dusenberg in the morning and will contact Mr. Sterling in that regard.

The foregoing would indicate that the Army had received no genuine winds execute message by 7:50 p. m., December 5.

The FCC night watch log for December 4, 1941,[61] contains the notation that at 9:32 p. m. "Lt. Brotherhood called to inquire if any other reference to weather was made previously in program intercepted by Portland. Informed him that no other reference was made." There is manifested here an interest by the Navy in the nature of a winds message on the evening of December 4 which is hardly likely if a true execute was received on the morning of December 4.

Further, it would appear logical that had a true winds execute been received on the morning of December 4 the FCC would have been requested to discontinue its monitoring activities. This, however, was not done and the FCC was still monitoring for a winds execute and actually intercepted such an execute (with respect to England) after the Pearl Harbor attack.[62]

10. Collateral considerations tending to minimize likelihood that implementing winds message was dispatched from Tokyo.

A. Referring to the message telephoned by the FCC to Brotherhood at 9:05 p. m. on December 4,[63] Safford testified before Admiral Hewitt[64] that this was the "false" message which appeared on this surface to use the "winds" code relating to Russia but which was a genuine weather broadcast. This message, Safford said, Brotherhood telephoned to Admiral Noyes and later *Kramer took one look at it and said it was not what was wanted and threw it into the waste basket.* He testified that this message was received * * * 12 hours or more after what he referred to as the "true winds message."

[59] Committee record, p. 9740.
[60] Committee exhibit No. 142-A.
[61] Id.
[62] See also testimony of Colonel Bratton, committee record, p. 12074.
[63] Committee exhibit No. 142, sec. 3.
[64] Hewitt inquiry record, p. 113.

Query: Why would Kramer be "wanting" a winds execute message 12 hours after Safford alleges Kramer had an execute message and had noted thereon "War with England, War with U. S., peace with Russia"?

B. In testifying before the committee, Justice Roberts stated he had no knowledge of the winds matter and no access to Magic. This would appear to be partially at least in contradiction of Safford's testimony that he last saw the winds execute among material assembled for the Roberts Commission.

Further, Admiral Noyes testified that he was directed to prepare a folder for the Roberts Commission, but it did not include a winds execute message and the folder was in fact supposed to contain no magic nor any reference to it.[65]

C. Safford's detailed recollection of the winds matter, as set forth in his statement, is in sharp conflict with his indefinite and somewhat nebulous memory as reflected by his testimony and the letters directed to Kramer during December 1943, and January 1944.

It should be noted in this connection that Safford testified before Admiral Hart [66] that the winds implementing message came in on the evening of December 3 and Kramer went down to get it. From all of the testimony it appears that Safford's position before the committee was assumed after a process of elimination of possibilities and reconstruction of a situation concerning which he had only a partially independent recollection.

D. Considering the tight reign maintained by the military in Japan and particularly the desire to clothe the movement against Pearl Harbor with utmost secrecy, it would seem highly improbable that the Japanese would tip off her war decision in a news broadcast by advising her London Ambassador of such decision 3 days before Pearl Harbor.

E. If a true winds execute was received and distributed on December 4 it would appear reasonable to assume that some record of the message could be found in the War or Navy Departments. Yet despite repeated searches there is no record whatever in either department of such a message. In this connection Safford has suggested that intercept No. JD–7001, marked "cancelled" in the Navy file of intercepts, may have been the missing winds execute. Such a premise, of course, presupposes a deliberate abstraction by someone of an official record from the Navy Department.

In evaluation of Safford's suggestion with respect to No. JD–7001, it should be noted that the file of JD intercepts was maintained by Kramer who has emphatically testified that no winds execute came into his section or was distributed by him. Further, Kramer has pointed out that there are several examples of canceled JD numbers in the file [67] and presented several reasons in testi-

---

[65] Committee record, p. 12620.
[66] Hart inquiry record, p. 361.
[67] This appears to be borne out by the record. See committee exhibit No. 142, sec. 6.

fying before the committee why a JD number might be canceled.

Significantly, a check of the Army file of intercepts for the period December 3–5, 1941, reflected that the Navy file contains all intercepts that are in the Army file.[68]

Conceding for purposes of discussion that a winds execute message was received in the form alleged by Safford, it will be noted that such message would not indicate *where* or *when* Japan would strike but merely her possible purpose to go to war. Bearing in mind the rather frank admission by Army and Navy officials that they knew war was imminent in the days before December 7, credence could scarcely be placed in the theory that the message was deliberately destroyed when it contained no information that was not admittedly already possessed.

Admiral Ingersoll, for example, testified before the committee that had a true winds execute message been received it would have been regarded as merely confirmatory of the implications contained in Japanese instructions to destroy codes contained in committee exhibit 1, inasmuch as instructions to destroy codes, particularly in the consulates, meant war. The testimony of several other witnesses, including Admiral Noyes and Colonel Bratton, is to the same effect.

11. The testimony of Col. Robert E. Schukraft, assigned to the office of the chief signal officer at the time of the Pearl Harbor attack, before the committee on February 19, 1946, is of particular pertinence to the testimony of Captain Kramer, set forth under section 3, *supra*. Schukraft testified that 2 or 3 days prior to Pearl Harbor Col. Rex Minckler brought to Schukraft's office a piece of yellow teletype paper (the carbon copy) which contained what appeared to be a winds execute message but that the message upon examination was obviously not a true winds execute. Further, Schukraft testified Colonel Minckler had indicated that the Navy had thought the message a true winds execute, Captain Kramer having seen the message and so thinking. He stated that he concluded very positively that the message was not a true execute of the Winds Code.[69]

12. The following officers have stated they have no knowledge of a message in execution of the Winds code prior to December 7, 1941:

Navy

Admiral Harold R. Stark, Chief of Naval Operations.[70]
Admiral Leigh Noyes, Director of Naval Communications.[71]
Admiral T. S. Wilkinson, Director of Naval Intelligence.[72]
Capt. Arthur N. McCollum, in charge, Far Eastern Section of Naval Intelligence.[73]
Admiral Joseph R. Redman, Assistant Director of Naval Communications.[74]

[68] See Army liaison memorandum dated January 26, 1946. Committee record, pp. 8965, 8966.
[69] Committee record, pp. 13093–13096.
[70] See Navy Court of Inquiry record, pp. 783, 872. Confirmed in testimony before the committee.
[71] Committee record, pp. 12605–12620.
[72] Hewitt inquiry record, pp. 398–401.
[73] Committee record, pp. 9124–9134.
[74] Navy Court of Inquiry record, p. 1103.

Lt. Comdr. George W. Linn, GY watch officer.[75]
Lt. Comdr. Alfred V. Pering, GY watch officer.[76]
Lt. Comdr. Allan A. Murray, GY watch officer.[77]
Lt. Frederick L. Freeman, assigned to section disseminating to ONI intelligence received from radio intelligence units.[78]
Capt. Redfield Mason, fleet intelligence officer, Asiatic Fleet.[79]
Commander Rudolph J. Fabian, Radio Intelligence Unit at Corregidor.[80]
Capt. Edwin T. Layton, Pacific Fleet intelligence officer.[81]
Capt. Joseph John Rochefort, in charge, Communications Intelligence Unit, Pearl Harbor.[82]

Army

Gen. George C. Marshall, Chief of Staff.[83]
Maj. Gen. Leonard T. Gerow, Chief of War Plans.[84]
Maj. Gen. Sherman Miles, Chief of G-2.[85]
Col. Rufus W. Bratton, Chief, Far Eastern Section of G-2.[86]
Col. Robert E. Schukraft, Chief, Radio Interception for SIS.[87]
Col. Rex W. Minckler, Chief, SIS.[88]
Brig. Gen. Thomas J. Betts, executive assistant to the Chief of Intelligence Branch MID.[89]
Lt. Col. Frank B. Rowlett, prior to Pearl Harbor attack a civilian technical assistant to the officer of the Cryptoanalytic unit, SIS.[90]
William F. Friedman, a cryptanalyst of War Department.[91]

Over-all observations with respect to Captain Safford's testimony:

13. As previously indicated Captain Safford has rather consistently testified that a true winds execute message was received prior to December 7. However, there are certain discrepancies in his testimony tending to show particularly that his recollection of the incident attending receipt of such an execute has not been definite and has been developed through a process of elimination.

    A. The following testimony, in relation to a winds execute, of Captain Safford before Admiral Hewitt reflects rather clearly his indefinite recollection of the winds matter and his efforts to reconstruct a "vague memory": [92]

> Captain SAFFORD. In the fall of 1943 it appeared that there was going to be a trial or court martial of Admiral Kimmel. It was hinted in the newspapers and various people in the Navy Department were getting testimony ready for it. I realized I would be one of the important witnesses, that my memory was very vague, and I began looking around to get everything that I could to prepare a written statement which I could follow as testimony. That was the time when I studied the Robert's Report carefully for the first

---

[75] Hewitt inquiry record, pp. 140–142.
[76] Id., at p. 148.
[77] Id., at pp. 433–441.
[78] Id., at pp. 149, 150.
[79] Id., at pp. 73, 78.
[80] Id., at pp. 73, 78.
[81] Id., at pp. 269–271.
[82] Id., at pp. 46, 48.
[83] See Army Pearl Harbor Board (Top Secret) record, pp. 35–39. Confirmed in testimony before the committee.
[84] Committee record, p. 4302.
[85] See Clausen investigation record, pp. 214, 215. Confirmed in testimony before the committee.
[86] Committee record, pp. 12068–12077.
[87] Id., at pp. 13093–13096.
[88] Clausen investigation record, p. 217.
[89] Id., at p. 194.
[90] Id., at pp. 225, 226.
[91] Hewitt inquiry record, pp. 515–520.
[92] Id., at pp. 112, 113.

time and noted no reference to the winds message or to the message which McCollum had written and which I had seen and I thought had been sent. And then I began talking to everybody who had been around at the time and who I knew had been mixed up in it to see what they could remember to straighten me out on the thing and give me leads to follow down to where I could put my hands on official messages and things so that it would be a matter of fact and not a matter of memory. I also talked the thing over with whatever Army people were still around at the time and had anything in this thing, and bit by bit these facts appeared to come together. The investigation was conducted, if you call it that, for the purpose of preparing myself to take the stand as a witness in a prospective court martial of Admiral Kimmel.

B. The letters directed to Captain Kramer by Safford and incorporated in the committee transcript also indicate an indefinite recollection of events prior to the attack on Pearl Harbor.[93]

C. In testifying before Admiral Hart, Safford stated:[94]

The "Winds Message" was actually broadcast during the evening of December 3, 1941 (Washington time), which was December 4 by Greenwich time and Tokyo time. The combination of frequency, time of day, and radio propagation was such that the "Winds Message" was heard only on the East Coast of the United States, and even then by only one or two of the Navy stations that were listening for it. The other nations and other Navy C. I. Units, not hearing the "Winds Message" themselves and not receiving any word from the Navy Department, naturally presumed that the "Winds Message" had not yet been sent, and that the Japanese Government was still deferring the initiation of hostilities. When the Japanese attacked Pearl Harbor, the British at Singapore, the Dutch at Java, and the Americans at Manila were just as surprised and astonished as the Pacific Fleet and Army posts in Hawaii. It is apparent that the War Department, like the Navy Department failed to send out information that the "Winds Message" had been sent by Tokyo. The "Winds Message" was received in the Navy Department during the evening of December 3, 1941, while Lieutenant (j. g.) Francis M. Brotherhood, U. S. N. R., was on watch. There was some question in Brotherhood's mind as to what this message really meant because it came in a different form from what had been anticipated. Brotherhood called in Lieutenant Commander Kramer, who came down that evening and identified that message as the "Winds Message" we had been looking for.

Yet in his statement and in testifying before the committee Safford has the message coming in on the morning of December 4, 1941, it being brought to him by Lt. A. A. Murray.

D. In testifying before the Navy Court of Inquiry Safford said:[95]

22. Q. Captain, in a previous answer you stated that the copy of the intercept using the winds code which you saw on the morning of 4 December 1941 indicated a break in diplomatic relations between the United States and Japan and Japan and Great Britain, and war between these nations. Was there anything in the establishment of the code originally which would indicate that a use of that code would indicate war as contrasted with a mere break in diplomatic relations?

A. The Dutch translation said "war." The Japanese language is very vague and you can put a number of constructions or interpretations or translations on the same message. In very important documents it was customary for the Army and Navy to make independent translations and the differences were sometimes surprising; that

---

[93] See testimony of Captains Kramer and Safford before the committee.
[94] Hart inquiry record, p. 361.
[95] Navy Court of Inquiry record, p. 748.

is, a difference in degree. The general facts would be alike. However, the people in Communication Intelligence and the people in Signal Intelligence Service and the people in the Far Eastern Section of Naval Intelligence, as well as the Director of Naval Intelligence, considered that meant war and it was a signal of execute for the Japanese war plans.

23. Q. Captain, I call your attention again to Document 3 in Exhibit 64 which is an English-language translation of the Dutch intercept. Was this your only source of information that the use of this code would indicate "a war decision" which is the wording used by the attaché in Batavia?

A. Mr. Foote's message to the State Department was even more specific. It said, "When crises leading to worst arises following will be broadcast at end of weather reports. 1. *East wind rain*—war with United States. 2. *North wind cloudy*—war with Russia. 3. *West wind clear*—war with Britain, including an attack on Thailand or Malaya and Dutch East Indies." This was apparently a verbatim quotation from the Dutch translation.

Significantly, in testifying before the committee Safford relies on Cincaf 281430 as the dispatch serving as basis for interpreting a winds execute message to mean war. It has now been conclusively shown that neither the Foote nor Thorpe dispatches were available in the Navy Department at the time Safford alleges an execute was received and interpreted to mean war; i. e. the morning of December 4, 1941.[96]

E. The testimony of Captain Safford taken in its entirety reflects substantial discrepancies as to where the alleged execute message was received. It was only at the time of submitting his statement to the committee that Safford stated definitely the message came in at the Navy's Cheltenham station.

14. Because of substantial discrepancies in testimony given in prior proceedings with respect to the question of whether a winds execute message was received in the War or Navy Department, the inquiry conducted by Admiral Hewitt went fully into the matter, among others, of determining if such a message was intercepted prior to December 7, 1941. Admiral Hewitt found:[97]

The interception of a "winds" message relating to the United States during the first week of December 1941, would not have conveyed any information of significance which the Chief of Naval Operations and the commander in chief, Pacific Fleet, did not already have.

No message in the "winds" code relating to the United States was received by any of the watch officers in the Navy Department to whom such a message would have come had it been received in the Navy Department. No such message was intercepted by the radio intelligence units at Pearl Harbor or in the Philippines, although intensive efforts were made by those organizations to intercept such a message. The evidence indicates further that no such message was intercepted by the British or the Dutch, despite their efforts to intercept such a message. Neither the Fleet Intelligence Officer of the Asiatic Fleet nor the Fleet Intelligence Officer of the Pacific Fleet nor the Intelligence Officer of the Far Eastern Section of the Office of Naval Intelligence, recalled any such message. The Chief of Naval Operations, the Director of Naval Communications, and the Director of Naval Intelligence recalled no such message. Testimony to the effect that a "winds" code message was received prior to the attack was given by Captain Safford, in charge of Op–20–G, a communications security section at the Navy Department, who stated that such a message was received on December 3rd or 4th, that it related to the United States, and that no copy could be found in the Navy or Army files. In his testimony before Admiral Hart, Captain Safford named, in addition

[96] See in this connection, committee record, pp. 9667, 9668.
[97] For Hewitt Inquiry report, see committee exhibit No. 157.

to himself, three other officers who, he stated, recalled having seen and read the "winds" message. Each of those officers testified that he had never seen such a message. The only other testimony to the effect that a "winds" message was received was by Captain Kramer, an intelligence officer assigned to Op–20–G, who said that he recalled that there was a message but that he could not recall whether or not it related to the United States or England or Russia. It may be noted that until he testified in this investigation, Captain Kramer erroneously thought that a "hidden word" message intercepted on the morning of December 7th had been a "winds" message.

CONCLUSION: From consideration of all evidence relating to the winds code, it is concluded that no genuine message, in execution of the code and applying to the United States, was received in the War or Navy Department prior to December 7, 1941. It appears, however, that messages were received which were initially thought possibly to be in execution of the code but were determined not to be execute messages. In view of the preponderate weight of evidence to the contrary, it is believed that Captain Safford is honestly mistaken when he insists that an execute message was received prior to December 7, 1941. Considering the period of time that has elapsed, this mistaken impression is understandable.

Granting for purposes of discussion that a genuine execute message applying to the winds code was intercepted before December 7, it is concluded that such fact would have added nothing to what was already known concerning the critical character of our relations with the Empire of Japan.

GEOGRAPHICAL CONSIDERATIONS AND NAVY AND ARMY INSTALLATIONS

Appendix F

GEOGRAPHICAL CONSIDERATIONS AND NAVY AND ARMY INSTALLATIONS

GEOGRAPHICAL CONSIDERATIONS

The Territory of Hawaii consists of a chain of eight principal islands.[1] The island of Oahu is to be regarded as of most importance by reason of the excellent enclosed fleet anchorage at Pearl Harbor and the commercial port of Honolulu. Pearl Harbor is located on the southern or lee side of Oahu, in a strategically and commercially important position in the North Pacific Ocean, 3,430 nautical miles southeast of Tokyo, approximately 2,000 nautical miles west to southwest of San Francisco, and 4,767 nautical miles east of Manila.[2]

The islands have a mild subtropical climate with moderate seasonal changes of temperature. They lie in the path of the steady northeasterly trade winds; therefore, the northern portions of Oahu and the immediately adjacent waters are characterized by fresh winds from a northerly direction. The force of the trades is broken by the configuration of the land so that so the south of Oahu the seas are relatively smooth.

Much of the moisture of the trade winds is deposited on the high peaks to the north, forming mist and clouds. Because of this, the visibility to the south of the islands is better than to the north. The northern fringe of the trade belt lies roughly about 300 miles to the north of Oahu, a belt which is characterized by low ceilings, poor visibility, squalls and rain.

The sea area around the Hawaiian Islands was, on December 7, 1941, divided into certain restricted fleet training areas where units and aircraft of the Pacific Fleet might carry out exercises and target practice. Two defensive sea areas were mapped off Pearl Harbor and Kaneohe, these areas having been designated by the President of the United States. Entry of all merchant ships, both United States and foreign, and of all foreign men-of-war was prohibited unless specific permission for such entry had been granted by the Secretary of the Navy.[3]

When the Japanese attacked Pearl Harbor at 7:55 on the morning of December 7, 1941, it was 1:25 in the afternoon of the same day in Washington, D. C., and 3:25 a. m., December 8, in Tokyo. In order to obtain the corresponding time in Washington and Hawaii, it is necessary to subtract 14 hours and 19½ hours, respectively, from Tokyo time. The time of sunrise on the morning of December 7,

---

[1] They are the islands of: Oahu, Hawaii, Maui, Kahoolawe, Lanai, Molokai, and Kauai, Niihau. See attachment No. 1.

[2] A nautical mile is roughly 1⅙ land miles. For a table of distances with respect to Pearl Harbor, see committee exhibit No. 6, item 2.

[3] For maps of the Hawaiian Islands and descriptions of the defensive sea areas, see committee exhibit No. 6.

1941, was 6:26 a. m., and morning twilight was at 5:06 a. m., both Hawaiian time.[4]

NAVY AND ARMY INSTALLATIONS [5]

NAVY

Pearl Harbor was the base of the United States Pacific Fleet at the time Japan struck on December 7, 1941, having been such since May of 1940. The island of Oahu was the headquarters of the Fourteenth Naval District which included the Hawaiian Islands, Midway, Wake, Johnston, Palmyra, and Canton Islands. Except for Pearl Harbor itself, other installations were characterized as "minor" naval installations and were naturally integrated in the over-all defense of the islands, of which Pearl Harbor was the focal point.

On the island of Molokai there was the Homestead Field Naval Air Base, which consisted of a runway, a warming-up platform and supporting installations.

On the island of Maui there was the Puunene Naval Air Base, which consisted of runways, a warming-up platform, and a CAA Territorial landing field. Also on Maui was the Maalaea naval emergency landing field, which consisted of two runways and other supporting installations.

On the island of Hawaii, the largest island in the Hawaiian chain, was located the naval radio station at Hilo.

On the most important island of the group, Oahu, there was a naval air station at Ewa, which consisted of a mooring mast, a landing mat, and supporting installations.

At the naval air station Kaneohe, on the opposite side of the island, was a landing mat and warming-up platform and supporting installations and also a seaplane base.

At Kahuku Point, up at the north end of the island, there was an emergency landing field.

At Lualualei was located a naval radio station—a transmitting station.

At Wahiawa, in the interior, was located a naval radio receiving station.

At Heeia, a naval radio transmitting station was located and at Wailupe a naval radio receiving station.

Referring to Pearl Harbor itself, it is to be noted that the only entrance is from the south by way of a channel which was blasted through the fringing coral reef that had formerly blocked entrance to the harbor. This channel extending to the harbor entrance proper was 375 yards wide and 3,500 yards long with a minimum depth of 45 feet. The entrance proper to Pearl Harbor is between Keahi Point and Holokahiki Point. From here the channel leads to the various lochs and passages which form the harbor. The major channels or the main channels and water in the vicinity of the major ships' berths had a depth of 40 feet. From the sea buoys to the large drydocks a portion of the channel had a minimum depth of 45 feet to provide for the entrance and docking of damaged vessels. The entrance to the harbor was closed by two protective nets where the channel through

---

[4] See committee exhibit No. 6, item 4, for a table showing comparative times and dates for Greenwich, England; Washington, D. C.; San Francisco; Hawaii; Tokyo; and Manila on December 6, 7, and 8, 1941.
[5] See committee record, pp. 50 et seq.; also committee exhibits Nos. 5 and 6.

the coral reefs was about 400 yards wide and the depth from 41 to 50 feet. The nets themselves consisted of a combined antitorpedo net and antiboat boom to seaward and an inner antitorpedo net without the boat boom.

The Pearl Harbor fleet base included every type of naval activity. Many of the installations operable at that time were new, having been built subsequent to August 1939. Major installations in operation were, at the Navy Yard, Pearl Harbor: one battleship dock, built in 1928; one battleship dock, under construction; one floating drydock, 18,000 tons; one large repair basin, supporting industrial establishments for repairs to anything afloat; one fuel depot with two tank farms above ground;[6] one submarine base with all services for war conditions; one section base, inshore patrol and harbor entrance control post; and, the administrative office of the Fourteenth Naval District which was inside the navy yard.

At the Naval Air Station—Ford Island, which is the large island at the center of the harbor—there was a large flying field, warming-up platform, sea plane parking areas, and supporting installations.

ARMY

On December 6, 1941, the Hawaiian Department included approximately 43,000 troops under the over-all command of Lt. Gen. Walter C. Short. The principal elements of the department were two Infantry divisions and supporting ground troops composing the beach and land defense forces; the Coast Artillery command, consisting of the seacoast and antiaircraft defense forces; and the Hawaiian Air Force.

In the Kauai district were located the Third Battalion, Two Hundred Ninety-ninth Infantry (less Companies K and L) and attached troops; Company C, Two Hundred Ninety-ninth Infantry; First Platoon, Signal Company Aircraft Warning; Air Corps detachment.

In the Maui district were the First Battalion, Two Hundred Ninety-ninth Infantry, less Company C and attached troops; Company K, Two Hundred Ninety-ninth Infantry (Molokai); Fourth Platoon Signal Company, Aircraft Warning; Air Corps detachment.

In the Hawaii district were the Second Battalion, Two Hundred Ninety-ninth Infantry and attached troops; camp detachment, Kilauea Military Camp; Fifth Platoon Signal Company, Aircraft Warning; Air Corps detachment.

On the principal island, Oahu, were located:

The Twenty-fourth Infantry Division (less Two Hundred and Ninety-ninth Infantry Regiment); Twenty-fifth Infantry Division; Hawaiian Coast Artillery Command; Hawaiian Air Force; Thirty-fourth Engineers; Eight Hundred and Fourth Engineer Battalion (Aviation); Eleventh Tank Company; Company A, First Separate Chemical Battalion; Hawaiian Pack Train. The Twenty-fourth Infantry Division was responsible for the ground defense of the northern half of Oahu, and the Twenty-fifth Division for that of the southern sector. Most of the components of these divisions were located at Schofield Barracks.

---

[6] A tank farm is a collection of fuel-oil storage tanks.

The Hawaiian Coast Artillery Command, under Maj. Gen. Henry T. Burgin, consisted of the following harbor defense units:

Fifteenth Coast Artillery Regiment (Harbor Defense).

Sixteenth Coast Artillery Regiment (Harbor Defense).

Forty-first Coast Artillery Regiment (Railway).

Fifty-fifth Coast Artillery Regiment (155 mm., tractor-drawn) and antiaircraft units.

Sixty-fourth Coast Artillery Regiment, semimobile.

Ninety-seventh Coast Artillery Regiment, semimobile.

Ninety-eighth Coast Artillery Regiment, semimobile.

Two Hundred and Fifty-first Coast Artillery Regiment, mobile.

Other large-caliber guns available for defense but manned by field artillery were two 240-mm. howitzers and thirty-two 155-mm. howitzers. The seacoast guns were installed principally in permanent fortifications. The fixed antiaircraft guns were emplaced generally to defend the seacoast artillery, and the mobile antiaircraft units were normally stationed at Fort Shafter, Schofield Barracks, and Camp Malakole.

The principal units of Maj. Gen. Frederick L. Martin's Hawaiian Air Force were the Fifth and Eleventh Bombardment Groups, the Fifteenth and Eighteenth Pursuit Groups, the Eighty-sixth Observation Squadron, and the Air Corps services. The Air Force was generally disposed on four fields—Hickam, Wheeler, Haleiwa, and Bellows.

For reference purposes in orienting the locations of various Army and Navy installations (as of December 7, 1941), the following illustrations are attached hereto:

1. Map of the Hawaiian Islands showing the disposition of Army forces.

2. Map of the island of Oahu showing Army installations, including airfields.

3. Map of the Hawaiian Islands showing United States naval installations in the Hawaiian area.

O

ILLUSTRATION NO. 1

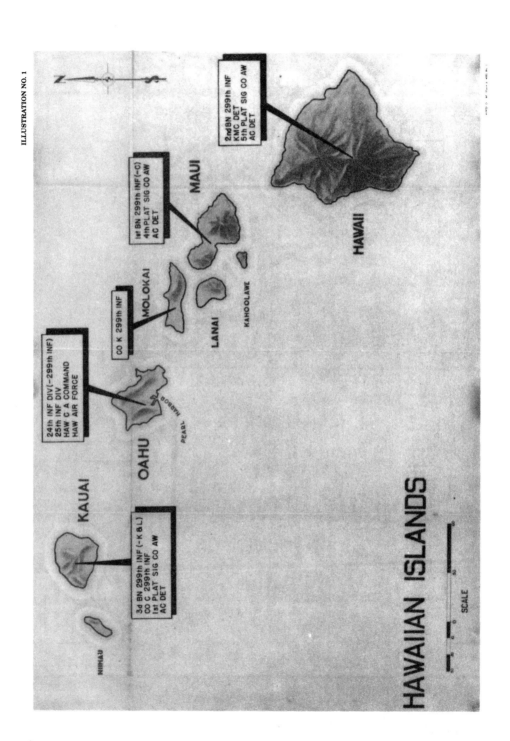

HAWAIIAN ISLANDS

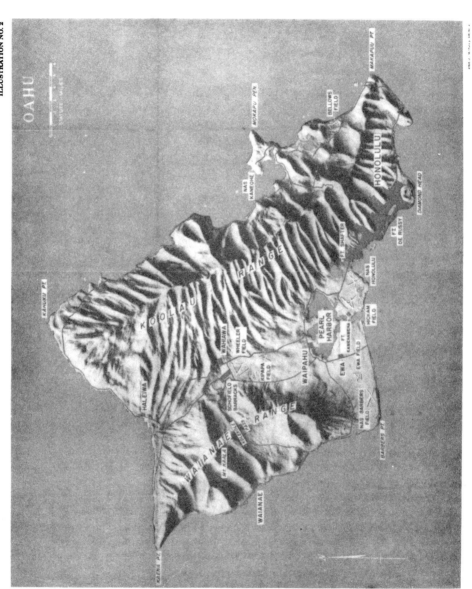

OAHU

497

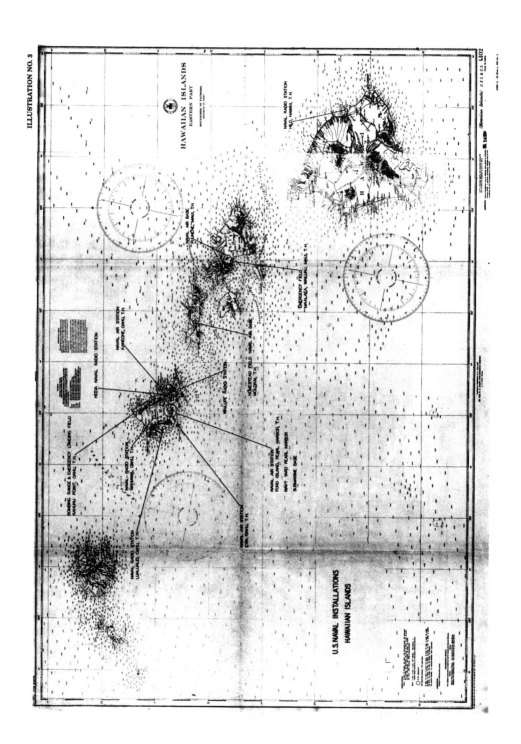

Memorandum
for the
Director of Central Intelligence

Memorandum for the Director of Central Intelligence

   Subject: Intelligence at Pearl Harbor

1. Pursuant to Senate Concurrent Resolution No. 27, Seventy-ninth Congress, (September 1945), a Joint Congressional Committee on the Investigation of the Pearl Harbor Attack was established to investigate the attack, and events and circumstances relating thereto.

2. In July 1946, the Committee Report was published, together with the additional view of one Congressman and the Minority Report of two Senators.

3. A study of the Committee Report has been made by the undersigned from the viewpoint of ascertaining the role, achievements, and shortcomings of intelligence in connection with the attack on Pearl Harbor. This intelligence study is attached herewith. No attempt has been made to examine the Committee Report from a military or diplomatic standpoint. Rather, this paper is restricted solely to the problems of intelligence.

4. For convenience, this study of the Committee Report has been divided into four sections as follows:
   Section A — Collection
   Section B — Research and Evaluation
   Section C — Dissemination
   Section D — Deficiencies, Conclusions and Recommendations
   　　　　　　　 of the Committee

5. The following are among the major conclusions and recommendations reached by the Committee:
   a. Intelligence work requires centralization of authority and clear-cut allocation of responsibilities.
   b. The armed services should:
      (1) Select officers for intelligence work who possess the background and capacity for such work;
      (2) Retain these officers on intelligence duty for an extended period of time;
      (3) Insure that officers with an aptitude for intelligence receive such assignments and do not have their progress impeded or their promotions affected.
   c. The restriction of highly classified information to a minimum

number of officials, while often necessary, should not be carried
to the point of prejudicing the work of an organization.

d. There should be complete integration of Army and Navy intelligence
agencies.

e. Congress should consider legislation fully protecting the security of
classified matter and amending the Communications Act of 1934
insofar as it handicaps our intelligence agents with regard to wire
tapping.

6. Nothing in the additional views of Congressman Keefe or the Minority
Report of Senators Brewster and Ferguson materially changes the Majority Report insofar as intelligence is concerned. All dates, unless otherwise indicated, are in the year 1941.

Chief, Legislative Liaison Branch

Section A — Collection

A considerable amount of information regarding Japanese plans, intentions, and capabilities was collected by the military and naval intelligence services, both in Washington and in the field, prior to Pearl Harbor.

The greatest source of intelligence information concerning Japanese plans was provided by the interception and decoding of messages from Japan to its diplomatic establishments. These intercepts were known by the code name *Magic*, and were provided by a joint operation of the Army and Navy. This operation was characterized by the Congressional Committee as "meriting the highest commendation" because of the "exercise of the greatest ingenuity and utmost resourcefulness" by the services.

To protect the security of *Magic*, it was necessary to pursue a policy of extremely limited distribution of the material. Thus it was possible to avoid alerting the Japanese to the fact that their diplomatic codes had been broken. Had the Japanese been aware of this fact, they would have changed their codes, resulting obviously in complete loss of *Magic* until the new codes could be broken.

The greatest volume of *Magic* traffic was of primary interest to the State Department, being diplomatic in nature, although certain elements of the information were of interest to the Armed Services. Many of the messages concerned the espionage activities of Japanese consular staffs, particularly regarding the location and movements of American ships and the status of military installations.

Detailed analysis of the intelligence secured through *Magic* is not required by this paper. However, it is interesting to note that the *Magic* interceptions included such messages (now much publicized) as the "winds" code, the "berthing" plan of Pearl Harbor, the "hidden word" code, the "deadline" messages, and the 14-part message of 6-7 December. In addition, as pointed out in the section of this paper on "Dissemination," messages were intercepted which showed the destruction by the Japanese of their secret codes and confidential papers.

Vital information was obtained by the Commander of the Pacific Fleet from the daily summaries prepared by the Radio Intelligence Unit at Hawaii which, through traffic analyses, identified, located and determined the movements of Japanese warships by their call signals and by radio direction-finding techniques. A similar unit was included within the Naval Command in the Philippines. The reports of the latter unit were considered the more reliable, and all Pacific radio intelligence reports were submitted to the Philippine Unit for evaluation. Copies of these evaluations were available to Kimmel, as were fortnightly intelligence bulletins from these sources by ONI.

Close liaison was maintained in Hawaii between the services and the FBI. The latter provided considerable information of significance, including (on December 6) the so-called "Mori Call," which was a transcript of an intercepted radio telephone conversation between a member of the Mori family in Honolulu and an individual in Japan. The transcript indicated that the latter was interested in such military information as daily flights of aeroplanes, searchlights, and ship locations in Pearl Harbor.

In addition to the sources of collection listed above, there was information to be obtained from the aircraft warning radar, which detected incoming Japanese planes on December 7th while they were still 130 miles from Oahu. (The failure to take advantage of this is now history.)

In addition, Washington recommended visual and photographic reconnaissance of the Japanese mandated islands, including troop concentrations in the Carolines and Marshalls. This recommendation for collection was not exploited.

The Committee also studied Japanese collection of intelligence, basing its resulting conclusions largely on post-VJ-Day reports of interrogations of knowledgeable Japanese. The following may be listed as among the main sources of Japanese intelligence:

(1)   Espionage;
(2)   Consular staffs;
(3)   Naval attachés of the Japanese Embassy in Washington;
(4)   Newspapers in the United States;
(5)   American public radio broadcasts;
(6)   Crews and passengers on ships which docked in Hawaii;
(7)   General information;
(8)   Foreign diplomatic establishments;
(9)   Commercial firms;
(10) Signal intelligence;
(11) Submarine reconnaissance in Hawaiian waters.

Early reports, by committees and boards investigating Pearl Harbor prior to the Congressional Committee, had supported the belief that one of the determining factors of the Japanese attack on Pearl Harbor was that the Japanese had the benefit of unusually superior intelligence. All early reports indicated the probability of extensive Japanese espionage activity in Hawaii. The Congressional Committee, however, concluded beyond a reasonable doubt that superior Japanese intelligence "had nothing whatever to do" with the *decision* to attack Pearl Harbor, and furthermore that Japanese espionage in Hawaii was not notably effective in securing the information necessary to support the attack plans. While interrogations in Japan indicate that one of the factors in the decision to attack Pearl Harbor over the weekend was the knowledge that the Fleet ordinarily came into the harbor on Friday and remained over the weekend, further interrogations and investigations in Japan reveal that, except for the consul in Honolulu and his staff, espionage agents played no major role in the plans for attack. It was therefore felt by the Committee that the role of espionage in connection with the Pearl Harbor attack has been magnified out of proportion to its significance.

As noted previously, much of the Japanese traffic intercepted by *Magic* was diplomatic in nature, but many of the intercepted messages concerned espionage activities by Japanese consular staffs, particularly as to the location and movement of American ships and the nature of military and defensive installations. However, Japanese interrogated since VJ-Day have placed little importance on intelligence obtained from the consulates. For example, the Japanese did not include the so-called "berthing plan" of Pearl Harbor (see "Research and Evaluation" section of this report) in listing information used by the attacking force at Pearl Harbor. This plan had been supplied by the consulate at Honolulu.

From newspapers and magazines published in the United States, the Japanese compiled material regarding America's war preparation, progress and expansion of military installations, locations and capabilities of aircraft and naval units, military strengths at Hawaii, Panama, the Philippines, and elsewhere.

In connection with items of general information, Admiral Wilkinson, former Chief of ONI, testified that "the Japanese for many years had the reputation of being meticulous seekers for every scrap of information...." In this connection the Admiral pointed out that the Japanese were also making investigations of naval installations at Seattle, Bremerton, Long Beach, San Diego, Panama, and Manila, as well as evincing an unusual interest in the presence of our Pacific Fleet and its detailed location within Pearl Harbor.

General information, in addition, included detailed bits of intelligence regarding the habits, strength, and security of the Fleet in Hawaii, which the Intelligence Section of the Japanese Naval General Staff had been amassing for years.

Of great interest is the fact that the Japanese placed little credence on reports from commercial firms in foreign countries. The Japanese regarded these reports as not important enough from the standpoint of intelligence to have a "special write-up, and were considered on their own merits."

The Japanese employed signal intelligence to deduce (from signals from American ships) the number of ships and small craft of the Pacific Fleet anchored in Pearl Harbor or out on training. The fleet training areas were also determined partially in this manner.

Commander Ono, staff communications officer of the Japanese striking force, kept close watch on Hawaiian broadcasts as the task force approached Pearl Harbor. It was felt that it could be determined from these broadcasts whether the forces on Oahu had any inkling of the impending attack. Since stations KGU and KGMB were broadcasting normally, Admiral Nagumo felt that American forces were still oblivious of developments. For several days prior to the attack, the Japanese force had been intercepting messages from our patrol planes. They had not broken the code, but by means of radio direction finders they had been able to plot in the plane positions, knew the number of patrol planes in the air at all times and that patrols were entirely in the southwestern sector off Oahu.

After sifting the information available on Japanese collection of intelligence material prior to Pearl Harbor, the Committee concluded that there were certain weaknesses in Japanese intelligence. This statement is supported by the fact that the Japanese estimates as to our air strength in Hawaii, made late in the fall of 1941, were thoroughly erroneous, and the margin of error was such as to make it impossible to credit them with superior intelligence. The Committee also felt that the Japanese did not have accurate intelligence as to our real naval weakness in the Pacific.

Section B — Research And Evaluation

The Congressional Committee investigating the Pearl Harbor attack reached the "indisputable" conclusion that "the attack on Pearl Harbor surprised the defending Army and Navy establishments."

General Marshall testified that the fullest protection for the Pacific Fleet was the major consideration of the Army. The secondary consideration was the protection of the Hawaiian Islands. The question then arises as to whether intelligence performed its role in this mission.

The Committee felt that the military and naval commands in Hawaii were "properly chargeable with possessing highly significant information and intelligence in the days before Pearl Harbor...." It also felt that this was true in Washington, where much information, particularly *Magic*, was available to the heads of the intelligence sections of both the services, as well as to the State Department. There also appeared to be the closest cooperation at the Secretarial level between Secretaries Hull, Stimson, and Knox.

It is the purpose of this section of this report to note briefly the major items of information available to intelligence officers of the Army and Navy for research and evaluation prior to Pearl Harbor, and the estimates resulting therefrom.

A letter from Admiral Kimmel to the Chief of Naval Operations, dated 18 February 1941, stated:

> I feel that a surprise attack (submarine, air, or combined) on Pearl Harbor is a possibility, and we are taking immediate practical steps to minimize the damage inflicted and to ensure that the attacking force will pay.

In March 1941, General Martin, commanding the Hawaiian Air Force, and Admiral Bellinger, commanding the Naval Base Defense Air Force, prepared a joint estimate foreseeing possible sudden hostile action in the Hawaiian area. This estimate included as possibilities, an air attack on the fleet, the arrival of Japanese submarines or a fast raiding force, with no prior warning to the defenders from American intelligence services. Thus it is evident that a possible surprise air attack on Pearl Harbor was in the minds of its defenders at an early date.

There was, of course, available for research and evaluation a mass of material obtained by *Magic*. As set forth in the section of this paper on Dissemination, the War Department did not disseminate *Magic* material to its commander in Hawaii. The Army did not feel its codes to be sufficiently secure for this purpose, though certain elements of information were of such a nature as to be of value to the field commanders, and though from time to time the

Navy did forward this material to the Pacific Fleet in the form of estimates or paraphrases. While the Committee felt that the decision not to supply field commanders with all of the *Magic* was a reasonable one, the feeling was also expressed that this material, insofar as it was pertinent, should have reached the field commanders in the form of operational estimates.

The Committee felt that the Japanese message of November 15 (translated December 3), referring to critical relations between the United States and Japan, and requesting that the "ships in harbor" berthing report be made irregularly, but at least twice a week, and directing that extra care should be taken to maintain its secrecy, should have raised the question as to whether or not this was highly important intelligence to the Pacific Fleet. While the Committee deems that the so-called "berthing plan" at Pearl Harbor and related dispatches could not be concluded to be a bomb plot, it felt that since a particular interest in the Pacific Fleet base was indicated, this intelligence should have been appreciated and disseminated to the commanding officers in Hawaii together with other available intelligence to assist them in making an estimate of the situation. It is interesting to note that no high ranking officers in Washington attached the significance to this intelligence which hindsight now makes apparent that it must have possessed.

One of the unfortunate circumstances in connection with *Magic* was the fact that several significant messages were not translated prior to the attack. One of these contained for the first time an inquiry from Tokyo regarding certain defenses of the Fleet in Pearl Harbor. The limitations of personnel and facilities both in Washington and the field, including the problem of transmission to Washington, was noted in the course of the testimony.

The Committee held that —

> The officers in the intelligence divisions of the War and Navy Departments had a *particular* responsibility with respect to the *Magic* intelligence. ... It was the duty of these officers to evaluate and disseminate the *Magic* in the form of estimates. ... This responsibility they failed to discharge with that high degree of skill and imagination which this intelligence warranted.

The testimony of Secretary Stimson bore out this view.

Information was available through *Magic* regarding Japanese instructions to its consulates to destroy codes, ciphers, and confidential documents. (See section of this report on Dissemination.) The overwhelming weight of the testimony by Army and Navy experts is to the effect that the destruction of codes and confidential documents under the circumstances prevailing in December 1941 meant war. The Committee took the position that Washington adequately discharged its responsibility in transmitting this information to Hawaii. The Committee points out that —

... with the failure, however, of Admiral Kimmel to read into this intelligence what it is agreed should have been self-evident to him, it is believed that in the future the intelligence as well as the departmental appraisal and estimated thereof should be supplied field commanders.

On 6 December, the FBI delivered to Army and Navy intelligence officers at Hawaii a transcript of an intercepted radio telephone conversation between a person named Mori in Honolulu and an individual in Japan. The transcript indicated that the latter was interested in daily flights of airplanes, particularly large planes from Honolulu, where the searchlights were being used, and the number of ships present at Pearl Harbor. Reference was made in the conversation to numerous flowers, which was presumed to be a code. The Navy determined that this information should be studied further by Japanese linguists. Admiral Kimmel was not informed and did not see the transcript until after the attack. The evening of 6 December it was brought to the attention of General Short and his G-2 by an assistant G-2, who indicated that a special agent of the FBI was alarmed by what he considered the military implications of the conversations in respect to Pearl Harbor. Both General Short and his G-2 indicated that the assistant was perhaps "too intelligence conscious" and that the message was nothing about which to become excited. The Committee felt that the Mori call pointed directly at Hawaii.

The fortnightly intelligence summary dated December 1, 1941, received by Kimmel from ONI, stated that it believed the major Japanese capital ship strength was in home waters, together with the greatest portion of the Japanese carriers. On December 1, Kimmel's daily summary indicated that the Japanese service radio call signs had changed at midnight, one month after the previous change, whereas the former Japanese practice had been to change their call signs every six months. On 2 December, a memorandum from the Fleet Intelligence Officer on the disposition of the Japanese naval force, together with a conversation between Kimmel and this officer, stressed the point that there was no reliable information on Japanese carrier divisions 1 and 2, consisting of four carriers. No information on carriers was available on 4 December. Admiral Kimmel received this intelligence, but accepted the estimate that they were probably in home waters. The Committee found that,

... recognizing all of the vagaries of radio intelligence analysis, however, it was still not in keeping with his responsibility as Commander in Chief of the Fleet for Admiral Kimmel to ignore the sinister implications of the information supplied through the Radio Intelligence Unit after he had been warned of war. In many respects the picture presented by radio intelligence was among the most significant information relating to *when* and, to a degree, *where* the Japanese would possibly attack.

In addition to this material, operational intelligence was available on the day of the attack itself. This included the reports of sighting and subsequent attack on a Japanese submarine in close proximity to Pearl Harbor, and radar detection of the Japanese raiding force over 130 miles from Oahu on the morning of December 7th.

Despite the foregoing, the estimate was made and persisted in that Hawaii was safe from an air attack, although the very assumptions made by the Army and Navy Commanders are implicit with the contemplation of an attack from without. General Short assumed the Navy was conducting distant reconnaissance. Admiral Kimmel assumed, on the other hand, that the Army would alert its aircraft warning service, antiaircraft guns, and fighter planes.

From the above, it is apparent that there was at least some cognizance in Washington and Hawaii of the possibility of a raid on Pearl Harbor. Much of the material available pointed to hostile action on the part of the Japanese, but in the mass of information available, many of the witnesses contended, a very small percentage pointed to Pearl Harbor as the point of attack. Granted that this point was so, and that those items of information which might have produced an estimate of attack on Pearl Harbor loom much larger by hindsight than they did at the time, the Committee felt that Admiral Kimmel and General Short were supplied enough information to make a correct estimate of the situation. That they failed to do. That there may have been other information which could have been supplied them, failed to modify the Committee's conclusion in this respect.

Section C — Dissemination

During the period preceding Pearl Harbor, there appears to have been a failure of proper dissemination of intelligence. This failure in dissemination lay not only between the Washington headquarters of the Army and Navy and their field commands, but also between the services themselves in Hawaii.

Admiral Kimmel's concern in connection with internal Naval distribution of secret material was set forth in a letter to Admiral Stark, Chief of Naval Operations, in February 1941, in which he stated:

> I do not know that we have missed anything, but if there is any doubt as to whose responsibility (as between ONI and Operations), it is to keep the Commander in Chief fully informed with pertinent reports on subjects that should be of interest to the Fleet, will you kindly fix that responsibility so that there will be no misunderstanding?

In response, Admiral Stark advised that ONI was fully aware of its responsibilities to keep the Commander in Chief of the Pacific Fleet adequately informed on matters concerning foreign nations and their activities. In addition, in April 1941, instructions were given various naval observers to include the Commander-in-Chief of the Pacific Fleet as an information addressee for all pertinent dispatches, and to furnish one copy of all intelligence reports directly to him.

The Army did not forward the substance of any intercepted Japanese dispatches to field commanders because of its feeling that the Army codes were generally not as secure as those of the Navy. As evidence of this, General Miles, War Department G-2 at the time of Pearl Harbor, testified that he was under the impression that the Navy would promptly disseminate such intelligence to General Short's headquarters.

A notable failure existed in the dissemination of intelligence between the Army and Navy commands in Hawaii. For example, the Army radar unit, which first picked up the incoming Japanese planes, plotted them back out to the north following the attack. Yet this information, which would have made an effective search for the task force possible, was not employed by either service. Admiral Kimmel stated he did not receive the information for two days.

A chart showing the position of the Japanese carriers was taken from a Japanese plane by the Army on 7 December. It was not shown to the Navy until the afternoon.

Admiral Kimmel stated that he did not supply General Short with information he had received from Washington concerning Japanese orders to destroy codes, ciphers and confidential documents, adding that, "I did not consider that of any vital importance when I received it...." General Short, on the other hand, complaining that he was not provided with this intelligence by the Navy, indicated that it was "the one thing that would have affected me more than any other matter...", and that if any of these dispatches concerning the destruction of the codes had been furnished him by the Navy, he would have gone into a more serious alert. The opinion of virtually all witnesses holds that the code burning intelligence was the most significant information received between 27 November and 6 December regarding the imminence of war.

The evidence before the Committee shows that although Kimmel received significant information on four different occasions between 3 and 6 December concerning the destruction of codes and confidential documents in Japanese diplomatic establishments, and that although he knew that the Navy Department had also ordered the destruction of its codes in our outlying possessions, he failed to convey this information to General Short. It is the Committee's conclusion that Kimmel's failure to supply Short with this intelligence was "inexcusable."

Despite Kimmel's personal failure (to inform Short), the testimony reveals that on about 3 December General Short's assistant G-2 learned from Navy sources that Japanese diplomatic representatives in Washington, London, Hongkong, Singapore, Manila, and elsewhere, were destroying their codes and papers. Further testimony shows that the assistant G-2 received similar information regarding Honolulu from the FBI. There is also evidence that this was communicated to General Short, although the Minority Report considers it an open question and the evidence is not decisive.

In making the finding set forth above, the Committee points out that the information on code destruction which Short received was not supplied him directly by the War Department.

Both Kimmel and Short have testified that they were wrongfully deprived of intelligence available to Washington through *Magic*, which would have completely altered their estimate of the situation and would have resulted in a proper alert and appropriate dispositions had they received it. In particular, there were four messages, or groups of messages, received through *Magic* which might have been particularly significant in Hawaii. The Committee is of the opinion that this intelligence should have been supplied Kimmel and Short (together with other available information and intelligence) to assist them in making their estimate of the situation.

However, the Committee further finds that, between them, both Commanders had considerable vital intelligence indicating a possible attack on Hawaii. They had, inter alia:

1. Correspondence with Washington and plans revealing the possible dangers of an air attack;

2. The warning dispatches from Washington;
3. The code destruction intelligence;
4. Radio intelligence concerning the "lost" Japanese carriers;
5. The "Mori" call. (See "Research and Evaluation" section);
6. The report of sighting and subsequent attack on a Japanese submarine in close proximity to Pearl Harbor (early on 7 December);
7. Radar detection of the Japanese planes over 130 miles from Oahu on the morning of 7 December.

Noting the erroneous assumptions which General Short and Admiral Kimmel made regarding each other's activities in Hawaii, and the estimates and actions which they took based on the intelligence available to them there, the Committee believes it problematical as to what steps Kimmel and Short would have taken had they received all the intelligence which they contend was withheld from them. As a result of this, the Committee finds that "the ultimate and direct responsibility for failure to engage the Japanese on the morning of 7 December with the weapons at their disposal rests essentially and properly with the Army and Navy Commands in Hawaii...."

However, it is the Committee's additional conclusion that the officers in the Intelligence and War Plans Divisions of the War and Navy Departments "had a *particular* responsibility with respect to the *Magic* intelligence;" that it was their duty to evaluate and disseminate *Magic* in the form of estimates. This responsibility, the Committee feels, these officers "failed to discharge with that high degree of skill and imagination which this intelligence warranted." The Committee further stated:

That the completely ineffective liaison between the Army and the Navy in Hawaii at a time when the fullest exchange of intelligence was absolutely imperative, dictates that military and naval intelligence, particularly, must be consolidated.

Section D — Deficiencies, Conclusions And Recommendation Of The Committee

In its final Section, the Committee devotes its attention to "Supervisory, Administrative, and Organizational Deficiencies in our Military and Naval Establishments Revealed by The Pearl Harbor Investigation." In this Section, the question is posed: "Why, with some of the finest intelligence available in our history, with the almost certain knowledge that war was at hand, with plans that contemplated the precise type of attack that was executed by Japan on the morning of December 7 — Why was it possible for a Pearl Harbor to occur?" The reactions of the Committee to this latter question are of sufficient interest to warrant their being quoted herewith verbatim insofar as they refer to intelligence:

1. *Operational and Intelligence work requires centralization of authority and clear-cut allocation of responsibility.*

   Reviewing the testimony of the Director of War Plans and the Director of Naval Intelligence, the conclusion is inescapable that the proper demarcation of responsibility between these two divisions of the Navy Department did not exist. War Plans appears to have insisted that since it had the duty of issuing operational orders it must arrogate the prerogative of evaluating intelligence; Naval Intelligence, on the other hand, seems to have regarded the matter of evaluation as properly its function. It is clear that this intradepartmental misunderstanding and near conflict was not resolved before December 7 and beyond question it prejudiced the effectiveness of Naval Intelligence.

   In Hawaii, there was such a marked failure to allocate responsibility in the case of the Fourteenth Naval District that Admiral Bloch testified he did not know whom the commander in chief would hold responsible in the event of shortcoming with respect to the condition and readiness of aircraft. The position of Admiral Bellinger was a wholly anomalous one. He appears to have been responsible to everyone and to no one. The pyramiding of superstructures of organization cannot be conducive to efficiency and endangers the very function of our military and naval services. [p. 254]

2. *Supervisory officials cannot safely take anything for granted
   in the alerting of subordinates.*

   ... Navy Department officials have almost unanimously testified that instructions to burn codes mean 'war in any man's
language' and that in supplying Admiral Kimmel this information they were entitled to believe he would attach the proper
significance to this intelligence. Yet the commander in chief of
the Pacific Fleet testified that he did not interpret these dispatches to mean that Japan contemplated immediate war on the
United States. ... The simple fact is that the dispatches were not
properly interpreted. Had the Navy Department not taken for
granted that Kimmel would be alerted by them but instead have
given him the benefit of its interpretation, there could now be no
argument as to what the state of alertness should have been based
on such dispatches. With Pearl Harbor as a sad experience,
crucial intelligence should in the future be supplied commanders
accompanied by the best estimate of its significance. [p. 254–255]

3. *Any doubt as to whether outposts should be given information
   should always be resolved in favor of supplying the information.*

   Admiral Stark hesitated about sending the "one o'clock"
intelligence to the Pacific outposts for the reason that he regarded
them as adequately alerted and he did not want to confuse them.
As has been seen, he was properly entitled to believe that naval
establishments were adequately alert, but the fact is that one —
Hawaii — was not in a state of readiness. This one exception is proof
of the principle that any question as to whether information should be
supplied the field should always be resolved in favor of transmitting it.

   ... ...

8. *The coordination and proper evaluation of intelligence in
   times of stress must be insured by continuity of service and
   centralization of responsibility in competent officials.*

   On occasion witnesses have echoed the sentiment that the
Pearl Harbor debacle was made possible, not by the egregious
errors or poor judgment of any individual or individuals but
rather by reason of the imperfection and deficiencies of the
system whereby Army and Navy intelligence was coordinated and
evaluated. Only partial credence, however, can be extended this
conclusion inasmuch as no amount of coordination and no system

could be effected to compensate for lack of alertness and imagination. Nevertheless, there is substantial basis, from a review of the Pearl Harbor investigation in its entirety, to conclude that the system of handling intelligence was seriously at fault and that the security of the Nation can be insured only through continuity of service and centralization of responsibility in those charged with handling intelligence. *And the assignment of an officer having an aptitude for such work over an extended period of time should not impede his progress nor affect his promotions.*

The professional character of intelligence work does not appear to have been properly appreciated in either the War or Navy Departments. It seems to have been regarded as just another tour of duty, as reflected by limitations imposed on the period of assignment to such work, among other things. The committee has received the distinct impression that there was a tendency, whether realized or not, to relegate intelligence to a role of secondary importance.

As an integrated picture, the Pearl Harbor investigations graphically portray the imperative necessity, in the War and Navy Departments, (1) for selection of men for intelligence work who possess the background, capacity, and penchant for such work; (2) for maintaining them in the work over an extended period of time in order that they may become steeped in the ramifications and refinements of their field and employ this reservoir of knowledge in evaluating data received; and (3) for the centralization of responsibility for handling intelligence to avoid all of the pitfalls of divided responsibility which experience has made so abundantly apparent. [p. 257–258]

....

10. *There is no substitute for imagination and resourcefulness on the part of supervisory and intelligence officials.*

As reflected by an examination of the situation in Hawaii, there was a failure to employ the necessary imagination with respect to the intelligence which was at hand.

Washington, like Hawaii, possessed unusually significant and vital intelligence. Had greater imagination and keener awareness of the significance of intelligence existed, concentrating and applying it to particular situations, it is proper to suggest that someone should have concluded that Pearl Harbor was a likely point of Japanese attack.

The committee feels that the failure to demonstrate the highest imagination with respect to the intelligence which was available in Hawaii and in Washington is traceable, at least in part, to the failure to accord to intelligence work the important and significant role which it deserves. [p. 259]

... ...

14. *Restriction of highly confidential information to a minimum number of officials, while often necessary, should not be carried to the point of prejudicing the work of the organization.*

The Magic intelligence was preeminently important and the necessity for keeping it confidential cannot be overemphasized. However, so closely held and top secret was this intelligence that it appears that the *fact* the Japanese codes had been broken was regarded of more importance than the *information* obtained from decoded traffic. The result of this rather specious premise was to leave large numbers of policy-making and enforcement officials in Washington completely oblivious of the most pertinent information concerning Japan.

The Federal Bureau of Investigation, for example, was charged with combating espionage, sabotage, and un-American activities within the United States. On February 15, 1941, Tokyo dispatched to Washington a detailed outline as to the type of espionage information desired from this country. The FBI was never informed of this vital information necessary to the success of its work, despite the fact that the closest liaison was supposed to exist among the FBI, Naval Intelligence, and Military Intelligence.

General Hayes A. Kroner, who was in charge of the intelligence branch of G-2, has testified that he at no time was permitted to avail himself of the Magic. And this despite the fact that to effectively perform his work he should have known of this intelligence and one of his subordinates, Colonel Bratton, was 'loaned' to General Miles to distribute Magic materials to authorized recipients.

While, as previously indicated, it is appreciated that promiscuous distribution of highly confidential material is dangerous, it nevertheless should be made available to all those whose responsibility cannot adequately and intelligently be discharged without knowledge of such confidential data. It would seem that through sufficient paraphrase of the original material the source of the information could have been adequately protected. Cer-

tainly as great confidence could be placed in ranking officials of various departments and bureaus of the Government as in the numerous technicians, cryptographers, translators, and clerks required for the interception and processing of the Magic."
[p. 261–262]

... ...

17. *An official who neglects to familiarize himself in detail with his organization should forfeit his responsibility.*

... Admirals Stark and Turner both have testified they 'thought' the commander in chief of the Pacific Fleet was receiving the Magic intelligence. Yet in a period of over 6 months, with relations between the United States and Japan mounting in tenseness and approaching a crisis, neither of these ranking officers determined for a fact whether the fleet was receiving this information.... [p. 263]

... ...

20. *Personal or official jealousy will wreck any organization.*

This principle is the result of the general impression obtained by the Committee concerning the relationship between the Army and Navy as well as concerning certain intraorganizational situations which existed. The relationship, understanding, and coordination between the War Plans Division and the Office of Naval Intelligence were wholly unsatisfactory. The War Plans Division, particularly, appears to have had an overzealous disposition to preserve and enhance its prerogatives...."

... ...

23. *Superiors must at all times keep their subordinates adequately informed and, conversely, subordinates should keep their superiors informed.*

In Washington, Admiral Wilkinson, Director of Naval Intelligence, and Captain McCollum, Chief of the Far Eastern Section of that Division, were not adequately and currently informed as to the nature of the dispatches being sent to our outposts emanating from the War Plans Division. Subordinate officials in both War and Navy Departments failed to appreciate the importance and necessity of getting to both General Marshall and Admiral Stark the first 13 parts of the Japanese 14-part memorandum immediately on the evening of December 6. Colonel French did not inform the Chief of Staff that he had been unable to raise the Army radio in Hawaii on the morning of December 7.

In Hawaii, Admiral Kimmel failed to insure that Admiral Bellinger, who was responsible for Navy patrol planes, knew of the war warning of November 27. Admiral Newton, as previously pointed out, was permitted to leave Pearl Harbor with a task force completely oblivious of any of the warning messages. General Short, construing the caution to disseminate the information in the warning of November 27 to 'minimum essential officers' in a too-narrow manner, failed to inform the essential and necessary officers of his command of the acute situation in order that the proper alertness might pervade the Hawaiian Department. [p. 265]

24. *The administrative organization of any establishment must be designed to locate failures and to assess responsibility.*

The Committee has been very much concerned about the fact that there was no way in which it could be determined definitely that any individual saw a particular message among the Magic materials. It does not appear that any record system was established for initialing the messages or otherwise fixing responsibility. The system existing left subordinate officers charged with the duty of disseminating the Magic at the complete mercy of superior officers with respect to any question as to whether a particular message had been delivered to or seen by them. [p. 265–266]

The specific conclusions and recommendations of the Pearl Harbor Congressional Committee with respect to Intelligence are of such interest that they are quoted verbatim from the report herewith.

The following are *Conclusions* with respect to responsibilities so far as they effect intelligence.

8. Specifically, the Hawaiian commands failed —

... ...

(b) To integrate and coordinate their facilities for defense and to alert properly the Army and Navy establishments in Hawaii, particularly in the light of the warnings and intelligence available to them during the period November 27 to December 7, 1941. [Page 252]

(c)   To effect liaison on a basis designed to acquaint each of them with the operations of the other, which was necessary to their joint security, and to exchange fully all significant intelligence. [Page 252]

... ...

(g)   To appreciate the significance of intelligence and other information available to them. [Page 252] ...

11.   The Intelligence and War Plans Divisions of the War and Navy Departments failed:

(a)   To give careful and thoughtful consideration to the intercepted messages from Tokyo to Honolulu of September 24, November 15, and November 20 (the Harbor berthing plan and related dispatches) and to raise a question as to their significance. Since they indicated a particular interest in the Pacific Fleet's base, this intelligence should have been appreciated and supplied the Hawaiian commanders for their assistance, along with other information available to them, in making their estimate of the situation.

(b)   To be properly on the *qui vive* to receive the 'one o'clock' intercept and to recognize in the message the fact that some Japanese military action would very possibly occur somewhere at 1 p.m., December 7. If properly appreciated, this intelligence should have suggested a dispatch to all Pacific outpost commanders supplying this information, as General Marshall attempted to do immediately upon seeing it. [Page 252]

The following specific *Recommendations* are made in the Committee report with respect to intelligence:

That there be a complete integration of Army and Navy intelligence agencies in order to avoid the pitfalls of divided responsibility which experience has made so abundantly apparent; that upon effecting a unified intelligence, officers be selected for intelligence work who possess the background, penchant, and capacity for such work; and that they be maintained in the work for an extended period of time in order that they may become steeped in the ramifications and refinements of their field and employ this reservoir of knowledge in evaluating material received. The assignment of an officer having an aptitude for such work should not impede his progress nor affect his promotions. Efficient intelligence services are just as essential in time of peace as in war, and this branch of our armed services must always be accorded the important role which it deserves. [Page 253]

That effective steps be taken to insure that statutory or other restrictions do not operate to the benefit of an enemy or other forces inimical to the Nation's security and to the handicap of our own intelligence agencies. With this in mind, the Congress should give serious study to, among other things, the Communications Act of 1934; to suspension in proper instances of the statute of limitations during war (it was impossible during the war to prosecute violations relating to the "Magic" without giving the secret to the enemy); to legislation designed to prevent unauthorized sketching photographing, and mapping of military and naval reservations in peacetime; and to legislation fully protecting the security of classified matter. [Page 253]